The Route of the Devon and Somerset Railway

The region of North Devon and West Somerset between Taunton in the east and Barnstaple in the west that was traversed and served by the Devon & Somerset Railway. There were stations at Milverton, Wiveliscombe, Venn Cross, Morebath, Dulverton, East Anstey, Bishops Nympton & Molland, South Molton, Filleigh and Swimbridge, and halts at Yeo Mill and Morebath Junction. With its northern terminus in the bay platform at Dulverton, the Exe Valley Branch then made its way southwards from Morebath Junction through Bampton, on its way to Exeter via Tiverton. Also seen heading away north-westwards from Norton Fitzwarren is the Minehead Branch. Taken from the 1960 edition of Bartholomew's Half Inch Contoured maps and enlarged by 25% to better show the detail.

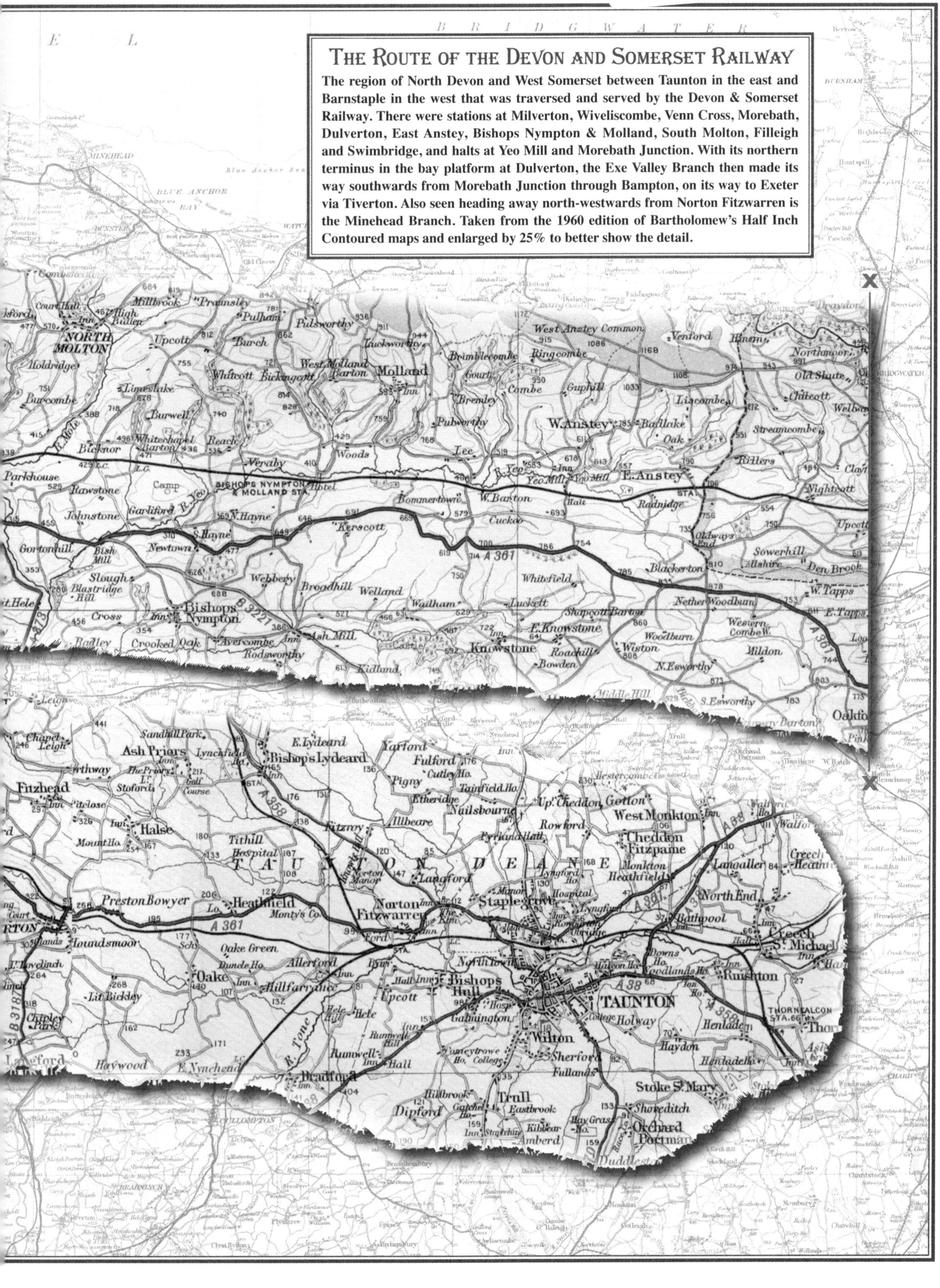

SPRINGBOURNE LIBRARY
HOLDENHURST ROAD
BOURNEMOUTH BH8 8BX
TEL: 01202 397115

29. 17 | 12/3/20
08. JAN 18.

1 - AUG 2019
12 NOV 2019

- You can return this item to any Bournemouth library but not all libraries are open every day.
- Items must be returned on or before the due date. Please note that you will be charged for items returned late.
- Items may be renewed unless requested by another customer.
- Renewals can be made in any library, by telephone, email or online via the website. Your membership card number and PIN will be required.
- Please look after this item - you may be charged for any damage.

BOURNEMOUTH LIBRARIES
WITHDRAWN STOCK
FOR SALE
SPA

Bournemouth Libraries

www.bournemouth.gov.uk/libraries

Class '43XX' 2-6-0 No. 6363 waits in the No. 3 Bay platform at Taunton with the 5.47pm departure to Barnstaple Junction on 29th August 1964. *Courtesy Tim Stephens*

FRONT COVER: Ex-GWR 'Mogul' No. 7304 calls at Dulverton station with a Barnstaple Junction to Taunton [illegible] **bay platform on the left.** *Neil Par*[illegible]

BACKGROUND: T[illegible] **se-up of one of the piers of Cast**[illegible] **oad.** *Author*

BOURNEMOUTH
410121797

Wiveliscombe from the south circa 1930, with the station just featuring on the far right. What this old postcard view clearly illustrates is the town's fleeting relationship with the railway, referred to on OS maps as the 'GWR Barnstaple Branch'. Arriving from the east, it glanced off Wiveliscombe's eastern edge, turning through ninety degrees to head due south. The town itself lies on the left-hand side of this panoramic view, with the buildings of Hancock's Brewery, by far the largest local employer, visible beyond the church. *Neil Parkhouse collection*

Published by LIGHTMOOR PRESS

© Lightmoor Press & Freddie Huxtable 2016

Designed by Neil Parkhouse

www.devonandsomersetrailway.co.uk

British Library Cataloguing-in-Publication Data. A catalogue record for this book is available from the British Library

ISBN: 9781911038 15 3

All rights reserved. No part of this publication may be reproduced, stored in a retrieval system or transmitted in any form or by any means, electronic, mechanical, photocopying, recording or otherwise, without the written permission of the publisher.

LIGHTMOOR PRESS

Unit 144B, Lydney Trading Estate, Harbour Road, Lydney, Gloucestershire GL15 5EJ

www.lightmoor.co.uk

Lightmoor Press is an imprint of Black Dwarf Lightmoor Publications Ltd

Printed in Poland

www.lfbookservices.co.uk

WIVELISCOMBE

THE TAUNTON TO BARNSTAPLE LINE

A HISTORY OF THE DEVON & SOMERSET RAILWAY

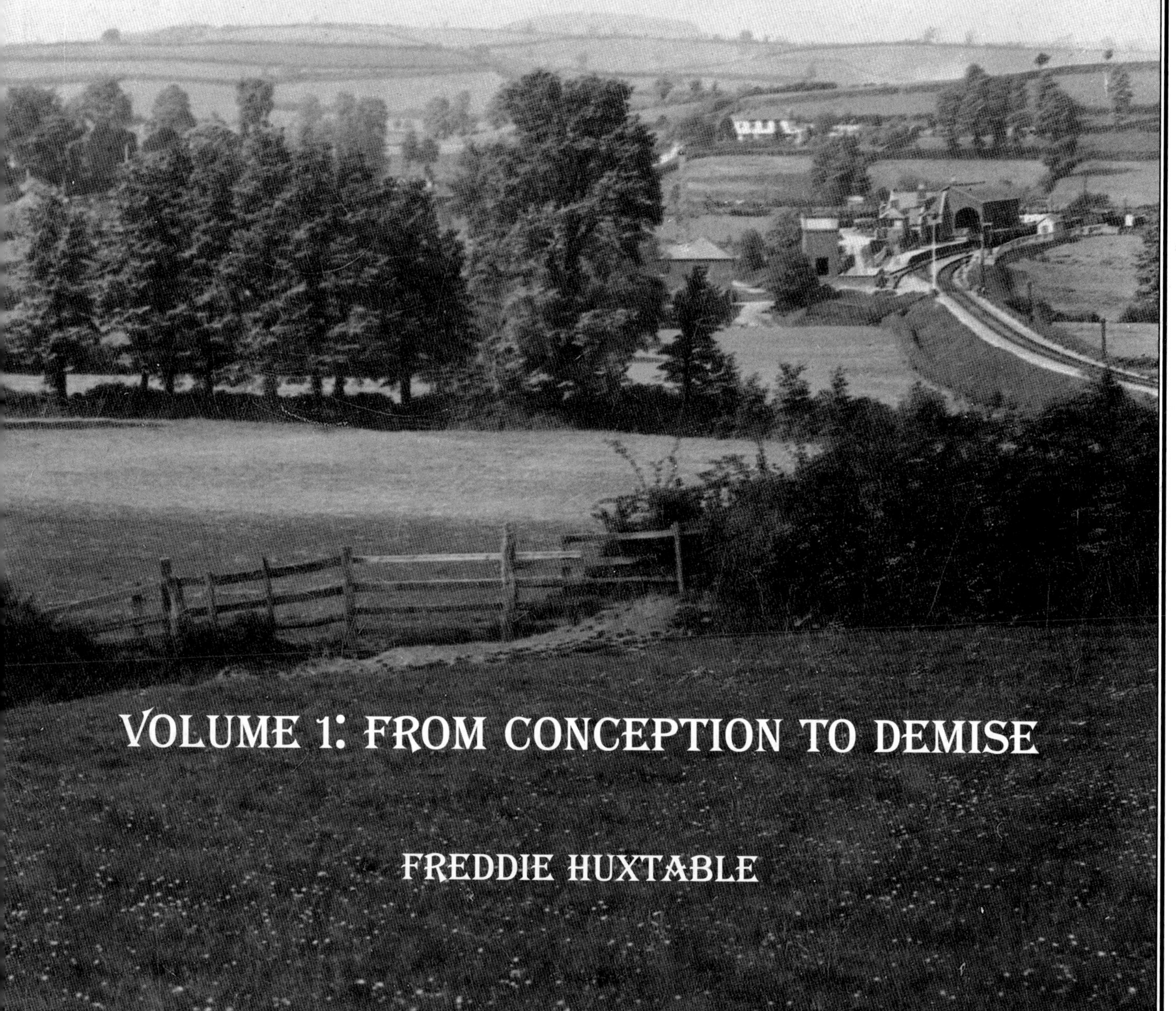

VOLUME 1: FROM CONCEPTION TO DEMISE

FREDDIE HUXTABLE

BR 'Standard' Class '3MT' No. 82008 was a regular performer on the Taunton to Barnstaple line in its later years and is seen here approaching Dulverton with an Up train on 9th September 1963. The rural beauty of this scene was typical of much of the countryside which the line traversed. *Derrick Joanes*

Contents – Volume 1
From Conception to Demise

FOREWORD

I am pleased to write this foreword given my family's association with early North Devon Railway projects in the 1840s and, of course, the Devon & Somerset Railway.

My Great Great Great Grandfather, the 2nd Earl, was involved in the initial North Devon Railway project of 1845. This scheme, which proposed a railway from the Bristol and Exeter line near Taunton to Barnstaple and down into Cornwall, never left the drawing board, despite having Brunel as its engineer. By the time the project was resurrected in the early 1860s, the 2nd Earl had died and his son did see the project through. He was on the provisional committee of the Devon (North) & Somerset Railway, along with the Earl of Carnarvon and Lords Poltimore and Clinton. The Bill for this proposed railway was deposited in Parliament in late 1863 and, with subsequent variations, in essence became the Devon & Somerset Railway that was opened in November 1873. The 3rd Earl was a director of the Devon & Somerset Railway Company in the early years thus continuing the family's link to the line.

The railway was a testament to the determination and perseverance of the promoters of the line, the Victorian engineers and contractors. The whole project took nearly ten years from the Parliamentary Bill stage until its opening to Barnstaple. From the start it was fraught with difficulties, such as financing problems – raising cash during a recessionary period in the economy, contractor problems (several were employed), cost over-runs necessitating restructuring on a number of occasions, engineering challenges, labour disputes and, of course, the North Devon weather ... All this resulted in an hiatus of about four years in the late 1860s when no construction work was done.

My family provided land at the Castle Hill Estate through which the railway was to run. The 3rd Earl offered to build a station at Castle Hill, which offer was gladly accepted by the railway company. He was also given a privilege; the ability to request (with notice) any train to stop at the station. Our family diaries from that time state that the woods planted to the north, along the railway line and up the coombes and goyles, were planted for the the joy of the railway traveller. Those now mature woods still enhance the landscape and still afford a splendid view from the North Devon Link road.

When it arrived, the railway opened up North Devon. Access to Ilfracombe meant that that town benefitted hugely in the Edwardian era and subsequently as workers in the Midlands and the North increasingly took their holidays in the area. The train was the only practical means of transport for many until the 1950s. The railway facilitated export of local products to the more populous areas of the country. Equally, goods arrived from the industrial areas and London. Whilst the railway played its part in the two wars, it suffered and needed investment.

It struggled finacially when it was the Devon & Somerset Railway but with the Great Western Railway takeover of the line in 1901, its future was brighter. There were piecemeal improvements in the early 1900s and again in the late 1930s, with major upgrading at most locations (including our own Filleigh station*). However, although the 1950s were good years for the economy, nationally the railways were suffering from under investment and the impact of the war. The 1960s brought Dr Beeching and his Reshaping Report. This condemned the Devon & Somerset Railway and it officially closed on 3rd October 1966, the last train running on Saturday 1st October.

So, after ninety-three years, all that effort put in by many in constructing the railway meant for nothing. A lot has happened in the last fifty years but the line is only a memory. The drive from South Molton to Barnstaple gives the traveller a glimpse of what it was like to travel along the railway and the beautiful scenery through which it passed. Some station buildings have been demolished, others converted to dwellings, some of the track bed has been returned to agricultural use, some parts are overgrown. Some structures, such as bridges and tunnels, remain almost ready for track and the next train. However, the real monument to the railway and those Victorian builders is fortunately on our land; the Castle Hill Viaduct still stands today as proudly as it always did, only now its five stone piers carry the North Devon Link road.

A number of local railway lines have had their detailed history recorded and published. Such a volume on this railway is conspicuous by its absence. The other publications on this railway have not yet done it justice in terms of a comprehensive, detailed and definitive history. The two volumes that will make up this history should fill that void. Freddie has spent nine years researching all facets of this railway, from its inception until today. It will be of interest to any one wanting to learn more about the history of North Devon and West Somerset, and those who like engineering and finance and, of course, to those railway enthusiasts who wish to understand the uniqueness of what was the Devon & Somerset Railway – the Taunton to Barnstaple line.

Eleanor, Countess of Arran,
Filleigh, January 2016

*Renamed from Castle Hill in 1881

THE FORTESCUE FAMILY

The Fortescue family descends from Sir Hugh Fortescue of Filleigh, who died in 1719. The second Earl (4th Baron), born on 13th February 1783, became a Whig politician and, in 1839, was summoned to the House of Lords through a writ of acceleration in his father's junior title of Baron Fortescue. He was Lord Steward of the Household between 1846 and 1851 and was also Lord Lieutenant of Devon from 1839 to 1861 (the year he died). The third Earl, his son, the 5th Baron, was born on 4th April 1818 and was also a Whig politician, holding minor office from 1846 to 1851 in the same government as his father. In 1859, he was also summoned to the House of Lords through a writ of acceleration in his father's junior title and he died in October 1905. Castle Hill House at Filleigh, built in the Palladian style by the 1st Baron Fortescue in 1730, remained the family seat until 1958 when the 5th Earl died and the property passed to his daughter, Lady Margaret Fortescue. Her daughter, Eleanor, Countess of Arran now lives there.

INTRODUCTION

Why, some may well ask, have I chosen to write a book on the long-closed Taunton to Barnstaple railway line? The next few paragraphs should help to explain why I embarked on a project which has taken nine years to research, compile and complete, at least to this point! I hope you feel it has been worthy of the time spent and goes some way to being the definitive work of this long-lost country railway.

My father was born at and lived for a number of years in South Molton. He met my mother when working at Dulverton and, in 1953, a few years after their marriage, they moved to Hatherleigh in West Devon. It was here that my railway memories began. My mother would take me for walks in my push chair and often we would venture past the old pig stys to the north of the village. It was risky, as these stys were then used as a dog kennels, inhabited by large dogs that barked and jumped aggressively at the slightest disturbance from passers by. Beyond the pig stys lay peace and tranquility, a narrow country lane and some tall iron 'walls'. Over these iron walls was the Torrington to Halwill Junction railway line and just every once in a while, the peace was broken by the coughing of a tank engine as it passed under the bridge. On this particular day, one such engine happened to pass under the bridge as my mother and I (in my push chair) passed over it. I was captivated by the spectacle; the noise and the smoke as it billowed under and over the bridge, then surrounding us like a mist, just temporarily, before dissipating into the sky.

After my father's death in 1960, my mother and I moved to Combe Farm, near Brushford, Dulverton. When in the farm's fields, it was possible to hear the steam trains whistling and working hard as they chugged up the long climb towards East Anstey. That was my first introduction to the Taunton to Barnstaple line.

The line was, in its remaining short life, to provide a personal link to London and other holiday destinations; we travelled on it to pick up the main line at Taunton – much easier than taking the car! In the final year of the line's operation we used it for the last time to get us to Chester for our summer holiday. At this time, my railway interests were encouraged by my uncles, Fred Hill (a former signalman at Exeter Central) and Ruben Rainbow (an inspector on the Central Line of the Underground), so there was some railwayman in the blood!

On Saturday, 1st October 1966, my mother and I went to a function in Brushford village hall. Towards the end of the evening, at about 10pm, there was a commotion outside; detonators were exploding there was cheering and a diesel horn sounded. The hall was situated above a cutting through which the railway ran and which was only a few hundred yards west of Dulverton station. It was the last train. My mother asked if I wanted to see it; I said '*No!*' – I still don't know why. Maybe I didn't want to witness the line's death throes but I still regret the decision not to see the last train. Maybe it was at that point I was destined to write this book, either as 'punishment' or as reparation of that decision not to see that last train.

In a sense that end was just the beginning of my affection for, and interest in, the railway.

We moved from Combe Farm to Brushford village in August 1967. It was at that time they were dismantling the line. In my school holidays I watched with fascination as the demolition trains trundled up and down the line near our Brushford home, with wagons containing the remnants of the Devon & Somerset Railway. I even remember hearing one such demolition train trundling down that same cutting by the village hall going towards Taunton, hauled by a North British 'D63XX' diesel-hydraulic. Off I ran to see it, maybe even to get the locomotive's number but I was too slow. By the time I reached the station bridge at Dulverton it had gone out of sight. However, what did not escape me were some of those remnants from the line. They fell into my possession, offered by the workmen dismantling the track and photographs of some of these items can be seen towards the end of the book. My passing interest in railways

Where it all began. The spot by the line in Brushford by the foot crossing near my then home, although it was a Fowler diesel not a Class '3MT' that was pulling the demolition train on that day in 1967. Here, Swindon-built BR 'Standard' Class '3' 2-6-2T No. 82008 heads towards Dulverton with a Taunton-bound train. ***Roger Joanes***

had, by then, turned into a hobby. With the line gone I felt it safe to explore the derelict station site and play with my friends up and down the bank in that very same cutting by the village hall; no trains to worry about anymore. That was until someone mentioned the adders that basked in the sun in that cutting. I stopped playing on that bank immediately and retreated indoors to build a model railway!

In a broader sense, the railway had shown me what lay beyond my localised world of Exmoor and West Somerset. Beautiful though that home area was and still is, I could see I had to venture beyond Taunton to what seemed a bigger, brighter world. Sadly, by the time I was making the bold step to travel east to London to go to university, the railway was not around to transport me those first twenty-four miles to Taunton.

My link to Dulverton was maintained by my trips home during university vacations. By then, my mother had moved to Northmoor Lodge and, coincidentally, as I found out later, Northmoor House was the home of John Locke, one of the early D&SR directors in the 1860s and '70s. When I started working in London as a trainee accountant in 1977, I still went back to Dulverton and the countryside but for less extended breaks. At that time, horse riding and tennis were my active pastimes and passions (football also featured but that was as a mere spectator!). When the West Somerset Polo Club was reforming in late 1989, I offered my services as Secretary and Treasurer. The club re-established itself in 1990 and its chosen new grounds were in the fields below Dulverton station, rented from the Carnarvon Arms Hotel; my close links to the old station were re-established. I had a happy six years playing there in the shadow of the station and the old railway line before moving my horses to London to play in the home counties.

Moving to near East Down in 1997, the weekend trips down from Ealing in London (the base during the week) inevitably took me along the A361; the North Devon Link Road as it is now known. This road from South Molton all the way into Barnstaple is largely built on the old track bed of the Taunton to Barnstaple railway line. So, with my weekend drives to North Devon, I began to regularly travel on that part of the railway I never travelled on as a child when it was open. Once again the line appeared in my life but in a different guise.

At home in North Devon, on those many wet weekends, I amused myself by building the model railway I always wanted, a representation of the Taunton to Barnstaple line focusing on Barnstaple Victoria Road (the end of the line where I now live) and Dulverton (where I was brought up). This inevitably led me to begin reviewing and studying my collection of books on the line to research layout plans, scenic effects, locomotive and stock workings.

The work on the model drew to a close after about ten years (well it looks complete but there are always things to do!). I then decided to use what little knowledge I had gleaned in building the model to start on my potential retirement project – the book of the line. This really took off in the autumn of 2006 when I met Ian Coleby at Bishops Lydeard on the West Somerset Railway (WSR). Ian was autographing copies of his excellent book on that line, *The Minehead Branch 1848-1971* (Lightmoor Press, 2006 & 2011). We got chatting and I asked him for tips, he helpfully sent me a comprehensive email on how to approach the detailed research and the rest is now history. As I started work on the book, collecting photographs, commencing the extensive research at Kew – just down the road from home in London (very convenient) – certain trivia stayed in my head. For example, the fact that Swimbridge had a milepost on its platform marked 204 from London (via Bristol of course). On setting off one day in the car from Ealing for my weekend break at home in Devon, I set the mileage recorder in the car as I drove away and then checked the mileage again as I passed the approximate spot of that old mile post; the car had recorded 204 miles – via the M4, the M5 and Bristol, of course!

So the line is still part of my life and this book was a project for me to learn more about my railway hobby, the local history of my area and its development, to the extent that was brought about by the coming of the railway. It is, as I like to say (and as my polo friends will understand), 'my line' and I am delighted to share my research with you whether your reason for reading the book is due to your railway interest, local historical interest or perhaps both. The book is also a celebration of the beautiful countryside through which the railway ran. I have aimed to illustrate this with some of the photographs selected for reproduction, a number of which show the trains in the landscape.

In writing the book I have met some interesting and helpful people, none more so than Denis Bending, the father of my good friend Martin, who kindly told me his stories, some of which I have recorded in these pages. Sadly, Denis passed away on 8th March 2008. Also Jim Elson, signalman at Venn Cross in the 1940s, whose stories and photographs have helped bring the line and book alive. So it was with some sadness that I heard that Jim passed away on 5th December 2012, aged 85, but I am pleased that the memories of Jim and others (see acknowledgements and credits) who worked on the railway are recorded here. I am also grateful to Lady Arran who has written the Foreword.

The Devon & Somerset Railway's original motto on the company seal was '*Labor Omnia Vincit*' ('Hard Work Conquers All'); that has been my life's work ethic and has served me well but was sadly, ultimately, less rewarding for the old railway as it only lasted ninety-three years.

As a final point, in the historical research I found reference to the North Devon Railway (prospectus issued 1845; engineer I.K. Brunel). Although never built, the route of this line would have commenced at Launceston, then on to Okehampton and Hatherleigh (actually right through my sister Rose's house!) to Barnstaple, South Molton, Dulverton and finally Taunton – the five places *en route* being closely associated with my family and their roots. I do hope you enjoy my story of the D&SR.

Freddie Huxtable
Ealing, London, 2016

A Sonnet to Devon

Thy pleasant valleys, groves, and swelling hills,
Clothe their verdant beauty, all must own
Unrivalled in the land. But not alone
Thy fair domain, romantic Devon, fills
The gazer with entrancement: there are thrills
Of feeling more intense-a finer tone
Pervades the raptured soul, as nobly prone
To share or kindle gladness, or the ills
Of darker hours soothe, with that sweet art,
Which pure and gentle spirits only know,
Thy matchless daughters hospitably smile
A welcome to the stranger, who shall throw
His farewell glance in pain, and find the while
Sweet home-feeling lingering in his heart.

Reproduced from the *Great Western Railway Magazine*, November 1891.

Acknowledgements

This book would not have been possible without significant help from many people. It is my best intention to list them all here and I hope there are no omissions. Where possible and appropriate, I have also credited them in the body of the book.

So my thanks go to the railwaymen whose stories enthralled me – Jim Elson (signalman), Brindley Prust (driver), Dennis Bending (parcels), Harry Kirkland (fireman), Melvyn Baker (fireman), John Howard (signal & telegraph engineer) and Mrs Joyce Stone (widow of Eric Stone, signalman). Other authors, especially Ian Coleby, who gave me such great guidance and encouragement at the start, but also Sue Farrington, Richard Derry, Richard Antliff, Mike Christensen OBE (who did a sterling job reviewing and providing technical input on the signalling chapter), Amyas Crump and Kevin Robertson. My long-standing friend Thomas Hayes, who amongst other things explored the closed Dulverton station with me in the late 1960s and walked those parts of the the line with me that could be traversed in the 2007-15 period. My long-standing friend Martin Bending, for promising to finish the book if I didn't and who provided useful guidance on railway matters and modelling. Special thanks are due to Lady Arran for agreeing to write the foreword, thereby creating that link between her family and the origins of the railway with my book. Credit is due to Karina Varma for designing the website (www.devonandsomersetrailway.co.uk) I am using to promote this and the following volume, as well as furthering knowledge of the line. Also to my mother, for her memories and Alison for her patience.

The photographers and those who have supplied pictures: Peter Gray, Peter Barnfield, John Spencer Gilks, the late Owen Mogg (Peter Triggs), the late Peter Treolar, Tim Stephens, Roy Denison, Gordon Bray, James G. Tawse, Stephen Derek, Hugh Davies, Roger Joanes, the late Michael J. Fox (Brian Stephenson), the late Ron Lumber (David Mitchell), Colin Caddy, David Burgess, Stephen Linney, Richard Antliff, David Burgess and John Alsop.

The modellers: Chris Nelder, Martin Bird, Mark Henshaw, Derek Garrett, Tony Hiscock, Douglas Grindlay, Jose Kimble, the Rev'd Canon Brian Arman, Maurice Sandell, Brian Morgan, Ian Harrison, Martin Tester and Norman Solomans.

Those who have helped generally, such as William Hancock, Wesley Wyatt, Graham Robertson, John B. Perkin, Ian Harrison, Mary Proffitt, Toni & Francois Jones, Rob Doidge, Derek Goodwin, Ken Morrish of the Grosvenor Church, Max Perry, Sylvia Manley, Stephen Jarvis, Mr & Mrs Anning (Venn Cross, goods shed), Mr & Mrs Wilson (Venn Cross booking office), Roddy Kane (Bathealton Tunnel) and Dr Sarah Blackburn (Dulverton goods shed). My grateful thanks too to Andrew Neale and Bob Schofield for their invaluable assistance in compiling the table listing the contractor's locomotives. Not forgetting my English teacher, Hilary Binding, who sadly died in December 2014 before seeing the publication of this work.

Those who have helped at a number of museums: Peter Treharne, at the West Somerset Railway Museum, Blue Anchor; Jenny Yendall, Alison Ricks, Andy Hedges and Phil Tonkin at the South Molton Museum; Ruth Spiers at the North Devon Museum, Barnstaple; North Devon Athenaeum, Barnstaple; Judith Elsdon and Patrick at Tiverton Museum; Elaine Arthurs at STEAM, the Museum of the Great Western Railway at Swindon; Laurence Waters of the Great Western Society at Didcot; Braunton Museum; Jan Ross OBE of the Dulverton Heritage Centre; and David Bird and others of The Railway Correspondence & Travel Society.

Significant research was carried out at the National Archives, Kew, the National Railway Museum, York, the Wiltshire Records Office at Chippenham, Somerset Archives & Local Studies at Taunton, at the Barnstaple Athanaeum and North Devon Records Office. The National Railway Museum proved invaluable for research and access, and the use of images from its photographic collection. Also Mr Warwick Burton of the Brunel University, Mowat Collection (3 Fairway, Clifton, York, YO30 5QA), the Lens of Sutton Association; Roger Carpenter; Robert Blencowe; Stephen Edge and David Holmes of the West Somerset Railway Association Journal; the Industrial Railway Society; and the Lynton & Barnstaple Railway and its associated magazine.

I am also indebted to the Signalling Record Society, the Great Western Study Group (and its Yahoo group members) and the Great Western Society, in particular Adrian Knowles.

Finally, I must specifically thank Lightmoor Press for taking on this project so enthusiastically and to Neil Parkhouse in particular for guiding a novice author professionally through the requirements of a publisher. He has further enhanced the book with some unique photographs from his own collection and given much assistance with additional information for many of the captions.

Whilst every effort has been made to make the appropriate credits, it is not the intention to miss out anyone, so if it transpires there is an omission please let the author or publisher know so the matter can be put right in the future. Every effort has been made to identify and credit images wherever possible. Where there is no credit it will be the author's own, where it belongs to a collection this too is noted. Should an error have occurred this is entirely unintentional and if notified will be corrected in any subsequent edition.

Footnotes

I would like to point out that the use of 'Devon & Somerset Railway (or D&SR)' and 'Taunton to Barnstaple line' mean the same thing to me and are used interchangeably in the script. In reality, very few people in later years ever referred to it as the Devon & Somerset Railway but I quite like the original name, especially as it links my two favourite counties.

There are a number of quoted phrases and paragraphs in the text, selected from original board minutes, contracts, newspapers, etc, from the Victorian era. I make no apology for using Victorian English, as it gives an accurate historical representation of the relevant topic.

Every effort has been made to accurately record and reproduce my research. It is, I suspect, inevitable there will be some errors, minor I hope but they are solely my responsibility. However, I shall be grateful to anyone who points out any such errors or indeed is able to provide further information on the railway and its operations. If there is a second edition any need for revision or amendment will be taken into account.

Finally, any references to time in this book are based on the 12-hour clock throughout. BR adopted the Continental 24-hour clock in 1965, just one year before the line closed.

CHRONOLOGY

KEY DATES RELATING TO THE DEVON & SOMERSET RAILWAY (D&SR)

1842 The broad gauge main line of the Bristol & Exeter Railway (B&ER) reaches Taunton.

1844 1st May; the broad gauge reaches Exeter.

1845 Brunel has a plan for a 'North Devon Railway' running between Taunton and Barnstaple and beyond.

1848 The first railway to enter Barnstaple, from Fremington, is opened (25th April).

1854 The Exeter & Crediton Railway is extended to Barnstaple (as the North Devon Railway).

1863 Plans for a railway between Norton Fitzwarren and Ilfracombe are resurrected.

1864 The Devon & Somerset Railway Act is passed by Parliament and the first sod is cut at Hacche Moor (South Molton); construction commences from the Barnstaple end of the line.

1866 The Norton Fitzwarren to Wiveliscombe section is staked out but construction is halted. The Devon & Somerset Railway (Capital) Act allows for replacement of 8,000 unissued ordinary shares to the value of £200,000 with new 5% preference shares and debenture bonds of £166,000.

1868 The D&SR undergoes its first scheme of arrangement, with £270,000 of 6% debenture stock being issued.

1870 Construction begins again after a period of nearly four years.

1871 On 8th June, the line is opened to Wiveliscombe (7$^1/_2$ miles).

1872 By February, broad gauge track has been laid between Barnstaple and South Molton. The Devon & Somerset Railway Act of 1872 is passed to secure a further £100,000 of capital to continue the project.

1873 On 1st November, regular train services begin between Taunton and Barnstaple.

1874 On 20th July, the Barnstaple to Ilfracombe line opens (London & South Western Railway (L&SWR), standard gauge). The Devon & Somerset Railway Act of 1874 is passed to secure a further £60,000 of capital to continue the project.

1876 The Great Western Railway (GWR) takes over operation of the D&SR. Morebath, East Anstey and Molland stations are given passing loops and there are improvements at Barnstaple.

1877 The D&SR goes into receivership but continues operation.

1881 The whole line is converted from broad gauge to standard gauge over the 'long' weekend of 15th-17th May.

1884 The Tiverton & North Devon Railway opens from Dulverton to Tiverton (1st August).

1885 The Exe Valley Railway opens through to Exeter (1st May).

1887 The connecting spur to Barnstaple Junction (L&SWR) is opened (1st June).

1888 The D&SR goes to the Court for a Scheme of Arrangement, which is approved. This capitalises outstanding loan interest payable on the debenture stocks.

1893 October, the Electric Train Staff is introduced on the line.

1901 The GWR purchases the D&SR.

1904 There are further improvements to the line; Swimbridge gets a loop and Up platform, Dulverton gets a new siding and signal box and Barnstaple a further goods siding.

1905 On 1st July, the connecting spur between the East and South Junctions at Barnstaple is opened and the GWR make other improvements to facilitate the running of more trains. Venn Cross gets a loop line and an Up platform.

1928 Electric Key token is introduced between Dulverton and East Anstey.

1930s The line has its halcyon days of holiday travel. Further track and signalling improvements are made along it in 1937 and the line adopts Electric Key token exchange, with Whitaker apparatus fitted to locomotives to facilitate token exchange at higher speeds.

1948 The railways are Nationalised.

1949 Barnstaple GWR renamed Barnstaple Victoria Road on 26th September.

1950s As the war years fade and prosperity returns to the people, holiday travel by rail increases and the line sees busy summer Saturdays, with through trains to and from Ilfracombe.

1960 On 11th June, Barnstaple Victoria Road closes to passenger traffic but remains open as a goods depot.

1963 The Beeching Report is published on 27th March. This schedules the line for closure in August 1965. Meanwhile, the Exe Valley line closes on 7th October.

1964 Freight traffic ceases at all intermediate stations, as does steam haulage on the line.

1965 The final year of summer Saturday through trains.

1966 The last passenger train runs on Saturday 1st October and the line is closed with effect from Monday 3rd October.

1967 Track lifting commences and is completed by the following year.

1970 Barnstaple Victoria Road goods depot closes and the track is lifted.

1988 Construction of the North Devon Link Road (NDLR) begins, resulting in the destruction of a number of D&SR bridges and the stations at Swimbridge and Filleigh.

1989 On 18th July, the NDLR opens at the Barnstaple end, its route from South Molton following the course of the D&SR.

2007 The West Somerset Railway (WSR) starts to reclaim some of the old D&SR trackbed at Norton Fitzwarren, towards the old Allerford road bridge, for a triangle to reverse trains.

2010 Ballast and track is laid on the old D&SR trackbed towards Allerford bridge.

2011 At the Norton Steam Fayre in August, diesel rides are given on the Allerford spur and a passenger carrying service of sorts runs on part of the route for the first time in forty-five years.

2012 The triangle at Norton is officially opened at the 25th anniversary Steam Fayre on Saturday 4th August and Allerford spur is operational. Locomotives begin to be turned on the triangle on gala days.

2014 At the Norton Steam Fayre on 2nd-3rd August, brake van rides allow passengers to travel on the Barnstaple chord and Allerford spur for the first time.

CHAPTER 1

A BRIEF HISTORY OF THE REGION SERVED BY THE DEVON & SOMERSET RAILWAY

Before embarking on a history of the development of the Devon & Somerset Railway, it is important to look at the area that was served by it and the main towns and villages, so that the line's 'worth' can be put into proper context.

DEVON

'When the sun shines in Devon we go out and welcome it.'
From *Glorious Devon*, a holiday book (1932)

Devon or, as it was once, Devonshire, is situated in the heart of the South West peninsula. It rains but that rain gives the county the lushness that is its label. It is the most consistently hilly of regions, with its trade mark deep and wooded valleys and is unique among counties in that it has two separate coast lines. The northern coast is rugged and barren, once the preserve of ship wreckers and smugglers, now of surfers. The southern coast line is the self-styled 'Devon Riviera', that title in itself being inviting as was presumably the intention. The weather seems to have been consistently better over the years in the south than the north but that does not seem to have deterred the holiday trade over the years which has long been one of North Devon's more important industries.

A brief summary of the area broadly served by the railway is best described from an extract of *Thorough Guides – North Devon and Cornwall*, published in 1892 (6th Edition):

> *'That portion of West Somerset and North Devon with which we are concerned is a country of deep wooded combes and glens and bright trout streams, and the thirty-odd miles from Minehead by Lynton to Ilfracombe are at least equal in beauty to any like distance in Great Britain. On the one hand is a coast-line singularly rich in colouring and varied in outline, and on the other for many miles the high rolling hills of Exmoor. Exmoor itself is wild and desolate. Speaking generally, its central parts are also uninteresting, but a walk or drive across it will be enjoyed by those who can appreciate a breezy moorland intersected by deep, occasionally well wooded and always stream-gladdened combes. Its outskirts are on all sides delightful, and the views to be had from such points as Porlock Hill, Dunkery Beacon and Ridge Head are not only wide but very beautiful.*
>
> *Exmoor is the home of the red deer which still roam wild over it. They are most abundant in the woods and combes about Dunkery Beacon, but the Badgeworthy valley and especially the Doone valley are as likely spots as any for a sight of them by those who do not join in their pursuit.*
>
> *... the climate of North Devon is not, as is often supposed, relaxing. On the contrary, in many parts it is distinctly bracing. The winters are as a whole less cold, and the summers less hot, than the central and south-east parts of England. The rainfall varies from 35in to 45in per annum, but this, though much more than the average of the Home Counties for instance, must not lead the intending visitor to expect any serious inconvenience during the spring or summer from wet weather. When, for example, it rains on Exmoor it rains in earnest, and after perhaps for some weeks the weather is unbroken. Even in those seasons that are showery there is the compensating advantage of seeing the green and ferny combes and glens at their very best. Devonshire should certainly be visited during the interval from May to October, as its beauties are largely those of wood and fern.'*

In order to encourage the potential traveller to the region, the guide goes on to indicate the distances and times to key destinations. For example: from London to Dulverton (184 1/2 miles and 4 1/2 hours) and Barnstaple (208 miles and 5 3/4 hours; Birmingham to Dulverton (158 1/2 miles and 4 3/4 hours) and Barnstaple (182 miles and 5 3/4 hours). So, by 1892, the railway had clearly been doing its part to help open up this beautiful region.

Ports in the Bristol Channel were served by boats from Bristol itself, as well as from much farther afield, including Liverpool, Manchester, Dublin and London. Before the advent of the railways, the sea was the most practical way to get provisions to the North Devon and West Somerset areas. The main ports were Bridgwater, Watchet, Minehead, Ilfracombe and Barnstaple. As will be seen, these places unsurprisingly featured in many of the early railway schemes and proposals for the region discussed elsewhere in this book.

The name Devon is derived from a Celtic tribal name, the Dumnonii, '*the people of the land*', which later developed (AD823) to the Defnas, which in turn led to Defnum (894), Defenum (897) and Defenun (in a charter of 955).

BARNSTAPLE

In the late 1800s, Barnstaple was a thriving municipal town and the commercial capital of North Devon. It is situated on the north bank of the River Taw, some eight or nine miles, as measured along the channel, from its mouth. As the 1892 guide says:

> *'Seen from the southern bank it has a particularly pleasing appearance and situation. The broad river, the long bridge, the lofty tower of Holy Trinity Church, are the prominent features, whilst behind the town rise the well-timbered slopes and gently-swelling hills that completely shelter it from the north. Though of great antiquity, Barnstaple presents now scarce a trace of its former self. In the time of Athelstan it not only existed, but its defences were dilapidated with age and were by him repaired. It retained its walls for many centuries; but in 1842 the last remnant of them was removed'.*

Barnstaple is over 1,000 years old. It was Abertawe to the ancient Britons, meaning standing in the mouth of the Taw (Taw meaning '*the silent one*'). In Saxon times it was known as Beardestaple (or Beardastapol), the stapol (meaning pillar or post) or market of Bearda. No one is really sure who Bearda was but he may have been a local captain of Egbert, King of Wessex. However, one other name for the town has subsisted, Barum – from the latin *Barumensis*.

King Alfred's grandson Athelstan had a wall built around the town to fortify it. It is not clear whether Athelstan granted Barnstaple the status of a Borough (circa AD930) but he did establish a mint in the town. By the Doomsday period (1086) there were around 350 people living in Barnstaple, a sizeable settlement at that time and it was one of the four Doomsday Boroughs of Devon (the others being Exeter, Lydford and Halwill), belonging to the King. By 1377, the population was around 1,000.

Given its location there was a natural connection to the sea and farming. Barnstaple was an important port as early as the 13th century, for trading in wool (from local fulling or tucking mills), shipbuilding and warfare (five ships from Barnstaple were sent to fight the Spanish Armada in 1588). Cargoes were carried between Barnstaple and the Welsh ports of Milford Haven, Carmarthen and Tenby, and included commodities such as whale oil, dried fish, wine, cheese, salt, pepper and ginger. In return came tin, barley, wheat and rye, leather, rabbit skins and sheep fells. By the 16th century, Barnstaple's population had risen to circa 2,000. Like several towns in the area, Barnstaple changed from Roundheads to Royalists a number of times during the Civil War, the Roundheads becoming ultimately triumphant. However, by the end of the 17th century, the town's anti-royalist leanings had virtually faded away. The plague came in 1646, resulting in a number of deaths. Four brothers found a bundle of old clothes while fishing in the Taw, caught the disease and died, and the epidemic spread. One Royal Charter was surrendered in September 1684, with another granted in the following October.

The roads in the area were little more than packhorse routes, over which were transported loads of wood, bundles of woven cloth, peat, coal, corn, hay, straw, lime, sand and yard dung. Leith carts and highland sledges (known as 'truckamucks') were the main mode of transport. Written communication was poor; letters would take twenty days to arrive. A foot postman was established and every Tuesday, starting at 7am, he would walk from Barnstaple to the Postmaster's House in Exeter. Arriving on the Wednesday, post would go forward to London and when the London mail arrived, the postman would head back, arriving in Barnstaple on the Friday night or Saturday morning. Carrying cost was 6d for a single page letter and 8d for a double page (there were no envelopes in those days). The roads had to be improved, so turnpike trusts were set up to collect tolls, the money raised going towards their rebuilding and repair.

In the 1700s, local merchants were still trading with Spain and France (as they had been since the Middle Ages), Newfoundland (since Elizabethan times) and the American Colonies (since the Stuarts). Barnstaple was exporting clothes, baize, kerseys and coarse cloths. America would send back deerskins, timber and tobacco. Baize was the principal manufactured product of the town in the 1770s and 80s. Marshall's description of 1796 is worth quoting:

> *'The town of Barnstaple is respectable. The streets are wider and better laid out than old towns generally are. Many of the houses are substantially built of brick. But the covering is the same mean-looking slate as that which is in use at Bideford ... the day is set for rains; yet the appearance of the country is delightful beyond description. Perhaps rain, as a varnish, mellows the view.'*

The Barnstaple Bank established in 1791 was the town's first, followed by the North Devon Bank in 1807. Barnstaple was potentially under threat from Napoleon as he assembled a fleet at Boulogne, resulting in plans to evacuate the town and surrounding districts, with escape routes east to Somerton or south to Dartmoor.

Robert Westacott's shipyard opened in 1804 and was originally located near what is now Rock Park. Moved by Robert's son William to Bridge Wharf, on the south bank of the Taw just to the west of the road bridge in the 1840s, the Westacotts built briggs, sloops and schooners at this substantial yard for owners in London, Liverpool and Wales.

West Country trading ketches at Rolle's Quay, Barnstaple, just prior to the First World War. Situated at the mouth of the River Yeo, where it empties into the Taw, the quay was built by John Rolle (1st Baron Rolle 1750-1842) in the 1820s. Beyond the two sailing vessels is Rolle Street Bridge, which was rebuilt in the 1980s, whilst the signal on the right is on the route of the narrow gauge Lynton & Barnstaple Railway. ***Neil Parkhouse collection***

Road journeys were tortuous in the early 1800s and it took fourteen hours to get to Taunton, where passengers travelling between London and Barnstaple would spend the night. Bristol was reached by the next night and London at 5.00pm on the third day. The first mail coach arrived in Barnstaple on 23rd September 1827 and, by 1830, Taunton was a mere eight hours away and London thirty hours. Timings improved; the mail coach could average 10mph (including changes of horses) and then took five hours to get to Taunton, Bristol in eleven hours and London in a day. The coach departed Barnstaple at 6.00am, with a four-horse team in charge, from either the Golden Lion (established circa 1760), or the Fortescue Arms (circa 1780). Also in the early 19th century, the town was connected to London by a daily (not Sundays) stage coach travelling via Tiverton, Taunton and Salisbury. A rival four-horse coach service from the Fortescue Hotel (Arms) via Crediton and Exeter was set up in 1831; leaving at 11.30am, London was reached by 4.00pm the following day. Plymouth was also connected by stage coach for three days of the week, on Mondays, Wednesdays and Fridays.

Barnstaple expanded rapidly in the period from 1821 to 1851 and the population grew with it, from around 3,500 inhabitants in the early 1800s to a reported 8,667 by 1851. With the capacity to export and import, trades in the town flourished, such as victualling, rope making, chandlery and candle making. A factory opened at Pilton in 1844, turning out agricultural gloves and gaiters. In 1855, the covered market was built.

Gas production began in Barnstaple in 1833 but the town was not the most hygienic place to live and got slated in an inspection report of 1841; subsequently, cholera claimed twenty-four lives in 1849.

By 1870, the wool trade was virtually at an end but some wool staplers were still in business; however, lace making had taken over, with factories employing around 350 people in the 1880s. The shipbuilding industry managed to last until the First World War. Other local trades at this time included pottery (the clay around the town was suitable and plentiful), brewing, baking, lace and glove making, and the dyeing of wool and leather (by fellmongers) from the sheep bred by local farmers. These pelts were used for boots and gloves. During the 19th century, factories developed for these industries, and iron founding and cabinet making were established. Charles Brannam established Brannam's Pottery in 1879, and pottery and lace making survived well into the 20th century; Brannam's sadly closed in 2005. In the 1800s, the pottery produced utilitarian ware such as drainpipes, bricks and tiles, developing its wares for the household market in later years. There were three iron foundries at one point, supporting the local shipbuilding and agricultural industries. Huxtable's plough works (latterly located in Alexander Road) made farm equipment, such as the renowned reversible plough, along with cultivators, chain harrows and hoes. Three generations of Huxtables (all called John) worked in the family business. It was their grandfather that invented the reversible plough and they took over the Lake Foundry in the town, this being subsequently sold to Norringtons of Exeter. The Derby lace factory was established by Mr Boden or Bowden in the early 1800s and employed 250 people by 1889. The Pilton glove factory was subsequently acquired by Messrs Dent & Allcroft who, by 1937, had two factories and 350 employees. These industries were all supplemented by the usual smaller tradesmen such as butchers, blacksmiths, wheelwrights, braziers, tinners, plumbers, masons, coopers, maltsters, grocers, tailors, milliners and gun, saddle, rope and basket makers.

The port of Barnstaple was also involved with the importation of timber from North America and lime from Wales, and continued to have a thriving coastal traffic until the Taw Estuary silted up in the early 1800s, preventing access to Barnstaple's riverside quays; they were only partially replaced by the opening of Rolle's Quay in the later 1820s.

Barnstaple was opened up to Exeter (and on to London) when the railway arrived in 1854 on the south bank of the River Taw. The town advanced its clocks by fifteen minutes to adopt 'London time'. Mail, newspapers and other commodities were now more easily despatched and delivered and, by the 1890s, there were four letter deliveries and two parcels deliveries per day.

GREAT WESTERN RAILWAY
ROYAL MAILS

From the Tiverton Road Station, via Tiverton and South Molton, to Barnstaple, Bideford, and Ilfracombe.

The Public are respectfully informed, the MAIL COACHES are despatched from the above Station after the arrival of the Trains as under, viz.:–

LONDON MAIL, after the arrival of the Night Mail Train, which leaves Paddington at 8.55 P.M.; Bath, 12.50 A.M.; Bristol, 1.25 A.M.; Bridgwater, 2.35 A.M.; Taunton, 3 A.M.; and Tiverton Road Station, 3.35 A.M.; arriving at Barnstaple at 8 o'clock in the morning, Bideford half-past 9, and Ilfracombe a quarter before 10 in the morning.

BRISTOL DAY MAIL, after the arrival of the Train which leaves Bath, Mornings at 7.15; Bristol (Mail Train), 8 A.M.; Bridgwater, 9.20 A.M.; Taunton, 9.40 A.M.; and Tiverton Road Station, 10.18 A.M.; arriving at Barnstaple at 3 o'clock in the afternoon, in time for conveyances to Bideford and Ilfracombe.

N.B. Barnstaple is 36 miles from the Tiverton Road Station; Bideford, 44 miles; and Ilfracombe, 47 miles.– Dated Jan. 15, 1845.

The Boer War caused an increase in taxation and trade declined, deepening the gloom around the country for a time. However, 1899 was a year of improvement, with trade flourishing and the staple industries being kept busy. Fortunately, the town was growing, with new houses being built in the Newport district.

In 1901, the population stood close to 9,700 (the national figure being 32 million). Barnstaple gained an electricity generating station in 1903 whilst, by 1906, cars were appearing and, by 1913, the town was described as '*peacefully prosperous*'. It had shared in a trade boom and an increase in visitors to the area during the holiday seasons, which were enhanced in by a heatwave in 1911 and in 1913 by fine and dry weather. Despite the losses of the First World War, Barnstaple continued to grow, with the population at around 14,000 in 1915.

In the period around the end of the First World War, Barnstaple was chosen as a place to build ferro-concrete ships, a project supported by the Admiralty, the ample gravel supplies in the Taw Estuary being one of the key reasons. However, after a couple of ship launches, of mixed success, the project was abandoned and the company converted to the Manufactured Concrete Works.

By this time, cars were also starting to become more accessible; the Barnstaple Motor Company was selling cars for £250-£330. By 1919, a bus service was running between Ilfracombe, Barnstaple, South Molton and Westward Ho!. By 1924, with motor transport growing, road improvements were necessary, such as tar spraying on main roads (side roads were still formed of crushed stone). In 1924, the *North Devon Journal* reported that '*over a thousand cars … pass over a main road leading to Barnstaple in a day*'.

Consideration was given in the 1920s to damming the River Taw to the south of Barnstaple but this plan had been abandoned by

Left: The Square, Barnstaple circa 1925, with a fine array of early motor cars in view. Most of these are likely to be taxis waiting for trade. Note, too, the motor garage in the left background. The clock tower was paid for by public subscription and built in 1862 as a memorial to Prince Albert, Queen Victoria's husband, who died the previous year. It has long been known by locals as 'the four faced liar', because all four clock faces give slightly different times; refurbished a few years ago, it was decided not to correct this as it is now part of local tradition!

Below: A slightly later view of the Strand, with the clock tower just visible in the distance. Buses and charabancs wait for passengers on the right and a lorry makes a delivery to E.M. Pow's confectioner's shop on the left.
Both Neil Parkhouse collection

1930, in which year Barnstaple chose to celebrate its millenary. Although the actual date (and year) was uncertain, the celebrations were arranged for Saturday 9th August to 12th August 1930 and comprised various festivities including military bands, a water carnival and fireworks.

Over the next thirty or so years, Barnstaple changed and grew, its population rising to between 16,000 and 17,000 in 1951, and to approximately 34,000 in 2015.

The Pottington district was made available for industrial development and factories opened there. Seven Brethren, on the south bank of the Taw, was converted from a rubbish tip to an industrial estate. In the late 1970s, work commenced on the Barnstaple Relief Road and Whiddon Valley Industrial Estate. The first stage of the relief road was completed by 1982 and Barnstaple was made more accessible in the late 1980s with the opening of the North Devon Link Road.

THE STRAND, BARNSTAPLE.

SOUTH MOLTON

There is evidence to show that the area around what is now South Molton was inhabited in the Bronze Age (circa 1900-750 BC). However, it appears not to have formed into a true village settlement until Saxon times (circa AD 700), when its population may have been in the region of 100-200 people. It grew little in the next three to four hundred years and, by the 11th century, South Molton (or '*Sut Moltona*' or '*Sud Moltone*' as referred to in the *Domesday Book*) was still a small village settlement. Within a century of the Domesday survey of 1086, South Molton had been granted Borough status by Gilbert de Turberville and, by 1302, with a population of 1,800, it had grown sufficiently important to have two burgesses in Parliament. It was at this time, in the mid-to-late 12th century, that South Molton commenced its development as a significant market town, albeit set back a little by the Black Death as was the case in many similar towns and villages. From the late 14th century, the town settled into its role as a cloth making centre and it managed to maintain its position during a stagnated economic period between 1350 and 1500.

South Molton was granted a charter incorporating the Borough by Elizabeth I in 1590 (which was renewed by Charles II in 1684), which gave the burgesses greater powers of self regulation and government, and enabled it to have weekly markets and an annual fair. Incorporation as a Municipal Borough was an important step in enhancing the town's status. It prospered in the period 1500 to 1640, when there was a national rise in demand for wool and the population grew due to the burgeoning woollen trade. South Molton was a centre for trade, merchants were based there and farmers brought their wool to trade at the market. It was a labour intensive industry and this increased the demand for food and goods in the area. The farmers were also dependent on grazing rights over land on Exmoor to maintain the supply of sheep and wool.

By the start of the 17th century, the population was most likely between 2,000 and 2,500 people. The major industry and source of wealth remained the wool and cloth industry and at the time there was a significant export market for these products.

In 1642, the Civil War touched South Molton. The war in Devon continued until April 1664, trade suffered and there was death through disease. Although the Royalist forces held most of the northern part of the county for the majority of the war, Fairfax had finally taken Devon for the Parliamentarians by April 1646.

The charter granted by Charles II in 1684 (renewing the one of 1590), gave the town the right to elect its own mayor and corporation and free its residents from the feudal duties and dues previously levied. This set the pattern of government for South Molton for the next 150 years. Trade in the town continued as before, being mainly agriculture and the wool and cloth industries. Whilst trading was still done through market stalls, retail shops began to open in the 1700s. However, most major dealings by farmers were done at the bi-annual cattle and horse fairs in the town. Farming was based on sheep, primarily providing wool for the local industry, but grass was cut and cereals were cultivated for both animal feed and sale.

During the 18th century, there was a gradual decline in the cloth industry, due to a failure to adopt new production techniques and also not adapting to changes in fashion, including the nature of the cloth produced. The export market declined and wages were high relative to other areas which were involved in such production. In this same century, the road network developed, along with coach services as the roads improved; London was twenty-four hours from Exeter in 1785. There was a twice weekly coach service from Tiverton to South Molton and Barnstaple, on Wednesdays returning Thursday evenings and then the same on Fridays, returning Sundays. The mail coach fares cost 4d per mile or £2. 10s to London, so it was an expensive means of travel. George Huxtable ran a stage wagon twice a week to Exeter in 1795 (leaving early on Mondays, returning late Tuesdays), costing 2s. 6d for passengers for a fifteen hour journey. At this time, William Warren also ran a wagon service from Taunton to Barnstaple, arriving at South Molton at midday on Tuesdays. The return trip from Barnstaple arrived on Wednesday evenings and left at 6.00am on Thursday mornings for Taunton.

In the mid-18th century, South Molton was prosperous, partly due to the death of Hugh Squirer who bequeathed the tolls of the markets and fairs in the town. The Guildhall was built at this time, followed by the Market House. North Devon had a typhus outbreak in 1741-42 and was ravaged by smallpox between 1750 and 1770, so population growth was hit by this.

By 1801, the population of the town was recorded as 2,753 (circa 2,200 being involved in manufacturing and 544 in agriculture). In 1835, Parliament passed the Municipal Reform Act and South Molton became part of this standard and democratic system, which was introduced nationally by the Act. The corporation became a town council of four alderman and twelve councillors. This change brought a new enthusiasm to the local government and life of the town. As the census shows, the population of South Molton steadily increased to 4,482 in 1851, largely due to the national increase in economic activity, being commercial, industrial and agricultural. By 1851, the businesses in the town comprised retail shops of many descriptions, along with small workshops and two woollen factories (employing over 300 people) and two tanneries.

A gas light company was set up in 1836 and a new sewage works began to function in 1869. By mid-December 1863, a new Pannier Market was built along with the Assembly Rooms. The market would turn out to be a good income earner and could seat 2,000 people for a meal. The Assembly Rooms could seat 400 people. In the late 1800s, the number of sheep in the area declined but the number of cattle increased and corn, green-crop and fallow acreage decreased. By 1870, farming was in depression caused by cheap imported grain (mainly from the USA), frozen beef from Argentina, and mutton and lamb from Australia and New Zealand. However, by 1871 (two years before the D&SR opened), the population had decreased to 3,978 and continued to decline to 3,340 in 1881, 3,126 in 1891, 2,848 in 1901 and 2,773 in 1911. This decline initially had an impact on road traffic. The Turnpike Trust set up by Act of Parliament in 1839 controlled five roads in and out of the town but, by 1870, the Trust was struggling financially and was wound up by 1882, a few years after the railway arrived.

The South Molton area had copper mines in the period 1860-1885 and a cloth industry but these never significantly changed the town in terms of size or prosperity, which maintained its identity as a typical west country market town that had first developed in the middle ages. A regular weekly market was established providing an outlet for surplus produce, this taking place in Broad Street and the Square.

If there was expansion and decline for South Molton in the Victorian era, then the 20th century brought a revival. The population had increased slightly to 2,843 by 1921 but the First World War had a dramatic effect on the town; it lost forty-seven men and it took about twenty years to shake off the impact of the conflict. However, tourism was a growing business by the 1920s and this was of benefit to the whole area. At the same time, the motor car was beginning to infiltrate life and several local traders adapted to cater for this new mode of transport.

The Old English Fayre was revived in 1930 and this provided funds to support the Cottage Hospital. The town first got its electricity in the 1930s from the Exe Valley Electricity Company, whilst the telephone had arrived a decade earlier but only a few businesses used it to start with; the market day at that time was still the focal hub of communication. By 1931, the population was 2,866, the number of inhabitants thus remaining relatively stable. At this time, the town's prosperity was seasonal, largely due to the requirement of casual labour in agriculture.

During the Second World War, South Molton accommodated evacuees from London and other cities, and hosted American soldiers, who were training locally on Exmoor.

The number of shops and traders increased in variety in the post war years, reflecting the changing local demands; a number of banks opened, a cinema was licensed, and a wireless and antiques dealer appeared. There was also a drift of the rural population to the town, so its numbers began to grow to reflect this. The new cattle market, located just off the centre of the town, was opened in 1961.

South Molton needed the railway. Various local projects promised rail connections to the town, like the abortive branch off the Taw Valley line (see the North Devon Railway, page 25). The nearest station in the 1850s and 1860s was South Molton Road (now Kings Nympton) on that line but it was a nine mile trek by road. In this period of time, South Molton began to lose out to nearby and better connected towns, such as Crediton and even Eggesford, where, on the second Wednesday of every month, there was a market and cattle sale at the Fox & Hounds Hotel near the railway. A cattle market also opened at Molland with the opening of the D&SR line and this too was competition for South Molton. The whole matter was compounded by the start of a twenty year depression in agriculture that reduced trade generally. So, arguably, it was more the late arrival of the railway that slowed or halted the town's growth. The railway also had an impact on the Turnpike Trust (referred to above) and also the local road carriers that worked to and from Barnstaple and Tiverton, as these declined from a reported ten in 1850 to two in 1866 and, by 1878, it seems the GWR carrier at the station was the sole representative.

South Molton's other industries were also in decline, such as woollen cloth making. The factory of Bawden, Cresswell & Bawden, set up in 1800, lost out in the 1830s to power looms. There were other factories (such as the two owned by W. Hitchcock) but these had closed by the 1890s. The tanners operating from the town struggled when railways reached the area and lost out to Eggesford and Molland. Mining was successful, although the limestone quarries struggled to complete with the cheaper stone brought in by rail. The four mines in the North Molton area producing copper and iron ore helped the town, with miners spending their wages in local hostelries. Somewhat surprisingly, perhaps, Devon is believed to have produced half the world's copper in 1855. Extracts from the Bampfylde Mine show that copper fetched nearly £10 per ton in the 1860-81 period. However, by the end of the century, cheaper imports of both copper and iron ore meant it was uneconomic to keep these local mines open (see the Mining section, pages 21-22).

The Square, South Molton looking west in 1930s. The Guild Hall with its clock tower and the entrance to the Pannier Market is on the left. The building in the centre is the Post Office, built in 1888; to the left of it, the road turns sharply to make its way south to Crediton and Exeter, whilst the road to the right heads more or less straight on to Barnstaple and Ilfracombe. Apart obviously from the motor cars, this scene remains remarkably little changed today. The station was poorly sited for the town, however, being about three-quarters of a mile away to the north. *Neil Parkhouse collection*

RIGHT: Dulverton High Street looking west circa 1890. The pony and trap would no doubt have made frequent trips to and from the railway station, some mile and a half distant. The route to it lay over the River Barle bridge, visible in the centre background, then south alongside the river to Brushford. Note the beer house on the right.

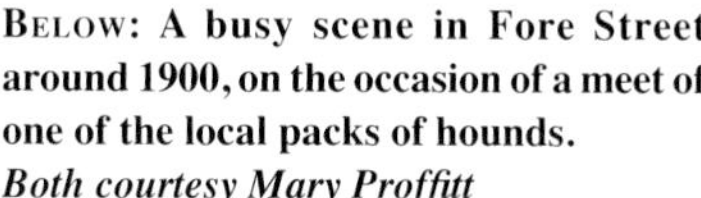

BELOW: A busy scene in Fore Street around 1900, on the occasion of a meet of one of the local packs of hounds.
Both courtesy Mary Proffitt

SOMERSET

Located to the east of north Devon, West Somerset shares similar geographical and geological features to its neighbour. Exmoor continues into Somerset with its characteristic moorland but the northern coast line of the county becomes less wild as it runs eastwards beyond Minehead. With similar woodlands and valleys, the area is primarily agricultural with cattle and sheep farms prevalent.

DULVERTON

It is understood that a settlement at Dulverton dates from the late Iron Age. The first Royal Charter was granted in 1278 and the town was a key location for trading wool, leather and iron. A second charter was granted in 1306 and this established a Thursday market. The Black Death in the 1340s halved the population and Dulverton suffered a long period of decline, until Henry VII granted a fresh and amended charter enabling weekly markets, two three-day fairs and a Piepowder Court* for the first time. The area had a range of industries, including spinning, weaving, fulling and grist mills, and tanneries. Dulverton again had a set-back in prosperity at the time of the dissolution of the monasteries in 1539. In 1555, John Sydenham of Combe applied for a charter on behalf of the people of Dulverton and this was granted in 1556, with William Babbington becoming Lord of the Manor until he sold it to Sydenham in 1558.

Dulverton's industries continued and those mentioned above were joined by harness and saddle-makers, boot and shoemakers, tailors, dressmakers and hatters. The essential butchers, bakers, chandlers, blacksmiths, wheelwrights and coffin-makers also plied their trades. The weekly markets continued to be the centre of this hub, as these brought in traders from further afield, with news and foreign goods.

Dulverton had 232 families in 1822 and was a market town, with roughly half its population engaged in agriculture, the other half in trade or manufacturing.

In the late 1800s, Lord Carnarvon, who was then Lord of the Manor, made the decision to move the cattle market from the town to a site near the (new) railway station at Brushford and the Carnarvon Arms Hotel, which he was building; the market opened on 5th August 1873. This spurred the locals to refurbish their homes to create accommodation for potential visitors brought in by the railway.

*A special tribunal in England organized by a borough on the occasion of a fair or market, which had unlimited jurisdiction over personal actions for events taking place in the market, including disputes between merchants, theft and acts of violence.

Outside of the town, hunting has played a key role since Iron Age times. King Harold made it his own and William I then claimed it, and Dulverton remained within the Royal Forest of Exmoor until 1279. It was then bestowed upon one of the Knight family, who was made Lord of the Manor. One of the main packs in the area was, and continues to be, the Dulverton East Foxhounds (now renamed as the Dulverton Farmers Hunt), kennelled at East Anstey. Dulverton was also a key location from which to follow the Devon & Somerset Staghounds, who were and are based at Exford but who held a number of meets during the season local to the town and the railway.

By the mid 1880s, the town had two main streets with well-built houses. Silk manufacturing had also been established by then. Cattle and sheep breading and rearing had been vital to the town's economy for many years and, by 1889, a monthly toll-free market was held on the first Tuesday of each month. There was work for the labourers and also those who provided support services, in the form of blacksmiths, wheelwrights, wagon-builders, millers, corn and feed merchants.

As the nation's prosperity spread and the tourist industry grew, Dulverton was able to offer more as the 'Gateway to Exmoor'. In 1928 the GWR publication *Somerset Ways* described the town thus:

'Dulverton, a low-built, sleepy township, claims to be the capital of moorland … Truly it is a valley of delight where the jumble of red homes and grey lies half-hidden in the woods. Dulverton is right on the edge of the moor, so it has less the essential moorland character than Exford has, which is why Exford in turn claims to be the capital of Exmoor.'

In 1934, the same publication expanded the description:

'… the adorable impetuous little river Barle rushes hurriedly through Dulverton … Dulverton is one of those places which have no relics of their history, and yet suggest an atmosphere of the past more successfully than many a town filled with medieval buildings.'

Dulverton had a set-back in August 1952, when the heavy rains that caused the Lynmouth flood disaster swelled the River Barle and surged down the Barle Valley, flooding the lower part of the town and damaging property.

By 1962, the population of the town was 1,464.

THE CARNARVON ARMS

The railway and the Carnarvon Arms grew together. The 4th Earl of Carnarvon (Henry Howard Molyneux Herbert) inherited his title in 1849 but came of age in 1852, at which time he took title to the lands. This included Pixton Park, between Brushford and Dulverton, which was built by John Dyke-Acland and became family property when the 2nd Earl married Elizabeth 'Kitty' Acland, John's daughter. Pixton was their country estate, whilst Highclere Castle in Hampshire was the principal seat. The railway had to cross the Earl's lands, so he began to take an interest in the venture. The D&SR needed to compulsorily purchase land affecting fifty-seven of his fields, one river, one mill leat, ten orchards, seventeen streams, four cottages, nine gardens, three dwelling houses, two offices, the parish school room and garden, a footpath, two pig houses, three woods, one furze, two coppices, a yard and out buildings, and a mowhay. Unlike his fellow peers, the Earl did not put up money, he looked to profit from the railway. Perhaps he had already invested in railway stocks elsewhere, so he was managing his risk. As a consequence, the plans for the cattle market and the Carnarvon

Dulverton station and the Carnarvon Arms Hotel, a view looking north circa 1900 and published as a commercial postcard a few years later. On the extreme right is the rear of the 1883 signal box, which was replaced by a new box at the end of the Up platform in 1904. However, this in turn was replaced in 1911, when the platforms were lengthened at the eastern end of the station. The single line running behind the Down platform led to a turntable, which was accessed from the west by a new siding after 1910. After crossing over the railway, the road (today the B3222) winds its way up the Barle Valley to the village of Dulverton, a mile and a half from its station. The conifer trees behind the hotel enclosed the cattle market established here by the 4th Earl of Carnarvon. The station was situated near the hamlet of Brushford, off picture to the left. ***Neil Parkhouse collection***

Arms were born. The livestock market was built first, located about 300 yards away from the station (towards Dulverton). It comprised two acres of grounds, with several enclosures, a yard for cattle, pens for sheep and an auctioneers stand and ring, all enclosed by fencing. He built it and staffed it at his own expense, and it was completed by 5th August 1873. This resulted in joyous opening celebrations, held in the goods shed at Dulverton. The market, operating on the second Tuesday of every month, with a monthly auction, was a great success. It had a dramatic effect on the existing market in Dulverton, which lost its importance. Although plans were in hand for the hotel by this time, the sheer volume of farmers attending the Pixton Market (as it was known) requiring refreshment and accommodation meant that the Earl had another potentially successful business venture to progress. The Carnarvon Arms, originally built as a sixteen-bedroom inn, with stabling for twenty horses, plus two cottages, was extended in 1906. The building stone was quarried at Kents (to the west of Brushford), whilst crushed stone for the drives and pathways came from Hulverton Quarry (also used for ballast by the railway) nearby.

The hotel opened on Tuesday 6th October 1874, with Mr James Nelder as its first landlord. Apart from the visiting farmers on market days, with the proximity of the railway, it was felt that the hotel could be a centre for those wishing to hunt with local packs, whilst the railway could provide transport for horses as well as riders. The Carnarvon Arms arranged a number of coach services such as the 'Tally Ho!' (to Lynton and Lynmouth) and the 'Wild West' (to Dunster and Minehead) to connect with the railway. The 'Tally Ho!' was subsidised by the GWR by 1890, to the tune of 10 shillings per journey – another attempt to compete with the L&SWR. Over the years, the hotel had a number of distinguished visitors, such as Alfred, Lord Tennyson and Prince Dhuleep Singh (son of Maharja Ranjit Singh, founder of the Sikh Empire).

Lord Carnarvon died on 5th April 1923 in Cairo, following the discovery of Tutankhamun's tomb; he had sponsored Howard Carter's exploration. On 4th February 1930, the Dowager Lady Carnarvon sold the hotel to the Nelder family. All other family holdings in Brushford were sold to tenants at this time, except Pixton Park which remained in the family until the death of Auberon Herbert in 1974. The hotel closed in 2001 due to the impact of foot and mouth on the business and was converted into flats for private use. More about the hotel's links with the area around Dulverton station can be found in Chapter 5.

WIVELISCOMBE

Wiveliscombe lies in the lee of the Brendon Hills, mid-way between Exmoor and the Vale of Taunton. An old market town, there is no mention of an urban settlement in the *Domesday Book* but it is likely that a small agricultural community existed at this time.

It has a strong agricultural heritage, primarily cattle and sheep farming. As a result of this, the town had a substantial woollen industry for 500 years, although the flatter surrounding landscape also supported some arable farming (mainly corn). There are records of a market in Wiveliscombe back as far as 1285, when King Edward I granted a charter for a fair or Pannier Market. Livestock sales were held four times a year and there were regular Tuesday and Saturday markets until the end of the 18th century, when only the Saturday markets remained. However, by the 19th century, market days were back to Tuesdays, the third one of each month being for the sheep and cattle auctions; major auctions were in February, May, July and September.

The Square, Wiveliscombe circa 1905, with a GWR delivery cart in front of the Town Hall. A *Kelly's Directory of Somerset* for 1902 does not list an appointed local cartage agent, so it is likley that this was a service operated directly by the GWR. *Neil Parkhouse collection*

A brewery was established in 1807 by William Hancock, this coming at the time the woollen industry was declining. Although the Hancock Brewery was closed in 1959, brewing returned to the town in 1980.

By the 19th century, there were a significant number of trades and industries in the town, partly due to the difficulties in travelling even to Taunton for basic provisions at that time. Thus the town was self-sufficient, because it had to be. Such trades and professions included saddlers, ironmongers, clothiers, tanners, dyers, bakers, a clock-maker, a wheelwright, solicitors, bankers, money lenders and others. The assizes were held in Taunton but the magistrates met locally. There was a slate quarry nearby at Oakhampton, which closed in 1880 but reopened in 1898, closing again, finally, just before the Great War.

Until the late 18th century, the town was not on any major through routes, so local lanes were the only means of access. The main road (or track) route to North Devon at this time was via Wellington and Tiverton. Under an Act of Parliament in 1786, the Wiveliscombe Turnpike Trust was set up, which led to the Barnstaple to Wiveliscombe road being turnpiked. In 1806, an Act was passed authorising the construction of a new road westwards from Milverton, through Wiveliscombe to Bullaford Gate, about six miles east of South Molton.

One of the engineers involved in building the railway, a Yorkshireman named Frederick John Littledale Rooke, attended the inaugural meeting of the Wiveliscombe Rugby Club in August 1872. He was elected the first captain of the club.

Despite its closeness to Taunton, Wiveliscombe was isolated until the railway came. Then, the Arnold & Hancock Brewery could compete with Starkey, Knight & Ford at Bridgwater. Cattle could be shipped further afield and other local produce such as rabbits, milk, butter and eggs could be sent to Bristol and London. However, in the early days, the feeder services from the farms and packing areas to the station was still by way of horse and cart. Indeed, it was the advent of the railway and the repeal of the 1865 Highways Act in 1896 that led to the development of a well known local business. Bessie Hill was a farmer's daughter and she helped her father by selling eggs, which she transported to the town. One day, a local grocer whom she supplied had a surplus of eggs and offered Bessie a derisory price. This spurred her into action and she contacted the provisions merchant in Bristol, a Mr Watkins, who was the outlet for her father's butter. She agreed to supply eggs to him as well and when his demand increased, Bessie's solution was to source them from other local farms and then transport them herself to the station with horse and cart for onward shipment to Bristol. In 1907, she married a local saddler, Thomas Langdon, but she carried on her egg business and this expanded into rabbits (with the wartime shortage of red meat) and, by the end of the war, she was sending about 1,500 rabbits a week to London, along with a significant quantity of eggs. The horses and carts were replaced in 1915 with a Model T Ford van. As a consequence, the Langdon Transport business was born and continues to this day, albeit from its base in Bridgwater.

TAUNTON

The name Taunton derives from 'town on the River Tone'. It is located between the Blackdown Hills to the south, the Brendon Hills in the west and the Quantock Hills to the north-west, in the area known as the Vale of Taunton.

The county town of Somerset was said to have been founded by Ine, King of Wessex in the 8th century. This was to control the local Britons who had reverted to tribalism following the collapse of the Roman Empire. A Saxon tribe known as the *Sumersaetan* then occupied the area (hence Somersetshire). King Ine constructed a timber stronghold which was destroyed in the Civil War twelve years later. The Normans built a castle at Taunton following the Conquest. By 1086, and as recorded in the *Domesday Book*, Taunton was owned by the Bishop of Winchester and was a prosperous manor. Despite occupation by Royalists during the English Civil War, the town was retained by the Cromwellians (who were in fact commanded by a local man, Robert Blake, who later became Cromwell's admiral and defended the town during the siege of Taunton from July 1644 to 1645). The Royalists got revenge later when they destroyed the town's fortifications and withdrew its charter. In 1685, James Scott, the 1st Duke of Monmouth, crowned himself King of England at Taunton during the attempt to overthrow James II, known as the Monmouth Rebellion. Judge Jeffreys lived in the town during the bloody assizes that followed the battle of Sedgemoor, in which Monmouth was defeated.

The town had received its charter of incorporation in 1627, which was renewed in 1677. However, it lapsed in 1792 and was not reincorporated until 1877. Taunton was known for its woollen industry and when this declined at the end of the 18th century, silk weaving took over as a major industry.

The Bridgwater & Taunton Canal was opened in 1827 and remained navigable until 1907. The Grand Western Canal reached Taunton in 1839, soon to be followed by the Bristol & Exeter Railway (B&ER), which opened on the 1st July 1842, providing a connection to Bristol and London. The line was extended to Wellington, opening on 1st May 1843, before reaching Exeter by 1844. On 27th March 1862, the branch line to Watchet opened.

EXMOOR

It is appropriate to provide a brief description of Exmoor (or Exemore as it once was). The railway arguably opened up this area to the tourist and although no station was located on Exmoor, as the line skirted the region there was a clear link. Largely untouched, the horse was the fastest means of transport and communication before the arrival of the railway, wheeled vehicles replacing pack horses and sledges in the early 1800s.

A Parliamentary survey in 1651 described the area as:

> '... *a mountainous and cold ground, much beclouded with thick fogs and mists and is used for agitating and depasturing of cattle, horses and sheep, and is very sound sheep pasture, but a very great part thereof is overgrown with heath and yielding a poor kind of turf of little value there, and a considerable part thereof lying upon the side of the combes lies near the rock and is capable only of being a sheep pasture, and the residue thereof being only some balls or hills if they were enclosed might be capable of improvement being a good soil.*'

Stretching from Porlock on the Bristol Channel in the north to Bray in the south (about 20 miles) and Martinhoe in the west to Dulverton in the east (about 35 miles), it was originally a vast area of moorland but this has been reduced over the years by cultivation. The Britons inhabited the area and built hill forts (remnants of which still remain today) but Roman incursion in to this part of Somerset is uncertain. However, Saxons came and then the Danes circa 997. It was a Royal Forest from Saxon times until 1818, being one of sixty-seven such regions in England. Although it is unlikely trees grew on large parts of the upper moorland (including that area still known as 'the forest' today), because of the altitude and climate, the area was designated for hunting (deer and wild boar) and had for a time its own 'Forest Law', which lasted until Edward I's reign (circa 1307), when the laws fell away. The whole of Devon had in fact been designated as a Royal Forest up until 1204, when it was disafforested by King John. The forest declined in Tudor times (1500s) and parts of it were leased in the 16th century.

Road access in the region was always poor. In 1653, it was possible to travel by road from Dunster to Barnstaple (via Exford, Simonsbath and Brayford) and from Lynton to South Molton (via Shallowford and Moles Chamber) but other roads were nominal.

A large swathe of the Exmoor Forest was bought from the Crown in 1818 by John Knight, an industrial magnate from Worcestershire. He embarked on a transformation of the moor and opened it up, building metalled roads and establishing mining enterprises, as well as a large agricultural estate. However, much of this development remained uncompleted at his death.

The Napoleonic Wars brought the first tourists to Exmoor, due to the restrictions imposed on foreign travel. Visitors went to coastal towns such as Lynton, Lynmouth and Porlock, access being by sea from Bristol. However, only the wealthy took holidays due to affordability and time – the working week was seven days until the six-and-a-half day week was introduced in 1871.

Exmoor was made a National Park in 1954 under the 1949 National Parks & Access to the Countryside Act and maintains its wide variety of beautiful scenery, from wooded combes and valleys to the ever-changing moorland, purple with the heather in the late summer, to bleak and foreboding in the winter. The area of the National Park is 692 square kilometres.

Mining in the North Molton Area

Towards the middle and late 1800s, there was a re-establishment of mining in the Heasley Mill area, to the north of South Molton, where there had been intermittent digging for centuries. The three main workings, the Bampfylde Mines (copper and iron), and the Crowbarn and New Florence iron mines, surrounded Heasley Mill – Bampfylde Mines just to the north, Crowbarn in Crowbarn Wood to the south-east and New Florence about one mile to the east, under the lee of Tabor Hill.

Mining on a small scale began in the 13th century. However, it is understood that large scale mine working was not undertaken until the 16th century, tunnelling being carried out without the use of explosives. It is recorded that German miners were specifically brought over for this work. In the 18th and early 19th centuries, some of the shafts were worked by horse 'whims' – a large winding drum upon a wooden frame, usually powered by one or two horses walking in a circle underneath the construction.The power of these wheels was later boosted by using water conveyed from other locations by leats. The coming of the steam engine was a further boost to the mines and their efficient operation, as their working was not reliant on fluctuating water power. Mine depths reached 90 to 112 fathoms.

During the 1870-90 period, large quantities of spathic iron ore were extracted, suitable for steel making by the Bessemer process. In 1874, Bamfylde Mine had four copper lodes producing ore valued at £17 per ton (when the West Country average was £5), along with manganese at £7 per ton; it was indeed a prosperous time, until there was a recession in the iron trade and the price of copper fell. Efficiencies of extraction, falling prices and the inability to raise capital funds to finance more powerful machinery were all contributing factors in the demise of the industry here. Florence Mine produced 38,386 tons of iron ore between 1873 and 1885, probably representing three-quarters of its production (per John Rottenbury in his thesis). This mine was finally abandoned in June 1894.

In 1871, William Bailey Hawkins and his brother Sydney, who were iron agents and who were working the Florence Mine with George Bush, were the first to consider a tramroad link with the D&SR. When built, it ran north up the Mole Valley from the D&SR, about half a mile east of South Molton station, near where the line crossed the River Mole. At Brinsworthy Bridge, about three miles from the

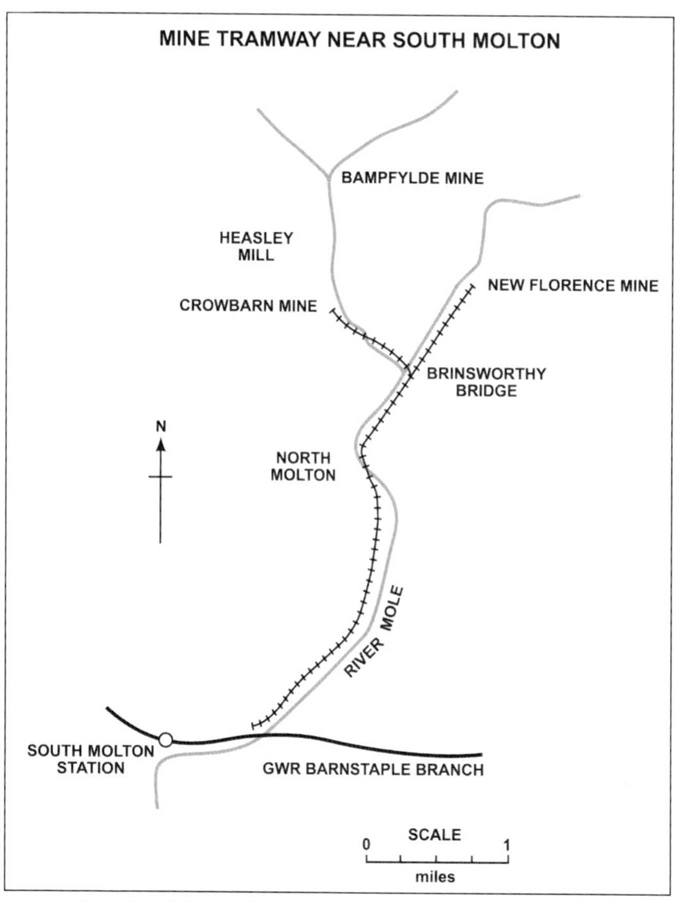

Above: Plan of the Florence Mining Co. tramway near South Molton.
Below: The transshipment wharf between the tramway and the D&SR, as shown on the 1889 edition 25 inch Ordnance Survey.

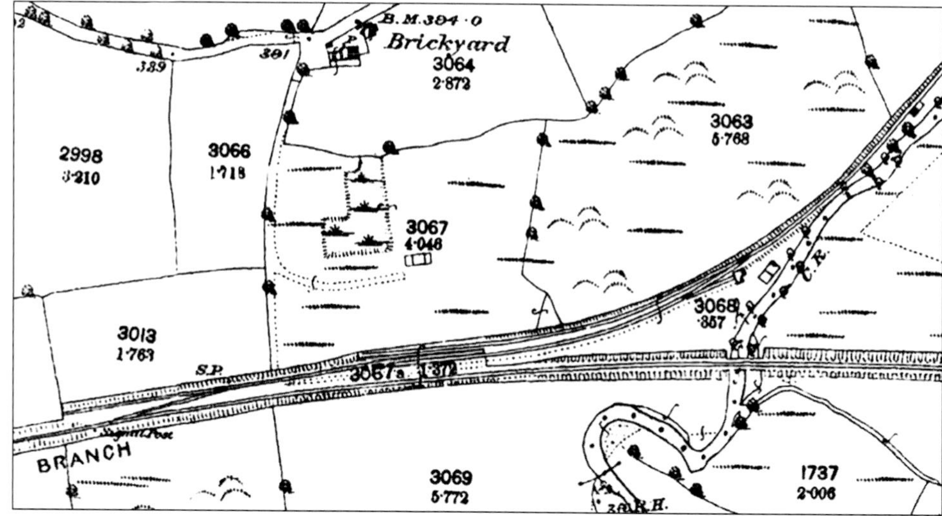

railway (north of North Molton and near where the two tributaries of the Mole meet) the tramway divided, one branch going towards Crowbarn Mine, the other to New Florence Mine.

Access to the railway allowed the mine owners to transport their ore to smelters around the UK and to ports for transshipment overseas. The tramway was horse-drawn and of 2 feet 6 inches gauge, with wagons being hauled up the Mole Valley, climbing from approximately 450 feet above sea level to around 900 feet. Loaded wagons heading down the valley often carried miners looking to enjoy their free time in the pubs of North Molton. The miners, known as 'Tributers', were mainly independent contractors and were skilled men, able to assess the quality of the ore to be extracted, their success or otherwise determining their financial rewards for the future. At times, up to 200 miners from Ireland, Cornwall and Wales could be present in the area, requiring serious policing after a few drinks!

Crowbarn Mine, south of Heasley Mill, was worked by open casting, unlike the others in the area. It is understood that Bampfylde Mine had been closed towards the end of the 18th century and again between 1820 and 1840 but it then operated fully until final closure circa 1894. The D&SR therefore had about twenty years of traffic coming off the mines north of South Molton.

The siding, located about half a mile east of South Molton station, gained Board of Trade approval (subject to minor rectifications) from Colonel Hutchinson in a letter dated 18th March 1874. The wharf complex comprised a single (broad gauge initially) siding with narrow gauge tramway sidings running either side. That to the north side was elevated above the railway siding to facilitate loading into D&SR wagons. The one on the south side was mainly for empties waiting to return up the valley but any materials bound for the mines could also be loaded here. Both the railway and tramway sidings appear to have had short headshunts ('blind sidings'). The signalling arrangements relating to the working of the wharf will be covered in Volume 2.

The Florence Mining Company was registered on 23rd December 1871 and built the tramway in 1874; the branch to Crowbarn Mine opened later, in 1877. The name then changed to the North Molton Ironstone Mines Company but the venture closed in 1879. However, it was soon reopened, the New Florence Mining Company being registered on 14th January 1880. The four-mile line was horse-worked for much of its existence but, in June 1880, John Fowler of Leeds supplied a small 0-4-2T for use on the tramway. Built to Works No. 3767, it had $5^1/_2$ins outside cylinders, so was tiny indeed. The branch to Crowbarn Mine had fallen into disuse by 1889, in which year the locomotive was sold back to its builders, whilst the main line of the tramway continued to be used until the mines were abandoned in June 1894, presumably having reverted back to horse haulage. John Fowler, meanwhile, swiftly regauged the 0-4-2T to 2ft 8ins gauge and sold it later in 1889 to Pike Brothers, who used it for hauling ball clay trains on their well known Furzebrook Tramway on the Isle of Purbeck in Dorset. The locomotive was given the name *Quartus* (Latin for 'Fourth' – the company named their engines in a sequence up to *Septimus*) and remained in use until 1934.

There have been subsequent attempts to reopen the mines, firstly in 1918, by the South Western Mining Syndicate. With the need for raw materials in the war effort, the Home Ore Department reopened the mines in 1942, facilitated by Canadian army engineers but flooding occurred and efforts were abandoned. In 1949, a further attempt was made by a private concern, their application being refused by the local planning authority. The mines remain inactive today and it is unlikely they will ever now be reopened, whilst much of the route of the tramway has been subsumed back into the land.

Ore was also carted to South Molland station, most likely from Marcia Mine, which was worked by the Marcia Haematite Iron Ore Mining Company from 1874 and produced 200 tons of iron ore in 1876.

IN SUMMARY

At the turn of the 19th century, North Devon and West Somerset were isolated. Those towns and villages situated along the coast, such as Ilfracombe, Lynmouth, Minehead and Watchet were, of course, accessible to an extent by sea. Travel over land was usually by coaches for passengers or packhorses for goods but the number of routes were limited and some of those, such as the east-west route along the coast, impassable in winter. Due to the nature of the terrain and the lack of industry, no canals were built in the region. The first transport links were turnpikes, roads built by public trusts which charged tolls for their use to enable upkeep and maintenance. One of the first major improvements for the West Somerset and North Devon area was the opening of the main railway line from Bristol to Taunton in 1842 and then to Exeter, thus allowing direct access to London in reasonable time, provided the traveller could make it to the railway in the first instance. In the 1840s, a horse-drawn coach service commenced linking Bridgwater to Minehead which, in the 1850s, was extended on to Lynmouth in the summer months. Once the West Somerset Railway (WSR) had opened to Watchet in 1862, this coach service operated from Williton and, with the subsequent WSR extension to Minehead in 1874, it then operated from that town. Three coaches were used to operate the service, named *Lorna Doone*, *Katerfelto* and *Red Deer*. Four horses pulled each coach, taking three hours to complete the journey, with additional horses being added to help the climb up Porlock and Countisbury hills; the fit and able passengers were asked to walk! The coach service was daily in the summer and weekly in the winter and ran until 1922, when it was replaced by a motor bus service.

The opening of the North Devon Railway in 1854 to Barnstaple led to further access into that isolated corner and was an improvment on the coach services that had been running for a few years. The potential for growth in tourism was already there and from the 1850s, the railways began to enable ever growing numbers of the population, especially from the cities of the North and the Midlands, to visit the seaside to escape from their long hours of work in slave-like conditions in the mills, factories and other industrial enterprises.

The arrival of the railway in Devon transformed life for the local people too. The stations along the Taunton to Barnstaple line supported agricultural communities, market towns and villages, and gave opportunities to the inhabitants to transport their produce, such as cattle, fish and rabbits, to larger markets in towns and cities across the country. Equally, exotic items such as oranges and bananas could be imported and distributed in the district. Coastal resorts like Ilfracombe would benefit from the developing tourist trade, these locations being available to the masses rather than a select few for their annual holidays or even summer Sunday and bank holiday excursions. This industry provided additional local employment, albeit some of it seasonal. People who worked on the railway had a variety of employment opportunities and also the ability to move away from their home town or village, perhaps temporarily but sometimes forever. Coal and other materials were more easily and cheaply transported. There was less of a need for local materials, such as thatch to use in house building, for example. So after years of isolation, the railways of the area and the D&SR in particular gave the local population the feeling they were connected to the rest of the country and that opportunities for the development of their businesses and life was at last a possibility.

Chapter 2

Lines Proposed and Built in the North Devon and West Somerset Areas

Before embarking on a detailed *resumé* of the origins, financing and development of the Devon & Somerset Railway, it is important to trace the development of railways generally in the region. Thus the D&SR may be seen as a piece of the North Devon and West Somerset railway jig-saw. Some of the earlier local projects were conceived and built in the 'Railway Mania' period, broadly 1844-47, when something in the region of 576 Acts of Parliament were passed and approximately 9,000 miles of railways were authorised nationally, although a great many were never built. The potential investment represented by these Bills and Acts was around £100 million, a substantial percentage of gross domestic product (GDP) at the time. There may not seem to be any obvious financial, commercial or other logical reason to what follows; this apparent lack of structure and planning was being repeated all over the country and Parliament was being swamped with Railway Bills.

Prior to 1844, the economy had suffered from a deep depression which had begun in 1837 but once this was over, optimism was in the air and there followed an upturn in the economy. Until 1860, railway companies were the only type of business that could raise capital from more than five people (a restriction imposed after the 'South Sea Bubble' collapse). Thus railways were the most favoured alternative to government stocks.

So, with interest rates dropping, investors started to look around for better financial returns and the developing railway companies seemed to provide this; returns for most railway ventures in 1844 broadly ranged between 6-8%. This apparent financial success, largely arising from investment in the main lines operating at this time, lured ordinary people to invest their whole life savings in any proposed railway venture, including those that were never going to get off the ground as they were financially unsound, impractical or just 'paper railways' – proposed to influence the stock market. Even Brunel at this time referred to those people caught up in the mania as being '*mad – stark, staring, wildly mad*'. In October 1845, the Bank of England raised interest rates, which precipitated some investors cashing out of railway stocks in order to put their funds in a more secure environment.

By 1847 the railway bubble had burst. Investors ditched shares for gold and there was a run on the Bank of England. The Government stepped in to pump money into the financial system to stave off worse news. The railway dreams were in tatters and as much as £230m was lost, this being equivalent to half of the country's national income at the time. The table below summarises the railway miles sanctioned and revenues in the relevant periods mentioned:

Parliamentary Session	Miles Sanctioned	Total Revenue
1845	2,700	£6.1m
1846	4,538	£7.5m
1847	1,354	£8.4m
1850	8	

Despite the economic trials referred to above, railway building did continue. The average cost of building a railway line in the 1840s was calculated at £31,000 per mile. By the end of the 1850s, total investment was put at £250 million, almost half of GDP. In the twenty years after the collapse of railway mania (therefore by 1865-7), the route-miles built had doubled from approximately 6,000 to 12,000. A combination of competition and over-confidence in the anticipated financial success of the ventures, resulted in many unnecessary or uneconomic branch lines being built. Also, those built were usually 'over-sold' at the prospectus stage, with anticipated revenues being overstated by traffic-takers and other costs being underestimated (whether land purchases or construction costs, which were doubled in some cases). By 1872, the total capital investment in railways had increased further and was in the region of £560 million.

In the light of this background, this section aims to briefly summarise the proposals for various railway schemes and their relevant undertakings in and around the North Devon and West Somerset area on, broadly, a chronological basis. However, as will be seen, the history of some of them is interwoven, whilst in a number of instances, delays occurred from the time of initial planning to receiving Parliamentary approval and then further delays in raising finance or in construction, so there is no obvious definitive chronological order. Inevitably, and rightly, this summary includes those lines that were proposed but were never developed beyond the planning stage. It is interesting to see what might have been and how different the railway map in the area might have looked had some of these plans come to fruition. One can also try to ascertain some commercial or other logic to the various proposals and observe the local rivalries that existed at the time, whether between different railway companies or varying local interests and other relevant groups. The bibliography sets out other major historical references relating to local lines which were built if the reader requires further and more detailed information.

Bideford & Okehampton Railway

The Bideford & Okehampton Railway, proposed in 1833, was essentially a high level line running along the top of the hills between the two towns. Its proposed route, twenty-one miles in length, was to be broadly halfway between the Okement and Torridge rivers in the west and the River Taw in the east, passing near Winkleigh at the Okehampton end and Yarnscombe in the north, where it turned west to Bideford. The commercial aim was to effect junctions with the Bristol Channel at the Bideford end and the English Channel at Exeter and Plymouth. The proposal included access by rail to the valuable iron ore mines at Haytor, along with the limestone and clay deposits from the Torrington area, and granite from Meldon, near Okehampton.

The capital requirement was to be £87,000 to be satisfied in shares of £25 each. The proposed engineers were Messrs Hopkins & Sons of Plymouth but despite efforts being made to raise the capital, they were unsuccessful and the line was not proceeded with.

A Bristol Channel to English Channel Railway Project

In September 1833, a prospectus was issued by an unknown person from Carhampton, which proposed a '*Rail Road*' from Minehead in the north, running towards and then via the River Exe valley to Tiverton and on to Exeter, near the southern coast. It did not proceed beyond this initial stage.

Taw Vale Railway & Dock Company

Under an Act passed on 11th June 1838, the Taw Vale Railway & Dock Company (TVR&DC) was authorised to build a $2^3/_4$ mile '*narrow gauge*' (*i.e.* standard gauge) line from Barnstaple to Fremington quay. However, initially very little happened and the powers of the Act expired after seven years. The promoters subsequently returned to Parliament in 1845 and, on 21st July, a five-year extension to the original time limit was obtained under the Taw Vale Amendment Act. The first sod was cut on 5th January 1846 and construction took two years. This was the first railway to enter Barnstaple, opening on 25th April 1848, albeit horse-drawn and goods only (coal and lime from Wales, brought by sea to Fremington, being the main freight transported). William Thorne, a local businessman, initially worked the line.

The TVR&DC had ambitious plans and developed a liaison with the London & South Western Railway (L&SWR), as will be seen below (in the sections on the Exeter & Crediton Railway and the Taw Vale Extension Railway). It continued to carry goods solely until 2nd November 1855, when the extension to Bideford was opened (see the section on the Bideford Extension Railway below) and it began carrying passengers.

Bristol & Exeter Railway

The Bristol & Exeter Railway (B&ER) was authorised by an Act of Parliament as a broad gauge line on 19th May 1836. Its engineer was Isambard Kingdom Brunel. The main line opened to Taunton on 1st July 1842 and had been extended on to Exeter by 1st May 1844, as a result becoming the most significant artery in the railway system of the South West and the Devon area in particular. A third rail was added to the broad gauge line and completed to Exeter by 1875, thereby allowing through traffic from the standard gauge lines of neighbouring railway companies. The B&ER's history and development is recorded comprehensively elsewhere so any further comments are beyond the scope of this summary. However, it is important to record that, the B&ER having found itself in financial difficulties, it was leased to the GWR for operational reasons from 1st January 1876. The GWR then took over the B&ER on 1st August 1876, under an Act of Parliament dated 27th June 1876.

Exeter & Crediton Railway

The initial scheme for the Exeter & Crediton Railway (E&CR), joining the Exeter Canal Basin with Crediton, was proposed in 1831, the primary supporter being Thomas Pring, a solicitor from Crediton. Although an Act of Parliament was obtained on 23rd June 1832 for the line, no construction work took place for three years and the powers lapsed. However, a new scheme was proposed in 1844, with the publication of a prospectus requiring £60,000 of capital. The railway was to run from the B&ER main line at Cowley Bridge (near Exeter) to Crediton. This new proposed plan for the E&CR, which received Parliamentary approval on 21st July 1845, was to construct a $5^3/_4$ mile broad gauge line between the two locations. Once construction commenced after passing of the Act, progress was rapid. This was despite the recommendation of the Board of Trade (BoT) committee, set up in 1844 to review all proposed railway plans for Devon and Cornwall in the railway mania period, which suggested a delay in construction of the E&CR, in order to assess which of the proposed schemes were the most suitable for local requirements.

The development of this short section of line became inextricably linked to an extension of it, from Crediton to Barnstaple (and then on to Bideford), proposed by a separate group of individuals. This was proposed under the title of the Taw Vale Extension Railway (TVER) and is described below.

The E&CR's development became very political and from 1844 to 1851 was a mixed period of construction and deadlock. The B&ER had made a provisional agreement in May 1846 to lease the E&CR (and the proposed TVER as well). However, the Taw Vale board considered the B&ER proposals but rejected them in September 1846. In December 1846, the TVER then turned to the L&SWR and a provisional lease agreement (on better terms than the B&ER lease) was made but this needed Parliamentary approval. The E&CR proceeded with the B&ER lease and discussed a possible opening date of the double track, broad gauge line on 22nd December 1846. However, at that time, there had been some recent dealings in E&CR shares (some for handsome profits) and that meant new shareholders were in attendance at the special meeting on 11th January 1847, at which the B&ER lease was formally rejected. At the next meeting (on 17th February 1847), some Taw Vale directors were voted on to the E&CR Board and a lease to the TVER (guaranteed by the L&SWR) was proposed. However, it was then revealed that a lease had already been granted to a Mr George Hennett by the E&CR board without any consultation. The L&SWR was upset by this and the battle had begun.

At an extraordinary general meeting on 12th April 1847, the B&ER directors were removed from the board and the lease to the Taw Vale considered and approved. Legal proceedings followed but the B&ER directors' claims were rejected. The B&ER and E&CR directors had also complained to the Railway Commissioners following the January meeting. The B&ER complaint in particular was about the nature of the new shareholders; namely that they were only nominees for the Taw Vale and the L&SWR. A statement subsequently issued by the L&SWR confirmed that they had indeed provided funds for such share acquisitions. However, the B&ER also admitted to purchasing some E&CR shares through one particular individual. The Railway Commissioners did not impose penal sanctions on the L&SWR, despite their guilt, and as a result the L&SWR then went on to obtain the lease of the E&CR.

By February 1847, the broad gauge line to Crediton had been built and was ready for traffic but the junction at Cowley Bridge had not been constructed. However, the L&SWR, with its 60% shareholding (largely through nominees), refused to allow the opening of the broad gauge line. Towards the end of 1847, the E&CR board had ordered that its existing, so far unused, broad gauge tracks be narrowed and, by December, they had been. The B&ER complained to the Railway Commissioners again regarding the narrowing of the gauge. Despite potential arbitration by the Commissioners, the E&CR then announced their intention to open the line by February 1848. This did not happen, because the Railway Commissioners had issued their Order earlier that month that the line should be built to the broad gauge. Time passed and, towards the end of 1848, it was still not open, even though the track was now laid throughout but to the standard gauge.

Several years then elapsed before the E&CR was eventually opened as a broad gauge line on 12th May 1851, the directors having opted to restore one set of lines to the 7ft gauge following the ruling by the Commissioners. The second line remained standard gauge, however, as traffic initially did not justify the cost of conversion of both lines. The E&CR also paid for the construction of the junction at Cowley Bridge.

The line was first leased to the B&ER for operation, initially for seven years until after the opening of the TVER line from Crediton to Fremington and was thus effectively operated as a branch of the B&ER from Exeter. The L&SWR subsequently acquired a lease over the line from 1st January 1862 and ran standard gauge train services from 3rd February 1862, by which time it was a mixed gauge line. At this point, the L&SWR were operating standard gauge passenger and goods services, and the B&ER broad gauge goods services to Crediton. Meanwhile, Thomas Brassey, a well known contractor of the era who often took shares in and worked under lease some of the lines he built, was operating passenger services from 1st February to 31st July 1862 on the broad gauge TVER line between Bideford and Exeter. From 1st August 1862 to 1st March 1863, these broad gauge services were run by the L&SWR using Brassey's rolling stock.

The E&CR continued its independence (despite the fact that the L&SWR had taken over the Crediton to Bideford section in 1864 as discussed below). The L&SWR's operational lease was extended in January 1869 for seven more years and renewed again in 1876. Then, to complete a somewhat complex picture, the L&SWR acquired the E&CR in 1879. The E&CR ran broad gauge goods trains between Exeter and Crediton until 1877. The broad gauge on the main line at Cowley Bridge was converted to standard gauge on 20th May 1892.

NORTH DEVON RAILWAY

The North Devon Railway (NDR) was borne out of proposals mooted in the early 1840s, for a line from the B&ER through Milverton, Wiveliscombe, Dulverton, South Molton, Barnstaple, Ilfracombe and Bideford. A number of meetings were held at the key towns in support of the proposals, one such being at Wiveliscombe on Wednesday 14th May 1844. Sir Thomas Lethbridge, Bart, took the chair, whilst Sir G.P. Adams, H.D. Harvey, Messrs P. & W. Hancock, F.N. Bower and J.B. Clarke formed the provisional committee. The minutes of the meeting highlighted the merits of the proposals; namely the link to London and the north of England and the opening up of an area with a population of more than 16,000. Further benefits derived from the potential transportation of coal from Barnstaple and Bridgwater, along with many thousands of tons of culm for burning the plentiful limestone of the area. It was agreed that a deputation of six individuals were to meet with the B&ER to put forward the merits of the railway.

A public meeting was also held at Tiverton on 18th October 1844; Mr Gamlen, the Mayor, was in the chair. A motion was put forward by Mr J. Heathcoat and seconded by a Mr Patch:

> *'That it is the opinion of this meeting that in the event of a railway being extended from the B&ER line of railway to Barnstaple and North Devon, the most desirable line in a mercantile, agricultural and general point of view, is by the way of Tiverton and Southmolton* [sic]*, and that the following memorial, expressing the opinion of this meeting, be signed by the Mayor on its behalf, and immediately forwarded to the directors of the B&ER Company.'*

The memorial went on to state that they were happy with the proposed B&ER branch to the town but they '*were anxious with regard to the B&ER proposals to connect Barnstaple with the B&ER by means of a projected line from Barnstaple to Exeter, by way of Crediton*'. The concerns were that this Crediton line would exclude cheap and direct communication with Bristol, London and the North for the North Devon towns.

There were references to the line being further extended to the '*mining district of Coombemartin* [sic]' and the port at Ilfracombe, which the Crediton line '*neither presents, nor admits to being accomplished*'. The resolutions were to be advertised in the Barnstaple papers, *Woolmer's Exeter Gazette* and the *Western Times*.

These discussions, proposals and meetings manifested themselves in an initial prospectus entitled 'North Devon Railway' and dated 30th June 1845. It listed a provisional committee of twenty-nine members, including Lord Politmore, Sir Robert Throckmorton and others. It proposed a railway from Tiverton to Bampton, Dulverton, South Molton, Barnstaple and Bideford, with a branch to Ilfracombe. The share capital requirements were £700,000 in 14,000 shares of £50 each. One of the proposed railway's 'selling points' was that the area between Dulverton and Barnstaple was becoming highly important as a mining district, with resources of copper, lead, manganese and other ores present.

It is presumed that this initial plan immediately attracted the support of the GWR, B&ER and South Devon Railway, as a revised prospectus was published soon after in July 1845.

The cover of the 1845 NDR plan. *Courtesy Somerset Archives & Local Studies*

This next venture was promoted initially with Lord Clinton as chairman. The share capital requirement of this extended project was increased to £1.75 million and was to be met by the issue of 70,000 £25 shares. In addition to Lord Clinton, there were some eighty other persons on the provisional committee, including almost all of the local individuals set out in the June prospectus (only a small number appear to have dropped out). The key committee members were The Right Hon. Earl of Fortescue (the then Lord Lieutenant of Devon), Lord Poltimore, Lord Palmerston, MP, Sir Robert George Throckmorton, Bart, Sir Thomas Lethbridge Bart, William Hancock of Wiveliscombe, Lt-General Sir George Pownell Adams, John Heathcoat, John Knight, Montague Beer, William Smyth, and Charles Russell, Chairman of the GWR and a number of his fellow directors, along with directors of the South Devon Railway (SDR) and Bristol & Exeter Railway companies. Brunel was to be the engineer. The prospectus stated that the '*Company is formed by an influential Local Proprietary, including the Promoters of the North Devon, Crediton and Barnstaple Railway Company*', as well as the three railway companies mentioned above.

The plans were developed with the support of local landowners and the GWR, SDR and B&ER into a very comprehensive scheme. Indeed, the prospectus suggested that the three railway companies were to subscribe for half of the share capital and join in the direction of the affairs of the company. The plans were deposited with the Somerset Clerk of the Peace on 30th November 1845.

Map of the Proposed North Devon Railway from the June 1845 Prospectus. ***Courtesy Somerset Archives & Local Studies***

This revised and extended proposal was for a railway running from a terminus at Launceston in Cornwall, via Okehampton, Hatherleigh, Torrington, Bideford, Barnstaple, South Molton, Brushford, Morebath and Wiveliscombe, to the B&ER main line at Hillfarrance, near Taunton (just south of Norton Fitzwarren). The Okehampton to Bideford stretch of this line was different from that proposed by the earlier B&OR scheme (see above), as the NDR line ran closer to the River Torridge to the west. In all, this line was to be 97 miles and 60 chains in length, with eight tunnels (the longest being 1,078 yards near Launceston and one of three tunnels proposed which were over or near 1,000 yards in length). There were to be three viaducts, the longest being 209 yards over the River Bray near South Molton, and several proposed branches. These included a branch of 6 miles to Tavistock (the triangular junction being at 10 miles 65 chains and 11 miles 40 chains from Launceston); the plan here was to join the existing line at '*Lidford*' (Lydford) and then on to Plymouth; a branch (at 25 miles 41 chains and 25 miles 57 chains from Launceston) to Crediton, 15 miles away, and then one to Tiverton (from near Morebath) for a distance of 8 miles and 28 chains. There were to be terminii at Tavistock and Crediton, whilst at Tiverton there was a further line proposed of 8 miles and 28 chains to the B&ER main line. At this time Tiverton was the third largest town in Devon, after Plymouth and Exeter, with a population around 10,000.

The proposed line was therefore to form a key artery in a comprehensive Devon railway system linking north to south and east to west. Indeed, it could have provided a viable alternative to the main line to the South West of England and would have been a shorter route to Barnstaple than that via Crediton (by about 20 miles), whilst also providing a direct link to South Molton.

Unfortunately, on 12th May 1846, a Parliamentary committee decreed that the scheme failed to comply with Standing Orders and therefore the Bill could not proceed. Lord Fortescue reported on 20th June 1846, when Chairman of the provisional committee, that the expenditure incurred on this project had amounted to £38,668 and that the undertaking was to be wound up. The North Devon Railway dream was no more and this left the way open for the Taw Valley Extension Railway to progress its plans to open up North Devon to the railway network as was referred to above (the E&CR

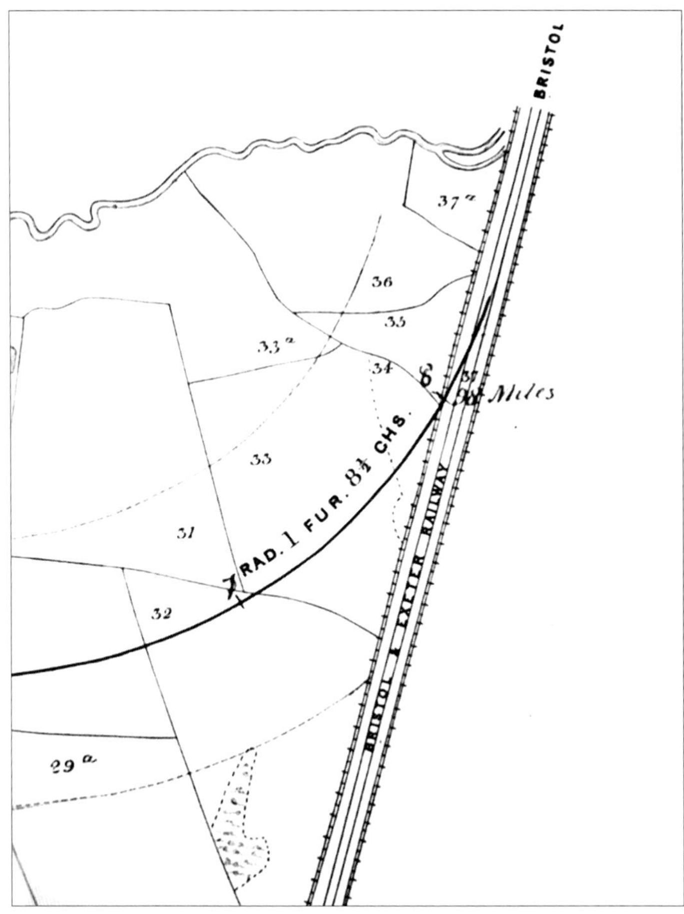

Extract from the NDR plan, showing the junction with the B&ER near Norton Fitzwarren. ***Courtesy Somerset Archives & Local Studies***

section) and will also be seen below. However, what was clear was the need for a railway to run between the B&ER, near Taunton, and Barnstaple, to benefit the district in between those two towns, its inhabitants and the agriculture and mining in the area.

As an aside to reviewing the actual proposals for the line, it is interesting to report some of the issues that were pertinent at the time. In particular, there was drafted a note to the provisional committee of the NDR and its engineer from the landowners and inhabitants of Bampton, who stated:

> '*... that in making the railroad from Southmolton* [sic] *to Tiverton with a branch line to Taunton you have in contemplation to make the two branches of the line to diverge from each other somewhere in the neighbourhood of East Anstey and to carry one such branch to Tiverton by way of Valdridge and Stuckeridge Bridge and Duvale and the other to Taunton by way of Exebridge and ... there will consequently be two parallel lines for a distance of more than 7 miles.*'

The memorandum goes on to suggest that for the sake of economy and practicability, a single line should be built by way of Valdridge, Oakford Bridge and Westbrook to a point a few hundred yards west of Bampton, at which the two lines should

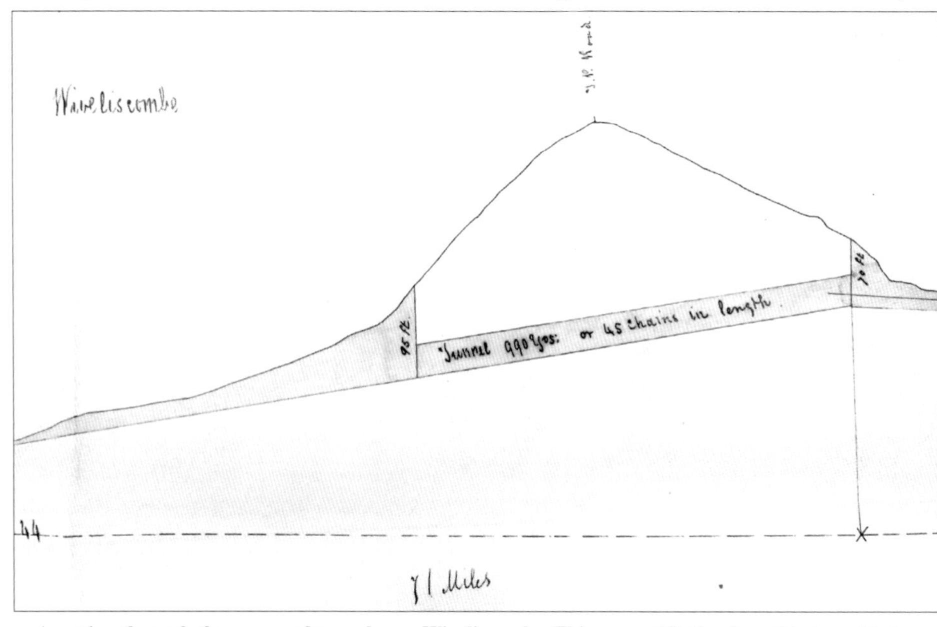

A section through the proposed tunnel near Wiveliscombe. This was not Bathealton, this tunnel being north of the line as built. ***Courtesy Somerset Archives & Local Studies***

then diverge, one heading to Tiverton via Duvale lime kilns (and Exeter Inn) and the other to Taunton via Shillingford and Wiveliscombe, thereby keeping just north of Bampton. They added that with 2,049 inhabitants, the consumption of 700 tons of coal per annum, the potential export of lime (circa 10,000 tons per year), and the weekly sheep and cattle market, both Bampton and the railway would benefit with the line passing though the village. The key issue about this line is that, unlike the D&SR when built, it ran along the top of the hills between Anstey and Brushford, via Allshire Farm, above Upcott Farm and down past Croft Farm, and running the Brushford side of Riphay Farm, before crossing the River Exe and on towards Morebath.

BRISTOL & ENGLISH CHANNELS DIRECT JUNCTION RAILWAY

A prospectus for the Bristol & English Channels Direct Junction Railway (B&ECDJR) was prepared in 1845, which proposed the establishment of a '*direct Line of Railway for Passengers, Goods and Commercial, Mining and Agricultural produce between the Harbour of Watchet on the Bristol Channel, and the Harbour of Bridport on the English Channel*'. The aim was to avoid the need to ship goods around Lands End (a '*dangerous and uncertain passage*') by providing a direct inland link and to provide a reasonably populated area (circa 150,000 people) with transport. It was also a more practical and cheaper option than a proposed ship canal between the two channels.

Whilst the direct line would have been 48 miles in length, running from Watchet to Taunton, then Hatch Beauchamp, Ilminister, Chard, Crewekerne, Beaminster and Bridport, there was also a proposed branch to Wiveliscombe. This would have left the B&ECDJR about half way between Watchet and Taunton, in the region of a farm house called Northam at Stogumber and terminated at Golden Mile Street in Wiveliscombe. The prospectus noted that the branch will '*avail itself of the North Devon Railway* [as referred to above], *to Taunton, and also Westward*' (and indeed the prospectus' title does refer to the continuation of the North Devon, Bristol & Exeter and Great Western railways).

The provisional committee numbered 114 persons and there were three who were directors of the proposed North Devon Railway: Sir Robert George Throckmorton Bart, Sir John Trevelyan Bart and Lieut-General Sir George Pownoll Adams. The initial capital requirement was £1 million, being 40,000 shares of £25 each. Mr C.B. Vignoles was to be consulting engineer and Messrs W.C. & R.W. Mylne engineers.

The line was not proceeded with and got no further than the Parliamentary Bill stage.

THE BRISTOL & ENGLISH CHANNELS CONNECTION RAILWAY

Originally known as the West of England Central & Channels Junction Railway, the Bristol & English Channels Connection Railway (B&ECCR) proposed a line from Stolford, where a new harbour was to be built, to Bridport and Lyme Regis. The capital required was to be £1.6m in shares of £20 each. Another 1845 scheme, it was a highly ambitious idea but it was also impracticable and as a result, never got beyond the initial stages in its development.

THE BRIDGWATER & MINEHEAD JUNCTION RAILWAY

The Bridgwater & Minehead Junction Railway (B&MJR) was proposed to connect Minehead with Bridgwater and the B&ER, where there was to be both facing and trailing junctions. Essentially, the line was to take the coastal route between the two towns and would have been 26 miles long. The commercial advantage was linked to the proposal of Minehead becoming a steam packet port for Ireland and in connecting this line with other local railways to facilitate access to the Bristol and English channels. This would have put Minehead in competition with Ilfracombe, which had similar ideas. There was a proposal for a short branch to Watchet, along with a further branch from Watchet to a terminus at Poole Town in the Parish of Luxborough on the Brendon Hills, this being for iron ore traffic. At the Minehead end, the line would have carried on beyond the quay to a new harbour to the west of the town. Support for the project came from Henry Luttrell of Dunster Castle.

Plans were deposited with Parliament in 1845 but the Act was not passed.

THE EXETER, TIVERTON & MINEHEAD DIRECT RAILWAY

The promoters of the Exeter, Tiverton & Minehead Direct Railway (ET&MDR) were in league with the B&MJR, with the channel-to-channel link in mind. The route proposed was from Exeter to Silverton, Tiverton, Dulverton and Dunster, and then to Minehead with an extension to Ilfracombe. It generated local interest but little else and certainly not the £1.6 million capital asked for.

THE MINEHEAD & CENTRAL DEVON JUNCTION RAILWAY

The Minehead & Central Devon Junction Railway (M&CDJR) was another proposed extension of the B&MJR, running from Minehead to Tiverton and Exeter, almost the exact route of the ET&MDR referred to above. Needless to say nothing further happened on this project and it faded away.

GREAT WESTERN EXTENSION ATMOSPHERIC RAILWAY

The Great Western Extension Atmospheric Railway (GWEAR), proposed in 1845 with a prospectus issued on 25th September, was to run from Exeter to Barnstaple and Ilfracombe, with branches to Bideford and South Molton. There were also improvements proposed to the harbour at Ilfracombe. Based on the Brunel design that was tried in South Devon at the time, it was a system of propelling trains by compressed air. It failed for mechanical reasons and the South Devon venture was abandoned and, in consequence, the GWEAR did not proceed.

NORTH DEVON EXTENSION RAILWAY

The North Devon Extension Railway (NDER) was another 1845 scheme, which proposed a line from Barnstaple to Combe Martin, just east of Ilfracombe on the coast but which again did not proceed.

SOMERSETSHIRE & NORTH DEVON JUNCTION RAILWAY

Plans for the Somersetshire & North Devon Junction Railway (S&NDJR) were deposited on 29th November 1845 and showed the line running from Porlock harbour along the coast to Minehead, then from Carhampton on to Williton, where it would have joined the proposed B&ECDJR near Castle Hill. There was also a proposed branch to Watchet. It is believed that this line would have run on to Bridgwater to join the B&ER (as referred to in the B&ECDJR prospectus discussed above, probably as an extension of that line) and also along the coast to Ilfracombe, with a branch to Barnstaple. A Mr Charles Fox was to be the consulting engineer and Mr John Hughes the engineer. Two tunnels were planned, one of 667 yards at Greenaley Point west of Minehead, the other of 902 yards (believed to have been under the Quantocks) at the eastern end.

Despite the depositing of plans, no Bill followed and the project did not proceed. In some ways this was not surprising given the nature of the coastal route, which would have caused a major engineering and financial challenge to bring the project into being.

SOMERSETSHIRE & NORTH DEVON
JUNCTION RAILWAY,
AND
PORLOCK HARBOUR AND DOCK
PLAN, AND SECTION.
CHARLES FOX, CONSULTING ENGINEER.
JOHN HUGHES, ENGINEER.
NOVEMBER, 1845.

Cover of Plan and Section for the S&NDJR. ***Courtesy Somerset Archives & Local Studies***

TAW VALE EXTENSION RAILWAY/NORTH DEVON RAILWAY & DOCK COMPANY

The development of this railway, originally proposed between Barnstaple and Exeter, was fraught with difficulties, not of an engineering kind but of politics and railway company rivalry. One such example was the 1845 broad gauge proposal as discussed above (see NDR), backed by the GWR, B&ER and South Devon Railway, which was clearly a rival scheme. In addition to this was the politics between the B&ER, the E&CR and the TVER backed by the L&SWR (as described in the E&CR section above).

The Taw Vale Extension Railway Act was passed on 7th August 1846, for the line from Barnstaple to Crediton; the gauge was not stipulated in the Act, being at the discretion of the BoT. The company subsequently looked to obtain authority by Act of Parliament for a branch line leaving the main line near Umberleigh to South Molton and an extension from Fremington to Bideford. This latter Act was passed on 22nd July 1847. Later that year, the TVER petitioned the Railway Commissioners to build the line to standard gauge. However, they ruled in early 1848 that the line should be constructed to the wider gauge because of convenience and the need to avoid a break with the broad gauge B&ER. This order did not apply to the E&CR or the Barnstaple to Fremington line. The TVER did not like the ruling so took a Bill to Parliament to authorise a standard gauge line and a lease for the L&SWR to operate it. The Bill failed in June 1848, along with the L&SWR lease. With these distractions there were delays in construction, so by the end of the decade little progress had been made and the future of the line between Exeter and Barnstaple was uncertain.

On 24th July 1851, the TVER was restructured and changed its name to the North Devon Railway & Dock Company (NDR&DC), under an Act of that title, which proposed a single broad gauge line be built. This is not to be confused with the 1845 NDR proposals above. The powers to build the branch to South Molton lapsed at this time and were not renewed, so this left that town still isolated from any railway. The Bideford extension was promoted independently in 1852 (see below).

By early 1852, construction had commenced again on the Crediton to Barnstaple route, with an injection of funds and a new contractor, Mr Thomas Brassey, who was one of the most successful and experienced contractors of the time. However, extreme weather hindered progress for a period.

Formally opened on 12th July 1854, public train services began on the broad gauge line from Crediton to Fremington on 1st August 1854. The single broad gauge line was worked with B&ER rolling stock until 28th July 1855. Thomas Brassey then provided his own locomotives and stock to fulfil his obligations under the lease (for seven years at £12,000 per annum rent). By 1860, the L&SWR were approaching Exeter from Salisbury and proposals were put and accepted for standard gauge track on the E&CR, North Devon Railway and Bideford Extension Railway. The L&SWR took over the lease of the NDR to Bideford from Thomas Brassey on 1st August 1862 (by which time the L&SWR had opened their line from Salisbury through to Exeter) and operated it using his rolling stock until the following year. Given the substantial involvement of the L&SWR in this project, the track was soon converted to mixed gauge beyond Crediton, with the first standard gauge train running through to Bideford on 1st March 1863.

The L&SWR was getting bad press over their resistance to the D&SR's proposals to reach Barnstaple. To mitigate this resistance, they proposed a line from the NDR to South and North Molton. The details of this potential detour are covered in Chapter 3, as it was integral to that line.

The L&SWR took over the North Devon and Bideford Extension railways on 1st January 1865. Despite this, regular broad gauge goods trains continued to run through from Crediton to Bideford on the mixed gauge line until 30th April 1877. This saved the transfer of goods to narrow gauge wagons at Exeter, given the Bristol to Exeter route was still broad gauge until and beyond this date.

On 30th June 1874, the E&CR obtained an Act of Parliament to double the line between Cowley Bridge and Yeoford, which line was brought into use on 1st June 1876. The L&SWR (Exeter & Crediton and North Devon) Act received Royal Assent on 13th July 1876 to purchase the E&CR, which was completed in 1879. This Act had a requirement to retain broad gauge services between Crediton and Barnstaple until 30th April 1877.

THE TIVERTON BRANCH

Perhaps primed by the NDR prospectus and plans to reach Tiverton, the B&ER opened its 4-mile, single track, broad gauge branch line from the main line near Sampford Peverell to Tiverton on 12th June 1848. At the time, hopes were expressed of extending this line into North Devon – in effect, a reverse proposal of the NDR's initial plans. The branch was converted to standard gauge in June 1884 but never extended.

BIDEFORD EXTENSION RAILWAY

The Bideford Extension Railway (BER) Act was authorised on 4th August 1853. It was a 6¹/₂ mile extension of the TVER/NDR&DC line from Fremington to Bideford. Opened to the public on 2nd November 1855, it was initially leased for operation by Mr Thomas Brassey who, as stated above, also leased the North Devon Railway and operated them as one. The L&SWR took over Brassey's lease on 1st August 1862. Following an Act of 25th July 1864, the L&SWR took over the BER with effect from 1st January 1865 (that is at the same time as taking over the NDR).

The line was originally built to the broad gauge but was converted to mixed gauge by 1st March 1863 and subsequently extended to Torrington on 18th July 1872. The broad gauge rails were eventually removed after 30th April 1877 (following Parliamentary approval to do so being granted on 13th July 1876), broad gauge goods trains running up until this date.

SIMONSBATH TO PORLOCK WEIR

This proposed line is included for completeness. John Knight, an industrialist, had acquired substantial parts of what was called the Forest of Exmoor, including mineral rights, in 1819-21. It is understood he considered the possibility of building '*a railroad*' as early as 1826, from Porlock on the coast to the Exmoor Forest, for the purposes of transporting quarry stones and minerals to specially built wharves at the harbour. However, he had to obtain permission from the Blathwayt Estate, through whose land the proposed line was to run but such permission was not forthcoming. The line would have run from Porlock Weir to Birchanger and via Hawkcombe into the Knight property on Exmoor.

The idea of a railway running from Simonsbath to Porlock was resurrected by Frederic Knight, John's son, in 1855. Frederic believed that his estate on Exmoor Forest and Brendon Common contained vast reserves of iron ore. With the apparent success of other companies on the Brendon Hills to the east, Knight agreed to lease his land to the Dowlais Iron Company. The mining lease was dated 25th March 1856 and was for a term of forty-three years. A key employee of that company, a Mr G.T. Clark, with railway engineering experience, visited Exmoor and worked with Knight to plan a route from Simonsbath to the coast – either Porlock or Lynton, as both offered ports suitable to transport any mined ore. Porlock was chosen and it was agreed that Knight would build the railway and Dowlais would supply rails and ironwork. A formal agreement to that effect was signed in December 1855. Knight started the work and applied to Dowlais for the rails in January 1859. However, by that time all mining activities had ceased and Dowlais made a large payment to Knight to terminate the lease. Knight argued that the railway contract was separate and that those terms should be honoured; Dowlais disagreed, saying that the cost was recoupable out of the royalties payable to Knight. Knight had in fact done few earthworks and although he made an attempt to form an independent company to complete the job, nothing had happened by 1865, when the lease from Blathwayt (which he had managed to negotiate for access to Porlock) expired. The lease was not renewed and the railway was not to be.

The route was planned to run from Porlock Weir, westwards along the coast to Worthy, then via two inclines lifting it up to 1,400 feet above sea level onto the coastal road (now the A39 between Minehead and Lynmouth). The inclines would have been worked by gravity, laden wagons going down pulling up the empties, rather like that at Comberow on the West Somerset Mineral Railway (see below). The track then ran for about 6½ miles on the level between Whit Stones and Warren Farm, via Larkbarrow and Alderman's Barrow, on a winding course. From Warren Farm, its proposed course is uncertain; perhaps the plan was to go to Exe Head (where there were proposals for canals) and then drop down to Simonsbath, with branches to the mines. The line would have been 14 miles in length and the wagons most likely horse-drawn on the flat, although steam traction was a possibility. When mining resumed briefly in the 1910-14 period, the ore was transported by steam traction engine running over roads constructed by John Knight.

SUMMARY – THE STORY SO FAR

This is a good point at which to take stock of developments. After some indifferent and false starts, and political posturing by various railway companies, the key railways in the North Devon area had been established by the late 1850s. In summary, lines ran from Bideford via Fremington (BER), through to Barnstaple (NDR&DC), then down the Taw Valley to Crediton (TVER) and from Crediton to Exeter (E&CR). The first (and at this time, the only) Barnstaple station was on the west bank of the River Taw, at what later became Barnstaple Junction. Exeter was by this time also connected to Bristol via Taunton, with the town of Tiverton being connected to the main line by a branch. Further, the GWR was pushing westwards towards Plymouth, whilst the L&SWR had also reached Exeter from London by 1860. However, no new lines were opened in the North Devon area until the early 1870s, starting with the Torrington extension of the BER referred to above.

WEST SOMERSET MINERAL RAILWAY

Initial proposals for a tramway linking Watchet and Withiel Florey Common were put forward by Sir Thomas Lethbridge (who was a principal shareholder in the Monmouth Iron & Coal Company) circa 1838. Development of the iron ore industry in the Brendon Hills having begun, its purpose was to carry the extracted iron ore down to the coast for shipment to Wales but no progress was made with the proposal.

By the early 1850s, the iron ore mines around Luxborough, Gupworthy and Raleigh's Cross were producing well and a number of ironmasters from South Wales got together to propose a railway to take the ore to the coast, to replace the horses and carts then in use. Thomas Brown, a partner in the Ebbw Vale Ironworks, leased the mines. A Bill was laid before Parliament in November 1854 and Royal Assent was received on 16th July 1855. This empowered the West Somerset Mineral Railway Company (WSMR) to build, within four years, a line from Watchet harbour via Roadwater and Brendon Hill to a terminus short of Heath Poult Cross, with a branch to Raleigh's Cross. The line was to be just over 13 miles long and standard gauge. Construction started in 1856, with the first sod turned at Roughmoor near Torre, just south of Washford; the line was completed to Roadwater by April 1857 and to Comberow by the November. The biggest challenge for the line's constructors was the Comberow incline, opened at the end of May 1858 although it was not complete at that time.

A 7 mile branch to Minehead, to gain access to the harbour there, was also considered at a meeting in November 1856. The West Somerset Mineral Railway Act of 1857 was passed to extend the railway 6 miles and 1,450 yards. This extension to Minehead would have created a triangle, which was to incorporate a northern loop of 660 yards length at Washford to enable direct running between Watchet and Minehead. This extension did not come to fruition, as Watchet harbour was rebuilt and access improved, after which it had sufficient capacity for the ore exports.

The line was authorised to carry passengers from 1865, including mine workers, although they had most likely been unofficially riding the trains before that date. Its main revenue earning purpose was always the transport of ore, so when local production dwindled as a result of a slump in the steel trade, the line's future fell in to doubt, and it closed to passengers and goods on 7th November 1898 without ceremony. The stock and locomotives were removed to Ebbw Vale. Local people did suggest to the L&SWR in February 1899 that the proposed railway from Bridgwater (the Somerset & Dorset branch terminus) to Stogursey should be extended to Watchet and then on to Exeter via the WSMR but nothing came of this. Various local businesses sought to use the redundant line but no agreement was forthcoming. However, it was reopened in 1907 by the Somerset Mineral Syndicate, with repair work commencing in July of that year. A former Metropolitan Railway locomotive, 'B' Class 4-4-0T No. 37, built by Beyer, Peacock, was procured as the motive power and this ran the public excursion arranged for 4th July. Sadly, the Syndicate was under-capitalised and the revival was short-lived, the line closing again for the final time in 1910. A Court Order was obtained to wind up the company on 16th April 1910.

In 1894, there had been suggestions for a light railway connecting the WSMR at Brendon Hill with the D&SR at Morebath but nothing came of this.

The track remained in place and, on 5th July 1912, an Australian firm (A.R. Angus Ltd) took a lease of the line between Watchet and Washford in order to test a new form of automatic train control. Further trials took place until 1914. Lifting of the track commenced in 1917 and was finished by 1918. The WSMR thus holds the dubious distinction of being the first line in the area to close.

WEST SOMERSET RAILWAY

An initial meeting regarding the West Somerset Railway (WSR) was held at Williton on 9th July 1856, with the intention of proposing a broad gauge line from Watchet, via Williton, to the B&ER main line either at Bridgwater or Taunton; the Bridgwater option would have required tunnelling under the Quantock Hills. A Wiveliscombe option was also proposed. The Reverend Llewellyn of that town suggested the WSR would run via Elworthy and Wiveliscombe to join the main line at Hillfarrence. Despite these options, it was agreed in principle that there should be a railway from Watchet. The commercial purpose of the WSR was to focus on the port at Watchet, which as we have seen was being used to ship iron ore out to Wales. It was considered that returning ships could bring back coal from Wales, which could then be transported by the railway to the West Somerset and North Devon areas.

At a meeting with Brunel on 1st August 1856, two deputations made their case, one for the Taunton route, the other for that to Wiveliscombe. Brunel commented on his preliminary surveys. The construction costs of the Quantock route were estimated at £6,000 per mile, with tunnelling at £75,000. In respect of the Wiveliscombe route, he regarded the construction as *'something fearful'*, including a number of tunnels which, in his view, rendered it impracticable. The vote fell in favour of the Taunton to Porlock route (but the Porlock extension was dropped almost immediately), with an anticipated construction cost of £8,000 per mile.

With the WSMR already established, it is not surprising to note that they raised objections to the WSR and its Bill; the WSMR wanted to keep the B&ER (who were to have running rights over the WSR) out of Watchet and protect its turf. A link was proposed in the Bill for the WSR line to join the WSMR line and operate a mixed gauge connection from Watchet to Washford. With the WSMR's standard gauge branch line from Washford to Minehead also proposed at this time and the WSR also acknowledging the potential of a line through to Minehead (and beyond to Porlock), it might have been that some agreement could have been reached between the WSMR and the WSR. However, the gauge issued raised its head again. In the end, the WSMR dropped their Minehead plans and the West Somerset Railway Act was passed in 1857. Construction commenced in 1859 and the line was formally completed on 14th February 1862. Built to the broad gauge, the line was opened from Watchet Junction, just west of Norton Fitzwarren, to Watchet and its harbour on 31st March 1862.

WATCHET & MINEHEAD RAILWAY/ THE MINEHEAD RAILWAY

Plans were deposited for what was initially known as the Watchet & Minehead Railway in November 1864. This was for a broad gauge line, separate from the standard gauge WSMR, to run to Washford, Blue Anchor, Dunster and Minehead. The Act received Royal Ascent on 5th July 1865 but with the financial crash of the following year, delays occurred in raising funds and in construction, and the statutory time allowed to build the railway ran out. A new Bill was eventually proposed (for the newly styled Minehead Railway) with a slightly different (cheaper) route than the 1865 proposals and this was deposited in Parliament at the end of 1870. Despite a WSMR objection, this Bill received Royal Ascent on 29th June 1871. Construction work started in January 1872 and was completed by 1874, with the railway opening on 16th July, albeit unfinished. This was the penultimate broad gauge line to be built and was subsequently bought by the B&ER in 1876, with the Minehead Railway being amalgamated into the GWR in 1897 and the WSR amalgamated in to the GWR in 1922.

OKEHAMPTON RAILWAY

Although slightly out of the North Devon region we are interested in, the Okehampton Railway (OR) gets a mention to pull together the threads of all the proposed lines covered in this area. The OR was incorporated on 17th July 1862, with the intention of creating a standard gauge route from Coleford Junction on the North Devon Railway, through central Devon to Okehampton. Powers were obtained to extend the line in 1863 through to Lidford [*sic*] to join up with the broad gauge Launceston & South Devon Railway, which ran to Plymouth. The line opened in stages, reaching Okehampton on 3rd October 1871 and Plymouth in May 1876.

NORTH DEVON & SOMERSET RAILWAY

Plans for the North Devon & Somerset Railway (ND&SR) were deposited on 28th November 1863. They showed a line commencing at Ilfracombe, thence to Barnstaple and then eastwards to South Molton, Brushford, Raddington, Chipstable, Wiveliscombe, Milverton and Oake, joining the B&ER at Norton Fitzwarren. It was to be 42 miles and 75 links from Norton Fitzwarren to the terminus at Barnstaple. Railway No. 1 was defined as running from Watchet Junction to Barnstaple. At Watchet Junction there was to be a chord line branching off to the north to join the West Somerset Railway (near the Norton Fitzwarren to Milverton road bridge). Referred to as Railway No. 3, it was 4 furlongs, 7 chains and 50 links long. The proposed route to Ilfracombe from Barnstaple was via Pilton, Marwood, Bittadon and Berrynarbor; not the easiest route to construct, it was known as Railway No. 2). At the Ilfracombe terminus there was to be a spur line leading to the harbour area; this comprised a line to Hele just east of Ilfracombe (Railway No. 4) and then from Hele to the Harbour (Railway No. 5). Eugenius Birch was to be the engineer.

Whilst the project was not proceeded with, this proposed line in a sense was the precursor to the D&SR. Leaving the Ilfracombe section to one side, the line as eventually built largely followed the route proposed under this scheme. There was subsequently a couple of deviations in the Wiveliscombe and Dulverton areas (plans for which were deposited on 29th November 1866) as will be seen in

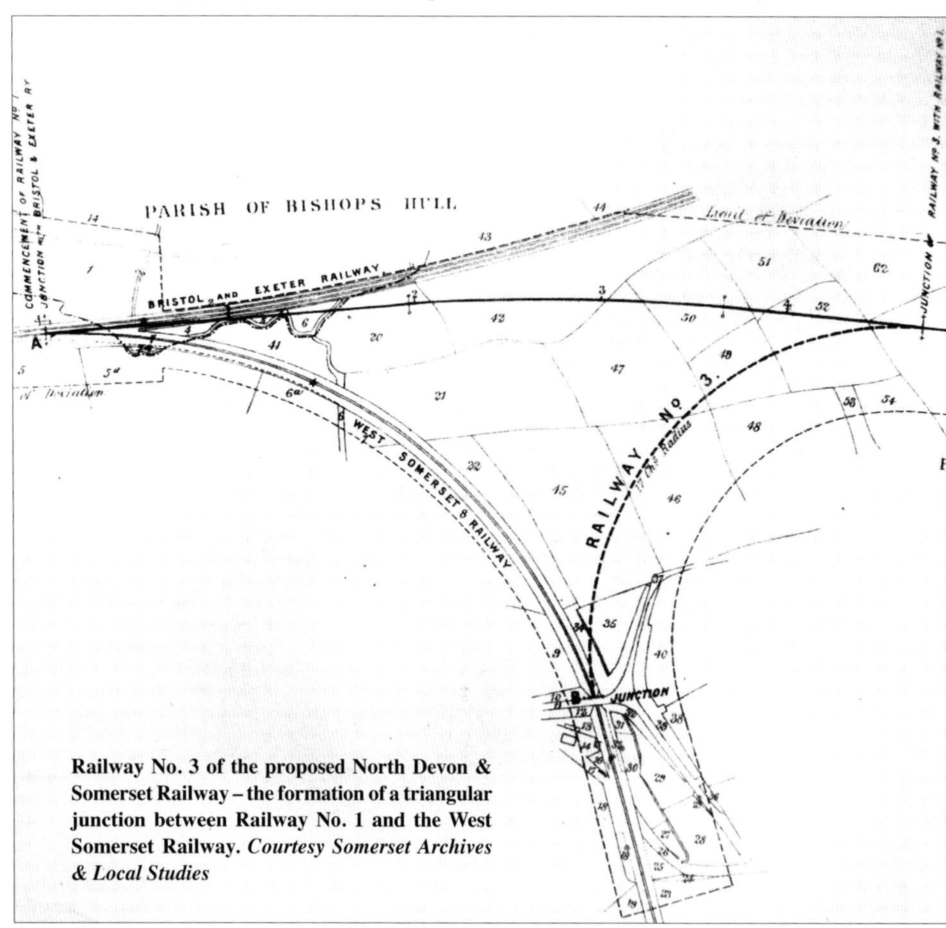

Railway No. 3 of the proposed North Devon & Somerset Railway – the formation of a triangular junction between Railway No. 1 and the West Somerset Railway. ***Courtesy Somerset Archives & Local Studies***

Chapter 3. Furthermore, it is interesting to note that the 1863 plans for the chord line to the WSR is indeed very similar to the one built by the heritage WSR in 2008-2012, as referred to in Chapter 5.

DEVON (NORTH) & SOMERSET RAILWAY

The prospectus for the Devon (North) & Somerset Railway (D(N)&SR) had similar objectives and route to the ND&SR reviewed above. The provisional committee – Earls Fortescue and Carnarvon, with Lords Poltimore and Clinton, and others, along with engineer Eugenius Birch and company secretary John McMillan – remained together to develop proposals for the D&SR. The D(N)&SR scheme was to connect Taunton with Ilfracombe via Milverton, Wiveliscombe, Bampton, Dulverton, South Molton and Barnstaple, stating that the area has been '*wholly neglected*' by the companies who had commanded the western district. The prospectus justified the route for two reasons. Firstly, the rich agricultural and mineral country in North Devon, which was isolated from the commercial world and from the sea-board. Secondly, opening up the country to the north of England and the manufacturing districts, and also also establishing a new route to Ireland, by which a saving of eighty miles of sea-passage would have been effected.

The prospectus also publicly announced '*their great desire to avoid a broad and narrow gauge contest*' and that they had had discussions with the B&ER and L&SWR to work together. This included working with the L&SWR for making the line from Barnstaple to Ilfracombe on the double gauge (broad and standard gauge), with mutual running powers and advantages.

The proposed capital was £600,000 in 24,000 shares of £25 each, with a deposit of £2 10s per share. No borrowing powers were proposed.

On 19th November 1863, the *North Devon Journal* published a notice for the Devon (North) & Somerset Railway. The proposals laid out were for four sections of line, running from Norton Fitzwarren to Barnstaple, Barnstaple to Ilfracombe, Ilfracombe to the Shipwright's Yard and for a chord line at Norton. The Bill was to be deposited before Parliament by 23rd December 1863. It seems that the two schemes (ND&SR and D(N)&SR) were, in effect, the same.

EXE VALLEY RAILWAY

Plans were initially deposited on 30th November 1863 and an Exe Valley Railway Company established. This line was originally planned to commence at Dulverton, in the town itself, and proceed down the valley of the River Barle for two miles before turning eastwards towards Morebath. At this point it would turn south and run down the Exe Valley through Tiverton and Bickleigh, with the objective of joining the North Devon Railway (that is the Exeter to Barnstaple L&SWR line) some three miles north of Exeter, at Newton St. Cyres, thence on to Exeter itself. The share capital was to be £100,000, with loans of £33,000. Its engineer was to be a Mr G.B. Bruce. This Exe Valley Railway Bill was covered in a House of Commons session in February 1865. There were a number of petitions from those based at various locations along the route, including the D&SR. It was regarded as '*badly laid out and designed*' and the Bill did not proceed beyond this point.

There was a variation to this original plan following the opening of the D&SR in 1873, when it was decided that the northern terminus of the proposed Exe Valley Railway should be Morebath station on the D&SR, not Dulverton town as originally proposed.

A second Exe Valley Railway Company was incorporated on 30th June 1874. It gained authorisation to raise funds and purchase land for its objective, to construct a line from Tiverton to Stoke Cannon, where it would join the Bristol to Exeter main line. After some negotiations, the B&ER took over the powers of the Exe Valley Railway Company in 1875 (coincidentally at the same time the Tiverton & North Devon Railway, below, was formed). At this point, the B&ER began lengthy discussions to amalgamate with the GWR so the Exe Valley project became a low priority.

On 1st January 1876 the B&ER was leased to the GWR and, from 1st August 1876 ,was amalgamated with it. Following the consolidation of the two companies, the GWR took over the Exe Valley Railway project and the line was eventually opened from Exeter to Tiverton on Friday 1st May 1885.

TIVERTON & NORTH DEVON RAILWAY

A meeting was held at Tiverton to elect members of the Tiverton & North Devon Railway (T&NDR) Company on 22nd September 1865, chaired by J.H. Heathcoat-Amory. The aim was to build a line from Tiverton through to Bampton and Dulverton. In the initial Tiverton & North Devon Railway Act of 1865, it was stated that '*the making of a railway from the Bristol and Exeter Railway, at Tiverton, to join the Devon and Somerset Railway in the parish of Morebath, in the County of Devon, would be of public and local advantage*'. However, a number of objections were raised and whilst the Act provided for a five year completion timetable, the attempt to progress the line failed.

Following the passing of an Act of Parliament, the T&NDR was incorporated on 19th July 1875, to construct a line from Tiverton (from the proposed Exe Valley Railway) to Morebath Junction on the newly built D&SR. Work started on 3rd May 1880 but the line was within two miles of Tiverton when financial problems halted construction. The GWR then intervened and they had the foresight to see that the T&NDR could be combined with the Exe Valley Railway

Looking east at Dulverton on 30th July 1963, as No. 7333 arrives with the 4.20pm service from Taunton to Barnstaple. No. 6327 waits at the Up platform with the 4.10pm train from Barnstaple Junction to Taunton, whilst in the bay on the right is Collett 0-4-2T No. 1450 with an Exe Valley train. The Exe Valley line left the D&SR at Morebath Junction, around a mile and a half to the east of here. *Stephen P. Derek*

to run trains through from Dulverton to Exeter. The T&NDR was a dogged and independent company, and it limped on financially, albeit with the GWR as the operator of its line, until February 1894, when it was eventually wound up. The initial planned opening date was 2nd July 1884 (ahead of the Exe Valley Railway). However, further delays to the opening of the line were caused by the need to rectify shortcomings highlighted by the BoT report in 1884. Opened as a standard gauge line on 1st August 1884, it meant that the route originally proposed in 1845 (part of the NDR) had finally been completed. Following the T&NDR opening, some nine months later the Exe Valley Railway opened and rail travel was possible from Exeter to Dulverton. After the demise of the T&NDR Company, the route became known and loved as the Exe Valley Railway.

THE ILFRACOMBE RAILWAY/ BARNSTAPLE & ILFRACOMBE RAILWAY

As already noted, various routes to Ilfracombe were proposed over the 1845 to 1870 period. The original North Devon Railway proposals incorporated such plans, as did the abortive North Devon & Somerset Railway and the Somersetshire & North Devon Junction Railway, all covered above. The main commercial driver here was Ilfracombe's location as a harbour and Packet station for South Wales and Ireland. At this time, Watchet was a thriving harbour but Ilfracombe saw the opportunity to exploit its more westerly location.

A prospectus was published in 1854 for a broad gauge line from Fremington, where it would cross the River Taw on a long bridge and then head north to Ilfracombe. Thomas Brassey would have been the contractor. The scheme did not proceed primarily due to the difficulties with the proposed river bridge and its impact on shipping on the Taw.

A further development occurred in 1859, when a group of individuals got together with the L&SWR to consider a route to Ilfracombe via Braunton and the Slade Valley. Progress was delayed by the L&SWR being distracted by the issues affecting the North Devon Railway, as described above. However, an Ilfracombe Railway Bill was put to Parliament in 1863, for a line leaving the North Devon Railway at Bishops Tawton, on the Exeter side of Barnstaple, and running up the east side of the River Taw, along the east of the town and then via Braunton and through tunnels to Ilfracombe, with a 1 in 33 gradient for 1 mile, 7 furlongs. However, the Bill was rejected; there was local opposition from an influential landowner, Sir William Williams, through whose land at Heanton Punchardon the line would have passed, so he proposed a *'cheaper and better'* line via Bittadon, further inland. This cheaper costing was disputed by the L&SWR.

A new Ilfracombe Railway Bill was put forward in the 1864 Parliamentary session, which amended the original line to go from Bishops Tawton via Bittadon, to the east of the Slade route to appease Sir William Williams. However, the D&SR raised an objection to this, as they were developing their own route to Ilfracombe, as an extension of their proposed Taunton to Barnstaple line. Local

The Barnstaple & Ilfracombe Railway opened to traffic on 20th July 1874 and this photograph of Barnstaple Quay station must have been taken around that date, probably very shortly before opening looking at the state of everything. The B&IR opened as a Light Railway, as clearly indicated by the trackwork in this view. Built on a very restricted site, it comprised a single platform on the Up side of the line, which adjoined the north end of the Taw Viaduct, and a stone-built, single storey station building with wooden awning. There was a small signal box, also named Barnstaple Quay, positioned just behind the photographer, but no sidings or other facilities. The station was renamed Barnstaple Town in July 1886 but was closed on 16th May 1898 and subsequently demolished, leaving no trace of it at all. It was replaced by a new station, opened on the same date and also named Barnstaple Town, which was sited 11 chains to the west. The move was necessary to allow space for an interchange with the narrow gauge Lynton & Barnstaple Railway. ***Neil Parkhouse collection***

support was with the Ilfracombe Railway and, as a consequence, its Act was passed on 25th July 1864 (the D&SR extension to Ilfracombe having been rejected in March 1864). This Act authorised capital of £210,000 being 10,500 shares at £20 each, with borrowing powers of £70,000. Five years were given for its construction. There was also provision for a tramway from the railway terminating on land abutting Ilfracombe harbour.

Following debates in Parliament, the compromise to the D&SR's objection to the proposed Ilfracombe Railway was for the L&SWR and the D&SR to become joint owners, the D&SR taking out the private subscribers. On 2nd June 1865, an Act authorized the acquisition, by the L&SWR and the D&SR, of the undertaking and property of the Ilfracombe Railway. However, problems developed, largely as a result of the poor state of D&SR finances and, as will be explained elsewhere, the project did not proceed. The D&SR was allowed to shed its commitments by virtue of the Devon & Somerset Act of 1867. On 25th June, the Ilfracombe Railway obtained an Abandonment Act, requiring discharge of all debts before dissolution. The D&SR's poor financial state delayed matters but eventually the GWR bailed out their commitment on takeover in 1901. This Ilfracombe Railway Company was eventually dissolved on 21st November 1901.

In carrying out a detailed review of the D&SR's development, it can be seen that the building of a railway between Ilfracombe and Barnstaple featured strongly and was closely linked. Indeed, further commentary is included in the detailed history and development of the D&SR below.

The Barnstaple & Ilfracombe Railway (B&IR) published its prospectus in November 1869, having enlisted the support of Barnstaple Corporation, the L&SWR and others. The route proposed was from Barnstaple station, across the River Taw and then via Braunton, the Slade Valley and on to Ilfracombe. Given the high level of popular support to this western route, the previous dissenter withdrew his opposition on this occasion and the eastern line supporters (via Bittadon) withdrew their Bill. This left the way clear for the B&IR and the Act received Royal Ascent on 4th July 1870. At last, a line to Ilfracombe was to become a reality.

Construction started in 1871. The B&IR was purchased by the L&SWR under an Act of Parliament dated 16th July 1874 and the line opened, single track throughout, as a Light Railway (with speed restricted to 25mph) on 20th July 1874. The trackwork was upgraded and the line ceased to be a Light Railway in 1887 and the track was doubled from Pottington to Ilfracombe soon after (1889-1891).

COMBE MARTIN RAILWAY & HARBOUR

Plans and sections were deposited in the 1886-67 session for a railway leaving the proposed D&SR line just west of Castle Hill Viaduct. The proposed Combmartin [*sic*] Railway & Harbour as it was titled wound its way north towards Stoke Berrah [*sic* – Beerah], Bratton Fleming, Challacombe and Blackmoor Gate. There it turned north-westwards to start its descent to Combe Martin, running via Kentisbury and Berry Narbor, before reaching the coast just to the west of Combe Martin Cove. The harbour was to be built on the east side of the cove.

The descent from Blackmoor Gate, at 1,000ft above sea level, was steep, so plans allowed for a reversing station above Combe Martin and a loop about one third of the way down to the terminus. It is presumed that the lead and silver mines then being worked in the area provided the commercial reasons behind the venture but it did not proceed.

BARLE VALLEY RAILWAY

The Barle Valley Railway plans were deposited on 30th November 1877, for a line to commence in a field 40 yards north of Marsh Bridge, about 1 mile north west of Dulverton on the River Barle. It was to follow the river northwards, winding along its east side up stream through the parishes of Dulverton, Hawkridge, Winsford and Withypoole [*sic*], to reach a terminus about 1 mile north west of Withypool village. The line would have been about 9 miles in length and required gradients of 1 in 44 and 1 in 50 at a number of points on the climb up the valley to Withypool. It was to be built to 2 foot gauge and the engineer was to be a John H. Miles. The commercial purpose was to link up with the Pennycombe Water group of mines (Blackland and Halsgrove) for iron ore transportation. The project was not proceeded with, presumably due to a lack of funding and especially as it seems there were no plans to link this proposed line to the D&SR at Brushford, thus necessitating double handling of goods and horses and carts to complete the link. It may have been that the promoters expected the D&SR to build a branch up to

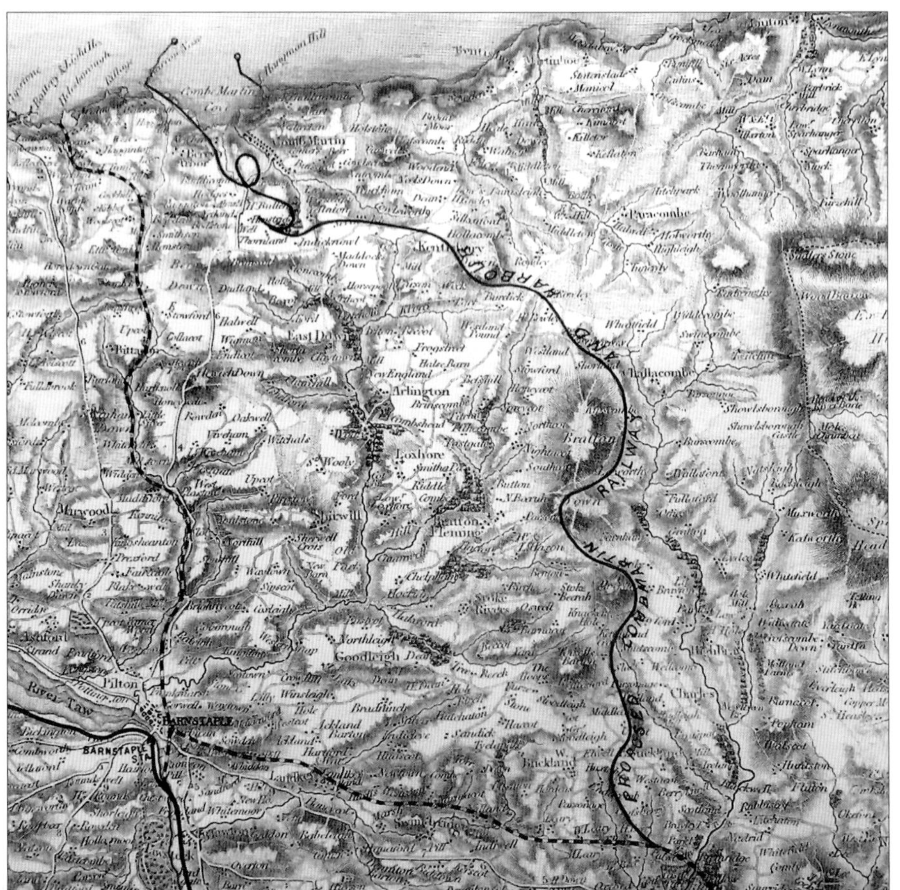

A map showing the full route of the proposed Combe Martin Railway & Harbour scheme. ***Courtesy South Molton Museum***

Dulverton to meet the proposed mineral line, although there is no record of this.

THE LYNTON RAILWAY COMPANY

A Bill was launched in 1879 for a 22-mile line from South Molton to Lynton. Apparently there had been previous abortive attempts to create such Bill. The prospectus was issued seeking capital of £72,000. This was done under the auspices of the the Devon & Somerset Railway and the prospectus stated:

'The new line will pass over an existing tramway belonging to the Florence Mining Company Limited. This Company has offered to take shares in the estimated value of their interest, and by way of this arrangement the cost of construction will, as a necessary consequence, be materially reduced.'

The plan was quickly dropped because of lack of support.

THE BRIDGWATER & WATCHET RAILWAY

In 1882, the WSR was suffering as the GWR had increased fares and there was dissatisfaction with the running of the services on that line. Proposals were developed by the Somerset & Dorset Joint Railway and the WSMR for a new railway running from Bridgwater to Stogursey and Watchet, where it would join the WSMR; there would also be a branch on to the Minehead Railway (with a proposal for running powers over that line). The aim was to thwart the GWR's monopoly in the area. The cost of building was estimated at £430,000 and a Bill went to Committee on 10th April 1882. Not surprisingly, the GWR objected and, despite the Bill being close to Royal Assent, it was withdrawn by the promoters. The link to the WSMR is referred to above in that section. A similar application was put forward in the 1884 Session but this too was withdrawn.

A comparable line was also proposed in 1899. The L&SWR were looking at a light railway to run from Bridgwater via Stowey to Stogursey and local inhabitants were trying to encourage an extension to Watchet, and then to continue that line via the WSMR to Exeter. Nothing came of the proposals. In the mid 1920s, the GWR were trying to encourage the Government to finance a Bridgwater to Watchet line to reduce unemployment but without success.

BRAY VALLEY RAILWAY

Following opposition from the GWR and the L&SWR, an 1883 Barnstaple & Lynton Railway Bill was dropped. This had proposed a line from Barnstaple to Lynton via Kentisbury. However, in 1884 there was an attempt to promote a line from Filleigh to Lynton via Bratton Fleming and Blackmoor Gate, the Combe Martin Railway & Harbour, sometimes referred to as the Bray Valley Railway and backed by local landowners. Once the GWR had removed its opposition, the 1885 Lynton Railway Act was passed, with approved capital of £83,000. The engineer was to be a Mr C.H. Meyer.

The section authorised for building was from Castle Hill (Filleigh) to Blackmoor Gate, which would have been a terminus. The railway would have been 10 miles, 6 furlongs and 2 chains in length and would have had severe gradients of 1 in 41, 1 in 45, 1 in 60 and 1 in 67 for stretches. It would have passed through the parishes of Charles, Bratton Fleming, Challacombe and Kentisbury, and was to pass near Cape of Good Hope Farm and the Friendship Inn (located at the junction of the Challacombe road with the South Molton to Combe Martin road). Powers were obtained to extend the line to Lynton in 1886 and, in 1887, a branch down to Combe Martin. The proposals did not proceed, as no capital was subscribed and no construction work was ever undertaken. However, the same promoters secured a new Act in 1890, which permitted abandonment of all proposed lines except the Lynton to Blackmore Gate section.

The *Lynton & Lynmouth Recorder Newspaper*, on 24th November 1885, reported these proposals in typically optimistic manner:

'The ambition of Lynton for the last twenty years has been to get a railway. On many occasions efforts have been made to promote it; sometimes in one direction and some times in another.

Surveys have been made to Ilfracombe, Castle Hill, South Molton, Dulverton, Watchet and Minehead, but they all ended in smoke until Messrs Turner and Toogood took the matter in hand and decided on Castle Hill – or as it now is called, the Filleigh-route. Barnstaple, being the capital of the district they tried first, in 1883, to run from that place but owing to opposition of the Great Western and South Western Railway Companies, that route had to be abandoned.

Being determined to prosecute the matter to the end they decided last year on adopting the Castle Hill line, which is much more easily made and worked than any other. Employing first-class engineers, they have succeeded in selecting an excellent line. Leaving Filleigh station it goes up the Bray Valley, over Bratton Down and by the Friendship Inn to a point near Blackmoor Gate, where there will be a station; thence to Tinworthy and around the base of Chapman Barrows, on the Paracombe

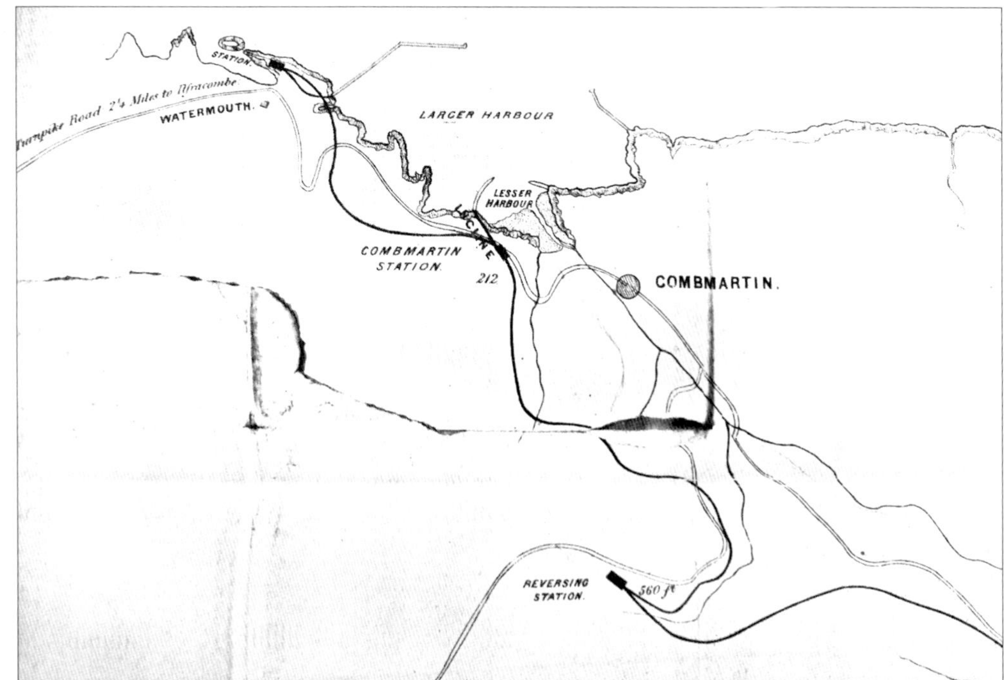

The proposed extension of the so called Bray Valley Railway's line to Combe Martin to some extent mirrored the earlier proposals of the Combmartin Railway & Harbour scheme. However, the BVR line was planned to carry on a further mile and a half to a terminus at Watermouth and also missed out the loop proposed for the earlier line, as the reversing station in the valley of the River Umber was at a much lower height, just 560ft above sea level; the line coming in is from Blackmoor Gate. ***Courtesy Somerset Archives & Local Studies***

side, to Ranscombe, and thence by Dean Steep to a point on Mr Baker's farm over Lynbridge, from whence a road will be made on the side of the hill to Lynton.

The total estimated cost is about £100,000 or £5,000 per mile, whereas former plans – badly conceived, we must admit – the good estimates never came below £7,500. A good deal of saving is effected by going up round the base of Chapman Barrows instead of crossing the Parracombe valleys as was intended in the former plans. A great proportion of land along the line will be given to the promoters gratis by Earl Fortescue, Sir Thomas Acland, Mrs Lock-Roe and others, and in no part will there be feeling exhibited but of friendship and goodwill.

As all our readers are aware, an act was passed last session for the part between Filleigh and Blackmoor Gate, so that operations may begin at any time and by the time that part is made, a further act will be obtained for the Lynton part, the plans having already been made for application next session; and by the time that is finished a branch will, we understand, be constructed to the port of Combe Martin.

In order that work might begin, Mr Turner has recently been in Lynton trying to get local support and he has met with extraordinary success, the total subscription promised in two or three days amounting to £20,000! This speaks volumes of what faith local people have in the undertaking. We believe Mr Turner is so well satisfied that he is going back to London to float the company at once.

That the line will pay we have every confidence. It will serve the whole district from Glenthorne to Combe Martin for the accommodation of thousands of visitors who come here in the summer and will have a considerable general traffic, particularly in lime and minerals when the Combe Martin branch is made and a tramway from Chapman Burrows out over the Forest to the mines. Possibly also a harbour of refuge may be made at Combe Martin, which would cause a great spring in the traffic between Devon and Somerset and Wales.

A favourable move is also going on at Barnstaple where the two companies [GWR and L&SWR] *are going to be united; this will enable constant excursions to be made between Exeter, Ilfracombe and Lynton. The Devon and Somerset Railway cost, we believe £23,000 per mile; the Ilfracombe line cost over £10,000 per mile and yet it pays 4½%. As the Lynton line will be made for £5,000 per mile, we feel satisfied it must also pay.*

It will serve the whole coast from Porlock to Combe Martin, all of which is now the favourite resort of tourists and visitors. When the district is developed as districts do after the advent of the railway, probably the only wonder will be that we remained so long eighteen miles from civilisation. As Lynton and district have given the promoters such help, we think it their duty to go ahead at once. When will the first sod be cut? Besides the benefit to the owners of coast lands, all owners of land along the line will be benefitted and the farmers too. We can therefore heartily wish the undertaking God Speed.'

In 1890, powers were sought to build a line from Blackmoor to Barnstaple and to operate all the lines electrically; the name adopted was the Barnstaple & Lynton Electric Tramroad Company. The Bill was passed in the Lords but it was not proceeded with in the subsequent session and the proposals died.

THE LYNTON RAILWAY

The potential of a rail connection to Lynton from Filleigh remained alive and, by circa 1894, Lord Fortescue, Viscount Ebrington (his son) and others were promoting an alternative standard gauge line to the 1885 proposals. The intention for this line was to run from Filleigh to Lynton via High Bray, Bratton Fleming, Paracombe and Martinhoe Cross. This apparently was shorter than

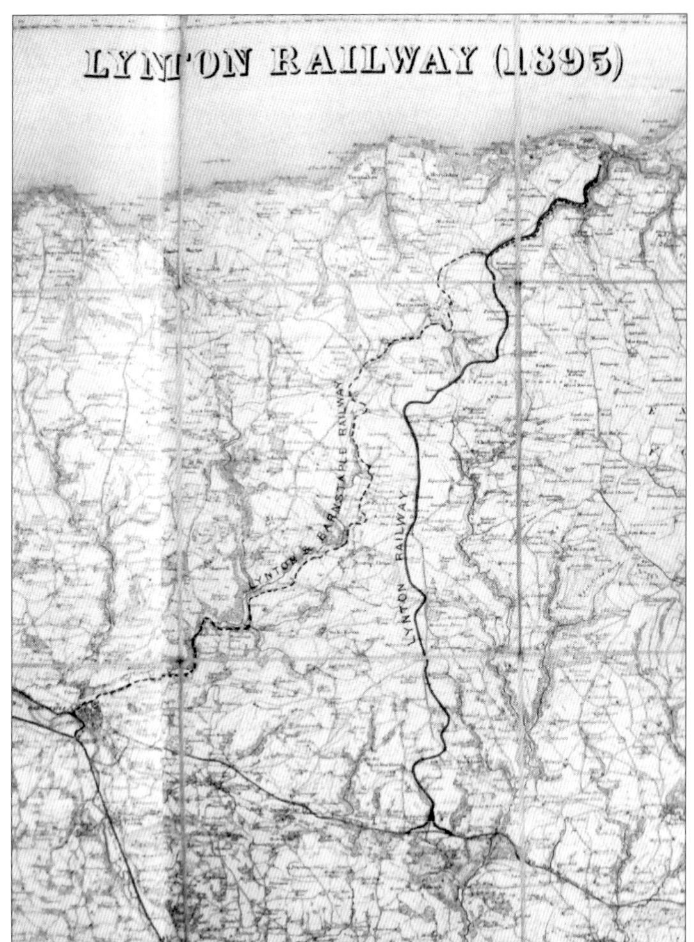

A map illustrating the potential route of the standard gauge Lynton Railway from Filleigh to Lynton, along with the proposed Lynton & Barnstaple Railway's narrow gauge line (the dotted line). ***Courtesy Lynton & Barnstaple Railway Magazine***

the previous Filleigh plan, as it would follow higher ground rather than run in the valleys and therefore required less engineering works. The plan was for trains to commence from Lynton and be split at Filleigh, with one part going to Taunton and the remainder west to Barnstaple. In some quarters, it was felt that this line was only proposed as a deterrent or obstacle to a narrow gauge line concurrently proposed by Sir George Newnes MP and others to run from Barnstaple to Lynton. There were merits in both lines and these were aired at a meeting of the House of Lords Select Committee between 19th and 26th March 1895. The narrow gauge scheme would link Barnstaple, the 'capital' of North Devon, with Lynton by a 19½ mile line. The gradients would not have exceeded 1 in 50 and the proposed cost was £50,410. A number of local communities would also have been served and it had the backing of 1,005 of 2,000 Barnstaple inhabitants. However, the proposed standard gauge route had a gradient of 1 in 40 for 11 miles and was to require share capital of £120,000 and loans of £40,000. Whilst this scheme was supported by the GWR (who would work the line), it served hardly any local population between the two key locations (4,873 versus 19,000) and there was concern over its use in adverse weather conditions. The standard gauge line had the advantage of being able to run passengers and goods through without transshipment, which the narrow gauge line could not claim. However, counter claims suggested the required share capital would never be raised for the standard gauge line, whereas Mr Heywood,

Chairman of the Urban District Council of Lynton, expressed that he had no doubt the narrow gauge line would raise the necessary money. Lord Fortescue had supported the original survey thirty years ago by contributing £200 and was now prepared to take shares in the venture to the value of his land (covering some 6 or 7 miles). The standard gauge line would also benefit tourism, the agricultural community and horse traffic during the hunting season. Tourists from Bristol, the Midlands and London would get to Lynton at least an hour and a half earlier by the GWR sponsored route. The GWR was even prepared to give the L&SWR access to the proposed line, despite the fact that detractors felt they wanted to keep another company out of Lynton. The concern was the Filleigh proposal was merely a 'block line' designed to keep others out. On 26th March, the Chairman of the Select Committee announced the rejection of the Filleigh Bill, leaving the way clear for the progression of the Lynton & Barnstaple Railway Bill.

LYNTON & BARNSTAPLE RAILWAY

As explained above, there were several attempts to reach Lynton, the earlier schemes all failing. However, the House of Lords Select Committee gave the Lynton & Barnstaple Railway (L&BR) proposals the go-ahead on 26th March 1895 and the Lynton & Barnstaple Railway Act was passed on 25th June, with authorised share capital of £70,000 for a narrow gauge (1ft 11$^1/_2$ins) line. Sir James Szlumper was consulting engineer, with Sir George Newnes as the first Chairman. The first sod was cut by Lady Newnes on 17th September 1895 and the line constructed and officially opened on 11th May 1898, with the public being able to travel this 19$^1/_2$ mile highly picturesque route for the first time on 16th May 1898. It had a short-lived existence, being closed by the Southern Railway in 1935.

BIDEFORD, WESTWARD HO! & APPLEDORE RAILWAY

The Bideford, Westward Ho! & Appledore Railway (BWH&AR) was incorporated on 21st May 1896 and opened in two stages; from Bideford to Northam on 21st April 1901 and Northam to Appledore on 1st May 1908. It was built to the standard gauge but was isolated from the Barnstaple to Torrington line, which ran on the east side of the River Torridge. The line was short-lived due to disputes with the local council and a difficult financial position, and it closed on 28th March 1917.

THE LYNMOUTH & MINEHEAD LIGHT RAILWAY

There was an earlier proposal in 1874 (see above) by William Dennis (engineer of the Minehead Railway) to extend the line from Minehead to Lynton or Lynmouth. This was put to B&ER directors, who expressed little interest in such a speculative venture.

However, two directors of the Barry Railway Company (Messrs Thomas and Thompson) joined with one director of the Vale of Glamorgan Railway and with George Luttrell of Dunster, and put forward a new proposal on 11th May 1898. The plan was to develop a steamship service from Cardiff to Minehead and to open up Exmoor to visitors from South Wales. Part of this plan was to build a railway line of 2ft gauge, running for 20 miles. It would have curved round the eastern side of Minehead from the GWR terminus, then broadly follow the route of the (now A39) road to County Gate, before swinging towards the coast near Countisbury and terminating 520 feet above the harbour behind the Tors Hotel in Lynmouth.

It would not have been as high as the L&BR (which was 250 feet above Lynton and 700 feet above sea level). As a consequence of the terrain, the railway would have required a number of trestle bridges and other substantial engineering works. Opposition was strong, not least from the newly opened Lynton & Barnstaple Railway, which feared competition. Sir George Newnes, Chairman of the L&BR, made his position clear at the celebratory lunch after the official opening of his line. He was concerned by the damage that may have been done to the beauty of the area by the incursion of the railway and the inevitable invasion of day trippers. Sir George even implied that his friend, George Luttrell, could not be aware of the full proposals otherwise he would not be supportive of them. Local landowners joined in, suggesting that the line would interfere with staghunting. On 9th August 1898, the Light Railway Commissioners met (under the provisions of the Light Railways Act 1896) in Minehead to consider the application '*for powers to construct a light railway from Minehead Pier to Lynmouth along the coast*'. Having heard the arguments (largely in favour of tourists and not local agriculture), the Commissioners declared that they '*did not consider that the present application should be entertained, for it was of the reason that it was not for the benefit of the country through which it passed*' (as reported in the *North Devon Journal*, 11th August 1898). Having failed in front of the Commissioners, there were never any attempts to re-introduce similar proposals.

WEST SOMERSET LIGHT RAILWAY

Somewhat surprisingly, a light railway proposal for West Somerset was laid out under the 1896 and 1912 Light Railways Acts in 1924. Plans were deposited in May for a line that left Bridgwater and was to run through the parishes of Cannington, Wembdon, Stogursey, Kilton with Lilstock and, finally, Kilve, where the terminus was to be located. The line was to be 11 miles, 5 furlongs and 9 chains in length but it never got beyond the planning stage and its commercial purpose is not clear. It may in fact be the same line that the GWR were trying to encourage the Government to finance in the mid-1920s; that is, to build a Bridgwater to Watchet railway as a means of reducing unemployment. It did not proceed.

IN SUMMARY

It would now be appropriate to summarise the North Devon and West Somerset railway map circa 1900. Numerous schemes had come and gone but, by 1908, the area was left with:

1. The Bristol & Exeter Railway (1842 to Taunton, 1844 to Exeter)
2. The Tiverton Branch (12th June 1848)
3. The Exeter to Bideford line, comprising the E&CR/TVER/NDR&DC/BER (12th May 1851 to 2nd November 1855)
4. West Somerset Mineral Railway (1858)
5. The Taunton to Minehead line, comprising the WSR/Minehead Railway (31st March 1862 & 16th July 1874)
6. Taunton to Wiveliscombe (8th June 1871)
7. The Okehampton Railway (3rd October 1871)
8. Bideford to Torrington (18th July 1872)
9. Wiveliscombe to Barnstaple (1st November 1873)
10. Barnstaple to Ilfracombe (20th July 1874)
11. Exeter to Dulverton, comprising the T&NDR/Exe Valley Railway (1st August 1884 & 1st May 1885)
12. The Lynton to Barnstaple line (11th May 1898)
13. Bideford, Westward Ho! & Appledore Railway (21st April 1901 & 1st May 1908)

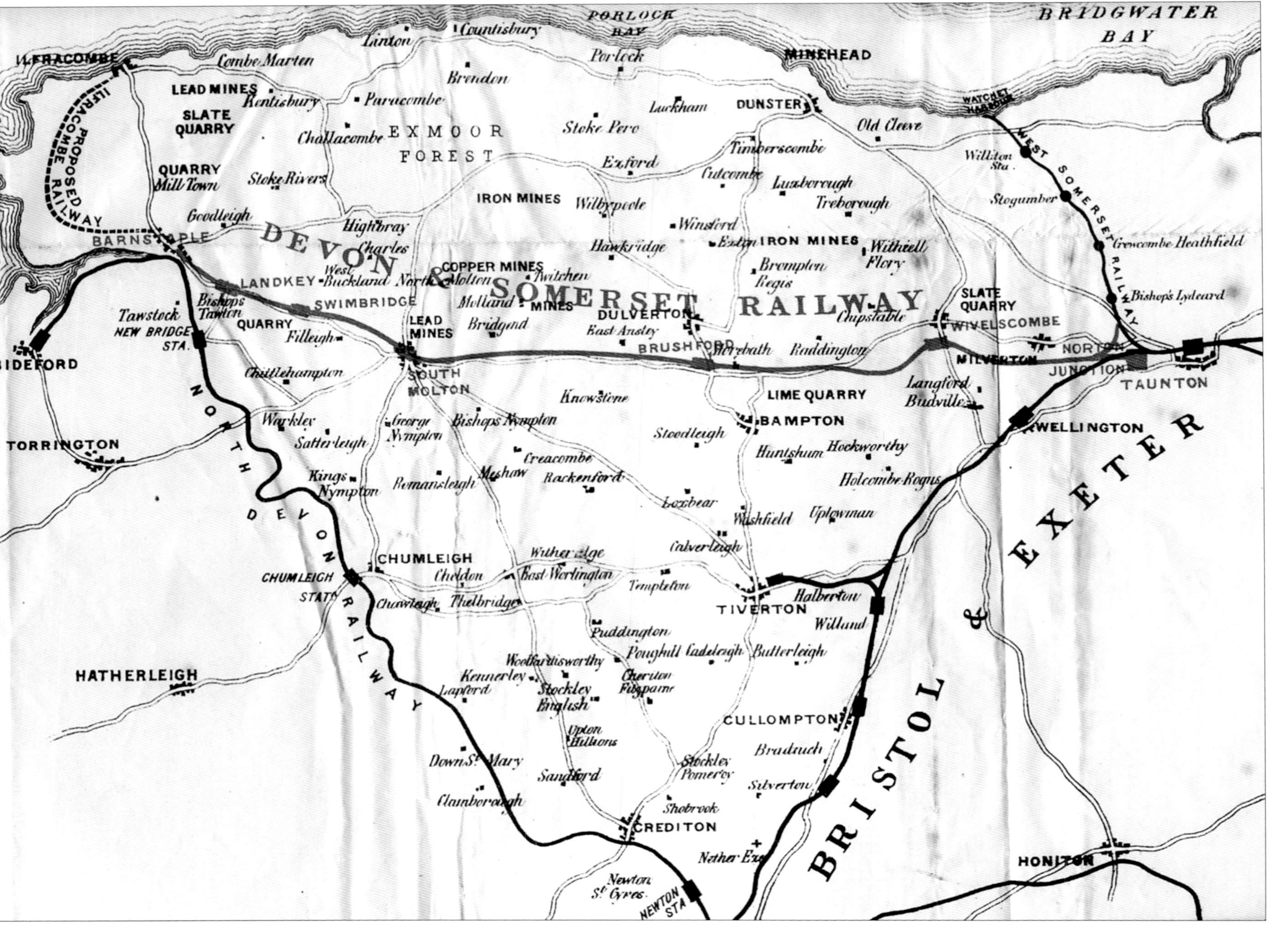

A map showing the proposed Devon & Somerset Railway route to Barnstaple. Note the spur to the West Somerset Railway (only open to Watchet) in the east. The '*Proposed Ilfracombe Railway*', as an extension of the D&SR, is shown as a black dotted line. The North Devon Railway at this point had reached Bideford. Note, too, the references to iron and copper mines, illustrating the '*rich mineral deposits*' potentially available in the area to be served by the D&SR line. *Reproduced courtesy William Hancock*

Chapter 3

The History, Construction, Development and Demise of the D&SR 1860-1966

The railway schemes that were proposed in the North Devon and West Somerset regions and the precursors to the D&SR, are described in outline in the previous chapter. The Devon (North) & Somerset Railway (D(N)&SR), which proposed a line between Norton Fitzwarren (Watchet Junction) and Ilfracombe in November 1863, was largely the template from which the D&SR, at least between Norton Fitzwarren and Barnstaple, was subsequently proposed, then put to Parliament and eventually built.

Whilst the D(N)&SR was in its gestation period, the *West Somerset Free Press* reported on 13th September 1862 as follows:

> *'It will branch off from the Bristol & Exeter Railway near Taunton, passing through Wiveliscombe, Bampton and Dulverton, through the Anstey Valley, close by the villages of Bishopsnympton* [sic] *and Molland and the hitherto neglected Southmolton* [sic] *and thence to Barnstaple-bringing Lynton a short hour's ride by coach-and terminating at Ilfracombe, the future packet station for South Wales, Ireland and Liverpool… It is said that a sum of money has been subscribed sufficient to make the line, and that no time will be lost in carrying it into effect.'*

The proposed railway between Taunton and Ilfracombe had also deposited plans but the Barnstaple to Ifracombe section was thrown out at standing orders in March 1864.

The Devon & Somerset Railway Bill

The D&SR Bill was presented to Parliament in 1864. During the debate, the *North Devon Journal* reported (on 2nd June) on the delaying tactics of the L&SWR, who were resistant to the D&SR having an independent line running though to Barnstaple. The L&SWR saw North Devon as 'their territory' and having reached Barnstaple also had their thoughts on a railway to Ilfracombe. As the paper reported:

> *'the issues are simply, – whether a vast tract of country, with a population of 100,000 persons, and possessed of inexhaustible agricultural and mineral resources, shall continue to be excluded from the advantages of free and facile communication with the great centres of commerce and manufacture – whether the towns abutting on the line shall be compelled to make a detour of 33 miles* [via Exeter] *in a journey to Bristol and the north of England for the special behoof of a grasping monopoly* [the L&SWR]*, which puts forth impudent and groundless pretensions that are at variance with the public interests.'*

The report went on to lambast the L&SWR, saying they had employed agents to convince a parliamentary committee that they were *'injured innocents'* who had spent large amounts of money in bringing rail to North Devon and should not to be deprived of the fruits of their investment.

This bad publicity was not good for the L&SWR and, by way of appeasement, they proposed an 11½ mile branch from the North Devon Railway (NDR) at Umberleigh to feed South Molton and North Molton, and join the proposed D&SR there. This was to prevent the D&SR building a direct line to Barnstaple and to allow the L&SWR to retain some control. Whilst it was generally felt that this proposed detour (resulting in an extra 4½ miles of travel) would never have been put forward by the L&SWR independently of the D&SR plans, it was a solution worthy of debate. The L&SWR dispute or resistance was really only over the last stage of the line, from South Molton to Barnstaple; they had no dispute over the development of the Taunton to South Molton section.

The *West Somerset Free Press* had previously reported (21st May 1864) on the House of Commons Select Committee debate over the so called North Devon Extension Bill and the D&SR. Mr Hope Scott (for the L&SWR), stated that, as the other line (the proposed D&SR) would touch neither North or South Molton, it would *'inflict permanent injury upon the latter place'*. Lord Fortescue reported that the Barnstaple and South Molton public were in favour of the direct line (D&SR), along with a majority in Ilfracombe. Further support came from Mr Knight and Lord Poltimore. The Reverend Karslake (rector of Meshaw) was supportive of the D&SR because of the direct communication to Taunton and Barnstaple, and was concerned that the B&ER would withdraw its financial support if the D&SR was not built through to Barnstaple. A number of Barnstaple merchants were also supportive. In addition, a Mr Watkins, a cattle dealer from Clifton (Bristol), proved that a cattle trade existed between Barnstaple and Bristol which offered further support to the D&SR. Mr Rodwell, QC for the D&SR, made the following proposal to the L&SWR:

> *'This line from Taunton to Barnstaple to be passed. The North Devon and Somerset to withdraw their opposition to the Ilfracombe Bill and assist in getting the best possible connection with the harbour at Ilfracombe. The D&S to have running powers over the line from Barnstaple to Ilfracombe, paying… for the cost of laying down the broad gauge. The above to be taken and considered as a whole.'*

Mr Clark, for the L&SWR said *'no arrangement had been come to, and there was no prospect of a compromise being arrived at'*. The Committee then deliberated and proposed that the D&SR Bill should be passed for the construction of the line to South Molton. The line of the L&SWR should be constructed from North Molton to Umberleigh, with them giving running powers to the D&SR to Barnstaple. A double line on the mixed gauge was to be laid on the proposed South Molton to Barnstaple route. The D&SR was to have separate platforms, clerks and agents at Barnstaple if they required them. The L&SWR requested time to consider the proposal. On the following Friday, matters proceeded and the L&SWR carried their bill for *'the construction of a branch from Umberleigh station to Northmolton* [sic] *through Southmolton* [sic]'.

The junction off the NDR at Umberleigh was proposed as a triangular junction (Umberleigh Junction), to allow for access in both the Exeter and Barnstaple directions. This line would have connected with the D&SR at Molton Junction, near South Molton. It was to be a single line of mixed gauge with the L&SWR and D&SR having joint responsibility for it. The section from Umberleigh to Barnstaple was to be solely L&SWR responsibility but was to be double track, with an extra broad gauge rail laid to accommodate D&SR services. Thus the plan was for trains to detour at South Molton in a south westerly direction to Umberleigh and then turn north westwards on to Barnstaple. However, despite these advanced plans, this proposed line never obtained the sanction of Parliament. Following a review of the submissions, the Committee of the House of Lords preferred the direct line to Barnstaple and so the route via Umberleigh did not proceed.

As with all Bills, the D&SR Bill had to pass through the House of Lords and it was hoped that they would see the benefits of their original proposals. The line was not an invasive scheme: '*it is designed to traverse a country that had no railway of any kind – to afford ready access to the markets to those who are now comparatively isolated – to promote the improvement of agriculture …*'. The *North Devon Journal* urged inhabitants to petition Parliament '*in right earnest*' and encouraged the support of landowners and noblemen. That latter reference was to include Lord Fortescue, acknowledging his potential personal benefit; the line passed though 6½ miles of his land, for which he would acquire shares in the D&SR. The report felt that his support, along with other landowners such as Lords Carnarvon and Poltimore, would add gravitas to the D&SR case. Given that North Devonians regarded Lord Fortescue as their natural leader, they '*earnestly believe that he will not fail them in this hour of their need*' – a powerful, emotive and persuasive case put forward by the *North Devon Journal*.

Despite the challenges and difficulties referred to above, the Devon & Somerset Railway Bill was presented to Parliament along with deposited plans for the House of Commons and the Lords to consider.

The B&ER board meeting of 2nd June 1864 confirmed their shareholders approval for '*a bill for making a railway from the B&ER to Barnstaple with branches*.' The B&ER were at this stage in provisional agreement to subscribe £100,000 in share capital in the D&SR – but to only pay when calls were made. In subscribing for £33,000 of shares, they would be able to appoint one member to the D&SR board, at £66,000 two directors could be appointed and three directors when the full amount had been subscribed. Even at this early stage, a working agreement was being negotiated and a four page Articles of Agreement, dated 20th June 1864, prepared; it stated '*The Bristol company at their expense may and will duly manage and regulate the Devon Railway and traffic thereon …*'. Thus the B&ER would operate the line for cost and in perpetuity. This working document also proposed that construction work was to be undertaken at least to Molton Junction (as referred to above) by the D&SR, with the Devon Company engineer responsible for overseeing the work but having a reporting obligation to the B&ER engineer. This working agreement is explored below in relation to the Act that derived from these initial Articles of Agreement.

DEVON & SOMERSET RAILWAY ACT OF 1864

The Act was passed 29th July 1864 (*27 & 28 Victoria c307*) and thus the D&SR Company was born with the proposal to construct a 43 mile broad gauge railway from Watchet Junction (subsequently Norton Fitzwarren), just west of Taunton, to Barnstaple; there was no detour at South Molton. The Act also allowed for a mixed gauge extension to Ilfracombe, which was to be a joint line with the L&SWR.

The Act stated that the capital of the company would be £500,000 in 20,000 shares of £25 each, one fifth being required to be paid up before any shares were to be issued. The power to borrow £166,000 on mortgage was also allowed by Clause 8. This borrowing ratio of one-third loans to share capital was the normal financing structure for such railways. All monies raised by the company was specifically stated to be applied only for the purpose of the company's undertaking. The number of directors was fixed between six as a minimum and nine as a maximum. The initial directors named in the Act were Lord Poltimore, Sir William Throckmorton, Bart, Arthur John Locke, John Thomas Nash, William Gould Smyth and William Hancock. There were powers of compulsory land purchase within the Act but such powers had to be exercised within three years of the passing of the Act (that is by 29th June 1867) and a requirement (Clause 21) that the railway be completed within five years (by 29th June 1869).

Clause 24 authorised a line (Railway No. 1) commencing by a junction with the B&ER at or near the point of the junction (Watchet Junction) of the WSR with the B&ER:

'in the Parish of Norton Fitz Warren in the County of Somerset, and passing through or into Bishop's Hull, Norton Fitz Warren, Hill Farrance, Oake, Heathfield, Milverton, Wiveliscombe, and Chipstable in the County of Somerset, Clayhanger, Bampton and Morebath in the County of Devon, Brushford and Dulverton in the County of

ANNO VICESIMO SEPTIMO & VICESIMO OCTAVO

VICTORIÆ REGINÆ.

Cap. cccvii.

An Act for making a Railway from the *Bristol and Exeter* Railway to *Barnstaple*; and for other Purposes. [29th *July* 1864.]

WHEREAS the making of the several Lines of Railway by this Act authorized would be of local and public Advantage: And whereas the several Persons in that Behalf in this Act named, with others, are willing, at their own Expense, to carry the Undertaking into execution on being incorporated into a Company (in this Act called "the Company") for the Purpose: And whereas the Railway by this Act authorized will communicate directly with the Railways of the *Bristol and Exeter* Railway Company (in this Act called the *Bristol and Exeter* Company), and it is expedient that Traffic Arrangements between the Company and the *Bristol and Exeter* Company be authorized: And whereas Plans and Sections of the Railway by this Act authorized, showing the Lines and Levels thereof, and Books of Reference to the Plans, containing the Names of the Owners or reputed Owners, Lessees or reputed Lessees, and Occupiers of the Lands to be taken for the Purposes thereof, have been deposited with the respective Clerks of the Peace for the Counties of *Devon and Somerset*, and those Plans, Sections, and Books of Reference are in this Act referred

[*Local.*] 52 *H* to

Somerset, East Anstey, West Anstey, Molland, Bishopsnympton [sic], *Northmolton, Southmolton* [sic], *Filleigh, Chittlehampton, Swimbridge, Landkey and Barnstaple in the County of Devon and terminating in the Parish of Barnstaple'.*

Railway No. 2 was essentially a chord line between the D&SR and WSR to form a triangle near Watchet Junction.

Clause 25 referred to the pending Bill of the Ilfracombe Railway and the need for the two engineers of the companies (D&SR and L&SWR) to liaise on the joint development of this line. Clause 26 stated the D&SR should be made in the broad gauge exclusively. This was despite the recommendations of the Gauge Commissioners in 1845, that all new railways should be built to the standard gauge. It was due to Brunel's efforts that a savings clause was added to the Gauge Act when it became law and the D&SR Act took advantage of this.

A completion bond was to be deposited with the accountant general of the Court of Chancery, based on the anticipated original completion cost of the railway. With the cost of completion anticipated at £650,000, the bond was calculated at £57,142 17s 2d. However, when part of the original proposed undertaking was not authorised and the total anticipated cost reduced to £500,000, this led to the bond element being reduced. The bond funds deposited would be forfeited to the Crown if the railway was not opened to the public in the appointed time (five years), as stated in the tortuous Clause 28.

The charges applicable for conveyance of passengers, animals and goods was set out in Clause 30 (*et seq*). By way of illustration, passengers were to be charged 2d per mile plus an additional 1d per mile if conveyed in a carriage owned by the D&SR Company (which was never the case, as we now know). Horses were 3d per mile (plus the 1d extra), cows were 2d per head per mile, with sheep, etc. being three farthings ($^{3}/_{4}$d) each per mile. Dung, compost, manure and coal was priced at 1d per ton per mile. There was also a maximum limit placed on the amounts that could be charged, namely 3d per mile for every First Class passenger, 2d per mile for Second Class and $1^{3}/_{4}$d for Third Class. Animals had similar *maxima* (as set out in Clause 33).

Finally, the Act acknowledged and outlined the agreements and arrangements that the D&SR and B&ER may need to enter into, given the intention of the D&SR to use the B&ER as its operator.

D&SR PROSPECTUS

Following the passing of the 1864 Act, a prospectus was issued for the D&SR to raise the capital stated. The provisional committee listed in the prospectus comprised forty-four members, including six directors: Lord Poltimore, Sir William Throckmorton, John Arthur Locke, William Gould Smyth, John Thomas Nash and John Henry Dillon. A number of local banks and local solicitors were also named. The Secretary was John McMillan and Eugenius Birch was stated as the engineer.

By today's standards, it was a short document of only three pages, outlining the benefits of the line in opening up the rich agricultural and mineral district of North Devon to other parts of England, and *vice versa* for the manufacturing districts in the north to have their products sent south. Also, a new sea route to Ireland could be established via Ilfracombe, saving 80 miles of sea passage. Support from landowners was emphasised, with some prepared to donate land gratuitously, others just selling to the railway for agricultural prices and taking shares in exchange. The prospectus even referred to the '*inexhaustible*' supply of iron under the Exmoor Hills (something that, as the section on mining in this book notes, the passage of time has shown to be optimistic at best!).

DEVON AND SOMERSET RAILWAY.

TAUNTON TO BARNSTAPLE.

FORM OF APPLICATION FOR SHARES.

No.

Gentlemen,

I request you will allot me Shares of £25 each in the Capital of the above undertaking, and I hereby agree to accept the same, or any smaller number that you may allot me, and to pay the Calls thereon as they may be made, and I hereby authorise and empower you to insert my name in the Register of Shareholders of the Company, for the number of Shares which you may allot to me.

I am, Gentlemen,

Your obedient Servant,

Name in full __________

Address __________

Profession or Business __________

Dated the ______ day of ______, 1864.

A copy of the application form that would have been used to subscribe for ordinary shares in the D&SR included in the prospectus. ***Courtesy Somerset Archives & Local Studies***

Following the passing of the Act, the first board meeting of the D&SR took place at noon on 4th August 1864, at 15 Parliament Square, Westminster, London. John A. Locke of Northmoor House, Dulverton was in the Chair. Directors present were Sir William Throckmorton (of Coughton Court, Bromsgrove, Worcestershire) and Mr Smythe. Mr R.M. Riccard, solicitor, was in attendance and acted as Company Secretary.

At the meeting, Lord Poltimore (of Poltimore Park, Exeter, Devon) was formally appointed chairman, John Locke deputy chairman, John McMillan secretary (on a salary of £400 per year) and Mr Eugenius Birch as the engineer. Other directors were Lord Fortescue (of Castle Hill, Filleigh) and John Dillon (instead of Hancock). Daniel Climie of Shrewsbury was appointed contractor.

It was also resolved that the agreements with the B&ER and Lord Poltimore, and the acts and proceedings of the provisional directors and officers up to the passing of the D&SR Act, were approved and ratified. It was confirmed that expenses incurred up to the passing of the Act totalled £42,000 and that Lloyd's bonds for £22,000 were to be issued.

The first half-yearly meeting of the company was held at South Molton Town Hall at 12 noon on Tuesday 4th October 1864. The first general meeting on 11th October ratified the appointment of the above directors but also included a Mr J.T. Nash (of South Molton).

Construction started towards the end of 1864. Lady Poltimore had cut the first sod at Hacche Moor, near South Molton, at the proposed site of the station on 4th October, on land donated by Sir Thomas Dyke Acland (see Appendix 6). It was quite an occasion, as the field was decorated with a temporary avenue of trees, along with flags and banners, and there was support from a huge crowd (reported as 10,000 in the *North Devon Journal*). This was the ceremonial start, the real construction commencing at Barnstaple, in a field below

Hawley House. The choice of Barnstaple as the starting place was purely practical, the transportation of plant to there being more straight forward than taking it to Hacche Moor, at that time almost in the middle of nowhere, with poor access roads. Stables were constructed for Climie's team of horses, along with a blacksmith's forge complete with modern equipment and a capacious saw pit. Wagons which worked between the wharves and the site were drawn by a team of four horses.

The *West Somerset Free Press* reported on 22nd October 1864:

'The engineering difficulties, we are told, are not very great. There will be two tunnels, one in the neighbourhood of Wiveliscombe, over half a mile long; the other at Memridge [sic] *Wood near Castle Hill which will be under a quarter of a mile. There will be a viaduct at Castle Hill under 100 feet high and some others of less magnitude. The broad gauge will be adopted and the Bristol & Exeter have entered into an agreement to work the line.'*

At the Board meeting of 3rd November 1864, an application to Parliament to extend the D&SR to Tiverton was confirmed. In December 1864, it was noted that the contractor Mr Climie had misappropriated funds and he was dismissed, subsequently being replaced by William & John Pickering & Co. Their appointment was subject to certain financial requirements, which included £100,000 of shares being subscribed by the B&ER and £100,000 worth of 5% preference shares being issued to the GWR. Pickerings were clearly concerned in committing to such a fledgling venture that they wanted the backing of the two more substantial organisations to secure their position and remuneration.

As matters progressed and with the D&SR now no longer proceeding west beyond Barnstaple, the requirement for the B&ER to subscribe for £100,000 of shares was removed. The proposed working terms were also revised; the B&ER was to work the line for 50% of gross receipts (along with rebates from the Great Western and Midland railways) rather than for cost. The lease to operate the line was proposed to be twenty-one years in length and along with this came the responsibility of maintaining the railway. This proposal was ratified at a meeting at South Molton on 28th February 1865, which also confirmed the removal of Mr Climie and the formal appointment of Messrs Pickerings as contractors (despite the removal of the potential investment by the B&ER in the venture).

It was at this time that concerns were first aired by the D&SR with regard to the proposed location of their Barnstaple terminus. It was suggested that it should be more centrally located in the town and the company began to assess the possibilities of extending the end of the line a short distance westwards to achieve this.

At the half yearly meeting of 28th February 1865, James Jerwood and George Robinson (public accountants) were elected auditors at 50 guineas a year.

THE ILFRACOMBE RAILWAY

Ilfracombe was the ultimate destination in North Devon for both the L&SWR and the D&SR and, as was discussed in the previous chapter, there were conflicts and competition over alternative routes, with promoters being thwarted in their attempt to reach the seaside town and harbour.

Although the D&SR's proposed extension to Ilfracombe was rejected in March 1864, they did not want to let the L&SWR have it all their own way. The Company's solicitor was asked by the Board in early 1865 to apply for an injunction to restrain the L&SWR from illegally proceeding with the IR. The fledgling D&SR was fighting back; it did not want to lose out on the potential prize – rail access to Ilfracombe.

HOUSE OF COMMONS, SESSION 865, 7TH MARCH 1865 – THE DEVON & SOMERSET (ILFRACOMBE RAILWAY) BILL

Set out below is a broad summary of the minutes of evidence heard in front of Frederick North, Chairman of the House of Commons Committee on 7th March 1865. In essence, the D&SR had proposed a Bill for an alternative line to Ilfracombe. This was objected to by the B&ER, the L&SWR and the Ilfracombe Railway Company, who had their own specific interests to protect. Mr Granville Somerset appeared as counsel for the promoters, with Messrs Denison and Millward for the L&SWR. It was put forward by Mr Millward that the lines proposed by the D&SR Bill and the Ilfracombe Railway Bill were nearly identical and it would be convenient if they were both considered together at this hearing, which was agreed to.

Commentary from the hearing of the Select Committee of the House of Commons on Railway Bills of 7th March 1865 is set out below, with John McMillan of the D&SR and Granville Somerset (barrister) for the D&SR.

Mr McMillan, the D&SR Company Secretary, had been involved in the railway since inception (autumn 1863), at which time the original Bill deposited was for a railway running from Taunton through to Ilfracombe. However, the portion between Barnstaple and Ilfracombe was thrown out on Standing Orders (February 1864). An agreement with the B&ER had been in place, to work the completed line from Taunton to Ilfracombe, a route of 53 miles.

The only parties interested in this current proposed undertaking were the D&SR and the L&SWR (the B&ER was not planning a share participation). The revised B&ER working agreement, signed on 6th March 1865, did not include working an Ilfracombe section and was virtually a fresh agreement. As the D&SR did not own any rolling stock, it was only the L&SWR that could operate the Barnstaple to Ilfracombe section. This of course raised the gauge question, as the change of gauge at Barnstaple would be an inconvenience to D&SR passengers, who would have to change trains and could not travel direct from London to Ilfracombe via the D&SR. The plan was to lay down standard and broad gauge rails between Barnstaple and Ilfracombe. The line thus required a mixed gauge but as the L&SWR ran broad gauge goods services between Exeter and Barnstaple, a precedent had been set. It was noted that the B&ER could have become joint owners of the Ilfracombe Railway but they chose not to exercise their option made available in the prior agreement. The D&SR did not have power to subscribe to the IR until Parliament sanctioned their Bill to do so.

It was agreed by the Committee that only one Ilfracombe Bill should pass; the parties were to determine which Bill that should be and that it should then be a joint Bill and a joint project of the two companies. The B&ER directors told the D&SR that they would recommend proprietors subscribe to their undertaking to the extent of £100,000.

For the whole Taunton to Ilfracombe route, the capital proposed was £866,000 (share capital £650,000, borrowing powers £216,000) but once the Ilfracombe section had been thrown out, this was proposed by the B&ER to be be reduced by £100,000. However, after consideration they remained committed to injecting that amount, so the B&ER working agreement of October 1864 was set out at cost price along with the £100,000 subscription.

In the earlier Bill, the line was to stop at South Molton and access to Barnstaple was to be via Umberleigh, the D&SR having running powers over that branch and then on to Barnstaple. However, the D&SR wanted full running powers to Barnstaple and as most of the traffic on their line was to come from Bristol and the north, it was undesirable to route it via Umberleigh.

There was nothing in the current Bill to allow the B&ER to work the line. The 1864 D&SR Act provided at Clause 3 '*for the connexion of the lines of the railway by this Act authorised with the lines of the North Devon Railway, so that the two railways may be worked continuously as if they were one railway*'. It was argued that unless the D&SR could traverse the line with the same engine and carriages, it was not a continuous line as provided by the Act, so the current Bill did not adequately provide for this facility. It was stated that the Bristol to Ilfracombe traffic was substantial and competition was with the steamers down the coast – three per week running in the summer. The continuous line would compete with the steamers and provide alternative transport. The line would give passengers a choice in getting to London, either via the L&SWR or the B&ER/GWR. The B&ER were adamant about having running powers over this Ilfracombe section and on the same basis as the Taunton to Barnstaple section (sharing 50% of gross receipts). This was proposed by James Cresswell, with Mr Somerset asking for some time to consider the request.

It was initially agreed that the Bill would stand and the D&SR and L&SWR would subscribe for 50% each of the capital.

The Chairman stated that the Committee entertained a strong opinion that facilities ought to be given to the public between Barnstaple and Ilfracombe, although their present impression was that they should not be inclined to grant running powers. He inquired whether there was any clause in the Bill giving the B&ER power to agree; there was not. The Chairman then firmly stated the B&ER would not get running powers granted by the Committee.

There was then an adjournment until the Friday. On 10th March, with Frederick North in the chair, Mr Manning stated that it had been agreed between the parties in the interim that, with the permission of the Committee, the Ilfracombe Railway Bill should be the Bill to be proceeded with, not that of the D&SR.

Following the hearing, a special general meeting of the D&SR was subsequently convened to consider the preamble and clauses of the Ilfracombe Railway Act, at which they were approved.

A shareholders meeting was held in London on 16th May 1865, to consider a Bill pending in Parliament, namely '*An Act of making a railway from the B&ER at Tiverton to the D&SR in the Parish of Morebath*', the proposal being to connect the D&SR to the B&ER at Tiverton. It was also at this time that the Exe Valley Railway Bill (1865) was thrown out, the D&SR having successfully petitioned with others against this independent proposal.

The Bristol & Exeter and Devon & Somerset Railways Act, 1865

This Act received Royal Assent on 26th May 1865 (*28 & 29 Vict. – Session 1865*), its purpose being to formalise the working agreement between the two companies that was legislated for in Section 40 of the D&SR Act. The schedule attached to the Act set out the revised and updated Articles of Agreement made on 6th March 1865 between the two companies, these cancelling the Articles of Agreement dated 20th June 1864.

In essence, this agreement stipulated the responsibilities of both parties towards the running of the D&SR. Namely that the Devon Company was to make and complete the Devon Railway as a single broad gauge line, with proper and sufficient sidings, junctions, stations, goods sheds and related facilities. The D&SR was to maintain the railway once it was opened for one year, after which it would become the Bristol Company's responsibility. If additional sidings or other works were required after opening, this was to be at the expense of the Devon Company up to the level of its authorised share capital and borrowings. The Bristol Company's obligation was to manage and regulate the Devon Railway and the traffic thereon, along with the officers and servants employed by them – including superintendents, inspectors, station masters, booking clerks, porters, engine drivers, guards, watchmen and workmen, and all other officers and servants (but not the Company Secretary, accountant or engineer). Their maintenance responsibilities after the first twelve months were to be overseen by the Devon Company and if the Bristol Company did not do what the Devon Company engineer thought was required, the Devon Company could carry out the repairs and then charge the Bristol Company accordingly. The Bristol Company had, at their expense, to provide all locomotive power, engines, carriages and other rolling stock, plant, stores, materials, etc, for the proper and sufficient working of the line.

All tolls, rates, fares and charges were to be fixed by the B&ER. When it came to revenue sharing, the schedule stipulated that '*The Bristol Company shall retain for their own use and benefit, one moiety of those gross receipts, and shall to pay the Devon Company for their own use and benefit the other moiety thereof*'. Thus the plan was to share gross receipts 50/50. There were agreements pending with the GWR and Midland Railway and any rebate due from them would be paid to the Bristol Company, and applied by them as follows, namely:

> '*Until, for any half-year, the gross receipts from the Devon undertaking amount to £18 per week per mile of railway opened for public traffic, the Bristol Company shall retain one moiety of every such rebate for their own use and benefit, and shall pay to the Devon Company the other moiety thereof for their own use and benefit; but whenever the gross receipts of the Devon undertaking shall for any one half-year amount to £18 per week per mile of railway opened for public traffic, the Bristol Company shall pay to the Devon Company the whole of every such rebate for their own use and benefit.*

The payments fell due for each half-year on 30th June and 31st December with payments required three months later, that is by the following March and September. The Bristol Company had to keep and render '*true and perfect*' accounts of all traffic to which the agreement related. There were two other significant issues: the agreement was in perpetuity and if the Devon Company was willing to dispose of the undertaking, railway and property, then the Bristol Company should have the right to acquire it under the same terms as any third party. In effect, that gave the B&ER a preferential opportunity to acquire the D&SR. As is normal, there was also an arbitration clause for disputes.

The D&SR and L&SWR Acquire the Ilfracombe Railway

The Act authorising the acquisition of the Ilfracombe Railway by the D&SR and L&SWR, received Royal Assent on 2nd June 1865 (*28 Vict. – Session 1865*). This in effect resulted from the House of Commons Hearing of 7th March 1865 (as referred to above), when it was agreed that the D&SR sponsored Devon & Somerset Railway (Ilfracombe Railway) Bill was to be withdrawn.

As both the IR and D&SR Bills were pending in Parliament during 1864, discussions were had with the L&SWR, for the L&SWR and D&SR to become joint and equal owners of the IR's undertaking. This was subject to the D&SR Bill being enacted, which of course occurred in July 1864. These earlier discussions resulted in heads of arrangement which provided for the D&SR (with prior consent in writing from the B&ER) to give notice in writing on or before 10th October 1864 to the IR and L&SWR if they wished to become joint and equal owners of the IR. The D&SR had duly given notice.

The IR proposal of 1864 was to have a single line of railway of mixed gauge throughout, with sufficient land alongside for a double line. There was to be a broad gauge connection with the D&SR, so the two railways could be worked continuously as if they were one line. The D&SR (and the B&ER if they so chose to join) would provide 50% of the capital, the L&SWR providing the other half, with joint control and management, and the provision of three directors each. They were to subscribe for 5,250 shares each at £20, requiring a contribution of £105,000 each. The L&SWR were to acquire or subscribe for further shares to make up their £105,000 within one month of the Act being passed. The D&SR had until three months from the passing of the Act to take up their shares and could do so by way of issue of further new shares or stock in the D&SR to the public. Any arrears of call for the IR was stated to bear interest at 5% per annum.

Provisions were laid out, amongst other things, for the smooth transition of traffic (of whatever nature) over the IR onto the D&SR and the L&SWR. Also, it was noted where further agreements would be needed, such as, maintaining, managing and working the line, the traffic, supply and maintenance of engines, stock and plant, employees, and fares and tolls, along with the distribution of receipts, etc.

When the IR Act became law, it was made clear that the B&ER did not exercise their option to become joint shareholders but the D&SR did, so they had a commitment to subscribe for the full £105,000 (their half share). The L&SWR had soon subscribed for £50,000 of shares, with £5,540 of shares (only) taken up by other subscribers.

At the 3rd Ordinary General meeting on 24th August 1865, it was resolved that the D&SR shareholders should not give authority to raise further capital for the purposes of the Ilfracombe undertaking. The D&SR then received a call on 5,250 shares at £2 per share by the IR on 13th September. John McMillan (D&SR Secretary) wrote to the IR saying the matter was to be dealt with but the D&SR did not send the cash. The D&SR directors were not prepared to encourage their shareholders to make further capital available for the Ilfracombe undertaking. They asked their solicitor to advise the company on its obligations to the IR. The current poor state of the money market meant that the D&SR was cash-strapped and was, at this stage, unable to honour its legal commitment to subscribe for the shares in the IR. With these delays in payment of the cash calls and the failure of the D&SR to fulfil its obligations, the IR had no option but to take legal proceedings against the Company.

100.–DEVON AND SOMERSET.

Incorporated by 27 and 28 Vic., cap. 307 (29th July, 1864), to construct a line from the Bristol and Exeter, at Taunton, to Barnstaple. Broad gauge. Length, 43 miles. Capital, 500,000*l*. in 25*l*. shares, and 166,000*l*. on loan. Arrangements with Bristol and Exter. Works in progress.

No. of Directors—9; minimum, 6; quorum, 3, *Qualification*, 500*l*.

DIRECTORS:

Chairman—The Right Hon. LORD POLTIMORE, Poltimore Park, Exeter, and Court Hall, Northmolton, Devon.

Vice-Chairman—JOHN ARTHUR LOCKE, Esq., Northmoor House, Dulverton, Somerset.

The Right Hon. Earl Fortescue, Castle Hill, Southmolton, Devon.
Sir William Throckmorton, Bart., Buckland, Berks.
William Gould Smyth, Esq., Fort House, Southmolton, Devon.
John Thomas Nash, Esq., Elm Cottage, Southmolton, Devon.

OFFICERS.—Sec., John McMillan; Eng., E. Birch, M.I.C.E., 43, Parliament Street, London, S.W.; Solicitors, Riccard and Son, Southmolton; Bankers, The West of England and South Wales District Bank, Bristol, with its branches.

Offices—15, Parliament Street, London, S.W.

Extract from *Bradshaw's Hand-Book* of 1870, showing the D&SR entry.

On 18th January 1866, a further call of £2 per share by the IR was made for the £10,500. Mr Sandars, a D&SR director, said he was authorised to offer the Board capital necessary to comply with the IR request, provided the B&ER, GWR and Midland rebates would ensure sufficient funds to pay interest on the capital so provided. A letter of 7th February from the B&ER, said they would accede to the request for payment of a rebate provided the GWR and Midland also did. A meeting was fixed with the Midland Company, who subsequently agreed to the payment of the rebate and that it was also extended to Ilfracombe traffic. However, the GWR was not yet ready to agree. The matter did not progress and the D&SR did not take up Mr Sandars' offer. So once again the D&SR had failed to pay its call. The L&SWR had paid all its calls and was keen to proceed with the project; indeed, the proposed Ilfracombe line had been staked out and some plans prepared. These were difficult times; Parliament had received a number of petitions relating to the D&SR from the B&ER, L&SWR, the Ilfracombe Railway and certain individuals. Also the D&SR had counter-petitioned against the Ilfracombe Railway. On 16th March, the Devon & Somerset Amendment of Acts Bill and the Ilfracombe Railway Bill were withdrawn, on the basis that the directors of the two concerns were to agree to settle their difficulties.

By October 1866, the IR solicitor had obtained judgements against the D&SR to serve notices on its shareholders, so that they could obtain an extension against them for non-payment of calls. As a consequence, three cheques were forwarded to the IR by certain shareholders. Messrs Pickerings then asked the Court to restrain the IR from taking further action against the D&SR, as they feared for their contractor's payments. This challenge was initially successful but the decision was subsequently overturned on appeal by the IR, leaving them in a position to prosecute certain D&SR shareholders. With the D&SR in a mess, the only practical option was for them to attempt to withdraw from the arrangements with the IR and have the Act of 1865 repealed. It was not going to be that simple; the IR refused.

The D&SR offered to place the Ilfracombe Railway in such a position as if the 1864 Bill had not been proceeded with but limiting the sum for costs to £10,000. The IR replied that they wanted a guarantee against the forfeiture of the Parliamentary deposit of £16,800. The contractors agreed to provide this, if a deal with the B&ER to acquire the D&SR went ahead. In the next move, the D&SR offered to indemnify the IR against the loss of the Parliamentary deposit of £16,800, if a D&SR Bill for repeal of the 1865 IR Act was passed by Parliament.

On 26th January 1867, the D&SR Secretary gave notice of a further call made on 10th January of £2 per share by the IR. There was also to be a petition to the L&SWR against a Bill to extend, on their own account, the time for completing the IR for five years and three years for the purchase of land. Writs were issued in March 1867 in relation to the IR. At a 13th May D&SR special meeting, consideration was given to a Bill to repeal certain provisions of the IR Act. The D&SR was clearly not in a position to commit funds to the IR.

All these disputes had a knock-on effect, as at this point the B&ER withdrew its Bill to purchase the D&SR, as it did not want to incur the additional financial commitment to settle the calls on the outstanding IR shares. Eventually, on 12th August 1867 (under *30 & 31 Vic. Cap. 172*) the D&SR obtained powers to shed its commitments to the IR, on the grounds of the inability to construct its authorised line from Taunton to Barnstaple and its inability to provide the required funds for the Ilfracombe line. In concluding this matter, it was proposed that the D&SR was to meet half the IR expenses and liabilities, whilst the Company could only leave the shareholders register by paying those obligations to the IR within three months. Parliament was also to be induced to reject the Bill promoted by the L&SWR and IR to extend the purchase of land and timing of works. Rejection of that Bill would practically defeat the progress of the undertaking at that time.

On 25th October, Mr F. Clarke, Secretary of the IR, provided estimates of liabilities amounting to £25,000, in addition to half the Parliamentary deposit of £16,800 (plus a further £2,000). However, funding that total obligation of £43,800 was still an issue for the D&SR.

The D&SR Board failed to procure funds to be deposited by 12th November in pursuance of the D&SR (Ilfracombe) Act, their only action being to convene a special general meeting of shareholders to lay before them the position of the company. This meeting was held at Taunton on 13th December 1867.

In view of the D&SR's intransigence and its objection to the L&SWR and IR Bill, the IR had no option but to seek formal abandonment of its project. As the Ilfracombe Railway (Abandonment) Bill was in progress, the D&SR Board agreed to oppose the Bill where clauses adversely affected their Company. The Bill became the Abandonment Act on 25th June 1868 (*31 & 32 Vic. Cap. 171*). Over three years of legal wrangling was almost at an end. However, the terms of the Act required a discharge of all debts before dissolution of the IR company, as expected. Again the IR brought writs against the D&SR shareholders so matters could be concluded. Although judgement was received for the payment by the D&SR of £11,492 4s (along with costs and interest at 4%) this remained largely unpaid for some considerable time. By June 1877, it was noted by the Board that the amount due to the L&SWR for the IR was £12,565 15s 7d. As will be seen later, when the GWR took over the D&SR in 1901 a settlement was made to the L&SWR of £1,500 cash and £1,570 nominal value of GWR $2^1/_2$% debentures, in exchange for £12,566 of D&SR 'C' debenture stock, issued by the D&SR in 1901 to settle their claim. This settlement then, in effect, enabled the financial commitment to be honoured and the dissolution of the IR Company all those years later.

BACK TO THE SUMMER OF 1865

The *West Somerset Free Press* of 27th May 1865 reported that Mr Pickering, the contractor, had visited Wiveliscombe on 18th May for the purpose of '*commencing immediately that part of the line between that town and Taunton*'. Mr Tyndall was also about to take up residence for three to four years as resident engineer. In addition, Messrs Pearce & Boucher had received orders to contract for poles, '*so as to erect there the telegraph at once*'.

In July 1865, it was resolved the D&SR would have offices at Taunton or '*some other equally convenient place in the county*'. By October, the Somerset county town was fixed as location for the permanent offices of the Company.

The contractor's contract between the D&SR and Messrs William & John Pickering was entered into on 19th July 1865. Under the terms, it was agreed that the contractors should pay certain costs, charges and expenses and other moneys for or on behalf of the D&SR, and execute the works. In consideration, the company should pay or satisfy the total authorised sum of £666,000; currently there being £50,000 cash (as a result of 2,000 'B' stock being issued to diverse subscribers), with £200,000 of the whole amount of 8,000 £25 Class 'A' shares, £250,000 in 10,000 £25 Class 'B' shares and the £166,000 residue by issue of mortgages of the Company still available for issue. The contract sum was apportioned as follows:

- £42,000 for fulfilment of obligations under Articles 1 and 2 (above); the money obligation
- £40,000 for acquiring land and buildings; the land obligation
- £39,000 for tunnels; the tunnel obligation
- £14,000 for fitting up of stations and other works; the stations obligation
- £531,000 for all other obligations under the contract; the general obligation

In August, the contractor was authorised to pay £42,000 to the promoters for the pre-incorporation expenses referred to above. Initial discussions were had at this time to improve the D&SR line at Barnstaple, by extending the terminus to a more central point and also crossing the River Taw and joining the existing North Devon line.

A letter from the D&SR to the B&ER of 30th August 1865, showed much satisfaction with progress of the line's construction and noted that '*some position of the line had been started between the Junction near Taunton and Wiveliscombe with a view to construction commencing there*'. However, it was the Barnstaple to South Molton section where contractors were mainly at work. The letter optimistically stated that the latter section would be ready for opening in August 1866 but aired concerns that no trains would be able to work through from Watchet Junction and that consideration should be given to opening all sections simultaneously. Understandably, the B&ER wanted completion from the Taunton end of the line and a link to the main line, so they could start revenue earning services at the earliest opportunity.

The *North Devon Journal* reported on 2nd November 1865:

'*On Saturday last* [28th October] *the friends of this undertaking* [D&SR] *were cheered by the arrival at the Barnstaple Station of*

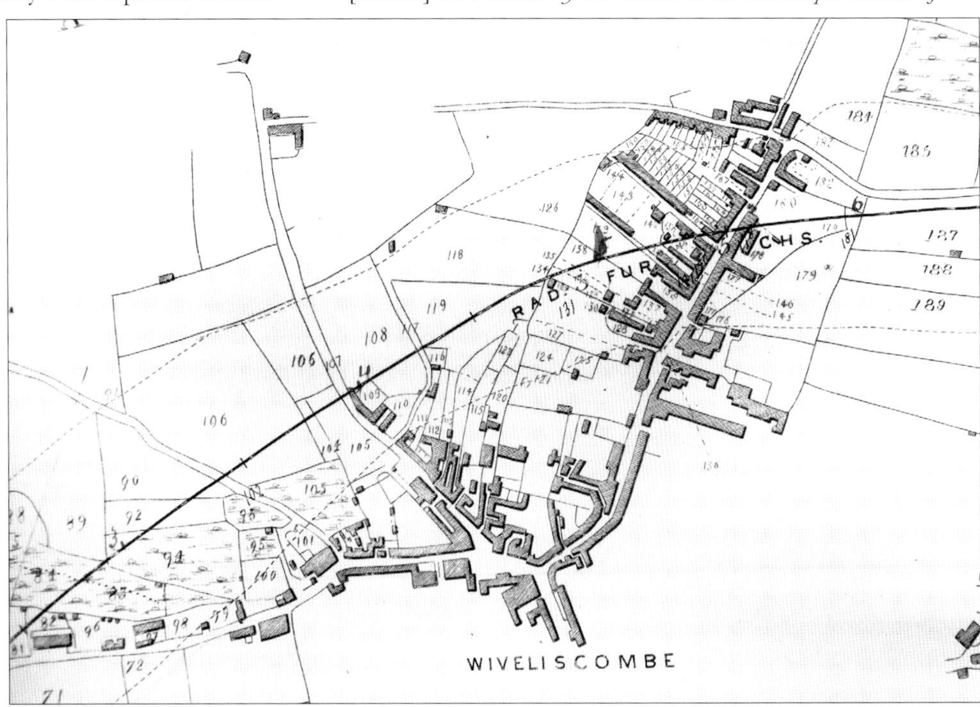

Plan showing the originally proposed route through Wiveliscombe. ***Somerset Archives & Local Studies***

the London & South Western Railway of the first engine intended to be employed on the works now in the course of construction. It is appropriately named 'Fortescue' *after the estimable nobleman who has been one of the most energetic promoters of the Devon & Somerset line. It required some skill and judgement to transport the engine from the station to the contractors' yard, a distance of half a mile over common roads; but every difficulty was surmounted and the object safely accomplished under the judicious direction and personal superintendence of Mr Heather, the contractors' agent. Temporary rails were laid and relaid over which the ponderous mass was drawn by a number of powerful and tractable horses and thus by patient perseverance, the work was done. We were pleased to notice to the honour of the South Western Company that their stationmaster and his staff cheerfully rendered every assistance in their power. The works on the Devon & Somerset line are progressing rapidly and satisfactorily.'*

Fortescue was a standard gauge locomotive and had arrived via the Exeter to Barnstaple line.

As can be seen from the map of Wiveliscombe, the line approved by the 1864 Act was to have kept north of the centre of the town, crossing Ford Road and Golden Hill near Newgate Lane on an embankment. At North Street, it was proposed that the line would be level for about 110 yards, which would have been the station site (now the car park). It would have then continued over North Street, under Jews Lane and over West Street, at which point the line was to enter a tunnel 1,045 yards long near Coate Farm, then emerging west of Fleed Farm. It was to have been 220 feet below the summit of Fleed Knapp and, at Waterrow, it was to cross the River Tone on a high viaduct about 70 yards south of the Rock Inn. The tunnel would have been a major engineering challenge and of substantial cost.

The application to Parliament for the proposed Barnstaple improvements were agreed by the Board on 3rd November 1865. Also reported was the contractor's proposal for a deviation of the authorised line, commencing east of Wiveliscombe (at 5 miles, 2 furlongs and 7 chains from Norton) and terminating by a junction with the authorised line near Dulverton (at 18 miles and 3 furlongs). The purpose of this was to reduce the costs of construction by following a different route. In addition, there were also powers in the said Bill to abandon an element of the authorised line between 41 miles and 5 furlongs to the

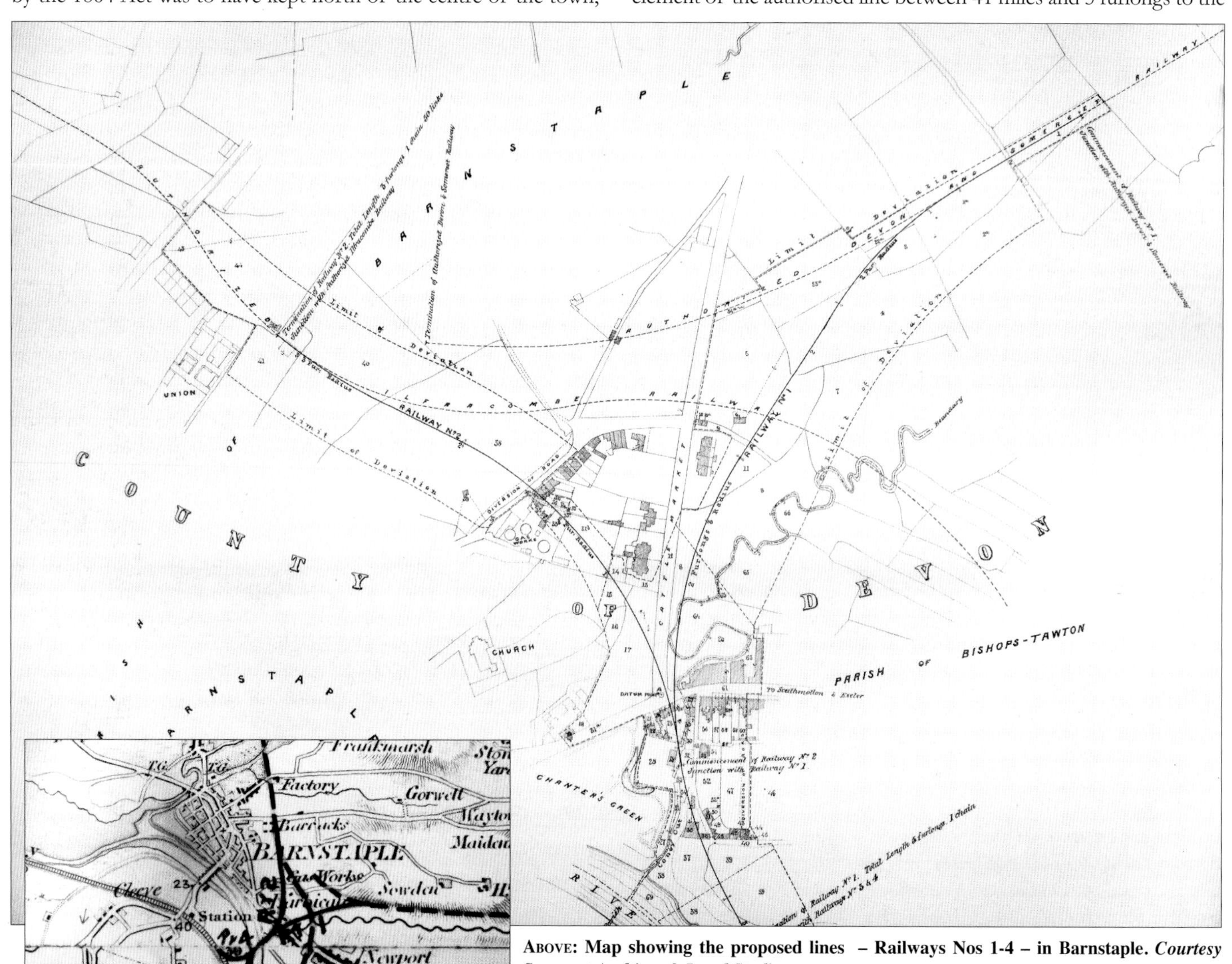

ABOVE: Map showing the proposed lines – Railways Nos 1-4 – in Barnstaple. ***Courtesy Somerset Archives & Local Studies***

LEFT: Map of Railways No's 1-4 as referred to in the Deviation Bill. The black dotted line to the right terminating just under the 'N' in Barnstaple was the authorised line. The black long dotted line running up the centre was the proposed Ilfracombe Railway. The other lines indicate the new railways linking the D&SR to the NDR and the IR. ***Courtesy Somerset Archives & Local Studies***

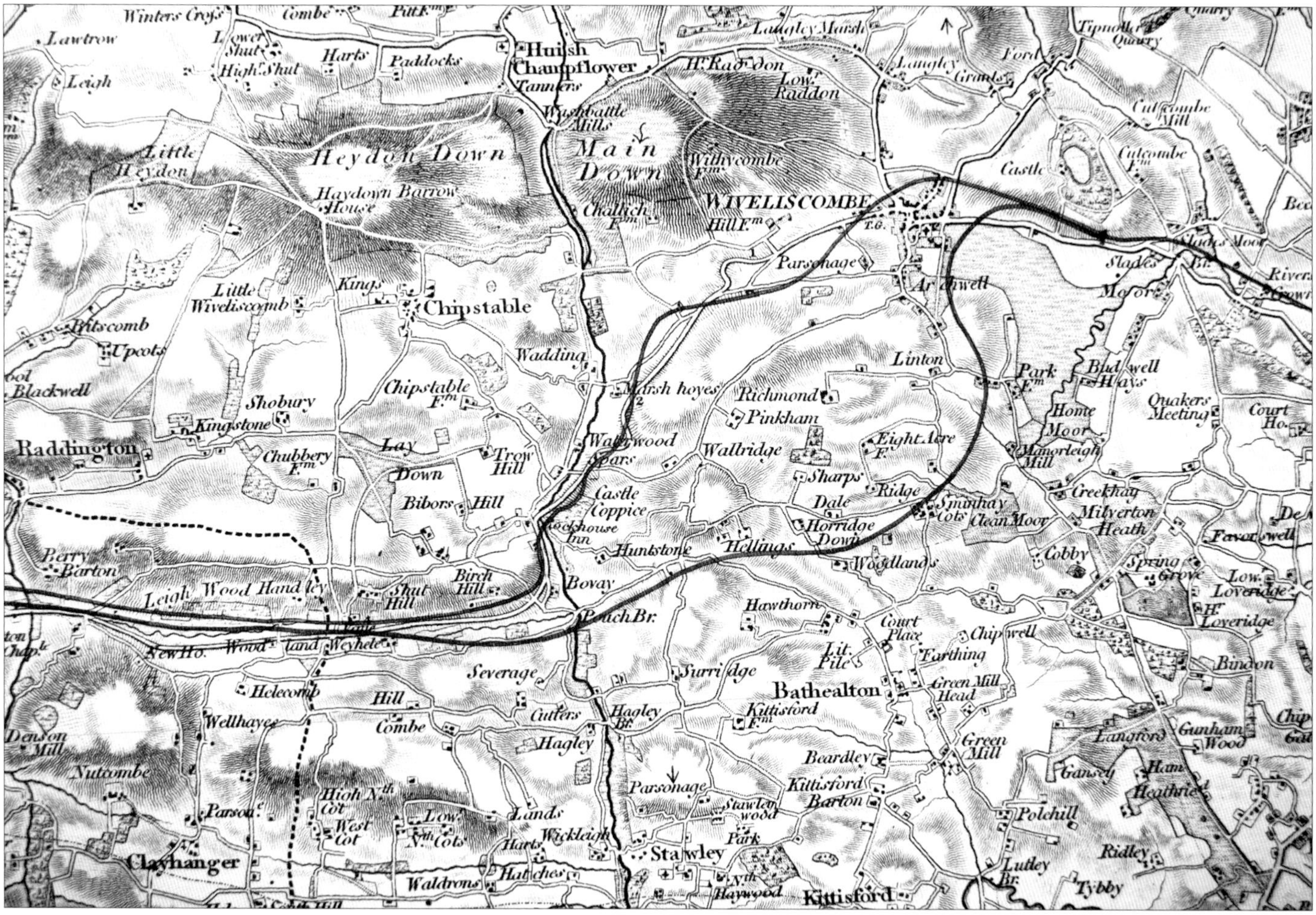

Above: The map showing the deviation of the line to the south of Wiveliscombe, from that originally approved by Parliament which ran through the north side of the town, in the section between there and Venn Cross to the west. These plans were deposited on 29th November 1866. ***Courtesy Somerset Archives & Local Studies***

Right: The next section of the deviation between Brushford and Venn Cross to the east, with the original route marked as A-A and the deviation as A-B. Also shown is the proposed junction with the Tiverton & North Devon Railway (C) and the subsequent realignment of that junction brought about by the deviation. Brushford was to be the site of Dulverton station when the line was built. ***Courtesy Somerset Archives & Local Studies***

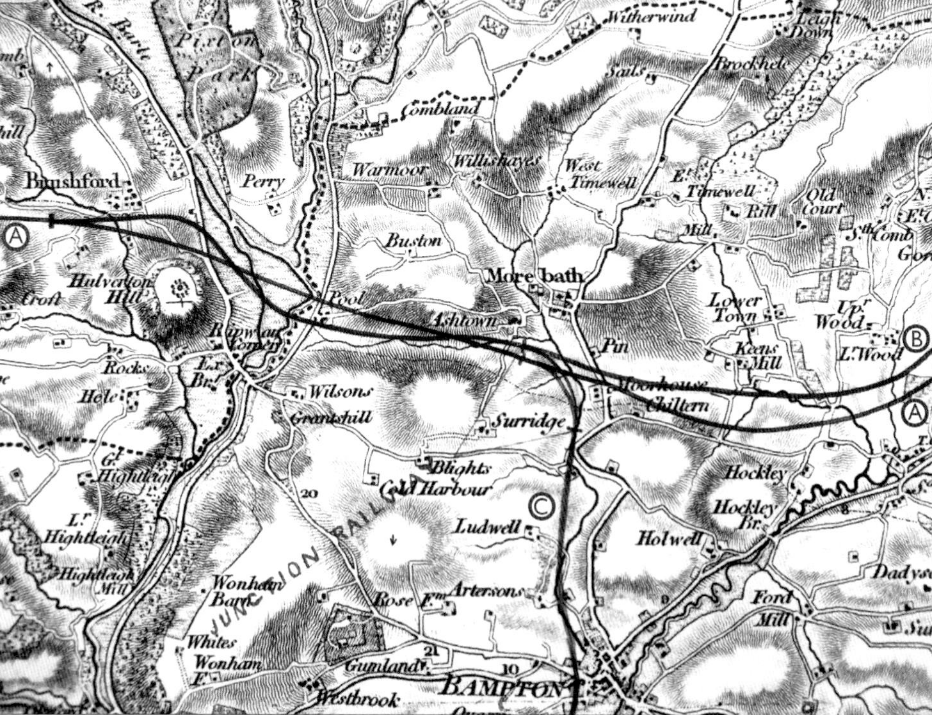

terminus at 42 miles and 75 links. However, the purpose of that abandonment was a plan to extend the D&SR a short distance and connect with the NDR in Barnstaple. There were four proposed lines; Railway No. 1 – at 41 miles and 5 furlongs, for 15 chains where the D&SR crossed the cattle market towards Bishops Tawton for 5 chains and 50 links. Railway No. 2 –from Bishops Tawton at the junction with Railway No. 1, terminating at a junction with the authorised Ilfracombe Railway (via Muddiford and Bittadon). Railway No. 3 – joining Railway No. 1 and crossing the Taw by a bridge into Tawstock parish, joining the current NDR at 38 miles 6½ chains on the west bank of the Taw. Railway No. 4 – as Railway No. 3 but joining the NDR at 39 miles 11 chains on the Barnstaple side of the North End Ticket Platform.

With the proposed deviations and potential development of the Tiverton & North Devon Railway, correspondence was had between the D&SR and T&NDR over the likely location of the junction between the two railways.

Also at this time a dispute arose with Mr McMillan, the Company Secretary. Although one of the promoters of the Company, he claimed salary and rent (of £450pa) on offices in Westminster for three years. McMillan retired on 31st December 1865 but this dispute ran into 1866, whilst Joshua Dean was appointed Company Secretary to replace him.

In order to facilitate the Company's Bills through Parliament, Lord Poltimore, Mr Moysey and Mr Sandars were appointed as the 'Parliamentary Committee'. It was also agreed that the half yearly meetings would now alternate between Taunton and South Molton.

In February 1866, the B&ER petitioned against the Wiveliscombe deviation referred to above, as they anticipated this would cause them to incur additional running costs due to the increased gradients and sharper curves proposed in the realignment.

Despite the legal distractions, land purchases continued. On 29th February 1866, a special meeting was convened exercising the powers under the D&SR Act to borrow, on mortgage, the £166,000 available under that Act. In addition, there was a move to cancel 8,000 shares at £25, as yet unissued and issue in their place 8,000 £25 shares with a preferential dividend of 5% per annum (Class 'A' stock). However, a new Act, the proposed Devon & Somerset Railway (Capital) Act of 1866 (see below), would be required for this.

On the construction side, the engineer reported in February 1866 that '*the Contractors have carried on the works with great spirit and energy*'. Between Barnstaple and South Molton, '*the whole of the earthworks, with the exception of one cutting and one embankment near South Molton has been executed and the tunnel at Castle Hill is being actively proceeded with at both ends.*' The contractor had also commenced work on the section eastwards from South Molton. In addition, the junction with the B&ER had been formed and about 3 miles of line towards Milverton was formed and ready for the permanent way.

The D&SR Deviation & Extension Bill was withdrawn from Parliament on 15th March 1866. This put paid to plans for the double junction with the North Devon Railway and a further connection with the Ilfracombe Railway at Barnstaple (Railways No's 1 to 4 as stated above). There were insufficient funds for these proposed works and with the IR dispute continuing such a connection was unlikely.

THE D&SR ARRANGEMENT OF CAPITAL BILL (1866)

On 18th May 1866, the Devon & Somerset Railway (Capital) Act, 1866 was passed, to '*authorize Arrangements of the Capital of the Devon and Somerset Railway Company*'. In the recital to this Act, it was stated that, to date, of the authorised capital under the D&SR Act 1864, shares only to the value of £107,100 had been issued, with none of the potential borrowings drawn down. The D&SR believed that funds for completing the railway could be more easily raised if £200,000 of unissued shares were cancelled and a new class of shares created *in lieu* of those cancelled. These new shares would have a preferential dividend, with the aim of being more attractive to investors.

The Act allowed for the changes, provided at least three fifths of the ordinary shareholders voted for the change in an Extraordinary General Meeting. Also, the new shares being issued were to have a preferential dividend not exceeding £5 per centum per annum. As was usual, the new shares could not be issued unless they were paid up to the extent of one-fifth of their subscription price. These new preferential dividend shares were designated Class 'A', the remainder of the ordinary shares being Class 'B'. It was also possible for any holder of the 'A' shares to give notice to convert them to 'B' shares – the number of 'A' shares then diminishing and the number of 'B' shares increasing by the new issue.

Mr Moysey, of Bathealton Court, near Wiveliscombe and a director of the B&ER, wrote a letter on 8th May 1866 to the directors of the D&SR, to stress that '*Wiveliscombe expects a considerable trade in lime and coal from Watchett* [sic] *and will export slate and beer*'. He was clearly concerned that the D&SR would abandon the through line, not intentionally but by non-completion of the heaviest of the work between Wiveliscombe and Bampton.

At this time, the B&ER agreed to indemnify the D&SR for the expenses incurred in respect of their petition against the Exe Valley Railway Bill that was in progress.

There was a Barnstaple station visit on Tuesday 26th June 1866, by the directors of the B&ER and D&SR to inspect progress and assess two sites; the one on the south side of the town was given preference by the directors and the town surveyor, as it was in the best interests of the inhabitants. It was also agreed the line would be opened from the Taunton end and the engineers of the B&ER and D&SR were to meet to agree the proposed deviation at and beyond Wiveliscombe. The B&ER also suggested that the D&SR should abandon all plans to form a joint station with the L&SWR, thus getting rid of a continuing dispute that was to require arbitration. So the next step was to apply to Parliament at the next session for an Act to empower the directors to purchase the land necessary to make an independent station, which in turn would relinquish for the present any steps towards creating a junction with the Ilfracombe line. It was agreed that a site about 44 yards north of the clock tower would best suit. It was in the centre of the town, close to main hotels and close to where the streets converge to cross the Taw by the long bridge, over which was the L&SWR station. If the D&SR station was built at that central location, then a junction with the proposed Ilfracombe Railway and the NDR to Bideford could be constructed relatively easily in the future.

In a letter of 29th June 1866, Messrs Pickerings stated that due to delays in settling rebates, they could not find the money to carry out the works and could not place the bonds for finance due to the then state of the money market (timing was poor because the Overend & Gurney Bank had collapsed precipitating financial problems nationally). Pickerings demanded backing from the B&ER, otherwise the contractor would have no option but to discharge the workforce from 15th July. The D&SR's reaction was to write and request the B&ER to guarantee the company's debenture bonds of £166,000. Problems also arose elsewhere, as a petition was raised by inhabitants of Norton Fitzwarren and neighbouring parishes regarding the junction of the D&SR with the Watchet line.

At a special general meeting of shareholders in July 1866, the cancellation of the £200,000 of ordinary shares was authorised, along with the issue of £200,000 of 5% preference shares instead and debenture bonds of £166,000, as proposed by the 1866 Act, in the hope that the stock would appeal to the public and alleviate the financial constraints.

The B&ER agreed to guarantee the debentures (and the interest up to 5% from the date of opening of the whole line) and also support proposals for the Barnstaple station site and the Wiveliscombe deviation, along with certain other financial terms. Mr Riccard, the solicitor, was charged with the responsibility of putting the Wiveliscombe deviation and Barnstaple extension Bills through Parliament in the next session.

At the 5th ordinary half-yearly meeting in August 1866, the directors reported '*that the works on your Railway have, during the past half-year, been carried on without cessation, and through a period of almost universal monetary difficulty*'. Preparations were being made for the building of Castle Hill Viaduct and the tunnel there was driven through to two-thirds of its length. Earthworks were nearly completed to Anstey summit.

The Norton Fitzwarren to Wiveliscombe section was well under way. Earthworks to Wiveliscombe were nearly completed and all bridges in a state to suggest this section could take the permanent way by the end of the year, with a considerable amount already laid. At the meeting of 28th September 1866, Mr Birch laid out the sites and plans for the stations: Barnstaple, Landkey, Swimbridge, Castle Hill, South Molton, Molland, Anstey, Morebath, Raddington Road, Pouch Bridge, Milverton and Norton. The Board's role was not easy and objections to the undertaking were received from inhabitants of Norton Fitzwarren, Brushford and Dulverton at this time. In support of the project, the rector of Brushford, Charles Sydenham, sold glebe land to the D&SR for the site of Dulverton station.

CHOLERA STRIKES WIVELISCOMBE
September 1866

A large number of navvies were imported into the district to build the line. One of them, James Tucker, was taken ill and was brought to Wiveliscombe to be treated by local doctors, Messrs Edwards and Fowells. They diagnosed cholera and within hours he had died followed soon by another navvy. One of the town's children then collapsed and died, leaving the town potentially facing an epidemic. However, the skill of the doctors and the chemist, Mr Knight, combined averted the crisis. Pitch fires were lit and kept burning on every street, particularly High Street the principal scene of the disease. Also doses of chlorodene were administered to those who had come into contact with the infected premises. Mr William Hancock, the founder of the town's brewing business, provided a house in the town as a temporary hospital. All the bedding used was subsequently burned. Five people died, but it could have been worse. The *West Somerset Free Press* of 8th September reported '*... the pitch fires lined the route of the funeral procession ... which showed hundreds of faces peering forth from the windows of Church Street ...* [they] *were too afraid to venture out into the diseased town.*'

By October 1866, the contractors were due £50,175 for the '*considerable quantities of rails, sleepers and materials for bridges between Wiveliscombe and Taunton*' that had been delivered to the site. There was no cash available to pay them, as the D&SR could not obtain subscriptions for £50,000 ordinary shares, so this debt was to be settled by issuing further securities to the contractors but not until the next meeting. Messrs Pickering's letter of 22nd October to Joshua Dean (Secretary) stated that work had stopped at the end of September, as a result of non-payment and default by the D&SR in not obtaining the promised agreement for the rebate of 10% from the GWR. Pickerings stated that their contractor's agreement was not binding unless the rebate agreement was fulfilled, otherwise the D&SR was in breach of their agreement. The D&SR were urged to conclude the GWR agreement by Pickerings, so that work could recommence. However, by this time local labour had been laid off, with the threat that work may have to be stopped until the spring. Negotiations continued; Pickerings agreed to pay for the cost of the Wiveliscombe (deviation) and Barnstaple (extension) Bills through Parliament and requested £10,000 debenture bonds in part payment of the £50,175. The D&SR Board refused unless Pickerings withdrew their claim for a cash payment of £33,900 as part of the £50,000 cash due to them (as above and under Article 27 of the contract). This Pickerings duly did in their letter to the Board of 20nd November 1866.

The D&SR was in a mess; work had stopped, the contractor had still not been paid and the raising of finance continued to be difficult because of market conditions. Something had to be done. At the meeting of 11th December 1866, there was a proposal to transfer the company to the B&ER and Mr Muggeridge explained that it was planned to introduce a Bill effecting this in the next Parliamentary session. Heads of Agreement for this transfer were drawn up on 12th December 1866. The proposed terms were:

> *'The B&ER to have a transfer of the Devon and Somerset line (with or without the deviation at Wiveliscombe) completed for £400,000 partially in 4 percent stock* [£225,000] *and partially in cash* [£175,000]. *The line to include the extension into Barnstaple and to include the new station there.'*

The railway was to be completed by the contractors for £150,000 (being part of the £400,000), to be paid in cash from time to time with a 10% reserve (retention). With this potential commitment from the B&ER, Pickerings agreed to waive the £33,000 cash element of the £50,000 due because debentures of £10,000 in part payment of certificate No. 5 for the £50,175 and certificate No. 6 for plant of £23,000 were proposed. At this same meeting, proof of Bills were read, one to extend the railway at Barnstaple, the second to make the proposed deviation and abandon a portion of the already authorised line, and thirdly, a repeal of certain provisions of the Ilfracombe Railway Acts of 1864 and 1865 (as referred to above).

Despite a lack of progress on the construction, land purchases at December 1866 were proceeding; Thomas Acland had given some land, and Lords Fortescue and Poltimore had received shares to the value of £4,000 and £186 respectively. Total land purchases in Barnstaple and at theTaunton end at this time amounted to £14,813 and £9,892 respectively. A letter written in late 1866 from a William Sanderson at West Buckland, near Filleigh, made reference to the proposed Combe Martin Railway & Harbour Bill. The *North Devon Journal* said that line would commence at or near the viaduct of the D&SR over the River Bray in the parish of Filleigh.

This is a good time to summarise the receipts and payments position for the company. As at 31st December 1866, the total loan stock issued was £55,000 (£111,000 being unissued). A further £39,000 was issued by 30th June 1867, making a total at that point of £94,000, with £72,000 remaining to be issued. With construction still on hold, this situation did not change over the next six months to 31st December 1867.

By 8th March 1867, it was decided that advice should be taken as to whether Pickering's contract of 1865 could be legally rescinded, with no claims on either side. Counsel's subsequent advice was positive, so steps were to be taken to rescind the contract. Heads of Agreement between the D&SR and B&ER as scheduled in the Bill were approved by the Board. However, this was inconsistent with the 1865 contractor's contract, as this proposed for all shares to be issued to the contractor, so new terms had to be agreed with them. The Board was under no illusion that if the B&ER did not give the aid proposed, the district would be without a railway and all capital expended would be lost, with shareholders still required to pay the calls that were due.

The D&SR directors entered into a tripartite agreement on 19th March with the B&ER and Messrs Pickerings to support the completion of the line. Under these terms, following completion (anticipated by 29th July 1869), the D&SR undertaking would be transferred to the B&ER. In essence the B&ER was to support the construction by provision of £400,000 in financing, £175,000 in cash and £225,000 of B&ER shares. This reflected the desperate

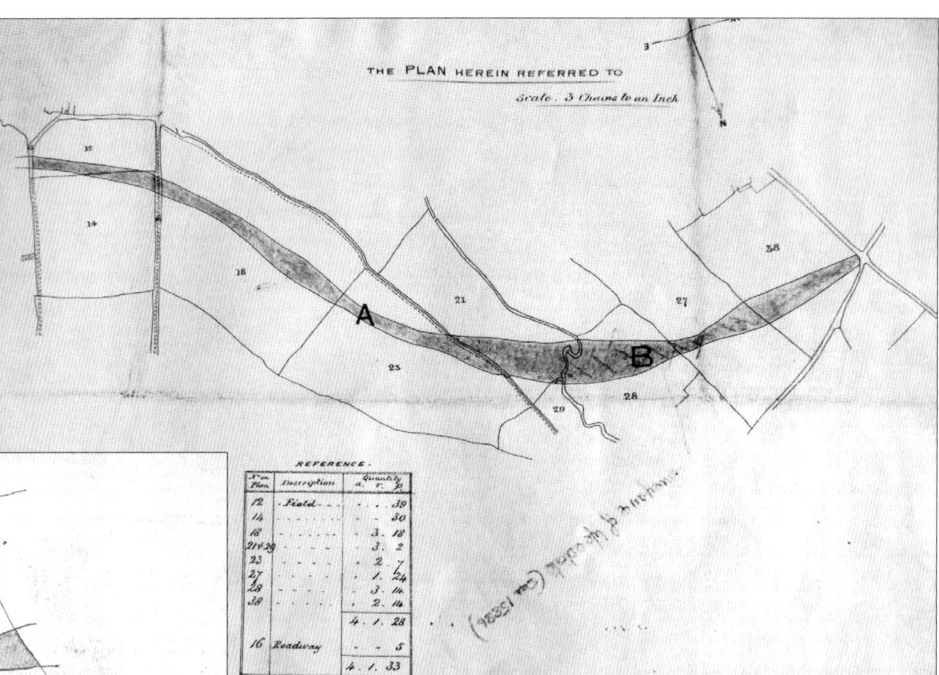

RIGHT: This stretch of land between Milverton and Wiveliscombe that was ear-marked for the railway was purchased by the D&SR from the trustees handling the will of the late Samuel Brown Esq. and was included with the conveyance document dated 6th February 1867. The shaded area is that which was to be bought. Each of the relevant fields are numbered and the total area claimed amounted to just over 4 acres. *Courtesy Wesley Wyatt*

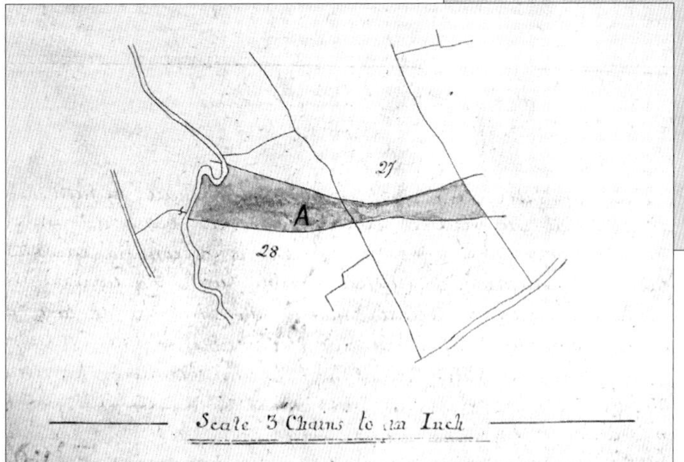

BELOW: This small section of land near Croford was again purchased from the estate of Samuel Brown. *Courtesy Wesley Wyatt*

state of the D&SR's finances and was their safety net to complete the railway.

Also on 19th March, Heads of Agreement were entered into between the D&SR and Messrs Pickerings. One of the recitals stated that:

> '... *the contractors have paid considerable monies to or for the use of the Devon Company; and have purchased and paid for considerable portions of the land required for the permanent use of the said railway and also lands for the purposes of temporary occupation, and have constructed considerable portions of earthworks, tunnels, permanent way, bridges and other works ...large portions of the said railway, together with the land for parts thereof, still remain to be completed and purchased.*'

The aggregate of monies expended by this stage was £308,800, of which £60,000 had been accounted for on mortgage, the balance being in shares issued to the contractors or their nominees, with some small portion having been paid in cash. The amount now due at this time under the original contract was determined to be £44,800 '*and no more*'.

It was agreed that the original contract of 19th July 1865 be rescinded and the performance bond cancelled and delivered up. Within two months, the D&SR was to pay to the contractors the sum of £44,800 due, if not paid in cash then by issue of a mortgage at 5% per annum. The contractors were then to proceed '*with all reasonable despatch*' to make and complete the D&SR by 29th July 1869 (or extended as agreed, if legislative sanctions were not obtained in the current Parliamentary session). The payments due to the contractor were to be made in cash based on monthly certificates given by the D&SR engineer, such amounts being payable within ten days following the production of the relevant certificates. If such dues were not paid, Article 9 stated that it was '*lawful for the contractors at once to discontinue their works and to remove their plant and materials and either before or after doing so to give notice ... to rescind the contract ...*'. If a further month elapsed with no payment, the contract would be rescinded and the contractors would be released from all claims and liabilities under it. Provided the contractors were paid and if they then failed in their obligations to complete the line in the stated time, the D&SR could possess all plant and materials, and be at liberty to proceed with the execution of the works or otherwise dispose of as they thought fit. Arbitration would settle any difference between the parties. A contract was to be drawn up to reflect these terms. The contractors were at liberty to to make deviations and alterations in the course of the line, along with changes to levels and gradients, as long as they were sanctioned by the D&SR engineer. The B&ER engineer would also inspect the works from time to time and if there was a dispute it was to be referred to the BoT.

At the 20th May meeting, a number of Bills were approved. One was in respect of deviations in the authorised railway, to make a junction railway and to abandon part of the authorised railway. Another was to extend the railway at Barnstaple and a third to authorise the transfer of the undertaking to the B&ER.

MORE D&SR ACTS OF PARLIAMENT

Passed on 15th July, the Devon & Somerset Railway (Deviation) Act of 1867 approved a deviation of the railway:

> '*of 13 miles, one furlong and 6.78 chains in length commencing in the Parish of Wiveliscombe, terminating in the Parish of Brushford and a junction railway 3 furlongs and 7.55 chains in length commencing from and out of the proposed railway in the Parish of Morebath by a junction with the lines of the Tiverton & North Devon Railway authorised under the 1865 Session.*'

The objective of this Act was to save the cost of tunnelling. There was a two year period for compulsory purchase of land and a three year timescale in which to complete the railway, *i.e.* by 1870.

On 12th August 1867, the Devon & Somerset Railway (Extension) Act (*30-31 Vic. Cap. 182*) was passed to enable the Company to extend their railway at Barnstaple and for other purposes. Primarily, it was to authorise an extension of the railway:

> '*6 furlongs 9.22 chains in length, commencing in a Field numbered 13*

on the deposited plans of the Devon and Somerset railway Session 1863-64, in the Parish of Barnstaple ... by a Junction with the authorised Devon and Somerset Railway at a point 41 Miles 3 Furlongs 2 chains or thereabouts from the commencement thereof, and terminating in the said Parish of Barnstaple at a point 2 chains or thereabouts, measured in a Northerly Direction, from the Clock Tower, known as the Barnstaple Albert Memorial.'

Thus the extension was to take the broad gauge line beyond its current planned terminus at Victoria Road to a more central location, that is '*to a first rate and convenient position in the square*'.

There was also the ability to raise a further £30,000 of ordinary share capital and an additional £10,000 to the mortgage borrowing of £166,000, specifically for the purposes of this Act (to acquire land, etc). It specified that the railway '*shall be completed within three years*', that is 12th August 1870, otherwise the powers would cease (the land was also to be purchased within two years). As was usual at this time, a sum of £2,400 (being 8% of the £30,000 being raised) was to be deposited with the Court of Chancery, such funds not to be repaid until the line was opened or half the capital was paid up and expended. If there was a breach of terms, the funds would belong to HM Exchequer. Also, the Act specifically obliged the D&SR to give not less than eight weeks notice before taking in any Parish houses occupied by persons belonging to the labouring classes as tenants or lodgers – such notices to take the form of placards, handbills or other notice on general view.

Mr Birch reported on 28th August 1867 that '*no progress in the construction of the line has been made since my last report*'. The permanent works were, with two exceptions, in good condition; the Board was notified of the state of insecure bridges where work was essential. Birch reported that, in July, there had been an issue involving the removal of forty '*muck wagons*' (spoil wagons) from the works by Pickerings, without authority (W.C. Floyd in the South Molton engineer's office originally drew this to Birch's attention). In order to counter this, Birch served the contractors with a notice of criminal proceedings. Also, landowners were complaining at the state their land was being left in by the unfinished works.

The table below is an extract from the D&SR Statement of Receipts & Payments on Capital Account to 30th June 1867, as extracted from the corporate records. These were '*Examined and found correct, 3rd August 1867*' by James Jerwood of Exeter and Geo Robinson, 10 Coleman Street, London (auditors).

DR	**RECEIPTS (£ S D)**
Per last half-yearly report	**309,822 10 0**
To Ordinary Share Capital	**10,800 0 0**
To Debenture Bonds	**39,000 0 0**
TOTAL	**359,622 10 0**
CR	**PAYMENTS (£ S D)**
Per last half-yearly report	**309,816 0 0**
By Contractors on account of Construction	**49,000 0 0**
By Balance at Bankers	**6 10 0**
TOTAL	**359,622 10 0**

The Bill introduced in Parliament by the B&ER to take over the D&SR received the sanction of the committee of the House of Commons. However, due to circumstances outside the D&SR directors' control, namely the B&ER deciding that to proceed with the purchase was undesirable, the Bill was withdrawn. This further set back raised a serious concern as to how the railway was to be finished by the D&SR as an independent company.

Claims by Mr McMillan, Riccard & Son and Mr Birch against the company were highlighted in the 25th October 1867 minutes. Mr Birch estimated assets (rails) at £40,000 and a bank loan with the West of England & South Wales District Bank could be considered for £20,000 with the rails as security. This would be partly in respect of those obligations and the share of the £43,800 estimated commitment to the IR as described above. Lord Poltimore suggested issuing debentures to the creditors, including the three claimants referred to above (as per minutes of 8th November).

At the next meeting on 19th November, a letter dated 16th from Mr Sandars (a director who could not be present) was read, stating '*the position of the company is a very anxious one*'. He continued that every act of the Board was being watched jealously by the L&SWR and criticised in the Court of Chancery. It was clear the line could not be finished except by applying to the Court. It would be dangerous to issue debentures to creditors on account of claims and there was concern over the legality of agreeing to the promoters claims of £42,000, so settlement of those monies was still outstanding. Mr Birch wanted a salary regardless of whether the works were continuing but there was no detailed plan of the line for the contractor, so it was difficult to justify issuing debentures to him!

In late 1867, work remained on hold but the poor condition of a bridge and highway near Molland, and a temporary bridge near Filleigh were highlighted. Mr Birch was anxious for the Board to place him in a position to have those bridges repaired. He also wanted an assistant to protect the company's interest on each section of the line but they could not afford to do so. Another contractor (William Jackson) offered to do the repairs for payment in debentures and was also prepared to submit a tender to complete the works. This offer was accepted by the Board and they subsequently forcibly dispossessed Pickerings. The turmoil continued as the directors then tendered their resignation at an EGM on 13th December. It transpired that the number of shareholders attending the meeting was inadequate and a quorum was not present, so the meeting was adjourned and the existing directors had to continue in office.

At the 18th February 1868 board meeting, with work still suspended and ruinous disputes with the L&SWR over the IR continuing, something had to be done. The directors agreed to file for a Scheme of Arrangement in the Court of Chancery for the adoption by the company under the provisions of the Railway Companies Act of 1867. Such proposal was put to the shareholders at an EGM and was passed and subsequently filed on 5th March 1868. The aim was to reach agreement with creditors and raise further loan capital to secure the completion of the works of the line.

One positive piece of news was confirmed by Mr Birch in his letter of 15th February; the insecure bridges had been fully reinstated. Mr Muggeridge, in a letter of January 1868, said that a new board should be formed of landowners and inhabitants of the district. Debenture holders declined to fund more money, the landowners' real estate was cut up by the contractors and the company was encumbered with decaying works. Advice from Mr Morris (of Ashurst Morris, solicitors) was to have a qualified engineer estimate the cost to complete the line and finish it, get capital and funds, and present this to the Court. Muggeridge suggested that landowners should provide funds of £500 and he would find another £500 to pay for an engineer (at £1,000 plus expenses).

At this time, debts due to Messrs Riccard, Birch and McMillan amounted to £17,805 and this was to cause a further issue.

On 31st March, a special general meeting was held to elect directors following the Court's confirmation of the Scheme. Also, the shareholders and stockholders had to assent to the Scheme between the company and creditors, and for raising loan capital. The promoters (who were still owed their £42,000), somewhat surprisingly, then changed their claims from settlement by debentures to settlement in cash and opposed the Scheme! Again the progress of the line was put in jeopardy. Mr Sandars stated that the promoters must accept 'B' debentures for their payment for matters to proceed. In this regard, it was proposed that Riccard be paid £2,000 plus £7,520 in 'B' debentures and Birch £2,000 plus £4,947 in 'B' debentures (potential settlement of part of these amounts are referred to below). The Board were at liberty to terminate the services of the solicitor or engineer at any time within six months of the confirmation of the Scheme. These terms were set out in a memorandum of agreement dated 31st March 1868 (and subsequently appended as schedule 2 to the trustee agreement with Reed).

By this stage, under the agreement of 19th July 1865, the amounts issued to the contractor totalled £3,000 in cash, £94,000 in debentures and shares (fully paid up) of £256,600, making a total of £353,600.

At the 6th June 1868 board meeting, a Works & Finance Committee was set up. Lord Politmore, Mr Sandars, Mr Locke and Mr Moysey were to enter into negotiations for the construction of the remaining works of the line and raising capital. A Land sub-Committee (comprising Lord Poltimore, Mr Locke, Mr Moysey and Mr Smythe) was formed to affect arrangements with landowners. This was potentially a big step forward for the Company. Furthermore, on 29th July 1868, the Scheme of Arrangement was enrolled at the Court of Chancery. The Scheme as approved stated the D&SR would create and issue new irredeemable 'A' debenture stock of £270,000 at 6% per annum, with a first charge over all assets. The existing debentures would be converted to 'B' stock, which would then rank behind the new A stock. The board of directors subsequent to the Scheme was confirmed to be not less than six and not more than eight. New contractors were to be appointed and '*two eminent railway contractors*', Thomas Brassey and Mr Wythes, were so named. It was stressed that the current Scheme would not raise enough funds to reach Barnstaple, so there needed to be scope and plans for issuing further capital. The current priority would be land possessions to progress the works, which would be acquired by issuing 'B' debentures to landowners (the largest had already agreed to this). No work had been done in the six months to the report of 28th August 1868, extending the inaction to around twenty-three months. A meeting of 28th August 1868 resolved that the debt should be issued to the full extent of the said Scheme, to facilitate completion of the undertaking.

Linked with the Scheme of Arrangement and under an indenture dated 13th November 1868, the company's lands were vested in the hands of trustees for the benefit of the debenture stock holders. It was stated that the trustees should always be directors of the company.

The Midland Railway rebate agreement, to encourage '*respective endeavours to develop through traffic*', was ratified on 6th November 1868. Applying to all types of traffic, it provided for a rebate of 10% (after working expenses) to the Devon Company, excepting if they paid a dividend in excess of 5%, in which case the rebate was not payable. The agreement would cease to operate if the interchange of traffic between the Midland and B&ER at Bristol was discontinued.

Mr Easton inspected the deviation of the line from Wiveliscombe to Brushford (a distance of 13 miles, 1 furlong and 6.70 chains), the land required for this being 92 acres at a cost of £8,600.

The promoters' claims were paid by issue of 'B' debentures and preference shares, whilst landowners were paid by 'B' debentures alone. Mr Sandars accepted 'A' debentures for his advances made to the Board

Eugenius Birch (1818-1884)

Eugenius Birch was born in Shoreditch, where his father was a grain dealer. Even as a boy he designed a carriage for the London & Greenwich Railway, placing the wheels beneath it rather than to the side. At age 16, he joined an engineering company, Bligh's, in Limehouse, East London. In 1837, he received a silver Isis Medal from the Society of Arts for his drawing of a marine steam engine. In 1845, he formed a general design engineering partnership with his brother and worked on railway, viaduct and bridge projects. He travelled to India to advise on the design and construction of the Calcutta to Delhi railway of the East Indian Railway Company. In addition to his work with the D&SR, he designed Exmouth dock, Ilfracombe harbour and Margate Pier. He built his last pier at Plymouth in 1884, the year he died, and was known as the 'Brunel of the British Seaside'.

for Parliamentary and legal expenses in sessions of Parliament in 1866 and 1867-68. 'A' debenture stock was issued to certain landowners for rent charges and land acquisitions. It was agreed at the meeting of the directors on 6th November 1868, that completion of the line to Wiveliscombe should be proceeded with immediately and tenders sought for the work. Messrs Relf & Scott were appointed to do the works, which was to be a single line built to the satisfaction of the D&SR and B&ER engineers. There was a requirement to maintain the undertaking for twelve months and they were to be paid in cash not shares. Birch ceased to be the engineer from 30th November 1868 but Riccard & Son were retained as solicitors.

	Issued at 29/6/1868	Unissued at 29/6/1868	Total (£)
Loan stock (1864 Act)	94,000	72,000	166,000
Loan stock (1867 Act)		10,000	10,000
Preference shares/ Designated Class A		200,000	200,000
Ordinary Share capital	272,700	27,300	300,000
Ordinary Shares (1967)		30,000	30,000
Total	366,700	339,300	706,000

Note 1: The amount of issued shares represents 10,908 at £25, that is £272,700, of which £256,600 had been fully paid at the date of filing the Scheme. The balance of ordinary shares was to be cancelled.

Note 2: The preference shares (at 5% dividend) were created under the D&SR (Capital) Act 1866 (8,000 at £25) and labelled 'A' shares, the ordinary shares being cancelled.

Note 3: The £30,000 additional share capital and £10,000 loan were raised under the D&SR (Extension) Act 1867 (in respect of purchase of additional lands and the proposed extension in Barnstaple). Although listed as still unissued at this date, in the event this was never issued.

In summary, the authorised share capital after the Scheme of Arrangement was as follows:

Stock	Authorised (£)
'A' debenture stock (new issue at 6%)	270,000
'B' debenture stock (formerly old debenture stock *i.e.* the £166,000 and £10,000)	176,000
Preference shares (issued, created out of ordinary shares)	12,000
Ordinary Share capital (£30,000 unissued)	290,700
Total	748,700

Note 1: The preference shares were issued to Messrs Riccard & Son, Birch and McMillan, as referred in the text.

Note 2: Of the £290,700 ordinary share capital, £260,700 was in issue and remained so (being £272,700 less the £12,000 Preference shares created). The £30,000 unissued was for the Barnstaple extension.

Note 3: The £10,000 Debenture stock (part of the £176,000) was not issued.

At this stage the estimate of future expenditure was as follows (no work was anticipated over the first six months to 30th June 1869):

• That suspended between Taunton and Wiveliscombe 20,000
• That suspended between Brushford and Barnstaple 45,000

SUB TOTAL £65,000

Works not yet commenced:

• Deviation Wiveliscombe to Brushford 155,000
• Extension at Barnstaple 30,000

TOTAL £250,000

Negotiations began for a loan of £200,000 (at 7% rolled up) to be repaid after two years. Lord Poltimore wrote on 25th February 1869, stating his wish to resign if the loan was not effected within six weeks.

At the 26th February 1869 10th half yearly meeting, the directors reported they had successfully carried through the Court of Chancery Scheme. This was the only means of saving the company from long, harassing and expensive litigation and relieving landowners from '*the annoying position in which they are unfortunately placed as the works are taking so long and are suspended ... The scheme provides ample security for the capital necessary to complete the undertaking, the general disinclination of the public mind and amongst capitalists to invest in railway securities, however, has prevented your directors from being able to carry out successful issue negotiations*'. With the advent of the Regulation of the Railways Act 1868 in the last session of Parliament, the first of many statements of account in the form required by that Act were prepared by the Company.

Under the articles (with reference to the 1868 scheme), the company was able to issue preference shares to the value of £12,000 and they were to be issued in lieu of ordinary shares held by Messrs Riccard (214 shares – £5,350), Eugenius Birch (159 – £3,975) and John McMillan (107 – £2,675). After the issue, the company's share capital would be £260,700 (the £30,000 difference above being the unissued element created under the 1867 Act).

An EGM on 18th March 1869 agreed to cancel £12,000 of issued share capital to create preference shares (as above) and to convert debentures to 'B' stock under the Scheme of Arrangement.

At the meeting of 23rd March, the company declined to proceed with the expected £200,000 loan. Mr Morris (solicitor) said that, in order to proceed with the loan, a statement of liabilities and securities for completion, and parties with whom negotiations had been unsuccessful, would be needed. By May, consideration was given to approaching landowners for money in respect of rent charges under the provision of the Improvement of Lands Act 1864. However, it was felt that it was not practicable to obtain rent charges up to £50,000 (a figure of £20,000 being more realistic). It was deemed unfair on the landowners, a number of whom had already contributed significantly to the company resources. At this juncture, Lord Carnarvon was highlighted in the minutes for not having taken a single share in the company.

With construction work still not recommenced and the clock ticking, the D&SR company made an application to the BoT on 27th May 1869 under the Railways (Extension of Time) Act 1868, to extend the works by two years from the time limit imposed by the 1864 Act (29th July 1869), following unanimous support from the shareholders at an EGM on the same day (£248,850 of value in favour and only £275 against). There was time given for any person or corporation to object to the extension by sending a written notice but, in the Board's opinion, no objection that could be sustained was brought. The enthusiasm and will was there to complete the project, despite the difficulties encountered so far and the work still to be done.

However, at the 3rd August 1869 half yearly meeting, the directors stated their regret that they were unable to enter into any contracts for the resumption of the works of the undertaking:

> '*The general disinclination of the public to invest in Railway Securities on uncompleted lines has prevented their raising any portion of the capital whilst the provisions of their scheme led them to hope ... and the directors have had no alternative but to abide by the course of events which they are unable to control. They will not relent in their endeavours to complete the line.*'

With no payments and receipts since the last half yearly meeting, the financial position remained '*just the same*'.

THE 1870S

Despite the advent of the new decade, old troubles remained; work was still stagnated and disputes continued. Pickerings were still keen to compete the project and were looking to get a loan to facilitate completion of the line in 1868. In a letter dated 21st January 1870 to the Board, the contractors stated their willingness to enter into a (revised) contract to complete the D&SR as a single line, on specified terms that required the Company to take actions, including:

• to settle all claims for land in respect of the original authorised line
• pay all unpaid purchase money and costs
• to purchase land necessary for the deviation authorised by the Act of 1867 along with costs
• completion of the line as authorised by the 1864 Act (subject to the 1867 deviation) to the satisfaction of George Parker Bidder (or other agreed engineer)
• extension of time (say three years) to complete the works
• original authorised line to terminate at Cattle Market Road
• to not include the works of the extension railway into Barnstaple as authorised by the 1867 Act

The price for this was the issue of 'A' debentures of £255,000 and 'B' debentures of £50,000, whilst any extra work required by the B&ER was not to be covered by the contractor.

Also, if part of the line were to open to traffic before its entire completion, all profits would accrue to Messrs Pickerings in addition to the contract amount. The Board asked the solicitor to negotiate with Pickerings but some of their proposals were not acceptable to the D&SR.

Meanwhile, the D&SR was not sitting back; consideration was given to looking at the use by the Post Office of the telegraph poles and wires between Taunton and Wiveliscombe, and Barnstaple and South Molton.

Also, the company had decided to look for a new contractor. Tenders were being received for completion of the line and one from Messrs Dierden & Mander was accepted subject to certain securities (as indicated in the minutes of 27th April 1870).

J. & A. Scrimegour were to be appointed to act as brokers in placing unissued 'A' debentures in April 1870. However, Cazenove, De Zoete & Gorton were waiting in the wings if Scrimegour did not accept. The task was to place £255,000 of 'A' debenture stock and £40,000 of 'B' debenture stock, which was to be applied for the new contractor's contract of 24th May 1870. However, when it came to issuing the prospectus, Scrimegour's name was not there.

Mr Birch, the engineer attended the board meeting on 11th May 1870 but was asked to withdraw; he did not. The Secretary then took steps to have him removed by a policeman, at which point he decided to leave the meeting of his own accord. It was stated that Mr Birch was '*incapable of efficiently superintending the finishing of the line*'. He was thus summarily dismissed as engineer.

Problems with recruiting new contractors continued; it was established that Mander's tender was made without the approval of his partner, Mr Knight, and Holden (another who had tendered) complained for not being chosen. As Holden withdrew from the fray, a Mr Leather (who put up Mr Holden's surety) appeared and offered his services. Then up stepped John Langham Reed, who was acting as guarantor for Mr Mander, and he requested to be named as contractor. With Mander's sureties declined and Knight's reluctance to commit his firm, a decision was made to appoint Mr Reed as the contractor on 24th May. A drawn out saga was over, and Leather and Mander were told that they were not going to be considered as another contractor had been appointed. At this point, monies for the construction of the line were vested in the hands of trustees (who had to be directors), these being Lord Politimore and the Earl of Fortescue.

A formal agreement between the D&SR and John Langham Reed was entered into on 25th May 1870, for the completion of the railway works. Lords Fortescue and Poltimore as trustees were authorised to sign the agreement on behalf of the D&SR. In association with the main contract was a declaration of trust, dated 24th May 1870, between the Rt Hon. Earl Fortescue, Rt Hon. Augustus Frederick George Warwick, Baron Poltimore (as trustees for the D&SR) and John Reed (contractor). In essence, this agreement was there to protect the funds for Reed to complete the line and get paid.

The outline of the terms of the trust deed were as follows:

- Messrs Combe & Wainwright (London solicitors) were to be paid
- any residue was to be invested in Government securities (the 'invested trust funds') and of this, £20,000 was to be set aside to pay annual interest until the railway was operational
- purchase or compensation money required from time to time
- a salary to be paid to Richard Muggeridge (Parliamentary Agent and Company Secretary), such amount not to exceed £1,000 along with office expenses not to exceed £1,000 and ,on change of company engineer, a sum not exceeding £5,000 and other sums set out in the memorandum of agreement dated 31st March 1868.

Any part of the gross receipts payable to the D&SR under the B&ER agreement of 6th March 1865 was to enure for the benefit of Reed and be applied to pay down any interest on the 'A' debenture stock.

There was a further agreement of 24th May 1870, between William McArthur and the D&SR in respect of a bond for securing the completion of the railway. The amount stipulated was £20,000 and was stated to be a penal amount for the due performance of Reed under the contractor's contract; William McArthur was surety for Reed. Should the railway and other specified works be completed to the satisfaction of the engineer and maintained for twelve months after completion, then the bond would be void.

There followed a report by a Mr Hassard as to the condition and cost of completion of the line from Norton Fitzwarren to Wiveliscombe and he was subsequently appointed as engineer, with Birch formally dismissed. So, after an hiatus of over three and a half years, construction was about to start again.

Further good news was received from the BoT, when their letter of 11th May stated that they were '*prepared to grant a warrant under the Railway (Extension of Time) Act 1868*'. However, this had conditions attached. An amount had to be deposited at the Court of Chancery and be retained as security for the completion of the railway for the time extension. This meant there was a risk of the Crown proceeding to recover the deposit or bond if the work was not completed on time. Messrs Charles Edward Stubbs and George Thomas Davy were willing to become sureties for the bond required by the BoT. A warrant was then issued on 31st May 1870 from the BoT, which enabled the time limit for building the D&SR to be extended. The original course of the line between Wiveliscombe and Brushford prior to the deviation authorised by the 1867 Act was to be abandoned. However, the time limits of the 1867 Deviation Act and 1867 Extension Act were also approved for extension to 15th July 1872 and 12 August 1872 respectively. If the railway was not completed and opened to passengers by these revised deadlines, there would be a default payment of £4,100 due. The BoT, having ascertained the state and condition of the D&SR company, saw reason to believe that the project could be completed in the extended times and ordered and declared the extension of time approved on 6th September 1870.

By 14th June, Birch had issued a writ. There was a cross action for negligence by the D&SR against him and the *Exeter Gazette* for libel. Hassard was charged with laying before the Board, by 24th June, drawings, schedules and plans for completion of the first stage of the railway. Also, Richard Muggeridge was formally appointed Company Secretary.

A review of the financial state of the company at the 30th June 1870 half-year makes for interesting reading. The total share capital was £272,700 (£30,000 still to be issued), to which can be added the borrowing powers by way of debenture and loan stock, as set out in the following table:

EXISTING AT	AT 5%	AT 6%	TOTAL DEB. STOCK	TOTAL RAISED BY LOAN & DEB. STOCKS
31/12/1869	94,000	13,930	107,930	107,930
30/6/1870	94,000	177,591	271,591	271,591
Increase		163,661	163,661	163,661

The total amount authorised to be raised by loans and debentures was £436,000. With £271,591 issued above the available borrowing powers at 30 June 1870 were £164,409.

This next table sets out the net cash position:

RECEIPTS/EXPENDITURE	£ s d	£ s d
Shares (to 31/12/69 and 30/6/70)		272,265 0 0
Debentures to 31/12/69	107,930 0 0	
Debentures to 30/6/70	163,661 0 0	271,591 0 0
Interest		3 0 3
TOTAL RECEIPTS		543,859 0 3
Authorised line of company to 31/12/69	373,546 0 0	
Half year to 30/6/70	23,653 18 11	
Ilfracombe Railway	6,645 10 3	
TOTAL EXPENDITURE		403,845 9 2
Surplus Funds		140,013 11 1
Represented by		
Investment in Consols and East India Stock	75,000 0 0	
At Bank	65,013 11 1	140,013 11 1

Of the £23,653 expended in the six months, £20,400 was spent on the contractors account but the railway was still a long way from completion.

An estimate of further anticipated expenditure at this time is summarised as follows:

SECTION	HALF YEAR TO 31/12/70	SUBSEQUENT HALF YEARS	TOTAL
Taunton to Wiveliscombe	20,000	nil	20,000
Wiveliscombe to South Molton	40,000	80,000	120,000
South Molton to Barnstaple	30,000	25,000	55,000
TOTAL	90,000	105,000	195,000

The financing of this anticipated spend of £195,000 was to come from:

- Cash and investments £140,000
- Additional stock to issue:
  A Stock – £92,409
  B Stock – £72,000
- Total £164,409*
- Overall funds anticipated. £304,409

Leaving a surplus of funds of £109,000 for other matters.
*The total loans and debenture stock available to issue at this point was £436,000, of which £271,591 had been issued by 30th June 1870 (£163,661 being issued in the six months to then out of the £225,000 'A' debenture stock from the public issue), leaving £164,409 in total ('A' and 'B') to issue under current borrowing powers.

At this time, £100,000 was taken to a trustees account '*to be applied by them in or towards the completion of the railway and works under the declaration of trust executed 24 May 1870*'.

JUNE 1870 – CONSTRUCTION BEGINS AGAIN

Richard Hassard, the engineer, reported on 3rd August 1870 that works on the line from Norton Fitzwarren to Wiveliscombe had resumed by the middle of June, with Mr Reed as the contractor. Two locomotives and a good deal of additional plant had been delivered on that portion of the line. The mode of junction with the B&ER had been arranged with their engineer. Stations at Milverton and Wiveliscombe were '*about being at once commenced*' and he saw '*nothing to prevent this portion of the line being ready for opening in October*'. At their 21st September board meeting, the B&ER directors again stressed their objections to the proposed alterations to the line, saying that the increased gradients and curves would increase the costs of working it; they had accordingly notified the D&SR of their right to claim compensation in the form of an allowance for those extra working costs.

Hassard went on to report that the second section of the line (Wiveliscombe to South Molton) had been set out on the ground, the necessary sections had been taken, and that plans required for the purchase of land were in preparation and would be soon handed to solicitors. On the third section (South Molton to Barnstaple), all necessary levels had been taken and the design for Castle Hill Viaduct was prepared and given to the contractor.

On 1st August, Lord Fortescue wrote to the Board offering to build Castle Hill station at his expense and to rent it for a reasonable sum; this proposal was accepted.

An engraving of Castle Hill House, the home of Lord Fortescue, which was published as a coloured lithographed plate in *County Seats of The Noblemen and Gentlemen of Great Britain and Ireland* by Francis Orpen Morris (1870). Built in 1730, it is now the home of the Countess of Arran, who provided the forward to this volume.

Hassard reported his concerns that the cost of building stations and the BoT requirement with respect to signals was likely to be in excess of the anticipated expenditure. It will be recalled that the contractor's contract stipulated a budget of £14,000 for the buildings.

The B&ER wrote to the D&SR on 26th September 1870, setting out the anticipated weekly working expenses of the line from Norton Fitzwarren to Wiveliscombe.

	£	s	d
Share of expenses at Norton Junction – signalmen, signals and stores	1	10	0
Inspector	1	13	0
Station work at Milverton and Wiveliscombe and working block	13	10	0
Stores and Stationery at Milverton and Wiveliscombe	5	10	0
Wages and clothing of guard	1	7	6

USE OF CARRIAGE STOCK:	PER MILE
First Class and Composite	1½d
Second Class	1¼d
Third Class	1d
Vans	1d
Horse boxes	¾d
Carriage trucks	½d
Sheets	1/16d
Covered wagons	7/16d
Open wagons	⅜d

The locomotives were to be coupled tank engines (or other such power that the B&ER saw fit to provide). Coupled tank locomotives for a train of not more than six vehicles were charged at 10d per mile and ½d per mile for each vehicle above six. Trains were to be arranged so that there was a 20-30 minute time for turning around at either terminus. Provision of water was to be arranged and provided by the D&SR. Also, there was a charge of 5% interest based on the cost of the locomotives used (which cost was £6,400). The use of Taunton station was to be charged at £150pa.

The B&ER reserved the right to receive compensation for the extra costs arising from the alterations in the curves and gradients from the Parliamentary plans. The D&SR accepted these proposals at their Board meeting of 5th October 1870, subject to the contractors' approval. At the same time, Mr Fox, the B&ER engineer, reported in correspondence with Hassard on the condition of timber sleepers and their creosoting. An independent inspector was to determine which sleepers should be rejected. A Mr Richardson was appointed as civil engineer by the B&ER and he was authorised to go and inspect the works between Norton Fitzwarren and Wiveliscombe (B&ER minutes 12 & 19, October 1870). Richardson reported back by 28th October and a copy of his report was to be sent to the D&SR, along with a letter referring to the '*unsatisfactory manner in which the works are being executed and giving notice that this company* [B&ER] *will not accept any portion of the line for working unless and until the defects be remedied and the portion proposed for opening* [Norton Fitzwarren to Wiveliscombe] *be*

A FATALITY

The *West Somerset Free Press* reported on 22nd October 1870 that a ballast engine on the D&SR knocked down a valuable bullock which had trespassed on the line. The property of Mr R. Brown, a farmer from Preston [Bowyer], the animal received such severe injuries it unfortunately had to be slaughtered.

LOCOMOTIVES USED ON THE D&SR CONTRACT

These photographs of the construction of the D&SR have been useful for crystallising recent research into the locomotives employed by John Langham Reed on the contract. There were three standard gauge 0-6-0 saddle tank locomotives used, all supplied by Fox, Walker & Co. of Bristol, which company was later taken over by Thomas Peckett. In addition, there were two steam cranes also supplied by Fox, Walker, an 0-4-0 vertical boiler engine built by Alexander Shanks & Sons of Arbroath circa 1872, an Aveling & Porter 12hp 4-wheeled engine of 1870, with wheels coupled by chains, and three broad gauge locomotives.

It had originally been thought that the three Fox, Walker 0-6-0STs were Works No's 17, 18 and 19, all new circa 1870, but it is now known that No. 18 was one of the steam cranes. However, further research indicates that the third of these engines is quite probably Works No. 16 of 1864. This engine is recorded as arriving in Sussex, it is believed in the summer 1880, for the construction of the southern extension of the line from East Grinstead to Lewes via Horsted Keynes in Sussex – the 'Bluebell Line'. Nothing was known of its history prior to that date but it was then owned by the contractor Joseph Firbank and was carrying the name *Taunton*. These engines often acquired names to do with contracts on which they were used and the temptation to link *Taunton* with the D&SR contract is great indeed, Firbank probably buying it at auction in September 1873 when Reed sold all of the plant off. This locomotive was one of Fox, Walker's 'A' Class, so is not the engine seen in the photograph here. Firbank also owned Fox, Walker No. 14 at the same time as *Taunton*, so further speculation suggests that Works No. 15 may well have been the second steam crane used by Reed on the D&SR contract.

The Shanks vertical boiler 0-4-0 is interesting because the firm only built a handful of locomotives between 1872 and 1877 and, as will be seen from the sale notes a little further on in these pages, clearly did not find another buyer immediately. However, it was eventually bought by Messrs Budd & Holt and used on the construction of the Malmesbury Railway, where it was photographed in the late summer of 1875. Of the Aveling & Porter engine, however, nothing else is known.

Three broad gauge engines are also believed to have been involved in the construction of the D&SR. The first was ex-Bristol & Gloucester Railway 0-6-0 No. 11 *Defiance*, supplied new by the Vulcan Foundry for that line's opening in 1844. In 1857, it was one of eight of the original eleven engines supplied new to the B&GR that were sold to the contractor Thomas Brassey, who having just built the North Devon Railway, agreed to lease and operate it. *Defiance* was acquired from the L&SWR, who had taken over the NDR in 1862, by Reed probably in early 1871, to use on ballasting of the Taunton to Wiveliscombe section of the D&SR (which opened first). In August 1870, in a report to the Board, L&SWR Locomotive Superintendent noted that *Defiance* was '*completely worn out and not worth repairs*'. The second engine was ex-B&GR 2-4-0 No. 2 *Industry*, built by Stothert & Slaughter in 1844, sold to Brassey in 1856 and renamed *Venus*. Again obtained from the L&SWR, Beattie had noted in 1870 that it was '*in fair order*' but he could see no further use for the engine, so recommended it be sold. Finally, Reed bought a broad gauge engine from Swindon in March 1873 but nothing further has been discovered about its identity.

This information is summarised in Appendix 2, along with details of orders for spares for the Fox, Walker engines delivered to Reed at locations on the D&SR in 1871-72.

BELOW: Milverton station nearing completion circa 1870, with one of the contractor's locomotives posed in front of the newly constructed station building. The goods shed also appears to be finished or very nearly. The signal box awaits details but part of the lever frame can be glimpsed through the centre windows. It was replaced by a brick built box, sited further along the platform, in 1903. The station building had an inset covered waiting area and thus did not require a canopy or awning. A second platform, on the Up side, was added in 1880. In the background and on slightly higher ground, St. Michael's church and the town of Milverton gaze down on the new railway below. Note the three rails, for mixed standard and broad gauge. The enlargement, OPPOSITE PAGE LEFT, clearly shows the locomotive, a Fox, Walker 0-6-0ST either Works No. 17 or 19 of 1870, to be standard gauge and standing on the narrower set of rails. However, the second enlargement, RIGHT, taken from the photograph on the following page, shows the same engine a little further back down the line but coupled to two broad gauge wagons. *Courtesy South Molton Museum*

Taken on the same day as the previous photograph, this view is looking west through the new stone arch – clearly built to span two broad gauge lines – carrying what was to become Station Road over the line. Note the B&ER disc & crossbar signal to the left (a second signal can just be made out at the far end of the platform – see enlargement opposite), whilst there is also a more complete view of the wooden signal cabin. ***Courtesy South Molton Museum***

completed to the reasonable satisfaction of this company's engineer'. The *West Somerset Free Press* reported at this time that the first section of the line would probably not be completed by the anticipated date (26th October) and was unlikely to be finished by Christmas, as there was still 10 miles of permanent way to lay, with the junction (at Norton) having just been completed. This was of great disappointment to Milvertonians, who were looking forward to the opening.

Under an agreement dated 10th November 1870, between Reed and Lord Politimore and the Earl of Fortescue (as Trustees for the D&SR), the contractor required a further advance of funds and as a consequence agreed to assign plant and materials to the D&SR to secure such advance. The entitlement was to receive funds equivalent to 50% of the value of plant and materials brought onto the D&SR premises. The value assessed amounted to £8,825 4s 8d, so the advance was agreed at £4,412 12s 4d out of the trustees account and the contractor assigned to them plant, machinery, engines, stock, horses, wagons and other materials. Such assets would be reassigned to Reed if the said sum was repaid by 10th April 1871. If the contractor defaulted in completing the railway under the terms set out in the 24th May contract, then Reed would pay interest at a rate of 5% per annum until the railway was completed and then the trustees could call in the £4,412, or recoup it (and any interest) out of the 10% retention under the contract; all plant was to remain on site during the currency of this or any other loan. The plant could be seized in the event of any breach of the contract and equipment between Norton Junction and Wiveliscombe, Yeo Mill and South Molton, and South Molton and Barnstaple were listed in the Schedule.

EXTRACT FROM SCHEDULE OF 10TH NOVEMBER 1870
LOCATION OF PLANT AND MATERIALS
List of Plant of Works between Norton Junction and Wiveliscombe

'Ten work horses, four trap ditto, ten sets of chain harness(new) ... four carts in good order, one dray for timber in good order, two Smith's bellows, two anvils, one vice, one set of stocks and dies, one set of Blacksmith's stools in good order, one crab, one set of blocks and ropes, two fifteen ton screw jacks ... sixty-eight waggons in good order, twenty waggons want repair, two side waggons in good order, one hundred and sixty new wheelbarrows, nine old ditto ditto, twenty-one broken ditto, five dobbins want repair, two trollies in working order, one trolley wants repair, six hundred and seventy left baulk timber, three hundred and twenty lineal yards temporary rails (40lbs per yard) say six tons, ten 28 feet centres (ribs), six nine feet ribs, four hundred and eighty five 3ins planks 16 feet, three hundred 6 ft timber lying in waggon at Junction, two hundred laggings, two hundred picks, sixty bars, twenty sledges, twenty jumpers, twenty devils, six long levers, one screw rail straightener, two locomotives, two spring carts with harness complete, sheds, buildings stables, Smiths shops ... at Wiveliscombe.'

A further request for a two-year extension of time to complete the line was registered on 29th November 1870. The B&ER were still unhappy with the '*imperfect character*' of the works and Mr Richardson was to be called in again.

On 31st December 1870, there was payment to John Reed of £33,964 3s 5d (and £10,000 made up of 'B' debenture stock). Following further funds received from the issue of 'A' debenture stock in the six months to 31st December, a further £115,000 was transferred in tranches to the trustees account, their responsibility being to safely invest the money until the contractor was required to be paid.

Further land purchases were made (cheques for £5,000 drawn were disclosed in the 29th October minutes) and the deeds of land deposited at the National Provincial Bank (the Company's bankers).

At the 5th January 1871 Board meeting, Mr Sandars resigned as a director on good terms and Lord Fortescue resumed his seat, whilst Mr Reed, was issued £30,000 of 'B' debenture stock. Building work on the Wiveliscombe section was proceeding and, on inspection by the engineers, they (Hassard and Richardson of the B&ER) indicated that the objections and reservations of their company had been satisfactorily dealt with.

In February, it was announced that some compulsory purchases of land had been made from Rowcliffe's, Messrs Rawles and the Earl of Carnarvon, £5,000 being expended in the January to April period. The Rev'd Nicholetts wrote to the Board to suggest the provision of a station at Chipstable. This seemed a strange request, as the course of the line line was some miles to the south of that village, following the deviations agreed in the 1867 Act.

By 16th February 1871, the engineer was reporting that the first section to Wiveliscombe was completed and that BoT approval was anticipated by the next Board meeting. He highlighted that the works had been greatly retarded by the severity of the season and the difficulty of obtaining ballast for the permanent way – little being procured from the cuttings on the line as was initially hoped. Ballast had latterly been carted from the Wiveliscombe area and some brought in by rail from Wellington. However, given that good ballast was to be found on other sections of the line, this difficulty was not expected to be repeated elsewhere.

The second section was being fenced in and earthworks and masonry were progressing. The shafts for the tunnel near Wiveliscombe (Bathealton) had been sunk to 85 and 50 feet, with steam engines provided and erected at them. The contractor was now opening quarries to construct the Tone Viaduct. In the East Anstey to South Molton section (about 8 miles), earthworks and masonry had nearly been completed.

On the third section, almost all the excavations and masonry had been executed and satisfactory progress made with ballasting the line. Castle Hill Tunnel had been driven through Bremridge Hill and the abutments and piers of Castle Hill Viaduct were considerably advanced.

At this time there were currently 1,100 men on site and seven locomotives at work on the construction of the line. Also, all the rails and fastenings necessary for completion had been delivered to the works.

On 25th February 1871, the *West Somerset Free Press* reported that two trains had been arranged to transport shareholders of the D&SR from Wiveliscombe to Taunton for the half-yearly meeting. Under the heading '*The Long-Expected Railway*' it stated:

'On Tuesday great numbers of the inhabitants were gratified with the sight of the first train running from the station at Wiveliscombe to Taunton. The occasion was the half-yearly meeting of the directors and shareholders of the Devon and Somerset Railway. To enable the shareholders resident in the town to attend this meeting, two trains were run to Taunton in the course of the day, and a return conveyed the passengers back to their homes. The Bristol and Exeter Railway Company kindly lent their first-class saloon carriage for the occasion, and afforded every facility for the conveyance of the ladies and gentlemen direct from the Wiveliscombe station to the Taunton station.The line was found to be perfectly smooth, and the ride was extremely pleasant; without the least mischief-a happy augury, we hope, of its future success. The distance of eleven miles was easily accomplished in twenty minutes, though no trial of speed was intended.'

Mr Fox (B&ER engineer) carried out a further inspection of the Norton Fitwarren to Wiveliscombe section and called for the D&SR's '*renewed attention to the incomplete and defective works*'. The B&ER wanted some protection against the additional cost of maintenance and he subsequently met with Mr Hassard and Colonel Yolland, the BoT Inspector, at his inspection on 18th March.

A letter from the D&SR Company Secretary (Mr Muggeridge) of 13th March 1871, gave notice to the Assistant Secretary, Railway Department, of the BoT that the railway '*be sufficiently complete for the safe conveyance of passengers on the seventeenth day of March and will be ready for inspection ...*'. Colonel Yolland carried out his inspection promptly, on 18th March, and reported as follows on 22nd March:

'I have the honour to state for the information of the Board of Trade, that in obedience of your minute of the 13th instant, I inspected on 18th instant, a portion of the Devon & Somerset Railway, 7 miles and 29 chains in length from a junction with the West Somerset Railway close to Norton Junction and Wiveliscombe station.

This line is single throughout, with the exception for short pieces of double track at the junction, and a further piece at the terminal station at Wiveliscombe. There are also some sidings at the only other station on the line, at Milverton.

The over-bridges have been constructed for a double line, but the under-bridges and the land have only been constructed and purchased for a single line.

The width of the line at formation level is 18 feet on the embankments, and 16 feet in the cuttings: the gauge is 7 feet and the width between the lines, when they are doubled is 6 feet.

The permanent way consists of a flat-bottomed rail in lengths of 24 feet stated to weigh 75 lbs to the linear yard, laid on cross sleepers, placed on an average, about 2 feet 9 inches apart, from centre to centre. The rails are fastened to the cross sleepers by fang bolts and dog spikes – there being 2 fang bolts to the sleepers next the joints, for each rail, and 1 fang bolt and a dog spike to each of the other sleepers under each rail.

The sleepers are of memel timber, rectangular, and measure 11 feet in length by 10 inches x 5 inches.

The ballast consists of a bottom layer of coarsely broken stones stated to be 13 inches deep on which the sleepers are laid, and which is covered in with gravel and broken stone.

The joints of the rails are fished with two plates, and four bolts with nuts at each joint.

The fencing is of larch. An engine turntable has been provided at Wiveliscombe station.

The steepest incline on the line is 1 in 60, and the sharpest curve, has a radius of 20 chains; but the Parliamentary Plans have been largely deviated from both, both as regards the lateral and vertical deviation from the authorised line, and also in the introduction of sharper curves than were sanctioned in order to diminish the cost of the works by lessening the depth of the cuttings and embankments. It is however stated that these alterations have been made with the consent of the proprietors of the adjacent lands. I am not aware whether the sanctions of the Board of Trade was obtained for these alterations.

There are 5 over and 6 under bridges. The largest span being that of an under bridge of 38½ opening on the skew. They are all constructed either with brick or stone abutments and with wrought iron girders on brick arches. The wrought iron girders are sufficiently strong, according to calculation, and in the under bridges they exhibited moderate deflections under a rolling load. The abutments of two or three of the bridges were slightly out of the vertical, but they have been long built and were apparently standing well.

This line has been many years in hand, and the fencing in many parts is weak: but it has been recently overhauled and may as repaired stand some years. In a few places the width of formation is not quite sufficient – and at others the slopes of the cuttings require dressing down: but altogether the line is fairly finished off, although it will be more expensive to work than if it had been constructed strictly in according to the deposited plans.

When I went over the line, some of the indicators at the facing points required [adjusting], *so as to show clearly when the moveable switch was not quite close to the stock rail. At Milverton Station the points leading out of the siding required alteration so as to be under the control of the signalman. At Wiveliscombe the facing points at the entrance of the station required to be interlocked to the down home signal by a lever in the box: and the up starting signal, interlocked with the down distant and home signals, so as to prevent contradictory signals from being given. I have however heard today from the engineer Mr Hassard that all I required has been done including the repair of some slight damage that was done to the engine turntable in turning a heavy engine, weighing 60 tons on it for the first time and of the putting in of a pair of catch points to prevent anything running into Wiveliscombe station from the unfinished line beyond it. The line is to be worked, I believe in perpetuity, by the Bristol & Exeter Railway Company: who should concur in the undertaking as to the mode of working, which has yet to be received from the Devon & Somerset Railway. As soon as satisfactory undertaking has been received, I am of the opinion, that the Board of Trade may sanction the opening of the first portion of the Devon & Somerset Railway between Norton Junction and Wiveliscombe Station, which I understand is to be worked on the absolute block system.'*

A subsequent reply following the inspection by Colonel Yolland stated '*The undertaking as to the mode of working the traffic is satisfactory ... The Board of Trade have no objection to the line being opened for public traffic.*'.

As the opening day approached, the B&ER was still concerned about ballasting and masonry, and the fact that some sleepers were not creosoted. Also, the steep approach to Milverton was highlighted but this was obviated by a new route. With the line about to be open and operational, it was decided that the company should appoint an accountant, whilst the Secretary was charged with writing to all shareholders who had defaulted on payments, to indicate that if the shares were not fully paid they would lose them. The issues between the B&ER and D&SR continued, so arbitration was proposed and a deed of agreement for working the line was submitted to arbitration, as reported on 1st June 1871, a matter of days before the line was expected to open. As the company's compulsory purchase powers for lands were due to expire on 15th July, urgent consideration needed to be given to what further lands were required between Wiveliscombe and Barnstaple, and Mr Hassard was to determine the notices to be served to the landowners as a priority.

The (temporary) working agreement for the line still had to be approved by both companies and negotiations continued until the minutes of the B&ER on 7th June confirmed that it had been signed and the seal affixed on 1st June. It enabled the B&ER to get out of the agreement after three years if the D&SR had not completed the line through to Barnstaple. It was temporary in the sense that the main articles agreed in March 1865 and the DSR and B&ER Act of 1865 underpinned this.

The seals of both companies were appended to a certificate on B&ER note paper, dated 5th June 1871, which stated the working arrangements as follows:

'This is to certify that the mode of working to be adopted on the section of the Devon and Somerset Railway, between Norton Fitzwarren and Wiveliscombe, is by Train Staff, in the mode described in the regulations of the Board of Trade, in conjunction with and in addition to the BlockSystem of Telegraph.'

THE LINE OPENS TO WIVELISCOMBE

On Thursday, 8th June 1871, the first section of the D&SR from Taunton to Wiveliscombe was officially opened for passenger traffic. There was only one intermediate station, that at Milverton and this was the main point of celebrations. The village was elaborately decorated and there was a double arch by the turnpike gate, with 'Success to the Devon & Somerset Railway' emblazoned on it in flowers. Two bands also played and rural sports were enjoyed. Quarter pound packets of tea were given to the oldest and poorest women in the parish and 300 pupils of the National School each received a penny.

The *West Somerset Free Press* reported on 17th June 1871 that the opening of the line passed off tamely at Wiveliscombe: '*The bells were not rung and although the shops were closed, very few persons could be seen on the streets, many of the inhabitants having gone into Milverton, where the event was being commemorated with great spirit ... even the Tolland and Lydeard St. Lawrence brass band was drowned up by a rival band of local performers ... and the result was anything but harmonious*'. This subdued feeling was due to the disappointment felt at the time taken to complete the first section of the line. The leading inhabitants of Wiveliscombe and Milverton were taken to Taunton in a saloon carriage and were entertained for lunch under a marquee erected on the lawn adjoining the residence of a Mr Daniel in North Town.

However, the most important point was that the persistence and dedication of the directors and promoters had paid off; the line was now open, even if only in part, and the first timetable showed six trains each way per day (*see Volume 2*).

With the line now partially open it is timely to summarise the loan stock issued as at 30 June 1871, which was as follows:

BY 30/6/1871	ISSUED	UNISSUED	PER ACT
B debenture stock (1864)	**154,390**	**11,610**	**166,000**
Loan stock (1867)*		**10,000**	**10,000**
A Debenture stock (1868)	**269,080**	**920**	**270,000**
TOTAL	**423,470**	**22,530**	**446,000**

***This amount was for the Barnstaple extension.**

John Reed was paid a further £59,281 3s 4d on account of six months construction work at 30th June 1871.

CONSTRUCTION CONTINUES, PROBLEMS CONTINUE

In a letter to the Board from John Reed (referred to at the 6th July Board meeting), it was his turn to express his concern that the £14,000 set aside for station works was insufficient. It was now anticipated that total costs for this work would exceed £34,000, whilst related land purchases were anticipated to cost £15,000. Any excess purchase price would have to be settled with stock but there was insufficient 'B' stock

A B&ER 4-4-0 saddle tank, possibly one of the Rothwell & Co. 1855-56-built engines, with a train at Wiveliscombe. This is clearly a posed view, most probably taken soon after the station had first opened in June 1871. Wiveliscombe was the terminus of the line until November 1873, when it finally opened throughout to Barnstaple. During this period a turntable was provided here and the engine was most likely turned before being photographed, hence the appearance of a train arriving from Barnstaple. As well as the station and train staff, some of those posing are likely to be contractor's men. *John Spencer Gilks collection*

to issue to Reed for this purpose. A total of £28,000 had been expended on land so far, along with expenses of conveyance of circa £5,000. Furthermore, three miles of land had not yet been acquired between Yeo Mill and the River Exe, for which the anticipated outlay was to be £25,000. Under the circumstances, it was proposed and approved that an application to Parliament be made for raising further capital.

It was at this time the B&ER acknowledged that it would be prepared to stop its trains at Castle Hill at the request of Lord Fortescue, upon sufficient notice by telegraph and by appropriate signal. Also, any passengers who were travelling to his residence, even if the train was not intended to stop there, could avail themselves of this privilege. This was a compromise as it was proposed initially that there would be a second, private, station at Castle Hill just for Lord Fortescue.

The B&ER complained of a shortage of siding accommodation at Milverton and Wiveliscombe, such that they were unable to stack coal and other merchandise. They suggested the purchase of additional land at Wiveliscombe but again finances did not currently permit such acquisition, with land at the high price of £1,000 per acre. Mr Moysey also referred to a complaint letter about the high prices charged by the B&ER for parcels and goods conveyed on the D&SR. Indeed, because of a dispute, mails were not carried on the line until 1876.

The engineer's report of 22nd July 1871 to the Board of the D&SR stated there were delays on the second section, due to obtaining possession of certain portions of land, unfortunately at the locations where the works were heaviest. However, work at Bathealton Tunnel was progressing well and the headings between the shafts had been met. About one half of the masonry of the Tone Viaduct had been completed and the iron works for the superstructure delivered to the site. The bridge over the River Exe was well advanced, with several road and accommodation bridges completed, or under construction – the masonry '*executed by the Contractor being of a very good and substantive class*'. The ballasting of the East Anstey to South Molton section was rapidly progressing.

On the third section, the works were almost finished. The viaduct at Castle Hill was partially complete; one abutment and three piers had been built to their full height of 100 feet. Four of the iron girders had been lifted into place and ballasting of the line was well progressed. Two small bridges still had to be completed.

Plans of all the stations and the accommodation (with the exception of the temporary one at Barnstaple) had been agreed with the engineer of the B&ER. Although the buildings were constructed plainly and '*without pretension*', the engineer confirmed that they would cost more than the £14,000 anticipated and that had been set aside for the purpose; more money would be needed. At this period, around 1,350 men, 120 horses, five locomotives and three fixed steam engines were present on the works. Mr Hassard's original engagement terminated on 31st July 1871 but a new contract was agreed at a rate of £160 per month until the whole of the line was ready for opening.

Item 16 of the B&ER minutes of 9th August 1871, acknowledged the opening of the D&SR as far as Wiveliscombe and highlighted that the statutory agreement for working the railway would only come into being once the full line was completed. However, the current arrangement for working it was on a scale of charges representing cost price, a temporary arrangement similar to that used on the Portishead Railway (which the B&ER also worked). For good measure, they reported that the D&SR mileage and receipts information was not

BELOW: Bathealton Tunnel west portal, circa 1871. The track here is solely broad gauge, so the contractor was clearly using a broad gauge locomotive during the construction as well as standard gauge motive power. The stonework of the portal looks complete and it may well be that the cutting was largely dug out by hand; note the barrow remaining on the left and also the rudimentary chute over the tunnel mouth, for tipping spoil directly into broad gauge wagons below. Hiding just inside the tunnel and perched sideways on board a broad gauge flat wagon is a horse-drawn van, better seen in the enlargement, LEFT; a couple of men can also just be made out, with a third sitting on the framework to the right of the portal. The main picture bears the photographer's imprint, bottom right: John Blizard of Taunton. We can speculate that the van is his, for carrying all the heavy equipment a photographer required at this time, that the wagon would have needed a locomotive to get here and that he was taking these pictures either on behalf of the contractor or the D&SR but clearly with their assistance. *Courtesy South Molton Museum*

Below: Castle Hill Viaduct in the course of construction, probably in early July 1871. Three of the five piers are complete and one of the lattice girder spans has been placed in position at the Barnstaple end (left). The boom of a crane of some description jutting up into the air between the second and third piers suggests that preparations for lifting the second span into place are well advanced. The enlargement, Right, showing work progressing on the unfinished piers is interesting, for as well as showing another of the lattice girder spans waiting to be lifted into position, there is a works to be seen behind. Nothing is shown of this on the 1888 25ins OS, nor can it been seen on the picture of the newly completed viaduct on page 67, so the assumption must be that the works was established here to assist in the building of the railway and, in particular, Castle Hill Viaduct, and that it was completely dismantled immediately on completion. *Courtesy South Molton Museum*

recorded in their traffic accounts. However, the 2 miles between Taunton and Norton Junction was included in their figures.

At the half-yearly meeting on 10th August 1871, the directors expressed their disappointment at the slow progress of the works, which they acknowledged were out of their and the contractor's control. However, they stressed that the '*soundness of the undertaking*' remained unaffected. Traffic on the opened part of the line was exceeding expectations but there were requests by the B&ER for additional yards and sidings in the vicinity of the stations to facilitate the expanding traffic, which would require additional financial outlay. The prices for land purchase had exceeded their estimated amounts. Also, landowners who had expressed a willingness to take the company's 'B' stock in payment of claims, could only accept money instead of stock as, following investigation of their title, their lands were stated to be under strict settlement.

It had also been necessary to improve station accommodation and adopt the '*expensive* (but perfectly effective) *system of Signals in use on the Bristol and Exeter Railway to secure uniformity of working*'. Again, a larger outlay than was anticipated had to be provided for this, so the directors had no option but to, reluctantly, take the necessary measures to increase their borrowing powers up to £100,000.

It was in August 1871 that William Thomas first made a request for a siding serving his lime kilns at Milverton; however, as providing this siding would be costly, it was decided that it could not be entertained at this time.

However, just two months later, on 2nd November, the engineer was reporting to the Board that the construction of a siding for a Mr Hunt at Milverton '*should proceed without delay*'. It was also noted that the rails supplied by Pickerings were of indifferent quality and, as such, it was likely a claim would be made by the D&SR against them. Regarding progress on the Wiveliscombe to Barnstaple stretch, Bathealton Tunnel had been driven through the hill to three fifths of its length, whilst the Tone Viaduct had one abutment constructed and three piers were built to girder level. With the other abutment to be completed within the next two weeks, the iron superstructure would then be put together. Work at Venn Cross Tunnel was behind schedule and to expedite matters a shaft was being sunk at the eastern end (and at this time was down to 20 feet). Masonry of the bridge over the River Exe was almost complete, with the girders lifted and fixed in place. Engine roads had been laid in cuttings at Nightcot and East Anstey, and the rate of progress was to be accelerated. The masonry of Castle Hill Viaduct was almost complete and five pairs of girders lifted and fixed in place, with one more girder remaining to be put into position. About 1$^1/_4$ miles of broad gauge rail had been laid from Castle Hill Viaduct towards Barnstaple. By this time, the plan of arrangements for the temporary passenger and goods station at Barnstaple had been agreed with the B&ER engineer. This work had not commenced, as more land was needed before being able to do so. The masonry at stations at Dulverton Road, South Molton, Castle Hill and Swimbridge was complete to platform level but the contractor needed to secure the arrangement for future payments before proceeding. There was excess clay in some cuttings and purchase of additional lands was needed. Also, there was a need to procure a supply of water to Dulverton Road station from the River Barle nearby.

The railway also had another casualty, as a Mr Easton sent a letter to the Board indicating that one of his sheep had been killed on the line on 30th September; the company denied liability. Plans were deposited for additional lands adjacent to the railway that were required in the parishes of Wiveliscombe, Bathealton, Milverton and Chipstable.

By the 5th December Board meeting, Bathealton Tunnel had 286 out of 462 yards pierced and the end faces commenced; the Tone Viaduct's masonry was completed to girder level; Venn Cross Tunnel was still behind schedule and extra effort was being made to catch up; and Castle Hill Viaduct's masonry was almost complete – iron work was lifted and fixed, and the railway over the viaduct nearly finished and ready to test within the next three or four days. Ballasting was in progress and about 5 miles of broad gauge track had been laid. More than 900 men were employed on the works at this time.

Mr Reed requested the second half of his funds (due within three months of completion of the Norton Fitzwarren to Wiveliscombe section) in a letter dated 27th October but the Board had not paid it by December and he had stopped work on the stations (with £14,660 having been spent). The Board agreed to advance £2,400 to complete the Barnstaple section. However, in consequence, Reed would get £65,000 for completion of all works, subject to the D&SR Bill for the next round of financing receiving sanction in Parliament.

By 31st December 1871, with the line to Wiveliscombe having been open for just over six months and work progressing on the remaining 36$^1/_4$ miles, the financial position was getting tight: a total of £424,760 of debenture stock had been issued (£153,169 in the previous eighteen months), with total capital receipts amounting to £700,261 (*i.e.* including ordinary and preference share capital). Expenditure on the construction of the line had reached £636,045, with almost 10% of that figure (£63,185) being incurred in the previous six months. Of that, £56,035 was for the contractor and £4,042 for land purchases or tenants' compensation. Cash (£20,722) and investments (£24,097) totalled £44,819, which when added to the balance of debentures then available to issue (£11,240) meant that £56,059 was all that was available to complete the construction to Barnstaple. The estimated expenditure beyond 31st December 1871 was stated as follows in the half yearly report, thus indicating a potential shortfall in financing of nearly £80,000:

	HALF YEAR TO 30/6/72	SUBSEQUENT HALF YEARS	TOTAL
Line in course of construction	**30,000**	**67,000**	**97,000**
Works yet to commence /in abeyance		**31,000**	**31,000**
Other items	**5,000**		**5,000**
TOTAL	**35,000**	**98,000**	**133,000**

On a more positive note, the total train mileage for the six months of operation to 31st December 1871 was 16,080 miles, being the equivalent of 2,218 train journeys over the 7$^1/_4$ miles of the branch.

The siding for Messrs. Thomas & Co. at Milverton was finally completed in early 1872, so they had rail access to the four lime kilns that they had recently erected at the site. Colonel Yolland reported on it on 14th February 1872:

> '*... the siding commences by a pair of facing points, somewhat less than 30 chains from and to the west of this station. The up home signal is placed close to, but west of the facing points and these are secured in their proper position by a lock connected both with this up home signal and the down starting signal from Milverton station, and that starting signal cannot be taken off until these facing points are closed against the siding and open for the main line.*
>
> *A catch siding has been provided with the points weighted to stand open for the catch siding and there are stop blocks and padlocks in addition to prevent any vehicle from leaving the siding: but I have suggested that the points of the catch siding should be locked by the up distant signal so that they shall stand closed to the main line and locked for the catch siding, when this up distant signal is taken off for an up train to reach the station.*'

Colonel Yolland charged the resident engineer to report back when the arrangements had been completed.

However, 1872 did not get off to a good start. The weather around the turn of the year was poor, one of the contractor's locomotives had broken down and operations at Bathealton cutting had stopped, although it was anticipated that the tunnel would be pierced side to side within ten weeks. Between East Anstey and Barnstaple, most of the work was done, apart from ballasting and track laying, but station works continued to be suspended. As an additional unwelcome 'surprise', the solicitors advised that land tax was payable by the D&SR.

On 6th February, a contract was entered into between the D&SR and Reed to complete the stations (see Appendix 5). However, the additional funds would be required before this work could progress.

By the end of February 1872, Richard Hassard was reporting that earthworks were nearly complete on the Wiveliscombe to South Molton section, except at Bathealton, Morebath, Nightcot [*sic*] and East Anstey. The delay at the last three places being caused by obtaining possession of the land, with further retardation due to the '*unusually wet winter*'. On a positive note, the East Anstey to South Molton section of 8 miles had been ballasted and was ready for the permanent way. Work at Bathealton Tunnel was progressing and it was anticipated that, in the course of a month or so, the remaining headings would have been met and the tunnel pierced from side to side. Also, the masonry of the Tone Viaduct was almost complete, with the ironwork of the superstructure being erected in place. Likewise, the River Exe bridge was complete with the exception of the parapets, and four-fifths of the the entire masonry of the numerous road and occupation bridges had been finished. The 27th February meeting referred to the '*Viaducts which are of considerable magnitude are now all but finished and they bear favourable comparison with similar constructions in any part of the Kingdom*'. It was also noted that the directors had by this time introduced a Bill in Parliament for increasing the capital of the company, to enable the discharge of obligations necessary to complete the undertaking; this to acquire additional land, capital raising and for other purposes, including the completion of the station buildings.

Inclement weather retarded the progress on the middle section but, despite this, 35,000 cubic yards of material had been excavated. By March, at Bathealton Tunnel the headings of 462 yards had been met and 200 yards of it had been lined with masonry and was complete. Venn CrossTunnel headings had been driven for 110 out of 230 yards and lining of that tunnel had begun. On 3rd March, Mr Hassard tested the girders of Castle Hill Viaduct with a weight of 100 tons on each span; it was reported that there was a deflection of $^1/_2$ inch and the girders recovered position immediately the weight was removed. Whilst the weight applied was not quite as great as that of two broad gauge locomotives, the deflections showed the girders were stiff and strong. Some of the cross bracing had not been put together as it should have been by the manufacturers and this was to be rectified.

The next D&SR Bill to increase the financing was in Parliament. It was seeking to raise £100,000, with the aim of discharging their remaining obligations necessary to complete the undertaking. The Bill was expected to progress after Easter and there was no known opposition to it. With the third section almost complete, Mr Reed requested £4,700 plus £10,000 of 'B' stock, the latter to be set aside for claims.

The Barnstaple to South Molton section, with the exception of a small amount of ballasting and sundry matters, was now complete, along with the broad gauge permanent way laid along its entire length. Optimism was in the air and the Board indicated that completion of the line was anticipated by the end of 1872 '*at the latest*'.

At this stage, some 950 men, 95 horses, seven locomotives and three fixed engines were employed on the works and it was believed that, by July (1872), it would be possible for engines to traverse the line from end to end. At the B&ER board meeting of 7th February, Mr Hall reported on the ability of Lord Fortescue to stop trains at Castle Hill. The draft was to be settled by solicitors with the proviso that twenty minutes notice in writing should be given for every stoppage. Meanwhile, Inspector John Goddard was reported and called before the B&ER board for his neglect of duty in connection with the block telegraph at Wiveliscombe; he was dismissed.

By 22nd March 1872, the contractor's maintenance contract had expired but the D&SR company was bound to maintain the line until twelve months following on from the B&ER running the first train. As a consequence, Mr Hassard put two gangs of four men in place, each with a foreman at D&SR expense. At this time, Mr Fowler (the arbitrator) enquired into the number of trains and the amount of traffic anticipated on the line. On establishing this he expressed his surprise at '*such useless expenditure*'. In consequence, the Board was to write to the B&ER to reduce the number of trains in order to reduce the working expenses.

East of the Exe bridge, completion of certain earthworks were retarded; urgent rectification of the embankments at Exebridge and Sminhay (near Wiveliscombe) was needed. West of the Exe, meanwhile, earthworks were now well progressed. The masonry at all the tunnels was nearly completed and the Tone Viaduct had its girders pulled across and erected in place. On the third section, pipe drains were needed '*here and there*' and a small amount of work was still needed at Castle Hill Viaduct. At the Board meeting of 4th April, a letter was read from the engineer which discussed the possibly of a change of the gauge – this being the first reference to that matter it seems. By May, the earthworks were nearly completed at Bathealton, Morebath, Nightcot and East Anstey. It was reported that 850 men were then employed on the works and it was also stated that there were $2^1/_2$ acres of surplus land to dispose of.

THE GAUGE WAR AND THE GAUGE ACT OF 1846

A Royal Commission was set up in 1845 to consider whether there should be one uniform gauge in the UK, the first hearing taking place on 6th August. The broad gauge was attacked by those in support of the standard gauge but was defended vigorously by Brunel and indeed, the argument was planned to be settled in a pragmatic way; a trial between a broad gauge and a standard gauge locomotive. Following the trials, the Gauge Commissioners reported to Parliament in 1846 and although Brunel's *Ixion* beat the standard gauge challenger in the trials, the Commissioners in effect backed the narrower gauge alternative as the national system. The conclusion to the report stated '*That the gauge of 4ft $8^1/_2$ins be declared by the legislature to be the gauge to be used in all public railways now under construction or hereafter to be constructed in Great Britain*'. Brunel wrote a thorough criticism of the Gauge Commissioners report, which, after some political lobbying by him, led to a 'savings' clause being added to the Gauge Act, as it became law on 18th August 1846 (*Public General 9 & 10 Vict., cl 57*). So whilst the standard gauge was established as the sole legal gauge of Britain, there was an exception such that '*any railway constructed or to be constructed containing any special enactment defining the gauge or gauges of such railway*' could pursue its own choice of gauge. Thus the *status quo* seemed to have been maintained – significantly for the D&SR, as the line was built in a gauge effectively condemned to death in 1846. However, it was not the last line to be built to this gauge, the final one, the St. Ives Branch in Cornwall, being built in 1877. When put in context, the D&SR was authorised by the 1864 Act and, at this time and when it was built, it did connect with the broad gauge at Taunton and therefore took advantage of the 'savings' clause in the Act to use the broad gauge.

As a result of the realignment of curves, gradients, etc, on the first section and following his examination, Mr Fowler awarded the B&ER a sum of £1,108 in respect of additional costs sustained. The D&SR was to pay such sum within one month (with each party paying its own costs), as per his statement of 25th April 1872:

'I find and award that the said portion of the D&SR has not been constructed in accordance with the terms of Article 1 of the said agreement of 6 March 1865 and there has been default in that behalf in respect of the curves and gradients, earthworks, formations, drainage, road-approaches, metalling, fencing and permanent way including ballast and that the damage and costs the B&ER have sustained and will sustain in respect thereof is £1,108, which amount of compensation is awarded to the B&ER and to be paid within one month.'

On 30th May, the *North Devon Journal* reported as follows:

'Several hundred tons of Railway Sleepers have been landed at our quay during the past week having been brought up in lighters into which they were transferred at Appledore from larger vessels that had brought them from Norway. They are being carried on to the terminus of the Devon and Somerset Railway, and taken up in trucks to the higher part of the line, at which works are said to be actively progressing; although it is said to be feared that the long wanted for day of the opening of the line and the restoration of the now almost suspended intercourse between Barnstaple and Southmolton, is yet in the distance.'

DEVON & SOMERSET RAILWAY ACT OF 1872

In the six months to 30th June 1872, most of the existing cash had been spent, including a further allocation of loan funds, mainly on construction and land purchases totalling circa £43,000. With the further estimated expenditure on capital account at this stage being £91,000 (£55,000 being lines in the course of construction, £31,000 for works not yet commenced and £5,000 other) there was a clear need for additional borrowing powers. The Devon & Somerset Railway Company Act of 1872 sought to raise an additional £100,000 of 'A' debenture stock to rank *pari passu* with the existing 'A' 6% stock. This would add to the £436,000 of total debentures authorised (of which £425,680 had been issued by 30th June 1872). When the Bill was passed the finances looked like this (Capital stock authorised or created but not yet issued):

A Stock (1872)	£100,000	
B Stock (1864)	£10,320	
Total		£110,320
Investments	£2,956	
Cash	£1,789	
Loan on plant	£12,500	
Total		£17,245
Potential total funds available		£127,565

The issued stock at this time was £155,680 5% 'B' debenture stock (1864) and £270,000 6% 'A' debenture stock (1868), totalling £425,680. The 1867 'B' debenture stock (authorised £10,000 for the extension into Barnstaple) had, by this stage, become time-expired.

On the operational side, the total train miles for the six months to 30th June 1872 was 15,819, a reduction of 261 trains from the previous six months. There is a possibility, not confirmed, that the first six months also included trains for the period from 8th June 1871, the date of opening. However, it could also reflect the reduction

The completed Castle Hill (or Filleigh) Viaduct resplendent in the Bray Valley countryside. Note that there is no sign of the works seen a few pages earlier in the construction view; it should be just behind the fourth and fifth piers, on the right. *Courtesy South Molton Museum*

ABOVE: Tone Viaduct shortly after completion in 1872, with some of the contractor's men posing on top. The structure was also variously known as Venn Cross or Waterrow Viaduct, the former after the nearest station and the latter from the hamlet it straddled. ***Courtesy South Molton Museum***

BELOW: These photographs of construction work are held in South Molton Museum in the name of Harry Greenfield Duguid, who worked as a civil engineer on the D&SR contract. He may have taken the photograph of the completed Castle Hill Viaduct on the previous page but most are demonstrably the work of John Blizard of Taunton. Duguid was only in his early to mid 20s when these pictures were taken, so it is likely that he was employed as an assistant, probably to the contractor, and his name does not feature in the D&SR minutes. This portrait of Duguid was taken in 1882, when he was 35. Little is known of his later career, although he became an Associate Member of the Institute of Civil Engineers. ***Courtesy South Molton Museum***

of trains suggested by Mr Fowler to save the B&ER operating costs.

It was confirmed at the 4th June Board meeting that plant on site could not be released, as it was needed for ballasting and other works. A complaint was received by Mr Fox (the B&ER engineer) regarding the platforms at South Molton being faced with timber – even though he, or his inspectors, had seen the work in progress, with the proposed masonry walls not being constructed. Mr Reed commented that the cost of rails had gone from £8 per ton to £14 per ton and the price of labour '*is increasing daily*'. Reed applied for an advance of £20,000 in respect of the station works but the the Board cut this back to £10,000 on assent of the D&SR Act of 1872. He agreed to complete the station work for £42,500 (which was the engineers estimate in his letter of 11th July).

The new issue of 'A' debenture stock was offered to existing proprietors and was largely taken up. Any surplus was to be offered to the public and £6,000 of stock was placed with Lord Poltimore, Sir William Throckmorton and Mr Moysey, to indemnify them against their loan of £4,000. At this stage, a deputation from the Mayors of Barnstaple and South Molton strongly urged the completion of the works to the Board.

In the August 1872 engineer's report, only earthworks at Sminhay and the Exebridge embankments remained to be completed. At this stage, only 3,500-4,000 cubic yards of soil had been moved, when it required 17,000 in total to be shifted in the period; three more months was estimated as the anticipated time for the completion of the earthworks. However, labour problems continued, workmen having left the site for the hay harvest, which, coupled with the difficulties of finding lodgings, was not helping the progress of construction, particularly near Exebridge.

Bathealton and Venn Cross tunnels were expected to be completed by November 1872. The Tone Viaduct and the River Exe bridge were virtually complete and rails being laid over them, whilst the permanent way was still being laid between South Molton and East Anstey. On the Barnstaple to South Molton section, only the stations remained to be completed. In this respect, all the plans and quantities had been furnished to and agreed with the contractor, who was planning to sub-let the construction. Signals were also now fixed at various stations.

At the board meeting on 8th August, it was reported that the earthworks hold-ups in the Exebridge area were to such an extent that there was a danger they could delay the opening of the line further, much to the frustration of the Board. Accordingly, they gave notice to the contractor to provide sufficient additional men to complete the works, otherwise the impact of the delay would be at his cost. The Board were optimistic that traffic in iron ores from the Exmoor district were expected to be large and that coal carried in would be considerable but this depended on the facilities for shipment. With good progress at Barnstaple and Wiveliscombe, plant was able to be released at those locations. Maintenance work was now being carried out by local tradesmen as it was a cheaper option. The B&ER directors resolved at their 11th September meeting that they would visit the railway on Friday 20th September (which Messrs Wall and Fox were to arrange).

By October 1872, Sminhay embankment (near Bathealton Tunnel) was progressing but 12,800 cubic yards of soil was still needed to be laid down, this being estimated at ten weeks work. The Exebridge embankment was about three weeks away from completion but Ashtown Cutting was suffering from slips. The earthworks between the Exe bridge and South Molton were expected to be finished in the next month. All station works were well progressed with the exception of Venn Cross but there was an extra cost to sanction at the temporary Barnstaple station. The contractors bill for extras had come to £20,086 and the engineer said this could not be sustained; £11,000 of this was for sleepers and rails supplied by the original contractor (Pickerings), which were damaged or of inferior quality and needed replacing.

The Board proposed to offer Mr Reed £20,000 and £5,000 in 'B' debenture stock to settle his claims and this was subsequently accepted. An 'A' debenture prospectus was to be prepared to get rid of the balance of the 1872 'A' stock recently authorised to the public.

The 6th November board meeting had no good news. The progress of work on the second section was low, with the exception of tunnelling. There had been two land slips at Venn Cross, because the slopes were excavated at too steep an angle, which the engineer had consistently pointed out to the contractor. Land at Venn Cross station still had to be acquired, so no work could be done there. However, work had been completed in the western part, with the exception of Nightcot and Anstey cuttings, where the bottoms had to be taken out. Certain masonry work at Morebath, Dulverton, Molland and South Molton stations was found to be unsatisfactory and the contractor was therefore required to make good.

By December, Venn Cross Tunnel had only about 160 feet remaining to be constructed and lined. At the western end of the line, cuttings were well advanced and permanent way materials were brought in from Barnstaple to the Exe bridge by rail. Also, an engine road had been laid into a ballast pit at Brushford, from which ballast was to be procured. It is believed that this is the quarry cut into Hulverton Hill, near the station, which is still visible today. By now, the poor quality station masonry, reported earlier, had been taken down and replaced. Over 1,000 men were now working on the line to push to completion.

The *West Somerset Free Press* reported on 21st December 1872:

> *'The benefits of a railway in this district have just been experienced. On Thursday 5th* [December 1872]*, a train arrived at Brushford Station on the Devon and Somerset Railway from Barnstaple with a consignment of coal to JA Locke Esq of Northmoor House. On Friday morning, carts and wagons might be seen on the road to Dulverton laden with this valuable article upon which the comfort of all classes so much depends during the cold weather.'* [given that the broad gauge permanent way was not laid in until early 1873 – see below – it is presumed a temporary connection was made for the purpose of this goods train].

By 31st December 1872, the debenture stock issued in the six months amounted to £84,940, taking the total to £510,620); £60,083 of this was applied to line construction (£54,237 for the contractor, £2,040 to land purchases and £1,255 to engineering).

Future expenditure estimates had been revised, with £27,000 anticipated to be spent on line construction in the six months to 30th June 1873, plus £6,000 after that. In addition, £5,000 was reserved for '*other items*', making a total future anticipated spend of £38,000. The total funds available at this time (being debenture stock, cash, investments and loan on plant) were £67,551.

Train miles for the six months to 31st December 1872 were reported as 13,818½ for passengers and 2,276½ for goods and minerals, totalling 16,095 miles, the equivalent of 2,220 train journeys. This shows an increase of 276 train miles over the previous six months but at a similar level to the same period in the previous year. The revenue account at this time is shown in the following table:

Half Year Receipts	**£ s d**
From B&ER	
– Passenger	**814 10 0**
– Parcels, horses, carriages and mails	**44 6 0**
– Merchandise	**897 10 6**
Total	**1,696 6 0**
Expenses	
Working expenses	**(1,790 15 5)**
Deficit brought forward	**(323 9 2)**
Deficit carried forward	**(417 18 1)**

At the 3rd January 1873 board meeting, there was a complaint from South Molton Council over the safety of Hill Town bridge at Molland station (renamed Bishops Nympton & Molland in 1876). This was basically making a political point, as the council had wanted the station on the eastern side of the parish and were not happy with its location.

With £80,000 of the 1872 debenture stock taken up, another £20,000 worth was to be authorised for issue at a special meeting. However, works continued to be retarded due to the incessant rain; there were landslips at the west end of Venn Cross Tunnel and minor ones, still, in Ashdown Cutting.

The board meeting of 4th February 1873 gave a substantive account of progress, noting that the excavations at Bathealton and Venn Cross cuttings should be completed by the end of February and then ballasting could take place. The tunnels were to be completed simultaneously with the earthworks. Between Venn Cross and Morebath, all earthworks were virtually complete. At Ashtown Cutting, 96,000 out of the 108,000 cubic yards of soil had been excavated, with two months more work anticipated to remove the remaining 12,000 cubic yards. A ballast pit was to be opened at the eastern end of the Tone Viaduct to help ballasting that part of the line. Nightcot and Anstey cuttings only had 3,500 cubic yards remaining to be excavated, with the rocks extracted to be used for ballast. It was anticipated that these cuttings would be completed by the end of the month. The broad gauge permanent way was at this time being laid between Nightcot and Yeo Mill.

As for the stations, at Venn Cross the goods shed masonry work had started and was 3 feet above rail level. At Shillingford [Morebath], the earthworks and masonry were almost complete, the station buildings and goods shed were roofed in and work was being done

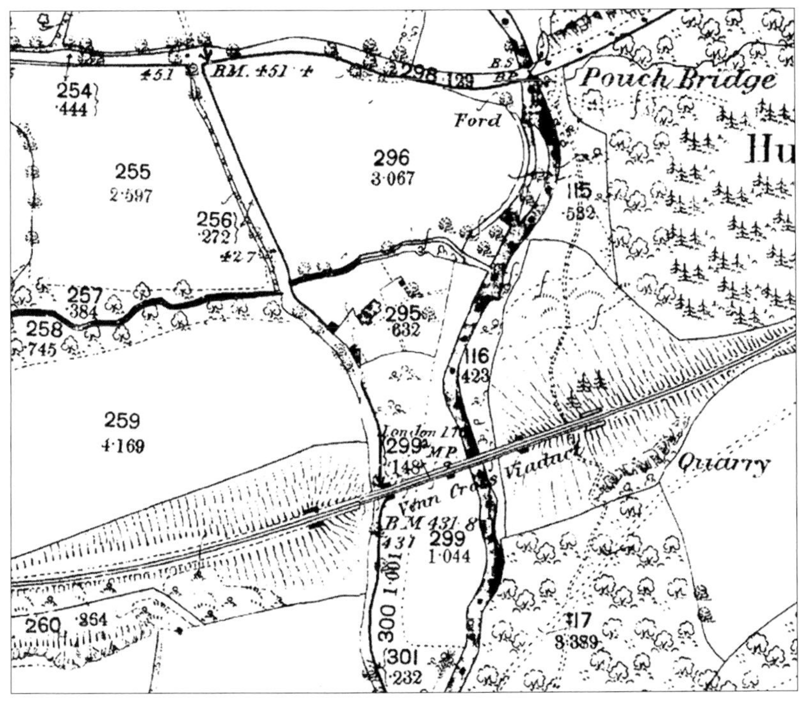

Extract from the 1889 25ins OS, showing Tone or Venn Cross Viaduct and the abandoned Pouch Bridge ballast quarry, opened by the contractor in early 1873, at its eastern end.

on the inside. At Dulverton, the earthworks were almost complete and road metalling and ballast had been provided. The masonry of the passenger platforms was complete and foundations for the goods shed had been put in. The passenger shed and dwelling house had been roofed in and inside work proceeded with. At East Anstey, the earthworks had been done, the masonry of the platforms built and the goods shed foundations were in. At Molland, the earthworks were compete, the approach road and yard partially metalled and the track ballasted. The masonry of the passenger platforms, station and dwelling house was nearly complete and the roof was going on. The goods shed masonry had also been commenced. At South Molton, the earthworks were nearly complete and the approach road was formed and metalled. Passenger and goods platforms were erected and the goods shed was nearly ready to receive a roof. The passenger station and dwelling house was roofed and internal work was continuing. At Castle Hill, the earthworks were nearly complete, and the approach road was formed and partially metalled. The waiting room and booking office were roofed in and the masonry of the dwelling house and goods shed were about half complete. At Swimbridge, the earthworks were nearly complete, with the approach road formed and metalled. The booking office and waiting room were roofed and the masonry of the goods shed nearly finished. Finally, at Barnstaple, the earthworks were nearly complete and the timber work of the passenger and goods platforms was erected in place. Half of the framing of the goods shed was up and timber for the remainder was sawn and on the ground. Framing for the station building was erected and it had been roofed.

There continued to be landslips, this time in cuttings between Norton Fitzwarren and Wiveliscombe; one was serious enough to threaten to stop traffic. However, the problem was alleviated after extra men were deployed to clear it. The substandard rails and fish plates provided by Pickerings were also still giving problems; they were giving way under traffic and this was an almost daily occurrence.

The engineer's report dated 10th February 1873 referred to the first section of line (Norton to Wiveliscombe) being satisfactorily maintained but due to some heavy landslips, consequent on wet weather, the maintenance costs had increased considerably. Hassard acquiesced with respect to his statement on the completion of the line by the end of 1872: '*I regret that my expectation in this respect has not been realised, as the unprecedented and almost incessant Rainfall of the past Autumn and Winter has much retarded the completion of the Line*'. There was another heavy landslip at the western end of Venn Cross Tunnel and a minor one in Ashtown Cutting. He did state that all other railways under construction had also been affected by the weather – small consolation given the continued delays in progressing this undertaking. As the opening of the railway in the early part of the year was now entirely beyond the control of those involved, he anticipated completion in about five months (that is by June/July 1873). By this stage, the earthworks at Sminhay and Ashdown Cutting were close to completion. West of the Exe bridge, about 5,000 cubic yards of excavation was still to be done but all the tunnels were complete, the face lengths being built or in construction. The viaducts were finished along with all the bridges, except '*three unimportant ones*'. The buildings and works at the various stations between Wiveliscombe and Barnstaple were by this time well advanced and some nearly complete. All that remained to be done, excluding station works, between the River Exe and Barnstaple was some ballasting and the laying of about 4 miles of broad gauge permanent way. Signals had been delivered and were ready for installation.

SALE OF CONTRACTOR'S PLANT

From the *North Devon Journal* of 27th February 1873:

'Important and Unreserved sale of MACHINERY and PLANT employed in the construction of the Devon & Somerset Railway now approaching completion. Messrs JS Gower & Co of London are favoured with instructions from Mr JL Reed, the contractor of the line to sell by auction at the Cattle Market, Victoria Road, Barnstaple on Wednesday, March 12 1873 and the following day at eleven for twelve o'clock each day, the first portion, comprising three valuable LOCOMOTIVES nearly new, by Shanks and others, two steam jib cranes by Fox, Walker and Co, set of self acting Incline Machinery, Quarry Cranes, set of winding Gear, 110 feet Pile Driving engines and Monkeys, Double & Single Purchase Crabs, 89 Earth Waggons, few tons of contractors rails, 10,000 Temporary Sleepers, large quantity of timber in bulk, Tunnel & Bridge Centres, Wood and Iron Skips, Wheelbarrows, Wheeling Planks ... etc'.

Progress was maintained at a good rate, as was reported in the 28th February 1873 board meeting. Sminhay embankment was now complete, communication with Wiveliscombe was made and ballasting commenced, whilst rails were soon to be laid in Ashtown Cutting. West of the Exe bridge, earthworks were complete and most of the rock had been removed from Nightcot and East Anstey cuttings. There was now only $1^1/_2$ miles of broad gauge track incomplete between Barnstaple and the River Exe. A scare about a bulge in Bathealton Tunnel had proved unfounded. Venn Cross passenger platform and house had not yet been started but the goods shed walls were up to 9 feet in height. Shillingford [Morebath] station was expected to be completed in the next month. At Dulverton, the internal works were nearly done and the goods shed was up to 9 feet in height. However, East Anstey had not progressed due to its isolated position and the difficulty in getting materials out to the site until the line was built. At Molland, the station building had been roofed and it was expected that South Molton would have its building work completed within one month. At Castle Hill, the buildings were nearly roofed and the goods shed half complete, Swimbridge buildings were nearly completed, and at Barnstaple the

It is believed that this is the contractor's quarry established at the western end of the Tone Viaduct in early 1873, track having been laid over the completed viaduct the previous November. Some of the quarrymen have stopped to pose for the cameraman, whilst others continue their back-breaking labour. One of the contractor's standard gauge locomotives, a Fox, Walker 0-6-0ST (one of three FW 0-6-0s that Reed used on this contract), stands at the head of a rake of spoil wagons being filled but note, too, the broad gauge wagons on the right; the wider gauge line on which they are standing crosses over the standard gauge just behind the engine and a second locomotive can be made out in the left background. The 3-plank open in the right foreground is a rare beast indeed, pictures of broad gauge private owner wagons being almost unknown. It is lettered for W. & J.E. Barnard of Reading, who were coal and coke merchants in that area. It is likely that they had disposed of their broad gauge stock by the time of this picture, however, as standard gauge wagons would have been far more versatile, the broad gauge lines in the home counties having largely been converted to mixed gauge by this date. Reed the contractor may well have bought it – and the other broad gauge wagons which appear in these views – especially for use in the construction of the D&SR line. Note the extremely rudimentary nature of the points in the foreground. Evidence of these excavations can still be found today, albeit now heavily overgrown. ***Courtesy South Molton Museum***

goods and passenger platforms and cattle pens were almost finished. The framing of the passenger station and waiting room was erected, with the roof on and felted. The goods shed frame was built and the roof was going on. In all, 900 workmen were on site. The contractor wished to purchase a broad gauge engine for completion of the ballasting at the east end of the line, which was to be funded from the proceeds of the plant which was about to be sold (now being surplus to requirements). Such locomotive would cost £750-£800 but be only of scrap value afterwards. However, approval was given and the locomotive purchased from Swindon. Cole, Chappel & Co. wanted land for coal sidings at South Molton, Sir Thomas Acland having land available with the Corporation of South Molton for this purpose. Approval was given to purchase rails for £200 for the Norton Fitzwarren to Wiveliscombe section to effect repairs. The half yearly meeting (also held on 28th February) disclosed that, with the exceptional character of the weather since last August and during the winter, the directors could not announce the entire completion of the works, which had previously been anticipated for January; it had been necessary to postpone the opening of the line for some few months longer. It was noted that the extra £20,000 of unissued 'A' debenture stock would be needed to secure completion of the line and subsequently the issue was approved at a special general meeting.

By the 2nd April 1873 board meeting, ballasting had been carried out between Venn Cross Tunnel and Wiveliscombe, and the permanent way was scheduled to be laid to the latter on Monday 7th April. The Shillingford to Exebridge section was then to be ballasted using material from the pit at Brushford, near Dulverton station. It was now anticipated that the line west of the Exe bridge would be completed by 10th May. On-going maintenance meant that the rails between Norton Fitzwarren and Wiveliscombe had been removed, cut to shorter lengths and replaced; about 20% of the rails previously laid were affected and had had to be replaced.

At the 1st May directors' meeting, Hassard's report stressed that he was not satisfied with the works. Work was not complete at the Wiveliscombe end of the line and delays ensued, mostly due to the workforce disregarding instructions. These stated that from the moment an engine could pass through Venn Cross Tunnel, no more ballast should be taken from Pouch Bridge (near the Tone Viaduct) to Wiveliscombe. Also, standard gauge engines should be used to haul rails, sleepers and bottom ballast from Wiveliscombe for the line west of Venn Cross, to complete work to Shillingford. The ballasting work between Shillingford and Wiveliscombe was to be carried out using two standard gauge locomotives. However, once broad gauge laying commenced west of Wiveliscombe, the remaining ballasting should then have been done by broad gauge locomotives. Despite this, the standard gauge engines were found to be hard at work between Pouch Bridge and Wiveliscombe, using ballast from the Pouch Bridge quarry. The yard at Wiveliscombe was full of rails and sleepers and no broad gauge had been laid west of that station. The broad gauge engine – presumably the one referred to earlier purchased from Swindon – was lying idle in the shed there.

By 24th May, the broad gauge had been laid between Barnstaple and the Exe bridge. Eastwards from there, a fair amount of work had been done as far as Wiveliscombe, $3^1/_2$ miles of broad gauge track having been laid and the line bottom-ballasted for the whole distance to Exebridge. About 750 men were employed on the works at this stage.

A deal was done with the Barnstaple Water Company to provide the anticipated 12,000 gallons of water per day to Barnstaple station at £50 pa (indeed, not surprisingly, the B&ER were insistent on this as their board minutes of 28th May showed). The deal at South Molton was £15 pa with the water company (there being a lower requirement for replenishing locomotives) but there was a delay by the contractor in ordering the fittings for water supply distribution at Dulverton and South Molton. Land purchases continued in the six months to 30th June 1873, £3,812 being expended, whilst extra horse hire at Wiveliscombe, on account of the turntable, amounted to £3 18s 0d!

In June, Reed laid on a special train from Dulverton to Barnstaple on a market day (Friday). It was primarily for landowners, farmers and tenants through whose lands the railway passed. The contractor's engine *Venus* hauled a motley collection of carriages but they were well decorated to celebrate this 'unofficial' occasion. The train stopped at all stations and picked up 200 passengers for the ride. Arriving at Barnstaple at 11.20am, they departed for the return journey at 7.30pm. Messrs Stannard (agent for the contractor, Reed) and Drysdale, and the Rev'ds Owen (East Anstey) and Bassett (Dulverton) were fortunate enough to ride on the footplate.

The securities issued (ignoring shares) at 30th June 1873 can be summarised as follows:

AT 30/6/1873	ISSUED	UNISSUED	AUTHORISED
1864 B Debenture Stock	164,298	1,702	166,000
1867 B Debenture Stock		10,000	10,000
1868 A Debenture Stock	270,000		270,000
1872 A Debenture Stock	99,867	133	100,000
Total	534,165	11,835	546,000

The powers to issue the £10,000 worth of 1867 'B' debenture stock had expired by effluxion of time.

Debenture interest due on 1st July could not be paid as the line had not opened and there were no traffic receipts. It was now anticipated the line would be completed by 16th August 1873.

At the 3rd July meeting, concern over a shortage of workmen was expressed. However, most of the line between Wiveliscombe and Exebridge had been ballasted and broad gauge track laid to a distance of $4^3/_4$ miles. Also, the B&ER had requested engine shed accommodation at Barnstaple and it was agreed to provide it at a cost of £1,200.

At the 1st August 1873 meeting, some good news was reported; the broad gauge was now unbroken between Taunton and Barnstaple. However, completion of ballasting was retarded by both locomotives having broken down and a shortage of workmen. Work was nearly finished at all stations and the D&SR Board was optimistic of giving notice of such to the BoT in the next three weeks. One concern was that nothing had been done on the provision of the engine shed at Barnstaple, which might cause a serious delay in opening the line. To overcome this, it was resolved that a wooden structure should be erected for the shed and this was to include accommodation for enginemen.

On 6th August 1873, an issue arose with certain locking apparatus connected with signals on the line at

LOCOMOTIVES FOR SALE

***The Engineer* advertised a sale to take place on 10th January 1873 at Wiveliscombe station: '*... a broad gauge locomotive, 16ins cylinders, 6-wheels coupled, about 27 tons empty, along with a small locomotive by Shanks, being 4-wheels coupled and 6ins cylinders.*' In an advertisement for a subsequent sale at Barnstaple on 12th-13th March, the Shanks locomotive appeared again, presumably unsold from the first sale. There was a further advertisement on 15th August 1873, which stated that J.S. Gower & Co. were to auction on 10th September (later postponed to 24th) three standard gauge 0-6-0 tank locomotives and a 12hp chain locomotive owned and used by Reed the contractor.**

Milverton, Wiveliscombe, Dulverton, South Molton and Barnstaple. A Mr Follett Charles Hennet, an engineer from Bridgwater who had supplied the equipment, had potentially infringed a Saxby's patent. It was agreed that Hennet was to replace the equipment or indemnify the D&SR from any damages and expenses that might arise. This related to forty-two levers, so it was agreed that £84 (£2 per lever) was to be deposited at the Bank of England in a joint account with Richard Muggeridge (D&SR Secretary) for two years. If there was no claim, the funds would be repaid and if they were insufficient Hennet agreed to indemnify the D&SR further (or remove the apparatus).

The *Illustrated London News* reported on Saturday 9th August 1873 that:

> *'The formal opening of the D&SR from Wiveliscombe to Dulverton took place on Tuesday* [5th August] *at the latter place. A large stock market was opened, for which the land had been given by the Earl of Carnarvon. A great number of nobility and gentry of the County sat down to dinner at which his Lordship presided. The line extends from Taunton to Barnstaple, a distance of 43 miles.'*

Reed ran special trains from Barnstaple to Taunton and Taunton to Dulverton. As the line had not been cleared by the BoT, the tickets were distributed free of charge by Mr Stannard. The Dulverton correspondent of the *Western Times* reported the event positively: '*The central portion of the Devon & Somerset line will produce quite a revolution in the social and business life of this district*'. The article went on to praise the Earl of Carnarvon's support for the venture. Dulverton goods shed was transformed for the lunch by the Pixton gardener and some lady helpers, a floor being laid and garlands made. Banners were displayed reading 'Success to the Market' and 'Long Live the Earl of Carnarvon'. Lunch was provided by Mr King of the Lion Hotel in Dulverton and his Lordship arrived shortly after 2.00pm and took his place at the head of the table as the '*ringing cheers of the visitors rent the air.*' About 200 guests sat down for lunch, which was followed by Royal toasts and speeches as was the usual Victorian means of celebration. The joyous occasion went on until nearly 9.00pm in the evening, at which point the trains departed taking guests back to Taunton and Barnstaple.

The B&ER Finance & Traffic Committee (F&TC) listened to a proposal on 12th August 1873 from Mr Wall (presumably the B&ER Traffic Manager) to have five trains per day (two fast and three stopping) on weekdays when the line opened throughout, with no trains on Sundays. On 22nd September, Wall's proposed fares were accepted by the F&TC.

Trains of passenger carriages were run over the line on 13th and 14th August between Taunton and Barnstaple and *vice versa* by the B&ER. Based on the minutes of the board meeting of 29th August 1873, these special trains ran from Bristol to Barnstaple with the purpose of a more careful examination of the works by the B&ER directors: '*the smoothness of the Permanent Way was the subject of general remark*'. The *North Devon Journal* reported on 14th August that this trial train ran '*yesterday* [13th] *and comprised of engine, van, saloon carriage and six composite carriages, the passengers and railway officials. The train arrived at Barnstaple from Taunton at 1-25, the stations being inspected on route. On their return the train pulled up on Castle Hill which is in the midst of some splendid scenery, and here luncheon was served in the saloon carriage. It is expected the line will be opened for traffic in about three months.*' A Mr E.J. Braund of Barnstaple was named as the driver.

On 19th August 1873, Richard Hassard wrote and confirmed that the works of the line were complete and top ballasting of some short portions was in progress. It was noted that the difficulty of getting suitable ballast had materially retarded its earlier completion, only broken stone being available on the whole length of line. The stations and related works were finished with the exception of '*some trifling matters of detail*' and the signals erected.

At the 29th August ordinary general meeting (the 19th half yearly meeting), the directors stated '*... that we ... have the satisfaction of reporting that the construction of the line in its entirety has been at length completed.*' However, an inspection by the BoT was necessary before the line could be opened to the public. The next meeting was to be at Barnstaple, so that the proprietors could travel the line and examine the works for themselves.

In the next two months, minor improvements were carried out, including the installation of an occupation crossing at Mornacott, near South Molton. Mr Hawkins wanted a siding at South Molton and it was suggested that rails not suitable for the main line could be used. The Mayor of South Molton was concerned about the D&SR's use of water and wanted a clause in the agreement to lessen the supply when it was appropriate to do so. The Mayor also proposed a public luncheon invitation to be held on opening of the line at South Molton. Roadways still needed to be finished, along with bridges, stations and the engine shed at Barnstaple before a certificate of completion could be given. By now, Pickerings' inadequate rails had been replaced. The issue of the extension of the line in Barnstaple was resurrected and was discussed at the board meeting of 7th October, with a proposal to make an application to Parliament for a renewal of the previous Act (the D&SR (Extension) Act of 1867).

The directors proposed that the next board meeting was to be held '*at such time and place as may be found most convenient, having reference to the opening of the line for public traffic*'. The B&ER looked at two proposed timetabling schemes; one with four Up and Down trains, the other with six trains in each direction. The latter option was chosen.

The opening of the line was getting ever closer but, even on 3rd October, Mr Hassard had to write to Lieut Col Charles Scrope Hutchinson RE stating: '*Owing to unforeseen circumstances the above line cannot be completed for your inspection by Saturday next* [4th] *and I shall be obliged if you can defer* [your inspection] *until Friday and Saturday* [10th-11th] *of next week*'.

The *North Devon Journal* reported on 9th October that the line was to be inspected by Government inspectors and were optimistic of announcing an opening date; '*we may hope that next week we will have the pleasure of naming the day appointed for the official opening*'. They further reported:

> *'A train went over the line on Tuesday* [7th] *and several gentlemen travelled by it, through the courtesy of Mr Stannard, the local agent for the contractor. It started from the town* [Barnstaple] *soon after 9am and traversed the whole of the un-opened part of the line to Wiveliscombe, returning at 4pm. Among the passengers was our Borough Member, CH Williams Esq, who is at present staying at Pixton on a visit to the Earl of Caernarvon* [sic]. *At Castle Hill's station the train took up Earl Fortescue and some members of his lordship's family; and at Northmolton* [sic] *Station Lord Poltimore, the Chaiman of the Directors of the Railway joined the train. It was the day of the Pixton and Dulverton monthly market, to which several gentlemen were accommodated from Southmolton* [sic]. *The ride was made most agreeable. All were in high praise the smooth and easy working of the line and all eager for the accommodation of its dedicated to the use of the public.'*

Lieut Col Hutchinson reported on 13th October 1873, in respect of his visit on Friday 10th and Saturday 11th October, on the new portion of line between Wiveliscombe and Barnstaple:

> *'this line ... is 35 miles 4 chains in length and is single throughout except at stations where there is an interval of 6 feet between the lines of the*

rails. The land has in some cases been purchased for a double line, and the over bridges have in all cases been built for same, but the other works have been constructed only for a single line.

The gauge is 7ft, the rails are flat bottomed and the permanent way is of the same character as that of previous parts of the line.

The stations are Venn Cross, Morebath, Dulverton, East Anstey, Molland, South Molton, Castle Hill, Swimbridge and Barnstaple, of these Dulverton and South Molton are arranged as passing places at all the stations the points and signals are interlocked. The steepest gradient on the line has an inclination of 1 in 58 and the sharpest curve a radius of 20 chains. There have been considerable deviations made from the sections as authorised by Act of Parliament but in no case has the steepness of the ruling gradient been increased beyond the authorised amount, nor have the landowners objected (as I am informed) to the alterations which have been made, and which have tended to cheapen the construction though they will increase the cost of the working of the line.

There are 22 bridges over the line, 43 under it and 5 viaducts. The overbridges are with 3 exceptions constructed entirely of brick work and masonry: 2 have masonry abutments carrying wrought iron girders with brick arches between them and a third is entirely of timber. Thirty three of the under bridges are built entirely of masonry and brick work the longest span being 21 ft – nine have masonry abutments carrying cast iron girders the longest span being 24 1/2 ft the remaining one of 4ft span has a timber top.

The Tone viaduct consists of 4 openings of 100ft each spanned by wrought iron continuous lattice girders resting on masonry piers and abutments; the Castle Hill viaduct is of similar construction to the Tone Viaduct except that the girders are not continuous, the openings are 6 in number and 100 feet each. The Exe bridge is one span of 70 ft similar in construction to the preceding viaducts, the remaining 2 viaducts consist of 2 openings each (the longest 28ft) where brick arches resting on masonry piers have been used.

The whole of these bridges and viaducts appear to have been substantially constructed and to be standing well. Those I was able to test with a rolling load of engines gave moderate deflections and the shams of the girders worked satisfactorily.

There are 5 tunnels on the line 450, 247, 38, 22 and 215 yards long respectively. With one exception [Castle Hill] *these are lined throughout with masonry. They are fairly dry appear to be generally standing well, and are large enough in section to allow a carriage to pass through with the doors open. There is a slight alteration in the form on the arch of the tunnel at 21.20* [Castle Hill] *which should be carefully watched.*

There are no public road level crossings. The fencing is almost entirely of post and rails. I pointed out to the engineer several cases in which some additions were wanted to make it secure.

The turntable has been moved from Wiveliscombe to Barnstaple, and there is one at Taunton where the traffic will be worked through to Barnstaple.

The following requirements came under my notice during the course of inspection

1 All the stations where it has not been already done the up and down signals should be made to interlock.

2 At the passing places by Wiveliscombe, Dulverton and South Molton a 2nd name board and shelter on the platform where it does not now exist should be provided. The starting signals should not interlock.

3 At Wiveliscombe station the down top points and the down starting signal should be interlocked with the up signals – at Morebath station the up distant signal should be lowered. At Dulverton station a chock block on the carriage dock should be interlocked with the up signals. At Molland station the two ends of the crossing should be connected with the same lever. At Swimbridge station the position of a crossover road should be reversed and the up signals should be interlocked with the blind siding points.

4 The string course in some of the over bridges projects too far and should be reduced so as to prevent it catching the carriage doors if open.

5 A hand rail is required on the top of the parapet wall of an under bridge close to Morebath and Molland stations and at the latter station the signal lever frame should be fenced round.

6 Transoms and straps to preserve the gauge are required in the bridges at 8 miles 4 chains and 15 m and 67 ch. Light ballast is wanting on several of the platforms of the bridges to guard against fire.

7 The ballasting at different places is not quite complete. The company is anxious to open the line on 1st November and as there will be ample time to have the above mentioned requirements (with the exception of the shelter sheds, which should be finished by 1 December) completed beforehand I am recommending the Board of Trade to sanction the opening of the Devon and Somerset Line between Wiveliscombe and Barnstaple upon receipt of a statement from the Engineer to the effect that these matters have been completed and also a satisfactorily undertaking as to the mode of working the line which I understand to be on the Ticket System supplemented by the Block System. This undertaking should be concurred in by the Bristol & Exeter Company who are to work the line.'

Lieut Col Hutchinson also said it was desirable that switch bars should be fixed in front of the the facing points at stations (other than the passing places) where trains would pass thorough at speed, as soon as they could be supplied. This was all reported back at the B&ER board meeting on 15th October. They proposed to send an official notification to the secretary of the D&SR, that the commencement of their working of the line was '*not to be taken as an admission on the part of the B&ER of its entire satisfactory completion in accordance with the agreement* [for the working of the line]'.

Hutchinson wished to re-inspect the line as soon as these requirements had been reported as completed but not necessarily before the opening. This he duly did and reported back on 8th December 1873, finding that most of his requirements set out above had been complied with. He commented that the shelter sheds at the three passing stations were nearly completed, improvements to certain fencing was still required and that it '*... was desirable that the engine shed signal interlocked with conflicting signals ... at Barnstaple station.*' Facing point switches were not in place but had been ordered.

On 24th October, a special train conveyed working staff to the stations and the next day a train comprising a saloon and five coaches was run over the line for the benefit of officials and reporters. This left Taunton at 11.00am and reached Barnstaple at 1.46pm.

THE RAILWAY OPENS TO BARNSTAPLE, 1ST NOVEMBER 1873

When the line opened beyond Wiveliscombe in 1873, there was much celebration, not least at Dulverton. The town was decked with flags, bunting and ceremonial arches, proclaiming 'Success to the Devon and Somerset Railway and 'May Dulverton Flourish', these being located on the River Barle bridge and raised by Messrs R. Hammond and J. Hildon. Lunch was provided to about 250 male parishioners at the Town Hall at noon, by Mr King of the Lion Hotel. At 4.30pm, 550 women and children had tea provided by Mr Bradley in the school room. A band played and the church bells '*sent forth merry peals*' during the day. In the afternoon, races commenced at Union House and in the evening a large bonfire was lit before fireworks concluded the celebrations. As the *West Somerset Free Press* related on 8th November 1873:

'Some of the flags were very large, having to be suspended on poles thirty

feet high to prevent their touching the heads of passers-by. Turning into Church Street, a painting of a huge viaduct with a train passing over it met the gaze, the passengers were waving their hats and the train marked 'Express' seemed to be going very fast.'

The *Illustrated London News* recorded the opening in its Saturday 8th November edition:

'The D&SR which connects the GWR system with West Somerset and North Devon was open to traffic last Saturday. The line is 43 miles long and is on the broad gauge. It has been 10 years in construction and has cost £21,000 per mile. A dinner in celebration of the opening was held in the evening – Captain Williams MP was in the Chair.'

The *Western Times*, however, was less enthusiastic about the opening:

'This long-awaited-for base of the railway triangle, the apex of which is Exeter and the two sides formed by the Bristol & Exeter and North Devon lines opened for traffic and travel on Saturday. It is not to be wondered at that the official parties made no noise about it considering the number of years it has been under hand, and how often public hope has been deferred … The inhabitants of this district – so purely rural – must bless themselves to think that so much has been risked and done to give them the benefit of a railway … No doubt it is a fine piece of agricultural country to the right and left of the line, which it will most beneficially drain as well as advantageously serve in other ways. Of the towns that lie in the vicinity it stays pretty clear, as Dulverton and Southmolton [sic]*, but it does not give them so wide a berth as to make access materially inconvenient.'*

At Barnstaple, the first train left without ceremony. The 7.40am departure was supported by the stationmaster and other officials, including those of the B&ER. The train comprised four '*established*' B&ER carriages and one new composite carriage. South Molton welcomed the train at 8.18am with a large crowd and the band of the 6th Devon Mounted Rifle Volunteer Corps playing the National Anthem. The first Down train arrived at Barnstaple at 10.30am.

The *North Devon Journal* also made the following comments at the time of opening:

'There can be no doubt that foremost among those gentlemen [who had played a part in the D&SR but were no longer connected] *is Mr John McMillan. A native of Southmolton, [sic], but now resident in London, whose zeal in the work the whole district was witness to for many years; and only second in value to Mr McMillan's labours were those of his professional friend, Mr Birch, the engineer. It would be ungenerous in the hour of final success, not to recognise the merits of those gentlemen in particular; and there are others, not so prominent as they, who might fitly be associated with them in thankful remembrance.'*

It is interesting to speculate whether the journalist was a friend of the two gentlemen as they had clearly left the D&SR under a cloud; despite that, there is no doubt they had played their part when associated with the railway.

South Molton also held their festivities but that was a few days later, on Thursday 6th November. The *North Devon Journal* again reported the occasion. A parade of 200 people went to meet the special train conveying directors of the B&ER, which was due to arrive at 12.30pm; there was a classic North Devon welcome – it was raining heavily! In addition, the 6th Devonshire Rifles were '*proudly piping their paeans of victory over all the difficulties which had been vanquished*'. The entourage included Blue Coat boys (with their white wands), the Royal Fortescue Lodge of the Manchester Unity of Odd Fellows, the Good Templars (carrying a scroll saying 'Total Abstinence Society'), civic officers '*in their gold laced dresses and grotesque looking hats*' and the Mayor, Mr John White, resplendent in gold chain and scarlet and blue robe. He greeted the guests at the station before the procession returned to the town, passing under a triumphal arch that led the way to East Street; banners were everywhere; the *North Devon Journal* described the scene:

'Entering the street, the visitor looked downward to receive from the mansion of Mr Alderman Smythe a 'Welcome to Southmolton', emblazoned in illuminated characters. Lining the way on both sides of the street leading up to the centre of town, which was also the centre of attraction, was a plantation of fir trees, charming in their greenness, which had been presented to the committee for the purpose by Lord Poltimore. The newly built villa of RM Riccard Esq., one of the solicitors of the line, standing at the corner of East Street, was clothed in scarlet and gold, and surmounted with a number of bannerets in the colours of all nations. The house of Mr JA Kingdom, just opposite, identified the occasion with 'Progress' a declaration of the past and a dictate to the future. Superintendent Wood, like a loyal servant, enshrined the initials of her Majesty in laurel leaves. A flag, declaring that 'Success attends perseverance', so summarising the history of the line, adorned the avenue leading to the Post-office. The houses of Mr Furse, Mr Sanders, Dr Fatherly and Capt. Dames were all enlivened with handsome flags. An immense Union Jack stretched across the opening to the road to Witheridge. The head quarters of the Odd Fellows, at 'Red Cow' were resplendent with a galaxy of trophies and ensigns. The Post-office told its loyalty and its public character by displaying the initials of the Sovereign. The West of England Bank was clothed almost from head to foot in a profusion of banners. The 'George Hotel' was congratulatory on the 'Success of the Devon and Somerset Railway'. The Town Hall mounted a Union Jack, and the Market-house repeated its 'Welcome!' to the Visitor. The National Provincial Bank displayed a handsome sheaf of shields inscribed underneath 'Libertas de Southmolton'.'

There were more banners including one near the station which stated '*South-molton bids you welcome!*'. The procession disbanded and focus was then on the Market Hall for the celebratory banquet. A number of distinguished guests attended: the Earl of Devon, Lords Fortescue, Poltimore, Portsmouth and Clinton, Sir Thomas Acland and the mayors of the various local boroughs. Lord Carnarvon sent his apologies. The luncheon served up '*soups of several kinds, and a plentiful cold collection, including joints of beef and mutton, poultry and game in variety, tarts and sweets, and dessert*'. Mrs Gould of the George Hotel and Mr Cole of the Unicorn provided the fayre. A number of toasts followed the luncheon. The Mayor of South Molton was praiseworthy: '*I think I may congratulate Lord Poltimore that he has at last brought the railway to Southmolton under the guardianship of the Bristol and Exeter Company. We are extremely pleased to see him here to-day, and to think that he has safely disposed of some of the difficulties which once lay in his path*'. Cheers resounded at the end of this and other speeches, and the jolly occasion came to a finale at 9.00pm with a public ball.

On 25th November, a dinner was given at the Castle Hotel in Taunton in celebration of the railway's opening. It was presided over by the head bailiff of Taunton, Mr H.J. Badcock, with Mayor Thomas May and other dignitaries from Barnstaple. They travelled

HENRY FROST

From the August 1925 *Great Western Railway Magazine*

'The death on, July 6 of Mr Henry Frost, retired engine driver, residing at Barnstaple, broke one of the most interesting links with the past in connection with railway work. Mr Frost who was in his 90th year, had been connected with the railway all his life, having started as a cleaner in his boyhood days, through the recommendation of the late General Sir Redvers Buller's father. He was the driver who was responsible for bringing the first train into and out of the Great Western station at Barnstaple when the "Devon and Somerset line" was constructed. The Rt Hon. J.H. Thomas, M.P., was at one time fireman on the engine driven by Mr Frost.'

A Down mixed passenger and perishables train at South Molton, bound for Barnstaple shortly after opening of the line in late 1873 – note there is no shelter on the Up platform. The locomotive is one of the class of eight 0-6-0 goods engines built for the B&ER by Stothert & Slaughter in 1849 and all rebuilt between 1858 and 1863. The first vehicle in the train is a 6-wheeled, iron-sided luggage or parcels van with guard's lookout in the roof, whilst the three two-tone liveried carriages comprise two Thirds and a First/Second Composite respectively. The fifth vehicle is a carriage truck complete with load and after that with the cupola on the roof is a meat van. The locomotive is standing alongside the original signal cabin, a timber hut perched on top of a wooden frame and note the banner signal on the left. Everything looks very new and the white paint of the signals and fencing is still bright. *Courtesy South Molton Museum*

up on the 10.30am from Barnstaple in a special carriage added there by the B&ER, returning on the 8.15pm train with a cheer from the assembled crowd.

The line was now open but work continued for the Board. The meeting of Thursday 6th November was held with Lord Poltimore in the chair, along with George Moysey and Captain Nash. Also in attendance was Mr Wainwright (Company Secretary), Mr Riccard (solicitor) and Mr Hassard (engineer). The report of the government inspection was laid before the Board, with the summary that '*the line had been opened throughout for passenger traffic between Taunton and Barnstaple on Saturday 1 November instant, but would not be available for goods traffic until Monday* [10th November]'. No certificates were presented by the engineer for the works, stations and matters raised by Col Hutchinson – namely alternations to signals – which had been done, whilst the contractor had been advised about the waiting sheds at Wiveliscombe and South Molton. The responsibility for maintenance was understood to be with the B&ER but Mr Fox, their engineer, believed the Norton to Wiveliscombe section was not. This difference was resolved by the December meeting, when the B&ER agreed to maintain the whole line.

The proposed Barnstaple extension was still a possibility and the potential site, at South Walk, which was a good location for a junction and an exchange with the Ilfracombe line, was visited and examined by Mr Hassard. However, he was concerned about the practicality of the extension and if it was to proceed, there should be no delay in building it. Improvements were to be made to the stations at Barnstaple, East Anstey and Morebath, and additional lands were to be acquired for this purpose. In part settlement of his bills, the contractor was allocated a broad gauge engine.

The B&ER recorded that the earnings per mile for passenger traffic in the first week of the line being fully opened was £6 10s 0d per mile.

At the 3rd December 1873 B&ER board meeting, it was reported that Mr Reed offered to sell an engine to the B&ER for £600. He was also to be supplied with a goods engine for ballasting on the D&SR, at a rate of £5 per nine hours and 10s per hour thereafter.

In the six months to 31st December 1873, a further £13,037 was spent financed by cash reserves: Contractor – £9,402 plus issue of £1,300 of 'B' debenture stock; land – £997; engineer – £640. The estimated future expenditure at that time was £40,000 – £20,000 for works not yet commenced or in abeyance and £20,000 for other items including land. The train mileage for the four month period 1st July to 31st October 1873 for the Wiveliscombe section was 10,875 miles, being the equivalent of 1,500 trains (9,338 miles related to passenger and 1,537 to goods and mineral trains). The revenue account at this time showed passenger and parcels income of £691 12s 1d and merchandise of £680 11s 4d, an overall total of £1,372 3s 5d, against costs of working the line and passenger duty of £1,235 9s 2d, so a small surplus to reduce the deficit brought forward. In this period, another Bill was also pending in Parliament for '*enabling the Devon and Somerset Railway Company to take Lands, to raise Additional Capital, and for other purposes*'.

Reed wrote to the directors in January 1874, stating that his cash expenses had reached £90,407 12s 6d and anticipating they would amount to £94,000. He had lost something in the region of £71,000

Another view of South Molton in late 1873, showing the station buildings on the Down platform in detail. Almost certainly again taken around the time of opening, the mortar in the stonework is still clean and white, and note the timber facing to the platform, constructed in this way presumably to save costs. The covered open waiting area is similar to that at Milverton, although here it adjoins the main building. *Courtesy South Molton Museum*

on the contract due to the inflation of labour and material costs after the commencement of the works.

The B&ER board heard correspondence between Hassard and Fox on 14th January 1874, in relation to the proposed claim by the B&ER for compensation in respect of the altered gradients and imperfectly completed works in the Wiveliscombe to Barnstaple section of the line. Messrs Combe & Wainwright (the D&SR's solicitors) had also written asking for an immediate reference to arbitration. However, the B&ER declined this until the unfinished works were completed (as the engineer had confirmed to Mr Hassard on 22nd December) but, in the meantime, Fox and Hassard were to consult on the differences if it was expedient to do so.

There was a substantive report by the directors at the 20th half-yearly general meeting on 6th February 1874 at Taunton. The line had:

> '*... been sufficiently completed to be opened to public traffic throughout from its junction with the B&ER line at Norton Fitzwarren near Taunton to Barnstaple a length of about 43 miles. The line opened for public traffic on 1 November 1873 and for goods traffic a few days later. Mineral traffic of which there is considerable promise will soon be commenced* [meaning Florence Mine]. *The season of the year and the heavy and continuous rains during November could hardly have been more unfavourable for the opening of a new line of railway but as postponement would have been attended with a risk of greater injury to the works from the action of the weather ... the directors deemed the most prudent course of action to be the opening of the line as soon at the Board of Trade had given their certificate.*'

With the agreement to share revenues with the B&ER and the relevant half-yearly amounts being paid in the following March and September, the company's payments were to be governed as follows:

- interest on the 'A' debenture stock at 6%
- interest on the 'B' debenture stock
- payment on the preference and ordinary shares.

Now that revenues were flowing, the cumulative interest overdue on the 'A' stock was agreed as a priority for payment. The directors confirmed that they had settled all accounts satisfactorily with the contractor and praised him for his '*perseverance and zeal with which amidst great and unforeseen difficulties he has fulfilled his obligations*'.

The directors went on to say:

> '*regret ... that the means at their disposal did not enable them to complete the line and stations so as to provide for the working of traffic in the most efficient manner which is essential to secure the punctual payment of the interest on the company's mortgage debt to the holders of A & B stock and some of the stations will remain unfinished and for the completion of these works additional capital must be raised.*'

Despite these comments, following the opening of the line, additional shelters were erected on the platforms at Wiveliscombe, Dulverton and South Molton, along with the signalling alterations required by Lieut Col Hutchinson. What remained to be carried out were additional passing places at Morebath, Molland and East Anstey stations, as required by the B&ER, and completion of the station at Barnstaple. On the day of opening, the maintenance of the first section to Wiveliscombe was taken over by the B&ER from the contractor, who was still responsible for the remainder of the line for one year. In this respect, Reed was awarded £1,000 as a fee for his extended maintenance time on the Barnstaple to South Molton section, due to the delays with the opening.

The B&ER wrote to the D&SR in February 1874, stating that cranes were required at South Molton and Barnstaple for stone and heavy castings. Also, slaughter houses were needed at Swimbridge, South Molton, Molland and Dulverton. There was a veiled threat here in that, if these facilities were not provided '*at once*', there was a risk the traffic would go to the L&SWR. The provision of an extra siding at Wiveliscombe was also agreed. Drainage works were also still on-going following a complaint by the B&ER, whilst water to South Molton was agreed to be provided by meter after 'Lady Day' (25th March), at 6d per 1,000 gallons; it was subsequently reported that the meter cost £12 9s 1d.

Traffic figures were of course being given at the Board meetings and these are summarised in Appendix 7. Hassard reported that the cost of the proposed additions at certain stations (listed above) would be £5,000 but the B&ER costed this at £3,000, so it was agreed it would be more commercial for them to carry out the work. Lord Carnarvon's agent, Mr Wall, wrote regarding the additional requirement of accommodation at Dulverton station and the clocks provided at Wiveliscombe, Dulverton and other stations were proving unreliable, so were to be replaced. Meanwhile, Lord Fortescue's solicitor wrote to highlight the '*inexcusable delay which has taken place ... and generally at the manner in which he had been treated ...*'. This was in relation to works and '*making good*' at the Castle Hill Estate, including such as gates on cattle arches, station ground to be levelled, carriage drives under the viaduct on both sides of the river to be protected and more. However, the engineer stated that whilst some were accommodation works (which was D&SR responsibility), some were not, so the Company was not responsible for the remainder.

It was reported at the B&ER board meeting on 18th March that four sheep had been killed between Norton Fitzwarren and Wiveliscombe, this being due to the decayed condition of the fencing. This could have been in place since 1866 when the line was first staked out but had not been adequately looked after.

As early as January 1874, there was comment in the *North Devon Journal* about the delivery of certain goods. The B&ER were sending goods brought in by the D&SR to Barnstaple and that were bound for Bideford on to their destination by turnpike road, when arguably it may have been cheaper for them to have gone via the L&SWR's North Devon line. Even the newly built Tinto Hotel at South Molton station was carting its consumables from South Molton Road station, 12 miles away by road, as this was cheaper than routing them just 10 miles along the D&SR.

Another subject of controversy was over the transshipment of coal, which was brought by ship into Rolle's Quay at Barnstaple for local distribution. However, as the quay was not connected to the D&SR's line, this meant that it would have to be transported by road to their Barnstaple station for loading into rail wagons, something which it seems the company was not prepared to do. Local distribution towards South Molton was facilitated by the turnpike road, which ironically ran close to the D&SR, whilst deliveries from Taunton to South Molton were made by rail by the B&ER, from their small port at Dunball Wharf, on the River Parrett just to the north of Bridgwater, which had been connected to the main line for working by locomotives since 1867. At the wharf, the transfer from ship to wagon was by crane, which resulted in less handling and thus less breakages. Furthermore, the B&ER were prepared to bear the costs of craneage at Dunball, estimated to be worth 5d per ton, which also therefore lowered the cartage costs.

A letter was written to the *North Devon Journal* and signed off '*One who knows*', comparing relative costs of delivery. For best Lydney coal it was 38s per ton delivered to the house at South Molton (other coal 35s), compared to 28s to deliver in Barnstaple. The writer felt this was '*reasonable*' for the extra distance involved but that Barnstaple would only provide the coal if the quay were connected to the railway. The port at Watchet was also cited as a possible inbound port for coal but with the favours given to Dunball by the B&ER it could not compete, despite it being one mile closer to all stations west of Taunton. On 18th February 1875, the *North Devon Journal* reported that Watchet was to appeal to the Railway Commissioners about the B&ER's preferential treatment for Dunball, on the basis that the railway gave a premium to this traffic in order to '*shut out the port of Watchet from the trade of those places*' – *i.e.* those stations on the D&SR). The differences in price per ton quoted in favour of Dunball were 11d to Milverton,

The B&ER's Dunball Wharf, seen here in GWR days circa 1908, was established in the 1840s by local merchants for importing coal; it was rail-served from opening but horse-worked for the first twenty or so years. The sidings, running in directly from the ex-B&ER main line, fanned out onto the wharf in the centre right background and also ran to a wagon turntable providing access to those running along the quayside, parallel to the River Parrett; this was positioned in the far left corner of the wharf, directly above the roofs of the houses forming Railway Crescent, in the centre of the picture. In the foreground, adjacent to Dunball Signal Box, a wagon turntable provided access via a flat crossing over the main line to a cement and lime works. The King's Sedgmoor Drain runs under the railway to the river on the left. Dunball Wharf lost its rail connection over fifty years ago but is still in use today by Hanson Aggregates for unloading dredged sand and gravel; it is the only part of the Port of Bridgwater still in commercial use. ***Neil Parkhouse collection***

17d to Wiveliscombe, Venn Cross and Morebath, 15½d to Dulverton and East Anstey, 1s 11d to Molland, 2s 6½d to South Molton, 1s 9d to Castle Hill [Filleigh] and 2s 1½d to Swymbridge [*sic*].

On 14th April 1874, the B&ER reported regarding plans for stables for twenty horses at Barnstaple. This was for the coach service to be inaugurated between the Royal Clarence Hotel in Ilfracombe and the D&SR station, to connect with trains to Taunton and beyond. There were three services to Barnstaple and four back, daily. Tickets could be booked at the Ilfracombe end at a new D&SR booking office near the clock tower. Four horses pulled the coaches, which covered the 12 miles in 1¼ hours. This gave passengers to Ilfracombe an alternative option to the paddle steamer from Portishead. The coach service, in direct competition with the Ilfracombe Railway once that had opened, lasted until 1887.

In the six months to 30th June 1874, a limited amount (£1,509) had been spent by the company, being largely Parliamentary expenses and land purchases. However, the estimate of future expenditure had increased again. Whilst works in abeyance were still costed at £20,000, outstanding liabilities, including land, was revised to £40,000 so £60,000 was the anticipated total expenditure. The mileage for the half-year was 82,941 for passengers and 27,330 for goods and minerals (total 110,271) – representing an unsurprising dramatic increase following opening of the line throughout. Mr Dymant was appointed by the Board to carry out an independent review of the traffic returns of the B&ER.

The B&ER continued to press the D&SR Board for the provision of additional passing places and station accommodation, the constraint, as always, being lack of funds. Steps were taken to remedy this.

The 21st ordinary half-yearly meeting, held on 28th August 1874, confirmed the sanction in Parliament of the 1874 Bill to issue £60,000 of debenture stock with the consent of three-fourths in value of the existing holders. This consent was subsequently given on 8th January 1875, at a Special General Meeting, sufficient consents being received by the 30th October board meeting. The purpose of the financing was to carry out improvements on the line, including the increased station accommodation and conveniences required by the B&ER as working company. This was deemed essential to the development and increase of the traffic in the district served by the line. These improvements were to be '*proceeded with haste*'.

The traffic receipts, as returned by the B&ER since the opening of the line, are set out in the following table, for the period to 30th June 1874:

	Passenger	Goods	Parcels	Total
Nov/Dec 73	1,934 2 0	1,276 5 3	105 1 7	3,315 8 10
January 74	741 8 0	483 14 2	33 2 3	1,258 4 5
February	793 6 4	491 18 10	29 2 0	1,314 7 2
March	955 12 4	883 8 9	51 0 4	1,890 1 5
April	892 15 10	625 9 4	74 17 1	1,593 2 3
May	1,698 10 8	952 11 9	156 10 3	*2,807 12 8
June	1,234 6 2	925 11 8	168 6 10	2,328 4 8
TOTAL	**8,250 1 4**	**5,638 19 9**	**618 0 4**	**14,507 1 5**

*** Barnstaple Cattle Show month**

The mileage for the half year to 30th December 1874 was 111,968 miles, with the passenger (85,627)/goods (26,341) split being in similar proportions (circa 75% to 25%) as the prior period above.

At the 23rd September B&ER board meeting, a letter from Mr Hassard was read regarding the plan to extend the line to a station in the centre of Barnstaple and to have a junction or interchange station with the Ilfracombe Railway. The B&ER Secretary was asked to write to the D&SR to stress the importance of extending the line and erecting a permanent station at Barnstaple. At this time, the B&ER was still unhappy with the general deficiency of accommodation at stations and resolved that expenditure not exceeding £3,000 be authorised for necessary outlays, provided the D&SR directors gave an undertaking that it would be repaid within six months of the passing of the D&SR's next financing Bill, with interest thereon at a rate of 5% per annum. All works would need to be executed to the satisfaction of the B&ER engineer.

The B&ER took over maintenance of the permanent way and works from the contractor as from 1st November 1874; Reed's contract expired actually expired on 20th October, so B&ER were asked to take up the responsibility from that date but they declined. Reed was thus asked to cover this gap period and, following B&ER engineer Mr Fox's report, was also requested to replace certain rails. A letter of 10th September 1874 referred to damage to the water supply near the railway bridge at Yeo Mill, which deprived residents of the usual supply from a spring in Mr Elworthy's field. Apparently, the contractor had taken away the original supply and laid clay pipes to a well; these had got damaged and, as a consequence, surface water mixed with the spring water. The site was inspected and the damaged pipes were replaced.

A B&ER letter of 30th September 1874 made a call '*to the necessity of providing without delay an improved and more central station at Barnstaple …*', which the D&SR Board acknowledged was serious and important. There were also continued representations from the B&ER for the additional passing places and station accommodation; Hassard prepared plans and estimates for their construction. The ambitious aim was to undertake the work in order for the improvements to be ready for the 1875 summer traffic. The Board meeting of 30th October indicated that a dividend would be payable to the 'A' stockholders at a rate of 1¾% for the half year (to 30th June), on account of interest (less income tax). It would seem from a report at this meeting that, in an effort to save costs, Reed had taken good rails out of sidings and swapped them with defective rails from the main line. Mr Fox, not surprisingly, objected to this and required Reed to replace them with new rails as his original contract had stipulated.

The B&ER directors had also recently resolved to replace the broad gauge lines of the D&SR with standard gauge. However, the D&SR directors were concerned that, as their Act prescribed that it was to be built to the broad gauge, any change of gauge would require Parliamentary sanction. The D&SR Board also considered a proposal by a Mr John Cock, who offered to build a slaughterhouse on his own land at South Molton, if the company would secure a small return per year. This was rejected by the Board.

By the 6th November 1874 board meeting, consideration was being given to a stock exchange quotation for the company. Mr Wall of the B&ER wrote to the D&SR over the extension of the line in Barnstaple:

> '*My company will feel that it is necessary to materially curtail the train accommodation which is at present given … we are placed at a considerable disadvantage by the present temporary inconvenient and insufficient passenger shed – it cannot be called a station – added to which is the great distance at which it is situated from the Town.*'

He further went on to confirm that the B&ER were incurring heavy losses working the line. Richard Hassard, in his letter of 5th November, said there was a proposal to extend the line from Cattle Market Road into Barnstaple and a Town Council resolution had been passed on the matter. The council had opposed an extension to Bear Street but had agreed to an extension to the Square by a modified route. This resolution was to be sent to the B&ER but, expecting opposition, the D&SR decided not to immediately proceed with the extension. They added that it would be to no advantage to either company, as within twelve months, a Bill for the necessary improvements at Barnstaple and a permanent passenger station there might be more advantageous than proceeding now.

It was reported in the *North Devon Journal* of 20th November 1874 that the traffic on the newly opened line was increasing daily. The innovation of market trains was a success; 200 people were brought to Barnstaple market on Friday 13th November, this being of clear benefit to the town. Also, new branches of trade were developing between the towns on the D&SR as a result of the opening of the railway and the open mindedness of the company.

Following the passing of the D&SR Act 1874, the authorised securities position (ignoring the ordinary and preference shares already in issue) was as follows:

AT 31ST DECEMBER 1874	ISSUED	UNISSUED	AUTHORISED
1864 B Debenture Stock	165,878	122	166,000
1868 A Debenture Stock	270,000		270,000
1872 A Debenture Stock	99,867	133	100,000
1874 A Debenture Stock		60,000	60,000
Total	535,745	60,255	596,000

At the meeting of 8th January 1875, the Board's attention was drawn towards two Bills going through Parliament. The first, for the Tiverton & North Devon Railway Bill, proposed a line from Tiverton forming a junction with the D&SR at Morebath. Whilst this was similar to the Exe Valley line proposed last session, it was to be standard gauge. The Bill had powers to enter into working agreements with the B&ER and D&SR. The directors stated that if the Bill was for a broad gauge line, there would be good reason to support it for the benefit of additional traffic over the Barnstaple to Morebath section, to avoid travel by the L&SWR. However, they declined to support the proposal due to the different gauge and the inconvenience and inefficiencies that interchange would bring. The other Bill was a B&ER one for laying down standard gauge on all lines worked by them. The Board felt that the cost of conversion should be a cost of the B&ER and a petition was lodged. Finally, new bankers, Messrs Cocks, Biddulph & Co. of Charing Cross, London, were appointed.

At the 9th March 1875 meeting, tenders were invited for the Barnstaple station work and the passing places. It was proposed (and subsequently agreed) that if the B&ER undertake to lay down the standard gauge line at their own expense within three years, to pay half or an agreed proportion of the proposed works and insert

A broad gauge 0-6-0 saddle tank locomotive at the head of a Down goods train at South Molton station circa 1880. The locomotive is either GWR No. 2060 or 2062, which were rebuilds of B&ER 0-6-0 tender engines of the class seen on page 76 – either No. 54 or No. 56. It is seen here with a Swindon Armstrong-era chimney, as fitted to broad gauge engines between 1876 and 1880. Note the waiting shelter on the Down platform, provided a few months aftert the line first opened. Station staff and the train crew hold the long pause required for the exposure of the photographer's glass plate. Note that the track was laid with cross sleepers, not the longitudinal 'baulk road' timbers normally associated with the broad gauge. ***Courtesy South Molton Museum***

a clause protecting the rights of the D&SR, then the Board would support the B&ER Bill. By the 7th May board meeting, a healthy cash balance of £9,563 16s 1d was reported. At the 4th June meeting, approval was given for the erection of a temporary shed at Barnstaple for accommodation of passengers, such cost not to exceed £100. Mr Reed's tender of £17,500 was accepted for new works (being covered by £6,000 cash and £11,500 of 'A' debenture stock). Lord Carnarvon had made a unilateral decision to build a hotel on the company's land; the Board wrote to him and then expressed surprise at not having received a reply to their letter, so correspondence between respective lawyers ensued. The erection of an office and fittings at Barnstaple in June 1875 cost £19 16s 4d.

At the 2nd July meeting, cash was reported as £12,568 3s 6d, after £19,207 of 1874 'A' debenture stock had been issued in the previous six months. The Secretary produced a prospectus bearing the name of G. Herbert & Sons of 73 Old Broad Street, London, inviting the subscription of £25,000 of 'A' debenture stock of the D&SR. The directors made it clear they had not authorised the prospectus – a fraud was being perpetrated at the expense of the D&SR! Purchases of land for £3,693 10s 3d for new works also came as a surprise to the Board, as it had not previously been mentioned.

On 7th July, the Board were not happy with the general state of the line and the maintenance carried out by the B&ER, being more of a slovenly appearance rather than dilapidation. Richard Hassard agreed to continue as engineer. Mr Riccard, the solicitor, was concerned about non-payment of a sum of £2,426, most of which related to fees for a land conveyance in 1872. He had been paid £15,000 in company paper for his earlier work but he had received no interest on the stock he held.

A report into surplus lands owned by the D&SR in 1875 made a number of suggestions as to what to do with it. For instance, at Chipstable, it was recommended that, if the land was sold, a strip 12 feet in width should be retained in the event of the line being doubled. Land at Brushford seemed to be interesting Lord Carnarvon but it was felt that it should be kept as it adjoined Dulverton station and may be required for sidings or a station approach or some such purpose. Meanwhile, at Barnstaple, part of the surplus land there would be required should the line be extended into the town. It adjoined Cattle Market Road and even if not used for the railway, it was realised that it may have strong commercial value going forward as the town developed. From all this, it is clear that the doubling of the line was still a consideration at this time, along with other potential improvements, albeit the original financing for the extension into Barnstaple had time-expired.

On 16th August 1875, the engineer reported that the contract for passing places at Morebath, East Anstey and Molland stations, the enlargement of Barnstaple station and the erection of a permanent goods shed in *lieu* of the current temporary arrangements had been give to Messrs Reed Brothers (John Langham Reed and George Daynell Reed). Already a considerable amount of work had been undertaken, totalling £1,750. At this time, an additional temporary shelter had been erected at Barnstaple station to provide for the usual tourist traffic.

At the 27th August meeting, the Board confirmed that brokers were asked to apply to the Stock Exchange for a quotation in the official list of each class of stock in the company. The D&SR noted it was prepared to accept £500 from Lord Carnarvon for the land on which part of the hotel was built, otherwise the hotel '*must be removed*'. It was also noted that, at the last session of Parliament, two Bills were introduced, one in respect of the B&ER (being that relating to the potential takeover by the GWR) and one for the Tiverton & North Devon Railway forming a junction near Morebath with the D&SR. It was agreed the directors would lodge petitions to protect the position of the D&SR in respect of both Bills and indeed this was subsequently confirmed. Lord Poltimore felt the line was now established and due to ill health was minded to retire at this time. However, in view of the B&ER/GWR pending Bill, he deferred his decision for twelve months. Mr Moysey stood down after ten years in office, to be replaced by Mr Montague Bere.

At the 1st October meeting, £5,830 10s 0d was received from the B&ER for traffic receipts to the half year ended 30th June 1875. The engineer reported that the earthworks for the double line at Morebath were almost complete, along with the new platform. Road ballast and metalling was deposited and one widened bridge abutment had been built. Earthworks for similar improvements continued at East Anstey. At Molland, earthworks for the double line was three quarters done, masonry for the passenger platform was half finished and the masonry for the abutments of the widened bridge was complete. However, work had been temporarily stopped on the bridge because of concerns from the Highways Board. At Barnstaple, three quarters of the earthworks were completed. The masonry of the passenger offices and the permanent goods shed (in *lieu* of the current temporary arrangement) were built to foundation level, whilst a considerable amount of the timber work had been assembled ready for erection when the buildings were sufficiently advanced. A cargo of rails and fishplates had arrived; the fishplates were at Barnstaple, the rails still on board a vessel in the river. The BoT report resulted in precautionary measures being put in place at facing points and signals at certain locations, at a cost of about £150 for each location (total £450). A further payment due to the contractor was settled by 'A' debenture stock of £1,000 and cash of £516. At the meeting of 2nd December 1875, the matter of the fraudulent prospectus raised its head again, as the Board had received a letter from a Mr Dykes claiming the return of his £500 subscription monies. He was politely referred to Messrs G.S. Herbert & Sons who had issued the prospectus.

In the six month period to 31st December 1875, £37,960 was spent on the line, funded largely from the issue of the new (1874) 'A' debenture stock; £52,093 worth of the stock had been issued by this date, with £32,886 of it in this six month period. The £37,960 was deployed as follows:

NARRATIVE	£ s d	£ s d
Construction	**8,265 0 0**	
Reed Bros Contract		
Settlement of Construction	**21,627 0 0**	
accounts Bond plus interest		
Waiting shed at Barnstaple	**93 15 0**	
Florence Mining Co signals etc	**400 0 0**	
Venn Cross telegraph apparatus	**4 5 0**	
Total Construction		**30,390 0 0**
Land		**3,722 18 0**
Engineering		**1,252 16 9**
Other		**2,594 09 01**
TOTAL		**37,960 03 10**

By this stage the estimate of further expenditure was down to a mere £10,300, all due to be spent in the next six months for land (£1,000) and additional works (£9,300).

Mileage recorded for passenger trains was 83,765 and goods 25,675, a total of 109,440 train miles, this total being down on the equivalent period in the previous year.

At the 7th January 1876 meeting, the Amalgamation Bill between the B&ER and GWR was brought to the Board's attention, along with the fact that the L&SWR was buying the Exeter & Crediton Railway and looking to remove the broad gauge on that and other lines in North Devon. Regarding the land used by Lord Carnarvon, Messrs Combe & Wainwright (solicitors) were authorised to take legal proceedings for the recovery of the acreage currently in the possession of Lord Carnarvon and his tenants.

By the time of the 3rd February 1876 report, the passing places at Morebath and Molland were complete, and had been inspected by Lieut Col Hutchinson and passed as satisfactory (BoT letter 8th January 1876). Works at East Anstey were far advanced, as were those at Barnstaple, where half of the sidings in the goods yard were laid. There was a delay in securing stone for the goods shed, so that was behind schedule but the roof was ready for erection once the walls had been completed. The new passenger offices there were due for occupation in the near future. The exceptional rains of the previous October had caused land slips in various of the cuttings, one of which had been sufficient to stop all traffic on the line for eight consecutive days. Whilst this was an inconvenience, the works of the line were not affected. The B&ER and GWR Amalgamation Bill was to be petitioned to protect the D&SR interests and there were land tax increases in the parishes of Milverton, Oake and Bishops Nympton. In respect of the disputed land on which the hotel stood, an offer was to be made to Lord Carnarvon to pay £200, with the added stipulation that he was only to use the road to the station and not to go through the station yard. Lord Fortescue was given land at Filleigh by the railway, which was presumably to cover for the reparation works referred to earlier.

Mr John Locke took the chair at the 25th February half yearly meeting. The general depression of trade in 1875 had affected traffic receipts, and the floods, suspension of traffic (as above) and unfavourable summer weather had diminished both tourist and regular passenger traffic. The GWR was focusing on controlling traffic in the west of England area and consideration was now being given to an amalgamation of the B&ER with the GWR with the Bill brought to Parliament. Again the D&SR directors' concern was to protect their company's position. Mails were first carried by the D&SR from March 1876, at an annual price of £200.

Hassard reported on 6th April 1876 that the works at Morebath, Molland and East Anstey were complete but the GWR had only just been given permission to run trains through the new passing loops. Barnstaple station and offices were now complete but the goods shed was one month behind schedule. The old passenger station and goods shed was to be sold to raise funds. At this time, the D&SR directors withdrew any opposition to the B&ER and GWR Amalgamation Bill, having established that their interests were protected. The Highways Board in Barnstaple had a complaint alleging injury to roads in the Bishops Tawton, Landkey and Swimbridge areas due to the carriage of heavy materials relating to new works.

By 5th May 1876, the new passenger station at Barnstaple was close to being handed over to the company. The goods shed had just 100 out of 1,346 cubic yards of masonry still to be built; this was completed by 1st June, with the roof half covered. There was a delay in completing the goods sidings and station yard works, because the old goods and passenger sheds, which were stored there, had not been sold and were taking up space; there had been no responses to an advertisement placed in the *North Devon Journal*. The possession of the old mileage siding at Barnstaple had not been given up to the company; the work had stopped and the Board was to write to the GWR about this. The total works at this stage amounted to £16,231 16s 5d. On inspection, Lieut Col Hutchinson decided that the works at Molland and East Anstey were not quite ready for approval, so he planned to revisit on 6th June and take in the Barnstaple works at the same time. However, at this visit, although everything was approved, the goods shed still remained incomplete and it would not be finished until 28th July. The total for the works had reached £17,558 by 6th July 1876, just over the anticipated cost.

IMPROVEMENTS AT MOREBATH, EAST ANSTEY AND MOLLAND IN 1876

A review of the contract outlines the new works that were intended to be carried out at Morebath in 1876. The surface of the new Up platform was to be covered with a depth of six inches of fine clean ballast or river gravel, to be well rolled and consolidated. A waiting shed 25 feet long and 2 feet wide, similar to that at Wiveliscombe on the Down platform, was to be provided and erected. The name board was to read 'Morebath for Bampton'. A block hut 12 feet by 10 feet, with stove and chimney, similar in construction to that at Milverton, was to be erected, containing a ten lever frame, along with the telegraph and instruments, all locking equipment and signals on the north side of the line. The bridge at the west end was to be widened to take the second line, which would include new masonry work.

Hutchinson reported on 7th January on his inspection of the new passing place at Morebath station. The construction of the loop line involved the widening of an underbridge, using wrought iron girders of the same strength as those carrying the original line. Point and signal arrangements, a new Up platform and waiting shelter had all been provided. However, the engineers had not received Hutchinson's letter confirming the date of inspection, so the coupling of the points and signals with the levers working them was incomplete and they could not be tested properly. He also noted some deficiencies:

- Through timbers should have been provided in the cranks working the points. It should not be possible to lower the Home signals until the points were bolted right for incoming trains and they should also be set tight before the starting signals could be lowered. A clock was required in the signal cabin.
- The outer rails of the curves at each end of the loop line required a more superior elevation.

Although the loop line at Molland should also have been inspected at this time, the report stated that '... *the work was so incomplete as to make it useless for me to visit it*'.

A further report, made on 6th May 1876 when visiting East Anstey, stated that the arrangements at Morebath were still incomplete and further recommended:

- No. 8 points should be set tight for Up trains before No. 2 Up Home signal can be given.
- No. 4 points should be set tight for Down trains before No. 3 Down starting signal can be given.
- No. 3 Down Starting signal and No. 2 Up Home signal should be interlocked.
- No's 3 and 10 Up and Down Starting signals should not be interlocked.
- A clock was still required in the cabin.

These matters had been satisfactorily complied with by the time of the report of 6th June 1876.

At East Anstey, the contract specified that the line was to be doubled by widening the cutting and embankment on the north side of the station. The walling, coping and gravelling of the new platform was to be similar to that built at Morebath and as the already existing East Anstey Down platform. The waiting shed was to be 25 feet long

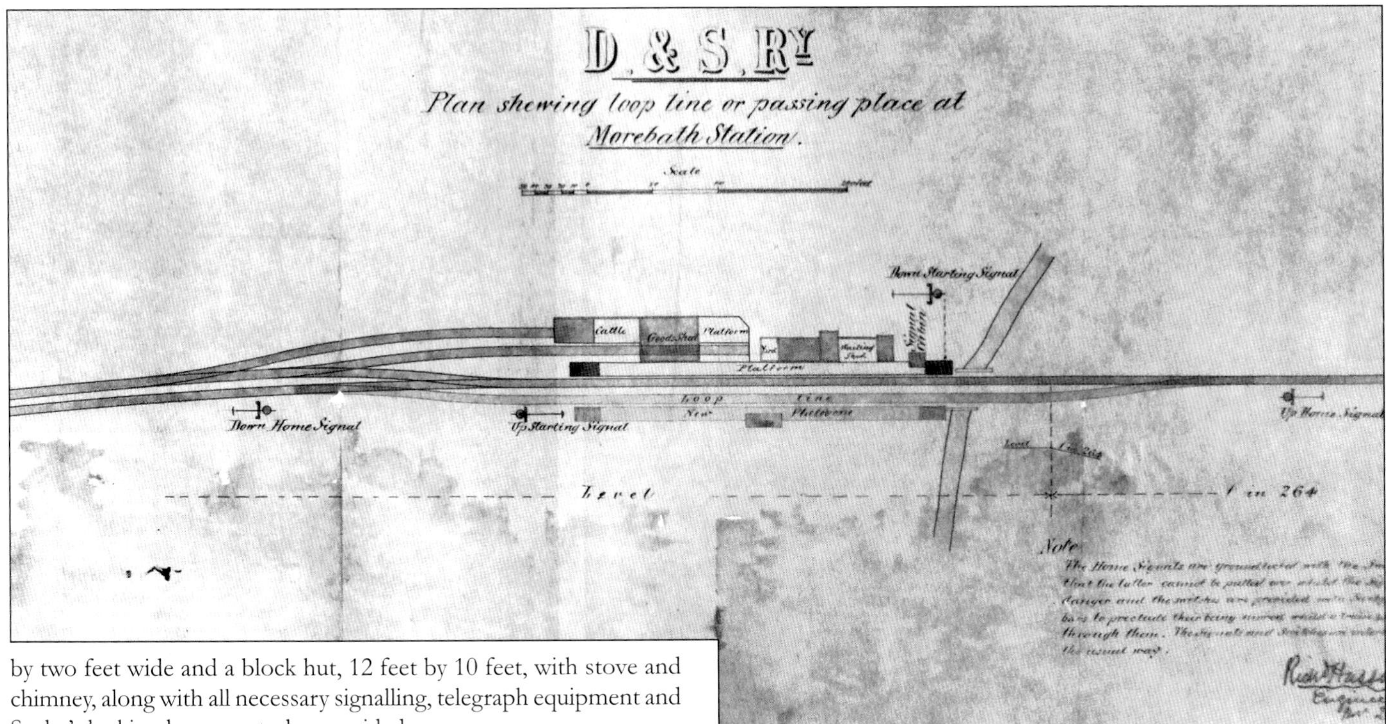

by two feet wide and a block hut, 12 feet by 10 feet, with stove and chimney, along with all necessary signalling, telegraph equipment and Saxby's locking bars was to be provided.

Hutchinson wrote the report of his inspection of the new passing place at East Anstey on 6th May 1876. He indicated that the facing points at the west end of the loop were 231 yards from the new signal box and, as a consequence, '*should not be worked from the cabin but locked tight (by a pulling and not a pushing action of the rod which now works them) for the up line before the up signals can be lowered and weighted to the right for the up line*'. The points at the east end of the loop were to be set right for Up trains before the Up Starting signal could be lowered and at the west end of the loop, the points should be free to move before the Down Starting signal could be given. Runaway points were recommended at the west end of the Up loop, where there was a falling gradient of 1 in 58 which continued '*more or less*' to the next station westwards. The lever to the points should be detached and kept in the cabin and a clock was to be provided in there as well. His subsequent report of 6th June 1876 confirmed the requirements had been complied with but that some adjustment was required to the runaway point. In addition to the loop, a new platform and waiting shelter were constructed.

At Molland, the contract stated the line was to be doubled on the northern side by means of an embankment and retaining walls. It stipulated that the stone for the walls was to be obtained from a quarry about one mile south of the station, owned by Sir William Throckmorton. The platform supports were to be of oak and memel timber, with yellow pine for the boards. The waiting shelter was to be 25 feet long by 8 feet wide, similar to that at South Molton. The contractor was to take down the masonry of the north face of the bridge under the railway adjoining the station and extend it in width. A block hut similar to those at Morebath and East Anstey was to be provided.

In the 6th June 1876 report, it was noted that the bridge at the east end of the station had been widened and had '*sufficient theoretical and practical strength*'. The points at the Down end of the loop did not close as well as they might and the bell crank timbers should be more

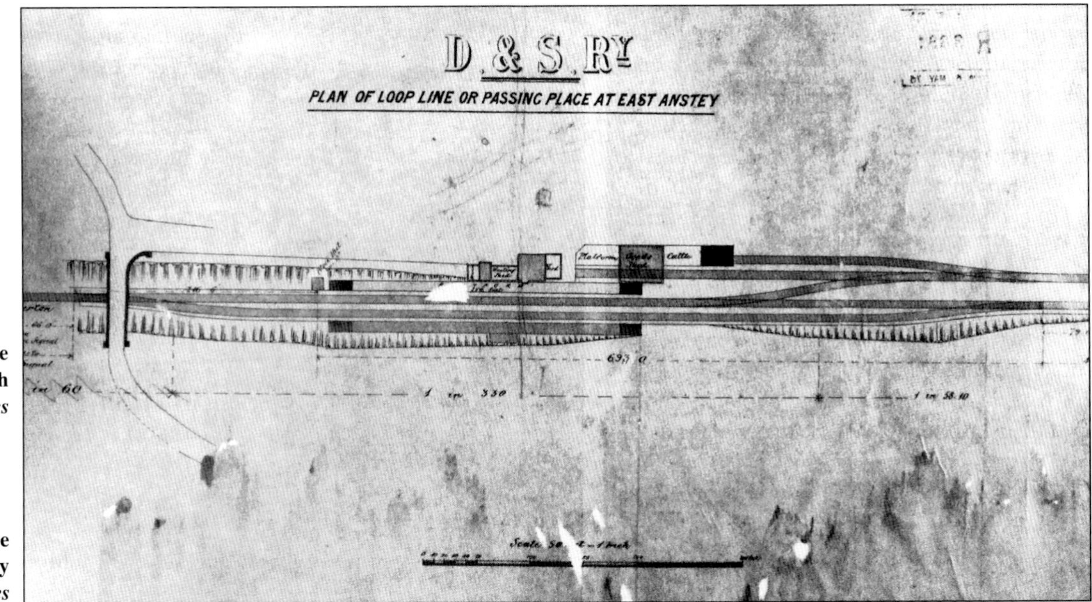

ABOVE: The engineer's plan of the new crossing loop at Morebath station. ***Courtesy National Archives***

RIGHT: The engineer's plan of the new crossing loop at East Anstey station. ***Courtesy National Archives***

firmly fixed in the ground. In addition to the passing loop, a platform and waiting shed were added.

Finally, there were the improvements to be carried out at Barnstaple, again as specified to the contractor in this new contract. The work here involved the construction of a new station and goods shed as previously noted, along with cattle pens, permanent way sidings, cranes and a turntable, and the making of metalled roads. The detailed specifications dealt with, for example, the removal of earth in expanding the site, the structure of the metalled road and the consistency of concrete mixes. The concrete and masonry for the seals of the 10-ton crane, 20-ton weighbridge and 13-foot turntable was to be made with Portland cement (concrete: 1 part cement, 5 parts shingle or gravel and the mortar to be 1 part cement and 3 parts of clean sand). The cranes, weighbridge and turntable were to be of the type used by the B&ER and manufactured by the Bridgwater Engineering Company. In respect of the new goods shed, initial work was to lay 9 inch, 6 inch or 4 inch glazed stoneware pipes for drainage. There were to be four 3-ton self-supporting cranes, with the chains tested to a strength of 4 tons. The walls of the goods shed and the platform for the cattle pens were to be of sound, flat-bedded rubble, with selected quoin stones of the same description, quality and finish as Swimbridge. The roof of the shed and offices were to be covered with Bangor Duchess slates.

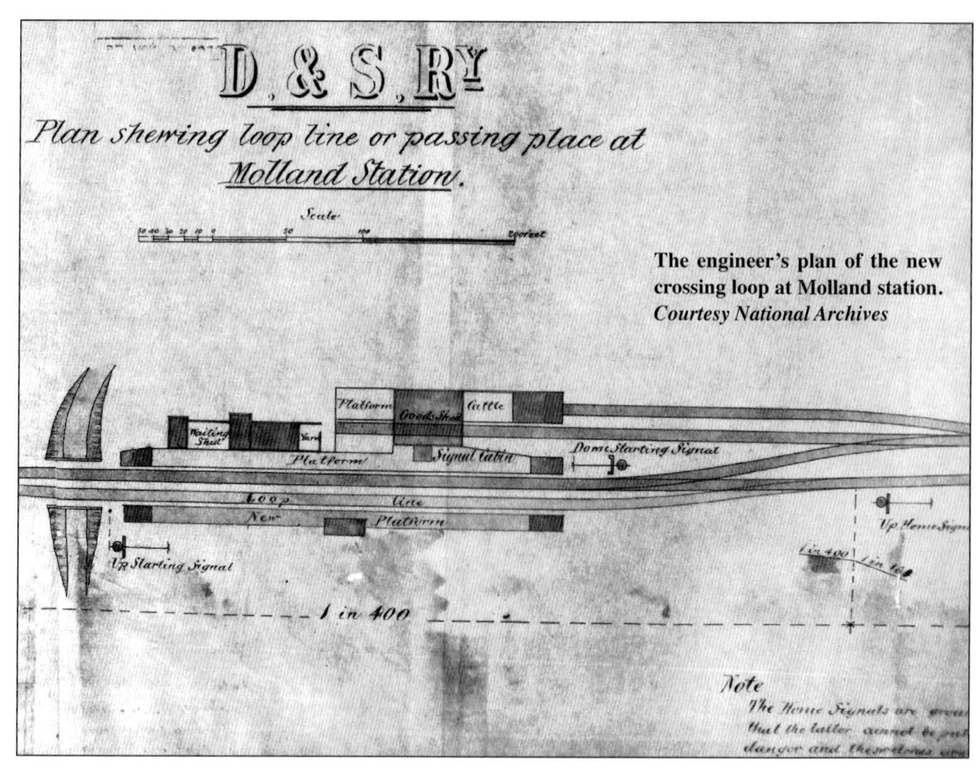

The engineer's plan of the new crossing loop at Molland station. ***Courtesy National Archives***

In regards to the additional sidings laid and the points to the passenger platform, which were altered in position, Hutchinson stated they were satisfactory but wanted to guard against collision between engines going to the shed and goods trains: '*it is desirable that properly interlocked signals for the engine shed and turn-table and new goods line should be put up*'.

Thus by the summer of 1876, the line's three original passing places had been increased to six with the addition of the loop lines at Morebath, East Anstey and Molland, whilst the layout and facilities at Barnstaple station had been much improved.

HALF YEARLY TRAFFIC REPORT 30/6/1876	GROSS EARNINGS £ s d
Passenger	6,182 3 1
Mails	100 0 0
Parcels	472 2 3
Goods	5,177 3 7
Rents	102 0 0
TOTAL	12,033 8 11

By July, the B&ER and GWR Amalgamation Bill had passed a select committee of the House of Commons. A Mr Dendle tendered £35 for the materials of the old goods shed, which offer was accepted subject to the items being removed within two weeks, the money being subsequently received. The Exe Valley Chemical Works had approached the D&SR for a lease of land adjoining Dulverton station for storage purposes but the company did not want to relinquish a hold on this as they might have needed it, so they refused.

As we have seen, the running rights of the D&SR were leased to the B&ER. However, the GWR was ultimately put under pressure to acquire the B&ER when its 'local' rivals (the Midland Railway and the L&SWR) acquired the Somerset & Dorset Railway. Not wanting to lose its route into the south west, the GWR had leased the B&ER from 1st January 1876 and amalgamated with it from 1st August, thus taking over the responsibility for services on the D&SR.

On 18th August, the engineer reported that all the new works referred to above had been completed and had been in operation for some time and no further works were in progress. The final costs for these improvements was revealed on 25th August as £18,315 8s 0d against the contract price of £17,500. The overrun was due to gas, water, additional signals not included in the original specification and extra works at Dulverton, namely a horse landing stage, carriage dock and fencing (totalling £31 4s 0d).

At this time, Sir William Throckmorton resigned from the Board and Lord Politimore ceased to be Chairman (to fulfil his aim to step aside), with Montague Bere taking his place. Mr Granville Somerset (who had been the company's counsel previously – see above) and Mr George Herring were invited to become directors.

The GWR, who had been working the line for the half year to 30th June 1876, complained about the inadequate water supply at Wiveliscombe; it would cost £650 to put this right, which the Board was unable to sanction. The planned 25th August half yearly meeting was postponed until 6th October due to the lack of traffic information from the GWR but it was reported that Barnstaple goods shed was at last completed. However, something of a financial crisis was now looming and influential shareholders were starting to revolt. A Mr Albert Grant (a Lloyd's bond holder for £10,000) obtained a judgement against the company for interest and costs of £1,267 9s 0d and presented a petition under the Railways Act 1867 for the appointment of a receiver. Others wrote to the Board suggesting they consider a sale to the GWR, Midland or L&SWR. By November's board meeting, the directors were having to look at the best means of reducing costs. Some railway land at South Molton had been taken by the Corporation of South Molton and '*planked off*'.

By 31st December 1876, the line had been in operation over its full length for three years and construction was complete, albeit minor improvements would still be made as the needs of both the railway and its users became clearer. Anticipated expenditure over the next six months was stated as £550 for land and £700 thereafter; future works were anticipated at £1,150. The capital account stood as follows:

NARRATIVE	£ s d	£ s d
Shares issued	271,582 10 0	
Debenture Stocks	593,685 0 0	
Interest	4,904 4 1	
Total inflow of funds		870,171 14 1
Expenditure on line	862,578 1 4	
Ilfracombe Railway	6,895 10 3	
TOTAL SPENT AT 31/12/1876		869,473 11 7
Cash balance at 31/12/1876		698 2 6

The statement of capital authorised and created by 31st December 1876 was analysed as follows:

ACTS OF PARLIAMENT	STOCKS & SHARES	LOANS	TOTAL
D&SR Acts 1864, Scheme (1868)			
'A' Debenture Stock (1st charge)		270,000	
'B' Debenture Stock (2nd charge)		166,000	
Preference Shares (3rd charge)	12,000		
Ordinary Stock	259,455		
Ordinary Shares not paid up	1,245		708,700
D&SR Act 1872			
A Debenture Stock (1st charge)		100,000	
D&SR Act 1874			
A Debenture Stock (1st charge)		60,000	160,000
TOTAL	272,700	596,000	868,700

At this point only £2,315 of debenture stock remained to be issued, being £122 worth of 'B' stock (1864), £133 of 'A' Stock (1872) and £2,060 of the 1874 'A' stock.

The train mileage for the half year to 31st December 1876 was 85,167 for passenger and 27,311 for goods and minerals, making a total of 112,478, an increase of 3,038 train miles (being 3% on the equivalent period for 1875).

At the 1st January 1877 meeting, the Secretary, Mr Muggeridge, was appointed as receiver as a result of the court order in the case of Locke *versus* Grant for the 'A' and 'B' debenture holders. On 4th January Mr John T. Nash resigned as a director. The receivership was extended to the whole undertaking by the Master of the Rolls by the time of the 23rd February meeting. A letter was received from the GWR referring to a claim for £75 by a Mr Wyatt of Croford, for a sheep that was killed at an accommodation crossing near his farm.

With total net earnings for the year being £14,133, it was agreed that the 'A' debenture stockholders would receive a 1 1/2% payment, the previous half year was recommended at 1 1/4 %. The general trading conditions were still depressed nationally and the weather was still poor. The directors were also communicating with the GWR to improve the carriage of goods over the line. Mr William Bailey Hawkins was interested in becoming a director; he had interests in the iron mines in North Molton and it was acknowledged that he also had experience in railway management, and would therefore bring useful expertease to the Board.

The 6th April meeting reported that the traffic receipts due from the GWR for the half year to 31st December 1876 amounted to £7,121 9s 5d.

At the 1st June meeting, the Board comprised Montague Bere QC as Chairman, John Arthur Locke, Arthur Barff, Granville Somerset QC, George Herring and William Bailey Hawkins. The appointment of a local agent was considered to look at means of generating an increase in earnings from the line; a commission of 5% to such an appointee was proposed. A letter to the GWR from the Rev'd Walter King was discussed. He was complaining about the '*dangerous proximity*' of the railway to the road between Wiveliscombe and Milverton, as his horses had been frightened. The directors decided that no action should be taken but a reply written stressing that in the six years the line had been open there had been no similar complaints.

It was noted on 18th June 1877 that there was to be a deputation to the GWR, comprising Messrs Herring and Bailey Hawkins to discuss the passenger services, Sunday trains, development of goods traffic, appointment of a local agent and the traffic to and from the Florence Mining Company siding near South Molton. The traffic returns for the half year to 30th June 1877 were down on the 30th June 1876 period and this caused considerable anxiety for the directors, who felt this was due to a '*want of energy*' on behalf of the GWR. However, the GWR declined to receive the deputation. In July, a Mr George Bush, a resident of George Nympton (near South Molton), was appointed the local agent and he was well versed in railway matters to review and propose what changes could be made to increase revenues. The 5% commission on such increases in earnings subject to a minimum fee of £100 was confirmed. However, one of his first jobs was to do a report on lands belonging to the company at each station and who was using the land and the level of rents payable.

The half yearly traffic report from the GWR showed total revenues of £11,620 15s 6d, of which the D&SR share was 50% *i.e.* £5,810 7s 9d. With the GWR delaying in the production of the half yearly receipts and traffic information, it was agreed to change the timing of the half-yearly meetings to accommodate their tardiness! It was proposed that 1 1/4 % be paid on the 'A' debenture stock for the half year to 30th June 1877.

A letter was received from the GWR, dated 29th November 1877, requesting that Castle Hill station's name be changed, as it had the potential to be confused with Castle Hill in West London (now West Ealing). Lord Fortescue was to be asked his view.

As at 31st December 1877, £59,957 of 1874 'A' debenture stock had been issued, £1,000 of which was in trust (with £43 being unissued, along with only £122 of the 1864 'B' Stock.

As regards the proposed deputation to the GWR, Swindon relented and eventually met the D&SR directors on 27th February 1878, with a view to seeking how to improve traffic on the line. However, these discussions developed into a possible takeover of the D&SR. There was further correspondence with the GWR on workings of the line, whilst they had also entered into correspondence with the Florence Mining Company over the sidings and the carriage of ore, and this continued for a few months. In March 1878, Mr Bush put forward his plans for a line from South Molton to Lynton, via Florence Mine and Moles Chambers, as noted in Chapter 2.

At the 5th April meeting, the rebate of £51 8s 0d from the Midland was noted. The GWR moiety for the half year to 31st December was £7,307 7s 0d, less £91 6s 10d in income tax. Mr R. Dymant consented to be auditor and Mr Edward P. Wolstenholme (barrister) to be a director. At the 1st June meeting, there was deadlock over the election of Mr Bere or Mr Bailey Hawkins as chairman, the other directors at this time being Mr Barff, Mr Somerset, Mr Herring and Mr Wolstenholme. At the subsequent meeting, on 5th July, Mr Locke attended and the vote for chairman was recast, with Mr Bere taking the chair.

The half year returns to 30th June 1878 showed total traffic receipts of £12,089 3s 3d, with £5,943 16s 10d allocated to the D&SR (*i.e.*

£6,044 11s 8d less income tax of £100 14s 10d). The summer period of 1878 showed a strong increase in revenues, indicating the success of the meeting with the GWR, as from June 1878, there were London trains, through evening services and other improvements including two Sunday trains. However, the Sunday trains had ceased to run by the 1st October timetable.

In October, it was reported that the South Molton & Linton [*sic*] Railway prospectus had been sent out with a letter to each bondholder and shareholder; the company was independent but the D&SR directors gave it positive backing. Substantial assistance was expected from the GWR and it was anticipated this new line would increase traffic further on the D&SR. Lynton was referred to by the directors as '*admittedly the most beautiful watering place on the North Devon Coast*' and as a consequence they felt that traffic expectations would be high. The directors hoped that the SM&LR would be successfully carried through, as it would add to traffic on their line. However, subsequent minutes showed there was only limited support for the proposal; the matter was first postponed (29th April 1879) and then it was confirmed there was to be no progress (31st October 1879). Instead, in order to facilitate traffic on the D&SR and link Lynton and outlying villages to the line, a coach service between South Molton and Lynton commenced on Monday 5th July 1880.

THE LYNTON COACH SAGA

An estimate of the cost of a coach service was prepared by George Bush of George Nympton. Broadly, it would be £1,340 to establish: 20 horses at £50 each, £220 for a coach (referred to as a '*brake van*') and spare, three sets of horse harnesses for £90, with clothing and stable utensils at £30. The coach was to leave Lynton at 8.30am to connect with the 11 o'clock train, so passengers could arrive in London at 6.00pm. The coach would return from South Molton at 3.00pm, connecting with the 9.00am departure from Paddington. Correspondence was entered into with the GWR coaching department at Barnstaple and they suggested that there should be a change of horses at the halfway stage, thus three sets of four horses would ordinarily suffice for the proposed service: two at Sandyway (the halfway point, to help on the hills), one spare at Sandyway and one spare at Lynton. The estimated running costs per week were Horses – £10 4s 0d, Coachman – £1 5s 0d, Guard (to attend to horses at South Molton) – £1 0s 0d, Stablemen (1 at Lynton/1 at Sandyway) £2 0s 0d. Ten horses were acquired for £450 from Pedrick & Brice in Exeter but there was difficulty in finding a coachman. The coach ran for the 1880 summer season but Bush complained that a lack of advertising had reduced takings and caused a loss to his business. In preparation for summer 1881, the GWR at Exeter wrote to Bush to see if the coach would run, informing him that it would be advertised if it did. The D&SR contributed £350 in July 1880. Lynton coach income accounted for on 28th March 1881 was £52 10s 0d. Minehead proprietors were now arranging for a second coach to work between Minehead and Barnstaple via Lynton and Ilfracombe. Bush suggested this would take traffic from the D&SR coach service and impact on passengers using the railway. He decided to sell his horses by auction but they only realised £352 16s 0d at Exeter, resulting in a £100 loss. He considered that he had been put at a disadvantage, with Mr Locke suggesting to the auctioneer that they could be '*given away*'.

The Tiverton & North Devon Railway (T&NDR) was proceeding at this time, a project that was also being looked at optimistically at bringing in extra traffic and revenue. Meanwhile, the Rev'd C.P. Quicke of Ashbrittle (near Bathealton) had written to the GWR to complain about the facilities at Morebath and Venn Cross stations.

At the 31st October 1878 meeting, Mr Granville Somerset resigned as a director but a Mr George Crawley of Brighton had been appointed to the Board by December. At this time, there was pressure to replace the solicitors, as some Board members wanted 'their man' to replace Mr Wainwright, 'the incumbent', but he had the support of Messrs Moysey and Locke. At the 17th December meeting, Montague Bere stated that he wished to resign as Chairman due to a lack of support but to retain his Board position; Mr Herring was then elected as Chairman. Lord Poltimore and Mr Locke were asked to go to London to remove Combe & Wainwright as solicitors to the trustees but they declined. In February 1879, Mr Wolstenhome wrote concerning an issue over cheques issued to certain bond holders and Messrs Scrimegour & Co. totalling £25,450; he wished to know who signed the cheques and who was present to witness that. Mr Bush reported on traffic: '*during the month of January the traffic on the line has been dull, although the returns for the week ended 25th* [January] *of this station* [South Molton] *are equal to the corresponding period last year*'. The new timetable had reduced train mileage by discontinuing the mid-day trains from Barnstaple and the 8.40pm from Taunton. Whilst the directors regarded the withdrawal of the mid-day train as acceptable, the withdrawal of the 8.40pm train was seen as inconvenient to the district. It would have been better if the first train of the day had been cancelled ('*which frequently passes this station empty*'). Combe & Wainwright were removed as solicitors for the company in the case of Locke *versus* Grant (as reported on 7th March 1879). Messrs Taylor & Hayles of Grays Inn were appointed in their stead.

The GWR renewed the agreement (originally set for 21st December 1881) with the Post Office for transport of mails on the line; this was to continue at the rate of £200 per annum.

At the 4th April meeting, the Midland rebate for the year ended 31st December 1878 showed passenger receipts of £939 14s 3d and goods of £200 12s 9d, a total of £1,140 7s 0d, less £627 3s 10d (55%), leaving £513 3s 2d, of which the rebate was 10% *i.e.* £51 6s 4d. The directors also expressed their regret at the postponement of the proposed railway to Lynton, as they were convinced the opening of the line would have added considerably to the company's receipts. Mr Muggeridge stood down as Company Secretary in April.

The half year to 30th June 1879 showed a decrease in all traffic compared to a year earlier, this being due to a great depression in trade, the wet season affecting tourist traffic and the closure of the iron mines temporarily. This slowness in trade and reduction of revenues continued for the next six months, despite the fact that some of the iron mines had re-opened. Mr John Wade was appointed Company Secretary on 4th July.

In December 1879, the GWR wrote to request a refreshment room at Barnstaple, which was to be financed at the same time as the narrowing of the line's gauge, and once built was to be let by public tender to the highest bidder. The sudden death of Mr George Crawley was also announced; this created a vacancy on the Board but it was decided not to replace him as they still had six directors.

Mr John Wade was appointed Receiver on 19th December 1879 by the Master of the Rolls in the High Court of Justice. This was to take effect from 1st January 1880, on behalf of the plaintiffs (that is the directors and the 'A' debenture holders) of '*all rents, tolls, fares, charges and other revenue and income* [that] *shall be payable by the GWR to the D&SR under the agreement of 6 March 1865 … and of the entire undertaking of the company*'.

At the 26th January 1880 meeting, the cost for narrowing the line was stated as £11,265 8s 9d. Mr Hawkins was charged with the responsibility of approaching the GWR to get it reduced but it was later reported at the 5th March meeting that this was unlikely to be achieved. At this meeting, Mr Herring was appointed Chairman with Mr William Bailey Hawkins as Deputy Chairman. Lord Potimore and George Moysey resigned as directors and were, as a consequence, disqualified from acting as trustees under the 1868

Scheme of Arrangement. The 2nd April meeting was informed that the anticipated bill for the refreshment room at Barnstaple was £1,676 10s 0d and there was also the cost of building a commercial slaughterhouse; the total, including narrowing the gauge, was not to exceed £12,941 18s 9d.

By summer 1880, Mr Grierson of the GWR was in correspondence with the D&SR in regard to the T&NDR and the interchange of traffic at Dulverton. The agreement between the three companies was approved, as noted at the 16th September board meeting. At this time also the agreement with the GWR for narrow gauging the D&SR was sealed, with Court of Chancery approval being given. The GWR then commenced preparatory works.

In October 1880, a Mrs Nelder had written to the Board about a refreshment room at Dulverton and a copy had been sent to the GWR.

An exchange of letters between the GWR and Lord Fortescue over the renaming of Castle Hill station was presented at the 6th January 1881 Board meeting. At the 4th March meeting, Messrs Bere and Locke referred to the *'great inconvenience'* which existed in working the railway, owing to the impossibility of getting information by telegraph to and from the various stations when trains were delayed on the line. The Secretary was to write to the GWR on this matter.

BROAD GAUGE

The GWR and B&ER were initially built to the broad gauge, that is a distance of 7 feet 1/4 inch between the two running rails. It was Brunel's idea and it was thought it would allow higher speeds and better comfort than the so called 'narrow gauge' (standard gauge) that was adopted throughout the rest of the country. Unlike standard gauge track, the broad gauge rails were generally not supported by sleepers running across the rails but by longitudinal timbers, with cross timbers at each joint and intermittently in between. The longitudinal timbers, 15 feet long, 15 inches wide and 5 inches deep, were laid flat and the rails screwed to them. Initially, 10-inch diameter piles were sunk into the ground at each cross-member but these were found to be too rigid when the ground beneath the longitudinal timbers settled and so were removed. This type of construction was known as 'baulk road'. However, as noted elsewhere, the D&SR was built in the conventional manner with transverse sleepers. The gap between double lines of broad gauge rails was 6 feet 2 1/2 inches.

THE CHANGE OF GAUGE 1878-1881

James Grierson, General Manager of the GWR, recommended to his Board in August 1878 that all remaining branches should be narrowed. The Company would thus being able to retire ageing rolling stock and avoid the need to transfer goods. This resulted in regular correspondence between the GWR and the D&SR directors, and a report was produced on 23rd October 1878 in respect of altering the gauge on branch lines north of Exeter. This stated that:

> *'The desirability of altering at an early date the gauge of these branch lines arises partly from the convenience that would be obtained in working the passenger, goods and mineral traffic, but more especially because of the difficulty experienced in keeping up sufficient broad gauge stock without constructing new vehicles which was first urged by the late Mr Armstrong as a reason for altering the gauge ...'*

A large percentage of the locomotive stock was ageing and certain classes of engine were in short supply. There were also complaints from Second and Third Class passengers that broad gauge carriages were poor compared to the more modern stock. At this date, the broad gauge fleet comprised 230 locomotives (130 passenger and 100 goods). The average age of passenger locomotives was 15 3/4 years (the age range being 10-30 years), whilst goods engines averaged 15 7/8 years (10-26 in range). There were 487 broad gauge carriages (299 being between 16 and 32 years old). Of the 3,519 broad gauge wagons, 2,401 were 10 to 38 years old, of which 1,181 were 23-29 years old.

The report summarised the stock requirements of the Barnstaple line:

Locomotives:	Passenger	5
	Goods	4
Total		**9**
Carriages:	First Class	1
	First/Second Composite	7
	Second/Third Composite	2
	Third Class	8
	Horse Boxes	2
	Other	1
Total		**21**
Average daily wagons required		40
Estimate total wagons required		120

The report stipulated that the 42 miles and 40 chains would require the sum of £16,593 13s 11d to alter the gauge, including locking equipment. This was out of an overall total of £69,258 referred to in the report for the conversion of eight lines (including the proposed doubling of the Yeovil line). At the 4th July 1879 board meeting, the D&SR directors stated that they would allow the GWR a return of 4% on the money raised for the purpose of narrow gauging, with a first charge on gross receipts prior to the division under their agreement. However, they wanted to restrict the expenditure to not exceed £10,000.

The following table is a summary of the costs of gauge conversion of local lines, as extracted from records held at the National Archives. The Yeovil figure is a net total, the cost of £9,950 being offset by the £5,672 value of materials removed, as the lines were already mixed gauge:

Branch	Length (miles/chains)	Cost of Alteration
Portishead	9.40	£8,432 16s 02d
Devon & Somerset	42.40	£16,593 13s 11d
Minehead	8.00	£3,134 12s 00d
West Somerset	14.49	£6,373 15s 08d
Clevedon	3.44	£3,946 18s 04d
Tiverton	4.57	£3,012 10s 02d
Chard	13.16	£6,932 06s 08d
Yeovil (mixed gauge)	19.75	£4,278 02s 10d
Sub total		£52,704 15s 09d
Doubling Yeovil Branch	7.18	£16,554 00s 00d
Total		£69,258 15s 09d

Regarding the D&SR the report stated:

> *'The narrowing of this Branch would be an inconvenience as regards passengers and luggage and parcels booked through by fast trains from London to Barnstaple and Ilfracombe, which are now taken through, but which would have to be transferred at Taunton if the gauge were altered and the importance from a passenger traffic point of view, of narrowing this branch, is not so great as some of the others.*
>
> *The transfer of goods at Taunton however, naturally operates prejudicially to the traffic, and as regards Cattle from Barnstaple to the neighbourhood of Northampton, Banbury and other narrow gauge destinations.*
>
> *The large amount of transfer thrown upon Taunton without any corresponding additions to the accommodation there has occasioned frequent delays and additional expense, and if the present arrangements*

were likely to be permanent, a large expenditure at Taunton, to provide additional transfer accommodation could not long be defended.

If the gauge is altered, the only additional accommodation which is contemplated to provide other than lengthening platforms and sidings consequent on the alterations of the gauge is at Milverton and Wiveliscombe, where increased siding accommodation is much needed and to make Milverton a crossing station.'

The discussions and correspondence that followed resulted in an agreement dated 31st July 1880, between the GWR and D&SR on the narrowing of the gauge. The next table shows the consequent cost of converting each station and certain other locations on the D&SR, followed by a breakdown of some the costs involved. At this date, Florence Siding and Thomas' Siding (near Milverton) were operational and so were included in the locking costs:

BARNSTAPLE BRANCH	ALTERATION – £ S D	LOCKING – £ S D
Narrowing branch	11,103 10 00	
Barnstaple station		345 14 04
Swimbridge		227 06 01
Castle Hill		265 07 00
South Molton		225 06 04
Bishops Nympton & Molland		172 10 04
East Anstey		347 17 04
Dulverton		344 05 00
Morebath		146 18 08
Venn Cross		174 00 04
Wiveliscombe	686 00 00	397 12 00
Milverton	1,326 00 00	345 00 00
Norton Junction (D&S part only)		244 11 02
Thomas' siding		135 01 04
Florence siding		106 14 00
SUB-TOTAL	13,115 10 00	13,115 10 00
TOTAL		16,593 13 11

BREAKDOWN – ITEM	COST (£)
3,400 chains main line @ 14s per chain	2,380
400 chains sidings @ 20s per chain	400
66 switches @ 25s ea.	82
74 crossings @ 10s ea.	37
148 guards @ 10s ea.	74
74 new crossings @ £15 ea.	1,110
1 turntable	20
1 engine table	70
1 engine pit	130
1 chain truck weighbridge,	
strengthening bridges and viaduct with beams under new rail	530
300 tons of rails @ £8 per ton	2,400
200 tons of fangs @ £13 per ton	2,600
4,000 sleepers @ 5s ea.	1,000
Ballast under new line	250
TOTAL	11,103

The GWR wrote to the BoT on 11th October 1880, expecting the gauge narrowing to take place in '*the present year*' and emphasising that the '*conversion does not involve any extensive alterations at the stations … It will of course be necessary to bring the alterations into use as soon as the gauge has been narrowed and before the actual completion of the whole of the works … and I assume that the Board of Trade will agree to this being done … the Company will give notice when the works are completed*'. They clearly wanted to minimise the disruption to services but had to write again on 4th May 1881, as the project was delayed.

The Board minutes of 29th April 1881 stated that the 16th-17th May had been set aside for carrying out the gauge conversion. The BoT gave sanction to this on 9th May 1881 and the work actually took place over a long weekend commencing on Saturday 14th and lasting until Tuesday 17th May. Thus the section from Norton Junction to Wiveliscombe had only ten years of use as a broad gauge line, whilst from there to Barnstaple was a mere eight years. That the work could be done so quickly was a triumph of forward planning and the mobilisation of large numbers of platelayers and permanent way staff from other areas.

Little detail is known about the conversion of the D&SR specifically but the normal process of reducing the gauge by cutting the transoms to the appropriate shorter length and then slewing one of the running rails to the reduced gauge width could not be used here. Presumably, for most of the line, a new line of chairs and running rail could be laid inside the existing track, the redundant rail then being removed later, although points clearly would have required more planning.

The last broad gauge train left Barnstaple on the night of Saturday 14th May, at which point the line was handed over to the engineers department. On Wednesday 18th, two standard gauge passenger and one goods train ran, with the full normal service being resumed the following day.

AFTER THE BROAD GAUGE

Around this time (April/May 1881), the Board received a letter from Mr Bush stating that surveyors were laying out a new line from Dulverton to Lynton, which would also join with the Exe Valley line at the former but little more was heard of this subsequently. The D&SR's problems continued; they were still plagued by claims (from Hassard, the engineer, Mr Hammett, a former local agent, and a Mr Cocks), and further surplus lands were to be released.

In April 1882, reference was made by the Board regarding further improvements to the line that would be finished by the summer, so that the '*road will be in first class order*'. In October 1882, the work on the T&NDR was reaching completion and the directors were optimistic of additional traffic arising from its opening. Further, the gauge narrowing had apparently led to an increase in traffic revenues of £797 18s 9d in the six months to 30th June 1882, compared with the same period in 1881. Of that increase, £490 was passenger receipts and £247 from goods.

In June 1882, Mr Herring was re-elected Chairman and Mr Bailey Hawkins re-elected Deputy Chairman. The GWR's plan of the proposed junction with the T&NDR at Morebath had been submitted and was approved.

In March 1883, there was correspondence with the GWR in respect of the irregular working of the Down goods to Barnstaple. The new bay platform at Barnstaple had not yet been brought into use, as it had not been inspected and approved by the BoT. At the April, meeting the cost of gauge narrowing was confirmed at £11,910 15s 5d and the GWR wrote to the D&SR receiver to pay its share to 31st December 1882, namely £297 15s 4d.

In early April 1883, the Board noted that the refreshment room at Barnstaple would be finished before the summer, thus improving passenger facilities at that station. The Board later reported that the licence to run the premises had been retained in the name of the stationmaster! The BoT report by Major General Hutchinson on gauge narrowing was received towards the end on 28th April. An issue with this was disclosed in a letter from the BoT to the GWR of 30th April 1883, stating '*until the rails have been altered in position on the Castle Hill and Tone viaducts and the requirements in the report have been complied with the Board of Trade cannot approve of the alteration of the gauge*'. Hutchinson's report (following his inspection of 31st March), highlighted the fact that the rails were laid on longitudinal sleepers secured to cross-girders with the rails placed vertically on the cross girder. However, in carrying out the regauging, one running rail over the viaduct had been left in position whilst the other was slewed over, thus creating an imbalance and an unequal distribution of weight; . He calculated this imbalance at 120 tons for one girder and 80 tons for the other. This clearly required rectification and the track would need to be repositioned in the centre of the road across the viaducts. Once completed he would give his approval to the regauging.

The charge for the carriage of mails was increased from £200 to £250 with effect from 1st January 1884, as proposed by the GWR and accepted by the Post Office.

In April 1884, the GWR had written with respect to putting in an approach road to the Down platform at Dulverton station and approving accommodation for the loading of horses. On 25th of the month, the GWR also wrote to the Assistant Secretary to the BoT to confirm '*the whole of the requirements contained in Major General Hutchinson's report … have been complied with, with the exception of the extension of Thomas' siding …*'; the reason for not altering this siding at Milverton was because the GWR had announced that they proposed to remove it in a month (to which the D&SR agreed). The final sanction of the BoT was now awaited and was duly received in Major General Hutchinson's letter of 17th May 1884.

Traffic reduced in the six months to 30th June 1884, due to the depressed economic conditions but, despite the continuing difficult economy, traffic returns in fact picked up for the next two half-year periods (compared to the previous year). The Board noted that the T&NDR had opened for traffic from 1st August 1884.

At the 8th January 1885 meeting, a memorial from the inhabitants of Morebath and district requested a new station at the junction of the D&SR with the T&NDR. Also, the Filleigh & Blackmoor Gate Railway Bill was in the offing. The D&SR wished to make a claim against the T&NDR for Dulverton station rents and land upon which their junction was laid. There was also tabled a proposed alteration to the Wiveliscombe station approach but whilst the directors had no objection, they had no power to authorise the expenditure of the company's money for such purpose.

The 29th October 1885 half-yearly meeting brought attention to the fact that the GWR had obtained powers to construct a short line at Barnstaple to effect a junction with the L&SWR (the Barnstaple Junction Railway). An agreement was made between the GWR and L&SWR to afford a link between Barnstaple and Ilfracombe.

A financial summary of the company at 31st December 1885 makes for interesting reading and analysis, as the following table shows:

CREDIT	£ s d	DEBIT	£ s d
Capital Account balance	**288 13 2**	**Cash at bank**	**503 18 3**
'A' debenture stock accrued interest	**179,004 0 3**	**Traffic a/cs due to Co.**	**7,386 11 6**
'B' debenture stock accrued interest	**103,290 5 2**	**Net Revenue (in debit)**	**274,867 6 9**
Interest and costs	**5,926 15 0**	**Bond suspense**	**15,926 15 0**
Construction debt (Bond granted)	**10,000 0 0**	**Judgments suspense**	**12,963 11 9**
Unpaid interest warrants	**14 18 1**	**Outstanding amount**	**14 6 10**
Sundry unpaid current accounts debited	**174 6 8**		
Judgments IR (£12,565 15 7) & R.M. Riccard (£397 16 2)	**12,963 11 9**		
TOTAL	**311,662 10 1**	**TOTAL**	**311,662 10 1**

The deficit on net revenue was £274,867 6s 9d, which, in effect, was entirely due to interest on the debenture stocks. With the total annual traffic revenues earned for that calendar year of £27,655, without any obvious or dramatic increase in this, it would have taken nearly ten years to pay off the existing accrued interest. This does not allow for the interest that would have accrued in the meanwhile.

The annual interest cost of the issued debentures at this stage was as follows:

'A' debenture stock £270,000 at 6% annual interest	£16,200
'B' debenture stock £166,000 at 5% annual interest	£ 8,300
1872 'A' debenture stock £100,000 at 6%	£ 6,000
1874 'A' debenture stock £60,000 at 6%	£ 3,600
Total annual interest servicing cost at 31/12/1880	£34,100

At this time, annual net traffic revenues due to the D&SR amounted to £27,655 (year to 31st December 1885) and so, leaving aside other costs of the business relevant to the D&SR, there was an annual short fall of £6,445 in servicing the interest alone. It was not until 1890 that traffic revenues went over £30,000 per year and not until 1900 that revenues 'peaked', immediately prior to the takeover by the GWR, at £35,744; just enough to service the annual interest due in 1880.

At the April 1886 meeting, it was noted that the extreme downturn in the economy was depressing trade but results, in terms of traffic revenues, were holding up. The construction of the Barnstaple Junction Railway had started and was progressing with a view to completion by summer 1886. However, this timetable proved optimistic, as the heavy nature of the works subsequently delayed progress. The line eventually opened on 1st June 1887, '*thus affording continuous communication by the company's system to Ilfracombe*' and, as a consequence, the GWR coach service between Barnstaple and Ilfracombe was discontinued.

BUILDING THE BARNSTAPLE BRANCH RAILWAY (1885-1887)

In 1884 the GWR threatened to build an independent line from the D&SR at Castle Hill (Filleigh) to Ilfracombe, by-passing Barnstaple, and a Bill was formulated to present to Parliament. The locals and Barnstaple Corporation opposed this proposal (a petition to the GWR Board dated 26th November 1884 was signed by around 150 individuals). As a consequence, there was consultation between Archibald Scott (the L&SWR Traffic Manager) and James Grierson (GWR General Manager), which resulted in the Bill for the proposed independent line being dropped. Consideration was then given to the construction of a loop line to connect the GWR station with the L&SWR near Barnstaple Junction and, as a result of those discussions, they agreed not to oppose the GWR Bill for this. There were two proposals for this line; one was to cross the River Taw and join the L&SWR just south of their station (Scheme 1). The other was to join the L&SWR at Pottington (Scheme 2), by a line that would have stayed north of the River Taw. Barnstaple merchants, traders and inhabitants supported Scheme 2 and wrote to the GWR on 19th December 1884, on the premise that their commercial interests were best supported by this line. However, those south of the River Taw saw it differently. The inhabitants of Bideford, Northam, Appledore, Clovelly, Hartland, Torrington Westward Ho! and Bude all independently made representations in support of Scheme 1. These were sent to the GWR in January and February 1885, stating that Scheme 1 would be '*most conducive to their interests and convenience*'. Fortunately, before the GWR directors made a final decision, the inhabitants of Barnstaple had also put their support behind Scheme 1. Their letter stated that the directors had come to the conclusion that Scheme 1 is the one that '*will afford the greatest amount of accommodation to the public and in this view the preponderating*

The GWR ran a coach service between Ilfracombe and Barnstaple and this is a Guard's Report for a journey on 26th October 1883. Note the trip took 1 hour and 40 minutes and all five passengers made the entire journey.

Great Western Railway. UP.

GUARD'S REPORT. ILFRACOMBE SERVICE. Oct 26 1883

1.40 P.m. o'Clock Break from ILFRACOMBE to BARNSTAPLE.

Stations.	Arrived. H.	Arrived. M.	Started. H.	Started. M.	No. of Passengers at Starting.	No. of Passengers taken up on the Road.	No. of Passengers set down on Road or at Barnstaple.	No. of Passengers set down at Barnstaple Station.	REMARKS.
									Horses Breakther
Ilfracombe			1	40	5				720
Two Potts Tollgate	2	5	-	-					331
Fry's Hotel	2	25	2	35					384
Mear Top Tollgate	3	-	3	-					292
Barnstaple	3	20						5	

Name of Driver: J. Hussell Guards' Signatures: C Lemon

opinion of the District appears to concur'. Scheme 2 was then abandoned. An extract of the GWR Board minutes of 25th March 1885 indicated that the L&SWR and the GWR were prepared to agree to 'Line No. 1' subject to satisfactory terms being agreed in a formal contract.

The relevant plan of the junction railway had been submitted to Parliament as reported at the D&SR board meeting of 30th April 1885 and the junction arrangements were finally agreed on 3rd July, with the GWR undertaking to use no other route to Ilfracombe. They were also granted the use of Barnstaple L&SWR station at an annual rent of £250 and payment of 8% on cost of extra accommodation provided.

Matters progressed so that the line from the GWR station to Barnstaple L&SWR was authorised under the Act of 31st July 1885. GWR Board minutes of 28th October 1885 stated '*... instructed to arrange without delay for the purchase of the lands required for the Barnstaple Branch line*' and tenders were then invited for the construction of the line. The '*Barnstaple Branch Railway*', as it was known in the contractor's agreement of 30th November 1885, was to be 1 mile and 29 chains in length. Under this agreement, works were to commence on or before 1st December 1885 and be completed by 1st June 1886, with a penalty of £100 per week for any delays. However, the D&SR Board subsequently commented (minutes of 28th October 1886) that '*the heavy nature of a portion of the works prevented the opening of the new line by the summer of 1886*'. In addition, there were debates over the height of the embankments and pedestrian access over the Taw bridge. Despite these distractions, the line was eventually opened on 1st June 1887.

The original tender for the works was drawn up by George Meakin, John William Dean and Thomas Wilberforce Davies, who were based near Merthyr Tidfill, Glamorgan. This was to provide all the materials and labour, except ironwork and woodwork, needed for the superstructure of the viaduct (Taw Bridge) and stipulated a tender price of £14,500. The contractor's agreement was drawn up between Messrs Meakin & Co. and the GWR, dated 30th November 1885, and stipulated that the line would run from a junction with the D&SR line, about 40 chains east of Barnstaple GWR station in the Parish of Landkey, and terminate at the junction of the L&SWR in the Parish of Tawstock, at about 13 chains south of the goods shed of Barnstaple Junction station. Construction of the actual railway junctions at each end was not included in the contract.

The contractors had the responsibility for the provision of plant, tools and machinery, and for the earthworks, waterways, drains and ballasting, to the extent it would be ready to receive the permanent way, then the laying of the permanent way and packing of the ballast. The contractors were to be provided with the sleepers, rails and other permanent way materials by the GWR.

The contract was fairly clear in terms of the build requirements, with the engineer overseeing the contractors' work. The land on which the line was to be built was provided by the GWR (and this included approach roads) but the contractor was responsible for clearing the land, removing houses and roads as appropriate, although this was at the GWR's cost. The earthworks were defined to include all excavations, embankments and surface forming (ballasting), as well as the diversion of streams, roads and bridges or their approaches. The depth of cuttings was stipulated to the extent that the bottom of them on completion were to be at least 6 inches below the formation level (but excavated to not less than 18 inches of the formation line) and they were to be kept drained of water during excavations. Also, on their sides, there should be oblique drainage channels cut to aid drainage, being not less than 18 inches deep and filled with large stones. Whilst the material excavated from the cuttings could be used for any of the embankments, the surplus spoil was to be

EXTRACTS FROM A MEMORIAL FROM THE INHABITANTS OF BARNSTAPLE TO THE GWR 1885

'Application is about to be made to Parliament by the GWR for two lines connecting the D&SR with the L&SWR, the one crossing the River Taw and forming a junction with the SW line near their station, the other running to and forming a junction with the Ilfracombe line, near where the Quay line branches off and we note that application is proposed for power to construct a railway from Castle Hill on the D&SR to Ilfracombe.

There is strong feeling in this Town and neighbourhood that if the line from Castle Hill is proceeded with it will be injurious to the interests of the Town and there would be no sufficient inducement to construct either of the other lines.

... the provision of a means of communication between the D&SR and Ilfracombe would be obtained by the construction of a junction line between the two railways at Barnstaple and by means of a line crossing the River the stations would be in convenient communication with one another even if it were not practicable to have only one station for all trains.

We consider that the injury to this Town would be irreparable if in consequence of a want of unified effort on the part of your two companies an independent line to Ilfracombe were to be constructed as while it would not afford that Town any facilities which it would not obtain if the Great Western trains ran over the existing line it would equally deprive us of the convenience to which we consider we are entitled.'

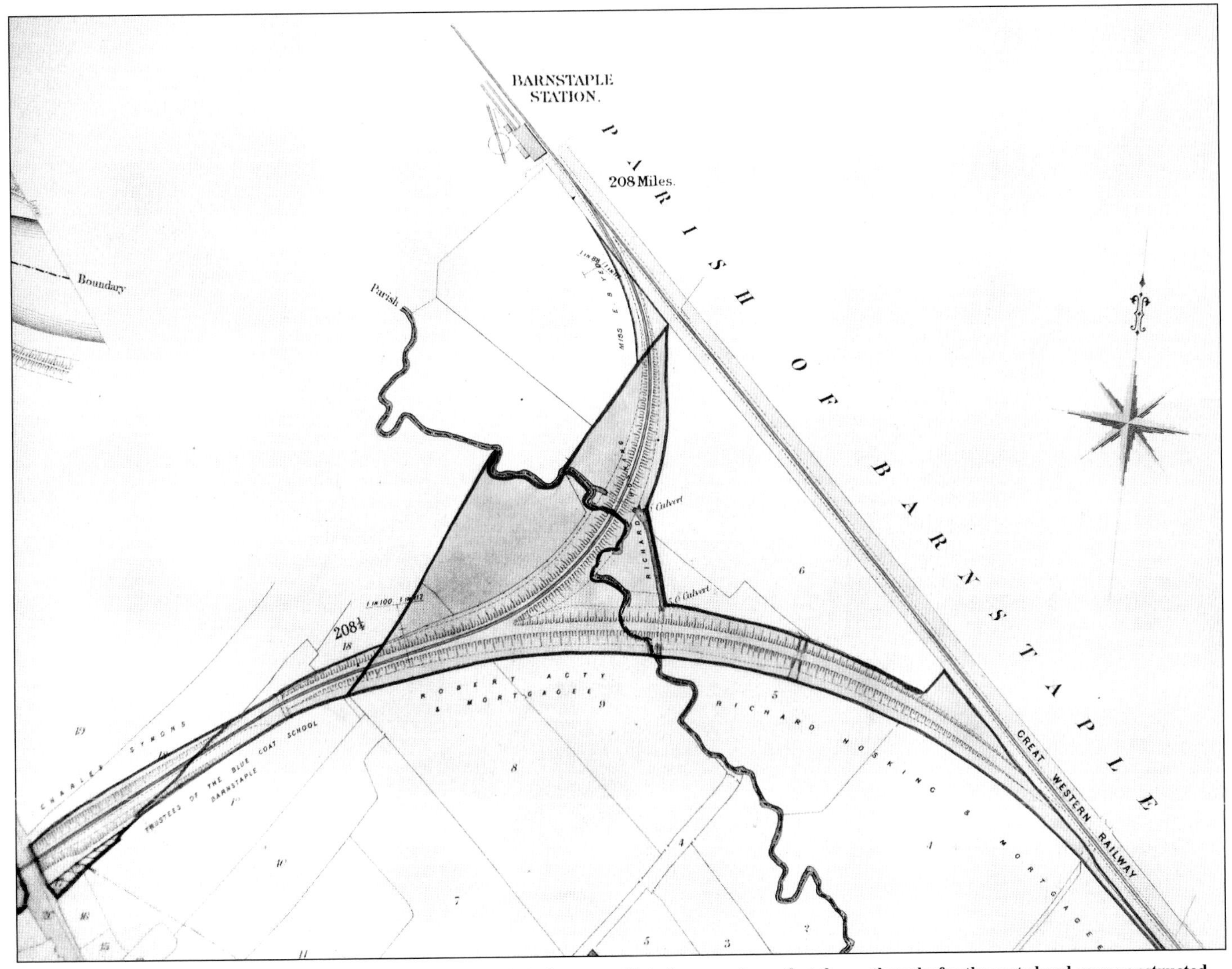

The Barnstaple Branch Railway as shown on the GWR 1887 2 chain survey. Note the map shows that the earthworks for the east chord were constructed at the same time, although in the event, this connection, permitting direct running to Ilfracombe, was not laid in until 1905. ***Courtesy National Archives***

disposed of (there was a penalty of 2 shillings for each cubic yard left behind). The embankments were to be built bigger than shown on the relevant drawings, so as to allow twelve months for settlement before the banks would be trimmed to size '*to form a solid smooth surface*' and sown with seed. Permanent cross-drains were made at every chain in the formation and more where the ground was naturally wetter.

The ballast for the formation could be obtained from excavations if it was of the appropriate quality, otherwise the contractor had to source it. Ballast would be course for the lower 12 inches, with fine ballast on top (or in totality if course ballast was not available). The '*clean and perfect*' ballast was to be laid on an '*uninjured and perfect formation*'. Any imperfect ballast was to be removed at the cost of the contractor.

Buildings were defined, as was brickwork, masonry, timber and iron constructions, such as bridges, viaducts, culverts and retaining walls. The building work was to be commenced immediately, as this would allow the structures to stand and settle before the earthworks were commenced. All building works were to be in brick (their size and type being defined in the contract, as was the mix of cement and concrete) unless specified. Roads were to be brought up to the bridges, drains aligned and proper materials were to be packed against the wing-walls of the bridges. In summary, the building works comprised three brick overbridges (at 36, 51 and 59 chains on the route), one ornamental underbridge (at 76 chains), the bridge over the River Taw and two occupation crossings at each end of the cutting.

The wrought ironwork was specified as Staffordshire iron (with no blisters or scales), having a breaking weight of 22 tons per square inch when tested in the direction of the fibre of the iron. The cast iron was required to be '*perfectly clean sound castings*', free from honeycombe or other defects. No. 1 Pig Iron was expected, being one-third Welsh/ Shropshire and two thirds Scotch [*sic*]. On completion, three coats of red lead or other approved paint was required to be added before rusting commenced. The structure of the Taw bridge is analysed further in Volume 2. Messrs Edward Finch Limited of Chepstow had the contract to supply the ironwork at £9 10s per ton.

The fencing was clearly defined to comprise straight, sound and well shaped split oak or sawn larch posts, free from bark, 7 feet 8 inches high and 16 square inches of cross section at the smallest and 18 square inches at best. These were to be placed 9 feet apart (centre to centre) and left 4 feet 8 inches above the ground. There were five horizontal oak or larch rails (at least $5^1/_2$ square inches of sectional area), clear of bark, to be fixed between the posts and supported by an intermediate small post of oak or larch sunk 1 foot into the ground, so as to keep out lambs, sheep, pigs and cattle. A ditch was to be cut near the fence for drainage.

LEFT: An unidentified Class '43XX' 2-6-0 hauls a Taunton-bound train tender first around the West Curve on 4th August 1951. The coaches may well have started from Ilfracombe but the locomotive will have been attached at Barnstaple Junction; after running round the train at the recently renamed Barnstaple Victoria Road station, the 'Mogul' can then proceed chimney first to Taunton. The nascent housing estate in the background has grown considerably since this view was taken. ***Roger Sellick collection, NRM***

BELOW: Another 'Mogul' about to pass under Newport Road bridge as it climbs out of Victoria Road on the last leg of its journey from Taunton to Barnstaple Junction. It has traversed the West Curve and passed South Junction Signal Box which can be seen behind the train. Note the L&SWR coaches.

As for the permanent way, the contractor was charged with ensuring '*the greatest accuracy must be observed in laying the rails perfectly straight*' on those sections which require it, to the 4 feet $8^1/_2$ inches gauge. The contractor was also to fix mile and quarter-mile posts and gradient posts in GWR style at the appropriate locations.

For such a short extension, there were a number of issues. Land had to be purchased, disputes arose in respect of certain pieces which had to be resolved and permission had to be granted for access over the River Taw by the Harbour Department.

Land purchases involved a number of vendors. Mr Charles Chichester of Hale, Bishops Tawton, sold just over 4 acres of land for £1,200 on 10th December 1885. Miss C.B. Yeo did slightly better, selling just over 1 acre for £550. Blue Coat School did a deal in June 1886 for a small corner of a good grazing field (rented at £8 per acre) for £220. A deal was also done with a Mr Tamlyn over land of a little more that 3 acres, where he was looking for a sale at £700 plus some capitalised rent (at £5 5s); the rent element was waived.

Mr Chichester had a minor dispute over land by the Taw bridge on the east bank of the river. The contractor had fenced the land to the bank in order to build the bridge and abutments but the river was left unfenced. As a consequence, Mr Chichester's cattle were able to stray from the south side along the river and into the park to the north of the construction site. There was a risk of cattle fouling the river and £5 was paid for Mr Chichester to erect a suitable fence and maintain it himself.

On 9th November 1885, the Harbour Department wrote and stated their concern over the rights and interests of the Crown in respect of the foreshore and river bed '*which will be interfered with*'. However, matters were resolved by 23rd March 1886, when the Harbour Department sent a letter confirming '*conveyance of certain foreshore and bed of the River Taw, which they* [the Harbour Department] *have granted to the Great Western Railway Company for the purposes of a viaduct over the River Taw*'.

There had been on-going correspondence with the Harbour Department and the Corporation of Barnstaple about an increase in the headroom for clearance under the bridge. The original allowance of 6 feet 4 inches was proposed to be increased to 9 feet 2 inches. The proposal from the Town Council was for the GWR to build a footbridge across the river, alongside the rail bridge but the GWR disagreed and a number of months of correspondence and debate followed. The likely cost of the footbridge was stated as £1,200.

The debate over the increased height of the embankment and bridge continued. The GWR considered that there were four options open to them:

1. To revert to the statutory levels of the earthworks and bridge.

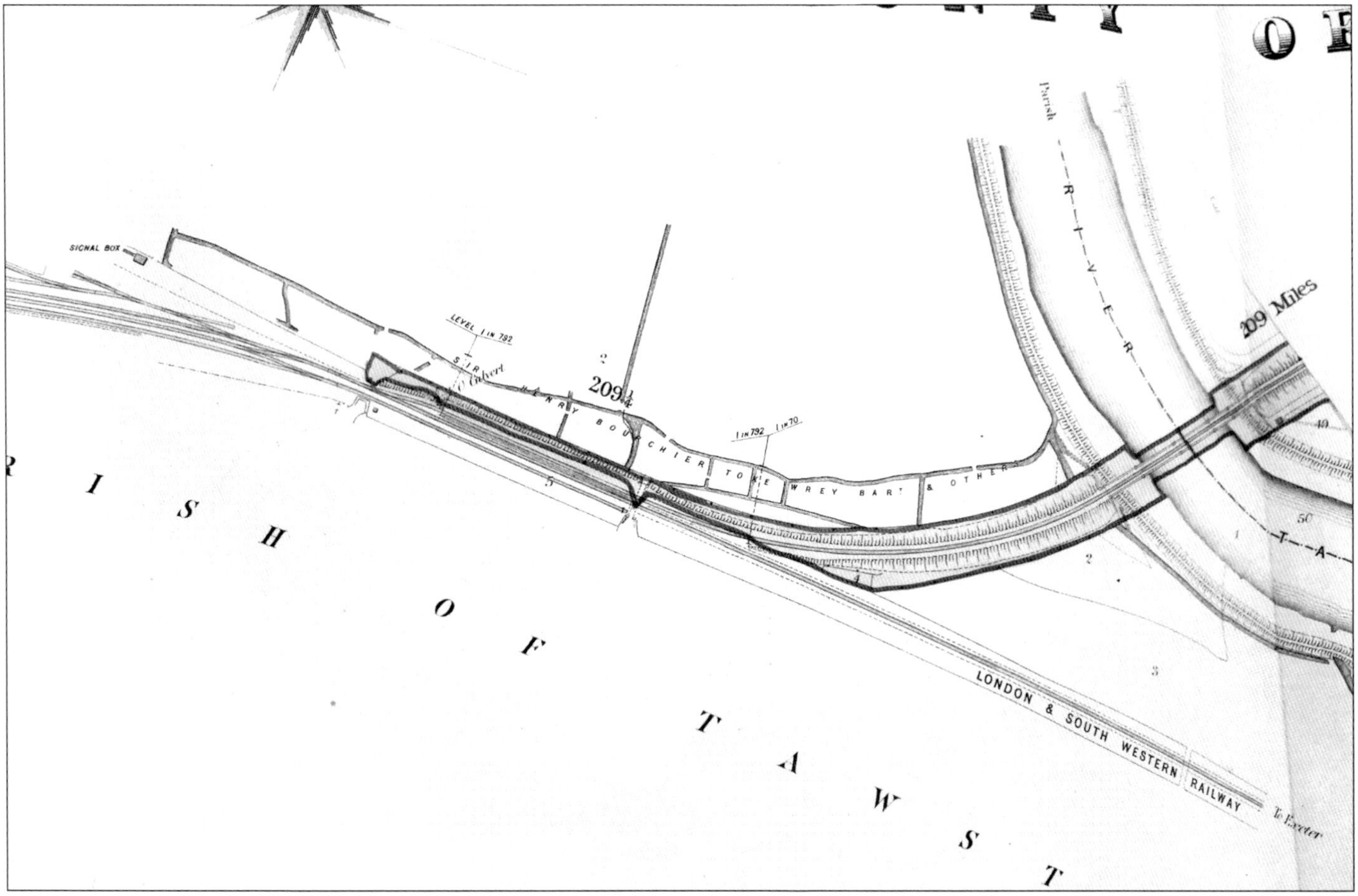

The Barnstaple Branch Railway and its connection to the L&SWR on the south side of the River Taw, with the bridge spanning it on the right. It survives today, carrying a foot and cycle path across the river. ***Courtesy National Archives***

Class '43XX' No. 5336 crosses the five spans of the Taw River Bridge on 15th August 1964 with the 10.17am Cardiff to Ilfracombe train. ***Edwin Wilmshust***

However, this would entail a loss of £5,000 of the £8,000 which it was believed would be saved by the proposed alterations.

2. To give public notice of the GWR's intention to make a greater deviation than authorised by statute, leaving the Corporation to apply to the BoT to decide the question of level of alteration permitted, as they were owners of the land.

3. To disarm the opposition by agreeing to the footbridge and then give the notices in outlined in No. 2 above.

4. To proceed with the works proposed, leaving the Corporation to take what ever steps they please (like application for injunction).

Having considered these options, the GWR proposed that No. 2 should be pursued and notices were duly placed:

'In PURSUANCE OF THE PROVISIONS for that purpose contained in the Railway Clauses Consolidation Act 1845 The Great Western Railway Company do hereby give notice that a Vertical Deviation is intended to be made in the levels of the Railway commencing in the Parish of Landkey in the County of Devon by a junction with the Devon and Somerset Railway and terminating in the Parish of Tawstock in the same county by a junction with the North Devon Railway of the London and South Western Railway which Railway the Great Western Railway Company are by the Great Western Railway Act 1885 authorised to construct and that such intended Deviation is entirely situated between a point four chains westward of the point marked in the deposited plans and sections referred to in the said Great Western Railway Act 1885 as four furlongs and a point two chains westward of the point marked on the same plans and sections as one mile and one furlong and does not at any point exceed nine feet beyond the statutory limit. Dated 27th day of May 1886.

FRED J. SAUNDERS Secretary to the Great Western Railway Company'

Extract from *The Barnstaple Times*, Tuesday, 1st June 1886.

Matters came to a head as a result of this notice of the increase in height (*'vertical deviation'*) of the line near the Taw bridge and the embankment leading to it (in fact the height was to increase by 4 feet on the east side and 2 feet on the west side of the bridge). It was published in at least two local papers, appearing in the *North Devon Herald* as well on 3rd June 1886. The 1845 Railway Clauses Act permitted certain deviations from plans (vertically 2 feet – although the D&SR had the statutory right to deviate to 5 feet and 10 yards horizontally) but what was being proposed was a vertical deviation which *'does not at any point exceed nine feet beyond the statutory limit'*. Not surprisingly, this sparked debate and controversy. The *Western Morning News* reported on 19th June 1886 *'that the scenic attraction of the grounds* [Rock Park, recently donated to the town by Mr W.F. Rock] *have been considerably injured and depreciated'*. As a consequence, the Town Council agreed at a special meeting on 16th June 1886 to oppose the GWR's application for the deviation and were also to appoint an engineer to help their cause, a Mr Joshua Thomas of Bristol. The council had concerns about the view of the River Taw looking up-stream from the park, as this vista would be blocked by the embankment and bridge. Also, there were potential drainage issues and a watercourse alongside the embankment to act as a storm drain was requested. They also suggested that a footway over the new river bridge should be considered, rather than the footbridge as originally proposed.

Allied to this there was also a reduction in the depth of the cuttings, the proposal being that they would be shallower than intended by 2 feet but this was in excess of the limit allowed under the Railway Clauses Consolidation Act of 1845. The key point here was that the railways passed under three roads in the Newport area of Barnstaple; the road heights would not be altered but the depths under the three brick bridges were 26 feet, 36 feet and 33 feet under the road (being 21, 31 and 28 allowing for the statutory deviation of 5 feet). Again the Corporation (who were responsible for road maintenance) initially objected to this but the GWR felt this objection was not sustainable.

Despite these distractions, the work progressed, being brought to completion and ready for inspection. The GWR confirmed on 18th May 1887 that the *'Single line of railway connecting the D&SR and the L&SWR at Barnstaple shall be worked by train staff and ticket in connection with the block telegraph'* and the Barnstaple Branch Railway was opened for traffic on 1st June 1887 (as reported in the board minutes of 7th July).

ROUTINE MATTERS

The board meeting of 29th April 1886 reported a land slip in the cutting near East Anstey station. In July 1887, it was reported that extra sidings were being considered at Dulverton and plans had been received in this regard. At the October meeting, there was a reference to a provision of a footbridge at Wiveliscombe but this was never authorised. The death of Montague Bere was reported at the 30th November 1887 board meeting. At the 7th June 1888 meeting, Mr Stephenson Robert Clarke was appointed as a director.

RESTRUCTURING (AGAIN) IN 1889

With the inability to service the interest on the debenture stocks and no obvious likelihood of a dramatic increase in traffic revenues to help cash flows, by the middle of 1888, the directors had no option but to seek assent from debenture holders, to go to the Court for a further restructuring under the provisions of the Railway Companies Act 1867. The proposed Scheme of Arrangement had received assents from holders of £132,712 worth of 'A' and 'B' debenture stockholders and the Board approved that the seal of the company be affixed to the proof of the Scheme, along with the declaration that the company was unable to meet its arrangements with creditors. The Scheme of Arrangement & Declaration was filed on 15th June 1888, EGM approval following on 17th July. There then followed an application to the stock exchange for the quotation of all new debenture stocks. At the 24th October half yearly meeting, the directors reported that the application to the Stock Exchange to list the 'A', 'B' and 'C' debenture stocks had been successful. At this time, the Board reported that £442,000 worth of assents had been received and this was nearly the requisite number for an immediate application to Court. Subsequently, there was confirmation that sufficient assents had been received as had the approval of the Court, so the Scheme of Arrangement could and did proceed; it was confirmed by 2nd February 1889, with enrolment in the Chancery Division of the High Court on 5th March 1889.

The new issue under the Scheme is summarised as follows:

1889 RESTRUCTRING	STOCK CANCELLED	NEW ISSUE (AUTHORISED)
'A' Debenture Stock	430,000	433,000
'B' Debenture Stock	166,000	430,000
'C' Debenture Stock		300,000
TOTAL	596,000	1,163,000

Total interest due at 30th June 1888 of £326,353 11s 2d was to be written off in pursuance of the Scheme of Arrangement in respect of 'A' and 'B' debentures as follows:

'A' Debentures. 202,328 11s 00
'B' Debentures 124,025 00s 02
Total. 326,353 11s 02

If this is compared with the 31st December 1885 position (page 89), where the accrued interest amounted to £282,294 then a further £44,059 of unpaid interest had been added to the arrears. The arrears of interest was to be converted to newly issued stock (see below).

The death of one of the D&SR's founder directors, John Locke of Northmoor House, Dulverton, was reported in the board meeting of 18th October 1888. His place on the Board was subsequently taken by Mr George Bush, on 25th April 1889. On a brighter note, the long-running claim by Mr Cocks (over conveyance of land at South Molton station) was settled for £90. An order dated 9th April 1889 was received in respect of Charles Rowcliffe (deceased), for settlement of value in respect of some land purchases in Bampton and Morebath parishes in the 1860s, under the Land Clauses Consolidation Act 1845. According to Mr Wade, the Secretary, in February 1872 Rowcliffe was offered a sum of £459 5s 0d in 'A' debenture stock in full discharge of his claims but this was disputed by his successors, hence the order. There was also £375 paid to the Courts in February 1871 under the said Act and Wade said that the D&SR were now entitled to have this returned.

At 30 June 1889 the restructured debentures were issued as follows:

	Issued	Unissued	Total
'A' Debenture Stock (1st charge)	432,000	1,000	433,000
'B' Debenture Stock (2nd charge)	428,957	1,043	430,000
'C' Debenture Stock (3rd charge)	248,817	51,183	300,000
Total	1,109,774	53,226	1,163,000

In addition, of course, the £259,455 ordinary shares and £12,000 preference shares remained in issue.

The new 'A' debenture stock was issued in substitution and satisfaction of the old 'A' debenture stock as follows:

– 1868 Scheme 270,000
– 1872 Act. 100,000
– 1874 Act. . . . . 58,957 (issued so far)
Total. £428,957

The total arrears of interest to be capitalised amounted to £511,896, whilst the amount to be issued as new 'B' debenture stock was £428,957. The new 'C' debenture stock was issued in part for the substitution of existing 'B' stock (£165,878) and the balance (£82,939) for (part) arrears of interest capitalised. Interest capitalised in 'B' stock (£248,957) and 'C' stock (£82,939) totalled the anticipated £511,896.

At the 53rd meeting on 23rd October 1890, the net receipts from the GWR for the year to 30th June 1890 was received and applied as follows:

Net Receipts to 31st December 1889 . . . . 8,510 14s 6d
Net Receipts to 30th June 1890. . . . . 6,452 17s 6d
Total. 14,963 12s 0d

'A' debenture stock 31st December 1889 . . . . 6,318 0s 0d
'A' debenture stock 30th June 1890 . . . . 6,318 0s 0d
'B' stock. 2091 3s 3d
Balance 236 8s 9d

Reverting to more mundane matters, the Board reported another land slip at East Anstey in April 1890. In August 1890, it was confirmed that the GWR had agreed to pay the proprietors of the Dulverton to Minehead stage coach a subsidy of 10 shillings per trip during the months of July, August and September, presumably as a means of encouraging traffic. With the financial restructuring complete, the Receiver was discharged with effect from 8th August and the final account passed and balance paid to the D&SR.

After the arrears of debenture interest had been capitalised, the financing structure looked like this at 31st December 1890:

CAPITAL	ORIGINAL	AS AT 31/12/1890	INCREASE
A Debenture Stock	430,000	433,000	3,000
B Debenture Stock	166,000	430,000	264,000
C Debenture Stock	nil	300,000	300,000
Preference Shares	12,000	12,000	nil
Ordinary shares	259,455	259,455	nil
Ordinary Shares not paid up	1,245	1,245	nil
TOTAL	868,700	1,435,700	567,000

The proceeds from the issuing of the stock was deployed as follows:
Expenditure incurred to 31st December 1890
for line open to traffic. 867,828 11s 1d
Ilfracombe Railway 6,895 10s 3d
TOTAL £874,724 01s 4d
Arrears of debenture interest capitalised 511,896 00s 0d
TOTAL £1,386,620 01s 4d

As a consequence, 37% of the stock issued was to cover for unpaid arrears of interest which had accrued over the previous twenty years or so – a clear indictment as to the lack of realistic and supportable financial return for the line. The numbers simply did not stack up.

At the 19th February 1891 board meeting, the directors agreed to a request from the GWR to have privilege priced tickets for adults at one quarter of the ordinary fare and one eighth for children.

The very severe weather of November and December 1890, which continued into the early part of 1891 and became known as the 'Great Blizzard', did not dramatically impact on the traffic return figures. On 10th March, the 7.35am train from Barnstaple was halted in a snow drift near Filleigh but was eventually released after three hours by a gang from Barnstaple and it proceeded to Taunton. The 9.20am train from Taunton failed to get through. Mr Campfield, the Divisional Superintendent, declared that no trains should run, so 11th March was a barren day, but the line was cleared that afternoon and services resumed the next day.

The net receipts for the six months to 30th June 1891, totalling £14,832 2s 3d was again applied to pay stockholders (as above). On 2nd July 1891, Mr Riccard's claim was settled for £100 plus £1,900 of 'C' debenture stock.

By September 1891, the Board comprised Mr Bailey Hawkins (Chairman), George Herring (Company Secretary), Arthur Barff, George Bush and Stephenson R. Clarke. Whilst it was agreed that interest on the 'A' debenture stock could be paid at 3% for the half year to 30th June 1891, the 'B' stock holders were only to get 0.5%. The proposal from the GWR for alterations at Dulverton, a siding at South Molton and improvements to the station master's house at Molland were rejected, as there were no funds to meet this expenditure. The Board added that the unissued 'C' stock was, under the terms of the Scheme of Arrangement, to be used to satisfy claims of creditors, not new works. By the 31st December 1891 meeting,

THE GAUGE CONVERSION 1892

Over the weekend of 21st-22nd May 1892, just over eleven years after the D&SR was narrowed to standard gauge, the main line and branches between Exeter and Truro were also converted. This required a significant movement of personnel and equipment ahead of the task and again when the job was completed. By reference to the *General Instructions* published at the time, it showed that approximately fifty-two workmen from the Barnstaple Branch were to help, travelling on 19th May on the 11.25am from Barnstaple to Taunton, where they would connect with the special workman's train from Bristol to Exeter. They returned on 24th May on the 11.05am from Taunton to Barnstaple service.

only a further £2,001 of 'C' debenture stock had been issued, £1,900 of this being to settle Mr Riccard's claim as referred to above.

At the 2nd March 1893 meeting, Mr Herring, who by then had become Chairman, announced his resignation due to other work commitments, Mr Bailey Hawkins resumed the chairmanship and Mr John Leonard Matthews was elected director.

In June 1893, a fall off in parcels traffic was noted, which was to be reported to the GWR. The total net receipts for the year ending 30th June 1893 was £15,013 19s 9d, these largely being applied to pay the 'A' and 'B' debenture holders, with £14 14s 8d being carried forward. For the next six months, the total receipts were down due in part to the on-going depression and the long coal strike. At April 1894, Mr John Henry Whadcoat (a large stock holder) made an offer to the Board to replace Mr Edward Wolstenholme as director.

At the 7th June 1894 meeting, it was noted that the GWR had written to announce that, from 1st July 1894, they would abolish differential Third Class fares and just charge 1d per mile for all Third Class passengers in the district. This had an immediate impact on passenger traffic returns, as can be seen from the summary analysis in Appendix 7. For the six months to 31st December 1894, there was a decrease of £716 16s 6d – being £10,359 0s 6d for 1893, dropping to £9,462 4s 0d at 31st December 1894. However, the D&SR Board hoped that passenger numbers would eventually increase to make up this shortfall. In addition, there were disastrous floods in the Taunton area which also knocked receipts.

NEW WORKS AT DULVERTON 1894

Lieutenant Colonel Yorke reported on his inspection: '*... the loop line at this place has been lengthened about 17 yards at the Taunton end and the station has been resignalled. The signal box is an old one but the frame has been relocked. It contains 16 working levers and 4 spaces ...*'. There was a reference to the possible relocation of the Distant signal but the report believed there was ample visibility, there being 1/2 mile before the signal was reached. The Up Distant signal was 900 yards from the station.

At the meeting of 4th October 1894, the proposed railway from Filleigh to Lynton was raised and considered. However, another scheme was highlighted in the 7th February 1895 minutes, with reference to the '*Barnstaple & Lynton Toy Railway*', a somewhat disparaging comment in respect of the proposed narrow gauge line, which had no link to the D&SR. As a consequence, the solicitor was requested to petition against the Bill and the GWR be informed. The Filleigh to Lynton railway even got as far as the GWR and D&SR discussing terms of working the line. At the 25th April 1895 board meeting, it was clear that the '*Toy*' railway was going to win, as the Lynton Bill was thrown out by a committee of the House of Lords.

On 20th May 1895, Barnstaple GWR station was decked out with bunting at very short notice for a visit by the Duke of Cambridge. He had been scheduled to travel on the 11.00am from Waterloo but missed the train and ventured west on the 11.45am from Paddington instead. The bunting, set up at the L&SWR station, was rapidly taken down and reinstated at the GWR one in time for his arrival there!

The 31st October 1895 board meeting had the directors receiving a memorial from the traders, agriculturalists and inhabitants of Dulverton and its neighbours, and a letter from the clerk of Dulverton Parish Council, as to the need for increased accommodation for goods traffic at their station. This was duly forwarded to the GWR and in reply they indicated that it was the D&SR's responsibility but, again, a lack of funds meant this would go nowhere. The external pressures on fares, such as the GWR having had to reduce all Third Class tickets from July 1894, also did not help the railway to service its obligations.

The half year to 31st December 1895 reflected an increase in passenger numbers: 122,822 passengers travelled, an increase of 2,382 over 1894, and receipts were up from £9,642 4s 0d to £9,913 7s 3d, an increase of £271 3s 3d. However, revenues remained lower than for the periods prior to the fares change. The passenger numbers were analysed as follows:

PASSENGER ANALYSIS 6 MONTHS TO 31/12/1895	NUMBER	PERCENTAGE
First Class	1,697	1.38
Second Class	2,447	1.99
Third Class	118,678	96.63
TOTAL	122,822	100.00

A more uniform scale of charges was adopted by the D&SR along the following scale from 1st May 1896:

CLASS OF TRAVEL...FARE
First ....Double the ordinary Third Class fare
Second – single....A Third Class fare plus 1/4 of that fare
Second – return...Price of a single Second Class fare plus 3/4 for a return

Whilst these initially resulted in a decrease of passenger receipts on the D&SR by £79 8s 0d for the period to 30th June 1896 – albeit goods increased by £369 14s 7d – there were increases for each of the years 1897-99 in passenger traffic.

At the 25th June 1896 meeting, a letter was shown, from the Parish Council of Wiveliscombe drawing to the GWR's attention the danger that existed at Croford owing to the close proximity of the D&SR to the highway. The council sent a plan of a proposed screen that could be provided at a cost of £80. Again the directors rejected the matter as they had no funds.

With the dire financial status being maintained and no hope of a recovery, at the 6th August 1896 Board meeting it was resolved that negotiations for the sale of the railway to the GWR be left to the chairman, Mr Bailey Hawkins.

The *Bristol Times* reported on 30th October 1896 the comments raised at the sixty-fifth ordinary half-yearly meeting of the D&SR shareholders. Whilst gross receipts for the half-year had increased by £292 13s 3d, this was accounted for by an increase in goods traffic of £369 14s 7d, with a consequent decrease in passenger receipts of £79 8s 0d, showing the impact of the GWR's fare reduction. It was acknowledged that the receipts would be absorbed by the debenture interest payments. This led to a question from a Mr Gilford of Bristol as to the state of negotiations for the D&SR to be absorbed by the GWR. Mr Bailey Hawkins stated that the negotiations had not reached a stage that could be disclosed to the shareholders; furthermore, they had stalled. There then followed a discussion on the difficulties of getting to Ilfracombe. There was criticism that the GWR did not stop enough express trains at Taunton, thus depriving the D&SR of traffic which would have enable passengers to get to Ilfracombe more directly. A discussion ensued about an alternative line to Ilfracombe '*through the valleys*' but it was acknowledged this would require extensive tunnelling so a more convenient route was being considered.

The 4th February 1897 board meeting was shown an application by Lord Fortescue for a siding at Filleigh, to serve a brick and tile works that he was about to establish near the station. Lord Fortescue was prepared to pay the cost and construct a loop line on his own land, '*enough to admit the separation of up and down traffic and easy access by GWR engines*'. The D&SR directors agreed to this proposal. On the other hand, the proposal by North Molton Council for a footpath to South Molton station was rejected, as there were no funds to meet the expenditure. However, the parish council subsequently agreed to do it themselves and pay for it but works then were delayed as the cesspool of the station drain had to be moved to an adjoining field and this had to be done at the Company's cost.

On 10th February, Stephenson R. Clarke resigned as a director to be replaced by Strachan Child Clarke. A modest increase in passenger recepits was reported at the 29th April 1897 half yearly meeting, at which it was also noted that the GWR were looking to make improvements to the service between Ilfracombe and Bristol. They were hoping to speed it up, to induce passengers to use the D&SR rather that the more circuitous and longer route via Exeter.

In 1898, an extended coal strike in the South Wales colliery district affected coal, coke and mineral traffic throughout the calendar year. This was, not surprisingly, reflected in goods receipts for 1898, with £15,193 recorded for 1897, down to £14,564 (a reduction of 4%) in 1898 but recovering again to £15,140 in 1899. It was specifically noted by the Board that goods receipts in the half year to 30th June 1898 were down by £394 8s 8d and in the subsequent period to 31st December by £290 9s 4d. The West of England Iron Co. complained of a lack of siding accommodation at Dulverton station on 10th March 1899.

Between June 1898 and 30th June 1901, £36,166 worth of 'C' debenture stock was issued to pay creditors (see below) leaving the final position as follows:

	ISSUED	UNISSUED	TOTAL
'A' Debenture Stock	433,000		433,000
'B' Debenture Stock	428,957	1,043	430,000
'C' Debenture Stock	287,114	12,886	300,000
Total	1,149,071	13,929	1,163,000

At the 12th January 1900 D&SR board meeting, the Great Western Railway Bill (Session 1900) was considered. Section 41 of the Bill was regarded as highly prejudicial to the interests of the stock, share and debenture holders of the D&SR, so the solicitor was to take all necessary steps to petition against it. Further consideration of the Bill was carried out by the Board as it progressed. This subsequently led to a special meeting, held on 30th March 1900, with Mr Bailey Hawkins in the chair, Arthur Barff, George Bush, Strachan C. Clarke and John H. Whadcoat as directors, and Messrs Taylor and Wade also in attendance. With John Whadcoat proposing and Arthur Barff seconding, it was resolved that the GWR terms of purchase of the undertaking be accepted as a satisfactory basis for submission to the stock and shareholders, subject to some modifications:

• that the figure of £40 in clause 3 be increased to £50

• that the figure of £38,500 in clause 4 be increased to £50,000 as follows:

£300,000 of debenture stock at £12. 36,000
£12,000 of preference stock at 4%. 480
£259,455 of ordinary stock at 2% .5,189
For winding up expenses and compensation to officers 8,331
Total £50,000

A review of the GWR board minutes of 5th April 1900, indicated that the D&SR had petitioned against the powers sought by them for the provision of additional station accommodation, sidings and other works on the line. In the course of the discussions over these matters, it had been suggested that the line should be acquired by the GWR and the powers sought be withdrawn to enable takeover negotiations to proceed. The minutes went on to note that the 50% gross receipts paid by the GWR to the D&SR for operating the line was at this stage sufficient to pay interest on the 'A' debentures in full, leaving a balance available for interest on the 'B' debenture stock which last year received 16s 9d, the remaining stocks and shares receiving nothing. A memorandum of certain terms which had been suggested for the absorption of the line was read and explained to the board, along with the views of the D&SR. The Chairman was authorised to continue the negotiations and '*to endeavour to bring about an arrangement for the acquisition of the Undertaking on terms which were generally indicated*'.

Noted in the GWR board minutes of 17th May 1900, the Chief Accountant had reported back on the D&SR discussions, that the issued capital of the Company at 31st December 1898 (and also at 31st December 1900 per the D&SR half-yearly report) was as follows:

'A' Debenture Stock (3%). £433,000
'B' Debenture Stock (4% non-cumulative) £428,957
'C' Debenture Stock (4% non-cumulative) £250,948
5% Preference Shares of £25 each £12,000
Ordinary Stock £259,455

Filleigh station in the 1890s, looking west towards Barnstaple from the bridge carrying the lane between Proutworthy and Knowslade over the line. The station is seen in its original form and remained thus until 1937, when it was significantly improved with the addition of a loop and new Down platform, whilst the Up platform was raised in height and extended eastwards up to the bridge. The small signal cabin just visible on the platform was replaced at the same time, by a standard GWR brick-built hipped roof box sited at the far end of the station, on the Up side. *Roger Joanes collection*

The D&SR's representatives agreed to recommend to their proprietors that they transfer the undertaking to the GWR and reference to the D&SR minutes of 12th July 1900 confirms this. At a Special General Meeting of the D&SR on 8th March 1901, in respect of the GWR Bill and takeover, the votes were 419,047 in favour and 4,023 against the take over by the GWR. This left only parliamentary sanction remaining, which was was unlikely to be refused and it passed a second reading in the House.

At the 14th June 1901 D&SR board meeting, a letter from the L&SWR in regards to the Ilfracombe Railway was read. It referred to the still outstanding claim by the IR and that an agreement was to be made with the two companies. This proposed that £12,566 worth of 'C' debenture stock be issued to the IR, to be accepted as full discharge under the Scheme of Arrangement of 1889.

The GWR Board approved an arrangement for the acquisition of the D&SR on the terms named to take effect from 1st July 1901 and authorised the inclusion of powers for this purpose in the GWR Company's next Bill.

The D&SR half yearly report at 30th June 1901 showed the final Revenue account summary as follows:

EXPENDITURE TO 30TH JUNE	£	RECEIPTS	£
GWR Moiety	7,963	Passengers	6,542
Moiety of Mid. Rly rebate	32	Parcels, horses, carriages, etc	1,714
Moiety of interest on cost of gauge conversion	129	Mails	125
General charges (auditors, traffic returns etc)	315	Merchandise, minerals, livestock	7,353
Income tax	387	Rents	193
Land Tax	25	10% rebate from Mid. Rly	64
Total	8,851	Fees	7
Balance to net revenue a/c	7147		
Total	15,998	Total	15,998

In addition, the half-yearly accounts to 30th June 1901 showed that £36,166 of 'C' debenture stock (4%) was issued as proposed in the GWR minutes above, such funds being designated to creditors in accordance with Clause 10 of the Scheme of Arrangement 1889.

An extract from the final half-yearly report of the directors at 30th June 1901 is set out below:

	1901 (£ s d)	1900 (£ s d)	INCREASE	DECREASE
Passengers	6,542 6 0	6,669 7 4		127 1 4
Goods	7,353 9 7	7,659 10 8		306 1 1
Parcels	1,713 11 0	1,332 7 11	381 3 1	
Mails	125 0 0	125 0 0		
Miscellaneous	257 7 1	238 2 11	19 4 2	
TOTAL	15,991 13 8	16,024 8 10	400 7 3	433 2 5

In summary, for the construction of the line, the total amount of capital that was authorised was £1,163,000 and after the debenture increase of £36,166 referred to above, the total raised amounted to £1,149,071. This left £13,929 as the balance and not able to be issued under Clause 4 of the Agreement of 25th July 1900. The allocation of total funds raised were split as follows:

AMOUNT EXPENDED:	To 31/12/1900	To 30/6/1901	TOTAL
On line open for traffic	£870,470 12s 2d	£36,166 0s 0d	£906,636 12s 2d
Working stock	nil	nil	nil
Subscription to IR	£6,895 10s 3d	nil	£6,895 10s 3d
Arrears deb. int. capitalised	£511,896 0s 0d	nil	£511,896 0s 0d
TOTAL	£1,389,262 2s 5d	£36,166 0s 0d	£1,425,428 2s 5d

The scary fact is the extent to which arrears of debenture interest were capitalised, indicating there were insufficient funds to service the debts from the D&SR company's share of revenues. This amounted to more than one third of total costs (actually 35.9%), including the capitalised interest or over one half of the actual expenditure on the line for it to open for traffic.

For a line of 42¼ miles this resulted in a total financing cost of £27,197 per mile, including the capitalised interest, or a more 'modest' £21,460 if that capitalised interest is excluded from the calculation.

The final D&SR directors were Chairman William Bailey Hawkins, Arthur Barff, George Bush, Strachan Child Clarke, John Leonard Matthews and John Henry Whadcoat. John Wade was the last Company Secretary.

TAKEOVER BY THE GWR IN 1901

The Great Western Railway Act of 1901 received Royal Assent on 26th July 1901. This Act conferred powers on the GWR (and the London & North Western and Great Central railways where there were joint interests) for vesting the Devon & Somerset Railway and other certain undertakings at that time, such as the Bridport Railway and the Windsor & Ascot Railway. The vesting date for the D&SR was 1st July 1901 (Clause 3), as anticipated by the GWR board in their minutes of 17th May 1900, the vesting being deemed to be an amalgamation between the two companies under Part V of the Railway Clauses Act 1863. The details pertinent to the D&SR were contained in clauses 64-70 and the Second Schedule to the Act .

The schedule refers to the agreement made on 25th July 1900 between the D&SR and GWR, which effectively dealt with the acquisition of the undertaking. The consideration for the sale and purchase is summarised as follows:

1. Release and extinguishment of all claims of the GWR in respect of the £12,942 of expenditure incurred under a certain agreement dated 31st July 1880 (the gauge conversion of the D&SR).

2. The issue of GWR stock to each of the 'A', 'B' and 'C' debenture stockholders of the D&SR as set out in Clause 66:

D&SR DEBS	EXCHANGE	INTEREST	GWR VALUE
A	£120 of GWR deb. stock for £100 D&SR 'A' debs	At a rate of £2 10s % per annum	519,600
B	£50 of GWR deb. stock for £100 D&SR 'B' debs	As above	215,000
C	£12 10s of GWR deb. stock for £100 D&SR 'C' debs	As above	37,500
TOTAL			£772,100

3. Payment by the GWR to the liquidator of the D&SR of £12,650 within fourteen days of 1st July 1901 (or after the appointment of the liquidator, if later).

With the value equivalent in GWR stock of £772,100, plus £12,650 and £12,942 (the amounts at 1 and 3 above), along with the £1,500 payable to the L&SWR, the total purchase price was thus £799,192. It will be noticed that the GWR debenture interest rate was 2.5% – a little less than that offered by the D&SR debentures but which in reality was largely an illusion due to the poor operational cash flows of the D&SR from the opening of the line.

As a consequence, all the land, buildings and property of every description, along with rights and privileges, were vested in the GWR, who were freed and discharged from all debts, liabilities and obligations of the D&SR existing at 30th June 1901. The liquidators retained the iron safe used for the custody of the books and papers, along with any money held, other than that relating to unclaimed interest and dividends on stocks and shares. Also, any amounts due by the GWR to the D&SR on revenue account – broadly sums due under the running agreements dated 6th March 1865 and as modified by the GWR agreement of 31st July 1880 – would also be retained by the D&SR.

The amount of £12,650 and any amounts due from the GWR on revenue account as referred to above would be applied to the payment of interest on the 'A' debenture stock for the half year to 30th June 1901. Any surplus would then be applied towards interest on the 'B' debenture stockholders for the same period. Any undistributed revenue of previous years (after administration expenses) should also be applied towards payment of interest on the 'B' debenture stock. Subject to this, the assets of the D&SR would then be applied as follows:

- payment of £5 per £100 (nominal) to the preference share holders
- payment of £2 per £100 (nominal) to the ordinary stock shareholders and £2 per £100 to the ordinarily shareholders
- payment of the costs of liquidation of the D&SR company
- payment of compensation duly voted to directors and officials for loss of office
- the surplus (if any) being rateably distributed amongst the holders of the ordinary stock and ordinary shares of the D&SR company in proportion to the amounts paid up

The GWR was also responsible from 1st July 1901 for fulfilling all rights and obligations of the D&SR on the acquisition of lands, the construction and maintenance of works, and payment of rent charges. The D&SR company was to hand over all deeds, land and property plans, Parliamentary plans and other documents related to title and land.

At this point, the Devon Company (as the D&SR was defined) was dissolved and the un-exercised powers of the company raising capital by creation of shares or funding by mortgages and debenture stock was extinguished. The winding up would be in such manner as if the Devon Company were registered under the Companies Acts 1862 to 1897 and a special resolution had been passed for voluntary winding up. It was the responsibility of the GWR, within fourteen days following the appointment of the liquidators, to pay the sum mentioned in the agreement – £12,650 – meanwhile holding such amount in trust for the liquidators.

Shareholders of the D&SR were not to become shareholders of the GWR on the amalgamation; they received nothing. The agreement was signed by Mr Bailey Hawkins, Chairman of the D&SR and John Wade, Secretary. Mr G.K. Mills, Secretary of the GWR signed on their behalf.

Messrs Bailey Hawkins and Wade were appointed as joint liquidators following an extraordinary general meeting on 30th August 1901, in respect of holders of the preference and ordinary shares and stockholders. The liquidators announced that the calculation of amounts due under the provisions of the said agreement were such that the holders of shares and stock should treat their investments as valueless. Nonetheless, there was a job to be done to wind the company up. The final statement of the liquidators' account was dated 3rd April 1904, so the whole process took just under three years. Part of the reason for this delay was due to the number of preference and ordinary stockholders (461 as registered) where no particulars of deaths or other devolutions had been recorded in the register. As a consequence, this required research and correspondence and the reference of a number of matters to the dead letters office. Also, certificates had been lost, so indemnities and personal interviews were required in the case of each holder who could not prove title.

All this extra work and the large and diffuse number of shareholders meant the liquidators had to apply to the High Court of Justice for Mr Registrar Hood to confirm their remuneration at £1,000.

Set out below is the liquidators' summary of realisations and application of funds to shareholders and creditors (disbursements). The total amount of paid-up share capital at the commencement of the winding up was £1,420,653 10s 0d.

LIQUIDATORS SUMMARY	INITIAL £ s d	FINAL £ s d
Total realisations	**24,062 11 5**	**24,071 18 9**
Total Disbursements	**19,638 11 9**	**23,187 12 1**
Net balance	**4,423 19 8**	**884 6 8**
Paid to liquidators account	**2,712 16 1**	

Of the final realisations, £12,650 was the amount from Clause 6 (arrears of debenture interest) of the 1901 Act paid by the GWR. The traffic account for 30th June 1901 was £7,385 6s 8d and £3,617 6s 6d was unclaimed interest, the balance being capital account credit/sundries. The main disbursements were £10,056 17s 3d as interest at 3% to the 'A' debenture stockholders for the half year to 30th June 1901, along with payment to the preference shareholders (£5 per £100 nominal) and ordinary shareholders (£2 per £100 nominal) which totalled £5174 0s 7d. The five directors each received £200, the chairman £500 and the traffic agent £200.

So the D&SR Company was no more but the railway was still there, entering a new era of ownership by the GWR.

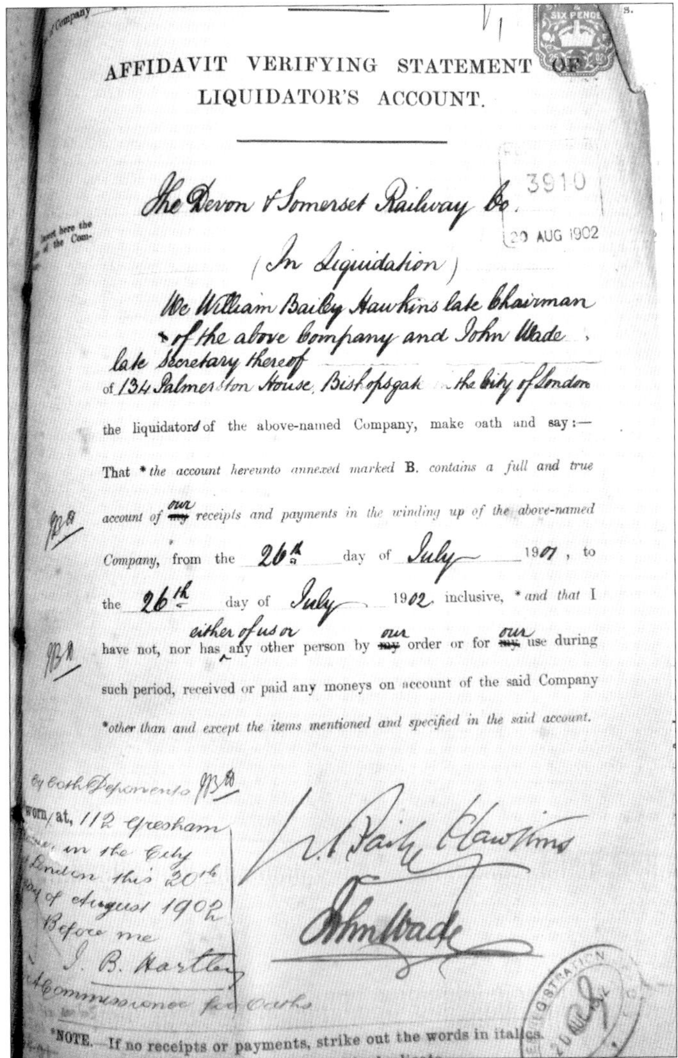
AFFIDAVIT VERIFYING STATEMENT OF LIQUIDATOR'S ACCOUNT.

The Devon & Somerset Railway Co. 3910 20 AUG 1902

(In Liquidation)

We William Bailey Hawkins late Chairman of the above Company and John Wade, late Secretary thereof of 134 Palmerston House, Bishopsgate the City of London

the liquidators of the above-named Company, make oath and say:—

That *the account hereunto annexed marked B. contains a full and true account of ~~my~~ our receipts and payments in the winding up of the above-named Company, from the 26th day of July 1901, to the 26th day of July 1902 inclusive, *and that I have not, nor has either of us or any other person by ~~my~~ our order or for ~~my~~ our use during such period, received or paid any moneys on account of the said Company *other than and except the items mentioned and specified in the said account.

by both Deponents WBH Sworn at, 112 Gresham House in the City of London this 20th day of August 1902 Before me J. B. Hartley A Commissioner for Oaths

W. Bailey Hawkins
John Wade

*NOTE.—If no receipts or payments, strike out the words in italics.

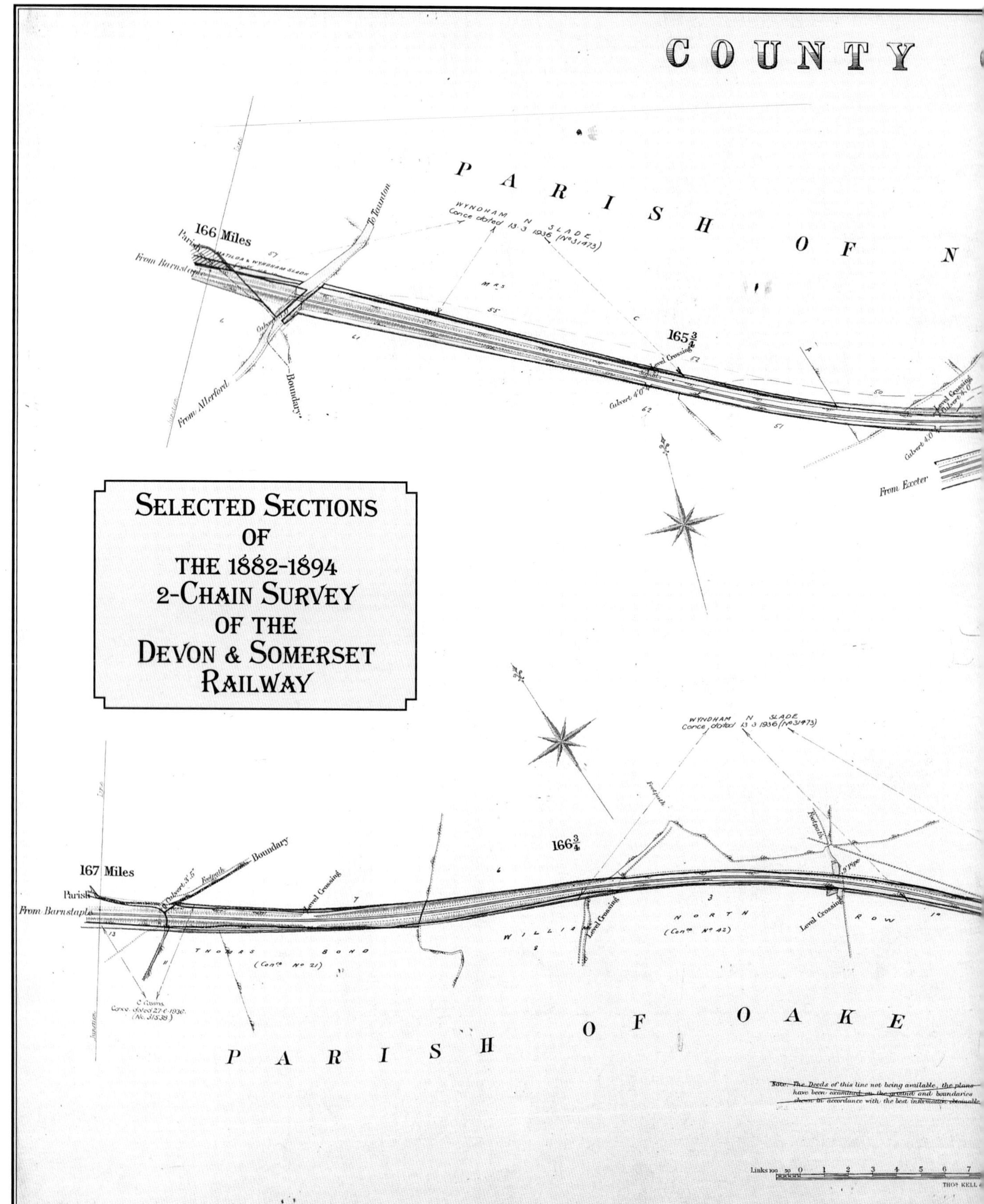
COUNTY
PARISH OF N
166 Miles
From Barnstaple
To Taunton
From Allerford
Boundary
165¾
Level Crossing
From Exeter
SELECTED SECTIONS
OF
THE 1882-1894
2-CHAIN SURVEY
OF THE
DEVON & SOMERSET
RAILWAY
167 Miles
Parish
From Barnstaple
Footpath
Boundary
Level Crossing
166¾
NORTH ROW
PARISH OF OAKE

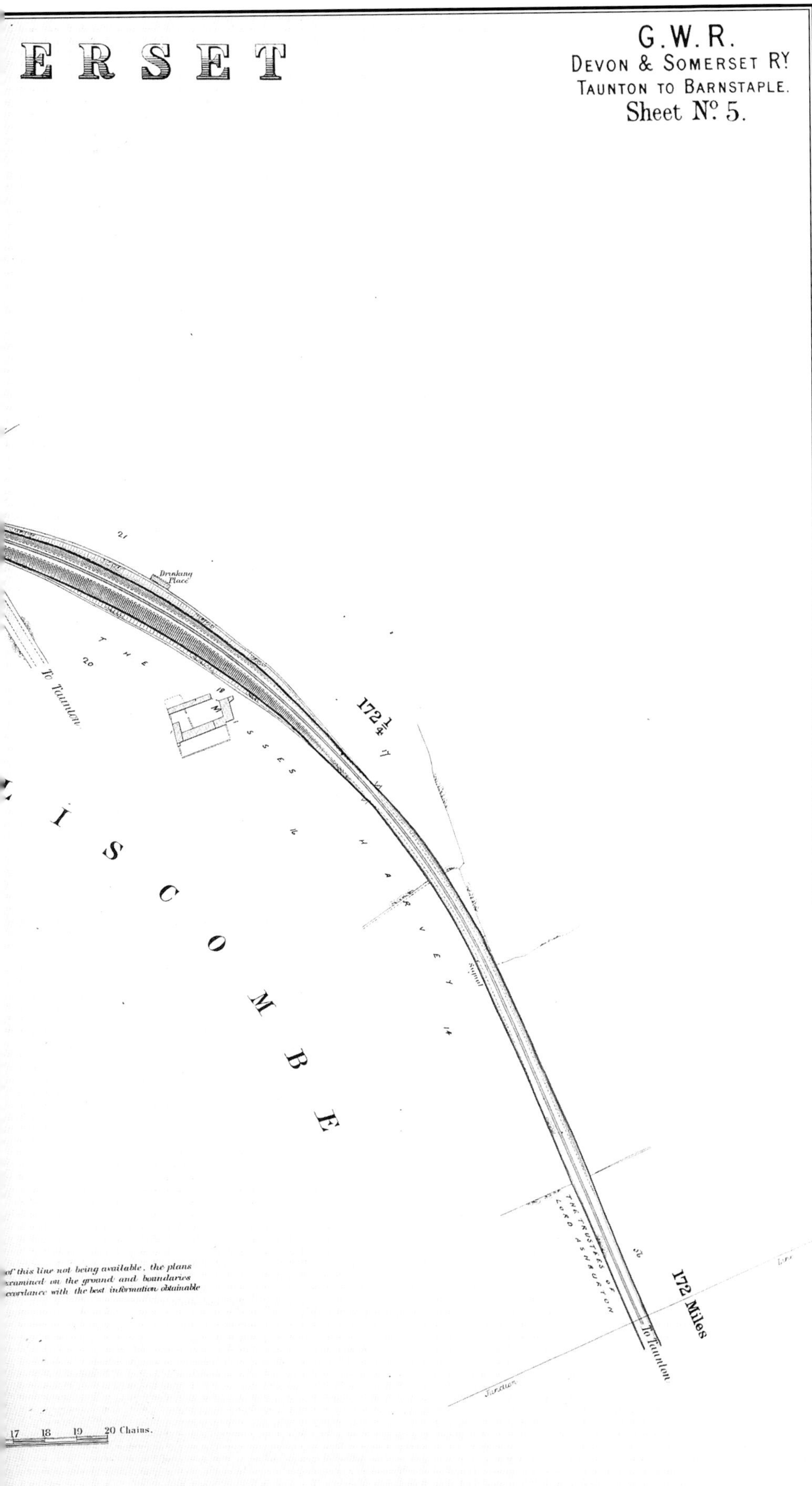

THE 1882-94 2-CHAIN SURVEY OF THE DEVON & SOMERSET RAILWAY

This particular 2-chain survey is noted by the National Archives as being carried out in the period 1882 to 1894. It provides detailed track plans of the stations and junctions along the route of the D&SR. On close inspection of certain of the sections, it can be seen that dates have been added in places up to the mid 1930s, mostly in regard to the ownership and boundaries of sundry small parcels of land but the track plans themselves have not been altered to take into account such as the early 1900s improvements, such as those at Wiveliscombe and Dulverton, for example. However, the 1887 Barnstaple Junction Railway is shown. The survey is detailed, indicating signals, mile posts, culverts, permanent way huts, etc, as well as the more obvious features and landmarks such as tunnels and bridges. Names alongside the railway indicate landowners. A number of D&SR directors owned land along the line and their names will be familiar after reading this chapter. The parishes through which the railway passed are also listed. Most of the station layouts were simple and had a common theme – a single through road goods shed, cattle dock, one other siding and often a headshut off the running line to feed back into the yard. The layouts became more complex and interesting with the improvements of the 20th century.

All sections courtesy National Archives

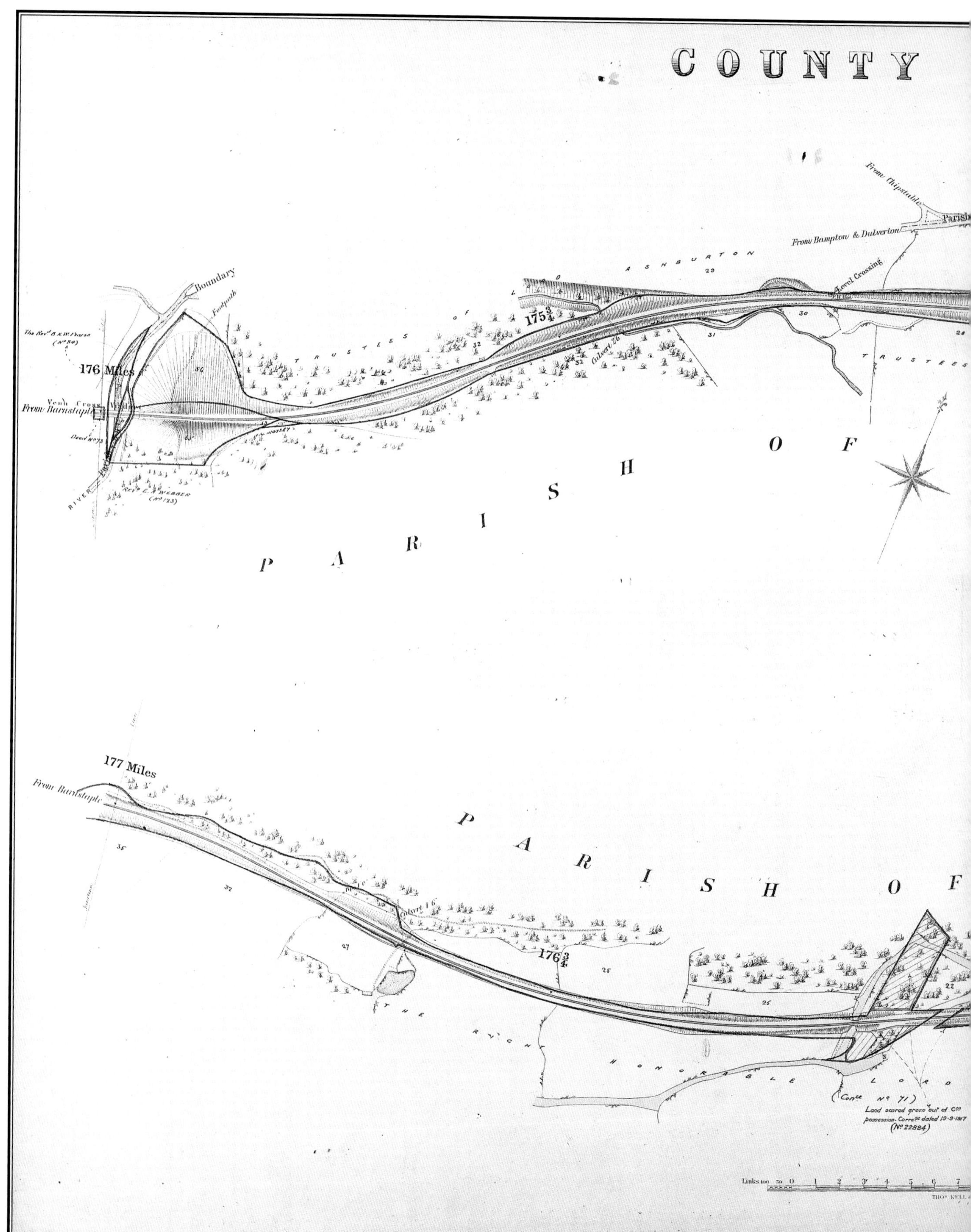
COUNTY
From Chipstable
Parish
From Bampton & Dulverton
Level Crossing
Boundary
Footpath
175¾
176 Miles
From Barnstaple
Culvert 26
TRUSTEES
PARISH OF
177 Miles
From Barnstaple
PARISH OF
Culvert 16
176¾
THE
HONORABLE
LORD
(Conce No. 71)
Land scored green out of Co's possession. Corresce dated 19-9-1917
(No 22884)
Links 100 50 0 1 2 3 4 5 6 7

SOMERSET

G.W.R.
DEVON & SOMERSET RY.
TAUNTON TO BARNSTAPLE.
Sheet No. 1.

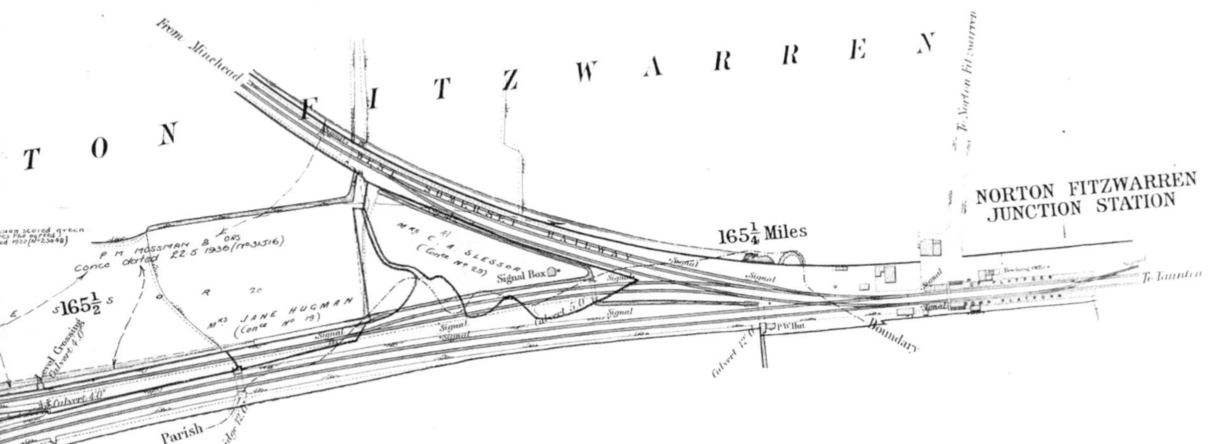

PARISH OF BISHOPS HULL

NORTON FITZWARREN JUNCTION

Note that, at this period, the D&SR branched off from the West Somerset Railway, at milepost 165¼, and not the main line. A small signal cabin controlling access to and from the Barnstaple Branch was sandwiched between the two branch lines; it contained six levers controlling two points and two bolt locks, with two spare. On the left of the top section, near milepost 166, is Allerford Bridge, carrying a lane from Allerford which joins the main road to Taunton at Norton Fitzwarren, and up to which the present day West Somerset Railway has now laid its spur (see Chapter 5). Norton Fitzwarren station was only two platforms at this time, located either side of the double track main line. Volume 2 will explore the growth and development of this junction and the station. The lower section, taking the line to milepost 167, was to be doubled in the 1930s, from the junction all the way to Milverton.

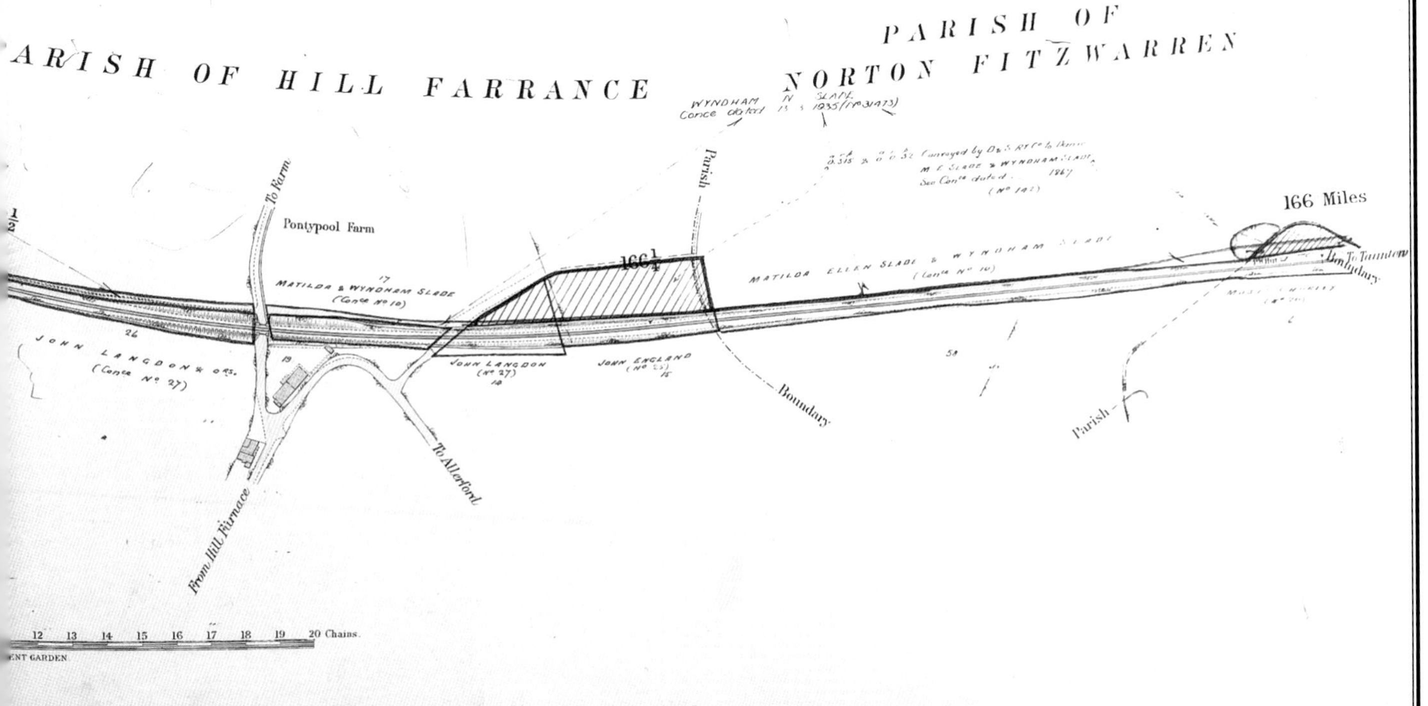

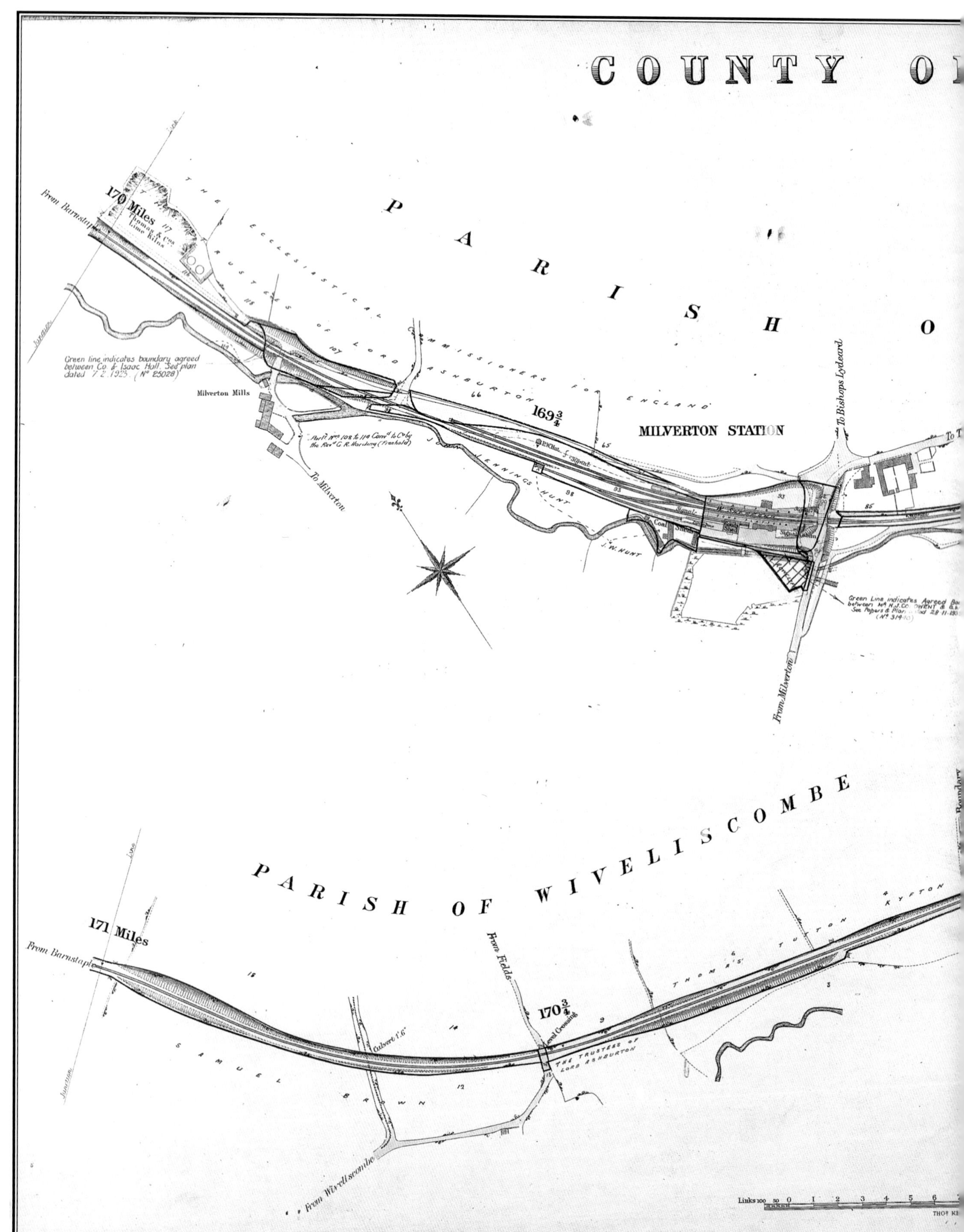
COUNTY OF
PARISH OF
170 Miles
From Barnstaple
Thomas & Cos Lime Kilns
THE TRUSTEES OF THE ECCLESIASTICAL COMMISSIONERS FOR ENGLAND
LORD ASHBURTON
Green line indicates boundary agreed between Co. & Isaac Hall. See plan dated 7.2.1923. (No 25028)
Milverton Mills
169 3/4
MILVERTON STATION
To Bishops Lydeard
To Milverton
JENNINGS HUNT
J. W. HUNT
From Milverton
PARISH OF WIVELISCOMBE
171 Miles
From Barnstaple
From Fields
170 3/4
Calvert
Level Crossing
THE TRUSTEES OF LORD ASHBURTON
SAMUEL BROWN
THOMAS' TUTTON
From Wiveliscombe
Links 100 50 0 1 2 3 4 5 6

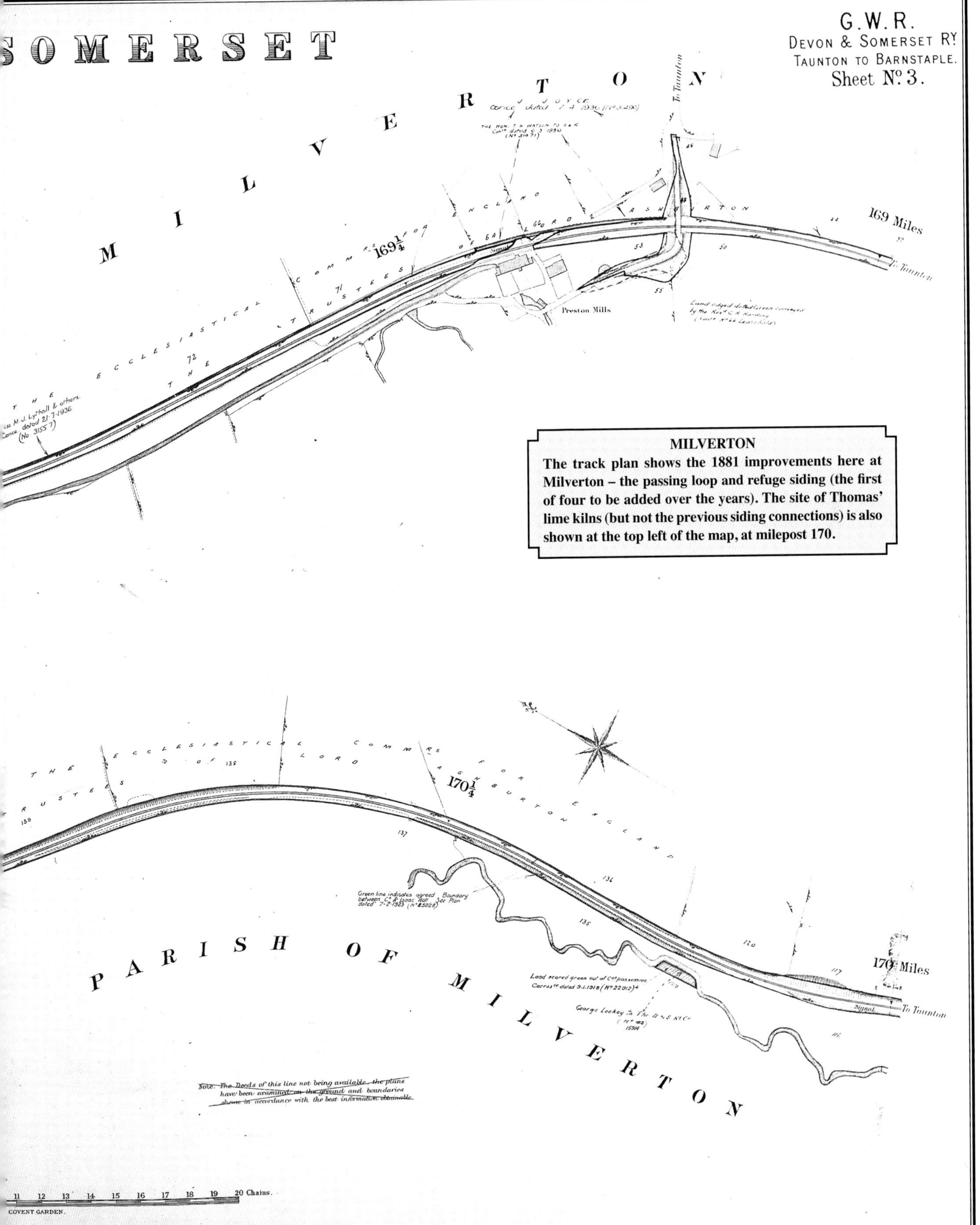

MILVERTON
The track plan shows the 1881 improvements here at Milverton – the passing loop and refuge siding (the first of four to be added over the years). The site of Thomas' lime kilns (but not the previous siding connections) is also shown at the top left of the map, at milepost 170.

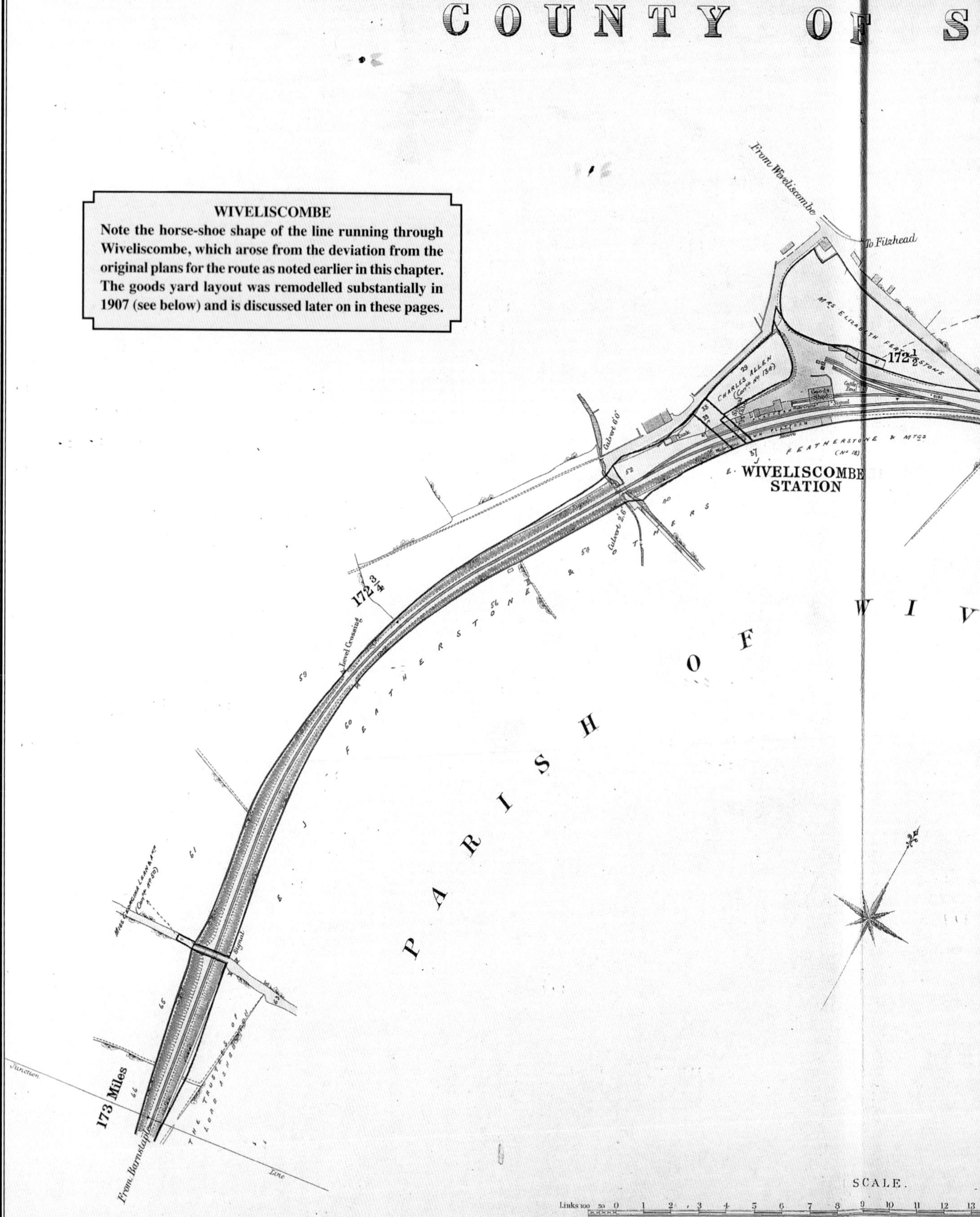

WIVELISCOMBE

Note the horse-shoe shape of the line running through Wiveliscombe, which arose from the deviation from the original plans for the route as noted earlier in this chapter. The goods yard layout was remodelled substantially in 1907 (see below) and is discussed later on in these pages.

SOMERSET

G.W.R.
DEVON & SOMERSET RY.
TAUNTON TO BARNSTAPLE.
Sheet No. 7.

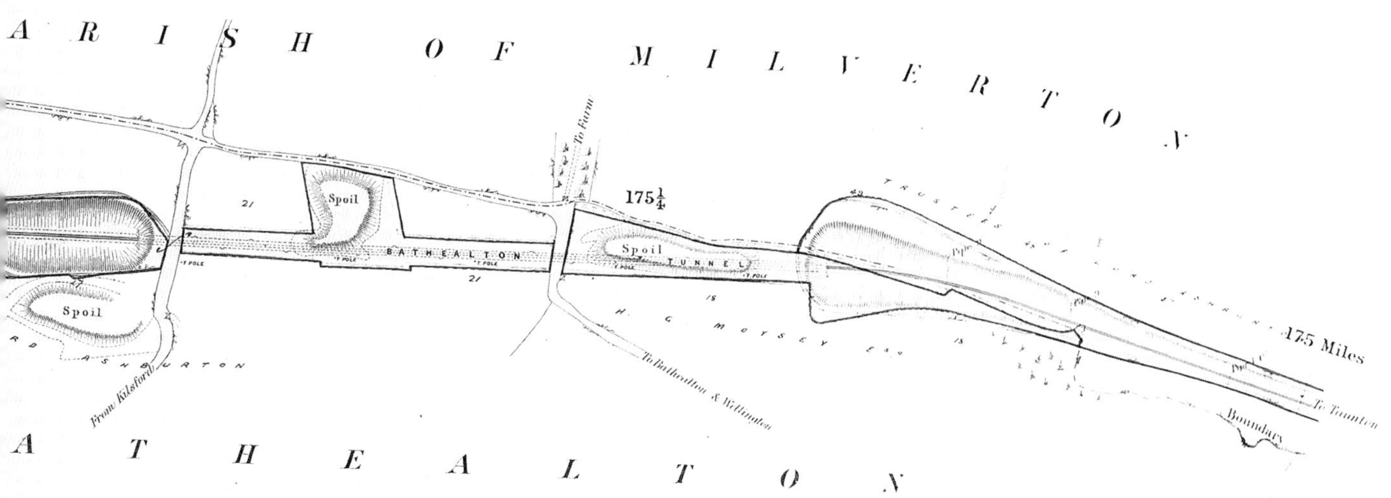

BATHEALTON TUNNEL

Note that Bathealton Tunnel was a straight bore and that the spoil heaps indicated on the map are still visible today. The Tone Viaduct (located at milepost 176) is split across the two sections of the survey on this sheer. Plot 35 just to the south of the line at the east end of the viaduct is the site of Pouch Bridge Quarry (see page 69); Pouch Bridge was the road bridge crossing the river a little way to the north of the viaduct. It is possible that the quarry indicated to the west of the viaduct on the section below is the one featured in the contractor's photograph on pages 70-71.

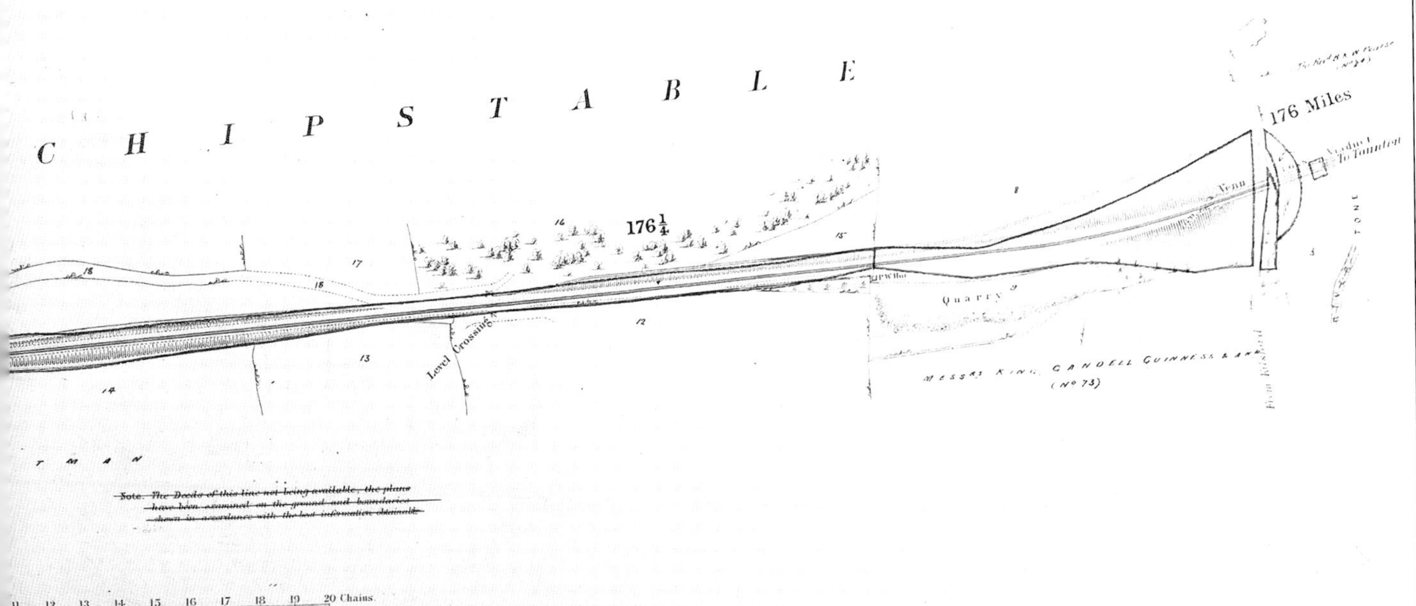

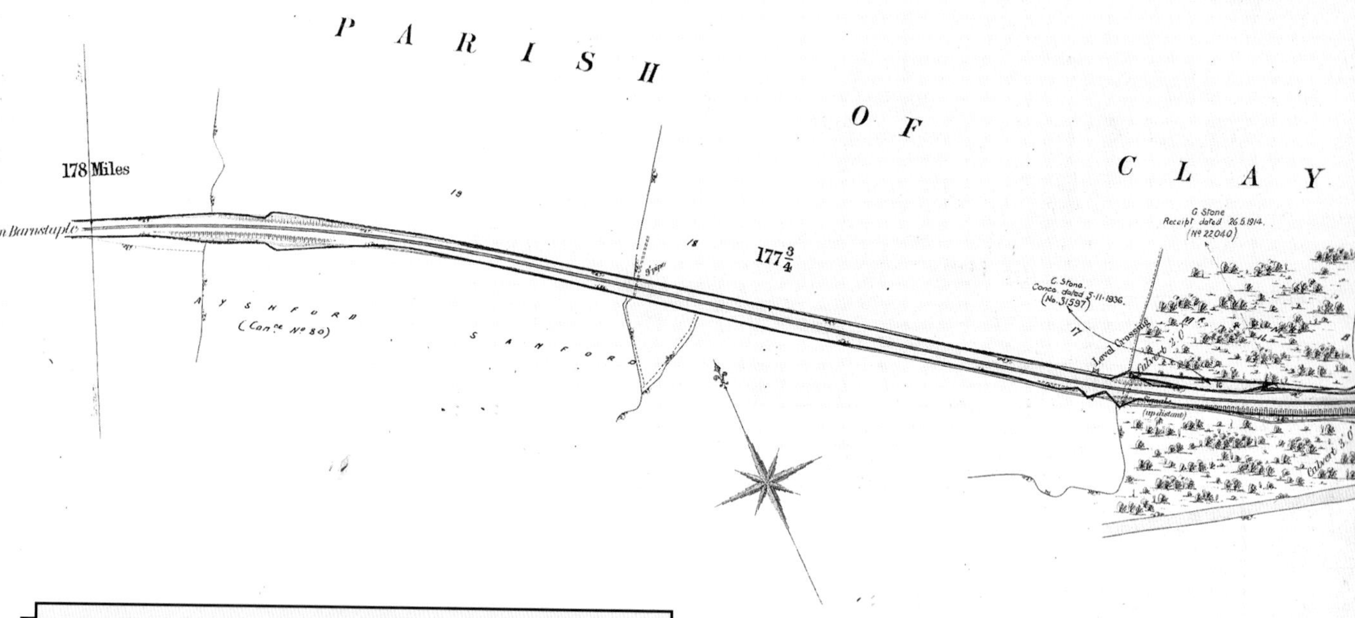

VENN CROSS

The location of Venn Cross station in a cutting at the west end of Venn Cross Tunnel is clearly shown here. The station possessed a simple layout with no passing loop and a most basic of goods yard at this time. Note the county boundary passing by the goods shed – Somerset to the east, Devon to the west. Note that the tunnel had a slight curve at its eastern end.

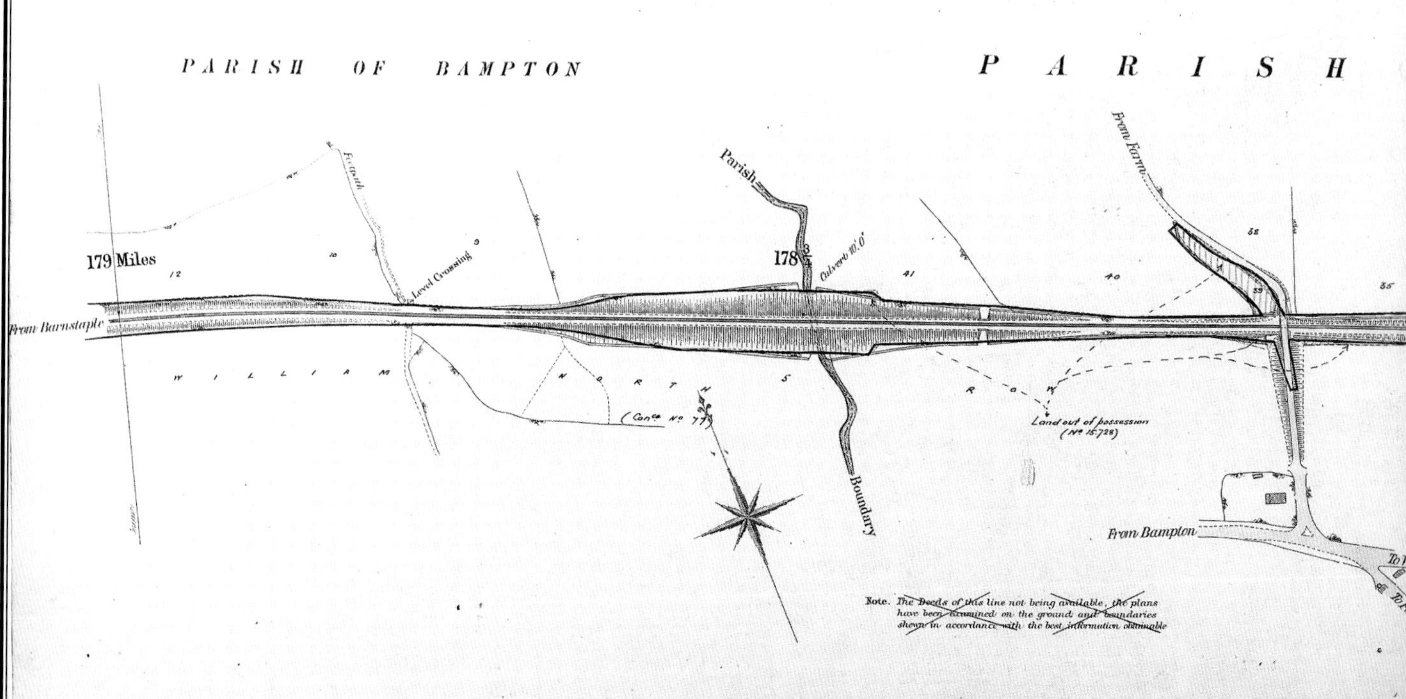

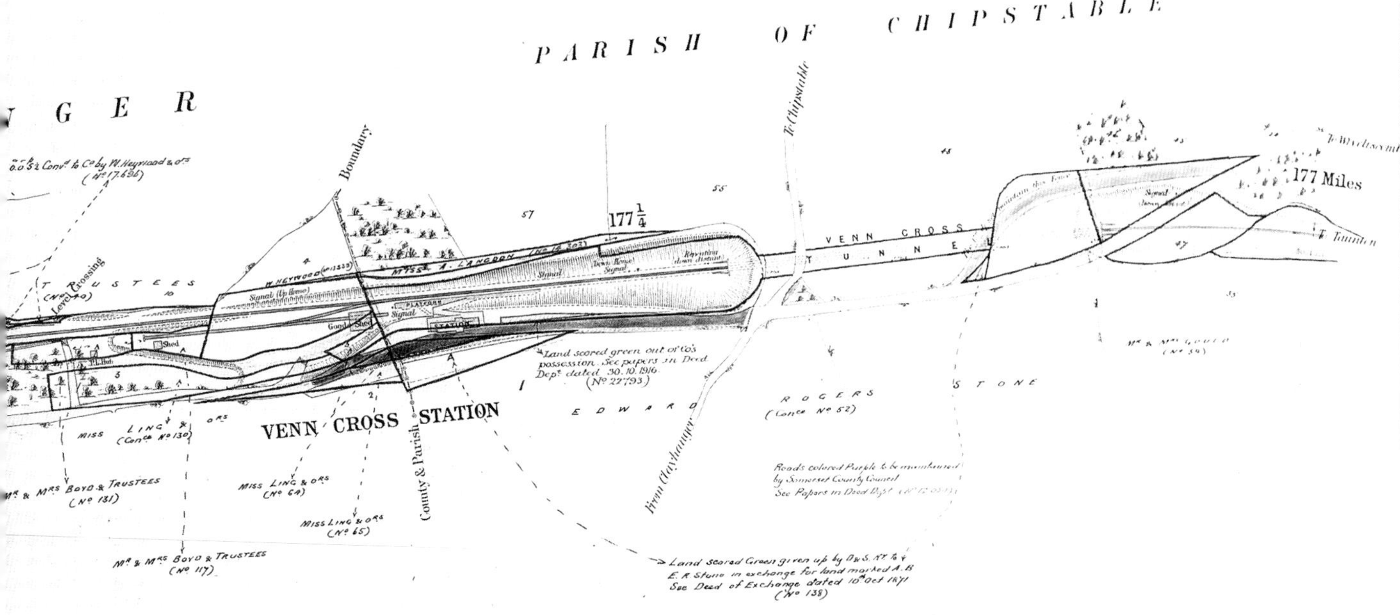
ON
COUNTY OF SOMERSET
G.W.R.
DEVON & SOMERSET RY
TAUNTON TO BARNSTAPLE.
Sheet No. 8.
PARISH OF CHIPSTABLE
GER
Boundary
To Chipstable
177 1/4
177 Miles
VENN CROSS TUNNEL
Level Crossing
TRUSTEES
VENN CROSS STATION
County & Parish
From Clayhanger
EDWARD
ROGERS STONE
(Conce No 52)
MISS LING & ORS (Conce No 130)
MR & MRS BOYD & TRUSTEES (No 131)
MISS LING & ORS (No 64)
MISS LING & ORS (No 65)
MR & MRS BOYD & TRUSTEES (No 117)
Land scored green out of Co's possession. See papers in Deed Dept dated 30.10.1916 (No 22793)
Roads colored Purple to be maintained by Somerset County Council. See Papers in Deed Dept
Land Scored Green given up by D & S. Ry Co to E. R. Stone in exchange for land marked A.B. See Deed of Exchange dated 10th Oct 1871 (No 138)

OF CLAYHANGER
To Chipstable
178 1/4
178 Miles
Level Crossing
To Taunton
THE RIGHT HONORABLE LORD PORTMAN
(Conce No 71)
From Brampton
To Wiveliscombe
11 12 13 14 15 16 17 18 19 20 Chains.
ST COVENT GARDEN.

COUNTY

P A R I S H O

180 Miles

From Barnstaple

Level Crossing

Culvert 2.0"

179¾

THE REVD. WM. P. BROWNE (No 51)

JOHN EDWARDS (No 56)

JOHN BARN

To Farm

From Turnpike Road

Note. The Deeds have been shown in

MOREBATH

Morebath station had changed since its opening, the passing loop having been added in 1876. Note the proximity of the road passing under the line at the west end of the station, which made the extension works of 1937, when the the loop and platforms were all lengthened, somewhat more complicated. The station was situated some way to the east of the village it purported to serve, being much nearer to Shillingford, although even this small community was around half a mile away to the south

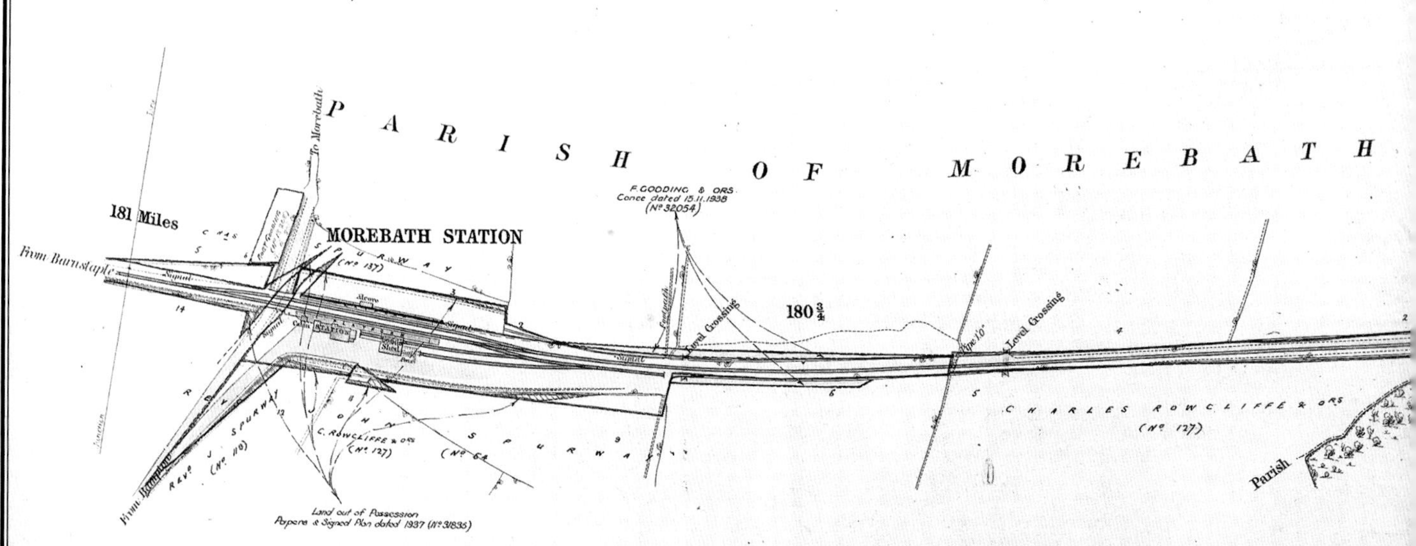

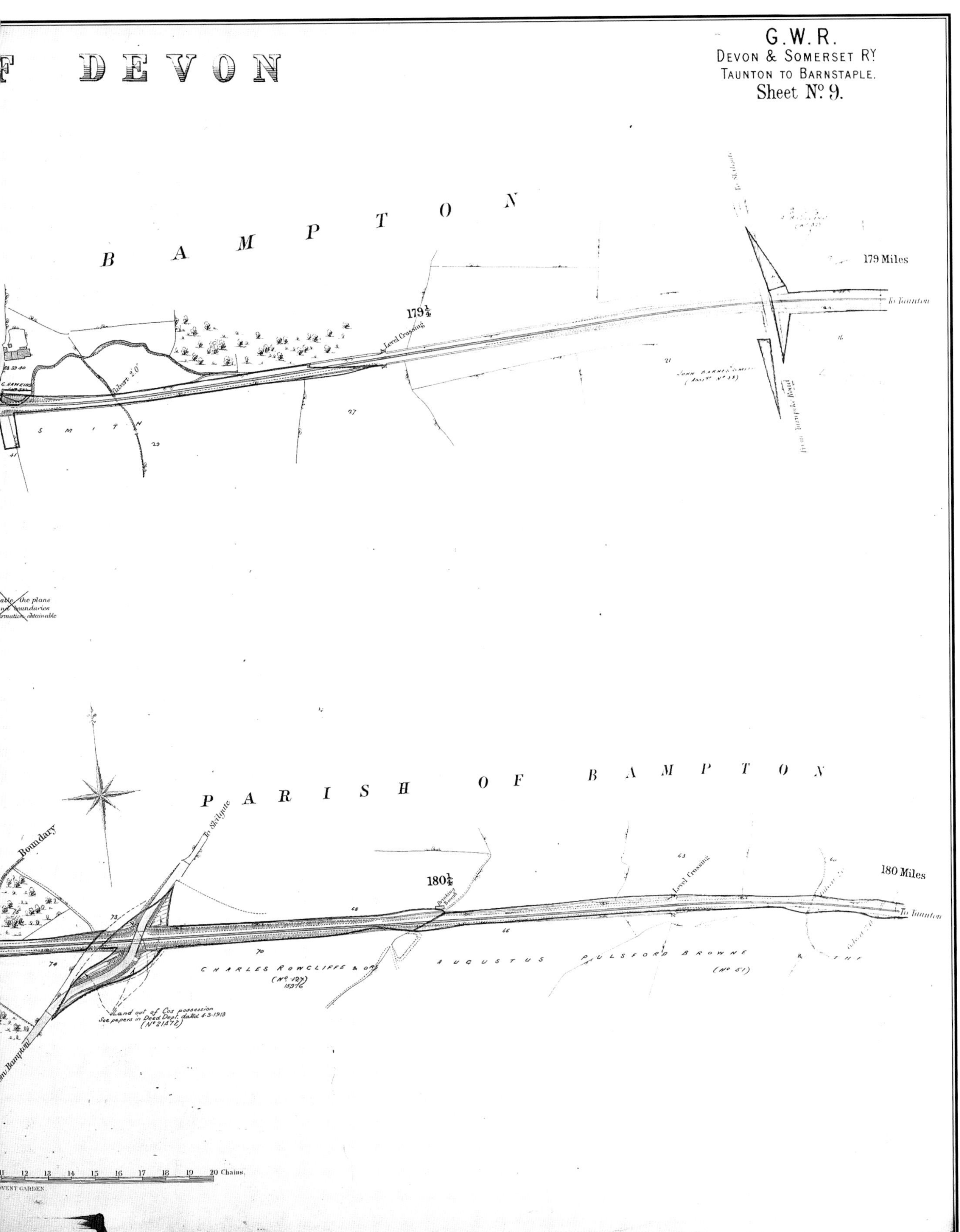
G.W.R.
DEVON & SOMERSET RY
TAUNTON TO BARNSTAPLE.
Sheet No. 9.
F DEVON
BAMPTON
179 Miles
179¼
Level Crossing
To Taunton
PARISH OF BAMPTON
180¼
180 Miles
Level Crossing
To Skilgate
Boundary
CHARLES ROWCLIFFE & ORS
AUGUSTUS PULSFORD BROWNE
Land out of Cos possession
See papers in Deed Dept. dated 4-3-1913
(No 21472)
20 Chains

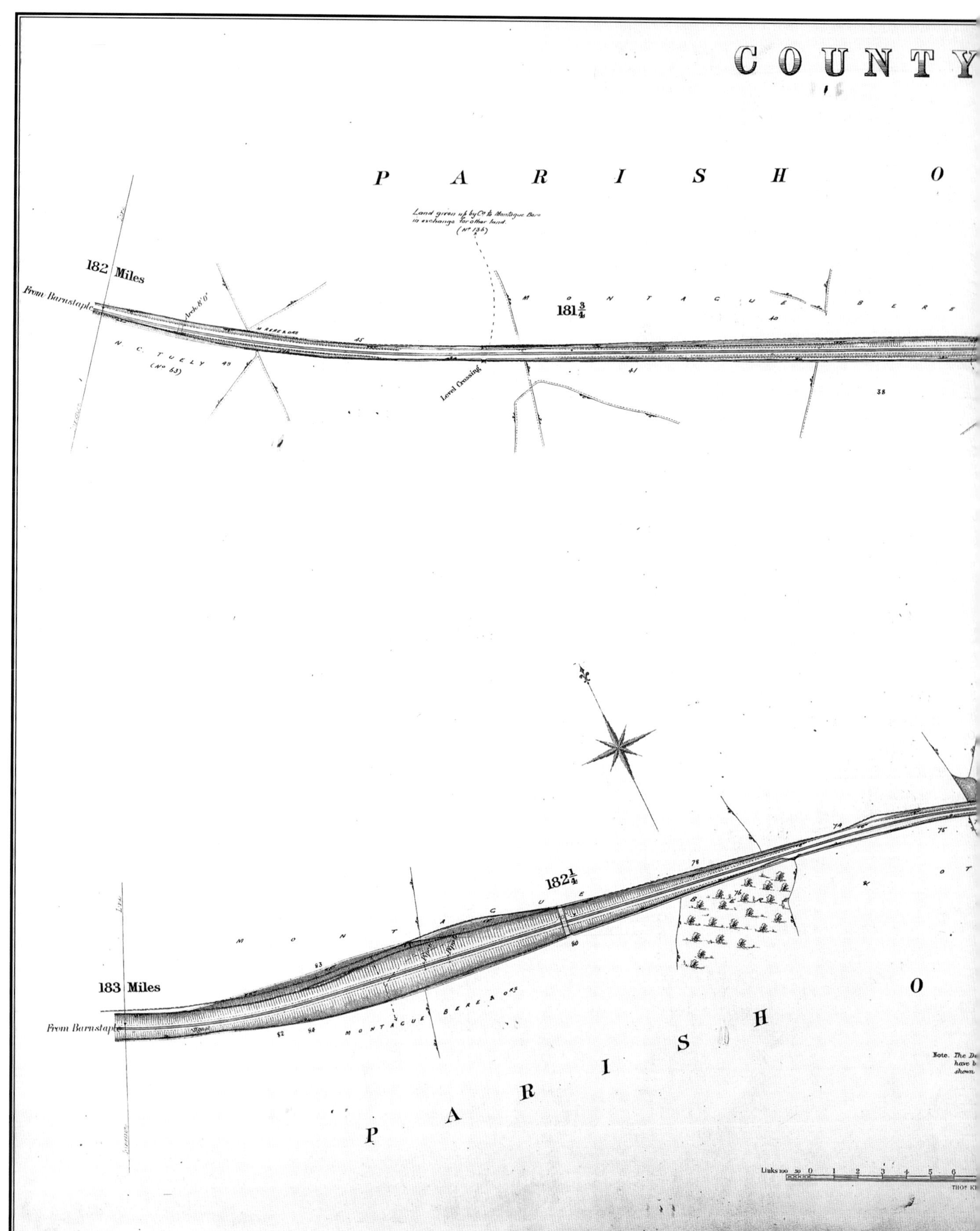
COUNTY
P A R I S H O
Land given up by Co. to Montague Bere in exchange for other land. (No. 135)
182 Miles
From Barnstaple
Arch 8'0"
1813/4
Level Crossing
N. C. TUELY (No. 63)
M O N T A G U E B E R E
182 1/4
183 Miles
From Barnstaple
M O N T A G U E
M O N T A G U E B E R E & Ors
O
P A R I S H
Links 100 50 0 1 2 3 4 5 6

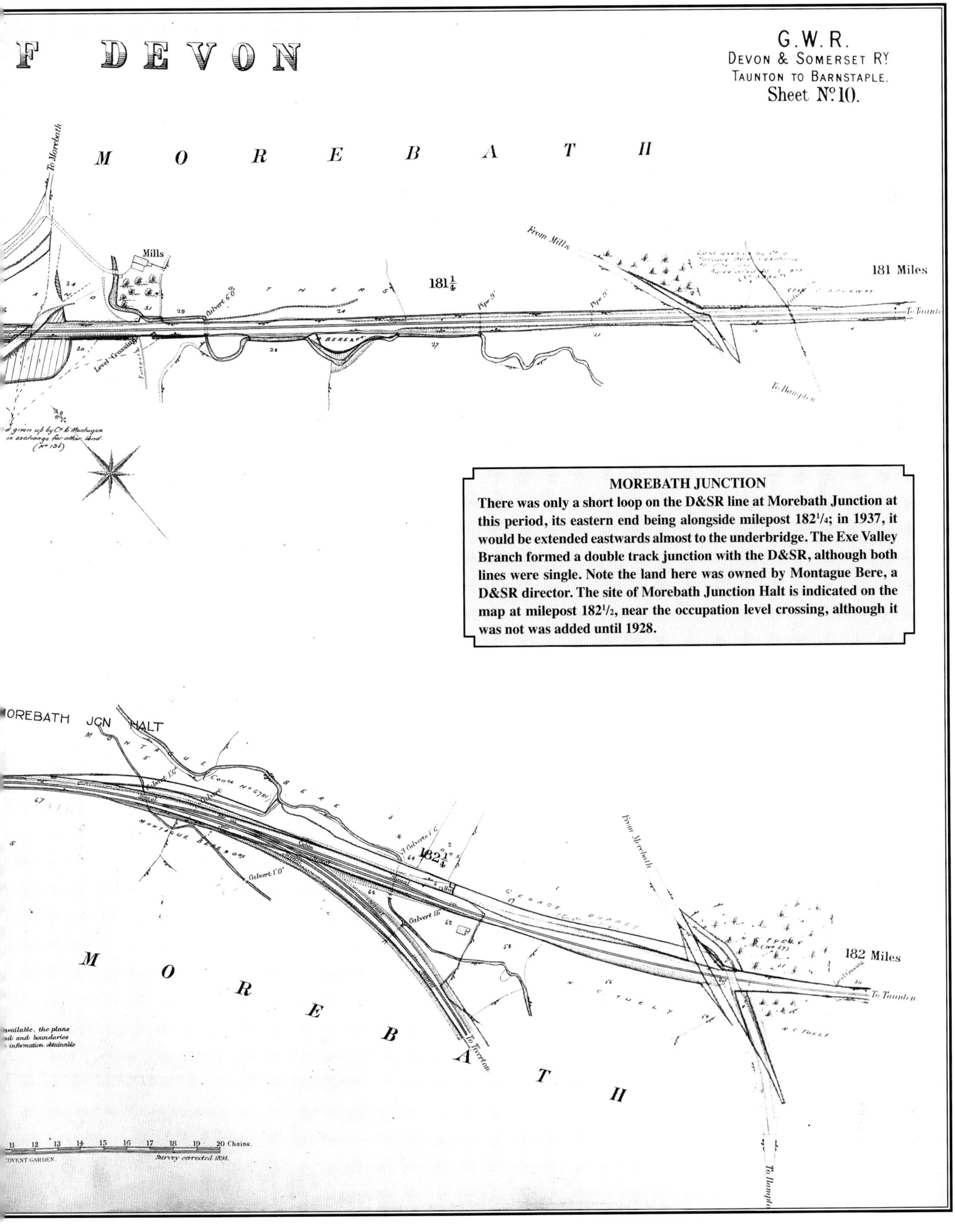

MOREBATH JUNCTION

There was only a short loop on the D&SR line at Morebath Junction at this period, its eastern end being alongside milepost 182¼; in 1937, it would be extended eastwards almost to the underbridge. The Exe Valley Branch formed a double track junction with the D&SR, although both lines were single. Note the land here was owned by Montague Bere, a D&SR director. The site of Morebath Junction Halt is indicated on the map at milepost 182½, near the occupation level crossing, although it was not was added until 1928.

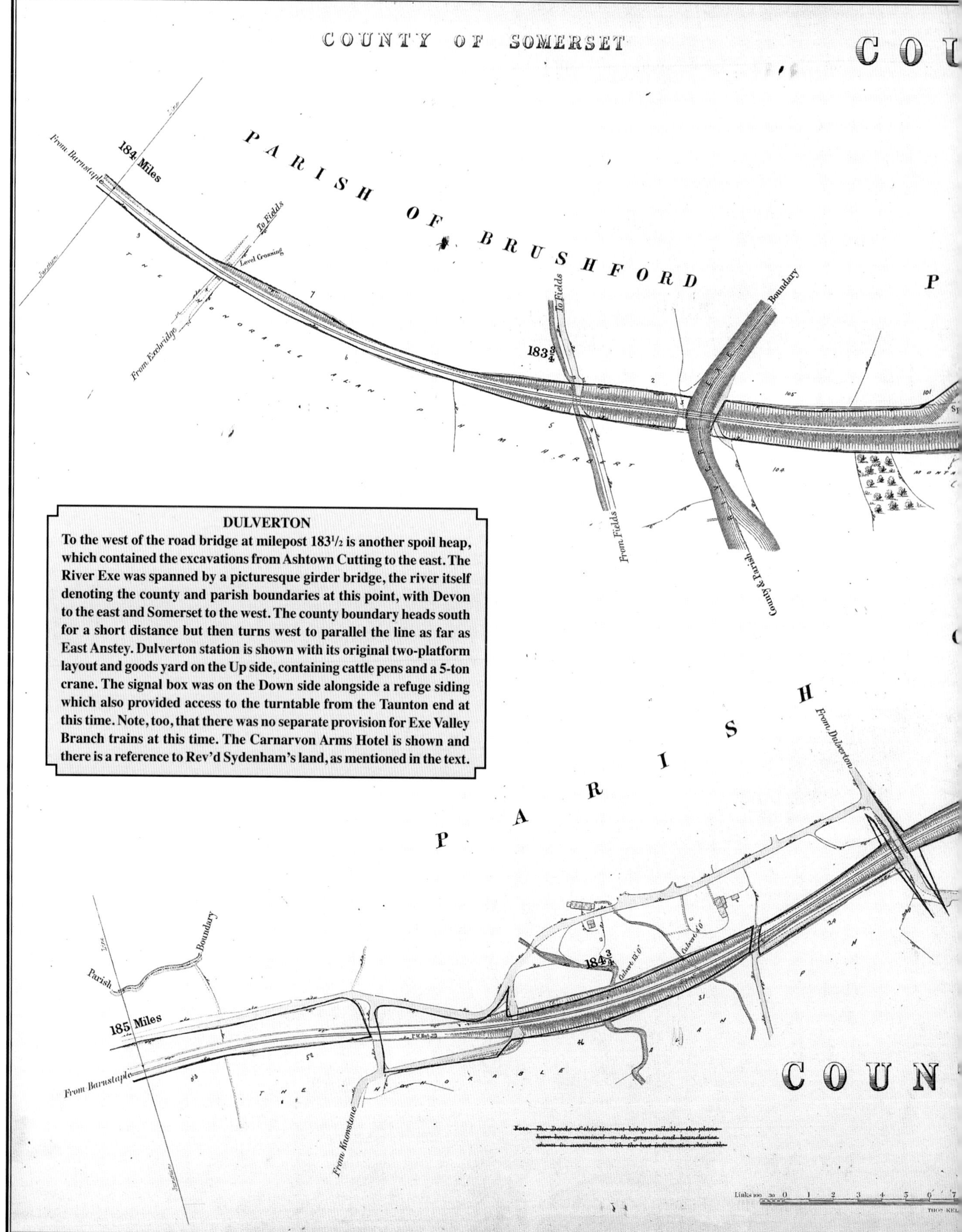

DULVERTON

To the west of the road bridge at milepost 183½ is another spoil heap, which contained the excavations from Ashtown Cutting to the east. The River Exe was spanned by a picturesque girder bridge, the river itself denoting the county and parish boundaries at this point, with Devon to the east and Somerset to the west. The county boundary heads south for a short distance but then turns west to parallel the line as far as East Anstey. Dulverton station is shown with its original two-platform layout and goods yard on the Up side, containing cattle pens and a 5-ton crane. The signal box was on the Down side alongside a refuge siding which also provided access to the turntable from the Taunton end at this time. Note, too, that there was no separate provision for Exe Valley Branch trains at this time. The Carnarvon Arms Hotel is shown and there is a reference to Rev'd Sydenham's land, as mentioned in the text.

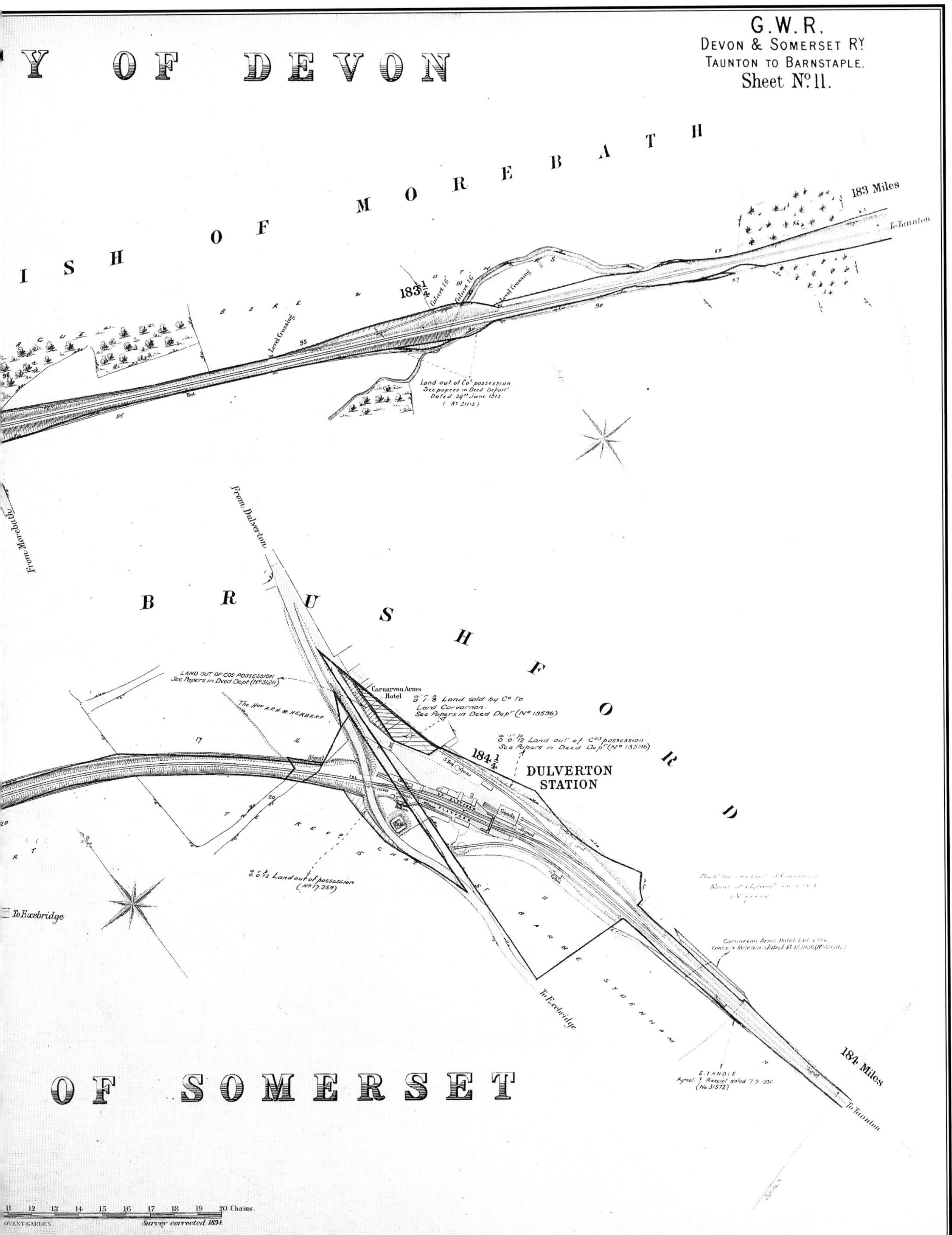
G.W.R.
DEVON & SOMERSET RY.
TAUNTON TO BARNSTAPLE.
Sheet No. 11.
Y OF DEVON
ISH OF MOREBATH
183 Miles
To Taunton
$183\frac{1}{4}$
Level Crossing
Land out of Co's possession. See papers in Deed Depart. Dated 29th June 1912. (No 21115)
From Dulverton
From Morebath
BRUSHFORD
LAND OUT OF CO'S POSSESSION See Papers in Deed Dept (No 31211)
The Hon A.P.H.M. HERBERT
Carnarvon Arms Hotel
Land sold by Co to Lord Carnarvon See Papers in Deed Dept (No 18596)
Land out of Co's possession See Papers in Deed Dept (No 18596)
$184\frac{1}{4}$
DULVERTON STATION
Goods
Signal
Land out of possession (No 17.259)
To Exebridge
Carnarvon Arms Hotel Ltd
To Exebridge
E. TANDLE Agreet & Receipt dated 7.9.1934 (No 31572)
184 Miles
To Taunton
OF SOMERSET
20 Chains.
Survey corrected 1894.

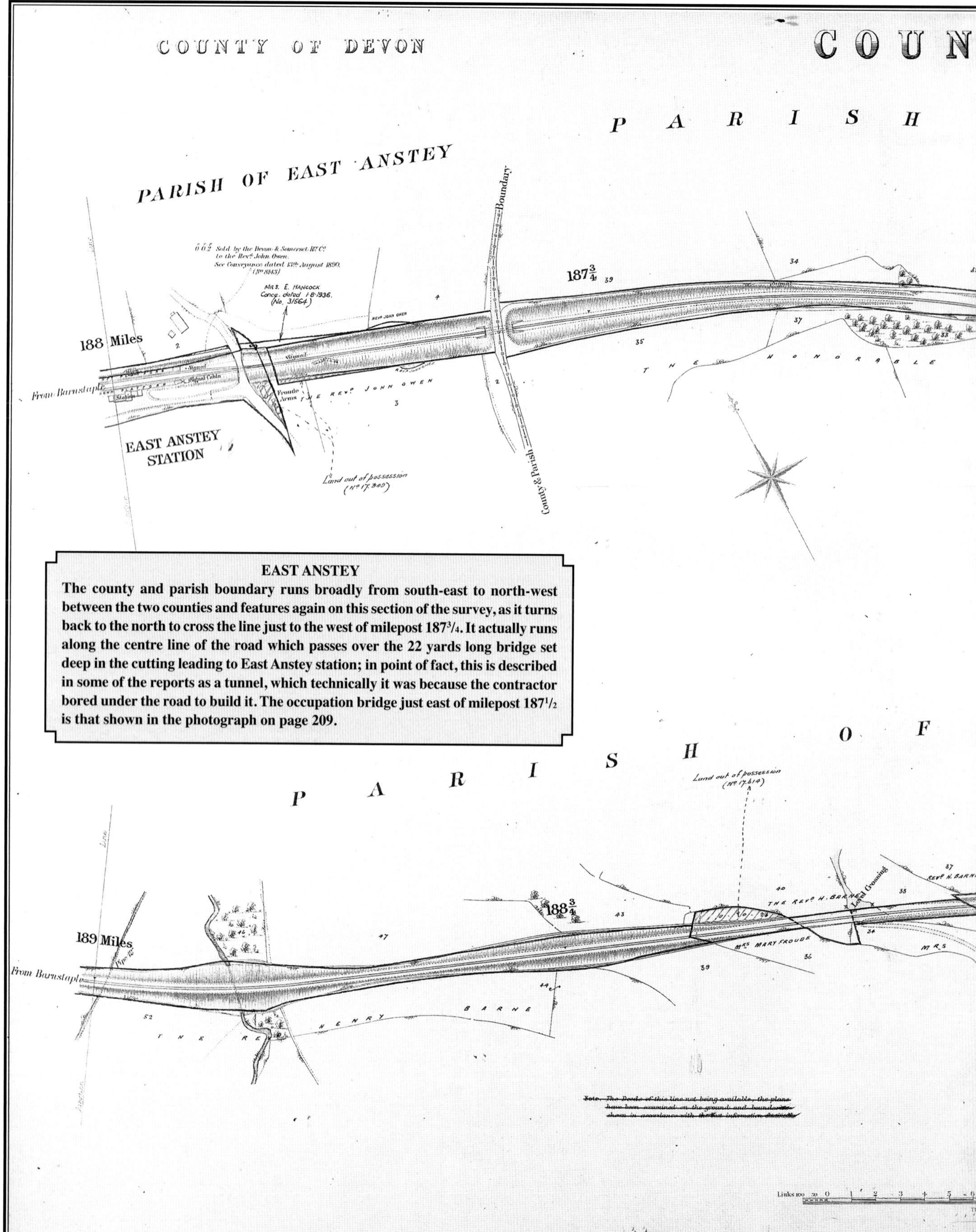

EAST ANSTEY

The county and parish boundary runs broadly from south-east to north-west between the two counties and features again on this section of the survey, as it turns back to the north to cross the line just to the west of milepost 187¾. It actually runs along the centre line of the road which passes over the 22 yards long bridge set deep in the cutting leading to East Anstey station; in point of fact, this is described in some of the reports as a tunnel, which technically it was because the contractor bored under the road to build it. The occupation bridge just east of milepost 187½ is that shown in the photograph on page 209.

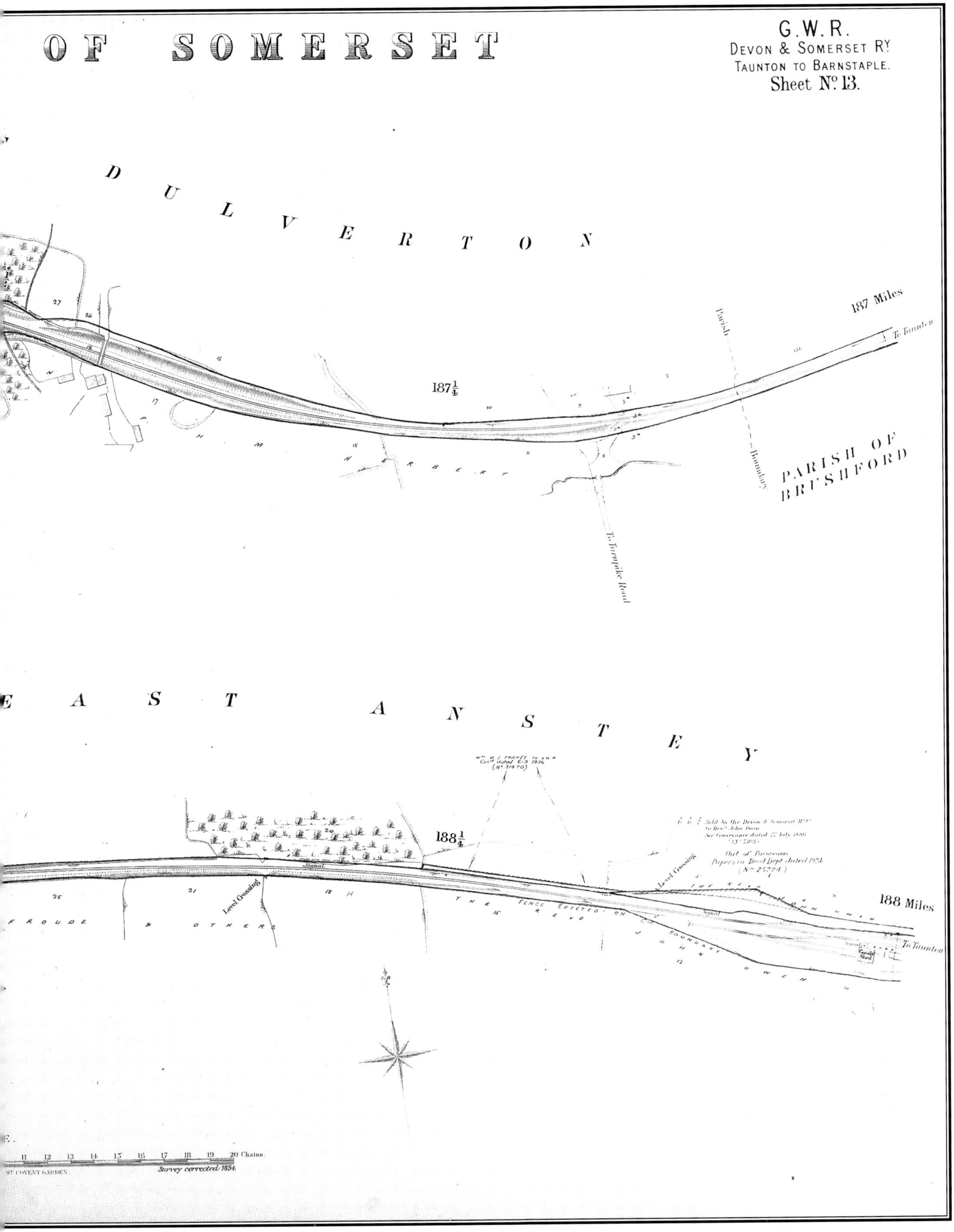

OF SOMERSET

G.W.R.
DEVON & SOMERSET RY.
TAUNTON TO BARNSTAPLE.
Sheet No. 13.

DULVERTON

187 Miles

To Taunton

Parish Boundary

187¼

PARISH OF BRUSHFORD

PHM HERBERT

To Turnpike Road

EAST ANSTEY

Mrs M. J. TRICKEY TO GWR
Cont dated 6.9 1936
(No 31470)

188¼

Sold by the Devon & Somerset RyCo to Revd John Owen
See Conveyance dated 22 July 1886
(No 7303)

Out of Possession
Papers in Deed Dept dated 1924
(No 25224)

Level Crossing

Signal

Level Crossing

188 Miles

To Taunton

FROUDE & OTHERS

THE REVD JOHN OWEN

FENCE ERECTED ON BOUNDARY

11 12 13 14 15 16 17 18 19 20 Chains.

ST COVENT GARDEN.

Survey corrected 1894.

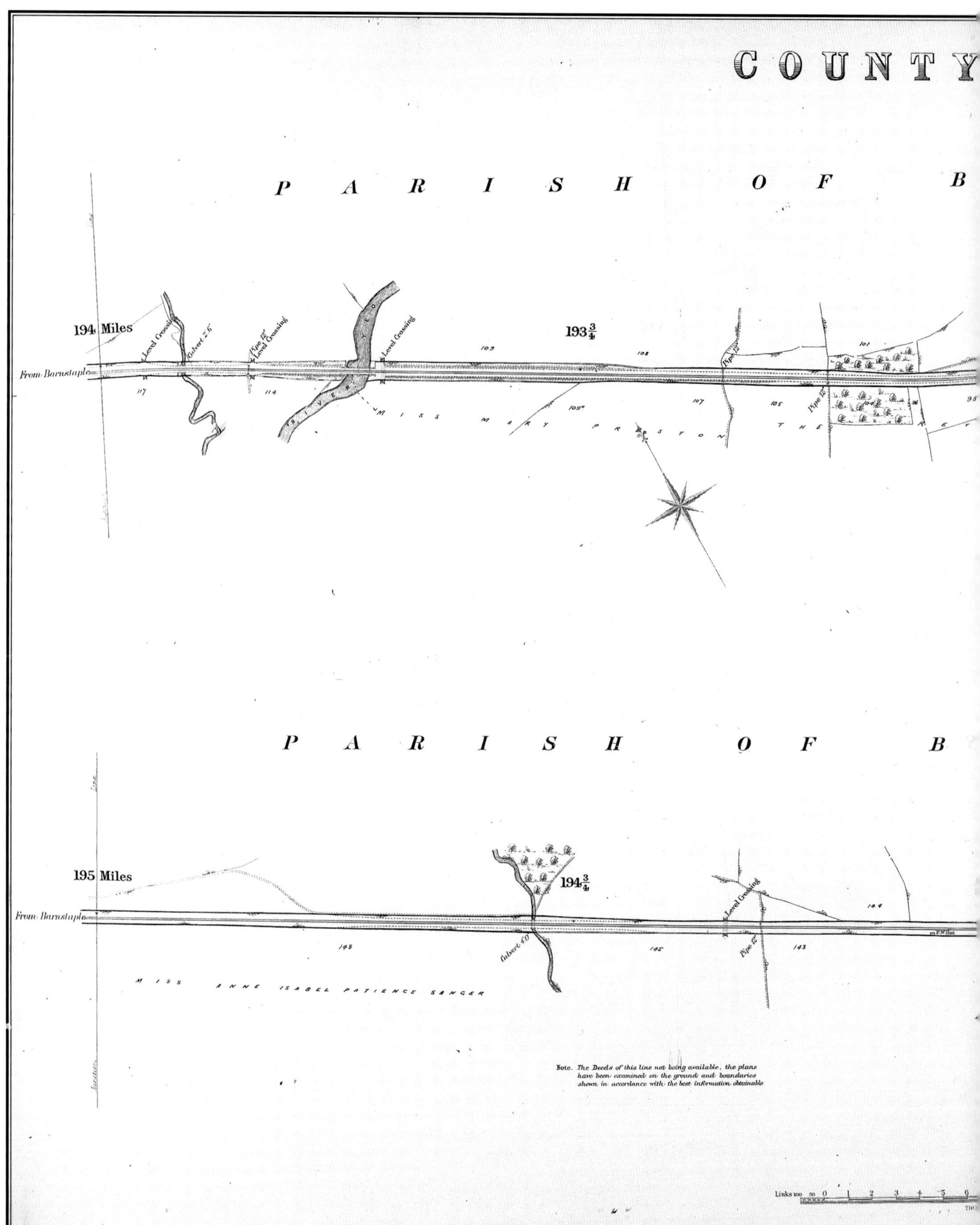
COUNTY
PARISH OF B
194 Miles
193 3/4
From Barnstaple
Level Crossing
Culvert 2'6"
Pipe 12"
Level Crossing
Level Crossing
RIVER YEO
MISS MARY PRESTON
THE REV
PARISH OF B
195 Miles
194 3/4
From Barnstaple
Culvert 4'0"
Level Crossing
Pipe 12"
MISS ANNE ISABEL PATIENCE SANGER
Note. The Deeds of this line not being available, the plans have been examined on the ground and boundaries shown in accordance with the best information obtainable
Links 100 50 0 1 2 3 4 5 6

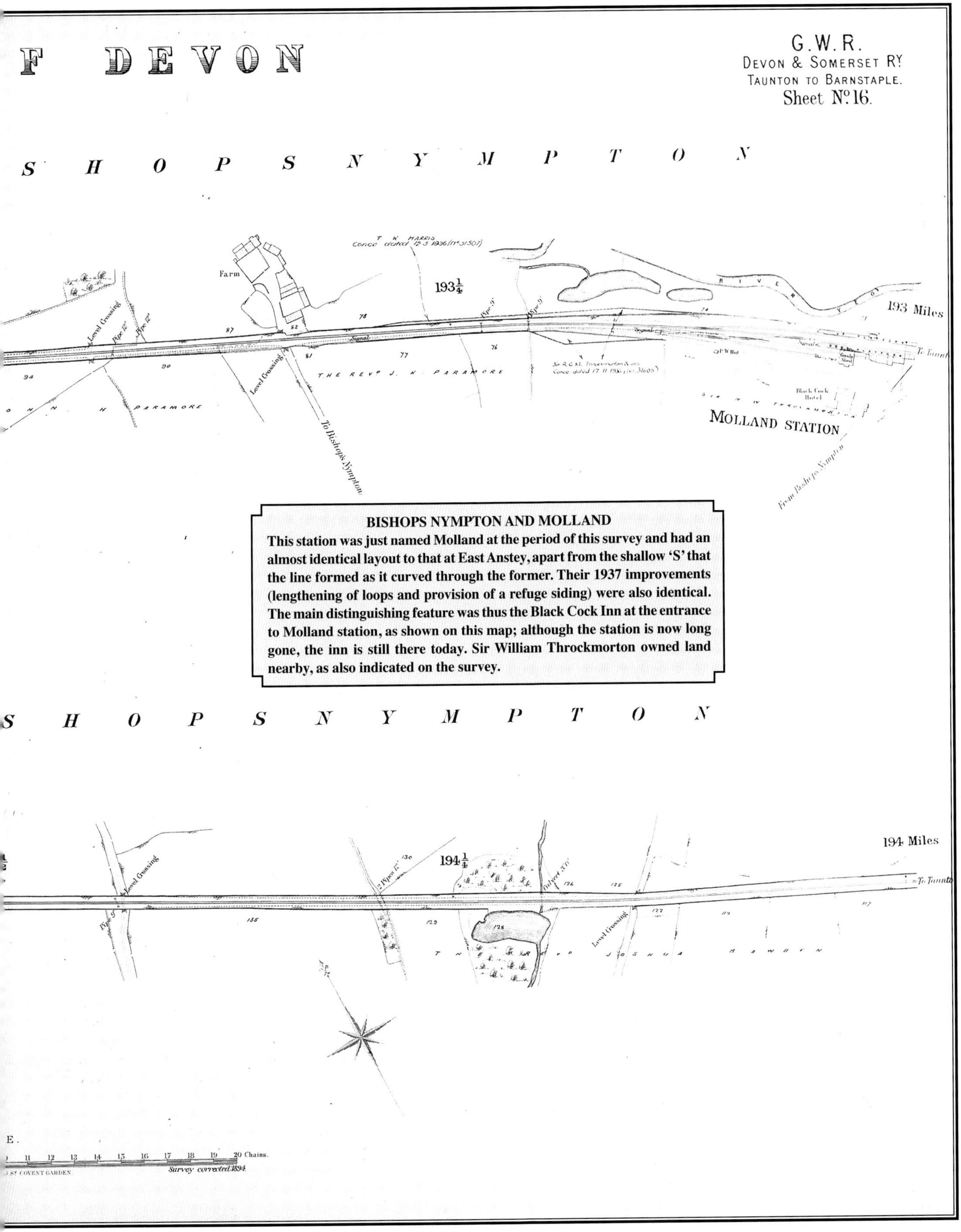

F DEVON

G.W.R.
DEVON & SOMERSET RY.
TAUNTON TO BARNSTAPLE.
Sheet No. 16.

SHOPS NYMPTON

193¼

193 Miles

MOLLAND STATION

BISHOPS NYMPTON AND MOLLAND

This station was just named Molland at the period of this survey and had an almost identical layout to that at East Anstey, apart from the shallow 'S' that the line formed as it curved through the former. Their 1937 improvements (lengthening of loops and provision of a refuge siding) were also identical. The main distinguishing feature was thus the Black Cock Inn at the entrance to Molland station, as shown on this map; although the station is now long gone, the inn is still there today. Sir William Throckmorton owned land nearby, as also indicated on the survey.

SHOPS NYMPTON

194¼

194 Miles

Survey corrected 1894

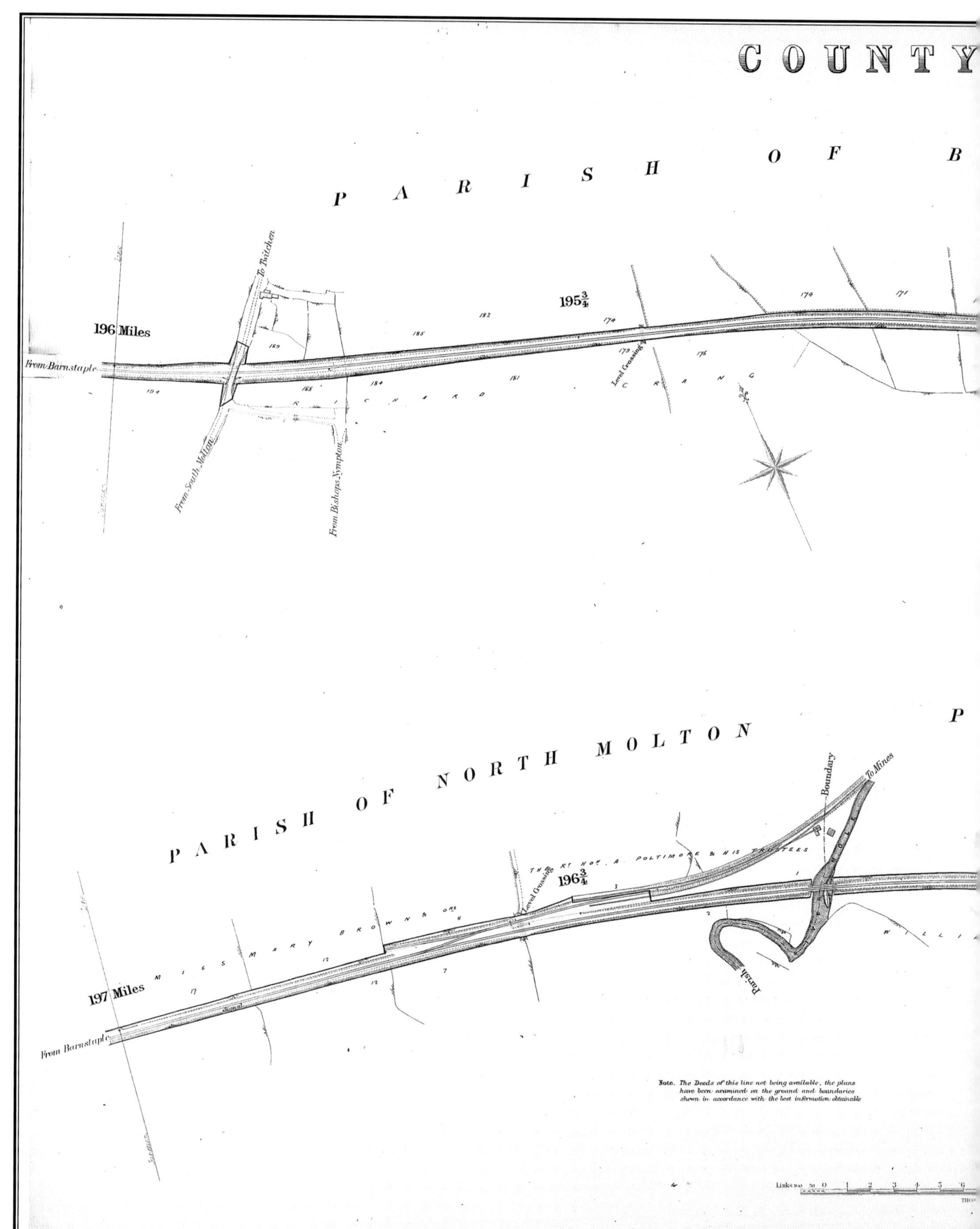
COUNTY
PARISH OF B
196 Miles
195¾
From Barnstaple
To Twitchen
From South Molton
From Bishops Nympton
Level Crossing
RICHARD CRANG
PARISH OF NORTH MOLTON
197 Miles
196¾
From Barnstaple
Level Crossing
MISS MARY BROWN & ORS
THE RT HON. A. POLTIMORE & HIS TRUSTEES
Boundary
To Mines
Parish
Signal
Note. The Deeds of this line not being available, the plans have been examined on the ground and boundaries shewn in accordance with the best information obtainable

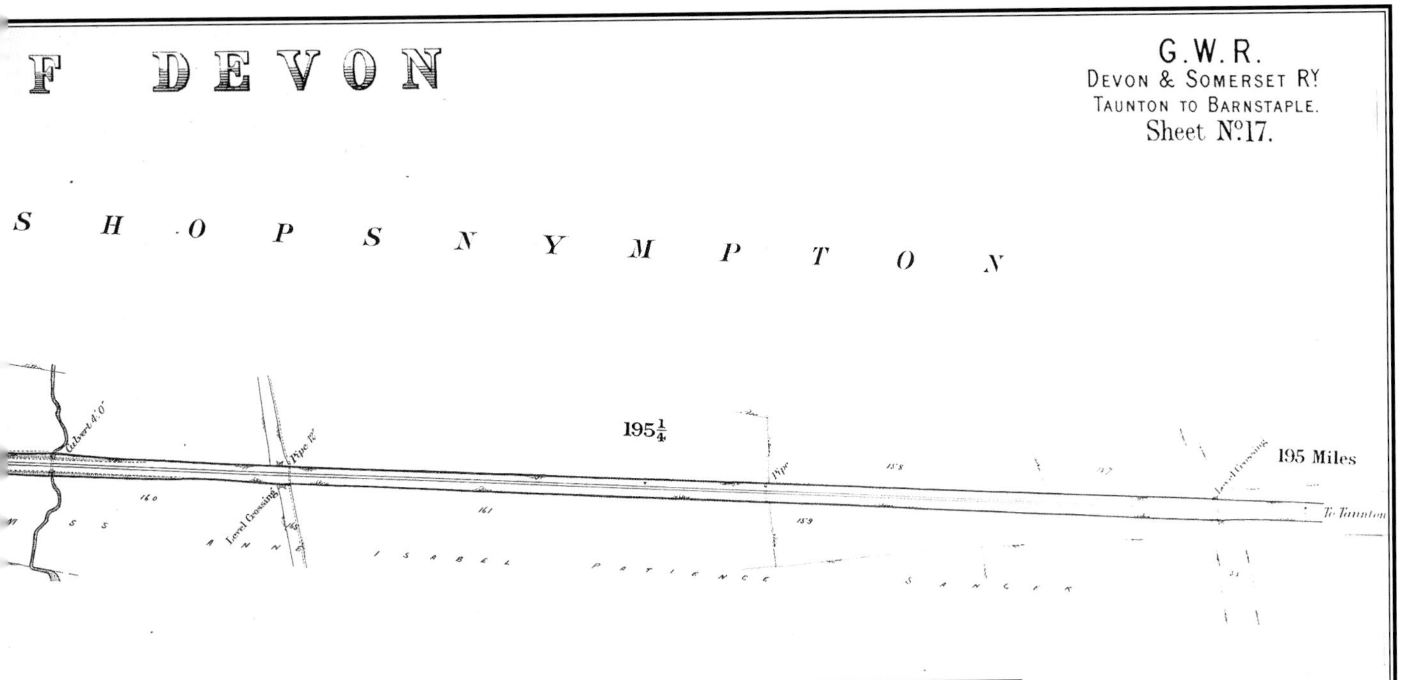

F DEVON

G.W.R.
DEVON & SOMERSET RY.
TAUNTON TO BARNSTAPLE.
Sheet No. 17.

S H O P S N Y M P T O N

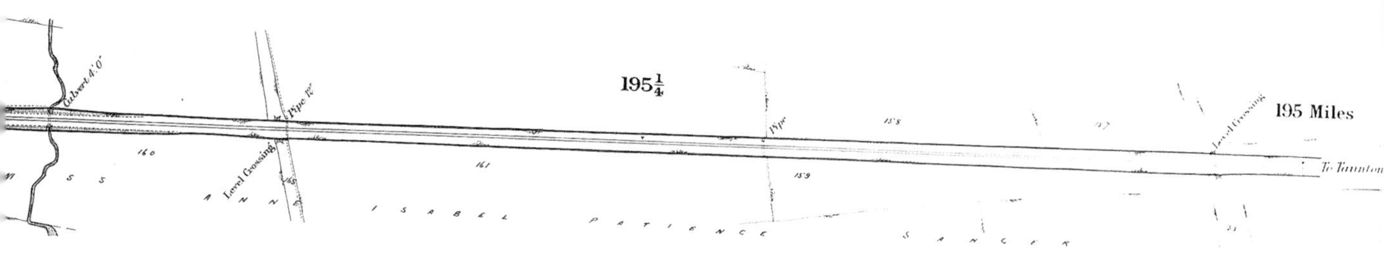

THE FLORENCE MINE TRAMWAY

Whilst these two sections of the survey were mostly plain line with few in the way of features, it does show the transshipment wharf with the Flornce Mine Tramway at milepost 196¾ and the simple track layout serving it, as described in the text on pages 21-22; arrangements at the wharf will also be covered in the Signalling chapter that will appear in volume 2. Note the River Mole, which paralleled the tramway for much of its route, snaking its way under the railway near the wharf.

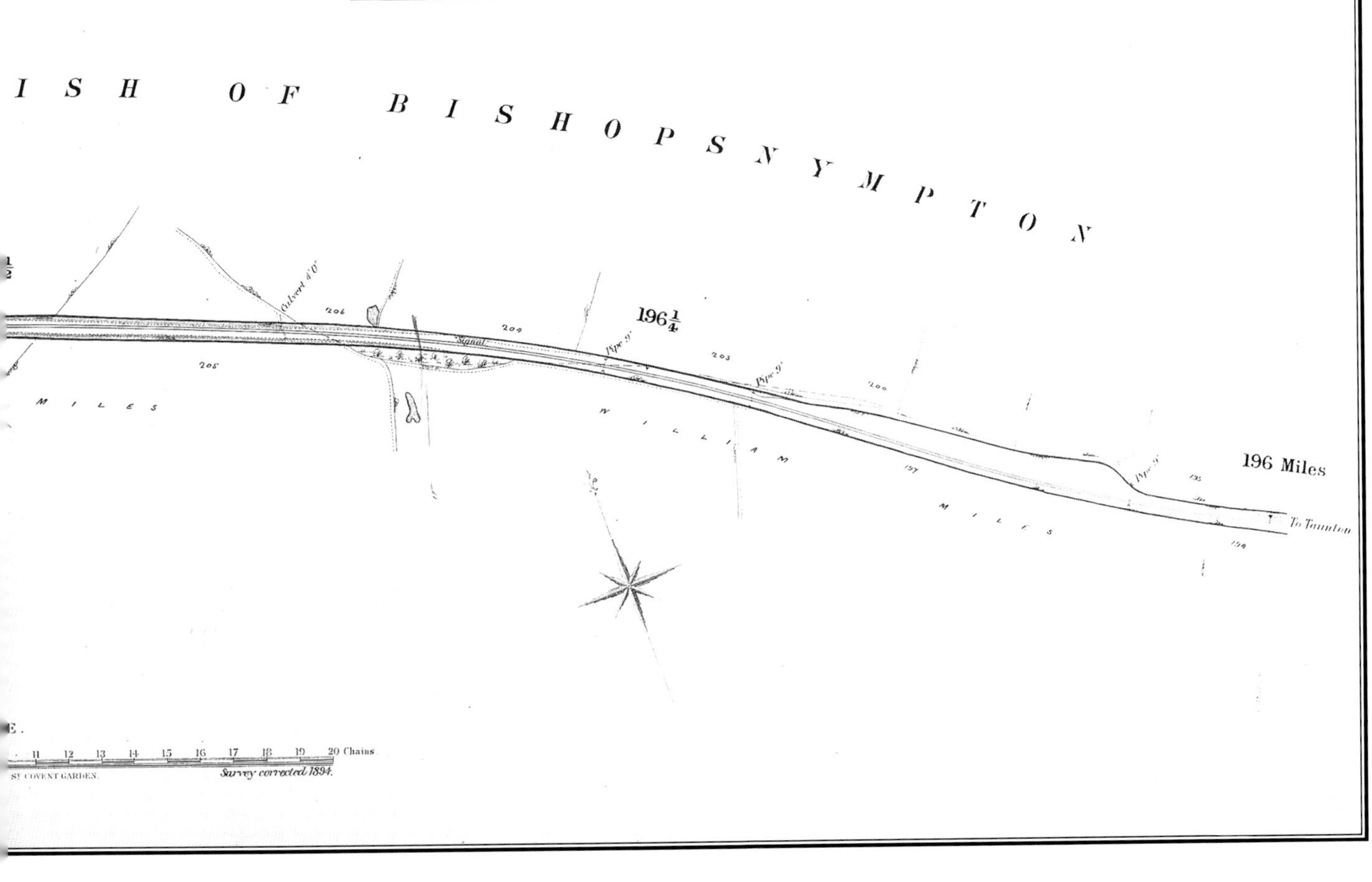

I S H O F B I S H O P S N Y M P T O N

Culvert 4'0"
Signal
196¼
Pipe 9"
Pipe 9"
196 Miles
To Taunton
M I L E S
WILLIAM MILES

11 12 13 14 15 16 17 18 19 20 Chains
Survey corrected 1894.

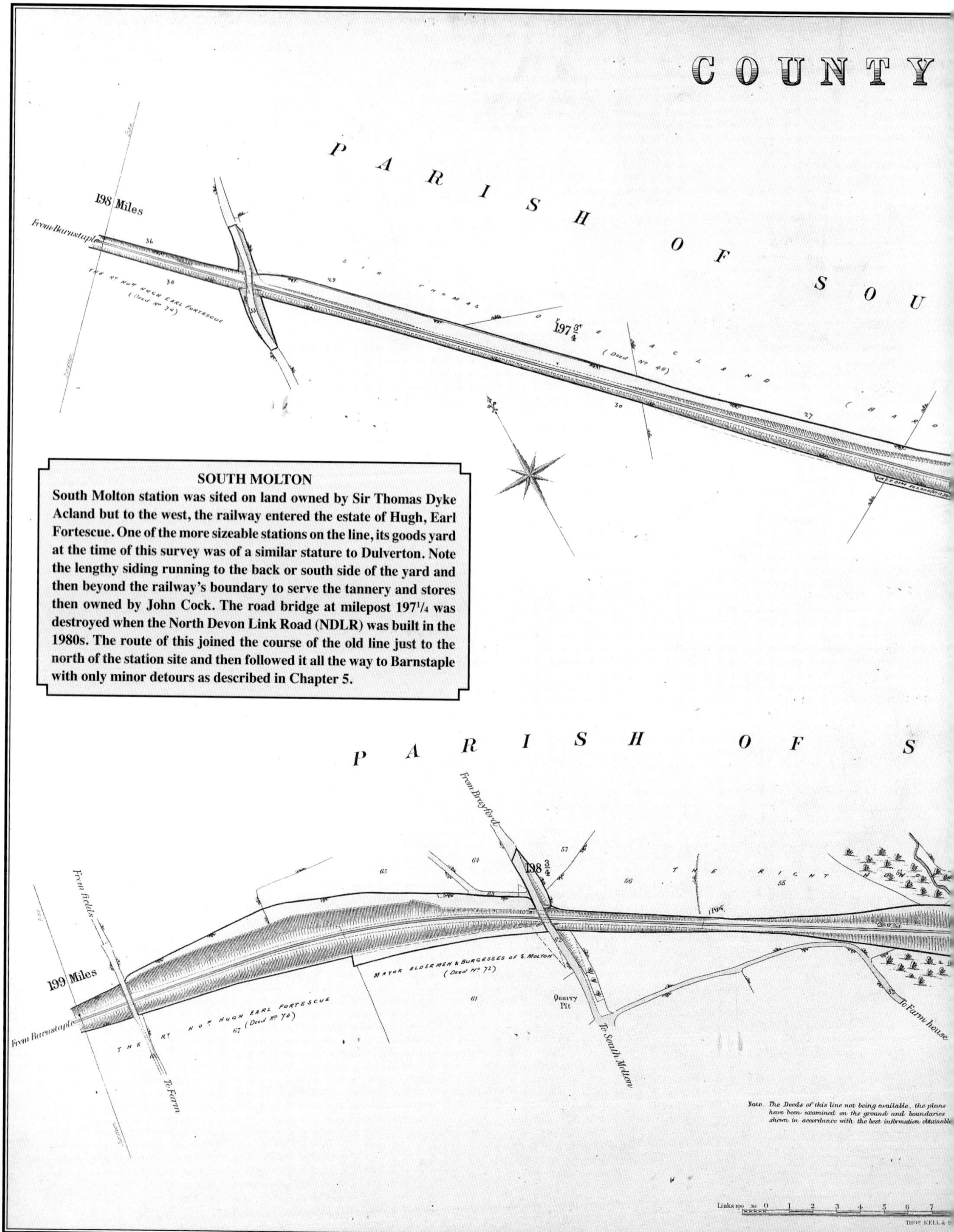

SOUTH MOLTON

South Molton station was sited on land owned by Sir Thomas Dyke Acland but to the west, the railway entered the estate of Hugh, Earl Fortescue. One of the more sizeable stations on the line, its goods yard at the time of this survey was of a similar stature to Dulverton. Note the lengthy siding running to the back or south side of the yard and then beyond the railway's boundary to serve the tannery and stores then owned by John Cock. The road bridge at milepost 197¹/₄ was destroyed when the North Devon Link Road (NDLR) was built in the 1980s. The route of this joined the course of the old line just to the north of the station site and then followed it all the way to Barnstaple with only minor detours as described in Chapter 5.

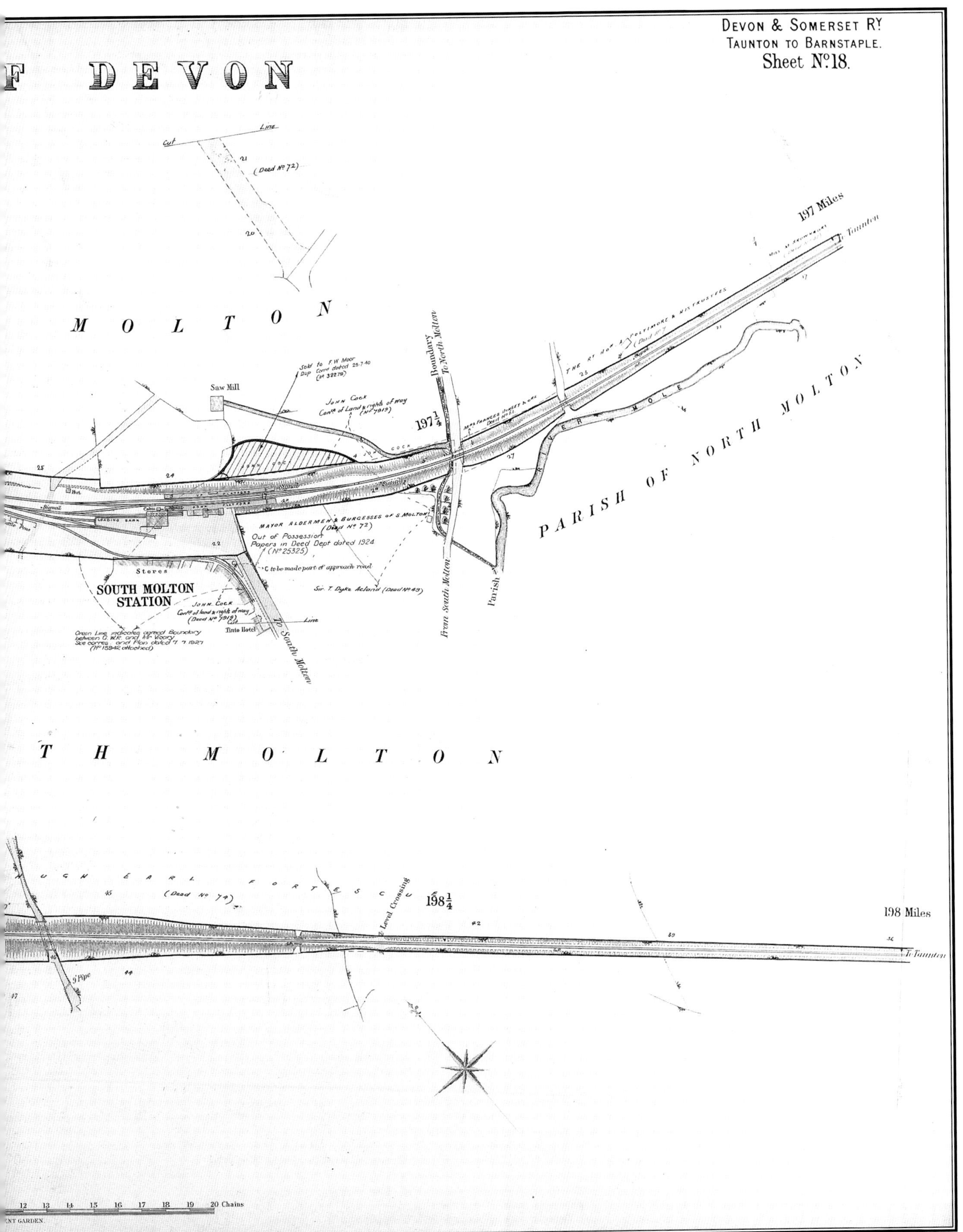
DEVON & SOMERSET RY
TAUNTON TO BARNSTAPLE.
Sheet No.18.
F DEVON
M O L T O N
Saw Mill
SOUTH MOLTON STATION
Stores
Tinto Hotel
197 Miles
197¼
198¼
198 Miles
To Taunton
PARISH OF NORTH MOLTON
RIVER MOLE
Boundary
To North Molton
From South Molton
Parish
To South Molton
Level Crossing
MAYOR ALDERMEN & BURGESSES OF S. MOLTON (Deed No 72)
Out of Possession Papers in Deed Dept dated 1924 (No 25325)
C to be made part of approach road
Sir T. Dyke Acland (Deed No 49)
JOHN COCK
TH MOLTON
(Deed No 79)
12 13 14 15 16 17 18 19 20 Chains

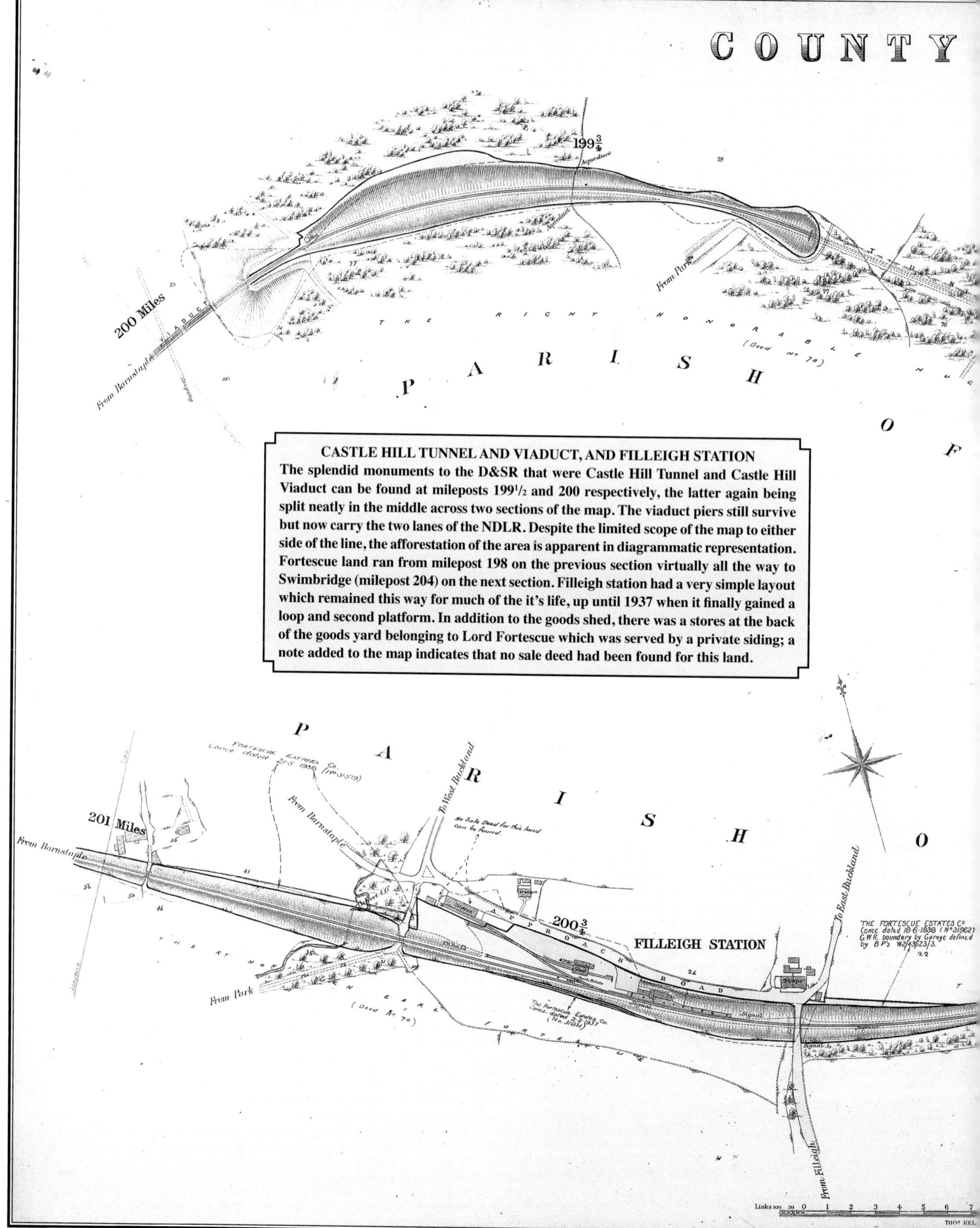

CASTLE HILL TUNNEL AND VIADUCT, AND FILLEIGH STATION

The splendid monuments to the D&SR that were Castle Hill Tunnel and Castle Hill Viaduct can be found at mileposts 199½ and 200 respectively, the latter again being split neatly in the middle across two sections of the map. The viaduct piers still survive but now carry the two lanes of the NDLR. Despite the limited scope of the map to either side of the line, the afforestation of the area is apparent in diagrammatic representation. Fortescue land ran from milepost 198 on the previous section virtually all the way to Swimbridge (milepost 204) on the next section. Filleigh station had a very simple layout which remained this way for much of the it's life, up until 1937 when it finally gained a loop and second platform. In addition to the goods shed, there was a stores at the back of the goods yard belonging to Lord Fortescue which was served by a private siding; a note added to the map indicates that no sale deed had been found for this land.

F DEVON
G.W.R.
DEVON & SOMERSET RY.
TAUNTON TO BARNSTAPLE.
Sheet No. 19.
199 Miles
To Taunton
199¼
FORTESCUE (Deed No 74)
To Keepers
From Park
SOUTH MOLTON
FILLEIGH
200 Miles
To Taunton
200¼
RIGHT HON.BLE HUGH EARL FORTESCUE (Deed No 74)
Parish Boundary
RIVER BRAY
Note. The Deeds of this line not being available, the plans have been examined on the ground and boundaries shown in accordance with the best information obtainable
11 12 13 14 15 16 17 18 19 20 Chains.
COVENT GARDEN.

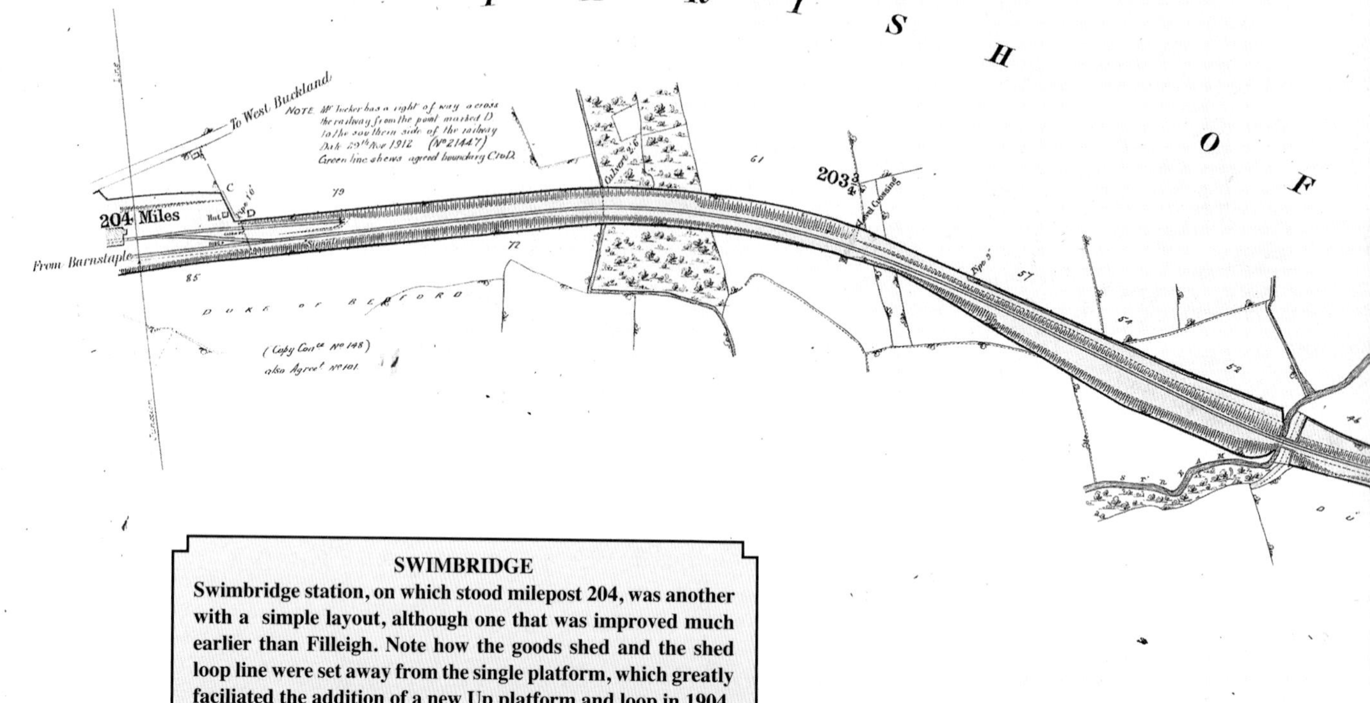

SWIMBRIDGE
Swimbridge station, on which stood milepost 204, was another with a simple layout, although one that was improved much earlier than Filleigh. Note how the goods shed and the shed loop line were set away from the single platform, which greatly faciliated the addition of a new Up platform and loop in 1904.

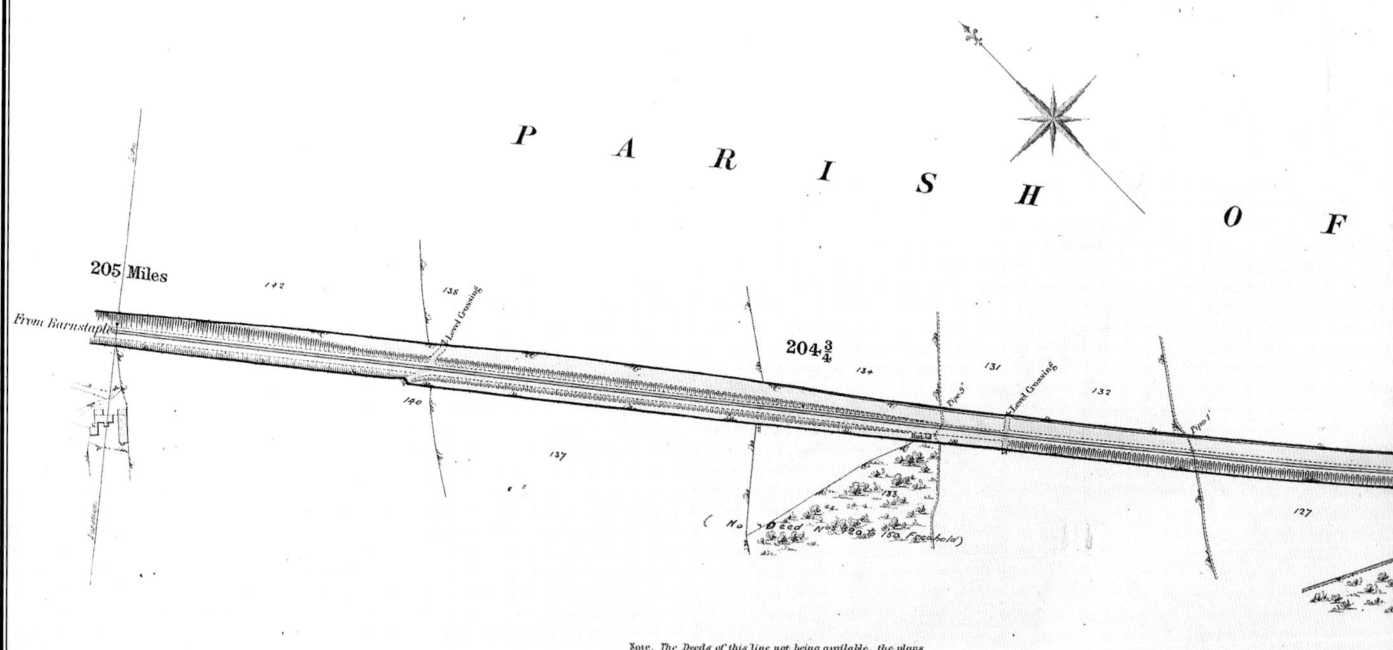

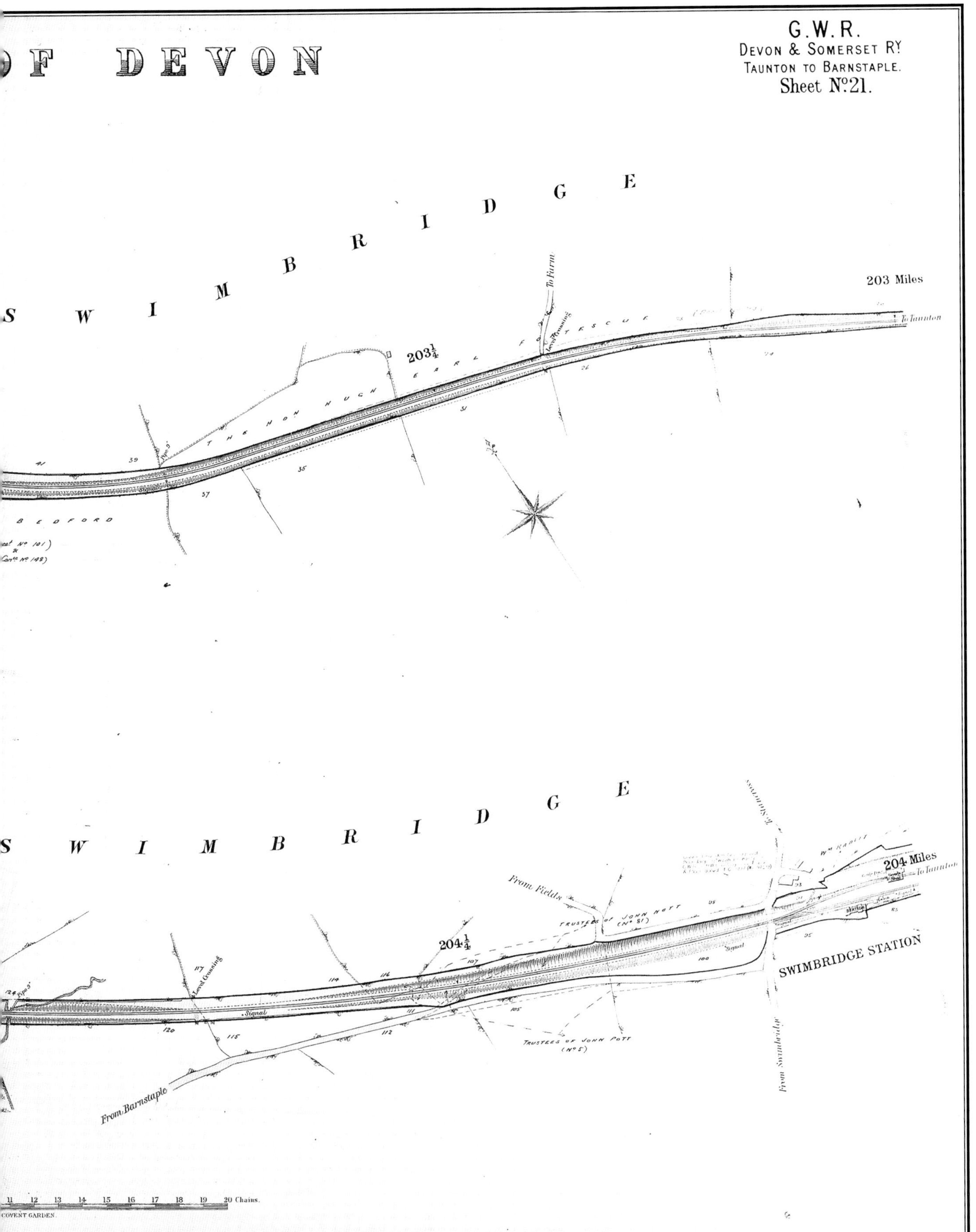

OF DEVON
G.W.R.
Devon & Somerset Ry.
Taunton to Barnstaple.
Sheet No. 21.
SWIMBRIDGE
203 Miles
To Taunton
To Farm
Level Crossing
203¼
The Hon Hugh Earl Fortescue
Bedford
SWIMBRIDGE
204 Miles
To Taunton
From Fields
Trustees of John Nott (No. 81)
204¼
Level Crossing
Signal
Swimbridge Station
Trustees of John Pott (No. 5)
From Barnstaple
From Swimbridge
11 12 13 14 15 16 17 18 19 20 Chains.
Covent Garden.

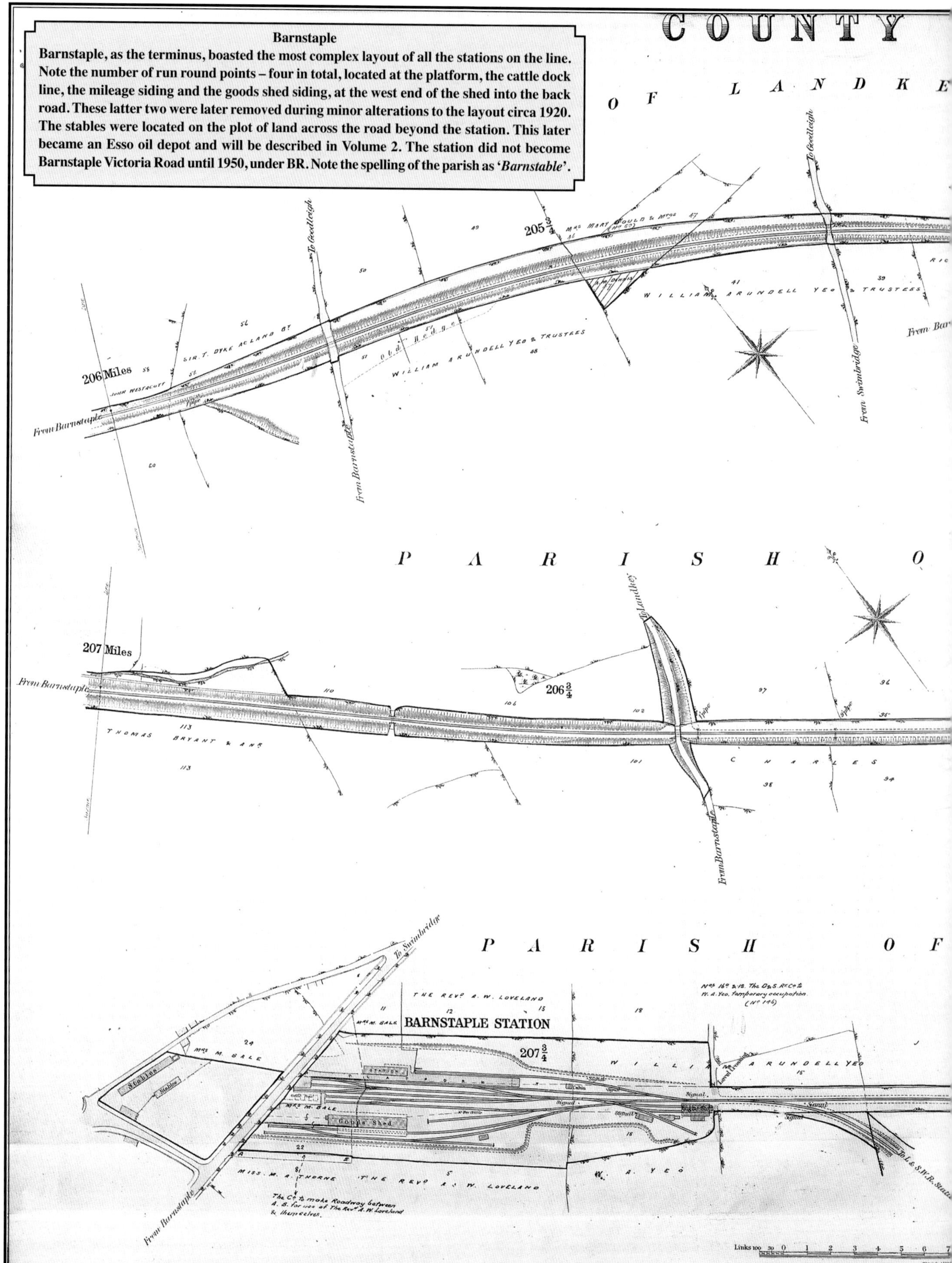

Barnstaple

Barnstaple, as the terminus, boasted the most complex layout of all the stations on the line. Note the number of run round points – four in total, located at the platform, the cattle dock line, the mileage siding and the goods shed siding, at the west end of the shed into the back road. These latter two were later removed during minor alterations to the layout circa 1920. The stables were located on the plot of land across the road beyond the station. This later became an Esso oil depot and will be described in Volume 2. The station did not become Barnstaple Victoria Road until 1950, under BR. Note the spelling of the parish as '*Barnstable*'.

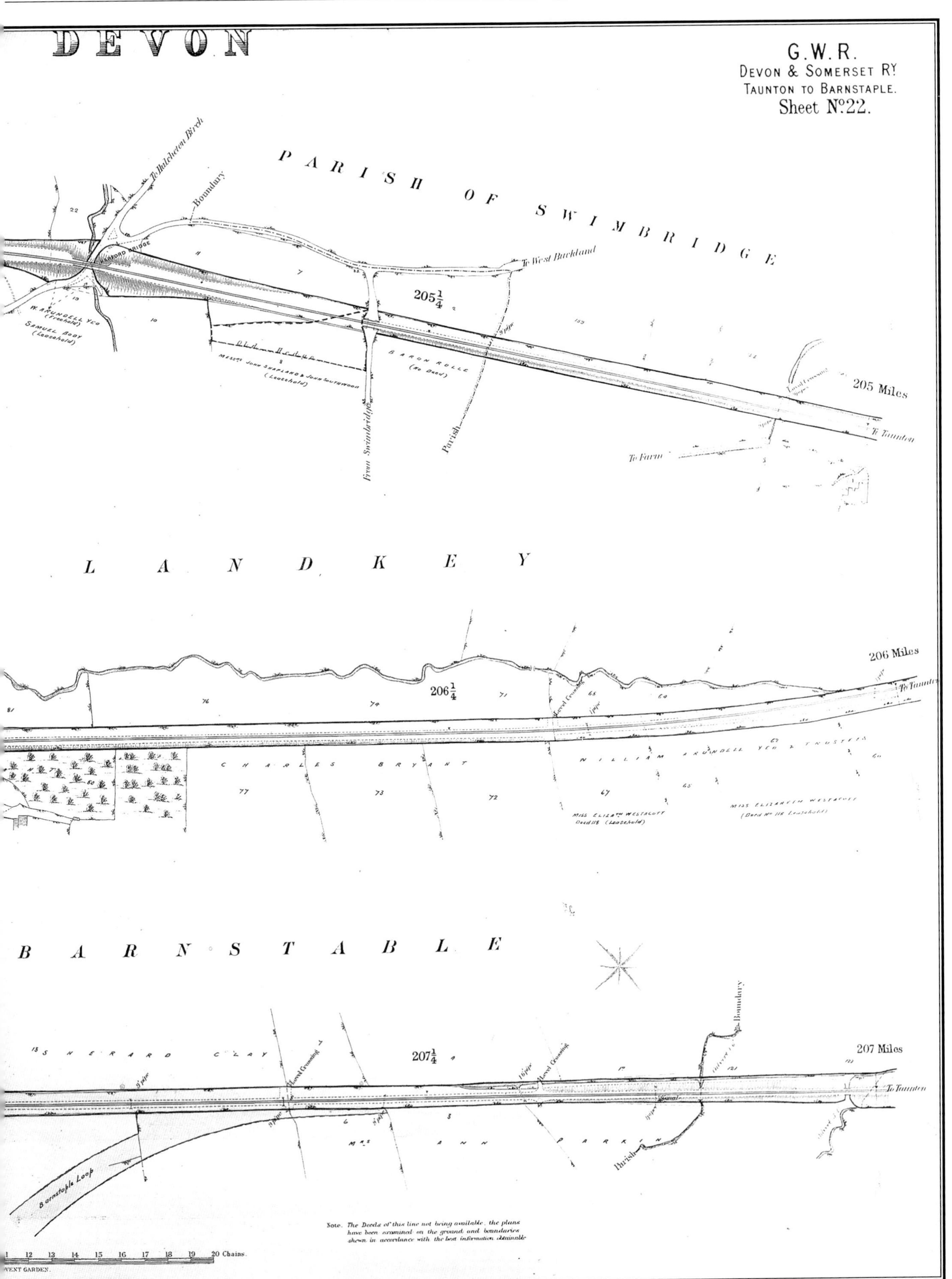
DEVON
G.W.R.
Devon & Somerset Ry.
Taunton to Barnstaple.
Sheet No. 22.
Parish of Swimbridge
Landkey
Barnstable
205 Miles
206 Miles
207 Miles
To Taunton
Baron Rolle (No Deed)
Charles Bryant
William Arundell Yeo & Trustees
Mrs Ann Parkin
Barnstaple Loop
Note. The Deeds of this line not being available, the plans have been examined on the ground and boundaries shown in accordance with the best information obtainable
20 Chains

South Molton station from an old postcard that was posted in 1908. The view makes an interesting comparison with the broad gauge picture on page 80 and shows that the the Up platform was widened after the gauge was narrowed and the Down platform face rebuilt in stone, whilst the end wall of the main station building has been slated to protect the stonework against the weather. As the station staff load some large baskets labelled 'SHEFFIELD' into the milk van on the rear of an Up mixed train, three well dressed young ladies pose for the photographer on the right. ***John Alsop collection***

FOUR-HORSE COACH IN 1902 – 'THE WILD WEST'

From 1st July to 27th September 1902, a four-horse coach started from the Beach Hotel in Minehead on Tuesdays, Thursdays and Saturdays, departing after the 9.09am train, returning from the Carnarvon Arms Hotel at 3.00pm the same day. The local fares were 5s 6d single, 10s return and 1s extra for a box seat.

LINE IMPROVEMENTS 1902-1923

Following its takeover by the GWR, the financial security of the line was no longer in doubt. It was now about the integration of the railway into the GWR network and carrying out improvements, as and when required, for the benefit of the service and those wanting to use the line. Therefore, the focus for the remainder of this chapter is of improvements and developments to the line rather than financing and survival.

It did not take the GWR long to focus on the line, with works at Dulverton being approved by the GWR Board on 9th October 1902, in the amount of £2,611, which were carried out in 1904 (see below). Also noted as approved in the GWR minutes was a contract for the repair of roadways and footpaths upon a bridge over the railway at South Molton. In addition, it was agreed on 12th April 1903 that additional sidings should be constructed there at a cost of £973. Other improvements followed and these are set out chronologically over the following pages.

MILVERTON

Milverton station gained its passing loop and Up platform in 1880, probably at the same time that the line was being narrowed from broad to standard gauge. The original timber signal box clearly still sufficed despite this expansion and thus remained in use for a further two decades, until it was replaced in 1903 by a new brick-built cabin, situated a little further along the Down platform, at 169 miles and 48 chains, next to the station buildings. Measuring 21 feet by 12 feet, the frame had 21 levers but was replaced by a larger one with 37 levers in 1936.

A postcard view from the rear of the Up platform at Milverton, showing the new brick-built, hipped roof signal box provided in 1903. ***John Alsop collection***

Many of the early general views of Milverton station were taken from Station Road bridge, so this photograph looking east from the Up platform around 1910 makes a welcome change. This platform was added in 1880 and the decorative barge boards on the timber-built waiting shelter on this side are very B&ER in style and there is much other useful detail in the picture to study. On a fine day and in a quiet moment between trains, the station staff have come out to pose for the photographer. The photograph was taken by William Samuel Chapman, who by this date was proprietor of the photographic studio established in Dawlish in the early 1860s by his father, William James Chapman. The firm were prolific publishers of photographic picture postcards from the early years of the 20th century through to the late 1930s, covering much of their home county as well as venturing further afield on occasion. They photographed many of the railway stations in Devon and may have had an interest beyond simply using the railways to get around. *John Alsop collection*

A Down passenger train at Swimbridge, not long after completion of the 1904 improvements. As built, the station had a single platform and a loop running through the goods shed with a siding running off it at the Taunton end. Fortuitously, there was enough space between these two lines to fit in the passing loop and new Up platform in 1904, which was built right up to the wall of the goods shed. However, the goods loop at this end of the station was realigned outwards a few feet to allow for some extra width to the platform and the provision of a waiting shelter; it then narrowed considerably to run past the goods shed. Note the B&ER style barge boarding on the signal box, which was extended to accept a larger frame. It is clear from the platform that it had rained shortly before the picture was taken. The train comprises mostly bogie clerestory roofed stock, with a 6-wheeled luggage or parcels van leading and headed by an elderly 'Standard Goods' 0-6-0; built in batches between 1866 and 1876, the engine would thus be at least thirty years of age. ***The Lens of Sutton Association***

SWIMBRIDGE

On 7th September 1904, Lieut Col P.B. Von Donop of the BoT reported on the new passing loop at Swimbridge, which had also gained a new Up platform. The platform was reported as 400 feet long, 3 feet high and a minimum width of 8 feet, and was provided with a shelter. It was stated that the points and signals were worked from the existing signal box, which had been extended and a new frame containing 21 levers (3 of which were spare) provided.

WIVELISCOMBE

Wiveliscombe station underwent significant change over the first decade or so of the 20th century. The first alteration took place in 1904, when the horse dock siding was added at the Down end of the station. It was accessed via a trailing connection from the Up loop line as, unlike many other companies, the GWR had a strong aversion to facing connections on main running lines. The point was worked from the existing signal box containing 14 levers (1 spare).

However, this was only for a short time as the signal box, situated on the Up platform, was replaced in 1906, by a new box situated just beyond the east end of the Up platform and opened on 20th June. Early photographs show that the old box remained in situ for a short while after construction of the new one, whilst the latter was not to remain in isolation for long. On 8th May 1907, authorisation was given to extend both platforms by around half their length again at the eastern or Up end of the station, this work being completed by the September. The Up platform extension was built around the new signal cabin, which had a brick base, thus giving the impression that it was built entirely of timber and situated on the platform, like the one it replaced.

At around the same time in 1907, the original three sidings in the goods yard were rearranged. The goods

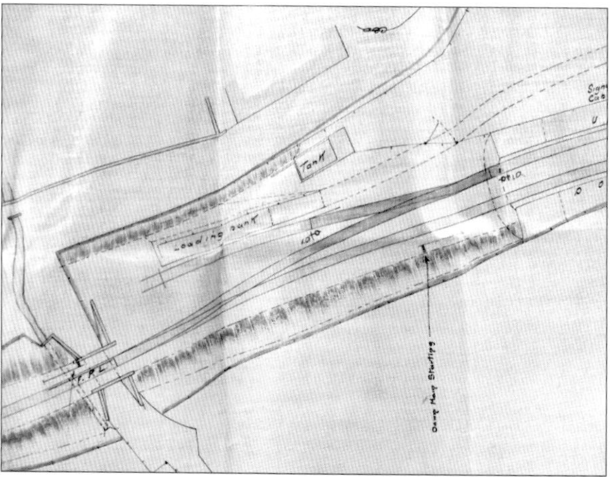

A plan of the new horse loading dock and siding installed at the Down end of Wiveliscombe station. ***Courtesy National Archives***

shed road remained as it was but the two in the yard were lengthened and the headshunt was removed to make way for a new siding. All of the sidings were rejoined to the Up loop line, which itself was lengthened at the Taunton end, via a new trailing connection.

Finally, in early 1911, the Up loop was extended at the Down end of the station.

RIGHT: A view west through Wiveliscombe station platforms in 1906. The new horse loading dock is hidden behind the barrow on the Down platform but its presence is indicated by the new signal just in front of the water tower, bearing a short Goods arm. This was later replaced by a disc signal positioned in between the running lines. *Author's collection*

A corresponding view eastwards, with both the original box, left, and the new signal box, centre right, in view. Taken before the platforms were extended, this photograph must therefore date from late 1906/early 1907. Note the brick base to the 1906 box, which was largely obscured when the Up platform extension was built around it. The base of the original box was retained, given a flat roof and converted for use as a store. *Author's collection*

DULVERTON

BoT Inspector P.G. Von Donop reported on 9th September 1904 in respect of the two new connections that were added on the Down station loop, one at the Up end of the station being a facing point for Down trains. The other, which was at the Down end of the station, was a trailing connection. Both connections led to new sidings laid in on the Down side of the line, along with a short terminal bay for Exe Valley line trains. The points and signals were worked from a new signal box with a larger frame containing 37 levers (1 spare), which was positioned at the far end of the Up platform beyond the goods shed, the old box having been located on the Down side, a little way off the Taunton end of the platform. The inspector confirmed the interlocking was satisfactory and so sanctioned the improvements. It was noted that the existing facing points at the Up end of the station had been experimentally fitted with an electrical locking arrangement and over the eleven months it had been in use, it had failed on two separate occasions, due to the contact rod becoming bent and failing to make contact. These failures made it impossible to lower the Down home signal and caused delays but there was no danger of any sort from the failure of the electrical apparatus.

Dulverton station from the road bridge circa 1907, after the alterations of August-September 1904. The new signal box can just be glimpsed through the footbridge, the one it replaced having been sited about where the 0-6-0ST shunting the new yard can be made out in the right distance. The sidings on the right were all new and clearly in use here for timber traffic. Note also the buffer stops marking the end of the new Exe Valley bay right behind the Down side building. The train at the Down platform, with a '517' Class 0-4-2T at the head, may be an Exe Valley service terminating here, after which the engine can run round its carriages and then reverse them in to the bay. However, the '517' Class did work passenger trains over the full length of the line between Taunton and Barnstaple, so it could equally be a D&SR line service. The station changed again in 1911, when the Up platform was lengthened and a new signal box sited on it a little further to the east, with the Down platform being lengthened and widened, and the Exe Valley bay extended to form a loop. Note the two Forest of Dean private owner wagons in the Up side yard, bringing house coal from Foxes Bridge and Parkend collieries, and also the array of horse-drawn vehicles waiting for passengers wishing to make the near two mile journey on to Dulverton town itself. The railway meanwhile, having curved to the right (southwards) out of the picture, then makes a wide turn to head east along the valley floor, before disappearing once again behind the roof of the Down side station building. This photograph is again the work of Chapman & Son of Dawlish and was published as a postcard. *Courtesy Great Western Society*

One of the earliest known photographs of Barnstaple GWR station, looking east from the buffer stops circa 1910. It is highly unlikely that the train at the platform has been hauled tender first all the way from Taunton; most probably it has been brought round the West Chord from Barnstaple Junction. The locomotive is a 'Dean Goods' Class 0-6-0 but coupled to an Armstrong tender. The Mex B cattle wagons give the clue that the livestock pens were situated just out of view on the right. The Cordon wagon in the middle of the picture carried gas to replenish the reservoirs in the gas-lit carriages; such vehicles were a common sight at terminus stations at this period, disappearing after the First World War as gas lighting in carriages was phased out. Note the plethora of enamelled advertising signs on the fence and station building, another once common feature. *John Alsop collection*

VENN CROSS

On 24th July 1905, Lieut Col H.A. Yorke, the BoT Inspector, reported that improvement works at Venn Cross had been completed on 17th July to a satisfactory standard and requested sanction from the BoT for their use. Previously, the station had comprised a single line with a point leading in to a siding on the south side at the Barnstaple or Down end, from which a second siding ran back through the goods shed. Now, a new loop line and Up platform had been constructed and the station converted into a passing place for passenger trains. At the same time, the old Down platform was raised and extended, and improved siding connections laid on the Up and Down lines, meaning that the small goods yard could now be accessed from both directions. It was noted that, owing to the gradient on either side of the station, runaway catch points were provided at the lower end of each loop line. On the new Up platform, a shelter and urinals were constructed and a new signal box was built on the Down platform, containing 22 levers in use and 7 spares.

BARNSTAPLE LOOP (THE EAST CHORD)

The GWR wrote to the BoT on 13th April 1905 in respect of the East Chord:

'It will be observed that the Junctions are to be laid as single line Junctions only, and I have asked that the Board of Trade will agree to dispense with the provision of double line junctions at the present time. It is not the intention to cross any trains at any of the three junctions, and all trains passing over the facing points at all three junctions will do so at such speeds as to admit of changing train staffs by hand. It is intended to use the new loop shown in red [the East Chord] *for two or three trains at the most, and for only about three or four months in the summer.'*

Lieut Col Yorke reported on 25th July 1905 that:

'The loop has been constructed so as to form a connection between the line from Taunton to Barnstaple (GW) and the line from Barnstaple (GW) and Ilfracombe so as to enable trains when desired to run direct to Ilfracombe without having to enter Barnstaple (GW) station. The loop is about 24 chains long and is single throughout. The radius of the curve is 20 chains and the line is practically level. The embankment was constructed many years ago [1887] *and is thoroughly consolidated. There are no bridges or works on the line … Two new signal boxes have been built viz Barnstaple East box containing 13 levers all in use and Barnstaple South box containing 11 levers and 2 spare levers.'*

The works were completed on 14th July 1905. Reference back to the map of the Barnstaple Branch Railway on page 91 shows the earthworks of the embankment for the East Chord and thus a long-standing commitment to building this loop.

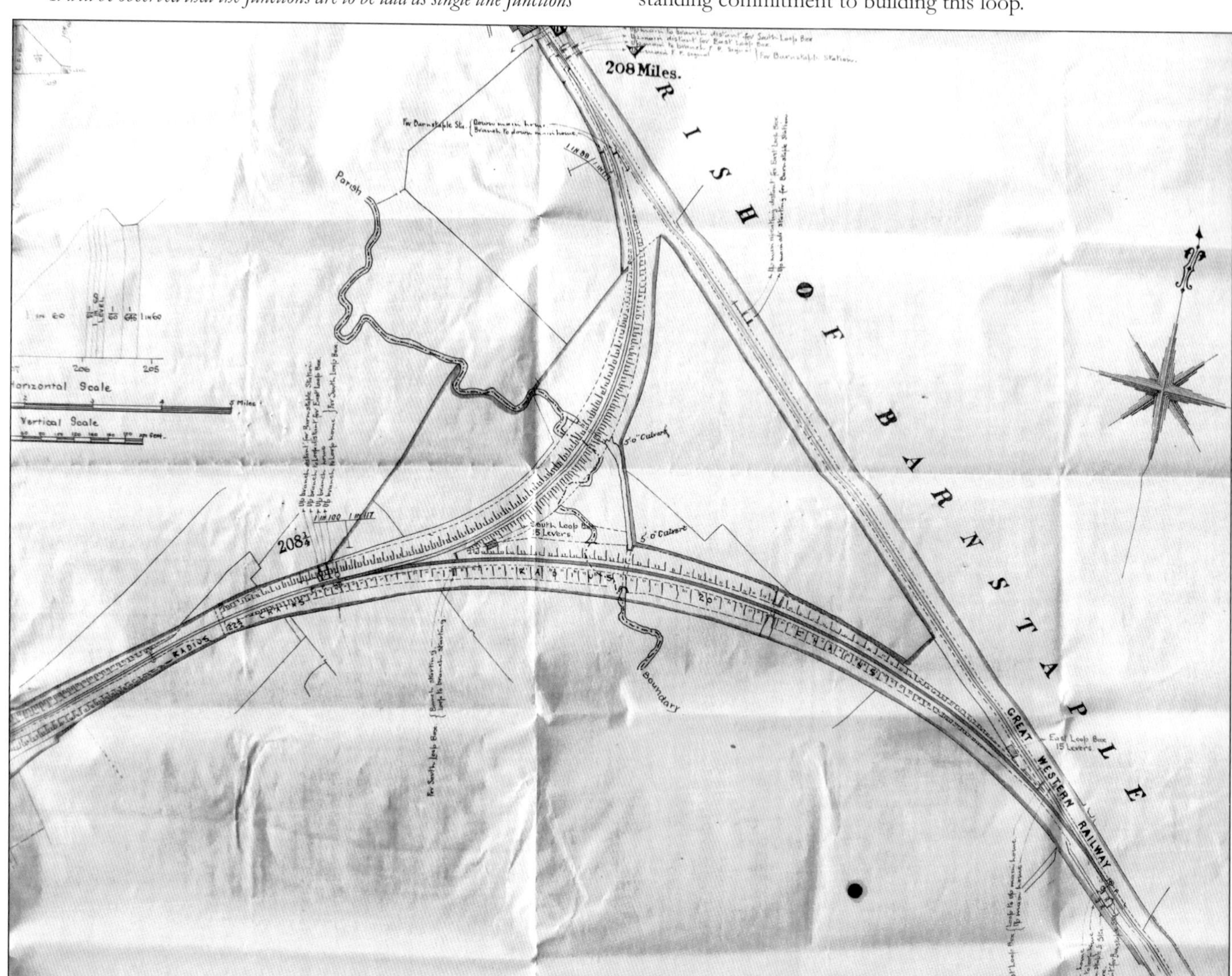

Plan showing the East Chord line finally added in 1905 and laid on earthworks constructed twenty years earlier. It permitted direct running for GWR trains to Barnstaple Junction and then on to Ilfracombe. ***Courtesy National Archives***

One of the ubiquitous GWR 'Moguls' leaving Barnstaple with an Up express circa 1932. The locomotive is just passing over the East Junction points but the East Chord, which finally opened in 1905, was used during the summer periods only. Clearly this photograph was taken outside of one of those limited times of operation, as the signal post on the left and the one behind the leading coach have had their arms removed. The East Chord was taken out of use in 1939 but reopened in 1960 when Barnstaple Victoria Road was closed. The train comprises a clerestory coach at the front and eight Collett coaches behind. The locomotive is probably one of the '53XX' series, built between 1916 and 1920 and fitted with cast iron chimneys. *A. Halls collection, courtesy National Railway Museum*

The single platform at Filleigh station in the years just prior to the First World War, looking east towards the bridge from which the picture on page 97 was taken. Its sylvan setting was clearly appreciated by the local staff, who had gone to some effort with the platform gardens and floral display. The waiting area had been partially enclosed by a timber and glass screen, which was also done at South Molton, whilst those at Bishops Nympton & Molland and East Anstey were bricked in completely but elsewhere, such as at Milverton and Wiveliscombe, they remained open until the end. Presumably the prevailing weather was a factor. Note, too, the 'S' and 'T' plates hung on the screen, where they would have been more visible than on the side of the small signal cabin that sufficed here at this date. ***The Lens of Sutton Collection***

THE OPENING OF THE CASTLE CARY TO LANGPORT LINE

Although not directly associated with the D&SR, the opening by the GWR in 1906 of a new so called 'cut-off' line between Castle Cary and Langport reduced the journey to the west by around 20 miles and avoided the need to go via Bristol. With the railway already in operation through Castle Cary (for Weymouth) and to Langport from Taunton (for the line to Yeovil, albeit this section had to be doubled), the new link was to transform services to and from the West Country. Opening on 1st July 1906, it also had a direct impact on the traffic on the Ilfracombe line, which was then only 203$^3/_4$ miles from Paddington (previously 225 miles via Bristol), whilst the L&SWR's route from Waterloo to Ilfracombe via Exeter was 226$^1/_2$ miles. It was reported that:

> *'in connection with the improved service to and from the West of England it is proposed to give good connections at Taunton with trains to Barnstaple and Ilfracombe. Passengers by the 11.40am express from Paddington, which will slip a carriage at Taunton at 2.15pm, will be due at Barnstaple at 3.57pm and Ilfracombe by 4.57pm. The 3.30pm express from Paddington will also slip a carriage at Taunton at 6.02pm and passengers will reach Barnstaple at 7.37pm and Ilfracombe at 8.25pm. In the reverse direction passengers will be able to leave Ilfracombe at 8am, 12.17pm and 1.25pm and reach Paddington at 1.35pm, 5.38pm and 6.45pm respectively. There will be other trains but these are the best services.'*

DULVERTON

Further improvement work took place at Dulverton in 1911, which comprised the extension of the Up and Down platforms, widening of the Down platform and the provision of a new passenger loop for Exe Valley trains at the rear (extending the short bay that had been added there in 1905), and the rearrangement of the connections. All of this necessitated the provision of another new signal box, sited on and further along the extended Up platform, towards Taunton, as well as a complete re-signalling of the station. The new box contained 42 levers in use, 2 spare and 10 spaces. Lieut Col H.A. Yorke, who carried out the inspection, was concerned that part of the new loop line was concealed from the signal box by the station buildings on the Down platform. In order to prevent the risk of an engine or vehicles, which might be standing on part of the loop line, being forgotten by the signalman, he recommended that fouling bars, controlling the signals entering the loop, should be placed on this part of the line. Yorke's letter sanctioning the improvements was dated 28th March 1911.

VENN CROSS

Von Donop reported on 21st April 1915 for works completed by the previous January at Venn Cross station. The points at the Down end of the loop were moved further out in the Down direction. Also, on account of the steep gradient on either side of the station, overrun

A slightly later view of Dulverton than that on page 134 and looking the opposite way, west towards Barnstaple from the footbridge, soon after the 1911 alterations had been carried out. The Down platform has been widened and the Exe Valley line now forms a loop around the rear of it but the most notable change here is the addition of a canopy to the main station building. The small crowd waiting on the platform are well dressed and the train of at least six bogie clerestory coaches is longer than for a normal weekday service, so this could be a Saturday shoppers train, with folk heading in to Taunton. At the head of the train is a 'Dean Goods' 0-6-0 and the coaches appear to be in the all over brown livery introduced in 1908. *John Alsop collection*

dead-end sidings were provided on both the Up and Down lines of the station loop and the position of the signals altered accordingly. The points and signals were worked from the existing box, containing a frame of 24 working and 5 spare levers; thus two of the spare levers shown in 1905 had been used for the overrun siding points. In a letter from the GWR (Frank Potter) to the Board of Trade, a reference was made to the proposed use of the dead-ends as overrun sidings but it was not practicable to make the dead-ends longer without large additional expense (which the circumstances scarcely warranted, as the precaution would only be for trains standing in the loop). The GWR stated that whilst it was not formerly their practice to provide over-run sidings in connection with crossing loops, they have done this at selected stations to give greater security and facilitate working in view of the gradients.

A circa 1930 view of Venn Cross station, with the loop, Up platform and waiting shelter on the right and the replacement signal box opposite, all provided in 1905. Beyond the end of the platforms, the loop had been extended in 1915, the points now being out of sight beyond the crest of the rise. The roof of the main station building can be seen at the top of the cutting on the left, with quite possibly what was the original timber signal cabin also to be seen, now in use as a garden house perhaps in the station master's garden. ***John Alsop collection***

BARNSTAPLE JUNCTION

Following the Grouping of the railways from 1st January 1923, the L&SWR became a part of the newly formed Southern Railway. An extra line and additional platform (No. 3) was provided at Barnstaple Junction station and opened on 23rd July 1924, facilitating arrivals from Taunton, which could now use platform 2 or 3 there.

THE CONCRETE SLEEPER EXPERIMENT

Taunton Division experimented with different types of concrete transverse and pot-sleepers during 1917-18, due to a timber shortage caused by the First World War. It is understood the Barnstaple Branch was one of those lines used in this experiment but the sleepers failed. Thirty-six transverse sleepers (measuring 8 feet by 8 inches by 6 inches deep) were installed on the line. Six lasted two years, six lasted seven years and twelve for nine years. The remaining twelve were removed after fourteen years. The sleepers had been subjected to a traffic density of fourteen trains per day at about 30 miles per hour (which it is understood was the speed limit for passing over them). Following these unsuccessful experiments and given the improvement of the timber supply, the use of concrete sleepers was not pursued at this time. A newer version were produced subsequently at Taunton in the early years of the Second World War (circa 1941).

THE 1924 STRIKE AND THE 1926 GENERAL STRIKE

In 1919, the National Union of Railwaymen (NUR) jointly with the Associated Society of Locomotive Engineers & Footplatemen (ASLEF) held a successful nine day strike against the reduction in the War Wage and the continuation of extended working hours. ASLEF called a second strike on 21st January 1924 but this time without the support of the NUR after a bitter fall-out between the two unions. Footplatemen were instructed to stop the trains wherever they were and cars were sent out by the union to collect their members, presumably leaving passengers stranded. As NUR members were not on strike, a reduced train service was able to be arranged. The

A general view of the Taunton concrete yard from the January 1918 issue of the ***Great Western Railway Magazine. Neil Parkhouse collection***

GREAT WESTERN RAILWAY.

NOTICE TO THE STAFF.

The National Union of Railwaymen have intimated that railwaymen have been asked to strike without notice to-morrow night. Each Great Western man has to decide his course of action, but I appeal to all of you to hesitate before you break your contracts of service with the old Company, before you inflict grave injury upon the Railway Industry, and before you arouse ill feeling in the Railway service which will take years to remove.

Railway Companies and Railwaymen have demonstrated that they can settle their disputes by direct negotiations. The Mining Industry should be advised to do the same.

Remember that your means of living and your personal interests are involved, and that Great Western men are trusted to be loyal to their conditions of service in the same manner as they expect the Company to carry out their obligations and agreements.

FELIX J. C. POLE,
General Manager.

PADDINGTON STATION,
May 2nd, 1926.

7765-5-26.

This poster appeal by Felix Pole to GWR staff was reproduced in the June 1926 issue of the *GWR Magazine*. *Neil Parkhouse collection*

strike lasted nine days again, until 30th January, and ASLEF were triumphant once more but it may have started to undermine the public's confidence in the railways.

The far more serious 1926 General Strike began in the coal industry, with railwaymen, dockers, lorry and bus drivers joining it on Tuesday 4th May. All local branch lines closed and there was very little traffic on the main line. The vast majority of goods were delivered at that time by rail, so food shortages became a distinct possibility. Whilst the Minehead Branch was one of the first to reopen, with a couple of trains running on the Friday, services on the Barnstaple line did not restart until the following Monday, when James Paige, a retired Paddington station master living in Taunton, volunteered to act as a guard.

Railway staff called off their strike activity on 13th May. However, the GWR deemed all strikers to have resigned and would only take those persons back that it had work for. Although the General Strike ended, the miners remained out on strike. Coal became in short supply, so it became rationed and the GWR reacted by reducing train services where it could.

The GWR Report on Branch Lines 1926

A comprehensive report on its branch lines was published by the GWR in March 1926. Fifty-three subsidiary branch lines (including the Exe Valley) were selected for review and for potential efficiency savings. Although the D&SR was not considered in this study, it makes for interesting reading on the costs and method of operating branch lines. The focus was on replacing steam traction by rail motors, a review of signalling and staffing (including hours of work) and the acknowledgement of road competition. In a sense, this was a precursor to the 1963 report *The Reshaping of British Railways*. A cost per mile chart was provided:

	Cost per mile
Main line (steam)	1s 11d
Subsidiary branch lines (steam)	1s 6¾d
Auto engines	1s 5d
Rail motors	1s 4d

It was acknowledged that it was difficult to assess contributing traffic revenues, that the layout of sidings was not conducive to mixed goods traffic and heavy goods trains would require steam traction. Heavy traffic (*e.g.* mileage traffic such as coal, grain and timber) was predominant on most branches, whereas general goods and perishables requiring quick transit would be a natural target for road competition.

In conclusion serious consideration was given to the closure of some lines, such as the Yealmpton Branch from Plymouth. In the event of such action being taken, it was suggested the trackwork should be retained for three years and maintained, thereby having the option of reopening the closed line if there were merits to doing so. Lines were looked at in terms of one eight-hour shift for operational purposes, thereby causing a reduction of trains to fit this schedule. The further replacement of steam hauled services by rail motors and auto trailers designed to be accessed from low level platforms was also considered. The saving projected for the Exe Valley line was £114 per year.

It is interesting to note that the Yealmpton Branch subsequently closed to passengers in 1930, although a service was reinstated from 1941 to 1947 as a result of heavy air raids on Plymouth during the war, the line having remained open for goods traffic.

Report into Electrification West of Taunton, Including Branches, 1927

A further report was commissioned by the GWR (following a board meeting on 1st May 1925) into the electrification of the main line and branches, including the D&SR, west of Taunton. In June 1927, Sir Philip Dawson, who was charged with the responsibility, passed his ninety-seven page report (including twenty-seven appendices) to Sir Felix Pole, the then General Manager of the GWR. The objective was to determine whether the expenditure involved in converting the lines to electric operation could be justified commercially. The report was in two parts; the first part looked at the lines themselves, whilst the second supplied maps, electric locomotive drawings (overseas types were used as example designs), train diagrams, track feeds, substations and various related technical matters. It was felt that not less than 120 miles should be converted and it was concluded that mixing traction (steam and electric) within each section was undesirable.

There is very little in the report that is specific to the D&SR, as it was an assessment of the applicability of electric traction to the area as a whole. One inherent disadvantage was that certain lines in the area were not owned by the GWR, so there would have been a necessity on certain services to change to steam traction, a case in point being the through services to Ilfracombe via Barnstaple Junction. However, the 1 mile and 25 chains of SR metals at Barnstaple was incorporated into the mileage calculations in the report. The efficiency of electric traction over steam was a key component of the report, such advantages being stated to include: an increase in the average speed for passenger and freight trains; quicker turn-round times (and less down time); easier to drive – better visibility and quicker preparation; lower cost and maintenance of locomotives; less deterioration; no need for coal and water supplies. Even in 1927, it was acknowledged that road motor services were serious competitors to the railways. The development of electrification on overseas railways was considered and designs of locomotives used abroad were illustrated.

The report divided the feasibility study into two parts: Scheme 1 (Penzance to Plympton and branches) and Scheme 2, the whole area (Taunton to Penzance) including branches. The D&SR potential conversion was considered in Section 4 of Scheme 2. Each section was anticipated to take two years to convert for costing purposes but the anticipated savings of electric over steam operation for Scheme 2 was £246,932. It is interesting to note that the report stated Taunton station should have four platform roads for this proposal to be properly implemented and operated, along with the provision of four tracks between Taunton and Norton Fitzwarren.

The most suitable arrangement proposed by the report was a high voltage continuous current overhead conductor system, although no actual voltage was stated. All the costs and benefits estimates were based on this proposal. The total anticipated capital expenditure for Scheme 1 was £1,755,185 and Schemes 1 and 2 £3,371,148. On the provision of line equipment, there were to be five standard constructions embodying five different sizes of conductor, simply referred to as 1, 2, 3, 4 and 5. Construction No. 2 was the one suggested for the D&SR, (along with, for example, the Helston, Newquay and Teign Valley branches and others). This was costed at £2,070 per single track mile, giving a total cost for all of Construction No. 2, a total of 141 miles and 79½ chains, of £293,927, of which the D&SR would have accounted for approximately £96,500, with its 46 miles and 52½ chains of running roads and sidings.

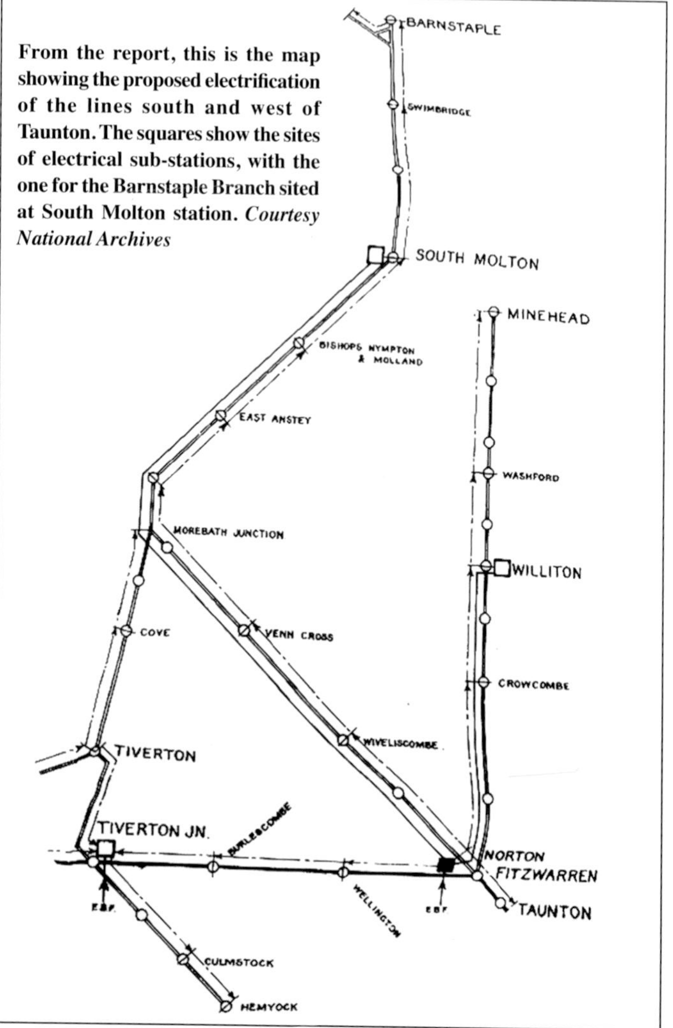

From the report, this is the map showing the proposed electrification of the lines south and west of Taunton. The squares show the sites of electrical sub-stations, with the one for the Barnstaple Branch sited at South Molton station. ***Courtesy National Archives***

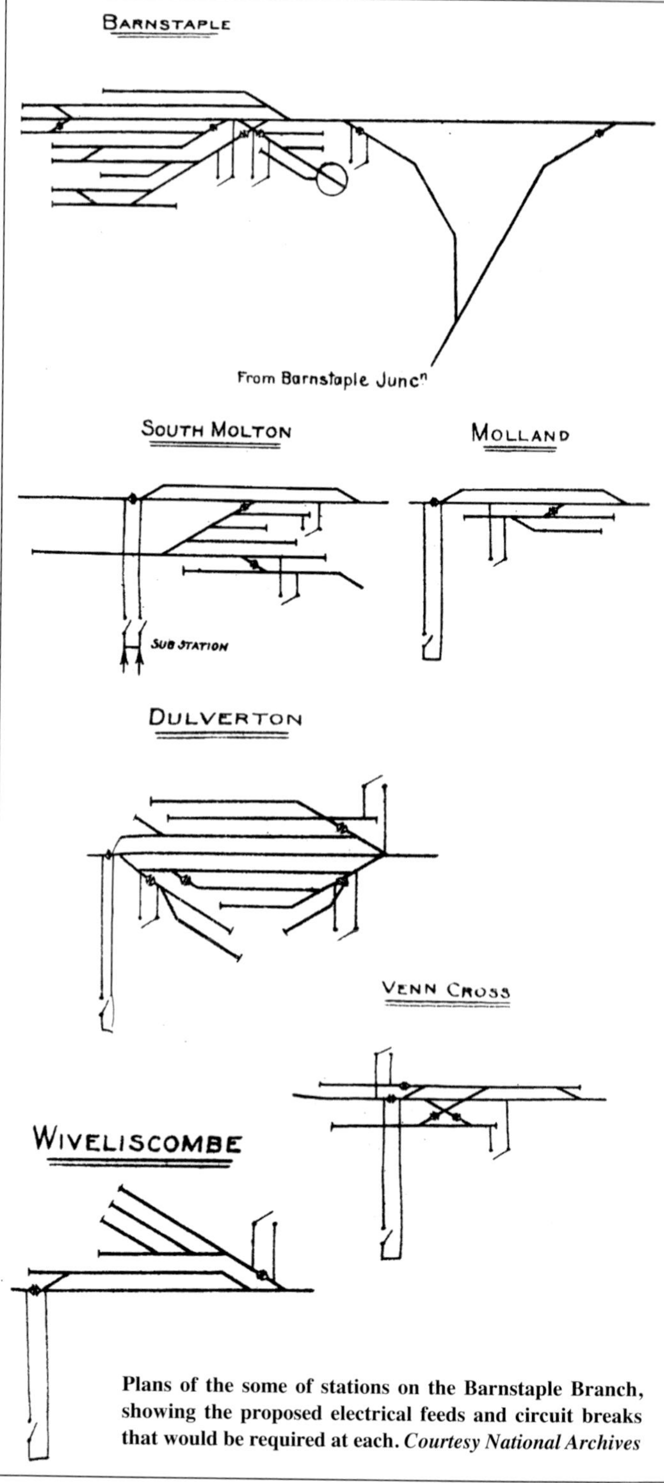

Plans of the some of stations on the Barnstaple Branch, showing the proposed electrical feeds and circuit breaks that would be required at each. ***Courtesy National Archives***

It is interesting to note here some other statistics from the report that were specific to the D&SR:

- Average daily traffic density in trailing-ton miles per mile of running track was 4,710 ton-miles, this being one of the more heavily loaded sections disclosed in the report

• Private siding roads 1 chain. Route miles GWR only 44 miles 32 chains

The cost of coal for locomotive use at Barnstaple was disclosed as follows:

Amount of coal delivered in 1925.......... 73 tons 8 cwt
Cost of coal at pit.......................... £86 4s 3d
Freight charges.............................. £7 0s 0d
Men's wages £2 3s 0d
Total cost............................. £95 7s 3d

The overall total coal delivered for the area covered by the report was 178,444 tons at a cost of £234,591 per year. The locomotive coal freight rates per ton for Barnstaple were 1s 11d in accordance with the above figures; estimated at 6s 1d, with commercial rates at 11s 0d. Barnstaple was one of the cheapest in the survey. However, given the inconsistency with the commercial rates in respect of all locations, doubts over the accuracy of the numbers were expressed and it was suggested that they may need to be reconsidered. Coal stocks normally held at Barnstaple were 17 tons.

Water supply costs/usage were recorded as follows:

Pumping Station	Repairs & Maintenance	Water (gals)
Dulverton	£318	5,547,750
Wiveliscombe	£123	1,878,000

The water supply required under electric traction would be 761,615 gallons at Dulverton and 257,818 at Wiveliscombe, a dramatic reduction in volumes.

Locomotive shed maintenance costs for Barnstaple are set out below, with Minehead also given for comparison:

	Barnstaple (£)	Minehead (£)
Building	5	3
Machinery and plant	187	74
Total	**192**	**77**

The equipment maintenance costs for the main line and Barnstaple Branch (and certain other heavily used branches) was estimated at £85 per mile for the 464 miles and 61¾ chains, giving a total of £39,506. For the D&SR's 46 miles, the figure was £3,910.

The cost of construction of the conductors, based on prices for steel, copper wire, cables, insulators, labour, etc, was £2,237 per track mile for the main line and the D&SR; the cost for the D&SR alone would therefore have been £102,902.

There were to be sub-stations at Norton Fitzwarren and South Molton, the land for which which would have required levelling, plus the installation of a water supply and of siding accommodation, at a total cost of £431 and £586 each respectively.

There was a review of the type of electric locomotives that might have been used and potential designs were disclosed in a separate section. The general purpose type was to be a four-axle (Bo-Bo) locomotive, the axles mounted in rigid frames with provision for 'play' in the axle boxes and the width of tread of the centre wheels to facilitate dealing with curves. Their rated capacity was to be circa 1,200-1,400 horse-power. It was anticipated the general purpose locomotives of the type that might have been used on the D&SR would have cost around £8,000 each, with express engines for the main line being £12,000.

In total for Scheme 2 (with Scheme 1 only in brackets) it was anticipated that fifty-six express locomotives (22) and 173 general purpose locomotives (91) would be required, with numbers 154-173 of the latter being spare locomotives.

A review of the proposed work diagrams indicates that seven locomotives were to be allocated to the Taunton to Barnstaple line. The diagram showed the use of one locomotive towards the end of the day (8-10pm) and then into the following day. The table below provides a summary of those anticipated duties:

Loco No.	Day 1 Evening	Day 2				
75	B-T	T-B	B-T			
80	T-B	B-T	T-B	BSJ-T	T-B	
81	T-B	B-T	T-B			
82	B-T	T-B	B-T	T-B	B-T	T-BSJ
83	B-T	T-B	B-T	T-B	BSJ-T	T-B
84	B-T	T-B	B-T	T-BSJ	B-T	
85	B-T	T-M	M-W-M			

B = Barnstaple; BSJ = Barnstaple South Junction; T = Taunton; M = Minehead; W = Williton

Several points of note arise from this:

• Seven locomotives were envisaged sufficient for summer Saturday passenger and goods services

• Two locomotives would be at Barnstaple overnight to start the usual first two Up trains

• Only one locomotive shared the duties with the Minehead Branch

• Certain through trains had their locomotives running to Barnstaple South Junction where there would be a change of motive power onto the Southern Railway section

• Taunton (and Barnstaple) turn around times were short

• Two locomotives would make six trips each, two five trips and two three trips, with one only making one trip on the branch.

The final analysis worth replicating is the summary of traffic densities on the branch compared to the overall (total and average). This does not accord with the first table as that covers all lines to be electrified:

Route Miles (RM)	Track Miles (TM)	Total*	Per RM*	Per TM*
42.71	48.67	203,000	4,750	4,170
498.38	699.08	4,340,000	8,710	6,200

The second line is the total
*** means Average day, trailing ton-miles**

The report made reference to an independent road motor service running between Taunton and Wiveliscombe at the time, by reference to potential/actual competition with the rail service.

The Norton Fitzwarren sub-station was to be under the control of attendants, whilst the substation at South Molton was to be semi-automatic.

There was a further report to the GWR regarding the potential for electrification of the main line and branches west of Taunton in February 1939, produced by Messrs Merz & McLellan, a firm of electrical consultants. This was clearly independent of the 1927 proposals above, with the later report envisaging a change of traction from steam to electric at Taunton, Exeter, Newton Abbot or Plymouth. It was a short-form report of sixteen pages and two appendices, and was precipitated by increasing coal prices (coal in 1934 was 12s 11d per ton and in 1937 17s per ton), as well as the cost of hauling it from South Wales to the west of England. This later proposal was for a Direct Current system, from an overhead line at 3,000 volts. This was double the voltage stipulated by the MoT in 1932, where DC systems were 750 volts third rail or 1,500 volts for overhead line. In addition, a number of bridges would need to be raised along with other infrastructure changes. In the final analysis, the return on net capital expenditure was concluded to be no more that 0.75% for the overall project, which was costed at £5,133,800. With such a low return on capital expended, the GWR decided not to proceed with the project and the idea was shelved on 24th March 1939.

SCENES AT DULVERTON STATION IN 1928

ABOVE: The station buildings from the bank facing on to the siding running to the cattle pens, with the Down side water column in the foreground. Note that the main building had been faced with slate, it is believed some time after construction but exactly when is not known. Presumably it was done for protection from the prevailing weather but it has been removed since closure of the railway and the original stonework is visible once more.

OPPOSITE PAGE TOP: The local GWR Country Delivery Service lorry in the station forecourt. Used for collections from and deliveries to all the outlying villages and hamlets, the agent, based at Milverton, was A. Lile and the driver seen here is Jack Vellacot.

OPPOSITE PAGE BOTTOM: There was a substantial timber traffic from the goods yard but a contemporary edition of the *Handbook of Stations* only notes one crane, of 5-tons capacity. The expalantion for the two seen here lies in the fact that the old one, on the left, was being replaced by the new crane on the right.

BELOW: Looking east towards Taunton from the end of the Up platform. The turntable in the Down side goods yard can just be discerned behind the water column, whilst a load of packages waits on a platform barrow in front of the main building to be collected by the next Up train.

All courtesy Dulverton Heritage Centre

RIGHT: Morebath Junction Halt, looking east towards Taunton. Note the sleeper construction of the face. In common with the other halts established on the line, it remained open until final closure of the entire route on 3rd October 1966. Morebath Junction Signal Box is just visible in the right distance. ***The Lens of Sutton Association***

BELOW: Specimen electric locomotive designs presented in the report. These came from the Paris-Orleans Railway. ***Courtesy National Archives***

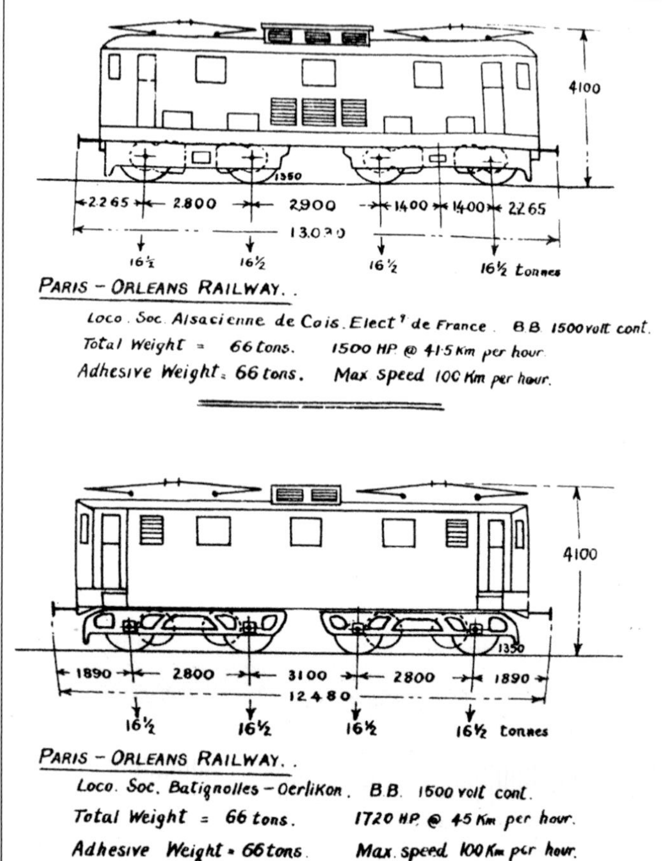

It is very much open to speculation as to whether the D&SR would have remained open had electrification taken place. Perhaps passenger and goods traffic would have increased with the modernisation. However, the DC system would have no doubt befallen the same fate as the Woodhead Route, whereby updating it was prohibitive on cost grounds, so it was closed. Even the latest 'Western Region' electrification scheme only incorporates the Paddington to Bristol and Swansea routes, whilst the rail connections in the South West peninsula are once again neglected. Over seventy-five years after the idea of electrification was mooted for the first time, it has still not advanced beyond the proposal stage.

OPENING OF MOREBATH JUNCTION HALT, 1928

Lieut Col A.H.L. Mount inspected the new works at Morebath Junction halt on 13th June 1932 (apparently in accordance with a minute of 30th November 1928). He reported:

> *'A high level platform 100 feet long and 8 feet wide has been provided on the north side of the railway, to the west of the junction of the Taunton and Tiverton lines. The new platform is formed of old sleeper walling, ash filled and surfaced. It is approached by long fenced footpaths, viz on the west side from an adjacent level crossing* [occupation crossing] *and on the east side, from a footpath across the fields. There is a shelter 12 feet by 8 feet and the platform is suitably fenced and lighted by oil lamps. The halt is served by 11 trains in each direction daily. The works are in good order …'*

He went on to acknowledge that additional facilities might be necessary if the neighbourhood developed. The GWR map showing the location of the halt had it at 1 mile and 36 chains from Morebath and 1 mile and 68 chains from Dulverton.

EARLY 1930S DEVELOPMENTS

The short-lived experiments with concrete sleepers after the First World War notwithstanding, wooden ones had always fulfilled the GWR's requirements but most were imported and as supplies became less plentiful and costs increased, they looked to an alternative. Steel sleepers were being developed and were considered for two reasons – cost and the labour benefits of manufacturing in the UK. There were a variety of steel sleepers available but the Guest, Keen & Nettlefolds (GKN) composite design was selected for trial on the GWR. Their design consisted of a plate $^3/_8$ inch thick, pressed to form a trough with a bead along the edge for strengthening. It was $9^1/_4$ ins wide by $4^3/_{16}$ ins deep, which spread to a width of 11ins by $3^1/_8$ ins deep some 16ins out from the centre for the remainder of the length, which was

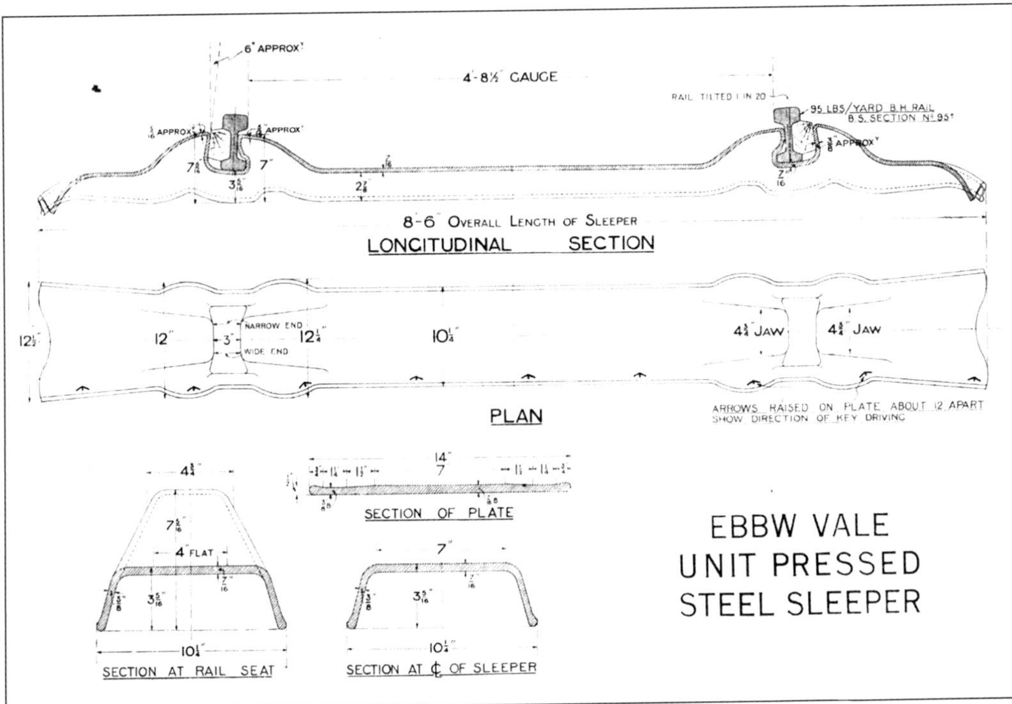

LEFT: A plan of a pressed steel sleeper, this a design produced by the Ebbw Vale Steel, Iron & Coal Co. Ltd, which was reproduced in the *GWR Magazine*. *Neil Parkhouse collection*

either 8 feet or 8 feet 6ins. The ends were turned down and splayed to a width of 12ins. The chairs were cast onto the sleeper, so chair bolts were avoided. In 1930, the GWR ordered 136,000 experimental steel sleepers, enough for 60 miles of track. This total was increased in 1931 and other non-GKN types were also experimented with.

It is understood the D&SR line was involved in this experiment and some steel sleepers were laid along it in the early 1930s.

BELOW: Shortly after leaving Barnstaple, 'Bulldog' Class 4-4-0 No. 3417 *Lord Mildmay of Flete* hurries along near Landkey, with a three coach train bound for Taunton in the early 1930s. The roofboards indicate that these are through coaches for Paddington, which will be joined at Taunton with a similar working off the Minehead Branch. The light loading further indicates that this is an 'out of season' service; during the summer, the number of coaches would be much greater, often loading to seven or eight. The locomotive was built in 1906 and was originally No. 3707 and named *Francis Mildmay* (he was a GWR director); it was renumbered in 1912 and its name 'updated' in July 1923, and was withdrawn in 1948. The incredibly neat track and lineside, a testament to the ganger in charge of this stretch, is in complete contrast to the tree-lined road that now occupies the route here. *Arthur Halls, courtesy National Railway Museum*

IMPROVEMENTS AT TAUNTON AND NORTON FITZWARREN

At the same time, between 1930 and 1932, improvements were carried out at Taunton station, coupled with quadrupling of the lines from Cogload Junction to Norton Fitzwarren, a distance of 7 miles, to cater for the growing holiday traffic at this busy interchange. This was undertaken by the GWR in conjunction with the Development (Loan Guarantees & Grants) Act of 1929. It resulted in the addition of Down and Up relief lines and Norton Fitzwarren station being rebuilt to acommodate these, with two island platforms serving the four running lines lines.

ABOVE: Norton Fitzwarren station looking south west towards Exeter around 1905, showing the original B&ER buildings, along with GWR additions such as the footbridge and corrugated iron lamp hut. Note the typical B&ER barge boarding to the main station building and the waiting shelter on the Down side, closely matching that see a few pages earlier at Milverton. The junction is just beyond the footbridge, with the line to Barnstaple curving right and then left beyond the post of the bracket signal; two other signals are visible in the distance, the furthest of which is on the D&SR line. The permanent way gang have briefly paused in their labours to pose for the photographer. *Author's collection*

LEFT: After rebuilding in the early 1930s, the station looked completely different. This view, looking in the same direction around fifty-five years later, on 25th August 1961, is looking along the slow line face of the Down side island platform, which was that used by Barnstaple line trains. The large wooden signal box that was provided to control the complex junctions here can be seen on the left. Note the nameboard, indicating that this was the junction for the Minehead and Barnstaple branches. *Michael Hale*

Class '43XX' No. 5337 approaches Barnstaple with a Down train circa 1927. The passenger stock is quite varied, with a four coach 'set' of 4-wheeled stock leading, comprising two five-compartment Composites flanked either end by a Brake Third. The final two vehicles are 8-wheeled bogie carriages, the rear one carrying roof boards, which suggests that these are through coaches for Ilfracombe which will have been dropped off at Taunton by a train originating from Paddington. No. 5337 was new in December 1917 and was one of sixty-five of the '53XX' Series converted to '83XX' in early 1928, which involved extending the bufferbeam forward by a foot and fitting a heavy casting behind it. This was done to reduce wear on the flanges of the front set of drivers on some of the twisting routes to be found in the West Country. The locomotive was also renumbered 8337 but reverted to '53XX' and No. 5337 in 1944. The modification had the effect of restricting '83XX' series engines to red routes only. A forty-three year career came to an end following withdrawal from Bristol St. Philips Marsh shed in October 1960. *Arthur Halls, courtesy National Railway Museum*

Above: Class '45XX' 2-6-2T No. 4590 climbs out of Barnstaple towards Landkey at the head of a varied Up goods train around 1928. The mixture of mostly box vans and open wagons begins with a Fruit D, followed by a Mica meat van, with an oil tank wagon fourth in line. The 'Prairie' tank was clearly still quite new here, having entered service in March 1927 and was withdrawn in October 1958.

Left: These historic photographs of GWR motive power hauling varied trains on the western end of the D&SR line all date from around the same period. Here, an unidentified 'Bulldog' Class 4-4-0 storms away from Barnstaple with a six coach train, again comprised of a rich variety of stock including both clerestory and elliptical roofed vehicles. The locomotive carries an oval cabside combined name and number plate, and also has straight frames and a slightly wider cab, which all marks it out as being one of the class in the number series from 3341 to 3360, all built in 1900.
Both Arthur Halls, courtesy National Railway Museum

RIGHT: Another unidentified 'Bulldog' Class passes Acland Wood near Barnstaple with a short Up stopping train comprising two 4-wheeled coaches – a Brake Third and a five-compartment Composite – and two clerestory roofed bogie coaches. The locomotive has a cabside numberplate and a curved two word nameplate, and is in the number series 3361 to 3380. A strong contender for its actual identity is No. 3363 *Alfred Baldwin*, renamed from *Baldwin* in 1903, which was certainly allocated to Taunton shed in the early 1920s.

BELOW: The final variant of the 'Bulldog' Class 4-4-0s were the 'Birds'. No. 3444 *Cormorant* was photographed a little further east on the same stretch of track, again with Acland Wood as a backdrop, hauling an Up local made up of four 4-wheeled coaches. Amongst a number of detail changes with the 'Birds', one of the most noticeable was their much deeper frames and they were also fitted with copper capped chimneys. New in May 1909 as No. 3734, No. 3444 was withdrawn in June 1951 from Taunton shed.
Both Arthur Halls, courtesy National Railway Museum

With what must have been close to the maximum load for the line, a 'Dean Goods' 0-6-0 trundles across Castle Hill Viaduct with an Up goods circa 1928. This splendid panorama from the south east side of the bridge, shows what a beautifully proportioned structure the viaduct was and how well it blended into its surroundings. Whilst it is pleasing to note that the piers have survived and found a new use, neither claim could be made for the North Devon Link Road bridge they support today. ***Arthur Halls, courtesy National Railway Museum***

ABOVE: A lovely action shot of a 'Bulldog 4-4-0 coming off Castle Hill Viaduct with a Down train, heading towards its next stop at Filleigh. The engine is another of the No's 3361 to 3380 batch.

LEFT: Whilst it is to be regretted that many of the locomotives featured in these views are not properly identified, the variations in the 'Bulldog' Class can help us pin them down a little. This is one of the ealier members of the class with curved frames, No's 3300 to 3340, built between 1895 and 1899. We can further narrow it down because the oval cabside name/numberplate, without the GWR coat of arms, puts it in the number series 3326 to 3340. The engine is seen on the Barnstaple Branch, in the cutting alongside the grammar school, heading towards Barnstaple Junction station with a train probably for Ilfracombe. The lead vehicle is a horse box. The bridge behind is believed to have carried a water main.
Both Arthur Halls, courtesy National Railway Museum

RIGHT: Yet another 'Bulldog' gathers speed as it heads away east through the cutting near Landkey on an Up local. Like the engine seen coming off Castle Hill Viaduct, this is one of the No's 3361 to 3380 series built in 1902-03.

BELOW: The last of the 'Bulldogs' to be featured in this section is identified, No. 3364 *Frank Bibby*, built in February 1903 as No. 3416 and named simply *Bibby* for the first two months of its career. The engine is seen heading away from East Junction, with the signal box just visible in the left background and again the lack of arms on the signal posts means this is outside of the summer period when trains worked directly over the East Chord. This is another Up local, comprising four 4-wheeled coaches and a bogie clerestory carriage. No. 3364 just made it into BR days, being withdrawn in June 1949. *Both Arthur Halls, courtesy National Railway Museum*

One of the '55XX' Series of Class '45XX' 2-6-2Ts, No. 5502 heads away from Barnstaple towards Swimbridge with a heavy load of eight bogie coaches. The lead carriage appears to be an older clerestory roofed vehicle with guards look-out but the rest appear to be all newer elliptical roofed stock. Interestingly, this particular view was taken during the summer season and the signals controlling the junction all have their arms attached. No. 5502 was new into service in May 1927, its first allocation being to Newton Abbott shed, so this view is likely to date from a year or so after that. The engine spent most of its career in the West Country and was withdrawn from St. Blazey shed in July 1958. ***Arthur Halls, courtesy National Railway Museum***

SWIMBRIDGE

The new works at Swimbridge station were inspected by Lieut Col A.H.L. Mount on 13th June 1932. A facing connection was laid at the west end of the Up loop, to serve the goods loop siding which was suitably trapped. This would have been a replacement point, as the goods loop had been *in situ* from the early days and remained after the provision of the Up passing loop in 1904 (see above). An additional backing signal was provided to control entrance to the siding. The new connection was laid with 97$^1/_2$ lbs rail and full facing point equipment was provided. The signal box frame now contained 17 working and 4 spare levers.

In 1933-34, the Minehead Branch underwent improvement, with additional loops and crossing places being added, along with the provision of Whittaker token exchange apparatus. It was therefore only a matter of time before similar work would be carried on on the D&SR.

Yeo Mill Halt from a passing train in the 1960s. *Peter Barnfield*

OPENING OF YEO MILL HALT

The residents of West Anstey and Yeo Mill got their wish when a one-coach length wooden platform was opened on 27th June 1932. Yeo Mill Halt was located 1 mile 51 chains from East Anstey and 3 miles 32 chains from Bishops Nympton & Molland (as set out on the official GWR map).

THE MAJOR LINE IMPROVEMENTS OF 1937-38

Under the provisions of the Railways (Agreement) Act of 1935, major improvements were carried out on the D&SR route in 1937-38. The work was preceded by an announcement in the December 1935 *GWR Magazine*:

'to facilitate the train-working on the Barnstaple and Minehead branches it is intended to carry out improvements which include the doubling of lines between Norton Fitzwarren and both Bishops Lydeard and Milverton. In addition, platforms are to be lengthened at Morebath, East Anstey, Bishop's Nympton [& Molland], *Dulverton and Filleigh stations and the loop lines at various passing places are to be extended. These arrangements will have the effect of reducing the time occupied by trains, and the holiday resorts served by them should benefit.'*

In addition to all this, improved points were laid in on the running line, of a more shallow radius to facilitate faster running for through trains at the intermediate stations. These improvements were supplemented by the provision of Whittaker automatic token exchange apparatus (which will be covered in detail in the chapter on signalling in Volume 2).

The works undertaken between Norton Fitzwarren and Milverton were described in detail in Lieut Col A.H.L. Mount's report:

'These comprise the doubling of the line between Norton Fitzwarren and Milverton, a distance of 4$^1/_2$ miles, and the re-arrangement of Milverton Station to suit the altered conditions.

There has been a considerable amount of re-alignment, but the bulk of the new track forms the up road; it has been laid throughout with 85lbs RBS material on Totnes ballast and mostly within existing boundaries. Fencing has been renewed where necessary with concrete posts and new wires with droppers, or strengthened with intermediate concrete [posts].

The rails are 45ft and 60ft long, carried in 40lb chairs, connected by 2-bolt fishplates, the sleepers being creosoted Baltic Fir throughout, 8ft 6ins x 10ins x 5ins, spaced 1ft 4$^1/_4$ ins at joints, 18 to the 45ft rail and 24 to the 60ft rail. Bottom ballast of stone has been laid in cuttings, ashes in bank, top ballast being 9ins deep and the whole depth below sleepers varies from 9$^1/_2$ ins to 1ft 0$^1/_2$ ins.

Steepest gradients are 1 in 53 for 6 chains and 1 in 66 for 41 chains; sharpest curvature is 25 chs radius. The general speed restriction for the branch is 55mph, and all single line facing connections at crossing places have now been relaid to 35 chs radius to permit a speed of 40mph.

The highest banks are 15ft and the deepest cuttings 13ft. There are two underbridges crossing a public road at 165m 75$^1/_2$ ch and an occupation road at 166m 31 chs by 20ft 9ins and 15ft spans respectively. There are three overbridges carrying roads.

There are 8 accommodation and 7 footpath level crossings; the former are provided with self-closing gates fitted with figure-four catches.

At Milverton, the layout at the east end has been altered to suit the double line; a trailing crossover has been laid on the 30 ch approach curve, cant being provided of 4$^1/_2$ ins for the maximum speed of 55mph, a check rail having been laid through the crossover owing to reversal of cant. The up advanced starter at this end of the station is 548 yards from the box released by line clear, with a track circuit in the rear of it and the down home is 19 yards, also provided with a train-waiting track circuit which locks the starter at Norton Fitzwarren.

At this end of the station, adjacent to the overbridge, there is a passenger level crossing and, owing to the shortage of view, a 'Stop, Look and Listen' notice board was erected on the up platform. It was agreed that the Company's standard "Beware of Trains" notice should be provided here on both sides of the line. Booking (on the down platform) amounts to only some 10 passengers a day, and there is little likelihood of development; in fact, traffic has much decreased in recent years, as at other stations on the line.

At the west end of Milverton Station, the single line facing connection has been relaid with 85lbs RBS material on ballast, the turnout being 35 chs radius with 1 in 10 crossing for 40 mph.

Besides a facing trap at the exit from the down line, (which permits of receiving two trains at the same time after check at the home signals), spring-slotted catch-points are provided; it was agreed that the instructions should prohibit shunting and the closing of the latter points until Out-of Section has been received from Wiveliscombe when an unfitted freight is involved.

The down main advance starter on the single line is 667 yards from the box, and a track circuit is provided in rear of it, which, when occupied, locks the starter in rear.

In the early 1960s, an unidentified ex-GWR 2-6-0 heads a Saturdays only train on the double track section installed between Norton Fitzwarren and Milverton in 1937-38 . Seven coaches was a good load for a 'Mogul'. ***Owen Mogg, courtesy Peter Triggs***

The box now contains a new frame of 27 working levers and 10 spaces, the up and down distant signals, 1,420 yards and 1,131 yards away respectively, both being repeated, arms and lights. Other repeaters are provided as necessary and the arrangements are generally satisfactory.

The locking is correct and the works are in good order and of substantial construction. Subject therefore to the remarks at A [Beware of Train notice] *and B* [shunting instructions] *I recommend that this doubling and the new facilities at Milverton be approved.'*

There were substantial improvements at all bar one of the stations on the line in this period, with Lieut Col Mount being kept busy with his inspections and his subsequent reports on these during June 1938. At about this time, the GWR and SR entered into an agreement where they proposed no further direct competition on the two lines to Barnstaple and therefore further expenditure beyond these improvements was not carried out. The exception was Wiveliscombe, which also bucked this latter agreement when the loop was lengthened by 88 yards and trap points installed in September 1939.

It was acknowledged that passenger traffic was light at most of the intermediate stations and footbridges were unnecessary but 'Beware of Trains' notices were essential at all locations. A summary of the substantive improvements from the relevant BoT inspection is set out below and it is interesting to note the focus on the addition of trap and catch points for safety, given the numerous and steep inclines. Also, at certain locations, reference is made to passenger numbers and a reduction them in the 1920-1938 period.

VENN CROSS

The loop at Venn Cross was extended at each end, to a total length of 750 feet clear, whilst the platforms were also lengthened by 90 feet at the west end but shortened by 70 feet at the east end, leaving them 365 feet in length. They were lit by vapour lights.

Facing traps were provided at the exit from each loop to permit

Looking east at Venn Cross on 29th August 1964, showing the shortened Down platform. Both platforms were reduced in length by 70ft at this end by simply removing the edges but were otherwise left intact so the foot crossing could still be used. ***Tim Stephens***

Up and Down trains to be simultaneously received after checking at their respective Home signals. The radius of the facing turnouts was 35 chains, permitting a maximum speed of 40mph and the leads were laid level. Switches were 30 feet and locking bars 50 feet as elsewhere throughout the branch. The Down facing points were adjacent to the tunnel mouth at the west end, the new crossing being at 1 in 16. The new Up Home signal was 320 yards from the signal box and the new Down Advanced Starter signal located 553 yards away from the box, with a track circuit in the rear.

The signal box remained situated at the west end of the Down platform and contained an old frame, re-locked, of 26 working and 3 spare levers. The report stated that automatic token apparatus had been provided '*as elsewhere on this branch*'.

MOREBATH

The loop at Morebath was also lengthened, particularly at the west end, to 750ft, with the platforms extended to 500ft. At the east end, a fully equipped facing connection was laid with a 1 in 20 crossing on an easy curve, with another facing connection outside it to give access to the goods yard. The lead on the facing points into the loop had a radius of 35 chains, with a 1 in 16 crossing. The platform extensions, at a width of 8 feet, were made of 3-inch timber decking carried on precast concrete trestles, with gas pipe hand-rail and three-wired fence. Lighting was by paraffin vapour lamps.

Facing trap points and trailing catch points were laid at the end of each loop; single line shunting was to be prohibited until the 'train-out-of-section' instruction had been given where unfitted trains were concerned.

A new signal box was built on the Down platform, which contained a frame of 25 working levers and 6 spaces. The Up and Down Distant signals were situated at 1,303 and 1,310 yards respectively from the box and were repeated (arm and light).

MOREBATH JUNCTION

At Morebath Junction, the main line loop was lengthened to 750 feet clear, with new facing connections and new track using 85lbs RBS rail. Each crossing was 1 in 20 with 2 inches cant, permitting a speed of 40mph entering the loop.

At the Taunton end there was now a facing trap in the Up loop and a trailing spring catch point in the Down loop. At the Barnstaple end, there was a facing trap and trailing spring catch points at the

A poor quality but unusual view of Morebath Junction from the Down loop, with a short goods train behind a Class '57XX' 0-6-0PT waiting to come off the Exe Valley line. ***Roger Joanes***

'Mogul' No. 7304 makes a brief stop at Morebath whilst on its journey from Taunton to Barnstaple on 9th July 1962. In the foreground, the simple and cheap timber platform extensions of the late 1930s are clear, whilst the signal box provided at the same time is also prominent. ***C.J. Gammell, courtesy Roger Joanes***

Class '43XX' 2-6-0 No. 6375 heads west away from Dulverton on 21st July 1961, with the 3.27pm Taunton to Barnstaple train. Note the three coaches are SR Bullied stock, indicating the blurring of regional boundaries following Nationalisation. Behind is the Carnarvon Hotel, along with the somewhat ornate roof of the cattle market building, with its clock tower and weather vane. No. 6375 was one of the batch of thirty-five of these 'Moguls' built in 1921-22 in Newcastle by Robert Stephenson & Co. Ltd. It was fitted with outside steam pipes in 1938. Note the tall Home signal positioned 'wrong side' of the line for sighting purposes. ***Michael J. Fox, courtesy Rail Archive Stephenson***

exit from the Down loop, the spring catch points protecting the Exe Valley Branch as well. It was again stated that the facing points should remain set until the 'train-out-of-section' signal was received from Dulverton, having regard to the rising gradient of 1 in 100 for $^3/_4$ mile after leaving Morebath Junction in the Down direction.

The Up facing connection was now immediately beyond the halt platform. The signals were altered and re-positioned; the Up and Down Distant signals were 1,216 and 1,290 yards respectively from the box, the latter being worked by motor. The box at this time then contained a second-hand relocked frame of 22 working leavers and 1 spare.

DULVERTON

At Dulverton, the loop and platforms at the south [Taunton] end were lengthened. the latter now extending to some 500 feet in length. The loop and goods yard facing connections were re-laid at the north [Barnstaple] end.

At the south end, the loop facing connection had a 1 in 16 crossing with 35 chains radius for 35mph running and there was a facing trap point positioned at the exit of the Up loop. At the north end, the loop facing point connection was on a curve and had a 1 in 20 crossing with $2^3/_4$ inches cant for 40mph running. Facing traps and spring-slotted catch-points were provided at the exit from the Down loop.

The Down Advanced Starter was 608 yards from the signal box and there was a track circuit in the rear exercising the usual control on the starting signals. New bracketed Home signals were provided at each end and calling on arms were provided in connection with operation on the back road (which was bi-directional).

The signal box contained an old frame, relocked, of 51 working levers and 3 spaces. The Up and Down Distant signals were 1,347 and 1,178 yards from the box, and their arms and lights were repeated. It was commented that the works *'are in first class condition'*.

EAST ANSTEY

Lieut Col Mount reported on 28th June 1938 in respect of the new works at East Anstey, which he had inspected on 17th June:

> *'These comprise the lengthening of the loop at each end to 750 feet clear, and the lengthening of the platforms at the east end 375 feet. The works have been carried out in accordance with the plan submitted.*
>
> *The station is at the summit and the line rises towards it in each direction at gradients of 1 in 58. The new facing connections are laid with 85 lbs RBS material on stone ballast, the turnouts having a radius of 35 chains, fit for 40mph.*
>
> *There are facing traps at the exit from each loop to permit of trains from each direction being allowed to approach at the same time after check at the home signals. There is 10 feet clearance between the loops and the platform extensions have been carried out in concrete block walling. Challow type paraffin vapour lamps are in use.*
>
> *There is no footbridge, but a barrow and passenger crossing exists at the west end of the platforms near the signalbox; 'Beware of Trains' notices should be provided, conspicuously displayed, and they should be illuminated at night* [A]. *The box contains a frame of 23 working levers and 6 spaces, and the signalling generally has ben re-modelled and brought up to date, all necessary repeaters having been provided. The locking was checked so far as time permitted, and the signalman had no comments to offer. The arrangements generally appeared to be satisfactory, and subject therefore to the remarks at A, I recommend that these new works, which were in good order, be approved.'*

BISHOP'S NYMPTON & MOLLAND

The loop facing connections at Bishop's Nympton & Molland were re-laid for 40mph running and the loop lengthened to 750 feet clear, most of this work being done at the west end. Facing traps were provided at the exit from each loop. With reference to the long rising gradient up to East Anstey, spring-slotted trailing catch-points were laid at the exit from the Up loop. Again, shunting for unfitted trains was prohibited subject to the 'train-out-of-section' instruction from East Anstey.

The platforms were extended westwards to 500 feet with a width of 8 feet. The platform extensions were carried out in concrete block walling on the Down platform and concrete trestling on the Up platform, with 3-inch timber decking.

A new signal box was built at the east end of the Down platform adjacent to the bridge which carried the line over the road. The box contained a frame of 24 working levers and 6 spaces. All necessary new running and shunt signals were provided along with repeaters, arms and lights as required.

A view of East Anstey station looking west along the Down platform circa 1960, with the line dropping away from the summit here in the right background, the loop having been extended in the late 1930s. Note the catch points notice board. ***Courtesy Great Western Railway Society***

A grin for the photographer from the driver of No. 6375, as he exchanges tablets with the signalman at Bishops Nympton & Molland station. The locomotive carries an 83B Taunton shed plate on its smokebox door, so is working back home. The concrete trestling used to extend the Up platform in the late 1930s can just be made beyond the end of the carriages, and the front of the new signal box built here at the same time can be seen in the left foreground. Despite the lengthened platforms, a footbridge was deemed not necessary *John Spencer Gilks*

The report acknowledged passenger traffic was light, being around 100 passengers per week, with fifty of those on market days. Thus the provision of a footbridge was deemed unnecessary, especially as the station master stated that he and the signalman protected the passengers when using the crossing.

The station was at this time lit with paraffin vapour type lamps.

SOUTH MOLTON

At South Molton, the loop was lengthened and connections at either end of it re-laid, with the consequential re-arrangement of signalling and the provision of facing traps and spring-slotted catch points at the exits from each. A spring-slotted facing trap was also provided at the trailing end of the Down loop, as it was also used for Up trains.

The new facing connections had 1 in 20 crossings and the cant was to allow for 40mph running. It was proposed in the report that the trailing catch points should not be closed for shunting on the single line until the 'train-out-of-section' signal had been received in respect of unfitted goods, whether Up or Down.

The signal box was reported to contain a new frame of 27 working levers and 6 spaces, the necessary alterations to the signalling having been effected. The Up and Down Distant signals (which were repeated) were at 1,394 and 1,160 yards respectively from the signal box.

The report commented on the use of the Down loop for Up trains and supported its continued use in that regard in view of the considerable passenger traffic from the 6,000 inhabitants of the town. However, by this time traffic levels were only a quarter of the 1923 numbers. Parcels traffic (including rabbits) had not decreased to the same extent and there was a saving of staff by continuing this two-way working on the Down line. In view of the method of working described above and the decrease in traffic, the provision of a footbridge did not have a strong case.

FILLEIGH

There were major improvements carried out at Filleigh, which had remained unaltered since opening. The station, which was situated in a cutting, was reconstructed with the provision of a passing loop 750 feet in length clear, and a new Down platform 400 feet in length and 8 feet wide with the Up platform raised in height to match. There was also a single line Up and Down goods loop added at the Barnstaple end. As the cutting comprised of shillet rock, a concrete block face walling was installed to support it at the Taunton end of the Down platform. The Up platform face was also realigned and both platforms were faced with concrete block walling. It was felt the provision of a footbridge was not necessary as the crossing of the line was supervised by station staff or the signalman.

At the east end, a facing trap point was provided at the exit from the Up loop, along with trailing catch points having regard to the rising gradient to South Molton. Again it was proposed an instruction be issued to prohibit shunting of unfitted trains on the single line without 'train-out-of-section' permission from South Molton.

At the Barnstaple end, at the exit from the Down loop, was a facing trap point. The Up goods loop (trapped at each end) was formed by a facing connection from the single running line at the Barnstaple end. A point motor at that site was worked by hand generator and was some 460 yards from the signal box.

The facing connections to the loops enabled 40mph running and automatic token pick-up apparatus was provided. The goods yard was served by a double compound or double slip point in the Up loop and a facing connection from the Down loop.

A new signal box was built at the west end of the Up platform containing 34 working levers and 10 spaces. Running and shunt signals were new throughout and track circuiting was installed on the goods loop (operating an indicator only), and between the goods loop facing points and the running loop facing crossover. Reference was made to the intermediate token instrument cabin, with a telephone at the west end of the goods loop facing points.

ABOVE: Filleigh station in 1939 just after the completion of the loop line. From left to right are Mrs Drew, J. Crockham (signalman), L. Hooper (station master) and C.H. Drew (signalman). ***Courtesy Roger Joanes***

SWIMBRIDGE

The loop at Swimbridge station was lengthened to 750 feet clear and the facing connections reconstructed to a radius of 35 chains to allow a speed of 40mph. Facing traps were provided at the exit from each loop to permit the simultaneous approach of trains in each direction (after checking at the home signals). Spring-slotted trailing catch-points were sited at the exit of the Up loop, having regard to the steeply rising gradient to Filleigh. As elsewhere on the branch, there was prohibition of shunting on the single line unless 'train-out-of-section' was received from the next box, at Filleigh. There were insufficient passengers to merit a footbridge at this time. However, it was suggested that in addition to 'Beware of Trains' notices that were to be provided at the west end of each platform at the existing barrow crossing, it was desirable to also erect 'Stop, Look, Listen' notices at the east end of the platforms by what was a public footpath level crossing.

The existing signal box now contained 24 working levers and 9 spaces. The Up and Down Distant signals were located at 1,100 and 1,426 yards respectively from the box, and the Up and Down Advanced Starter signals were 600 yards each from the box, with track circuits in the rear of the relevant starters.

THE YEARS TO CLOSURE

Following the major upgrade of the late 1930s, very little happened of significance over the remaining years of the line's existence. One change involved the East Curve at Barnstaple, which was closed

RIGHT: Looking west between trains at Swimbridge in the early 1960s, with the 'BEWARE OF TRAINS' notices placed here in the late 1930s warning passengers to take care when crossing the line, with traffic levels again not justifying the provision of a footbridge. The bridge carried the lane to the hamlet of Yarmacott, just off to the right, the station being sited roughly half way between it and Swimbridge. ***Courtesy Great Western Railway Society***

at the end of the 1939 summer timetable, so ending direct through running to Barnstaple Junction and Ilfracombe. All trains thereafter ran via Victoria Road until it closed to passenger traffic (as discussed in the next chapter) on 12th June 1960, upon which the East Curve was reopened to allow direct running to Barnstaple Junction station.

The line played a significant role during the Second World War (see Volume 2) being well used in this period but, like the rest of the rail network, failed to receive the maintenance it deserved afterwards. No additional sidings or track improvements were carried out because of or during the war.

After Nationalisation, British Railways' task was to rationalise the many duplicated facilities at locations such as Barnstaple so as to make best use of resources. As a result, from 1948, full wagon load freight was concentrated at Barnstaple Junction, thereby leaving the ex-GWR goods yard to deal with general merchandise, sundries and oil. The fleet of delivery and collection road vehicles were from then based there, with the station having been renamed Barnstaple Victoria Road by British Railways in 1949.

The only major alterations carried out in the late 1950s were in respect of certain signalling changes and replacements; the chapter on signalling in Volume 2 will have more specific information on this.

British Railways instigated boundary changes to the regions during the 1950s and, as a consequence, Barnstaple Victoria Road and the Barnstaple chord lines were transferred to the Southern Region on 1sr February 1958. The Southern Region/Western Region boundary was set at East Junction.

Once Beeching had announced his review of the rail network in 1962, the likelihood of any further investment in the Taunton to Barnstaple line became non-existent and the final phase of its history is covered in the next chapter.

Although taken from the end of the Down platform at Dulverton, this is close to the driver's eye view from the footplate of 'Mogul' No. 5336, bound for Taunton with the 12.20 service from Ilfracombe on 27th June 1964. In the right distance, the Down Home bracket signal can be seen, the lower right-hand arm being for Exe Valley trains heading into the bay platform; the entrance to this and to the goods yard on the Down side are also visible on the right. At this point the train will be heading south as it leaves the station but it will shortly turn east (left) and then, near where the trees can be seen behind the Up Starter, cross the River Exe and start the steady climb into Ashtown Cutting. ***Michael J. Fox, courtesy Rail Archive Stephenson***

CHAPTER 4

DECLINE AND CLOSURE

Britain gave the world railways. Within the UK, the growth of the national network opened up the country, facilitating the movement of goods, minerals, provisions and people. In the early days of railway development, there were few suitable alternative modes of transport and therefore little competition. The period that became known as 'The Railway Mania' and beyond saw lines financed and constructed that would never make money. However, there must have been an argument that this railway development had a social role to play in the days when alternative forms of transport were not available. This social role continued when the internal combustion engine arrived in the early 20th century but even then it would be another fifty years before the motor car became common place and a clear alternative and threat to rail travel.

Following the outbreak of the First World War, to help the war effort the railways were taken in to Government control (but not management) from 1st September 1914, being run on their behalf by a Railway Executive Committee (REC) consisting of experienced railway managers. Compensation for the railways was allocated on the basis of each companies' net receipts during 1913 but this was so all Government traffic was conveyed without charge and was given priority; this traffic was substantial.

The REC was formally disbanded in 1919 but the railways were clearly significantly the worse for wear after the long years of hostilities. On 23rd September 1919, a new Act formed the Ministry of Transport (MoT), to which the railway responsibilities of the Board of Trade were transferred. The REC was succeeded by the Railway Advisory Committee (RAC) and this led to the Railways Act 1921, passed on 19th August, and the subsequent Grouping (as it became known) of a number of independent railway companies into the so called 'Big Four': the London & North Eastern Railway (L&NER), the London Midland & Scottish Railway (LM&SR), the Southern Railway (SR) and finally – and the only company to survive intact albeit with the addition of various other smaller railways – the Great Western Railway (GWR).

It might be argued that, from the early 1920s up until the Second World War, the railways in Britain were in their heyday and possibly the finest in the world. In a sense, an opportunity was lost following the Grouping. Some rationalisation of the network might have been considered by the 'Big Four' but this opportunity to improve efficiency and remove duplication was not really taken in the years after 1921. At this time, railway company operations were extensive; they owned docks, hotels, local bus routes and lorry distribution networks from most stations, so could offer a fully integrated transport service.

The number of private haulage contractors grew after the war years, because the Government sold off surplus army equipment at reasonable prices, which these new operators used to set up in business, albeit mostly with only one lorry but they offered competition. A new system of freight charging was introduced in 1923, whereby these were fixed by qualified tribunal based on 1913 revenues. However, the railways were still required to carry certain traffic at uneconomic rates. Railways had to maintain the permanent way at their cost but road hauliers could, in effect, use their infrastructure, the roads, for free, thus having a significant competitive advantage. The 1933 Road & Rail Traffic Act organised the licensing and control of goods road vehicles and freed railways from restrictions for quoting special rates for special services; thus the railways could attempt to fight back. However, they still had to remain the 'common carrier' (a left-over from the Victorian era), which meant that they were obliged to transport any form of commodity; everything from small packets, perishable fruit and similar, to complete farm removals and circuses, even if such transportation was uneconomic. They also had to publish their prices, which the road hauliers did not have to do. As a result, the road hauliers undercut the railways and they lost business. The railways could not further undercut the hauliers as that was 'undue preference' and prejudicial to existing rail customers, who had to pay the original prices.

Following the declaration of hostilities on 3rd September 1939, which preceded the start of the Second World War, the Government again took control of the railways for the duration of the conflict. This time the guarantee set was not based on the revenues of 1939 but the average revenues for 1936 and 1937, which were of course lower (and inadequate). Once again the infrastructure and equipment took a battering and, after 1945, reinstatement of the railways to their pre-war state would have required a significant investment at a time when the war effort had drained Government coffers. It was not a priority given the other reparations that were needed and this period became something of a watershed, as that investment was not made.

The decline in rail traffic generally, and the loss of importance of the D&SR line in particular, commenced after 1945. This was partially caused by the continued growth of the road haulage industry, as well as the excessive wear and tear the system had received coupled with the under investment during and following the war years. Provision of an integrated transport policy by the Government at this time may have helped but they never developed one. Given the country's difficult economic and financial situation, measures were adopted to run the railways in a less expensive way than previously but there was also political interference. This commenced with the Transport Act of 6th August 1947, which brought Nationalisation and the formation of British Railways (BR) by the Labour Government on 1st January 1948, although there was probably no other realistic alternative at the time. Certainly, it was a move supported by most railwaymen at the time.

During the 1950s, as the economy improved, the trade unions became stronger and with the threat of strike action in their armoury, were collectively a force to be reckoned with. In 1955, there was a national rail strike over a pay dispute called by ASLEF. This ran from 28th May until 14th June and brought British industry to a stand still and although the NUR continued to work and keep some passengers and freight on the move, public confidence in the railways was damaged. This strike arguably precipitated the move by passengers and freight to the roads, and many of those customers did not return to use the railways in the future. This, coupled with the removal of restrictions on road operators and the low cost of petrol, gave those operators a further competitive edge over the railways and would have helped move freight away and onto the roads. Even at this stage, the designation of 'common carrier' was still retained by the railways, until removed by the Government in 1957, albeit by then too late to be of benefit.

In 1958, the Western Region (WR) of BR announced that it wanted to withdraw goods facilities from local stations. Under the plan, those were in future to be concentrated at Taunton for the area served by the D&SR. From the Taunton depot, customers would be served by road delivery. In 1964, at the time goods facilities were being withdrawn from the line, the freight concentration scheme became a reality at Taunton. The best example was the opening of the coal concentration depot, which dealt with around 500 tons of coal a day, arriving in rakes of 21-ton hopper wagons.

In October 1959, a Conservative Government was returned at the election and Ernest Marples was appointed Minister of Transport in Harold Macmillan's cabinet. Unfortunately, Marples was a 'roadsman', having an interest in a road construction company, Marples Ridgway, and he was keen to develop a motorway network in the UK. Unsurprisingly, this was where Government infrastructure funds came to be allocated and not to the railways. Given the parlous financial situation of the system generally and the lack of investment, the rail decline continued nationally. This was despite the 1955 Modernisation Plan (published on 25th January), which proposed the building of substantial quantities of new stock and equipment for the existing system – new diesel locomotives, for instance, and new marshalling yards. These changes were to be introduced over a fifteen year period and were costed at around £1.24 billion. However, this plan envisaged that the railways would operate the same way; there was no allowance made for changes to the scope or mode of operation and it was this fundamental operational change which was really needed. It was apparent within a few years of the publication of the Modernisation Plan that it was not enough to reform the railways and their finances. The Government had to take further action and so to quote the Prime Minister, Harold Macmillan, on 10th March 1960:

'First the industry must be of a size and pattern suited to modern conditions and prospects. In particular, the railway system must be remodelled to meet current needs, and the Modernisation Plan must be adapted to this new shape.'

By this time, increases in car and motorbike ownership, with the consequential reduction in railway passengers, was also taking its toll on rail receipts. The number of cars registered in 1938 was 1.94 million; by 1954 there were 3.1 million and this increased to around 6 million by 1961 (and, for reference, 13 million in 1970). Between 1953 and 1958, various railway branches, comprising a total of just less than 1,000 miles, had been cut back for financial reasons. There was even a proposal in 1959 to close the whole rail system. The key fact of life was that rail costs were rising faster than income; the cost of the ill-thought out Modernisation Plan and the high capital debt from Nationalisation, as well as rising staff costs, did not help and further coupled with fares and freight charges being frozen and declining revenue, it meant that something drastic had to be done.

An independent advisory panel, the Stedeford Committee, chaired by industrialist Sir Ivan Stedeford, was appointed to examine the structure and finances of the British Transport Commission (BTC) as a first step. The BTC, under the Chairmanship of Sir Brian Robertson since 1953, had been set up under the 1947 Transport Act to oversee all transport undertakings. Among the Stedeford panel members was a Dr Richard Beeching, a physicist, engineer and technical director at ICI. The panel's recommendations were never actually published but they were reflected in a White Paper to Parliament in 1960, entitled *Reorganisation of the Nationalised Transport Undertakings*. This called for a restructuring of the BTC, with the railways being run by a proposed new body, the British Railways Board (BRB). It stated:

'Sweeping changes will be needed. Effort and sacrifice will be required from all. The public will have to be prepared to face changes in the extent and nature of the services provided and, when necessary, the prices charged for them.'

Financial targets were also proposed by the panel, which would inevitably result in further cuts to rail services. In 1960, the railways were £67.7m a year short of covering their running costs and this gap was growing annually, rising to £86.9m in 1961.

Action had to be taken to stem the losses and an attempt made to return the railways to profitability. Marples appointed Beeching as Chairman of the BTC on 1st June 1961, succeeding Sir Brian Robertson. He was to be paid the same salary as at ICI, £24,000 pa. The Transport Act of August 1962 abolished the BTC with effect from 1st January 1963, replacing it with the BRB and Beeching became its first chairman, a post he held until 1965, when he resigned. It might be argued that his was a strange appointment; it was for a defined period of five years (until 1966), which led commentators to believe he was a 'surgeon' for a specific job – to cut-back the system. Also, he was not a railwayman, so he did not have a detailed knowledge of the inner workings of the railway business. However, he was known for his analytical mind and skill at solving business problems. Perhaps this independent and external view was what was needed. The financial objective was set in the 1962 Transport Act (at Section 22), which stipulated that the new board should run the railways so that its operating profits were '*not less than sufficient*' for meeting running costs. It was clear, therefore that the railways were no longer a special case for the government to fund at all costs and be there for 'social duty'; they had to compete on equal terms with other businesses. It was Dr Beeching's primary responsibility to achieve profitability for the railways, so on his appointment in 1961 he commenced work on his legendary report.

On Wednesday, 27th March 1963, the infamous 148-page so-called 'Beeching Report', *The Reshaping of British Railways*, was published at a price of 1 shilling.

On publication, Marples commented '*The board's lucid analysis and bold proposals fully accord with the Government's expectations*'. This statement raises a suspicion that the whole issue and process was politically motivated and Marples was at the heart of it. Not surprisingly, the Conservative Government accepted Beeching's report after the House of Commons debate in April 1963 and promised that the axed rail services would be replaced by cheaper to operate bus services. Despite the fact an election was looming, the Conservative Government pressed ahead with implementation of the report. Harold Wilson, the Opposition Labour Party leader at the time, saw a political opportunity and stated publicly that he would reverse the cuts if Labour were to be elected. The Labour peer, Lord Stonham (at one time elected as a Labour MP for Taunton) was sceptical of the numbers used to support Beeching's analysis, saying that '*unfortunately none of them can be really checked*'. He further felt it had '*been brutal surgery allied to mishandling so foolish as to appear deliberate*'. However, his blame was really levelled at the Government, not Dr Beeching, as Lord Stonham called for postponement on all rail closures until the cost to the economy as a whole could be determined. By this he meant cost in terms of lost jobs, extra cars on crowded summer roads and the cost of necessary road improvements, for example. In a TV

The two-volume Beeching Report, *The Reshaping of British Railways*. Part 1 set out the proposals, Part 2 contained the maps showing traffic flows, proposed closures and new liner train routes. *Courtesy National Railway Museum*

interview between Lord Stonham and Dr Beeching, conducted by the BBC, Stonham referred to '*phoney figures*' on which the analysis was based, with Beeching being '*an angry man*' who could not support his figures. Beeching countered eloquently; the one-week's survey gave vital conclusions and was true but no closure was based on this survey alone. Indeed, he accused Lord Stonham of '*systematic distortion*' of his report. If the debate had been a boxing match, Beeching did well and would have probably won on points. Other bodies, such as the National Council on Inland Transport (represented by local councils), came out and condemned the proposals, as did the County Councils Association. The country was in uproar and 'Beeching Must Go' slogans and banners appeared throughout the land. However, it must be remembered that Beeching could not close lines, it was only the Government that could do this.

Whilst the report was in progress, the intentions in relation to the D&SR specifically were made apparent during the two-year gestation period. It must be remembered that the report's aim was not solely to 'butcher' unprofitable branch and feeder lines:

> '*... we should expect the provision of railways to be limited to routes over which it is possible to develop dense flows of traffic, of the kinds which lend themselves to movement in train load quantities and which, in part at least, benefit from the speed and reliability which the railways are capable of achieving.*'

Its real thrust was to reshape the network to concentrate on those activities and services for which rail transport could provide the most efficient means of transportation and to return the industry to profitability. The focus would be on mainline city-to-city/town-to-town passenger services and freight hubs. In analysing the traffic types the report stated:

> '*in the passenger field, stopping trains are by far the worst loss-maker. These trains, which derive little advantage from the speed of rail movement, are known to be very lightly loaded and to run, very largely, on routes which carry little traffic of any kind.*'

Almost a specific description of the D&SR it seems. However, with the focus on mainlines, there was no consideration of the likely social consequences of the proposed closures to the local lines which fed into the main network. Apparently, 6,056 route miles (36% of the network) carried only 1% of passengers and 41% of the 4,300 stations produced less than 1% of passenger receipts. The impact of the report would result in a total reduction of around 5,000 of the 18,000 route miles of the network, being mainly cross-country routes and rural branch lines. The plan was to be implemented over seven years.

Under the Transport Act of 1962, any services listed for closure had to receive at least six weeks notice by BR and alternative travel arrangements had to be provided. Furthermore, objections could be raised by individuals and local authorities to the relevant Transport Users Consultative Committee (TUCC) specifically set up to register public objections in the cases of personal hardship (not because the financial numbers were suspect or wrong). The relevant local TUCC would consider those objections and also consider whether a public enquiry should take place. The receipt of an objection would result in a suspension of the closure plans until the objections had been heard by the TUCC

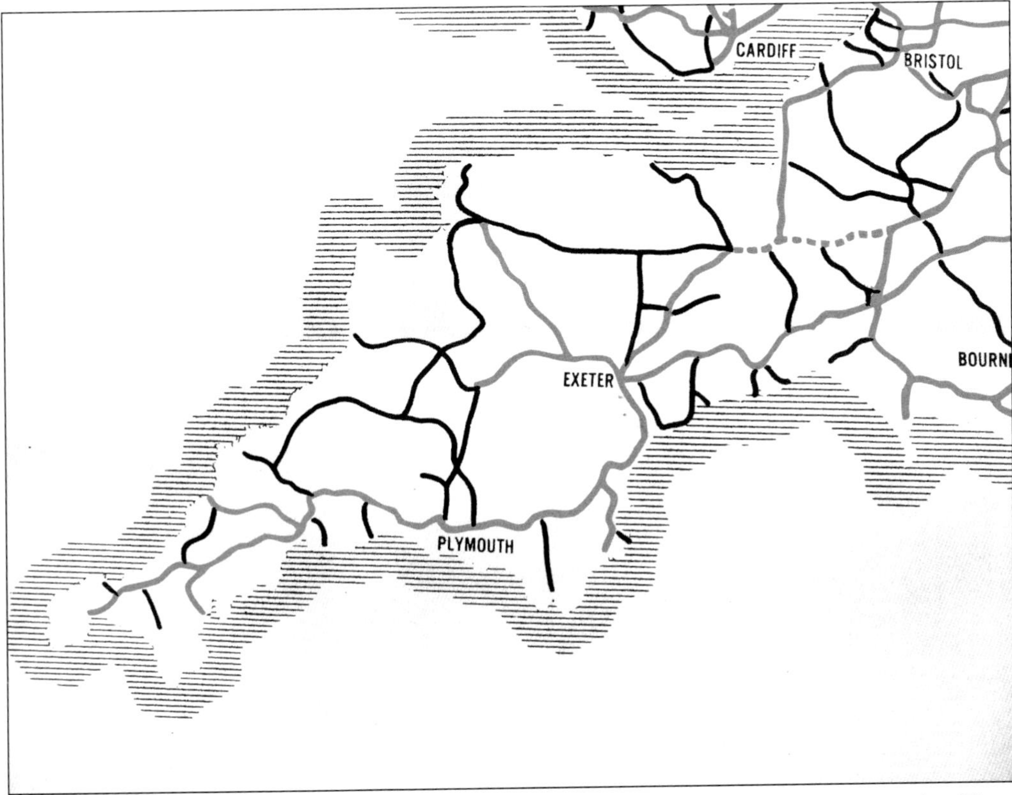

Detail from one of the maps in Beeching's report – Map 9: Proposed withdrawal of passenger train services. The ominous black lines show the destruction of rail connections in the South West. *Courtesy National Railway Museum*

and then the Minister of Transport would have the final decision on whether the proposed closure should proceed and, if the relevant line was to close, BR would then issue the closure notice.

Not surprisingly and sadly, there was no place in the Beeching retention strategy for the Taunton to Barnstaple line and the entry in the report at Appendix 2, Section 1, *Passenger Services to be Withdrawn*, page 106, listed the line's fate. Individual stations for closure were listed in Section 3, pages 109-121. As can be seen from the map (above) Beeching proposed closure of all lines in North Devon, other than the Exeter to Barnstaple route, and it is perhaps here that some criticism can be levelled at certain aspects of the report. Given the shortage of time allocated to producing it, the main criterion used to measure a station's and a particular line's profitability was that of originating revenue and the data was collected in a seven-day survey over the week ending 23rd April 1961 (two weeks after Easter). There was no computer modelling then! What this survey of course did not allow for, particularly in the D&SR's case, was the data in respect of all the passengers that used the line on travelling from northern and Midlands cities and London to holiday resorts in North Devon during the holiday season. It is acknowledged that such traffic was seasonal and there would always have been the risk that passenger numbers would have naturally declined with the growth in popularity of the car and the availability of affordable overseas holiday options. However, the number of tickets issued by Ilfracombe, Barnstaple and Dulverton, for example, would be far less than the volume of passengers that would have originated elsewhere and travelled in trains along the line to get to their North Devon holiday destinations. Indeed, looking at the detail in the report, it was only Barnstaple and Dulverton that produced station receipts of more than £5,000 per year. Most stations on the line provided fewer that 5,000 passengers per year (again Dulverton and Barnstaple were the exceptions). On the freight side, Victoria Road provided greater than 25,000 tons per year, with Dulverton and Wiveliscombe providing 5,000-25,000 tons. The remaining stations produced less than 5,000 tons per year.

Under Beeching's calculations 7,000 passengers per route mile was a sufficient break-even number to sustain a diesel multiple unit (DMU) service. The DMUs could run at 55d per mile (with rail buses and rail cars costing a lot less) but average branch line revenues were 2d per mile. The route from Barnstaple to Taunton was direct and the most obvious route to go 'up-country', rather than using the old L&SWR line down to Exeter, which added 22 miles to an up-country journey. The D&SR line may have been single track along most of its length but passing places were more than adequate and with the use of Whitaker automatic token exchanges, a higher speed for through trains could be maintained. The fact that these advantages did not seem to support the retention of the line leads one to believe there were other factors at influence with this proposed closure; the significant and numerous steep gradients perhaps. Often cited are the costs of repair and maintenance that would have been necessary to the substantial viaducts at Castle Hill and Waterrow. Indeed, there was a rumour that the Tone Viaduct at Waterrow had been damaged by the valve gear of a Churchward 'Mogul' running over it in 1960 and as a result would prove too expensive to repair but this clearly did not stop trains running over it for another five or six years! The North Devon Railway Report (see below) referred to the Tone Viaduct in 1963 as being '*in a critical condition*'. Clearly as stated above, the cost of repair and maintenance of the D&SR line was ultimately a major factor in its downfall and its social role did not appear to have any merits in the Beeching analysis, as his was a purely financial one based on current (at 1961) passenger usage.

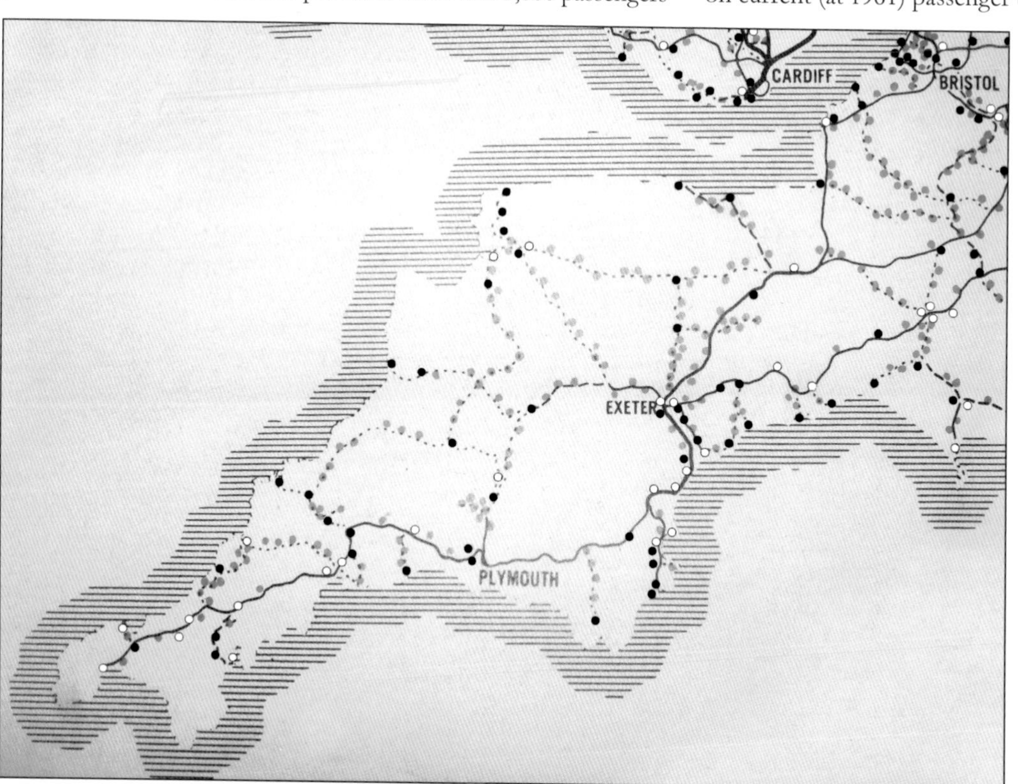

An extract from Map 3 in the report, showing the distribution of passenger traffic station receipts (in £s). The original is in colour so has been modified slightly for black and white publication. The white dots show where revenue exceeded £25,000 per annum, whilst black dots were stations over £5,000 and the grey dots less than £5,000 per year. With the exception of Barnstaple Victoria (which had a greater revenue than Barnstaple Junction) and Dulverton, the D&SR stations were all grey. ***Courtesy National Railway Museum***

There was also concern over the manipulation of train services, changing times so that connections could not be made, along with the removal of some through trains, all of which reduced the line's importance and made it of less use to those wishing to travel. It was also shown that bus services were better suited and more economical in handling lower densities of passengers, such as was found in rural areas.

So having looked at the general thrust of Beeching's report, which focused primarily on financial issues, it is important to see how the local community directly affected by these proposals reacted to them and what steps were taken to fight for the line's survival.

The *Western Morning News* reported on 30th March 1962 that Mr L.W. Ibbotson, the Assistant General Manager of the Western Region of BR, had written to Mr Edward du Cann, the Taunton Conservative MP, indicating that the Taunton to Barnstaple line would be considered for closure for reasons of economy. This letter was issued in response to a letter from Mr Du Cann to Dr Beeching. It had been known for some time that the Exe Valley line was under scrutiny by officials, whose job it was to reduce the heavy losses being incurred by BR's Western Region. However, the inclusion of the Taunton to Barnstaple line was a surprise and controversial, especially given its importance in serving isolated communities and providing a direct route to North Devon for summer holidaymakers.

Ibbotson stated both the D&SR and the Exe Valley line were under investigation and that:

'whilst in all such cases the possibility of achieving remunerative working will be fully explored, it is only fair to say that both are likely to be the subject of withdrawal proposals within the next few months. In the event such proposals being formulated and submitted to the South West Area Transport Users' Consultative Committee [SWATUCC], *copies of relevant memoranda will at the same time be sent to you and to Dulverton Rural District Council.'*

Only the previous evening, Mr Ernest Marples the Minister of Transport had reiterated that '*the process of dealing with hopelessly uneconomic branch line services must go on*' – a reference to the closure of certain branch lines in Cornwall but nonetheless an ominous message to others as well. There was an assurance that any hardship to users would be fully examined before closures occurred. With the Transport Bill before Parliament, the SWATUCC was required to report to the Minister on every opposed passenger line closure. Clearly any such case made would have to be good, as any financial loss would continue to be borne by the taxpayer. The SWATUCC was one of a number of area TUCC's set up under the Central Transport Consultative Committee (CTCC), as established under a 1947 Act. Members comprised representatives from commerce, industry, agriculture and local authorities with an independent chairman and BTC representatives. TUCCs, having received representations from the public and other interested local bodies, could then make recommendations to the BTC and the CTCC. Ultimately, a minister could force the Commission to follow those recommendations. The key remit was to consider '*hardship*' to the region in the case of a proposed closure. This was a restriction brought in by the 1962 Transport Act , which reduced their broader remit under the original Act.

It was in late 1962 that the North Devon Railway Action Committee (NDRAC) was formed and this, of course, was in advance of the publication of Dr Beeching's report. The purpose of this Committee was to evaluate the likely social consequences of railway closures in the area, and it included representatives of nearly all the local authorities and other organisations. It contributed funds to a fact-finding enquiry to report on the railway situation in the area, which was directed by Mr David St. John Thomas, the well known railway historian and co-founder (in 1960) of David & Charles. The 32-page North Devon Railway Report was published in 1963. It focused on all the local lines: Exeter to Barnstaple, Barnstaple to Ilfracombe, Barnstaple to Torrington, Torrington to Halwill and Taunton to Barnstaple. As a general observation, it noted that receipts from the conveyance of passengers and goods covered less than half the cost of running North Devon's railways. However, it emphasised that the area's removal from the railway map would cause widespread economic and social hardship; fewer tourists would visit, newly-retired people would look to retire in other areas, the long-standing unemployment problem would continue and North Devon would run the risk of being isolated from the rest of the South West.

The local population was not helping the situation, however, as the report emphasised, noting that '*road transport is chosen almost automatically for passenger and goods journeys*' to, from and within the region, unless the railways provided a specific advantage. Even passengers arriving at Taunton from London, for example, could be collected by car and arrive in Barnstaple before the scheduled connecting train, given that this would still take the best part of 1½ hours to travel the 44 miles. However, this of course assumed that the car was immediately available and travellers didn't require it to have set off from Barnstaple at least one hour before the train was due to arrive at Taunton! The report stated that if the railways of North Devon were to play an active part in the area's future, they would need to reorganise radically. Perhaps they had not been given the chance to survive; steam had only just been replaced by diesel multiple units and other potential savings methods (*e.g.* a reduction of staff numbers) had not really been implemented. Indeed, at a local TUCC inquiry into the D&SR, the BRB had stated that dieselisation had been examined and would not make the service remunerative even under the cheapest working methods. There was a fear the TUCC's were mere stooges of the BRB.

One of the specific problems with the D&SR was that passengers in the area were leaving the railway in favour of local bus services, which was particularly the case between Taunton and Wiveliscombe, and South Molton and Barnstaple. However, the railway was vital for the isolated villages in between. The report further stated that the maintenance costs of the tunnels, bridges and viaducts could take all the receipts of the branch if it were to be kept open for another ten years. This was despite the fact that cost-savings had already been introduced, including the closure of Barnstaple Victoria Road as a passenger station, removal of through goods traffic (which was re-directed via Exeter), Morebath becoming an unstaffed halt and, from June 1963, the last Down train connecting with the 4.30pm from Paddington rather than the 6.30pm, so that signal boxes could be closed earlier and staff wages saved. Despite these savings, BR stated that the revenue from passenger services on the line covered only about 10% of the costs of about £80,000 per week. The details are set out in the table below. As these costs were fixed, they would still be incurred despite the complete cessation of goods traffic (as planned), a drastic reduction in signalling and the introduction of DMUs.

The report included a passenger traffic census conducted on Tuesday 7th May 1963. The first Tuesday in May was chosen as a typical quiet day, not influenced by market days, weekend use or other potential distortions. All the local lines were surveyed and the D&SR was the third busiest with an average number of passengers at 11.42 (just over half of those on the Barnstaple to Exeter line in first place). The results of passengers joining and leaving at each station in the course of the day are set out below:

STATION	PASSENGERS JOINING	PASSENGERS LEAVING
Taunton	119.5	116.5
Milverton	10.5	10
Wiveliscombe	35.5	28.5
Venn Cross	5.5	14
Morebath	4	5
Morebath Junction Halt	2	4.5
Dulverton	54	34
East Anstey	10	5
Yeo Mill Halt	0	1
Bishops Nympton & Molland	4	3
South Molton	10	10.5
Filleigh	2	2
Swimbridge	4	5
Barnstaple Junction	27	49

As always, the outline figures are only part of the story. It is important to highlight that the first train to Taunton carried more passengers than all the remaining five arrivals of that day. This was partly due to the fact that a total of sixty-four passengers (more than half the arriving at Taunton) travelling from Dulverton and Wiveliscombe were going to school or work. One train carried just one passenger and, on seventy-one occasions, trains stopped at stations on the line without anyone joining or leaving.

On summer Saturdays, the D&SR carried considerable through traffic. Of the 35,000 or so holidaymakers that travelled to Ilfracombe by train in 1962, about 75% came in the three summer months, mostly traversing the Taunton to Barnstaple line. However, Beeching was focused on efficiency; he could not see the reason for having reserve coaching stock being idle for significant parts of the year and then only being used on as few as ten occasions in the summer timetable. Outside of the summer months, the line's importance was mostly local, although it had the earliest morning service from Barnstaple to connect to London and the last return. Dulverton was stated to be the busiest intermediate station on the route, with over a 1,000 passengers and a similar number of parcels per year. South Molton still had its goods, namely fertiliser, animal feed-stuffs and coal. Beeching's view was that 17,000 passengers per week were needed for a line to be viable, whilst other commentators believed a line could be sustained with 8,000 passengers per week but the D&SR was not even close to achieving that figure.

As regards the conveyance of goods, large merchants with steady business had by this stage more or less deserted the railway, because the train services and charging structure were geared to smaller, irregular consignments. Thus the railways had lost the very type of business they were seeking to attract. The report underlined that local industrialists, and agricultural and other merchants were dissatisfied and were able to demonstrate that the railway service had not adequately met their requirements. Furthermore, their criticism particularly concerned the railway's delays in considering complaints and suggestions. This did not help the railway compete with the road hauliers, which offered highly competitive charging and efficient services. This swing to road haulage may have been facilitated by the area's under-employment, so labour to drive lorries was cheap and plentiful. The report envisaged the situation getting worse for the railways, as larger road hauliers were, in time, likely to absorb the smaller local operators who were still distributing from their nearest railway station, thereby cutting off further revenues once they were taken over.

It was recognised that, as a result of the proposed local railway line closures, the area's economy and competitive position would be weakened. Also, hardship and inconvenience would be suffered by a number of individuals. The chief objective had to be protecting the area's economy but hardship was going to be difficult to prove as this had to be '*positive hardship*', as laid out in the 1962 Transport Act, not just mere inconvenience. Issues such as the holiday trade (particularly the impact on Ilfracombe's economy), road traffic, attracting new residents to the area, industry, school children (isolating West Buckland School, near Filleigh, for example), employment and agriculture were all considered.

When looking at individual hardship, the Taunton to Barnstaple line was a classical illustration. Dulverton, for example, had buses to Tiverton and Minehead but nothing west to east. The areas served by the stations at Venn Cross, Morebath and East Anstey at the time had buses on only one or two days of the week. No buses served the localities of Morebath Junction Halt, Yeo Mill Halt and Bishops Nympton & Molland. It was acknowledged that even substitute bus services could not fully replace the trains, as it would hinder those people who worked away and returned home for weekends, and would also inconvenience those wishing to make a day trip to the capital. One of the benefits of retaining the line could have been no better illustrated than over the bad winter of 1962-63, when it was kept open whilst local roads were closed, enabling isolated parts of Exmoor to receive much needed and essential supplies.

When all the evidence was gathered, the North Devon Railway Report concluded that the drastic reduction of the region's railway system would cause '*widespread dislocation and accelerate the area's depopulation*'. However, the current losses in operating the lines had to be reduced and it was further stated that it was not possible to justify the retention of two routes to Barnstaple for through traffic. At paragraph 3 of the 'Conclusions and Recommendations' chapter, the D&SR was condemned. So not only had Beeching suggested the axe but this locally sponsored report saw no benefit in retaining the line either. As a consequence, it had little, if any, hope of survival. Paragraph 3 noted: '*In view of the extremely heavy cost of maintenance, the poor condition of several vital engineering works, and the scarcity of both through and local traffic, this line should be closed, subject to the immediate implementation of the vital points (4)-(9)*'.

In essence, these '*vital points*' covered improvements to the Exeter to Barnstaple train service, charging goods from North Devon as if they were conveyed on the shorter D&SR line (not the extra distance via Exeter) for ten years, improvements in bus services, A361 Taunton to Barnstaple road improvements (such as by-passes at Milverton and Wiveliscombe) and the retention of King's Nympton station (on the Exeter to Barnstaple line), with a regular bus service to South Molton.

The bus service proposals are worth exploring. The Taunton to Wiveliscombe bus route was proposed to be extended to Dulverton, via Bampton, with at least three daily journeys each way – an early service to take workers, school children and those wishing to catch an early London-bound train, along with bus connections to the 2.30pm and 4.30pm London trains. It recognised that it was impracticable to run a bus service the whole length of the Taunton to Barnstaple line, parallel to the railway, as this would be slow and ineffective; stops at Dulverton and other villages would require detours off the main A361 Taunton to Barnstaple road. The Dulverton to South Molton 'gap' was to be bridged in two ways; priority was to be given to passengers in the district on the Royal Blue bus service run by Southern National on the A361 and a local bus operator was to link South Molton and Dulverton via the small villages in the East Anstey and Molland area.

In June 1963, British Railways published a statement of annual losses made by passenger train operation (only) in North Devon, which was included as an appendix to the North Devon Railway Report. It stated that the losses could be substantially reduced with the use of diesel traction. The relevant figures for the D&SR are reproduced below:

NATURE OF EXPENSES	AMOUNT (£)
Movement expenses	**57,700 (181,200 miles)**
Terminal expenses	**8,800**
Track and Signalling expenses	**16,100**
Total	**81,800**
Earnings	**8,610**
Deficit	**73,190**

The Ministry of Transport prepared several lists of lines to be closed and this was sent to the Cabinet Office in September 1963. At No. 2 was the closure proposal for the Taunton to Barnstaple

Junction route, with publication already announced on 20th June 1963. The comments noted that the '*line runs the whole width of North Devon. Opposition can be expected to be highly vocal*'. They were not wrong!

As momentum gathered for closure, significant efforts were made to obtain a stay of execution and possibly even a full reprieve from closure. The SWATUCC held a public inquiry at Dulverton in November 1963, where over 100 objectors to the closure attended. Their objections ranged from general cases of hardship to one possible fear that Exmoor would be sent back to the era of the Doones! As part of this gathering, Chris Nelder built a mock-up of a railway locomotive from odds and ends; a cistern for the boiler, an old oil drum for the chimney. The 'Dulverton Express', as it was labelled, was parked outside the town hall. It was constructed as a fun-ride at the school fete but it had this additional use and carried the legend 'Beeching can't ban us!'. This, reported in the appropriately named *Devon & Somerset News*, clearly summarised the mood of those on the edge of Exmoor. The reality was that the line offered little additional benefit to those who lived near Taunton but there were others in the Exmoor region for whom the railway was their only link with the outside world – it was essential. This was no better illustrated than by W.J. Fenwick of the *Western Morning News*, who published on 15th November 1963 a series of interviews with families who were to be affected by closure of the line. He chose well because those he interviewed lived in the West Anstey/ Molland area and used Yeo Mill Halt, arguably the most isolated part of the line and in an area not well served by main roads either.

The Cockram Family lived and worked at Whitley Farm near Molland. The farm was isolated; there was no telephone, no mains electricity and the moorland virtually reached the back door. They owned no large car but, as they needed to get to South Molton a few times a week and East Anstey on market days, the train was the only practical way and Yeo Mill Halt was the nearest station. There was no easy access to or from their farm, only a rough track on which to walk. Once they reached the metalled road, the halt was still two miles away down narrow country lanes. The railway was their link to the outside world. This had become very apparent in the previous winter (1962-63) when snow drifts cut the area off but the trains kept running. If the line was to be closed for good and replaced by a bus service, this would run on the main road at least another mile further south from Yeo Mill Halt, too far away for the Cockram's to use it. As Mr Cockram said at the time, '*We'll just have to 'bide home here, I suppose*'.

Another farm worker, a Mr Sturgess, actually signed the petition which persuaded the railways to open Yeo Mill Halt thirty-one years previously in 1932. He and his wife lived at a cottage in West Anstey still lit by oil lamps and they would be cut off from their children, who had moved away to London and near Tiverton; again the bus would be inadequate for them.

Mr Mildon [*sic*, most likely Milton see Volume 2] from West Anstey had a car but still preferred the train to get him to Taunton market, especially after one such road trip which took him nearly four hours. His support for the line's retention was on the basis that out of a population of 128, with an average of four or five people using the train each day, this was a good percentage, maybe as good as in some large towns.

Generally, it seemed by this stage people were resigned to coming to terms with the potential loss of their railway and overall they felt that, provided the bus service was adequate, in this case linking South Molton to Dulverton, then it would meet most of their requirements.

An argument was submitted to the SWATUCC by Devon County Council that the new bus service should not be a short-term fix to plug the gap arising from the closure of the line, for it only to then fade away after a few years. If road improvements were needed for the buses, then they should be made and the railway kept running until such time as the bus service was itself properly running.

It was almost as if closure of the D&SR was inevitable and momentum was gathering. The Labour Government was returned in the 1964 election and, despite the continuing furore over the railway closures at the time, Harold Wilson, now in power, was unable to halt the closures already sanctioned, although he still sought to honour his pre-election pledge to stop major closures. However, it was a political 'hot potato'. The Transport Secretary of the time, Tom Frazer, gave serious consideration to his role in stopping closures in a note to Harold Wilson on 21st October 1964 but concluded that the Transport Act 1962 gave him no authority to reverse those already agreed and that he would only reconsider major closures once a national plan for road-rail co-ordination had been worked out. Ultimately, the cost of retention of these railways to the taxpayer had to be considered and such lines were seen to be not sustainable in the longer term. One might say, somewhat cynically, that as the number of employees in the road transport sector at this stage outnumbered those in the railways by five to one, this may also have been an influencing factor. Surprisingly, under Labour, the closures continued at a faster rate than under the previous regime. So there was to be no respite for the D&SR and many other lines, and it was closed in 1966, 44 miles out of the total of 750 miles of railway closed that year. Transport Minister, Barbara Castle's Transport Act of 1968 came too late to save the D&SR and a number of other local West Country routes.

Dr Beeching produced his second report on the development of railway trunk routes in 1965 but he then returned to ICI, as always intended, if perhaps a little earlier than originally envisaged. Richard Beeching was made Baron Beeching of East Grinstead in 1965 (Queen's birthday honours list), retiring from ICI in 1977; he died on 23rd March 1985.

History has proved that some of the closures were unjustified, whilst others did not yield the anticipated savings. However, without some dramatic action the railways as they were structured could not sustain themselves. Whilst railways engender romance and sentimentality, the practise of having a stationmaster, porter and signalman as a minimum at most stations and a train crew of three persons was arguably a luxury, especially given the efficiencies in train operation today. Should more consideration have been given to reducing costs, cutting back on certain expenses in an attempt to make a line profitable or at least make a greater contribution to overall costs? Against this, though, there is always the concern that there was a Government agenda to cut back the rail system in the 1960s and all Beeching's report did was to allow them to do this. Beeching did not address the real impact of contributory revenue from branch lines to main lines and it was never established how long it would take for the purported savings to work there way through to 'the bottom line'. Also, it is not clear whether the actual savings made from the cuts were then subsequently compared to the anticipated savings. Finally, Beeching used average costs for track maintenance, train operations and staffing, along with an assessment of renewals of structures and earthworks required to maintain services over a five year period. It is questionable as to whether this was right, being an over simplification leading to erroneous decisions. A proper management assessment and a look at the 'bigger picture', not just the raw statistical data and theoretical techniques, would have given the whole exercise more credibility and left it less open to criticism, particularly by posterity. If computer modelling, as used today, had been as well developed then, then maybe the conclusions would have been different. So Beeching's task was purely a numbers game without real regard to other social and cultural costs. The haste with which the cuts were implemented was also not ideal. As is always the case, its more than about the numbers!

It is perhaps only in the last few years that the railways have blossomed, some forty to fifty years following the Beeching cuts, and it is ironic that some lines that were closed in that period are now being reopened because the potential rail traffic levels demand it and the road system is creaking.

Rationalisation of the D&SR

With a view to making economies on the line, freight had largely ceased at all stations by 1964. This was facilitated by the advent of Taunton's coal concentration depot at this time, thus removing local coal traffic on this and other branch lines. The last through passenger trains along the line from Ilfracombe to Wolverhampton and Cardiff ran during the summer period of 1965 but by this stage rationalisation had already begun.

As the spectre of closure loomed, it is interesting to chart the decline of the stations and trackwork. The line remained broadly intact until the early 1960s, with the track in a good state of repair, free from weeds and well maintained at this time. However, closure by stealth then followed, decay setting in rapidly as rationalisation proceeded at a pace after the publication of Beeching's report, with the once neat stations being left unattended and neglected. Set out below is a broad summary of the various stations' rationalisations, with the presumed objective of saving costs, prior to final closure (this is further covered in the signalling section in Volume 2).

A Birmingham Railway Carriage & Wagon Company-built DMU, with Driving Motor Second No. W51328 leading, waits in the bay at Taunton on 1st October 1966, the last day of the passenger service over the D&SR line, with the 13.28pm service for Barnstaple Junction. ***The late Owen Mogg, courtesy Peter Triggs***

Norton Fitzwarren

Norton Fitzwarren station was closed to passengers on 30th October 1961. On 30th August 1964, the Up crossover linking the D&SR Up line to the main line at Norton Fitzwarren was taken out of use, following which Up branch line trains could then travel directly on to the Up relief line. However, it was still possible to reach the Barnstaple Down line from the Down relief or Down main lines. The Barnstaple

'Warship' Class diesel hydraulic No. D858 *Valorous* with a West of England express is seen overtaking a 2-car DMU bound for Barnstaple Junction on the four track section of the main line just to the east of Norton Fitzwarren on 17th September 1966. ***The late Owen Mogg, courtesy Peter Triggs***

Branch was taken out of use on 3rd October 1966 and all the track lifted during 1967, the final section between Milverton and Norton being lifted by 18th November.

Milverton

The back goods siding at Milverton had been removed in 1944 but the remaining siding running through the goods shed and the Up refuge siding were taken out of use when goods services to the station ceased on 30th September 1963 and were recovered on 8th May 1964. The double track to Norton Fitzwarren remained in use until closure, along with the crossing loop at the station and as a result, the signal box only closed when the line closed.

Above: Two BRC&W Co. twin car DMUs, with Driving Motor Brake Second No. W51314 leading the first pair, speed towards Norton Fitzwarren on the double track section through the flat fields of Taunton Deane near Oake on 14th August 1965.

Left: North British Loco 'Type 2' No. D6332 pulls away from Milverton on 4th September 1965.

Below Left: Another NBL 'Type 2', No. D6324, with box headcodes, departs from Milverton on 30th July 1965.

Below: In the Up direction, NBL No. D6328 works its way back to Taunton on 4th September 1965.
All the late Owen Mogg, courtesy Peter Triggs

LEFT: On 19th June 1965, the driver of No. D6332 exchanges single line tokens with the Milverton signalman, collecting that for the next section to Wiveliscombe. The train is a summer Saturday service bound for Ilfracombe. *Roger Joanes*

OPPOSITE PAGE TOP: Later on the same day, No. D6332 was photographed at Wiveliscombe, returning along the line but this time with a short train heading all the way around the Bristol Channel to Cardiff. This early in the summer season, two coaches would suffice; it would be later into the school summer holidays period when loadings would increase to six or seven coaches. The Down platform was clearly becoming rather grass grown by this date but there were still plenty of flowering plants making a display on the Up side. *Roger Joanes*

RIGHT: A single railcar unit arrives at Milverton with a Barnstaple to Taunton service on 25th October 1965. The vehicle is Gloucester Railway Carriage & Wagon Company-built Driving Motor Brake Second No. W55016, which had entered service in May 1958. *The late Owen Mogg, courtesy Peter Triggs*

OPPOSITE PAGE BOTTOM: 'Mogul' No. 6345 pauses at Venn Cross with a Taunton-bound train on 5th September 1964. Note the fenced off platform and the missing platform slabs. New in 1923, No. 6345 was in its final few weeks in traffic, being withdrawn from Taunton shed by the end of the month. *Michael J. Fox, courtesy Rail Archive Stephenson*

LEFT: A Derby-built 3-car unit, with Driving Motor Second No. W50901 leading, pulls away from Milverton bound for Barnstaple Junction in 1965. The DMU was already over seven years old, having been new in to service in February 1958. *The late Owen Mogg, courtesy Peter Triggs*

WIVELISCOMBE

At Wiveliscombe, one of the goods sidings (the middle road) and the horse dock siding were taken out of use on 19th May 1964. By this time, the station had a run-down appearance, with grass and weeds growing on the Down platform. Goods services continued until 6th July 1964, using the three remaining sidings. The crossing loop was also retained, with the signal box closing with the line.

VENN CROSS

The edging tiles and supporting materials for about a carriage length at the Taunton end of both platforms were taken away in the early 1960s and fenced off for passenger safety. Goods services at the station ceased in September 1963, the Up refuge siding and the goods yard sidings (including the crossover point into the yard) being taken out of use on 24th June 1964. The crossing loop remained, as did the signal box, until the line closed.

BR 'Standard' Class '3MT' 2-6-2T No. 82001 coasts into Morebath station with the 4.20pm Taunton to Barnstaple Junction train on 30th May 1964. With just a single line remaining here and no sidings, the signal box had been out of use for over a year and was now just an empty shell. By this date, following the closure of Morebath Junction Signal Box on 29th April 1964, the section was from Venn Cross to Dulverton. ***Ron Lumber, Dave Mitchell collection***

Looking west from the end of the disused Up platform in 1965. Note that the signal box had now been removed completely. ***Peter Barnfield***

MOREBATH

The station layout at Morebath was effectively destroyed in 1963, when the Up loop and all sidings were take out of use on 2nd March. Just a single line through the station remained, so the signal box was closed at the same time. The frame and locking room equipment and all internal fittings were removed, leaving just the shell of the box and an all round general scene of desolation and depression at the station, which thereafter became an unstaffed halt.

Right: An unidentified North British Loco 'Type 2' pauses at a desolate and depressing Morebath station with a two-coach Up train in 1965. This class of locomotives were all numbered in the 63XX series and are today commonly referred to as Class '22', although this is the British Railways TOPS classification introduced between 1969 and 1973, by which time all of them had been withdrawn. Hampered by their relatively low top speed, they were eminently suited to secondary passenger duties, such as on the Taunton to Barnstaple line, and freight work. The widespread closure of branch and secondary routes led directly to their early withdrawal. *Roger Joanes collection*

Below: The road approach to the unstaffed station in May 1965, with the main building on the left. *Peter Barnfield*

Morebath Junction

The Exe Valley Branch had closed on 7th October 1963, following which the track was recovered. The loop was taken out of use on 29th April 1964, leaving only a single set of rails, the old Up line, for two-way running. The signal box also closed at this time.

A view of the former Morebath Junction from the 3.50pm Barnstaple to Taunton train on 29th August 1964. Although the Exe Valley Branch had been closed for nearly a year by this date, the track remained in situ apart from the junction points. The Down loop had also been dismantled, although some of the sleepers remained in the distance. *Tim Stephens*

ABOVE: Rationalisation at Dulverton, with evidence of track lifting having begun. The horse dock siding in the left foreground had been removed, as had access to the turntable in the Down yard but the cattle dock line, the bay loop, the siding next to it and the coal yard siding all remained *in situ*, along with the Up yard sidings. 'Mogul' No. 7337, with the 4.03pm Taunton to Barnstaple train, is crossing an Up service on 27th June 1964. *Michael J. Fox*

LEFT: By May 1965, Dulverton had been further being run down. The coal yard and goods siding had been lifted but at least part of the Exe Valley bay loop still remained, as did the outer siding on the Up side. With rail-borne deliveries having ceased the previous year, the coal yard would now be receiving deliveries by road lorry from the recently opened freight concentration depot at Taunton. A railcar sidles into the Down loop with a Taunton to Barnstaple service. *Peter Barnfield*

DULVERTON

At Dulverton, the turntable road and middle siding (next to the Exe Valley bay platform) were taken out of use in April 1964, presumably as a consequence of the Exe Valley line closure some six months earlier. Goods services ceased on 6th July 1964 and the layout was further reduced with all of the remaining sidings being taken out of use and recovered, such that all that remained of the layout by August was the passing loop and the cattle pen/loading dock siding. The final piece of rationalisation prior to closure took place on 31st July 1966, when the Down loop was taken out of use (although not lifted) and the Up line operated as a single track through the station for the last two months of the line's life. The signals had their arms removed and, as a consequence, the now redundant signal box was closed. The cattle pen/loading dock siding was retained as an engineer's siding, its final use being during the recovery of the track from the line after closure. There is no evidence of a manual ground frame being installed here to work this last siding, so it is presumed that the signal box was opened by the train crew as necessary.

ABOVE: A few minutes after the previous view, the railcar is seen departing for Barnstaple. From this viewpoint, it is not easy to spot the evidence of track rationalisation at first glance. On the Down platform, a barrow is in use to wheel away a sack dropped off from the railcar. *Peter Barnfield*

RIGHT: On 30th September 1966, the penultimate day of services, a Barnstaple-bound twin-car DMU waits alongside the Up platform, the Up loop being the only line in use by this date. The signal box was now out of use and the signal arms removed. The cattle dock siding was now the only other piece of track that still remained here. *Roger Joanes*

LEFT: The 4.40pm Taunton to Barnstaple service coasts into Dulverton on 29th August 1966. Of note here and in the second photograph below – with closure only a little over five weeks away – is the general condition of the station structures, which appear well looked after, with the paintwork in good condition, whilst the track also looks very well maintained. Evidence, perhaps, of money being spent unnecessarily to further justify shutting the line? *R.A. Lumber, Dave Mitchell collection*

BELOW: After a brief stop, the twin-car DMU heads away to East Anstey. The detail of the waiting shelter is clear to see here. Although still August, the platforms are wet from a recent rain storm. Note the point rodding still in place, although that on the Up side was redundant. It is believed that the points to access the cattle dock siding could still be worked from the signal box as required. *R.A. Lumber, Dave Mitchell collection*

EAST ANSTEY

At East Anstey, goods services ceased in September 1963. The Up refuge siding and the goods yard sidings were taken out of use on 16th March 1964 but the passing loop remained and the signal box closed with the line.

With the signal box just glimpsed on the right, a three-car DMU departs East Anstey on its way to Taunton on 26th June 1965. ***Roger Joanes***

A LAMENT from the ANSTEY VOLUME of the *WOMEN'S INSTITUTE JUBILEE SCRAPBOOK* 1965

'The single line winds its way up one of the steepest gradients in the country from Dulverton to* [East] *Anstey. Under one bridge and then another, and the one line swells into two, between the two bare platforms. At night two Tilley lamps swing in the wind, casting weird shadows and quite failing to light the name* [East] *Anstey, small and rusting on its post. The late traveller alights doubtfully at this lonely place, wondering if he has arrived anywhere. But there are some buildings – a signal box, ticket office and even a waiting room, and further down a goods yard and siding. For this was once a busy little station, lifeline to a large farming community and market. But now the line is doomed – the Beeching Axe is poised to fall, and 1965 may well be its last year. Already the staff has almost vanished – somewhere a boy may be found to sell you a ticket; but he also works the signals, receives the parcels – goods are already a thing of the past, so is the fire in the waiting room; last year's fag ends still litter under the seats. And the dear old puff-puff is superseded by a busy practical diesel, which rolls in and out four times a day each way. The moss is growing on the platforms and as the diesel grunts its way down the straight towards Barnstaple through the lovely intimate country of North Devon, there is a great sadness in the knowledge that soon this line, like so many others, will be empty and useless.'

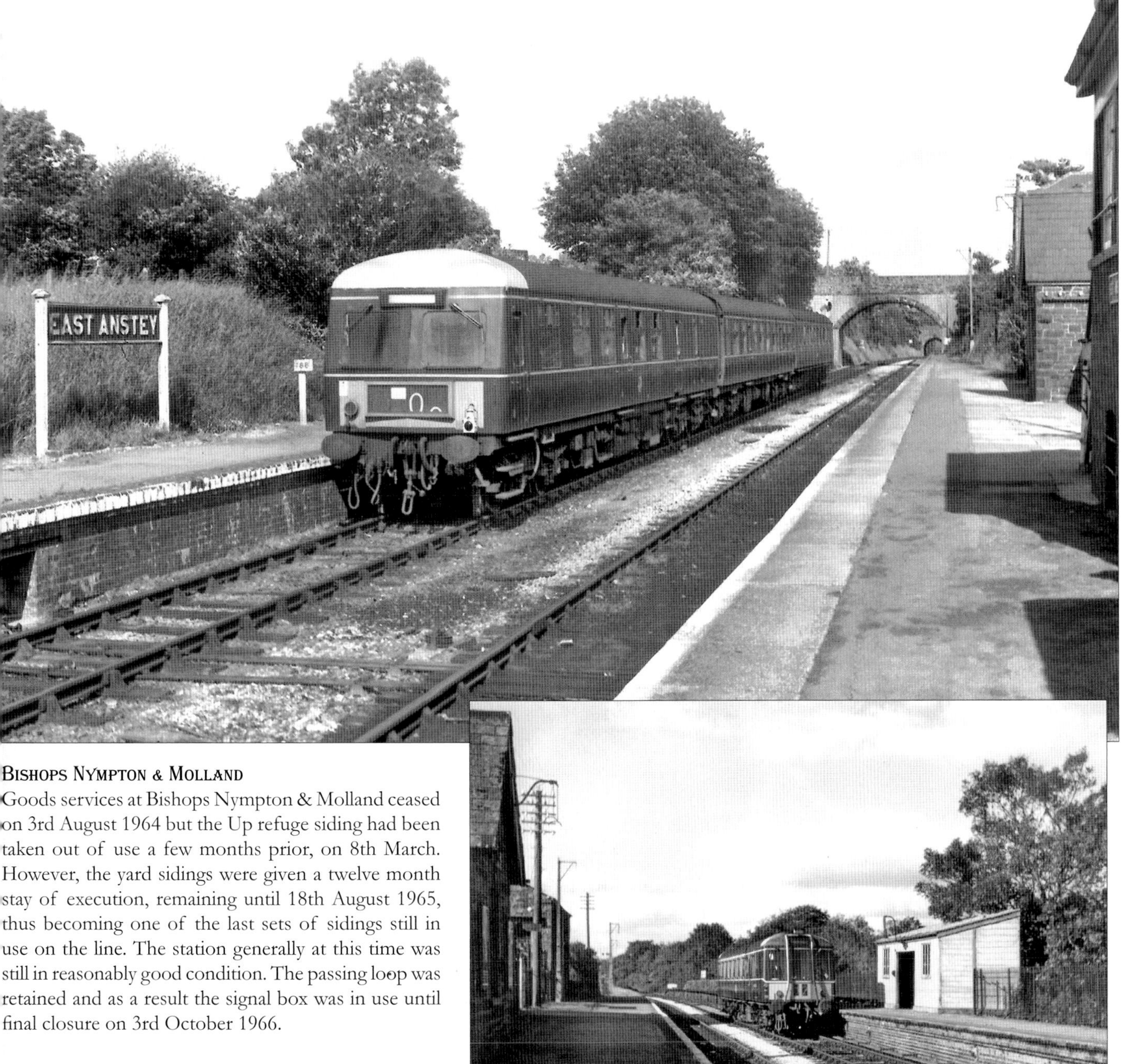

BISHOPS NYMPTON & MOLLAND

Goods services at Bishops Nympton & Molland ceased on 3rd August 1964 but the Up refuge siding had been taken out of use a few months prior, on 8th March. However, the yard sidings were given a twelve month stay of execution, remaining until 18th August 1965, thus becoming one of the last sets of sidings still in use on the line. The station generally at this time was still in reasonably good condition. The passing loop was retained and as a result the signal box was in use until final closure on 3rd October 1966.

Gloucester RC&W-built railcar No. W55000, the first of its class, stops briefly at Bishops Nympton & Molland whilst on its way to Taunton on 16th October 1965. ***Roger Joanes***

A three-car DMU forming the 5.55pm Barnstaple Junction to Taunton service departs from Bishops Nympton & Molland on 24th September 1966. Having exchanged single line tokens with the driver – collecting that for the section from South Molton and handing over the one to East Anstey in its stead – the signalman waits for the unit to clear the boarded crossing before making his way back to his box. There is little sign in this view that closure was just a week away, the final day of operation being Saturday 1st October, although the official date was Monday 3rd October. ***R.A. Lumber, Dave Mitchell collection***

SOUTH MOLTON

There had been an oil depot at South Molton, served by two wagon turntables and a kick-back siding but the Private Siding Agreement had been terminated in 1944; the kick-back siding was not removed until July 1959. The timber part of the Down platform (the eastern end) had been barricaded off by 1963 on safety grounds. Goods services ceased on 3rd August 1964 and all remaining goods sidings were taken out of use on 3rd February 1965, leaving only the passing loop operational. Again this was enough to ensure that the signal box stayed open until the line closed.

A view east from the entrance to the goods yard at South Molton on the last day, 1st October 1966, showing that the point accessing it had been left in place. Note the ends of tie bars in the end wall of the goods shed; clearly the building had needed strengthening at some stage. ***Owen Mogg, Peter Triggs collection***

FILLEIGH

At Filleigh, the private siding to the Fortescue Estate good shed and store, which had operated without a Private Siding Agreement, had been removed circa 1945. The Up goods loop was taken out of use on 20th December 1961, whilst the Down loop and remaining sidings were taken out of use on 6th September 1964, just one month after goods facilities at the station ceased to be provided (see diagram on page 146). This left only a single line running through the Up platform, rather similar to when the line was opened. As a result, the signal box was no longer needed and this closed on the same date in 1964 and was gutted soon after. The whole station area, somewhat like Morebath at this time, became forlorn and unkempt.

A Barnstaple-bound DMU pauses at Filleigh station in the last few months before closure. ***Blake Paterson***

SWIMBRIDGE

From June 1962 to 1964, the station became the terminus for the daily goods train, unless it was required to run on to Barnstaple Junction. Goods services here ceased on 3rd August 1964 and it is understood that the loop siding through the shed was then used as a storage line for, most likely, condemned wagons for a short period. The siding was taken out of use on 18th November 1964 and subsequently removed but the passing loop remained along with the signal box until the line closed.

Ex-GWR 'Mogul' No. 7337 pauses at Swimbridge with a 6-wheeled milk tank wagon and five coaches bound for Barnstaple on 9th July 1962. Again notice the crosses of half a dozen tie bars visible on the end wall of the goods shed. As noted above, the daily pick-up goods from Taunton had begun terminating here from the previous month, which carried on until the cessation of goods services on the line just over two years later. ***C.J. Gammel, courtesy Roger Joanes***

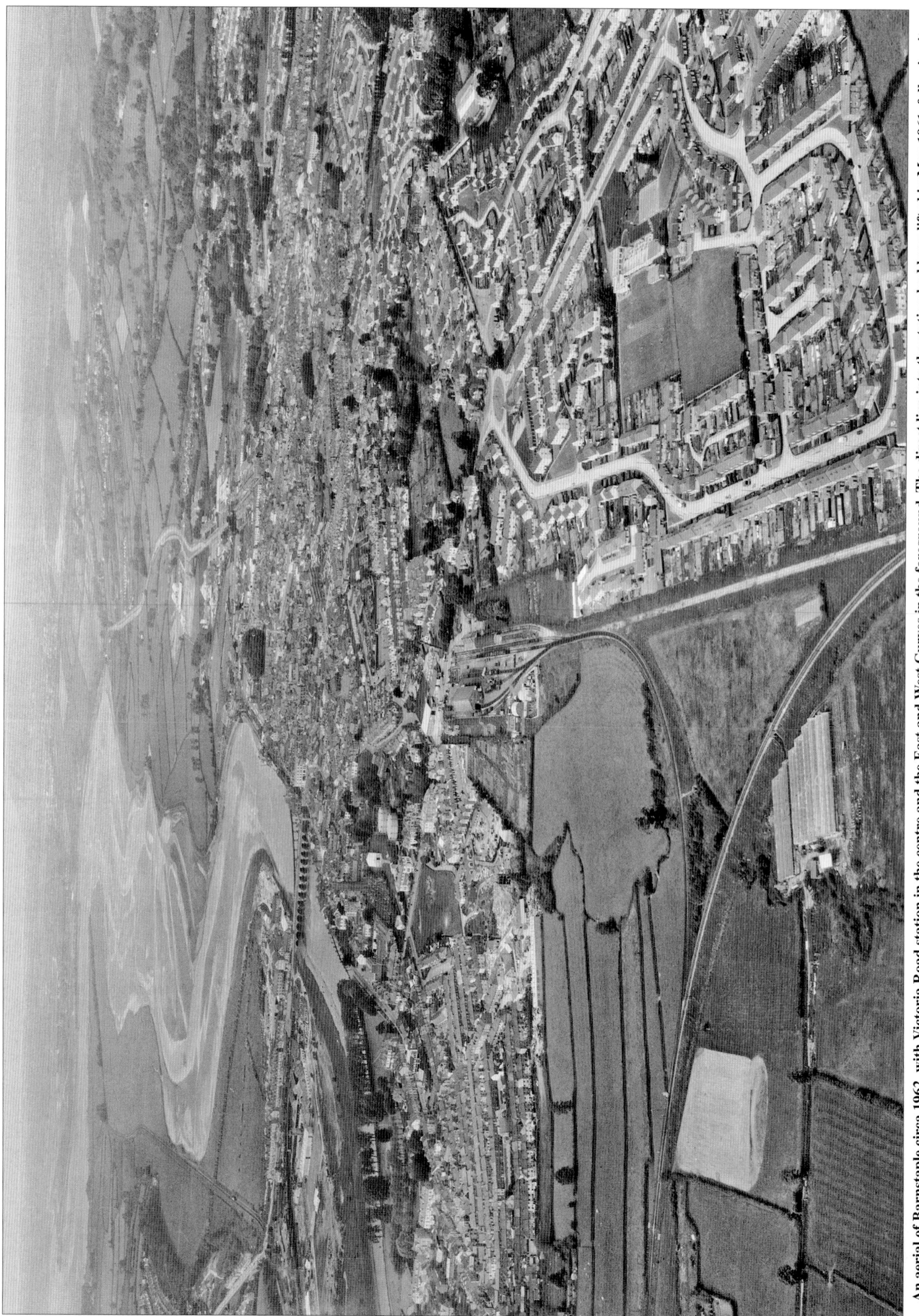

An aerial of Barnstaple circa 1962, with Victoria Road station in the centre and the East and West Curves in the foreground. The direct line into the station had been lifted in May 1961, following its closure the previous year. Just visible at the junction of the two chords on the left is the ground frame which replaced South Loop Signal Box in June 1960. Barnstaple Junction station can just about be made out in the far left distance, with the line to Torrington heading in a straight line to the left (south) of the Taw Estuary. The two bridges carrying the road and the Ilfracombe line respectively across the river can also be seen, with the latter initially following the twists and turns of the Taw on its right (north) bank. Note too the gas works on the far side of Victoria Road. *Aerofilms/Historic England*

An aerial of north east Barnstaple circa 1962, with the suburb of Derby top right. Victoria Road station features bottom left, now just a goods depot but with its track layout still intact. Victoria Road itself runs past the end of the station to the roundabout in the centre. ***Aerofilms/Historic England***

BARNSTAPLE CHORD LINES

Having been out of use since the end of the 1939 summer time table, as mentioned earlier, the East Curve was re-opened on 13th June 1960 on the closure of Barnstaple Victoria Road to passenger trains. It was closed for the second and final time on 3rd October 1966, with the track being recovered in December 1967. The direct route in to Victoria Road from Taunton was closed at the same time that the East Curve was reopened and the track had been lifted by May 1961, although the terminus continued to receive timetabled goods trains from Taunton after that date, presumably via the West Curve, with the locomotive having to run round its train at Barnstaple Junction. This changed from June 1962, when the daily D&SR line goods train was terminated at Swimbridge for the final two years or so that it ran, apart from the occasional load for Victoria Road. After that date, the goods service was worked solely from Barnstaple Junction, with the West Curve being operated as a siding from June 1960 until the cessation of goods services to Victoria Road in March 1970; it was officially closed on 30th May 1970. Both the East Loop and South Loop signal boxes had been closed on 12th June 1960, the former completely and South Loop being reduced to a ground frame, in which guise it lasted until being taken out on 3rd October 1966. Incidentally, the boxes had been renamed by BR on 11th March 1950, having been named East Junction and South Junction respectively by the GWR.

BARNSTAPLE VICTORIA ROAD

Rationalisation at Barnstaple Victoria Road had begun in the early 1950s. The engine shed was closed from 1st January 1951 and its sidings removed on 26th July 1953. By this date, general goods traffic for the town was being dealt with at Victoria Road and plans were afoot to close the station to passengers but this took another seven years to implement. It did enjoy one brief final swansong before this occurred, being lavishly decorated on being used for a visit to Barnstaple by Queen Elizabeth II and Prince Phillip in May

LEFT: Barnstaple Victoria Road station on 27th March 1965, with the platform now occupied by pallets laden with sacks. In this essentially agricultural area, they are likely to contain either fertiliser, animal feeds or corn seed. *Richard Maund*

BELOW: The revised closure notice for the line, issued in late 1965 and carrying details of the replacement bus service and also correcting a minor mistake in the Minister of Transport's consent letter. *Melvyn Baker collection*

BRITISH RAILWAYS BOARD TRANSPORT ACT 1962

PUBLIC NOTICE

WITHDRAWAL OF RAILWAY PASSENGER SERVICE

TAUNTON – BARNSTAPLE JUNCTION

With reference to the Transport Minister's Consent published on 10th September, 1964, to the withdrawal of the passenger train services between Taunton and Barnstaple Junction, the Minister has issued revised Consents as follows:

AMENDMENT DATED 5th APRIL, 1965

I am directed by the Minister of Transport to refer to the Ministry's letter of 10th September, 1964, conveying consent to the discontinuance of all railway passenger services between Taunton and Barnstaple, involving the discontinuance of all railway passenger services from the stations and halts at Milverton, Wiveliscombe, Venn Cross, Morebath, Morebath Junction, Dulverton, East Anstey, Yeo Mill, Bishop's Nympton and Molland, South Molton, Filleigh and Swimbridge (hereinafter referred to as "the consent").

2. The conditions subject to which the consent was given included the requirement that certain alternative bus services should be provided to run near to certain stations and halts between South Molton and Dulverton. The Minister has received representations from the Devon County Council to the effect that by the use of a different route each of the five daily bus services required by the consent to be available between South Molton and Dulverton when the closure takes place, should call at Bishop's Nympton and Molland station, Yeo Mill halt and East Anstey station.

3. The Minister has considered the Council's representations and has come to the conclusion that it would be desirable to vary the conditions attached to the consent so as to provide, as the Council have suggested, for each of the daily bus services to call at the places at present served by the railway between South Molton and Dulverton.

4. Accordingly the Minister in exercise of his powers under section 56 (11) of the Transport Act 1962, hereby varies the conditions of the consent as follows:

The conditions set out in paragraph 3 of the Ministry's letter of the 10th September, 1964, shall have effect subject to the modification that paragraph 2 of Part II of the Annex to that letter shall cease to apply and shall be replaced by the paragraph set out in the Annex to this letter.

ANNEX

2. Services on Monday to Saturday between South Molton and Dulverton, with stops at Blackcock Hotel (for Bishop's Nympton and Molland), Yeo Mill, East Anstey station and Brushwood Cross (for Dulverton station), as follows:

ex South Molton — Dulverton
approximate starting times 6.30 a.m., 8.50 a.m., 1.05 p.m., 4.15 p.m. and 6.50 p.m.

ex Dulverton — South Molton
approximate starting times 7.35 a.m., 10.05 a.m., 2.05 p.m., 5.18 p.m. and 7.50 p.m.

AMENDMENT DATED 29th SEPTEMBER, 1965

I am directed by the Minister of Transport to refer to the Ministry's letter of 10 September, 1964, conveying consent to the discontinuance of all railway passenger services between Taunton and Barnstaple, involving the discontinuance of all railway passenger services from the stations and halts at Milverton, Wiveliscombe, Venn Cross, Morebath, Morebath Junction, Dulverton, East Anstey, Yeo Mill, Bishop's Nympton and Molland, South Molton, Filleigh and Swimbridge (hereinafter referred to as "the consent").

I am to say that a small error appears in Part II of the Annex to that letter. Paragraph I of Part II included a requirement for a bus service on Tuesdays and Fridays only leaving Taunton for Dulverton at approximately 9.15 a.m. This time was intended to be 9.15 p.m.

Accordingly, the Minister, in exercise of his powers under section 56 (11) of the Transport Act 1962, hereby varies the conditions of the consent as follows:

The conditions set out in paragraph 3 of the Ministry's letter of the 10th September, 1964, shall have effect subject to the modification that in paragraph I of Part II of the Annex to that letter the time "9.15 a.m." shall be replaced by the time "9.15 p.m.".

I am, Sir
Your Obedient Servant
J. H. H. BAXTER
Assistant Secretary
Ministry of Transport

The Secretary
British Railways Board
222 Marylebone Road
London, N.W.I

1956. With passenger services into the terminus ceasing on 12th June 1960, the station signal box closed at the same time. Further rationalisation of the track layout took place around 1966, when the long cattle siding and the carriage siding were taken out of use and removed. This left a four-siding layout, with the platform road and bay platform line still intact, along with the run-round loop, the mileage siding, goods shed road, crane road and the back road. The wooden station buildings were not maintained and began to deteriorate; they had gone by the late 1960s, with the platform overgrown with weeds and only the shed siding and one other remaining. The National Carriers Ltd (NCL) freight railhead distribution depot for parcels and smalls traffic closed on 5th March 1970.

Steam operation on the D&SR ceased with the end of the summer timetable in 1964, by which time goods services on the line had finished too. Passenger services were taken over by diesel multiple units and railcars, with the 1965 summer through passenger workings being the preserve of North British 'Type 2' diesel-hydraulics.

THE FINAL YEARS AND CLOSURE

The Taunton to Barnstaple Junction line was originally scheduled for closure in August 1965. However, it remained open after this date because the Minster of Transport made it a condition of closure that alternative bus services had to be provided. The Western Region was not helping passengers either at this time. As the *Railway Observer* noted, the early morning train from Barnstaple was operated by a single railcar and by the time it arrived at Taunton it would be crammed full of passengers, a deterrent to using the line if ever there was one. The main obstacle to closure, namely the lack of suitable replacement bus service, was removed when the South Western Traffic Commissioners reviewed licence applications from the Southern and Western National bus companies (whose application was apparently suggested by BR) and Mr W. Terraneau, a private contractor from

South Molton, to provide that alternative.

The process of substituting the train with a bus service had not been entirely straightforward, as there also had to be some road improvements. Whilst most had been completed, the Castle Hotel turning in Bampton on the A361 road had not and this prevented the buses serving the village of Morebath until such work was done. This meant Morebath inhabitants had a 1½ mile walk to the nearest bus and so Devon County Council objected to the granting of licences. It was suggested that BR might co-operate with a local car hire firm to take the villagers to the bus route. Even Robin Maxwell-Hyslop, the MP for Tiverton, appeared in person to raise an objection, proposing that the line be kept open until the works were completed. He was concerned that the Morebath inhabitants, with virtually no local facilities, would be badly disadvantaged with the loss of the railway and no replacement bus service.

Despite this, the applications were granted and the bus licence affecting the Taunton to Dulverton section was of a temporary nature for twelve months, so that it could be amended to serve Morebath when the roadworks at Bampton were completed.

When the 1966 summer timetable was published, to commence on Monday 18th April, there were no Taunton to Barnstaple services shown. A supplement to the working timetable was subsequently produced, which showed six trains per day running in each direction on weekdays and Saturdays. Summer Saturdays from 18th June to 3rd September in that final year had nine Up and Down trains.

By September 1966, two- and three-car DMU sets were working the line. A Birmingham Railway Carriage & Wagon Company twin-car unit, comprising Driving Motor Brake Second (DMBS) No. W51313 and Driving Motor Second (DMS) No. W51328, along with a Derby Works three-car DMU, comprising DMBS No. W50824, Trailer Second Lavatory (TSL) No. W59580 (built at Swindon Works) and DMS No. W50877 were noted working from Barnstaple on 21st September, based on details published in the *Railway Observer*. The RO also recorded Derby-built twin-car unit DMBS No. W50088 and DMS No. W50130 working from Taunton on the same day. However, on the penultimate day, 30th September, only twin-car DMUs operated. Also on this day, the 11.10am Taunton to Barnstaple service was delayed for nine minutes due to the late running of the 8.30am from Paddington, with which it connected. It had regained its scheduled time by the end of the journey largely due to speeds of between 64-68mph at a number of locations and, apparently, an incredible 72mph on the final leg between Swimbridge and Barnstaple (a speed that would be breaking the law today driving the North Devon Link Road with its 60mph limit!). It is worth noting that the working timetable for that period stipulated that '*The speed of all up and down trains between Norton Fitzwarren and Barnstaple Junction must not exceed 60 miles per hour and must further be restricted to a lower speed shown below*.' [basically restrictions into and out of stations and over the viaducts]. In this case it was the 60mph restriction that was exceeded.

On 29th September 1966, just two days before the last train was to run, the *Western Morning News* reported that apparently a last-minute move was afoot to save the D&SR from closure. A body, the South-Western Economic Planning Board, had recently been set up and its brief was to review the whole of the railway proposals for the South West. However, the decision to close the Taunton to Barnstaple line was taken before the board was set up and this caused difficulties. Mr John Scoble, the Chairman, tried to argue that the Council's views had no standing in law, as they [the board] were never formally consulted on the Taunton to Barnstaple line closure, but without success.

The last train was due to leave Barnstaple Junction station at 7.04pm on the evening of Saturday 1st October 1966 and was due to return to Barnstaple by 10.42pm. It was expected to carry 350 passengers, of which 150 were guests of Barnstaple Round Table (a special booklet and ticket being issued for the occasion). In the end, close to 400 passengers made the trip. There was optimism that the last train would be steam hauled but this was not a practical proposition so DMUs were used instead – a three-car unit plus two twin-car sets to make a seven coach train.

ABOVE: The cover of the commemorative booklet produced for the occasion of the final train.

LEFT: Ticket for the final train, which was red with embossed black ink lettering. Note the fare of 16 shillings. *Derek Goodwin collection*

At Barnstaple there was a civic send-off, with the Mayor, Alderman William H. Wilkey and the Rt Hon. Jeremy Thorpe, MP for North Devon, on the train. The non-travelling members of the public coming to pay their last respects were apparently issued with platform tickets. Riding in the cab of the DMU was 83 year-old Mr Albert Doran, who was a driver himself on the line in steam days and who had apparently made an offer to the BR Area Manager to drive the train but was declined. The driver was Mr Lionel Cox of Taunton for the Barnstaple to Taunton leg. The DMU was adorned with a headboard stating '1873 Last Train Excursion 1966, Barnstaple to Taunton'. The local British Legion band also travelled on the train and on the return journey they played at each of the stations and halts on the line. Many passengers joined the train as it called at the intermediate stations, including Ada Williams, Lady Mayoress of South Molton. Mr Tim Keigwin, the prospective Conservative MP, joined the train at Yeo Mill Halt, the nearest station to his home at West Anstey.

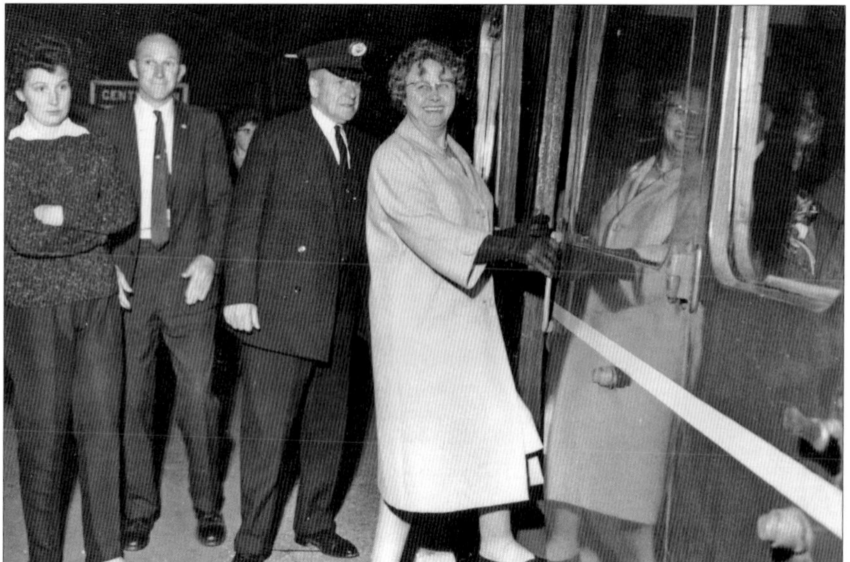

South Molton Lady Mayoress, Ada Williamson about to join the last train at her local station on 1st October 1966. ***Gordon Bray***

As the train arrived at Taunton it was welcomed by 300-400 people, including the official welcoming party of Mr H.V. Ellis, Deputy Mayor of Taunton, Mr D. Kennedy, chairman of Taunton Round Table, Mr S. Berry, chairman of the Minehead Round Table and Mr J.W. Passmore, chairman of the Round Table's Area 37. Taunton Round Table had wanted a piper to play a lament as the train departed for the last time. Unfortunately, a piper could not be found but, perhaps more appropriately, a hunting horn was sounded. Detonators exploded and this, along with the people in attendance, gave the train a lively send off on its way back to Barnstaple for the final time. Mr Rex Lock of Barnstaple was the driver for the return journey.

With the British Legion Band playing at each stop, it was no surprise that the train arrived at Barnstaple Junction 45 minutes later than the planned 10.42pm. Passengers sang *Auld Lang Syne* and danced the polka on the platform, and the wake did not conclude until after midnight. The age of the Devon & Somerset Railway was over, just short of its 93rd birthday.

Scenes at Dulverton were somewhat subdued, where some even felt (perhaps with a glimmer of optimism) that the line might be re-opened given the uncertainty over the alternative bus service. However, a 'special notice' was chalked up on the Dulverton sign board which summed up the mood of the occasion.

SPECIAL NOTICES
THIS IS THE
END OF
THE LINE
THANK YOU FOR YOUR
PATRONAGE OVER THE
PAST 93 YEARS
GOOD-BYE
FROM THE STAFF

Sadly such scenes of lamentation were being repeated in other parts of Devon and Cornwall that night as the Okehampton to Bude line closed along with the Halwill to Wadebridge line. These may have been L&WSR lines in the past, with the associated rivalry with the GWR, but that night their fate was indistinguishable from that of the Taunton to Barnstaple line.

Soon after closure, Edgar Hicks, a Western Region official at Taunton, organised a recovery train for collecting seats and other easily moved items from the stations. It was now inevitable the wrecker's trains would soon start to claim the line but, prior to this, there was at least one other recorded 'excursion' onto the branch, by an unidentified North British Loco 'Type 2' on 7th February 1967, hauling an inspection coach and one ordinary carriage. It was reported in the *Railway Observer* that up to fifty dignitaries/officials had cause to make the trip.

By the summer of 1967, dismantling of the line was in full swing. The demolition contractor's were George Cohen, Sons & Co. of Kettering. As motive power during the demolition, they used a John Fowler diesel mechanical 0-4-0 with a slightly off-centre cab, No. ED3. It was one of only two Fowler locomotives in service in 1967, the other being No. ED6 and both were withdrawn in September 1967, so this was clearly No. ED3's final outing; it was cut up by Cohen's in June 1968. It produced 150bhp and had a vertical 4-cylinder engine, with 15,000lb's maximum tractive effort, weighed 29 tons and was built at Fowler's Leeds works for the Engineering Department of the London Midland Region in 1949. Its early career included five years at Castleton Engineers depot, before moving to Lenton depot in Nottingham in 1955. It was transferred to Bedford in early 1964 for use on engineering trains based at Bedford Belfast Pit Sidings and was bought from BR by Cohens in 1965.

Dismantling started in the west at the Barnstaple end and moved eastwards. Dulverton became a railhead for the demolition and the cattle dock line was used to store the bogie flat wagons for carrying the rails and other paraphernalia. The wagons used to carry the remnants of the line were a mixture of bogie bolster flat wagons and open wagons (most of which had 'Cond' [for condemned] written on their sides). North British 'Type 2's were employed on moving the wagons from the railhead back to Taunton. Sadly precious few photographs seem to exist of the demolition trains in action.

So was Dr Beeching right with his proposals? In purely financial terms he probably was as far as concerns the closure of the D&SR, given the low level of direct passenger receipts and high maintenance costs, although the hardship of those living on the route should have perhaps been considered further given the general isolation of the area. This, along with a serious rationalistion of the line, maybe even after a 'mothballing' period, might have saved it. However, as noted above the demolition crew came in soon after closure and began the task of dismantling everything; there was no stay of execution like the Ilfracombe line had for a period of years whilst a preservation group tried, albeit in vain, to raise funds to purchase that line. The D&SR, scenic though it was, was never considered for preservation; in the early era of such projects, a line of that length would have been a huge and probably impossible challenge at that time. If we look at the railways today, they are a shadow of their former selves almost everywhere; fewer sidings and running lines, whilst virtually every passenger train is a unit capable of being driven from either end. The fate that has befallen the Exeter to Barnstaple 'Tarka Line' would almost certainly have been mirrored on the D&SR if it had survived. The Tarka Line is now little more than a long siding with just two passing passes, at Crediton and Eggesford, operated usually by a two-car unit that rides like a bus. There have been no freight services on it for many years.

However, at least the Tarka Line is well patronised and supports a (broadly) hourly passenger service on weekdays, preventing that part of North Devon from being totally isolated from the rail network. Would the D&SR have been as successful today, if it had stayed open or would it always have come down to one route or the other to serve Barnstaple? I believe the D&SR could have been equally successful but the lost decades for rail in the 1970s and 1980s would undoubtedly have seen one of them closed. There are many, however, who believe that the wrong line was closed in terms of the town's accessibility from the rest of the UK and it is possible, too, that the Ilfracombe Branch may have survived if it had been on the end of what was a more direct route from London, the Midlands and the North. Perhaps the ultimate 'proof' of its viability as a route is the fact that much of it was rebuilt as part of the A361 North Devon Link Road in the 1980s, including the construction of a new road bridge on the original piers of Castle Hill Viaduct. However, whilst it no longer exists, at least the D&SR can be remembered as it was and not as a very long siding with a few passing places and a 'rattling bus' for a train.

An aerial view of Dulverton station and Brushford village in 1966 or early 1967. It is difficult to be certain if this was before or after final closure; Goodlands, the local coal merchants, continued to operate from the yard for some after the railway had closed, whilst the signal arms had been removed some time before services ceased. The B3222 road crosses the railway as it makes its way north towards the Barle Valley and Dulverton. ***Aerofilms/Historic England***

ABOVE: A second aerial view of the area around Dulverton station, taken on the same occasion but looking west towards East Anstey. The River Barle flows from right to left across the foreground, whilst the railway curves away from the station to head up the shallow valley of the River Brockey. ***Aerofilms/Historic England***

RIGHT: The following short series of views were taken in late 1967, after track lifting at the station had been largely completed. This first picture is a useful study of the pump house, which was tucked into the bank on the Down side adjacent to the road bridge and is looking across the remains of the running lines. ***Courtesy Chris Nelder and the Dulverton Heritage Centre***

RIGHT: Another useful detail study, taken from the long loading bank that ran the length of the siding that ran into the yard from the Barnstaple end on the Down side. The livestock pens feature prominently in the foreground and note the sleepers and chairs stacked on the Down platform awaiting removal.

LEFT: A close-up of the footbridge, taken from the Up side and looking across the Down platform, with Goodlands Ltd's coal yard and offices visible in the background. Goodlands were coal and builders merchants, whose main depot was in Tiverton. The coal business was later bought out by national distributer Charringtons Solid Fuel, now part of CPL Ltd, whilst the builders side was sold to Sharp & Fisher of Cheltenham, who are now owned by Travis Perkins.

RIGHT: The view from the footbridge looking south across Grant's Hill towards Tiverton. The railway meanwhile curves to the left in the middle distance, to head east over the River Exe to Taunton. The rails were still in place just beyond the ends of the platforms and the signal box still looks in remarkably good condition. Like the footbridge, above, it appears to have been repainted only a couple of years prior to closure.
All courtesy Chris Nelder and the Dulverton Heritage Centre

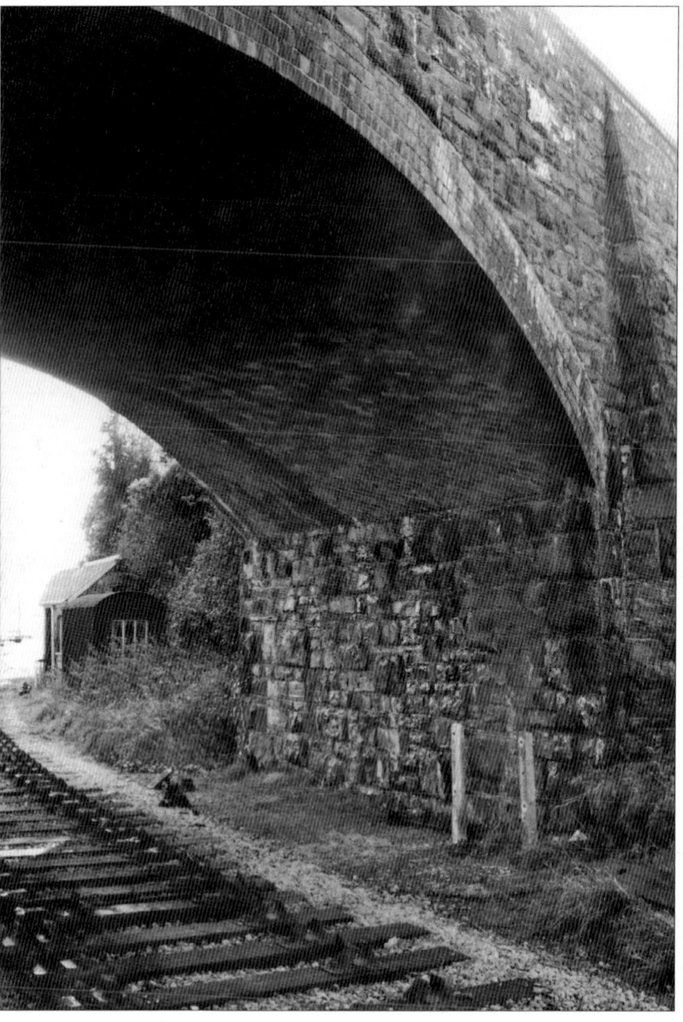

ABOVE: Detail of the stonework and underside of the arch carrying the B3222 over the railway, looking east with the pump house and an adjacent black painted corrugated iron hut also in view.

TOP: A close up of the Barnstaple end of the signal box, showing the door into the locking room. The access steps were sited at the other end of the box.

ABOVE: Looking through the bridge arch at the platforms and station buildings.

LEFT: The remains of the Down side goods yard from the long loading dock, with the turntable pit in the foreground. The turntable was removed in 1964, having fallen out of use following closure of the Exe Valley Branch. As can be seen, it was small in size and only suitable for 0-4-2 and 0-6-0 turning tank engines.
All courtesy Chris Nelder and the Dulverton Heritage Centre

Scenes on the D&SR after track lifting had been completed. TOP LEFT: The track bed near Wiveliscombe. TOP CENTRE: Bathealton Tunnel, east portal. TOP RIGHT: Looking across the Tone Viaduct. ABOVE LEFT: Milverton station. ABOVE RIGHT: Venn Cross goods shed. ***Courtesy Richard Antliff and Amyas Crump***

A sad scene of dereliction and decay at Barnstaple Victoria Road in the late 1960s, shortly before final closure in 1970. Note the poor state of the wooden station building by this date and the debris strewn across the platform road and adjacent loop line. This view should be compared with that on page 105, when the station was in its heyday. The line to Barnstaple Junction can just be seen curving to the right in the centre distance. ***Courtesy Kevin Robertson***

RIGHT: Diagram from the Taunton Civil Engineer's Office (date stamped by the WR Chief Civil Engineer's Office at Paddington on 2nd December 1959), showing the piecemeal rationalisation at Filleigh station. The Up goods loop (at the Down end) was removed in December 1961, whilst the sidings and Down loop were taken out in September 1964, with the Down platform and signal box being closed at the same time. ***Amyas Crump collection***

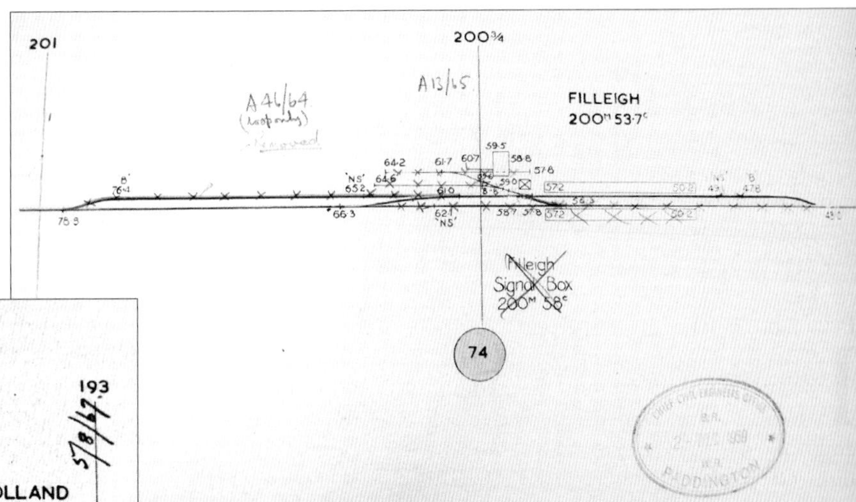

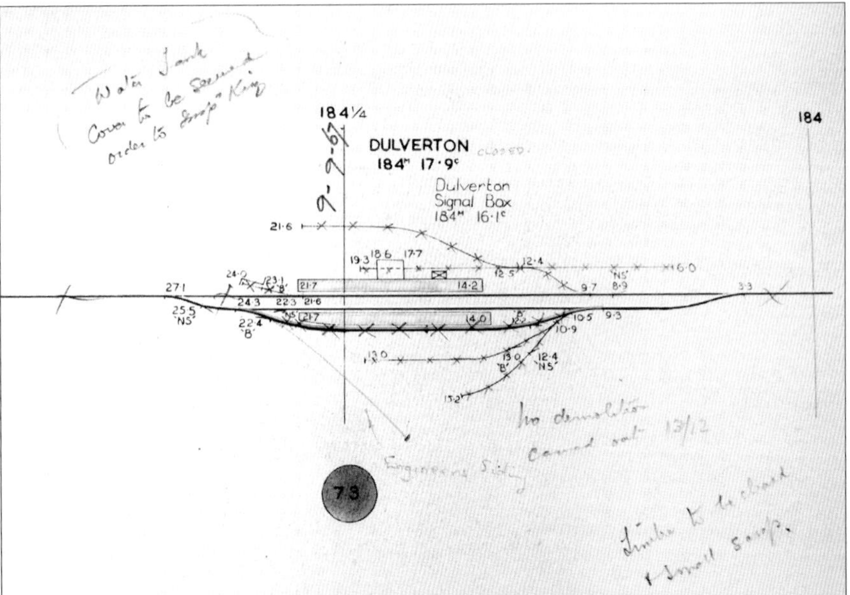

Three further diagrams from the Taunton Civil Engineer's Office, which detail the progress of track lifting at various locations on the D&SR. Lifting commenced at the Barnstaple end working back to Taunton; by 15th July 1967, the track had been lifted to mile post 197½, just outside of South Molton. ***All Amyas Crump collection***

LEFT: By 5th August, track lifting had been completed at Bishops Nympton & Molland but the bridge at 192 miles 79 chains had not been removed.

BELOW LEFT: Track removal at Dulverton, was completed on 9th September. Note the engineer's siding (by the cattle dock) is shown pencilled in, although photographs clearly show it was still *in situ* in 1966.

BOTTOM: Track lifting to milepost 172¼, just to the east of Wiveliscombe, had been completed by 28th October 1967.

TABLE OF TRACK REMOVAL DATES

DATE	LOCATION	MILEPOST
15.07	West of South Molton	197¼
22.07	West of Bishop's Nympton & Molland	196
05.08	Bishop's Nympton & Molland	193
12.08	West of East Anstey	190½
19.08	Just west of East Anstey	188¾
26.08	West of Dulverton (Combe Drive gate)	186¾
09.09	Dulverton	184¼
16.09	Ashtown Cutting*	183¼
30.09	Morebath	180½
21.10	Tone Viaduct	176
28.10	Just east of Wiveliscombe	172¼
02.11	Just west of Allerford Bridge	166
18.11	Norton Fitzwarren Junction	165¼

*** Just west of Morebath Junction Halt**

Information extracted from annotated diagrams from the Taunton Civil Engineer's office, courtesy Amyas Crump

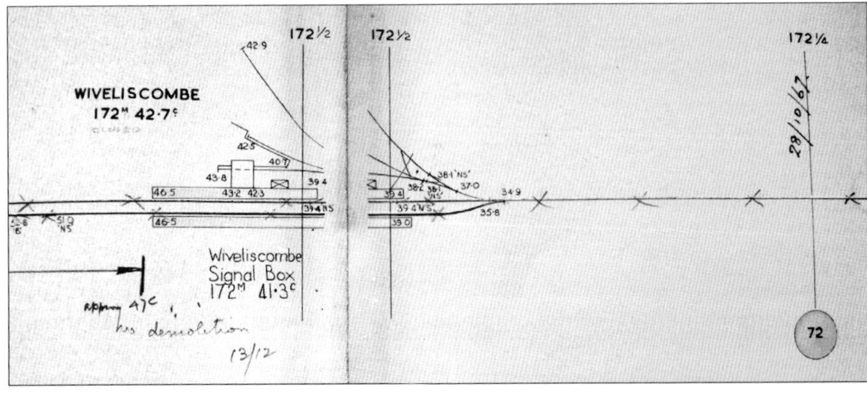

CHAPTER 5

THE INTERVENING YEARS 1966-2016

PROPOSALS FOR USE OF THE TRACKBED

In April 1969, the Exmoor Society became concerned about the future use of the now disused and dismantled Taunton to Barnstaple line. British Railways usually gave the relevant local authority the first option to buy the property (trackbed), often dismantling bridges, buildings and other infrastructure first. Chairman of the Society S.H. Burton drew attention to the fact that BR could cause irreversible damage before the trackbed could be secured for bridleways and footpaths, for example, especially given the complexities of the planning procedure that needed to be conducted. The grand plan was for an Exmoor-Dartmoor bridleway with spurs to more isolated locations, whilst the buildings would provide stabling and other facilities for visitors who would be encouraged to leave their cars behind. One such proposed 'greenway' was to start at Norton Fitzwarren and continue for at least 21 miles to East Anstey along the old D&SR trackbed, where it would link with the Exmoor-Dartmoor bridleway. It was even suggested that if the Taunton to Minehead railway closed (it was still then open, pending closure in 1971) a complete circuit could be made back to Norton Fitzwarren. The Exmoor Society commissioned the Dartington Amenity Research Trust to prepare a feasibility report (being their contribution to European Conservation year, 1970). They suggested that the conversion of both lines would give a number of potential uses such as walking, cycling, riding and picnicing, as well as being available for schools and university groups. However, the venture did not progress.

In October 1971, the *Railway Observer* reported that a consortium, representing the South Molton and Barnstaple branches of the National Farmers Union (NFU), had purchased 25 miles of the line between East Anstey and Barnstaple, involving 170 acres. The aim was for the land to be sold on a non-profit making basis to the farmers through whose land it passed. During the intervening years, various private purchases of the land occurred as outlined later in this chapter.

One specific example is the conveyance of land forming part of the Taunton to Barnstaple line from the British Railways Board (BRB) to Mr James Richard Dinham Wyatt, dated 15th June 1974 and comprising 4 acres 3,410 square yards. A schedule to the agreement confirmed that the original conveyance was on 7th February 1867 (by Trustees of the late Samuel Brown to the D&SR) and 21st September 1870 (Mrs Sarah Edbrooke to Trustees on behalf of the D&SR).

The *Somerset County Gazette* reported on 12th January 2001 that Jackie Ballard, the MP for Taunton, was to take to the skies in a tracker plane to assess the feasibility of reopening the Taunton to Barnstaple railway line. Dick Joy, a parish councillor in North Devon and rail enthusiast, put forward the proposal, which included opening the stations at Wiveliscombe and Dulverton, as this would boost the North Devon economy and the environment. Mrs Ballard was keen to have a look but was recorded as saying '*There are several questions, such as what it would cost to re-route and replace the old line. It looks as though it would be incredibly difficult and expensive ... it may be a non-starter*'. Indeed, the idea of resurrecting the line died soon after.

At a Railfuture committee meeting in October 2005, the subject of re-opening the line was again raised. After some debate, no one wished to support either the original route from Dulverton to Wiveliscombe and Taunton, or an alternative via Tiverton (at which point it would have then joined the Exeter to Taunton main line). The main reason given was that the population of the whole area was too small to support traffic on the line and too much of the trackbed would need to be restored. In December 2005, Railwatch published correspondence regarding the suggestion of re-opening the line between Barnstaple and Tiverton. However, it was then confirmed by Gerard Duddridge that Railfuture Devon and Cornwall had never promoted the re-opening of the line, whether via the old route to Taunton or any proposal to re-route the line via Tiverton, as the old route '*has largely disappeared*'.

THE WEST SOMERSET RAILWAY AND THE ALLERFORD TRIANGLE

By 2007, the West Somerset Railway (WSR) had commenced one of its development projects. The plan was to create a triangle at Norton Fitzwarren in order to turn locomotives or, indeed, a complete train. The project was actually undertaken by the West Somerset Railway Association (WSRA), rather than the WSR itself.

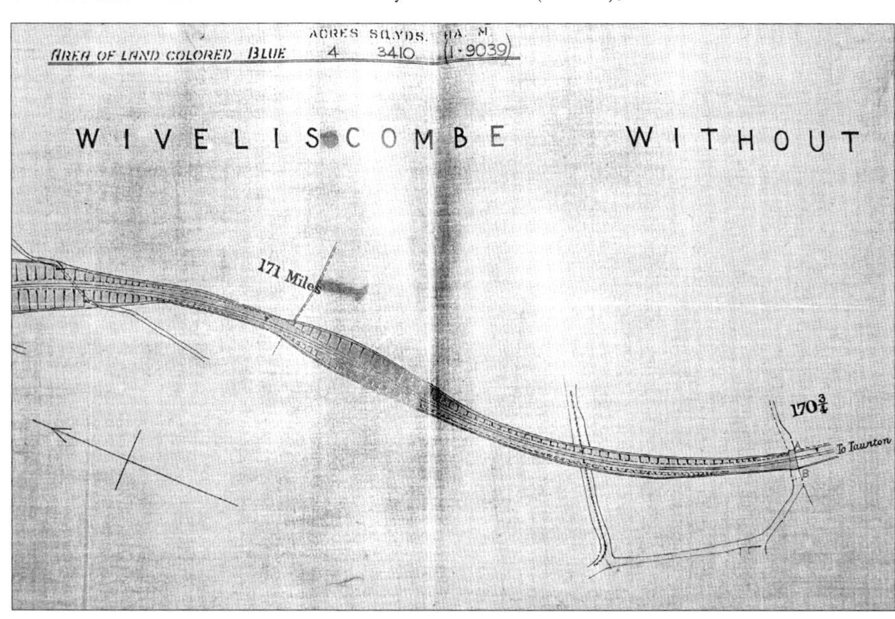

An 1880s plan of the land that was conveyed to Mr Wyatt in 1974. ***Courtesy Wesley Wyatt***

This project required the acquisition of certain fields (33 acres) between the Minehead line at Norton Fitzwarren Junction, the (old) A361 road bridge and the trackbed of the Taunton to Barnstaple line from the junction towards what was the Allerford road bridge (before former milepost 166). Most of the 1/2 mile of trackbed at the start of the D&SR had previously been acquired in the 1990s, with no particular plans in mind, by two private individuals, Messrs Dick Wood and Ian Jonas, who were members of the WSRA. The reason for acquiring and using the trackbed towards Allerford bridge was to create a spur off the proposed triangle. One side of the triangle (the East Chord) was to run more or less parallel but inside the WSR running line. The West Chord would branch off the WSR at the A361 road bridge and curve westwards towards to join the Allerford spur. The third side of the triangle was from the junction between the Barnstaple and Minehead lines at milepost 165 1/4, back towards Barnstaple, with the intended spur running towards Allerford bridge beyond this. The 'inner triangle', as so described, was needed to avoid encroachment on to Network Rail property and metals when turning trains, as any spur off the main running line would have been too short to allow room for anything other than a locomotive and support coach to use the east side of the triangle.

The WSRA made their intentions public in 2004 and David Holmes volunteered his professional services for the development and procurement of the project. Initial planning work then commenced later in 2004, with planning approval granted on 14th April 2005. The initial rail connection was at Allerford Junction, just north of the A361 road bridge, with about 380 metres of track being laid back under the bridge on the old double track section of the WSR in the winter of 2005-6. Early in 2006, an agreement was reached with Network Rail to unload spent ballast at the site, being close to their Fairwater Yard track maintenance depot. This provided two advantages: the first was the ability to use the old recycled ballast on the triangle, whilst the second was that the WSRA would be able to sell on what they did not require themselves to help fund the project. In addition, provision of reusable sleepers and rail for the triangle was included in the agreement. It was at about this time that Derek Head took over the project from David Holmes and he became responsible for day-to-day matters. Ground preparations were made for the high output ballast cleaners (HOBCs) and related matters and this was completed by December 2006. Work on the main HOBC contract started in January 2007, along with construction of the triangle, the next section being the track leading to the East/West chord divergence and the HOBC unloading site on the West Chord. By the end of 2007, the embankment and trackbed had been completed as far as Orchard Junction (so named as there was an orchard to the north of the Allerford spur). Part of the East Chord embankment had also been built and was at this stage just short of the old Barnstaple trackbed. Subsequent to this, new track (to a length of some 620 metres) was laid to Orchard Junction where a point was installed. HOBCs began to unload on the triangle in August 2007. Scrub clearance commenced with the cutting back gang operating near the site that was to be named Barnstaple Junction (see below). Early 2008 saw a slow down in work, largely due to inclement weather. At this time, negotiations were in train with Network Rail to acquire a short section of the trackbed that was not owned by Messrs Wood and Jonas. By August 2008, at the time of the Norton Steam Fayre, part of the new West Chord running from the A361 road bridge was built, ballasted and the track laid. Over the coming months, the embankment on the old double track section to Milverton was cleared of scrub. This was a major job so a flail machine was brought in, which left a thick layer of debris that had then to be cleared. To quote from the *WSR Journal* (David Holmes) in early 2009:

> *'The weekend of January 3rd/4th was one of the coldest for a long time (on Saturday the temperature never climbed above zero!) yet it did not stop the Cutting Back Gang undertaking one of its biggest tasks for quite a while as we tackled some serious growth blocking a drainage ditch alongside the Barnstable* [sic] *line at Norton. The ditch collects water from the fields to the south* [north] *of the track bed as it runs down toward the River Tone. It is doubtful if any management had been carried out for many years and the ditch bed had become completely overgrown and blocked with coppiced willow which threatened in places to block the ditch completely.*
>
> *... In two days we were able to disentangle and remove all the bushy top growth from a length of approximately 200 metres leaving the root systems to be pulled out using an excavator (hopefully during February 2009). On the second of the two days we were joined by the Association Permanent Way Gang and a tractor who, between them, dealt with a large area of bramble, elder and buddleia clearing the way for the final section of the track bed.'*

By early spring of 2009, almost the entire formation was cleared and graded. This included a reduction in the incline up to the old Allerford road bridge. As part of the original formation had moved, this was reinforced with a length of gabion baskets. The West Chord by this time had had track in place for some time and the East Chord had been lightly ballasted. About 300 yards of the Allerford headshunt was lightly ballasted just before Christmas 2008 and this was followed by ballasting of the Barnstaple Chord heading back towards Taunton.

Little track laying occurred in the early part of 2009. However, by the end of the summer, the long Allerford headshunt was ballasted and rail laid for 200 metres (out of a total of 300) westwards towards the old Allerford bridge. By the end of 2009, the Barnstaple Branch had been ballasted in readiness for double track again. With the provision of extra ballast, a decision was made to increase the height of the formation on the Allerford section, in order to eliminate a long dip between Orchard Junction (where the West Chord joined the Barnstaple section) and the Allerford bridge abutment. This required the raising of track that had already been laid on the headshunt by between 12 and 18 inches. A further delivery of concrete sleepers in October 2009 were laid out towards the Allerford bridge in single-track formation on the north side (Up line as was) of the line, leaving room for a second track to make the spur double track in due course.

The Norton Fitzwarren platform required planning permission, which was duly granted in May 2009, then built, approved by the inspector and became operational for the first time on 1st August 2009, at the annual Steam Fayre, with a DMU shuttle service to Bishops Lydeard. Contracts for the missing section of the trackbed were at long last exchanged with Network Rail on 24th September. Thus the WSRA had ownership of all the old trackbed at last and could go on to complete its project.

The cutting back and track maintenance gangs were then brought in to work on the newly acquired old Barnstaple line section.

Over the Christmas period in 2009, the bullhead rail available for the Allerford spur was laid on the sleepers and the track plated, keyed-up and packed to level. The track was still slightly short of the former bridge (about 50-60 yards) but sufficient rail was in place by this time to use the triangle when the remaining works were completed. The work continued on the old Up formation between Orchard Junction and culvert No. 4 on the Barnstaple track bed. The concrete sleepers, some 400 for flat bottom rail, were by now available and ready for laying on this section. The triangle earthworks had now been

Concrete sleepers awaiting positioning on the Allerford spur in May 2009. The wagon is 'parked' on the West Chord line. ***Author***

completed and the entire layout ballasted. At this stage, about three quarters of a mile of track were still to be laid to complete the triangle.

By the start of 2010, the civil engineering work was virtually completed, apart from the provision of stone topping which could only be laid after the track was in position.

Although not directly affecting the Taunton to Barnstaple section, the weekend of 6th-7th February 2010 saw the permanent way gang instal a point for the West Chord to the East Chord. The exact position was set by global positioning satellite.

Ballasting of the new spur took place on 1st May 2010, utilising a Class '08' diesel shunter and five hopper wagons. At the conclusion of operations, the Allerford spur and the track along the South Chord to Orchard Junction was fully ballasted and awaiting the tamper. Railway Support Services ballast tamper No. 73315 arrived on 20th May 2010 to complete the job, following which this section was passed for traffic. Recycled ballast amounting to some 200,000 tonnes was used for the whole project.

At this time, the Chairman of the WSRA set up a vote to name the new pointwork that was laid on the running line near the boundary with Network Rail. The result was announced at the AGM, with Barnstaple Junction the most popular name (13 out 37 votes); West Somerset Junction (6 votes) was second some way behind and Devon & Somerset Junction third (3 votes).

Whilst the Allerford spur is 300 metres long, the spur leading back to Taunton is only 150 metres and this would limit the length of a train to be used on that section to four or five coaches and an engine, thus restricting commercial use by Network Rail.

Further pointwork and track continued to be added to the triangle during 2010, including a short stub at the Taunton end acting as a trap point to protect the main line.

On 14th July 2010, the Network Rail ultrasonic test train was the first working to traverse Barnstaple Junction, the duty falling to Class '31' No. 31106. A deadline for completion had been set by the rail regulator of the end of September 2010 but, due to the weather causing rail delivery complications, it had had to be extended.

However, by November 2010, work on both the West Chord and the Allerford spur was complete. Her Majesty's Railway Inspectorate visited and granted permission for passenger train use of the two new sections of line.

Meanwhile, the section between the two chord lines was prepared and sleepers laid awaiting rails; these started to be laid along the Barnstaple formation between Orchard Junction and Barnstaple Junction by early 2011. At the same time, the final point between the East Chord and the Barnstaple section had been laid, leaving only rail to be added to complete the triangle.

In conjunction with the track laying, a token instrument was installed at Allerford Junction and a new token circuit was also installed to connect the new Allerford instrument panel to the one at Bishops Lydeard Signal Box. This enabled the 'one train working' arrangement previously in place between Bishops Lydeard and the main line to be abolished and replaced by 'no signalman token working'. The plan ultimately is to have eight tokens to work the system.

On Thursday 22nd March 2011, BR-built 'Pacific' No. 70000 *Britannia* became the first steam locomotive to be turned here, utilising the larger triangle on this occasion.

A month later, on 29th April, an important milestone was reached, when tracklaying on the former Barnstaple formation was finished, with the final concrete sleepers placed, rails trimmed and drilled, and fishplates fitted. A ground frame was put in at Barnstaple Junction in the late summer of 2011 and, as a result, the section to Orchard Junction was then complete. Once the Barnstaple Chord had been ballasted and tamped, the whole of the outer triangle was ready for use. At this stage, the East Chord formation remained bare, with about 360 yards of plain track required to complete the inner triangle. The stub sited at Barnstaple Junction was completed in the summer of 2011 and the whole of the outer triangle had been ballasted and tamped. Diesel shunter No. D3462 with five ballast wagons then top-ballasted the South Chord.

The first 'official' use of the Allerford spur came during the Norton Steam Fayre in 2011, when a Sentinel diesel shunter gave rides and driving opportunities, although it was still incomplete. However, the final 280 feet of track and the buffer stops had been laid in by December 2011.

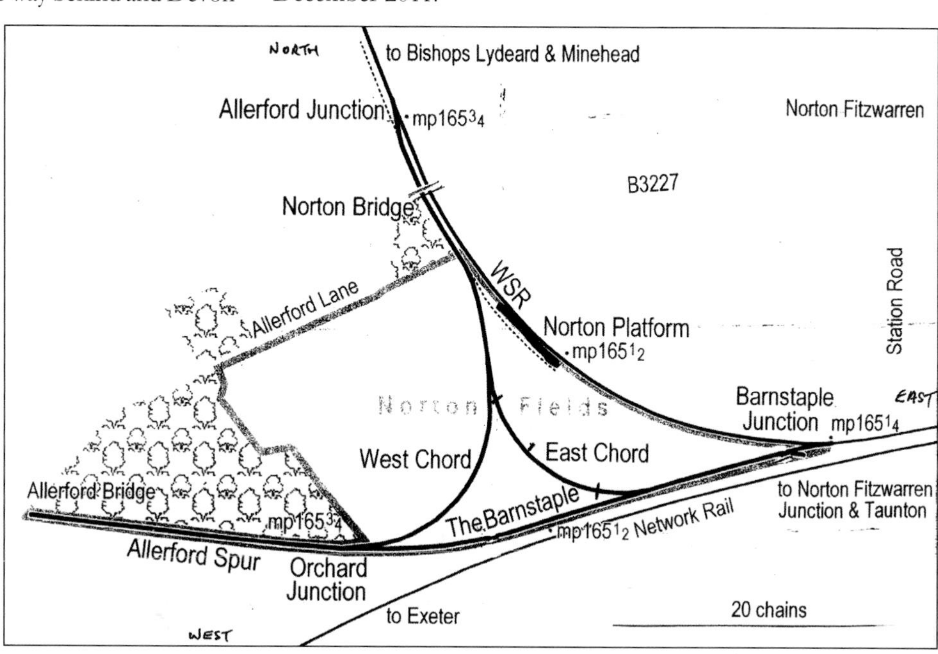

This plan of the completed triangle was put on display at Bishops Lydeard station in August 2012.

ABOVE: 'Hymek' No. D7017 has just broken the tape to formally open the triangle on 4th August 2012.

BELOW: A driver's eye view along the Allerford spur.

BELOW RIGHT: Looking along the Barnstaple Chord, which follows the former Up line. The Taunton-Exeter main line is to the right. ***All author***

Further work took place on the East Chord in the winter of 2011 by which time only 450 feet of track was required to complete the curve. By March/April 2012 the additional flat bottomed rail had been delivered and laid, and the inner triangle was complete. The final connection of the East Chord at the junction with the West Chord was made on 7th April 2012. The fitting of point levers and top-ballasting and tamping was done by May 2012, RSS Tamper No. 73307 fulfilling the duty.

The triangle was officially opened at 3pm on Saturday 4th August, 2012. Hymek D7017 of the Diesel and Electric Preservation Group, the longest-serving operational locomotive on the WSR, broke the ceremonial tape. Special guests included Councillor and Mrs John Edney, Chairman of Somerset County Council and Mr Richard Chandler, the High Sheriff of Somerset and his wife.

It was subsequently agreed that the Allerford spur would be increased by 7 metres in length, a minor extension but significant in that the spur could then accommodate a complete HOBC train which had a locomotive at either end. This work was carried out in the latter part of 2013, being completed by the volunteer permanent way gang by 19th October. The extension allowed the complete HOBC train to be turned on the triangle if so desired. Work involved the levelling of and compacting of the existing stone bed beyond the existing stop block (as shown in the above photographs) whilst maintaining the existing gradient. The stop block was removed to accommodate this extension and relocated at the end of the extension which is now virtually up to the bridge.

At the Norton Steam Fayre of 2nd-3rd August 2014, the Barnstaple line was in use again. The Peckett 0-4-0 saddle tank *Kilmersdon*, painted in Somerset & Dorset Joint Railway deep blue livery, trundled up and down the Allerford Spur and the Barnstaple Chord giving brake van rides. Passengers embarked at a temporary platform and it is arguable therefore that this was the first passenger service to use the line since 1st October 1966.

Left: Another August 2012 cab view along the Barnstaple Chord. The site of Norton Fitzwarren station in the right background, as denoted by the footbridge. Joining in the left foreground is the East (inner) Chord. Room was left for a run-round loop on the old Down line and some ballast is in place but, to date (2016), this has not been added. ***Author***

Below: A view from the footbridge at Norton Fitzwarren, as a Freightliner Heavy Haul Class '66' runs on to the Barnstaple Chord with a High Output Ballast Cleaning train in 2013. Network Rail now has several of these Plasser & Theurer HOBC trains, which are capable of moving under their own power when in operation but are loco-hauled to and from sites. The wagons at the front sieve and remove spent ballast, whilst those towards the rear replace it with clean new material. The old ballast is then dumped at sites such as this here at Norton Fitzwarren for possible re-use or recycling. ***Stephen Jervis***

Below: Under moody skies on Saturday 2nd August 2014, the 0-4-0ST ***Kilmersdon*** **hauls a brake van ride along the Barnstaple Chord during the Norton Steam Fayre of that year. Built by Peckett & Sons of Bristol in 1929 (Works No. 1788), the locomotive spent most of its working life at Kilmersdon Colliery, Radstock, apart from a couple of short spells at the nearby Norton Hill Colliery in the 1950s. It 'retired' in 1973 when Kilmersdon closed and was bought for preservation the following year. However, the S&DJR livery, whilst looking very smart, is not authentic (Kilmersdon was actually on the GWR route through Radstock, not the S&D line) and the name is a post-preservation addition too.** ***Author***

West Somerset Railway
Bishops Lydeard to
ALLERFORD BRIDGE
(Barnstaple Branch) via Norton
Special Return Souvenir Ticket
C 3 8 3

The overall cost of the project was in the region of £500,000 and was, at the time and may still be, the largest brand-new construction project undertaken by by an English heritage railway. A significant contribution was made by volunteers (of a clerical or manual nature) who helped with all aspects of the project. Also, the deal that was done with Network Rail over the storage of ballast and the provision of spent ballast for use on the site, along with used concrete sleepers and old rail, significantly helped with keeping the costs down.

So whilst the likelihood of the line ever opening again beyond Allerford Bridge is almost nil, all has not been lost as track has been laid on part of the old Barnstaple line and locomotives at least will run again on that section. Never say never but the sheer effort, manpower and cost of resurrecting the entire Devon & Somerset Railway will undoubtedly mean that Dr Beeching has had the last word on this scenic cross country route, as he did on so many similar lines. A review of the Campaign for Better Transport website in 2011 indicated that the Taunton to Barnstaple railway line was on its list but it is doubtful that anything further will happen in this regard.

In the summer 2015 edition of the *L&BR Magazine*, as part of the support for the reinstatement of that line and sustainable tourism in the North Devon area, it was proposed that:

'To work in partnership with the Tarka Line (Part of the Devon & Cornwall Rail Partnership), the Lynton Cliff Railway, Filer's Bus Service, the WSR and other public transport providers to offer a comprehensive rail and bus public transport service from the Taunton area via Exeter and Barnstaple and back to Taunton, with its connections to London, the Midland, the North and South Wales.'

The D&SR would have gone some way to completing a railway triangle, had it still been in existence.

Ironically, in September 2015, a motion by Councillor Ian Roome to a full meeting of the North Devon Council called for support for a daily through train from Barnstaple to London, commencing at 7.00am to run via the Tarka Line, thus removing the need for those in Barnstaple to drive to Taunton or Tiverton Parkway to catch an early train to London. However, it will take a special effort to convince operator Great Western Railway (formerly First Great Western) that such a plan would be beneficial – or indeed South West Trains, who could equally run a through service from Barnstaple to Waterloo via the ex-L&SWR route. A clear case of watch this space.

WHAT REMAINS OF THE STATIONS, STRUCTURES AND TRACKBED OF THE D&SR

A mixed fate befell the various stations and structures along the railway. Following the line's closure, with effect from Monday 3rd October 1966 (with no Sunday service, the last trains had actually run on Saturday 1st), track removal began soon after and ended in 1967. The timetable of track removal is outlined in the previous chapter. However, set out below is a broad summary of the fate in respect of each station, halt and major structure on the line. As a general principle, the station sites and the trackbed were initially offered to local councils and then sold on to private purchasers. A significant proportion of the line today is in private hands, so access to those parts is only possible with appropriate permissions. If the line is walked today, there is a mixture of sections that have been totally obliterated by being ploughed back into farmland, some walkways, some roadway or farm track and, of course, some remaining untouched and overgrown. However, unlike some old railways, there are no official cycle paths, bridleways or footpaths on the main stretch between Taunton and Barnstaple, with the exception perhaps of the short stretch of trackbed between Brushford (Dulverton station) and Nightcott.

TAUNTON

In common with most major stations today, Taunton is a shadow of its former self, comprising four through lines, with their respective platform faces, and one working bay (at the Bristol end). Following closure of the Barnstaple Branch in 1966, Minehead Branch trains used the Barnstaple bay until that line too closed in 1971. Having been used intermittently after that for parcels and wagon, coach and locomotive storage, rails still remain between those bay platforms but it is now rarely used. The old Up side arrival bay (platform No. 8) has long had its rails lifted and the area between filled in with debris. However, there is continued optimism that this bay will be reinstated with arrivals from the WSR, if that ever extends beyond Norton Fitzwarren to reach Taunton again. Little remains of the once extensive goods yards, locomotive sheds and other facilities that once existed here and the redundant railway land that has not yet been redeveloped is likely to be so in the near future. One exception is the old GWR water tower, in red brick with cast iron tank on top, which still stands forlorn, alongside the Taunton & Bridgwater Canal, surrounded now by modern apartment blocks.

TOP: The remains of the Barnstaple Branch arrival bay (the old platform No. 8) in August 2008, devoid of track and now partly filled in.
MIDDLE: The Barnstaple Branch bay with still extant but rusting rails. The redundant depot area to the right has since been reclaimed.
BOTTOM: Taken a few weeks earlier, with a shine still on the rails, this view is looking from the departure bay towards Forty Steps bridge and Norton Fitzwarren. Compare this scene with the frontispiece taken around forty-five years before. ***All author***

NORTON FITZWARREN TO WIVELISCOMBE

Norton Fitzwarren station, although not strictly part of the D&SR, was closed on 30th October 1961, prior to the closure of the line to Barnstaple, and was subsequently demolished. Various track rationalisations have taken place over the years and at the time of writing, only a single line connection to the West Somerset Railway remains, along with a relatively modern replacement footbridge spanning the site of the former station.

ABOVE: A view of Norton Fitzwarren Junction looking east from the footbridge in August 2013, with a First Great Western HST about to thunder past.

RIGHT: The remains of the former Railway Hotel at Norton Fitzwarren, which were scheduled for demolition at the time of this picture.

LEFT: All that remained of Allerford Bridge in 2008. ***All author***

RIGHT: Blagroves Bridge in 2008. The line was double track at this point but nature has largely taken over. ***Author***

LEFT: Just outside Wiveliscombe and photographed in April 2011, the road bridge to Castle now lies half submerged in the surrounding landscape. ***Author***

As already noted, the first part of line to Allerford Bridge has been reclaimed for use by the WSR but beyond and most of the way to Milverton, the route has been reclaimed back into the land. Blagroves Bridge stands as an isolated monument to the railway on this stretch. The trackbed remains at Preston Bowyer and in part has been used as a footpath to Milverton.

Nothing remains at Milverton, the station site having been obliterated when the by-pass (the old A361, now the B3227) was constructed in the early 1970s, opening in 1975.

On towards Wiveliscombe, the route has again largely been absorbed into the agricultural land, with one or two obvious features remaining, such as the stone bridge leading to Castle. Although now partly buried and surrounded by green fields, it is still visible from the B3227 road. At Wiveliscombe, the bridge over the old A361 at the east of the station was demolished to allow for road improvement works.

RIGHT: The road approach side of Wiveliscombe station buildings in April 2011. The whitewash is fading a little but the buildings were still in use.

BELOW: Wiveliscombe goods shed pictured on the same visit.

LEFT BOTTOM: A substrantial and well preserved stone-built bridge between Wiveliscombe and Bathealton. The cars give a useful idea of scale.

RIGHT BOTTOM: The gated eastern portal of Bathealton Tunnel in 2009, with nature making the approach to it ever more difficult. ***All author***

In Wiveliscombe, Station Road now leads to an industrial estate and the remaining station buildings are part of it. The main building was taken over by an industrial concern (Staceys) and was used as offices. The goods shed and associated provender store next to it were also in industrial use. Although most of the remainder of the site has been redeveloped, it is still possible to see a small section of platform on the Up side on which the station buildings stand. The original iron platform fencing is also still in place on part of the site.

In 2014, Staceys found themselves in financial difficulties and the fate of the station became uncertain as a possible residential development site. Consequently, members of Wiveliscombe Civic Society commenced work on seeking a listing for the original station buildings and goods shed from English Heritage. At the time of writing, the application had been rejected because the buildings were deemed not of sufficient unique architectural quality to merit preservation and their fate thus remains uncertain.

WIVELISCOMBE TO VENN CROSS

Beyond Wiveliscombe some of the earthworks and bridges have been removed but the course of the line can still be traced to a degree. Just off the Wiveliscombe to Bathealton Road, a house has been built on the trackbed, near where a road bridge was demolished. However, at least one stone bridge remains in good condition on this stretch.

As the line climbs to Bathealton Tunnel, some of the trackbed has been removed but it is still evident within half a mile of the eastern portal, albeit somewhat boggy and with fallen trees across the cutting. The tunnel itself is fenced off at the Taunton end and is not a welcoming sight.

The west portal is inaccessible. Part of the track down from it is in use as a footpath but this diverges off the embankment just before the abutment of the viaduct and leads down into Pouch Bridge Quarry and the Tone Valley below.

The Tone Viaduct is no more, the metal girder spans having been removed many years ago for maintenance and safety reasons. They are understood to have been claimed by a local farmer, leaving us with the tantalising thought that they may be preserved in some farm structure or lying abandoned somewhere awaiting re-use. The three stone piers of the viaduct remain standing, redundant like industrial chimneys and looking a little out of place between the trees and countryside.

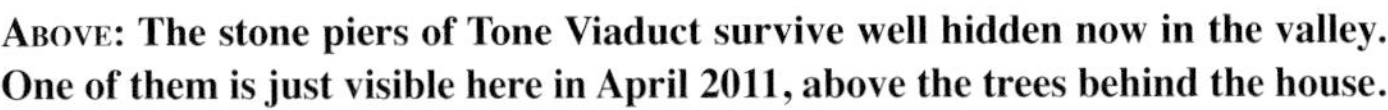

Above: The stone piers of Tone Viaduct survive well hidden now in the valley. One of them is just visible here in April 2011, above the trees behind the house.

Above Right: Just off the viaduct and to the south of the line, the overgrown site of an old quarry is still visible in the summer of 2011.

Right: Unusual motive power on the Taunton to Barnstaple line in summer 2011.

Below: Venn Cross Tunnel east portal, April 2011.

Below Right: Venn Cross Tunnel western portal May 2014. Note the gate, a Network Rail health and safety initiative added in 2011. ***All author***

The line up to Venn Cross is barely passable for most of the section but for a number of yards just before the eastern entrance to Venn Cross Tunnel, the trackbed is used as a farm track. The tunnel itself remains in good order.

Following closure, Venn Cross station site was initially the home of a building contractor and was used as a scrap yard by Mr Tony Towers. When the neighbouring B3227 (former A361) road was widened, the station site became a dumping ground for spoil and the area between the platforms filled in; cars and other scrap items are buried under some of the spoil. Mr and Mrs Eric Stone bought the station house property in 1977-8 (he had been a signalman at Venn Cross) and sold it in 1986.

The station building, former stationmaster's house and goods shed have all been converted for residential use since the line closed and remain so used, the goods shed being named *The Engine House*. With the realignment of the road, the old station buildings are now set back from the road and, due to the landscaping and tree growth, it is easy to drive past the location and not even realise its former use. One or two other railway features such as gates and fences remain, whilst signals (not the originals) have been incorporated as part of the garden landscaping.

The Venn Cross Gardens are occasionally open to the public. Kevin and Samantha Anning bought *The Engine House* in 2000, and Pat and Bill Wilson moved into the station house in 2006. The Anning's garden comprises three acres of lawn and herbaceous borders, a woodland area and three ponds. The Wilson's garden is formed between the two still visible platforms edges in the cutting and the west portal of the tunnel forms the unusual backdrop to the garden. Thus the two contrast each other in layout and foliage.

TOP: A scene of dereliction at Venn Cross station in December 1977. ***Courtesy Mr & Mrs Wilson***

ABOVE: The road frontage to Venn Cross station buildings looking east in April 2011. The far apex roof is a modern extension to the original building. The road now just provides access to the old station site, the realigned B3227 running past about 25 yards beyond the hedge on the right. ***Author***

BELOW: Still just recognisable for what it once was, the old goods shed has been converted to a dwelling and the surrounding gardens beautifully landscaped. ***Author***

TOP: A view from the top of the tunnel portal looking west towards what was the platform area. The unique location has created a natural landscape for a colourful range of plants and trees. ***Author***

ABOVE: The slope from the Down platform to the station buildings now forms a garden path. Note the original railings are still ***in situ. Author***

BELOW: The approach to Venn Cross in April 2011, with the old goods shed in the middle distance. The Distant signal in the foreground is not original nor is it in an original signal location but it forms a suitable and pleasant feature in the landscaped garden. ***Author***

VENN CROSS TO DULVERTON

On the down grade between Venn Cross and Morebath the trackbed remains largely intact, with part of in use as a farm track but overgrown elsewhere, with cuttings and the low embankments being virtually impassable.

There are three overbridges in the section towards Petton, clearly built for double track. Two are stone-arch construction, whilst the third is an occupation bridge.

Morebath station buildings and goods shed were converted not long after the line closed into dwellings and have remained so ever

Right: A tree-lined section of trackbed, looking almost ready for rails to be relaid!

Rar Right: An occupation bridge between Venn Cross and Petton. It is of a different design to two other overbridges on this section of the line, which are simple stone arches. This bridge has stone abutments and would have been built with a wrought iron span but has clearly been rebuilt with a concrete deck at some stage. *Both author*

since. In 2010, the station buildings consisted of two residential properties, named *Pixie Laughter Cottages*, both with extensions to the original structure. One family had been living there for twenty-five years at that time. The gap between the platforms has been filled in to create the garden areas. The goods shed now also comprises two dwellings and the external stone work has been rendered and painted cream. The original metal station gate still hangs at the entrance to the station yard and the remains of an 8ft high concrete lamp holder are still present by the side of the gateway.

From Morebath and through to the site of Morebath Junction Halt, the line is overgrown and as it approaches the road bridge to the east of the halt, has been partially reclaimed back into farmland or rough grass areas.

As Morebath Junction Halt was unstaffed halt with just a platform and a shelter, no use has been made of the site. The shelter is long gone but the two concrete posts that once supported the nameboard are still visible amongst the trees. The remains of the solid and broadly intact concrete platform can be seen alongside a farm track which follows the course of the line to an area of rough land. Beyond this and in the area of the former junction itself, the ground has been levelled and turned into a flat, well looked after field, belonging to a house situated between the course of the diverging Taunton to Barnstaple and Exe Valley lines, both of which course are still clearly visible. Morebath village itself, just on the hill above the former halt, has grown in size but is still small. There has been some limited house building towards the halt itself but it remains as isolated as ever, now protected and disguised by trees and overgrowth.

The remains of Morebath Junction Halt in 2011. Tree growth obscures the site of the junction from here, in a field around the corner. *Author*

Above: Morebath station building is today named *Pixie Laughter Cottages* but the section beyond the second window is a later, albeit sympathetic, extension. This November 2010 photograph should be compared with that on page 177, which shows the original building without this extension.

Below: Just glimpsed in the right background of the picture above, Morebath's former goods shed is almost unrecognisable in its new guise as two dwellings. *Both author*

Carrying on from here towards Dulverton, the route is accessible for a few hundred yards before reaching an occupation bridge in the deep Ashtown Cutting. At this point there is some some significant tree growth on the trackbed through the cutting and out the other side onto the embankment leading to the Exe River Bridge, such that it is now impassable. The trackbed remains overgrown but just

ABOVE: A hidden gem; an occupation bridge in Ashtown Cutting in 2011.

ABOVE: The eastern Exe Bridge abutment photographed not long after the removal of the iron girders in the late 1960s. *Courtesy Francois Jones*

BELOW: The same abutment in 2011. *Author*

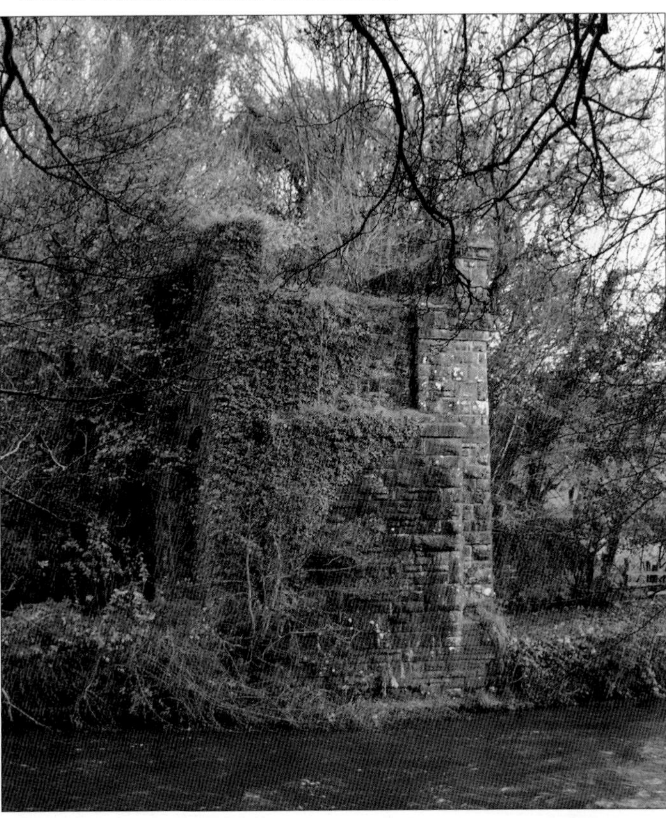

passable from the A396 road underbridge, on the short stretch to the Exe River Bridge. The iron girders spanning the river were removed not long after closure, thus making it impossible to cross the river at this point, but the handsome stone abutments still remain. Just to the south of the bridge, the river feeds the extensive ponds of the Exe Valley Fishery, which had been established here by the early 1890s.

Beyond the bridge, the trackbed remains as a footpath to Dulverton station but this is is now fenced off as a private area for the residents of the converted station buildings, goods shed and a new property built on the site.

Dulverton station site contained a plethora of buildings, including the station master's house, the booking hall and waiting room, goods shed and provender store. The island platform and its waiting room were demolished soon after closure but the main Up platform was retained, albeit truncated beyond the goods shed. It is interesting to relate the history of the station following closure, as it was probably the least straightforward of all transfers into personal ownership from BR or the local council.

The site was eventually taken over by Mrs Toni Jones, proprietor of the Carnarvon Arms Hotel but it was not a simple process. The stationmaster had moved out before the line closed and at that time, Mr Owen and Mrs Toni Howells (who in 1980 became Mrs Jones following her husband's death in 1974), approached BR to attempt to rent the main station house and waiting room area for use as accommodation for some hotel staff. BR would not entertain the initial approaches. When the line closed, Mr and Mrs Howells sought to buy the site, essentially to protect their interest given that the land adjoined the hotel. BR again refused. Following closure of the line the site was subsequently sold by BR to Somerset County Council (SCC). Mr and Mrs Howells then recommenced purchase negotiations in the early 1970s. As a consequence, SCC agreed to a lease of the site for twenty-five years on 15th February 1974, for payment of ground rent. It was agreed that the Carnarvon would be solely responsible for the upkeep of the buildings in addition to the payment of the ground rent. Three staff flats were made out of the accommodation and a hard tennis court built on the old trackbed at the western station throat in 1974. A subsequent approach by Mrs Jones (as she was then) to SCC to purchase the site was made and agreement in principle reached but the Council did not wish to sell the land by the road bridge, as they were considering straightening the B3222 by cutting off the corner of the road and demolishing the bridge. This land retention restriction was not acceptable to Mrs Jones and the deal fell through. Finally, and twenty years into the lease, on

ABOVE: Dulverton station forecourt in the 1980s. *Courtesy Jose Kimber*

poor condition having been stored there for some years), most likely removed from the old goods shed office when that was redundant and the new office built in 1905.

In landscaping the garden and improving drainage for the shed's new use as a dwelling, the owners discovered a parallel row of bricks forming a deep pit in the ground opposite the shed in the old goods yard area, towards the cattle dock. It was clearly not an old drain and was most likely the old engine pit that was located just before the turntable when that was originally accessed from the Taunton end, prior to the station improvements of the early 1900s.

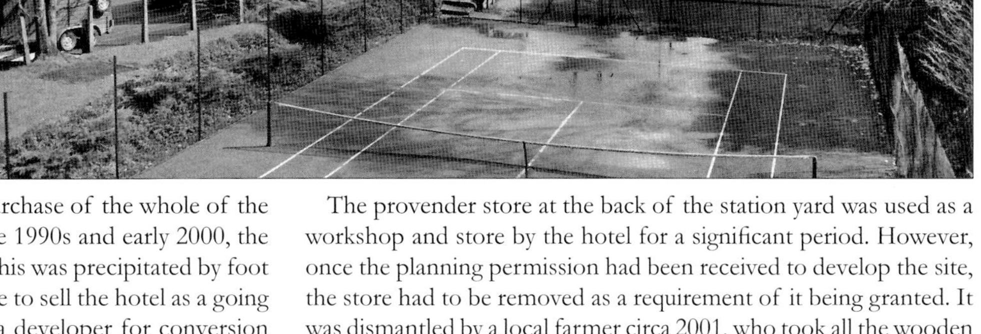

ABOVE: The road facing side of Dulverton goods shed in the 1980s.

RIGHT: A general view of the station site in the 1980s. Note the provender store still in situ on the left; it was later removed for reuse on a local farm, where it still survives today. The tennis court in the foreground was built on the track bed at this end of the station.
Both courtesy Jose Kimber

BELOW RIGHT: The rail approach to the station from the Taunton direction in early 2011. The new house features at the far end. ***Author***

12th May 1994 Mrs Jones secured the purchase of the whole of the station site for about £70,000. In the late 1990s and early 2000, the Carnarvon's business was declining and this was precipitated by foot and mouth in 2001. Mrs Jones was unable to sell the hotel as a going concern so it was sold in June 2002 to a developer for conversion into flats. The developer was offered the tennis court on the station site but did not take it. Mrs Jones subsequently obtained planning permission for the development of the stationmaster's house, along with the goods shed and a new dwelling at the west end of the site, for eventual onward sale.

Dulverton goods shed survived after closure but was largely neglected, although it was used for a while as a store for a traction engine owned by Mr W.E. Hazel. The brick goods office at the western end of the shed was converted into a hairdressers called 'Buffers' in the late 1970s, remaining so under the initial proprietor until 1986 and then beyond that date for another hairdressing tenant. Following the granting of planning permission to Mrs Jones, the house conversion work on the goods shed was carried out during 2007-8 by the new owners (Mr & Dr Blackburn). At that time, the ironwork (hinges, strapping, bolts, etc) on the goods shed doors was reclaimed by the West Somerset Railway Trust for use on the goods shed doors at Bishops Lydeard station (now the Gauge Museum). Unfortunately, the redundant doors were removed from the shed during the renovations and lay idle in the station yard until they were cut up and some of the wood was used to make raised garden beds for the new owners – an ignominious end for them after all those years but they had decayed beyond repair. In constructing the dwelling out of the goods shed, the contractors had the challenge of removing the foundation of the platform mounted crane, which was a mass of concrete. In addition, a cellar was discovered under the platform in the shed. This contained old paperwork (unfortunately in

The provender store at the back of the station yard was used as a workshop and store by the hotel for a significant period. However, once the planning permission had been received to develop the site, the store had to be removed as a requirement of it being granted. It was dismantled by a local farmer circa 2001, who took all the wooden sleepers supporting it and the corrugated iron cladding and rebuilt it on his farm.

The final part of the 2003-4 development was the construction of an additional and reasonably substantial residential property at the Barnstaple end of the station on the Up platform and on the site of the tennis court. The entrance to this property and the stationmaster's house is now through the old entrance to the goods yard (opposite Goodlands as it was at the time of the railway, now Travis Perkins builders merchants) and along the old loading dock, which has been resurfaced with tarmac.

One other building, the old weigh-house at the entrance to the goods yard, remains intact externally and has been used as a store.

ABOVE: Dulverton in 2008, with repairs underway on the station building and the goods shed converted into a residential property. The new house is out of view to the left and note that the tennis court had been removed. ***Author***

Thus whilst some of the original buildings remain, the station is now a landscaped residential complex, whilst the former Carnarvon Arms Hotel has been converted into flats. All quite a difference from the heyday of the railway but the quality of the original Victorian building and its railway origins are still clear to see for all those who pass by the on the B3222, over the stone railway bridge which has fortunately survived SCC's 1970s proposals to demolish it

DULVERTON TO BISHOPS NYMPTON & MOLLAND

Beyond the bridge at Dulverton station throat, the cutting is filled in all the way up to the next bridge at the top of Brushford village. However, the trackbed is now a walkway from the old pedestrian crossing gates near the church (the spot where I used to watch the engineers' demolition trains run towards Dulverton), all the way up to Nightcott.

The bridge which carried the line over the narrow lane near Nightcott village has been removed, whilst the trackbed beyond and towards Nightcott Tunnel has been neglected and become overgrown with trees. The approach to the tunnel mouth is again an obstacle course created by fallen trees. The tunnel is not fenced off but is private property.

The trackbed between Nightcott Tunnel and East Anstey is now private property but partially passable and part used as a farm access track to a number of nearby dwellings. The cutting between the two Anstey bridges is overgrown with trees and virtually impassable.

ABOVE: The narrow and height restricted bridge at the bottom of Brushford old village; the road leads up Langaller Hill. ***Author***

ABOVE: The eastern portal of Nightcott Tunnel, looking west in 2008. The tunnel is a mere 44 yards in length and remains in remarkably good condition.

RIGHT: Looking back out out of the tunnel east towards Dulverton, showing the many fallen trees which present even the most determined explorers of old railways with quite a challenge in reaching here.
Both Author

Left: This occupation bridge between Nightcott Tunnel and East Anstey still carries a farm track over the empty trackbed.

Below Left: By the spring of 2014, the cutting to the east of East Anstey had been cleared, revealing the old trackbed once again.

Right: East Anstey station platforms from the road bridge in spring 2012.

Below Right: On the same date, the smartly refurbished station building is seen from the road side.

Bottom Right: Again on the same day, this is East Anstey goods shed, which in common with other surviving such buildings on the line, has been converted for use as a dwelling.
All author

In the late 1960s, the abandoned station site and buildings at East Anstey looked a sorry sight, rather like at Venn Cross. However, the station building and the goods shed were not long after converted in to dwelling houses. The trackbed between the platforms had been left untouched, with trees and undergrowth taking over and, consequently, for a long period it looked like some of the isolated overgrown sections on other parts of the line, rather than a disused station. However, as can be seen from the accompanying photographs taken in 2012, this area was subsequently cleared of foliage, so the imprint of the Up and Down platforms have become visible once again from the road bridge.

On leaving the station area, the route is now impassable and belongs to a farm, only opening up as a private farm track just over half a mile from East Anstey. It continues as a private track for the remaining mile down towards the site of Yeo Mill Halt, passing though a stable yard just before reaching it.

The wooden platform and shelter at Yeo Mill Halt no longer exist and the site is now part of a garden belonging to a bungalow which has been built, since closure, to the side of the course of the line. The bridge which carried the railway over the road has been removed to allow easier access for larger vehicles and reduce maintenance costs.

The route of the line between Yeo Mill and Bishops Nympton & Molland station is largely preserved as a farm track and in a good enough state that sleepers and rails could almost be laid on the surface and reballasted. However, just before reaching the old station at Bishops Nympton & Molland, the trackbed has become overgrown, whilst the bridge at the station throat carrying the loop and running lines over Hilltown Hill Lane has been removed, again to facilitate access and reduce the costs of maintenance.

ABOVE: Surviving concrete fence posts gradually keeling over near the site of Yeo Mill Halt.

LEFT: A beautifully rural view of countryside typical of that which the line traversed for much of its route. The site of Yeo Mill Halt is just off picture to the right.

BELOW: The ghost train! In 2014, low hanging mist creates the impression of exhaust from a passing steam locomotive along the Yeo Valley.
All author

Bishops Nympton & Molland station site has been well preserved. The stationmaster's house survives and the station buildings, which have been converted into a dwelling, along with the adjacent Black Cock Inn. The platforms are still there in part and a garden area has been made between them. The goods shed has also been converted into a residence.

ABOVE: Bishop's Nympton & Molland station in 2008, looking east along the rear of the former Down platform towards the goods shed.

ABOVE RIGHT: Coal staithes in the goods yard still in use in 2008.

BELOW: A close-up of the former goods shed. The road wagon entrance is still apparent in its glazed form and the solid beam lintel on the right of the structure indicates where rail access was from. *All author*

BISHOPS NYMPTON & MOLLAND TO FILLEIGH

The route of the line between Bishops Nympton & Molland and South Molton starts as a farm track. On the way to Mornacott Farm, it becomes overgrown for a short distance, converting back to a farm track all the way up through Whitechapel Moors. In the fields below Whitechapel Manor, the trackbed has been returned to grass pasture as far as Brockam Bridge. Beyond the bridge and virtually all the way to the camp site just outside of what was South Molton station, the line is overgrown, boggy and waterlogged in parts and virtually impassable. Near where the line crosses the River Mole, over which the bridge remains intact, earthwork remnants of the old Florence Mine tramway can just about be seen, despite having it closed some 100 years previously. A detour up the Mole Valley will reveal disconnected sections of the old tramway, whilst in the Heasley Mill area the old mine workings are still evident.

ABOVE: The twin arches of the River Yeo Bridge, about half a mile west of Bishop's Nympton & Molland station, can just be made out through the trees.

RIGHT: The stump of a signal post still in the ground near the site of the transshipment wharf with the Florence Tramway. *Both author*

Returning to the route of the D&SR, the North Devon Link Road (NDLR) now severs the course of the line as it approaches the site of South Molton station. Just before the station, the stone bridge which carried the railway over the South Molton to North Molton road was demolished for road improvements when the NDLR was built and a new junction was formed for access to both villages.

South Molton is perhaps the most unfortunate station on the line. The station buildings survived well beyond closure and were in use by a cement company. It is understood that they were to be listed but, before the consent came through, the station house and adjoining buildings were razed to the ground in a very short period of time in 2003. The goods shed still remains and this, plus the remainder of the station site, adjoins the relatively new Pathfields Industrial Estate.

During the demolition of the station buildings, a complete set of parcel way bills for the period 1876-77 were discovered.

ABOVE: Looking along the Down platform towards Filleigh in the late 1980s. The buildings were in remarkably complete condition, with the wood and glass screen front to the waiting room still intact. *David Burgess*

ABOVE: South Molton station buildings in the late 1980s. *David Burgess*

RIGHT: A view just prior to demolition, with ivy having very much taken over. *Courtesy, South Molton Museum*

ABOVE: Construction work nearing completion on the North Devon Link Road at South Molton in the late 1980s, showing the new junction for North and South Molton villages. The station buildings and goods shed can be seen on the right. The route of the line towards Taunton bears off to the left and is bisected by the new road as it climbs the hill to the skyline top right. Behind the photographer, the next section of it is built on the trackbed. *David Burgess*

TOP: **The eastern portal of the 319 yards long Castle Hill Tunnel in 2010. It was named Bremridge Tunnel on the 1889 OS.** ***Author***

ABOVE MIDDLE: **A view of the viaduct piers looking west in the 1980s, during the twenty or so years when they were 'out of use'.** ***David Burgess***

ABOVE: **Scaffolding surrounding two of the piers in the late 1980s, as work progresses on the new deck being built on them.** ***David Burgess***

RIGHT: **A spectacular view looking up from the valley floor, with work nearing completion. The 10ft extensions to the piers were sympatheticlaly done, to the extent that it is not easy to spot the 'join' from this angle it is also possible to see the two new concrete piers that were built at the eastern end after removal of the original abutment. The width of the new deck in comparison to the piers is also very apparent.** ***David Burgess***

Heading west from South Molton, the route of the NDLR now occupies the old trackbed for much of the way. About half a mile from South Molton is Aller Cross roundabout, where the B3226 and the A339 meet with the NDLR. This is the South Molton to Brayford road and it is understood that the bridge which once carried it over the railway line is buried underneath the roundabout. The NDLR now diverts slightly northwards for a short way and, consequently, a short section of trackbed remains, running behind North Aller Farm, under an occupation bridge and down the old embankment towards the eastern portal of Castle Hill Tunnel; it is, however, private property. The tunnel is not fenced off and is still used for access by the Castle Hill Estate for shooting and farming purposes.

Once out of the tunnel, the trackbed in the cutting soon disappears beneath spoil created by the construction of the NDLR and then once again beneath the road itself, as it heads towards the Bray Valley and Castle Hill Viaduct. A number of old railway viaducts in Great Britain have found further uses after closure of the lines which they carried but it is believed that Castle Hill may be unique for a structure of this height and size, in that the original piers were left standing after the iron spans were removed but were then later reused to support the concrete deck of the NDLR. They were increased in height by about 10ft and the new road bridge built on top. The original abutments were removed, with a new one built at the Barnstaple end and that at the Taunton end replaced by two short piers built of concrete. The road deck is considerably wider than the railway spans which the piers originally carried.

ABOVE: A view from the north side looking east, showing the supports on the tops of the piers which hold the new deck. *David Burgess*

ABOVE RIGHT: The new Castle Hill Viaduct in 2010, looking north up the Bray Valley. *Author*

RIGHT: A view of the new viaduct taken shortly after the North Devon Link Road had first opened for traffic in 1988. Cars speed across the new deck, their drivers possibly having very little regard for the fact that the piers beneath them had once carried trains running between Taunton and Barnstaple across the floor of the Bray Valley below. *David Burgess*

LEFT: Looking north up the Bray Valley again but this time from the deck of the new viaduct. Castle Hill House lies around half a mile to the south and west of here, behind the photographer's left shoulder. Its elevated position ensures that successive generations of incumbents, the current of which is the Countess of Arran, have long enjoyed the view up the Bray Valley, including the railway viaduct from the early 1870s and now its road replacement. *Author*

RIGHT: Filleigh station on 31st July 1972, as just sold by British Rail. ***Roger Joanes***

BELOW RIGHT: The station shortly before demolition in June 1987. ***Roger Joanes***

BOTTOM LEFT: The remains of the buffer stop circa 2009; it has now been removed. ***Author***

BOTTOM CENTRE: The station nameboard now resides outside Filleigh village hall. ***Author***

BOTTOM RIGHT: A view of the NDLR as it approaches Filleigh station site, looking east towards Castle Hill Viaduct. ***Author***

The trackbed from the viaduct to Barnstaple now forms the route of the NDLR right the way through to what was Victoria Road station.

The next stop was Filleigh, where the single storey station house also constituted the main station building. In addition, there was an open waiting shelter and ladies waiting room. The post of stationmaster ended at Filleigh in the late 1950s, when these duties were taken over by the Swimbridge stationmaster, so the house became vacant. Initially, a Filleigh signalman lived there but when the box closed and the signalman moved out, the stationmaster's house was let to a member of the public by BR in its existing state. There was no mains water, this being provided by a well and no mains electricity (in fact the district had only obtained electricity for the first time in the 1950s), oil lamps and gas lamps being used prior to this. A small coal fire and stove provided the heating and cooking facilities. The tenancy was relinquished in the early 1970s and the property remained empty for a year. The whole station and platform site was then bought from BR by Mr Roger Joanes and his family, who moved into the stationmaster's house during 1972.

He refurbished the house, incorporated the other station buildings into his property and installed an electricity generator before converting to mains electricity in the 1980s. He also resuscitated the old Calor gas lighting system which the signalman had use of but the subsequent tenant had allowed to fall into disrepair. The Joanes family lived there happily until it became clear that the course of the old railway line might serve to be the new North Devon Link Road.

Despite a public enquiry and an uncertain period of eighteen months to two years, he and his family were forced to leave by compulsory purchase order served by the Ministry of Transport. They moved out to the southern side of South Molton in the summer of 1987 to allow the bulldozers to move in; the station buildings were demolished one week later. The NDLR now runs right through the station site and the stone overbridge at the east end of the station was replaced by a modern concrete structure.

The signal box was gutted and stripped of its instruments in about 1965, and was demolished soon after, along with the goods shed. However, even today, part of the outbuildings remain. The sheds at the back of the goods yard belonging to the Fortescue Estate and have been converted into accommodation for shooting parties. Even part of the old buffer stop remained at the back of the (old) siding for some years later following closure but it has now been removed.

LEFT TOP TO BOTTOM: Stages in the disappearance of Swimbridge station site. For many years after closure, the platforms were all that remained, along with the bridge from which the first view was taken. The next two pictures show work in progress on the NDLR, whilst the final view is taken from the new road bridge that replaced the railway bridge. The unsuspecting motorist would find nothing here today to indicate the previous history of the route. ***Bottom author, Rest David Burgess***

FILLEIGH TO BARNSTAPLE

The situation was different at the next station, Swimbridge, but the ultimate outcome has been the same. The station buildings and goods shed were demolished soon after closure but the platforms remained for another two decades. The site was taken over by Devon County Council, who used it as a highways depot for road materials for a period of time. However, the site was obliterated when construction began on this section of the NDLR, including the bridge at the Barnstaple end of the station which had also survived until this time. The stationmaster's house was situated on the Barnstaple side of the bridge, on the top of the cutting. At the time the road was built the owner was offered the opportunity to have his house shored up by a retaining wall but he opted for compulsory purchase so it fell to the same fate as the platforms and bridge, and was demolished.

Barnstaple Victoria Road remained operational as a freight depot until 5th March 1970 but its days were then numbered. Whilst the NDLR follows the route of the line virtually the whole way from South Molton to the eastern outskirts of Barnstaple, the A361 road then turns south towards Bideford just before where the East Chord used to branch off at East Junction to reach Barnstaple Junction station. Additional road improvements here have seen the trackbed in the station area converted into a new road, named Eastern Avenue, whilst the rest of the site has been redeveloped for commercial and retail use. However, although the platform buildings were knocked down soon after final closure, part of the platform edge and base still remains and can be seen bordering the pavement along Old Station Road.

The platform surface and the station approach (that was) now form part of the SWEB Energy (previously the South Western Electricity Board) depot, as does the old bay platform line which was filled in to increase the area available. The goods yard area was developed for commercial use and is now known appropriately as the Great Western Industrial Estate, containing various industrial and business units. The area where the engine shed once stood is now bisected by a road leading to the suburb of Newport and is partly overgrown, being sandwiched between a small retail park and Eastern Avenue. The chord line embankments to South Junction have been partly obliterated but enough is left to ascertain their course, whilst part of the area in the old triangle between them has been made into a park.

Still standing proud in its original position but now surrounded by the more modern industrial units that fill up the old goods yard site is the old stone-built goods shed. This is now well preserved and externally retains most of the original features. The outer goods doors have been replaced by windows and the inside was gutted. The building is now a place of worship for members of the Grosvenor Church and has been since 1995. Prior to this and apart from a period used as a store for scaffolding, it lay redundant and derelict from the date of closure of the freight depot in 1970 and was an eyesore. It was on the market to be sold but could not find a buyer at the then asking price of £250,000. This money would have bought a solid stone building, the remains of the goods platform in the shed, rubbish and rubble everywhere, and a roof in poor condition. The railway offices at the end of the shed had been badly vandalised, with windows smashed, toilets and wash basins broken, walls blackened by fire and burnt floorboards. Ivy and brambles were growing through the windows in places. The existing landlord went into receivership as the Grosvenor Church were commencing their negotiations on the property. After initial negotiations, an offer price of £105,000 was accepted by the receiver and the existing tenant paid £35,000 to get out of the lease, so the property was secured for £70,000. However, a few months of uncertainty followed, as the owner tried to stop the sale going through but, eventually, the purchase was completed in 1993.

Construction work began with re-roofing, along with refurbishment of the offices. There were some interesting discoveries during this period.The ground was soft under where the goods loading/unloading platform in the shed was sited, reflecting the fact that true ground level was 16ft down. What the Victorian contractors had done was to support the goods platform on sleepers built up to this height and then extended the length of the building. The sleeper walls were found by the structural engineer to be in a good enough condition to carry the raft of reinforced concrete that was needed to consolidate the soft ground under the platform site. Further complications arose when two cracks in a water pipe were found. The pipe carried a small stream under the building, also 16ft down. The first crack was directly under the building, the other by the back of the railway bank. Deep excavations were made and the pipes replaced to allow the stream to flow freely again. An old broken petrol pump was also discovered on the bank near the shed, beneath which was a large petrol tank. The fire brigade were called to test it for petrol and fumes but none were found. However, the tank had to be sealed with concrete slurry to ensure it was safe. Bulldozers were used to clear the mass of brambles, trees, stinging nettles and ivy that formed an impenetrable mass of vegetation behind the shed on the back road and the embankment slope on which the site was built.

The goods shed is now surrounded by a car park and it is understood that the tarmac was put down on top of some of the old rails in the goods sidings but no proof of this has been found.

It is also appropriate to report that, in 1997, Barnstaple Town Council gave its first 'Best re-use of an old building' award to the new church, with the planning chairman declaring the reconstructed building as '*a remarkable transformation*'.

TOP: The approach to Victoria Road, taken from the entrance to the engine shed site (behind the photographer), with the SWEB Energy premises on the right. The goods shed is just visible in the middle distance.

CENTRE TOP: The 42 yards of platform edge that still remains.

CENTRE BOTTOM: Looking towards the buffer stops, with the SWEB depot fencing delineating the edge of the platform. The white van is on the site of the run round loop, with the location of the old cattle and carriage sidings just to its left.

BOTTOM: A side elevation of the old goods shed, now refurbished and in use as the Grosvenor Church. The old road access entrances are clearly visible.

BELOW: The eastern elevation of the goods shed. ***All author***

Of the line leading round from Victoria Road to Barnstaple Junction, as previously noted, about two thirds of the East Chord is now beneath an industrial and retail estate but the rest is a foot and cycle path, as is the whole of the West Chord. This continues through Newport to Rock Park and over the Taw Bridge.

Of the three original brick-built bridges between South Junction and the Taw Bridge only two remain, those carrying Landkey Road and Runsam Road respectively. The surface of the cycle track has been raised above the original trackbed height and this is very apparent with the latter. The route has been partly infilled at Newport (where the third bridge was removed) and a section of embankment has been removed near the Park Community School but beyond this the embankment leading to the Taw Bridge remains intact, albeit partly overgrown. The Taw Bridge now carries the cycle way over the river.

Beyond the bridge there is now scrub land where the line used to approach and join the L&SWR route from Exeter.

THE WATER PIPELINE

It is understood that around 10 miles of water pipeline was laid beneath the railway trackbed from the River Yeo at West Anstey down to near the Exe railway bridge where, just upstream from it, South West Water had constructed a weir and a pumping station. The purpose of this work was to enable water to be pumped to North Devon in an emergency such as a drought.

ABOVE LEFT: Looking north along the cycle and foot path towards South Junction with the bridge carrying Landkey Road ahead.

LEFT: The loading gauge would definitely need adjustment here at the second bridge, which carries Runsam Road over the pathway but that has been significantly raised up above original trackbed height at this point.

BELOW: The rusty iron spans and support columns of the Taw Bridge in May 2011, which was happily retained for use by cyclists and walkers. ***All author***

THE NORTH DEVON LINK ROAD (NDLR)

The first suggestion for a major trunk road to link North Devon with the M5 (which was then still to be built) came in 1967, within a year of the Taunton to Barnstaple line's closure. The *Railway Observer* reported in April 1967 that the Devon county surveyor had approved a suggestion that the line should be converted to a new trunk road. His report was forwarded to the divisional highways engineer at the MoT for consideration. Aside from these formalities, there were long public debates for a number of years about the merits of such a road. In November 1975, the Tiverton and South Molton councils voted against the plans. Two years later there was an open debate between Barnstaple traders, who were in favour of the road proposals, and Lady Margaret Fortescue of Castle Hill, who was against. Press reports hinted at secret surveying at night of the old railway line. There was a public enquiry at South Molton in January 1979 at the Guildhall and as time passed the likelihood of such a road grew stronger, subject to funding. By 1988-89, construction of the road was well underway. The link road was built in three parts; Tiverton to South Molton; Landkey and the Barnstaple by-pass; and South Molton to Landkey, which was last section to be completed and opened on 18th July 1989.

Originally it is understood that the NDLR was to be a dual carriageway and its original course was to the south of the Castle Hill Estate. However, once changed to be single carriageway, a decision was made to route it largely via the old railway. Some of the construction was directly on the D&SR trackbed and some not but, in essence, it was there to replace the line and to open up North Devon, making it accessible for tourists and commercial operators like it never had been before. The future economic success and development of the area is now determined to some degree by this road, a role that the D&SR played when it opened in 1873.

As already noted, the road cut through the site of Swimbridge station and then ran on to Barnstaple via Landkey, requiring the demolition of several old structures essential to the railway. Most noticeably was the three-arch stone bridge which carried the railway over the road to Birch and Gunn. This was removed by March 1988, with the new road bridge being commenced the following month and by winter it was virtually completed. Once around the curve bypassing Landkey, the new road ran straight down the trackbed into the east side of Barnstaple.

Today, North Devon is not served well by train, with Ilfracombe in particular being all the poorer and isolated due to the loss of its railway. Barnstaple is still served by the old L&SWR route, much reduced in stature but at least that runs a regular service to Exeter and is thriving. The irony is that the fastest route to London by rail today is via the North Devon Link Road to Tiverton Parkway and then by train from there!

EPILOGUE

It is a testament to Victorian construction methods and materials that so many structures remain today on the D&SR, such as river bridges, culverts and so on, that have had minimal maintenance over the last fifty years. The most significant of these are the piers of Castle Hill Viaduct, which now carry the NDLR and all its traffic. Perhaps these should now be considered as a monument to the line and those who built it, a few of whom lost their lives in bringing an essential connection to an isolated area for such a short space of time, a mere ninety-three years.

In researching this book I have come across many stories and anecdotes. However, there is one apt farmer's quote that was told in the formative years of the railway, related to me by Mr Wesley Wyatt of Wiveliscombe and attributed to a Mr Alfred Poole of Chipstable:

'One day turnips will grow on this line again.'

Perhaps not literally but with the reclamation of so much of the trackbed for agricultural use, especially around the Wiveliscombe area, the quote has turned out to be somewhat prophetic.

pot the station? Molland village was ypical of a number of the communities erved by the D&SR, in that the line ran ear them rather than through them. This 960s aerial view is looking west, with no ign of the line. The railway is actually in e valley in the far left distance, some wo miles away, not very well positioned or the benefit of passengers. *Aerofilms/ istoric England*

Appendix 1: Maps of Lines Proposed and Lines Built 1830-1925

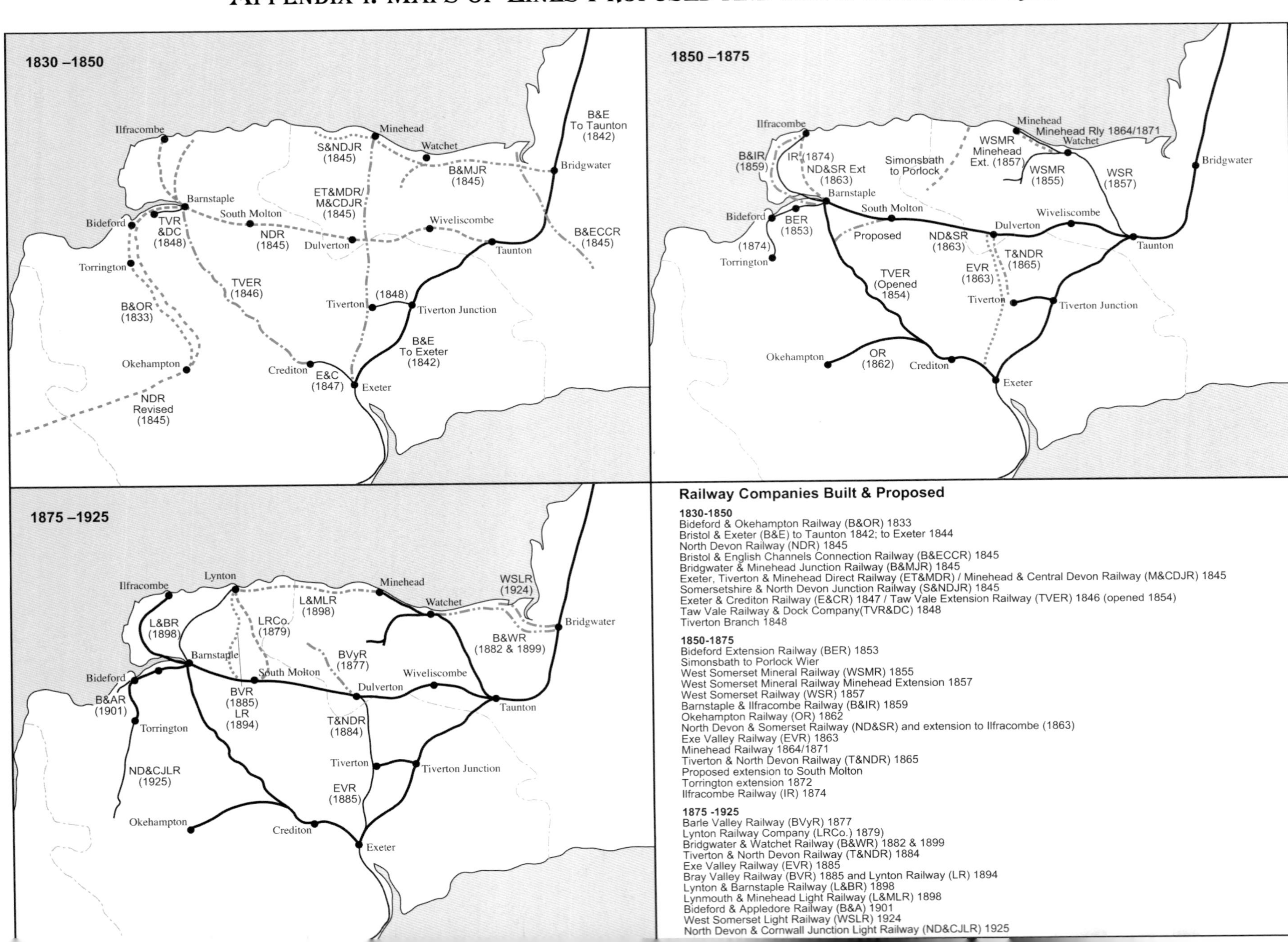

Railway Companies Built & Proposed

1830-1850
Bideford & Okehampton Railway (B&OR) 1833
Bristol & Exeter (B&E) to Taunton 1842; to Exeter 1844
North Devon Railway (NDR) 1845
Bristol & English Channels Connection Railway (B&ECCR) 1845
Bridgwater & Minehead Junction Railway (B&MJR) 1845
Exeter, Tiverton & Minehead Direct Railway (ET&MDR) / Minehead & Central Devon Railway (M&CDJR) 1845
Somersetshire & North Devon Junction Railway (S&NDJR) 1845
Exeter & Crediton Railway (E&CR) 1847 / Taw Vale Extension Railway (TVER) 1846 (opened 1854)
Taw Vale Railway & Dock Company(TVR&DC) 1848
Tiverton Branch 1848

1850-1875
Bideford Extension Railway (BER) 1853
Simonsbath to Porlock Wier
West Somerset Mineral Railway (WSMR) 1855
West Somerset Mineral Railway Minehead Extension 1857
West Somerset Railway (WSR) 1857
Barnstaple & Ilfracombe Railway (B&IR) 1859
Okehampton Railway (OR) 1862
North Devon & Somerset Railway (ND&SR) and extension to Ilfracombe (1863)
Exe Valley Railway (EVR) 1863
Minehead Railway 1864/1871
Tiverton & North Devon Railway (T&NDR) 1865
Proposed extension to South Molton
Torrington extension 1872
Ilfracombe Railway (IR) 1874

1875 -1925
Barle Valley Railway (BVyR) 1877
Lynton Railway Company (LRCo.) 1879)
Bridgwater & Watchet Railway (B&WR) 1882 & 1899
Tiverton & North Devon Railway (T&NDR) 1884
Exe Valley Railway (EVR) 1885
Bray Valley Railway (BVR) 1885 and Lynton Railway (LR) 1894
Lynton & Barnstaple Railway (L&BR) 1898
Lynmouth & Minehead Light Railway (L&MLR) 1898
Bideford & Appledore Railway (B&A) 1901
West Somerset Light Railway (WSLR) 1924
North Devon & Cornwall Junction Light Railway (ND&CJLR) 1925

APPENDIX 2
CONTRACTORS LOCOMOTIVES USED DURING CONSTRUCTION OF THE D&SR

W. & J. PICKERING CONTRACT 19/7/1865 – WORK SUSPENDED 29/9/1866 – CONTRACT TERMINATED 13/12/1867					
MANUFACTURER	WORKS NO.	YEAR	NAME	TYPE	NOTES
Hunslet Engine Co. Ltd	3	1865	*Fortescue*	0-6-0ST	New to Pickerings. Later to John Aird & Sons, Nottingham

JOHN LANGHAM REED CONTRACT 11/5/1870-1/11/1873					
MANUFACTURER	WORKS NO.	YEAR	NAME	TYPE	NOTES
Fox, Walker & Co.	No. 15	1870?		5 Ton Steam Crane	Possibly new for Devon & Somerset Railway Contract. Unspecified spares sent to Reed at Wiveliscombe 9/11/1871
Fox, Walker & Co.	No. 16	1870?	*Taunton*	Class 'A' 0-6-0ST oc	Built same time as FW No. 14, both were with Firbank later. The description of this engine matches a photograph in a book on the Bluebell line and the name would appear to link it with the D&SR contract. Later Firbank contracts it was on include: 1880 Bluebell Line contract, Horsted Keynes to Lewes section 1877-1886 GWR Contracts (unspecified) 1894-1899 MS&LR London Extension, Finchley Rd.-Marylebone 1896-1899 GNR Beeston-Hunslet Branch, Leeds
Fox, Walker & Co.	No. 17	1870?		0-6-0ST oc	Possibly new to Reed for D&SR contract 1870-1873. Unspecified spares sent to Reed at Wiveliscombe 9/11/1871*
Fox, Walker & Co.	No. 18	1870?		5 Ton Steam Crane**	Possibly new to Reed for D&SR contract 1870-1873. Unspecified spares sent to Reed at Wiveliscombe 9/11/1871*
Fox, Walker & Co.	No. 19	1870?		0-6-0ST oc	Possibly new to Reed for D&SR contract 1870-1873. Unspecified spares sent to Reed at South Moulton Road [*sic*] station 12/3/1872*
Vulcan Foundry		1844	*Defiance*	Broad gauge 0-6-0	New to Bristol & Gloucester Railway, their No. 11. Later became Midland Railway No. 266, then 366 and 466 respectively. Sold 1857 for £1,000 to Thomas Brassey who built, leased and operated the North Devon Railway until takeover by the L&SWR in 1862. On 24/8/1870 Beattie reported on condition of BG engines inherited from Brassey: Defiance '*completely worn out*', recommended breaking up. To Reed (on hire?) possibly early 1871, for use in ballasting Taunton to Wiveliscombe section
Stothert & Slaughter		1844	*Industry*	Broad gauge 2-4-0	New to Bristol & Gloucester Railway, their No. 2. Later became Midland Railway No. 269, then 369 and 469 respectively. Sold 1857 to Thomas Brassey for use on NDR and renamed *Venus*. Beattie noted 24/8/1870 '*in fair order*', recommended sale. To Reed (on hire?) c1871, presumed for use in ballasting Wiveliscombe to Barnstaple section.
				Broad gauge 0-6-0	16ins cylinders, 27 tons empty. Bought Swindon Works 3/1873 for use in ballasting Wiveliscombe to Barnstaple section but reported laid up in goods shed at former place for five weeks shortly after. Offered for sale 10/1/1873 (*The Engineer*)
Alexander Shanks & Son		1872?		Vertical boiler 0-4-0	c1873 to T. & C. Walker for use on Somerset & Dorset Railway's Bath Extension. c1875 to Messrs Budd & Holt for use on construction of Malmesbury Railway
Aveling & Porter		1870		4w tank geared	Chain coupled, 12hp

* The information on spares orders copied by Ken Plant from an old manuscript order book at Pecketts Works, believed to have been made for Edwin Walker.
** The IRS record FW No. 18 as an 0-6-0ST (*Industrial Railways and Locomotives of South Western England*, Roger Hateley, 2011).

NOTE: The information contained in this list and on page 56 differs from – and in places corrects – some of that published previously but represents the latest research into the locomotives used in the building of the D&SR line. Reed definitely had three FW 0-6-0STs and two FW 5-ton steam cranes on this contract, confirmed by the subsequent sale of plant notices but there is still conjecture about their works numbers. FW No. 16 *Taunton* has not previously been connected with this contract but the name given to the engine would seem to indicate it now as a highly likely contender. The information identifying FW No. 18 as a 5-ton steam crane was supplied to Andrew Neale from a Birmingham Locomotive Club source (the BLC was the forerunner to the Industrial Railway Society) via Maurice Billinton. However, this is still very much a work in progress and much remains to be confirmed or, as with the 'mystery' broad gauge locomotive bought from Swindon, identified.

Appendix 3
Summary of Contractor's Agreement (1865)

Summary of the original contractor's agreement dated 19th July 1865, between Messrs William and John Pickering and the Devon & Somerset Railway Company. This was the initial agreement spelling out the relevant terms – a single line built to the broad gauge, with sufficient sidings, turnouts and passing places, station houses and accommodation, goods sheds, turntables, loading banks, cranes, water supply apparatus and signals and electric telegraph. All to be built to the satisfaction of the D&SR engineer but subject to the the inspection of the B&ER engineer. If there were differences between the engineers, the dispute was to be referred to a competent civil engineer to arbitrate. If additional works and siding space were required by the B&ER, this was to be a cost to the D&SR and if there was a dispute, an impartial civil engineer would arbitrate with the Board of Trade being the final decision maker. The contract contained its main terms in Articles 1 to 61, along with a schedule of specifications. The key Articles are summarised below. The specifications are substantially reproduced as it gives a true insight to the building of a railway in the Victorian era.

Articles

1. Contractor is responsible for paying all costs, charges and legal expenses etc incurred by the promoters in and about the preparation and promotion and establishment of the Company and applying for and obtaining and passing of the Act which amount to £11,900 [and to Mr Climie] are agreed to amount to £42,000 and all other costs (other than future acts of Parliament) up to the engineer and the Board of Trade confirming the railway is ready for opening.
2. The Contractor having paid £22,950 will, on execution of the contract, pay to the Company or to their order £7,050 in acceptance at two months and £12,000 being the residue of the £42,000 (as in 1 above) by transfer or delivery to them or nominees of as many shares of par value as when fully paid will amount to £12,000 (to bear interest at 5%) such shares to convert to preference shares as soon as they can be issued.
3. Contractor will pay all other costs/charges in cash when incurred by the Company and certified.
4. The sum bound to be paid to the engineer for costs charges and expenses will be £1,500 for the period 30 July 1864 to 30 July 1865. After that £2,000 per annum until the line is ready.
5. a/b/c relating to interest.
6. The railway is defined.
7. Reference to the schedule.
8. Contractor is to enter into contracts on behalf of the Company to purchase lands as agent.
9. Contractor to pass land contracts to solicitor to investigate title and complete purchase.
10. Purchase price for land to be agreed by Contractor. Contractor is not at liberty to acquire any land for yearly rent.

11/12. Company and Contractor are bound by negotiations/arrangements and Contractor will pay for all purchases for land buildings and property.

13. Company will put in force any powers in the Act required to purchase land.
14. Contracts to procure and purchase lands should occur as soon as possible.
15. The lands to be purchased must be sufficient and proper for the railway as expressed in the agreement between the D&SR and B&ER.
16. The works specified in the schedule (see below).
17. Reference to Article 4 of the D&SR/B&ER agreement.
18. All works to be done under the supervision of the engineer and the B&ER engineer from time to time.
19. Railway to be opened and fit for public traffic at times set out in the schedules.
20. Contractors to indemnify Company against any liability for claims by landowners.
21. Contractor's indemnity against other claims during execution of works and any time thereafter before expiry of one year after completion of the railway, including misfeasance, default, neglect on execution of the word by the contractor.
22. Contractor not bound to purchase lands, buildings or other property to provide materials or works unless in accordance with the agreement.
23. Deviations to the line are to be agreed between the engineer and Contractor, levels gradients and sections (all subject to Board of Trade approval) must be settled by the directors. Any savings are to the benefit of the Contractor. The engineer is not to make additions to the works without the Contractor's consent.
24. If part of the railway is completed the Contractor can use it for his benefit/purpose and own cost if approval is granted.
25. Contractor will keep the railway in good and substantial repair and good working order to the satisfaction of the engineer.
26. All surplus land and buildings and property acquired by the Contractor can be disposed of by the Company for the benefit of the Contractor once the line is open on behalf of the Company. Any disagreement as to what is surplus is to go to arbitration.
27. Payments to the Contractor. The £666,000 'Contract Sum' is analysed as follows:

    £50,000 Cash
    £200,000 by whole of 8,000 Class A stock
    £250,000 by issue of £10,000 Class B stock
    £166,000 by issue of mortgage at 5%

28. The shares are to be issued as and when the contract requires.
29. The mortgage is issued when required and the Company is legally able to do so.
30. £50,000 can be applied to purchase land or by issue to the Contractor or nominees of the A or B stock.
31. All A and B stock issued is taken at par and deemed fully paid up in respect of the contract sum.
32. The contract sum is apportioned as follows:
    a) £42,000 for fulfilment of obligations under Articles 1 and 2 (above); the money obligation
    b) £40,000 acquiring land and buildings; the land obligation
    c) £39,000 for tunnels; the tunnel obligation
    d) £14,000 fitting up of stations and other works; the stations obligation
    e) £531,000 for all other obligations under the contract; the general obligation
33. The Company Secretary shall deliver certificates of amounts paid to the contractor from time to time for the money obligations.
34. The solicitor has an obligation to declare the fulfilment of the land obligations.
35. The engineer is to deliver certificates when requested by the Contractor of the tunnel, station and general obligations.
36. The engineer is to have regard to the schedule of tunnel costs and the £39,000 referred to above.
37. For performance of the general obligations the company engineer by agreement with the Contractor shall divide the £531,000 by the number of miles in the whole length of the railway (approx. 43) exclusive of so much as comprises tunnels. Such sum then being attributable to earthworks and works of the Articles and permanent way and any other works they think fit [The cost per mile was therefore anticipated at around £12,600].

38. The engineer is to deliver no more than monthly separate and distinct certificates of obligations on account of the amount in 37 above.
39. The engineer should have regard to mileage under the general obligations.
40. The Company will advance on execution of agreement £40,000 for plant (as part of the £531,000), such sum to be set off against certifications.
41. When the Contractor has fulfilled the land obligations to the satisfaction of the engineer there is to be delivered a written certificate of the balance of the £40,000 payable to the Contractor.
42. Likewise the tunnel obligations and the balance of £39,000.
43. Likewise the station obligations £14,000. Costs are not to exceed £14,000.
44. Likewise the general obligations.
45. Within seven days of delivery of the certificate the Company will pay or satisfy to the Contractor the amounts specified based on the relevant obligations in a) to e) of Article 32.
46. The Company has the option to make payments in cash in excess of the £50,000 instead of shares or mortgage (and to decrease the proportion of shares etc to be issued).
47. Contractors to use their influence to retain the company directors in office.
48. Mr John McMillan to be Company Secretary.
49. Messrs Riccard to be solicitors.
50. Mr Eugenius Birch the present company engineer and not to appoint another engineer without the consent of the Contractor.
51. Any new engineer should be appointed from a list of names to be furnished by the Contractor and be a member of the Institute of Civil Engineers.
52. Company will apply to Parliament at the cost to the Contractor to issue the 5% Preference Shares for £200,000 provided for in the Deed of Arrangement for creating those Preference Shares.
53-61. Generic articles.

Specifications to the Pickering D&SR Contract for Construction (19 July 1865)

The contract covers all materials, labor [*sic*], plant, tools and machinery necessary to construct a single line railway being of a distance of 42 miles and six furlongs in respect of earthworks, tunnels, buildings, bridges, viaducts, waterways, roads, level crossings, drains, temporary and permanent fences providing material for and forming the ballast ready to receive the permanent way, rails, materials for and erection of station buildings and all other works of every description whether temporary or permanent and for maintenance of the same for the period defined.

The Contractor is to provide a surety to enter into a Bond to the amount of £15,000 conditioned on the due fulfilment of the contract according to all the terms and conditions of this specification.

There should be a perfect setting out of the line and regular curves to such general levels, gradients and slopes as are shown on the plans. The Contractor to provide stakes to set out the line.

Permanent Fence (to separate the land from the works)

A good post and rail fence to connect with the wing walls of any bridges, the Contractor to maintain and be responsible for the fencing. Posts to be made of straight sound and well-shaped split oak or sawn larch, free from bark, 7 feet 8 inches in length at least 16 square inches of cross section at the smallest (average less than 18 square inches) to be placed 9 feet apart and 4 feet 4 inches above the ground. Mortices to receive the ends of four horizontal or larch rails 10 feet long (5$^1/_2$ square inches of sectioned area, not less than 6$^1/_2$ square inches on average) with bark stripped off. The intermediate small part of oak/larch to support the fence must be firmly and substantially fixed and maintained to effectively exclude lambs, sheep, pigs and all other cattle and to protect the adjoining land from trespass.

A ditch or drain must be cut next to the fence (but not to interfere with existing water courses). The materials excavated from the ditch will be used for forming a mound in the space between the edge of the ditch and railway slopes. Excess earth for the mounds must be used for slopes or carried to embankments.

Earthwork and Rockwork

In unsoiling a surface, the whole of the topsoil was to be excavated but not to interfere with ditches the best soil selected to soil the slopes. Where the ground near the surface is wet or soft this is to be removed to form a proper base. The formation of slopes of cuttings are to be made to specifications.

Cuttings

Refer to the longitudinal sections of the plans.

They are to be 17 feet wide at the foundations level and increase in width where the engineer so considers but not to exceed 21 feet. Where there is to be a bridge over the line the cuttings shall be formed to such bridge at the full width for a double line of railway being gradually reduced so as to secure the slopes in the lengths of a chain. Water from side ditches must run down slopes by half-barrel calvert drain and pipes (or other efficient method agreed by the engineer). The railway to be kept perfectly well-drained.

The slopes to be drained by oblique drains cut into the slopes not less than 18 inches deep at intervals directed by the engineer – filled with large stones or drain tikes. Stream down slopes should be led by drain pipes into side drains at the bottom of the slope.

Retaining walls can be used and be trimmed and soiled in the manner for embankments.

The bottom of cuttings are not to be excavated within 9 inches of the formation line (unless the foundation is rock) and subject to the engineer and must not cut up the ground on which the line will be carried and needs to be perfectly well-drained. In no case shall the steps or bottom of the cutting below formation level be excavated for ballast or other materials. Additional materials (soil etc) need to be obtained by widening the nearest cutting.

Embankments

To be formed based on the longitudinal cross sections.

To be 18 feet wide at formation level. Extremities to be widened in a distance of 1 chain to 21 feet at the formation line where an embankment joins a cutting. The whole of the embankment to be formed of good materials and must allow for settlement so to be raised up initially to allow for same. Lumps must be broken and the surface neatly trimmed and beaten down. Rye grass and clover seeds should be sown as soon as the weather permits, to keep well drained. The surface must be properly trimmed and formed before laying ballast and there is to be no tipping into the embankment or forming ballast foundations in wet weather.

Earthworks must be properly formed against bridges etc. the side drays on the upper side or sloping grounds shall always be well formed in advance of the embankment/earthworks. Any spoil banks are to be neatly trimmed. All hedges or banks within the fence to be removed and ditches filled to the ordinary level of the ground (except where drainage is required).

Tunnels

Contractors to confine their operations to the width of 1 chain upon the surface of the ground over the intended tunnels and that width to be fenced in with temporary fencing, which is to be removed when the work is completed and not replaced. The surface of the ground over the tunnels except the spoil banks must be reinstated and left in original condition.

The Contractor to provide machinery and other apparatus to pump and keep dry and ventilating during the works. Headings to be drawn through the tunnel in the direction of the centre line.

Contractor may sink working shafts on the centre line of the tunnel at places where the engineer directs, be at least 9 feet clear in diameter and lined with bricks if deemed necessary by the engineer. All rock cutting must be trimmed to an even surface. On excavating the tunnel Contractors should not advance beyond completed brickwork or masonry by more than 12 feet (unless special permission is given by the engineer) and be restricted further if unsafe or inexpedient.

Unless not required by space ahead of the brickwork the excavation should be supported by the usual modes of timbering, sills, props, shores, bars and boards (dimensions of which to be approved by the engineer). All spaces must be filled in solid hard materials as the masonry proceeds.

If the material through which he tunnel is advancing is unsound then the timbers may be left in place. All spaces must be closed and carefully filled in with dry materials only leaving the timber with the permission of the engineer. If withdrawing bars or other parts of timbering care is needed where ever streams of water may occur. Chimney drains must be left behind the walls and be provided with outlets at the level of line of rails (and prevent such water loosening the ground).

If any increase in dimension is given to excavation without the consent of the engineer through carelessness or neglect, the Contractor must make good. The tunnel must be ballasted throughout its length and full width and match the normal ballast width one chain from the tunnel entrance.

If it is found necessary to use powder [explosives]or blasting, great care should be taken in providing proper and safe magazines in order to avoid accidents. No powder should be stored on the works unless in strong tin or iron boxes made of suitable form with covers and in blasting no straws or other dangerous means be resorted to.

The fronts of the tunnels must be constructed of brickwork or fitted rubble masonry (as shewn in the drawings). If the latter the coping and the quoin and arch stones are to be of ashlar. The arch stones and quoins are to be each in one stone and in the dimensions of the drawings. The edges are to be tooled for a width of 2 inches.

If the front of the tunnel entrances are not dry then stones and drainage is to be put behind the back of the walls. Recesses are to be made at 40 feet from centre to centre. The abutment walls are to be constructed either of brickworks or good solid well-built rubble masonry, the footings in this latter case to be built of large flat bedded stone. All interior tunnels masonry and brickwork to be pointed as the work proceeds.

A drain should be formed the whole length of the tunnels and 40 feet beyond each end with regular fall to the side ditch or drain pipe at the mouth of the tunnel and with necessary openings to receive the drainage of water from the tunnels.

Ballasting

To be laid on a perfect formation surface with clean and approved ballast. Contractor must ensure the ballast is properly laid and maintained. The ballast is to be obtained at the Contractor's own cost from excavation of cuttings etc. Only areas shown in the plans can be excavated.

Ballast must consist of stone or gravel or any other hard coarse materials not affected by wet or frost (and to be approved by the engineer). Ballast to be laid to a depth of 18 inches, the lower 12 inches may be formed of larger lumps but not exceeding 20 cubic inches, the upper not to exceed 2 cubic inches. The slope is to be $^{3}/_{4}$ to 1 as shown in the cross-section, with coarse material over the drain pipes. Whenever material is met with in the progress of the works and is found 'fit for purpose' it shall be used at once for ballasting (or set aside for future use). If a cutting has a ballast floor it can be left but it is not to be excavated below the formation surface of the cutting. Precautions are to be taken to prevent spread ballast being trodden down or unnecessarily worked over by horses or men. The Contractor must leave the ballast in a good state at the end and any large amounts appearing should be broken up.

General Instructions as to Buildings, Roads and Waterways

This includes everything, including tunnels, culverts, etc.

There must be at least 15 feet 9 inches clear height from the level of permanent rails in all cases to the underside of the arch allowing for resettlement and if not the rebuild would be at the expense of the Contractor.

As for buildings, particularly those under the railway, shall be constructed of materials and the manner specified and are to be proceeded with immediately on the land being acquired and the engineer considers it practicable in order to give the longest time before earthworks approach them. Roads etc up to and under bridges are to be formed in accordance with 'Public General Railway Acts' or as directed by the engineer or by special Act authorising the construction of the railway.

All overbridges to be constructed for a double line, underbridges for a single line. It also defined how roads would be built (with stone used for metalled roads).

Where level crossings are required for occupation roads there should be provided two good and substantial oak gates 9 feet in the clear when opened with ironwork posts and fixings completed are to be fixed either side of the railway continuous with the fencing.

Approaches to the crossing is to be made up to the gate with an inclination of not less than 1 in 16 unless specified (drainage is to be under the crossing and not to be interrupted). Unless specified all buildings to be of brickwork.

Before forming an embankment against wing walls and overarches and abutments of bridges, viaducts etc and must be carefully packed.

Materials

Stone – for ordinary fitted rubble work is to be of the best quality of selected stone of the district or other good building stone to be sound, clean and free from cracks and defects.

Bricks – Bridgwater stock quality

Lime – best quality Blue or hydraulic lime or Watchet lime

Sand – fine with no soil

Mortar – 1 portion of dry lime and $1^{1}/_{2}$ to 2 of sand, the lime to be slacked and carefully screened through a screen not coarser than 4 measures to the inch and thoroughly mixed with sand and water in a pug mill or edge stones.

Cement – Portland cement used for foundations, arches and retaining walls

Concrete – 5 parts of clear gravel (no loam or clay) with small gravel and sand as well as stone chippings mixed with sharp sand and one part hydraulic lime. Lime to be mixed with gravel and water and sand thoroughly in a pug mill. Concrete to be spread in layers not exceeding 9 inches thick all over at one time then well trodden and pinned down and another layer added. Masonry and brickwork if built on concrete is not to take place until 24 hours has elapsed. The engineer can decide to use concrete under bridges or to substitute for masonry.

Timber – all must be Baltic red pine for permanent construction of buildings or white pine (if approved) being straight sound and free from sap. Creosoted under pressure (using ordinary process of creosoting) not less than 35 gallons of creosote used for each load of timber. Underground would be creosoted first then all other exposed wood creosoted. English oak of the best quality to be used.

Cast iron – best pig iron No. 2 cast iron

Wrought iron – scrap or cable iron or Staffordshire iron of approved brands

Workmanship

Masonry – 'tilted rubble', face stones not less than 8 inches in thickness 12 inches in breadth, need not be squared except to a depth of 3 inches on face, each stone to be 12 inches in depth at some point but not less than 6 inches depth at the shallowest point. Flat exterior face. To fit well against each other, with smaller stones filling the gaps to avoid thick mortar joints. Bonding stones behind the facing stones are to be up to 2 feet in depth. All wing wall pieces must be carefully bound into abutments. Stones in arches must be prepared with a flat bed and properly radiated throughout the entire thickness of the arch. Masonry of barrels of stone culverts and of other works not permanently visible (except for tunnel masonry) is to consist of good random rubble well bonded, no small stones to be used. The whole of the masonry to be built with mortar. Ashlar shall be neatly tooled all over, with samples submitted for the engineer to approve.

Brickworks – bricks bedded sound, well pressed into beds so as to squeeze the mortar out and leave the joints thin. Once mortar is set in exterior points of masonry and brickworks and joints carefully raked out and pointed with Roman cement or mortar. If weather is bad pointing is to be left until such time as the engineer may direct.

Timberwork – must be squared (unless underground). Ironworks must be carefully fitted. Bolt holes to be of the right size no play, the washer up against the wood to be of sufficient thickness. Bolts to be of the correct length. Piles driven out of line or damaged shall be withdrawn and replaced. No pile is considered driven if it moves $^{1}/_{4}$ inch under the blow of a monkey 20cwt falling 12 feet (unless special circumstances and the engineer deem this degree of resistance unnecessary). Roadway lancing must be true and even at edges and level. A good coat of creosote or tar if covered in earth.

Planking is to be spiked to timbers with 10 inch spikes.
Ironworks – cleaned from rush and one coat of paint, fixed and then not less than 3 coats of paint applied.
Cast iron works – clean and sound and have castings free from air.
Wrought iron works – approved quality of boilers late and free from blisters and scales and other defects. Size and dimensions based on drawings. Rivet holes punched perfectly, hills to correspond perfectly. Angle irons if required must be done with an easy bend.

Stations

The design of the stations have not yet been determined. They will consist of passenger booking offices, waiting rooms, ticket platform, goods sheds, lodges, engine houses, points and crossings, turntables, sidings (in excess of permanent way herein after mentioned) and all such necessary and contingent fittings etc. The cost thereof to the Contractor including all hydraulic cranes, pumps, tanks, reservoirs, station signals, signal houses and any other appliances that may be required to complete the stations is not to exceed £14,000.
Excavation – to the depths shown on the drawings, beds to trenches kept hard and level and any icy water drained before masonry or brickwork is commenced.
Materials – passenger buildings and engine house are to be stone. Goods sheds brickwork and timber carcasses framing covered with weatherboarding.
Roofs – framed with timber, covered with slate. Dressings of doors, windows etc of dressed stone.

Drains cesspools etc, brickwork or random rubble, masonry properly bonded. Air spaces formed and air gratings of cast iron 12 inches by 6 inches provided and inserted neatly in exterior walls. Chimneys, all fire openings with brick fenders for front hearths. Flues, shafts built in cement to the necking finished with stone caps. Chimney bars to be of wrought iron. Windows and door frames to be properly bedded and pointed round with lime. Stoves and grates to be properly set with fire bricks. External doorways next to the railway are to have 3 inches of York or cement stone paving continued under them. Internal paving to be 3 inches in thickness.Booking offices and principal waiting rooms to have polished slate chimney pieces. Goods office chimney pieces to be of stone.

Floors of urinals are to be laid with slate at an inclination as to admit perforated slates being laid upon for underwashing.
Carpented works – sound and well seasoned yellow pine of Quebec or Upper Port growth or Memel or red pine free from sap, knots etc.
Timberwork – carcass framing for goods sheds etc to be done in accordance with drawings. Principal posts are to be accurately seasoned and firmly honed into an oak sill. Timbers are to be carefully picked and uniform. Two piers of bond timbers are to be inserted in the walls of such of the rooms and are to have wall linings. Roof trusses and rafters were all specified. Roof timbers were to withstand three times the anticipated weight load.
Joiner's work – deal ash and battens must be sound. External door frames 5ins by 4ins. Internal doorways 1ins by 4ins grooved to receive plaster. All doors to be four-panelled, accurately hung, strong hinges, good locks and fastenings. WC's adjoining ladies to have Spanish Mahogany seats and risers with deal dovetailed barriers, the Mahogany to be French-polished. The deal should be fixed with screws to facilitate removal. Cisterns to contain 100 gallons of water for one closet, 200 for two.
Office fittings – a deal moulded clock bucket is to be provided and fixed at each booking office [*presumably a moulded case for a wall mounted timepiece, the mechanisms being bought separately*]
Plumbers' work – hips and ridges to be leaded, valley gutters to be lead. All flat roofs laid with milled lead. A service pipe is to be laid from cistern to urinals to be arranged and perforated so as to wash the surface and channels thoroughly, with a stop cock and lever handle
Plasterers' work – laths used for internal work are to be straight lash and half-heart of fir (Baltic), laths free from sap, ceilings plastered. Walls of booking offices are to be rendered on masonry. Waiting rooms finished for papering. Porters rooms, store rooms and closets finished with rough shicco. Plasterer to satisfy himself all is properly prepared.
Painters' work – four coats if external wood or iron. Internal to be 3 coats of pure zinc paint. Manufacturers approved by the engineer only to be used.
Joiners work in booking offices to be grained in imitation of [Wainscott] by a good grainer in accordance with samples. Booking offices, superintendent rooms and waiting rooms are to be lined and papered.
Glaziers' work – patent plate glass weighing 26 ounces to a foot for booking offices and waiting rooms. For goods shed and engine houses patent flattened sheet glass of 26 ounces to a foot.

Permanent Way

The permanent way to comprise 42 miles and six furlongs on main line and half mile on the branch line [to join the WSR] together with 10 percent additional in sidings and stations and in passing places. It is to be a single line throughout, double line at certain stations and passing places, laid on transverse sleepers placed at distances not to exceed an average of 2 feet 9 inches from centre to centre. The contract to defray the entire cost of making a junction with the B&ER and WSR which the said companies will make on behalf of the D&SR.

The £14,000 for station works is to include turntables, switches, points, crossings, capstans, signals etc as maybe required and approved by the Board of Trade.
Sleepers – perfectly sound American yellow pine lower port timber or Baltic timber from Memal or Danzig or larch fir of the very best quality, stored in stacks in yards (subject to inspection at all times). To be creosoted. Not to be less than 11 feet in length, 10 inches in width and 5 inches thick.
Rails – to present the exact form of the stumped template furnished to the Contractor. Length 24 feet 6 inches, 21 feet 9 inches, 19 feet and 16 feet 3 inches [width not exceeding 10% of 18 and 15 feet lengths]. Ideally weigh to average 75 lbs per lineal yard (but not less than 74lbs and not more than $75^1/_2$ lbs per lineal yard). A number of rails will also be required measuring 2 or 4 inches shorter than the 21 feet or 24 feet [not greater than one in 10 to be of the shorter length]. Rails to be rolled sound and perfect. Those with cracks or imperfections to be rejected. Rails to be sawn and be perfectly square at the ends and to be perfectly straightened when hot. Great attention must be paid to the fitting of nuts and bolts which must be tight and when screwed up must be left horizontal and the nuts placed on the inside. The fish plates to have 4 bolts to each mint of $^7/_8$ inches diameter, nuts being neatly finished square. The bolt heads to be round with square shoulders. Rails to be bolted to sleepers with $^3/_4$ inch bolts passing through the base of the rails and screwed into wrought iron plates $3^1/_2$ inch square placed on the underside of sleepers. The number of bolts should be as follows

24 foot rail – 7 bolts
21 foot rail – 6 bolts
18 foot rail – 6 bolts
15 foot rail – 5 bolts.

Rails to be also spiked with spikes of an approved form to the sleepers. 4 spikes to each sleeper, except where bolts occur in which as spike is to be opposite every single bolt.
Creosoting – timbers when dry are to be put into preserving tanks. Creosote to be warmed when used, pressure brought up to 120lbs per inch and left for not less than 8 hours with the pressure not allowed to fall to enable the timber to be thoroughly impregnated. 35 gallons of the best quality creosote to be used with 50 cubic feet of timber.
Workmanship – sleepers to be laid with the heart of the wood down and at right angles to the rails. Care is needed in handling and transport. Any injured timber, including split ends, is not to be used. Before laying the timber the Contractor must trim and level the ballast under the sleepers to a general uniform surface, hollows filled and lumps of ballast trimmed. Where there needs to be headroom the timbers must be laid so a minimum of 16 feet over the centre of the line above the rails.

The Contractor must follow the lines and curves and general directions given by the engineer. Where curves are less than 20 chains radius, rails will require slight bending, this maybe affected by a screw press or by striking the outer flange on a curving anvil. The rail must be permanently set to the form required before being laid. Where the line is straight, rails must be level. Where there is a curve the outer rail must be elevated (such elevation determined by the engineer). When being laid timber and chairs must be clean and properly set out and fixed with spikes; rail must only be secured if properly straight (otherwise refixed). The rails to be fixed so the gauge is exactly 7 feet in the clear, using the gauges at hand to ensure proper fixing. After the rails are laid the line should be well packed and sleepers brought to a perfect level or to the right cant.

42 mile posts and 171 quarter mile posts should be provided and placed at proper distances to the side of the railway. The former being 6 feet long and 12 inches broad and 6 inches thick. The latter being $5^1/_2$ feet long and 8 inches wide and 4 inches thick. They to be fixed 2 feet into the ground. To be made of wrought iron with 2 coats of paint and have proper figures marked. Gradient posts are to be fixed at every change of gradient.

Maintenance – after passed by the Government inspector the Contractor shall for 12 months thereafter maintain and keep the works in complete repair and at the end leave it in a state to the satisfaction of the engineer.

General stipulations – The Contractor and engineer (with the approval of the Board of Trade) shall have the option of making alterations in Parliamentary or contract plans (the benefit of any savings accruing to the Contractor).

All works to be carried out and completed in compliance with and prescribed by the General Public Railway Acts in force at the time and any special Act authorising the railway. The whole works are under the supervision of the engineer. The Contractor takes responsibility for sufficiency of scaffolding, planking, dams, tools, implements etc. The Contractors are to make good any matters not caused by the D&SR or its directors in the period of construction and a further 12 months.

If the Contractor becomes insolvent the D&SR can take the works wholly or in part out of the Contractor's hands and to apply or use all machinery which has been paid for under the engineers certificates. Negligent execution or use of bad or doubtful materials (as confirmed by the engineer) is the responsibility of the Contractor. If the Contractor does not deal with the issue immediately they can be suspended from all proceedings or the matter can go to arbitration.

Contractor must do his best to avoid injury to or improperly interfering with the use of paths, roads, canals, water courses or deviations of the same. Drains and watercourses must be properly and effectively diverted and led to new streams, channels etc to secure and maintain the existing drainage or irrigation.

No work is to take place on a Sunday (unless absolutely unavoidable and confirmed by the engineer).

The Contractor is to prevent (to this best of his power) the introduction of the Truck system upon the works (that is where there is no control over the men by inducement or by market or mode of payment). Men to be paid in cash at least once a fortnight and on no account shall the whole or any portion of wages be paid or any advance made to men by tickets or orders upon victuallers or in any way what so ever except cash. If there is a risk the peace of the neighbourhood is likely to be disturbed or security or proper progress of the works endangered by reason of men being left unpaid the Company may pay arrears of wages as may be due on the next payday and charge the same to the account of the Contractor.

Period of completion

To be completed and ready to be opened for public traffic and given up to the Company on or before 29th day of July 1869. Contractor required to complete the work within 18 months from commencement of the works. If not completed the Contractors will pay damages to the Company in the region of £7-10 per month per mile not fit to be opened and during the period up to 29 July 1869 to the extent any part remains incomplete.

APPENDIX 4
SUMMARY OF CONTRACTOR'S AGREEMENT (1870)

Summary of key issues and terms of the contract between the D&SR and John Langham Reed for the completion of railway works, dated 24th May 1870.

An acknowledgement of the scheme filed in the Hight Court of Chancery under the provisions of the Railway Companies Arrangement Act 1867 on 5 March 1868 was made. This providing for the creation and issuing of Debenture stock to an amount not exceeding £270,000, called A debenture stock, with interest at 6% per annum. The monies so received to be applied against the said scheme and then at the discretion of the directors to complete the railway. Existing debt would be converted to B debentures.

The contractor agreed to purchase land and the D&SR directors agreed the first priority is to complete the railway.

The railway was to be completed as a single line to be done in accordance with plans deposited for the purposes of the D&SR Act of 1864 and the D&SR (Extension) Act of 1867 under the guidance of Richard Hassard (engineer) and to the reasonable satisfaction of the B&ER engineer. Stations and incidents thereto shall not be required to exceed £14,000 in the whole.

The contractor shall complete said railway and render it 'fit for opening' so far as Wiveliscombe within four months of the commencement of the works and shall complete the said works from South Molton to Barnstaple and also the short branch connecting the railway with the Watchet line within eight months of recommencement of the works and the entire railway by 6th June 1871. The contractor was to maintain the line for one year after opening. The contractor could deviate the line as laid down in the plans and the two Acts and vary gradients with the engineer's prior approval. If this required Parliamentary sanction then this was to be at the contractor's expense. The line was also to be extended into Barnstaple to meet Cattle Market Road. If the engineer felt additional time was needed for the works he could approve an extension to the time of completion. Any savings on outlay are to accrue to the contractor but use of improper materials or workmanship would not be allowed.

Whilst plant, materials and buildings are to be assigned over to the contractor to be used by him, he is not at liberty to sell them until such time as the railway is completed for public traffic (and were also surplus to the company's use). The contractor is to find scaffolding, labor [*sic*], services, implements, utensils, machinery, power, etc necessary for the full and safe expeditions.

The contractor shall purchase or complete the purchase of land sufficient to enable the said railway to be spanned with bridges for a double line and shall if necessary set back fences and clear the same for that purpose and shall purchase land sufficient for the works incidental to the railway and shall make such compensation to owners/occupiers of the land.

The contractor shall be liable to pay for extraction rights, clay, rubble, stone, gravel or matter from the site and be liable for any damage which ... shall be occasioned by diversion or interruption of any rivers or streams, water courses, roads, streets or operations connected therewith. The contractor agrees to indemnify the D&SR in respect of all such damage and every penalty to be incurred under sections 23, 54, 57 and 58 of the Railway Clauses Consolidation Act 1845.

If the contractor has to pay in cash for land a sum greater than £15,000 the D&SR will pay the contractor in B debentures (in addition to the £40,000 B debentures to be paid in any event).

The contractor is responsible for replacing any roadway or bridge on a private road where the existing structure is made 'impassable or dangerous' by the works. He would be required to make good at his own cost. This would also apply where there was injury or damage caused by flood, storm, tempest, fire, trespass or other means.

The D&SR will issue script certificates of A debenture stock of aggregate nominal value £255,000 and will appoint brokers to convert these to cash and pay reasonable expenses. The directors would pay the costs of the scheme out of the proceeds and place true residual amount in the hands of the Trustees to be applied by them in or towards the completion of the said railway and works. The contractor shall be entitled to request the Trustees to invest the funds in suitable stocks or securities as he thinks fit, subject to the approval of the Trustees. The money paid to the contractor would be at a rate of 90% of the monthly amounts of the works done, including materials and within seven days of receipt by the Company Secretary of the engineers certificate of value. The 10% retention being released when the engineer is satisfied and certifies that the railway is completely finished and in proper order for traffic, payment being due three months thereafter. There was requirement to pay 90% for new materials and 50% of plant brought on site as 'contractors plant'.

The contractor required the company to issue to him scrip certificates of £40,000 B debentures as part of the price irrespective of the engineers certificates. Stocks could be issued at the contractors request as follows:

£10,000 immediately
£10,000 on the line opening to Wiveliscombe
£10,000 on the line opening to South Molton
£10,000 on the entire line opening to traffic.

Owners of land required for the purposes of the railway should consent to the issue of B stock in lieu of cash. If the B stock is not all so applied Reed can keep the surplus. However, if there is insufficient B stock the contractor has to make good the shortfall out of his own resources.

All materials and work done not to the engineer's satisfaction is to be repaired or replaced. If fourteen days elapsed before said rectification, the contractor would pay damages too.

The engineer may require the contractor to provide at all times such number and quantity of efficient workmen, agents, horses, engines, buildings, huts, machinery, power and plant of every kind as he thinks expedient for the satisfactory progress of the works.

The contract would be determined if the contractor goes bankrupt and if he is in breach of works. If such happens all monies owed and plant and engines, materials, etc shall be forfeited by the contractor.

The surplus land not required for the purpose of the railway is the property of the D&SR.

Appendix 5
Summary of Contractor's Agreement to Complete the Stations (1872)

Contract between the Devon and Somerset Railway and John Langham Reed to Complete the Stations, dated 6th February 1872.

Reference was made in the recitals to the stations and incidents thereto not exceeding a price of £14,000 as computed at the prices in Loxtons book, or other prices approved by Francis Fox, the B&ER engineer. The railway was to be fit for opening to Wiveliscombe within four months of commencement and the remainder of the line and the branch to the Watchet line within eight months and the entire railway and works completed by 30th June 1871. In addition, where the Contractor had to pay cash for land purchases in excess of £15,000, the Company would pay the Contractor in B debenture stock (in addition to the £40,000 B debenture stock payable to him in any event).

The part of the line between Norton Junction and Wiveliscombe was complete and open to public traffic but the other portions of the railway were not completed in accordance with the contract. In default the D&SR directors have called upon the Contractor to make good to the holders of A debenture stock the dividends now accruing and to July [30th June 1872].

The Contractor had already laid out a sum of money, exceeding the said sum of £14,000 and only part of the said stations are completed and a large number remain to be built and a considerable sum of money is required to complete the same.

The land already paid for amounts to £29,000 and the costs of conveyance a considerable sum. A further £5,000 in B debenture stock could be issued to the contractor for land in excess of the £15,000.

The Contractor has declined to proceed further with the station work until further monies have been provided for that purpose (he wanted to recoup the excess out of the £15,000 cash and B stock). The Company has given notice that they intend to apply to Parliament in the next session to obtain further capital and on this basis, subject to the Bill in Parliament, the Contractor could proceed to complete the stations.

The terms agreed are:

1. Contractor shall immediately after the passing of the said Act and having raised sufficient sum in cash for the purpose of the works shall proceed to make and complete all proper and sufficient junctions, stations, station houses, station accommodation and fittings, goods sheds, waiting sheds, engine sheds, turntables, points, crossings, loading banks, cranes, water supply and apparatus, junction and other signals and all other requisite works and conveniences including electric telegraph and proper and sufficient cottages where requested by the Board of Trade at level crossings, if any, to the satisfaction of the engineer.

2. Contractor shall complete the entire railway and works together with said stations by 1 January 1873.

3. Contractor shall pay or cause to be paid the interest and dividends due and payable in respect of the A debenture stock payable in January and July 1872 and will pay the Company Secretary's salary and other office expenses during the course of construction.

4. Company shall issue scrip certificates and take steps to convert to cash and pay the Contractor £65,000 in cash.

5. Contractor to be paid monthly 90% of the amounts and value of the work done within 7 days of receipt of the certificate by the engineer. The balance due, one moiety being payable once the engineer certifies the line is completely finished and in proper order for traffic. The other moiety within three calendar months of completion.

6. Contractor to proceed to build the stations as set out in 1 above subject to the amount being raised by the Act.

7. On completion, the Contractor gets balance of the £65,000 remaining in the Company's hands subject to the retention.

8. If Royal Assent to the Bill to go to Parliament is not granted everything herein shall be null and void.

In summary the passing of the Act to secure more capital was vital to complete the railway.

Appendix 6
Cutting the First Sod – North Devon Journal 6th October 1864

'After the conclusion of the half yearly meeting on 4th October 1864 there was a procession to the site of Hacche Moor. At 2 o'clock a call from the bugler summoned the 6th Devon Mounted Rifles to assemble in the Square, in front of the Market House. The procession started in the following order:

6th Devon Mounted Rifles
Contractor's Horses, 14 in number, tastefully decorated with parti-colour ribbons
Wollcombers' Banner (Bishop Blaze)
Band of the 6th Devon Rifle Volunteers
Banner: 'Prosperity to the Town and Trade at Southmolton'
Six Tri-colour Banners
Band of 6th Devon Mounted Rifles
Police and Constables (two and two)
Town Crier
Mace Bearers
The Mayor and Chaplain
Alderman and Town Council of Southmolton
The Mayor, Aldermen and Town Council of Barnstaple
Gentlemen of the Town and Neighbourhood (two and two)

The procession extended for a quarter of a mile and was accompanied by a promiscuous crowd of every sex and age, who hurried on to the site of the ceremony.

On reaching the ground a most enchanting scene opened to view. A large space had been railed off and a tier of seats erected for the accommodation of ladies, from which a fine view of the proceedings was obtained. The approach to the enclosure was marked by two rows of small flags; and over the entrance was a neat triumphal arch, with the company name on one side and the motto on the other.

The arrangements were under the sole direction of Mr E.T. Trenery, the contractor's agent supervised by the engineer.

Lord and Lady Poltimore drove to the ground in dashing style, the Mounted Rifles forming a guard of honour; They were hailed with hearty cheering. In the centre of the area was a platform on which was placed a mahogany barrow, with massive solid silver mountings, and a splendid silver spade richly chased; executed by Messrs Mapins Brothers. These were presented to her Ladyship by Mr W. Climie (nephew of the contractor) on behalf of his uncle. Both articles were inscribed 'Presented to the Right Hon. Florence Lady Poltimore on the occasion of cutting the first sod of the Devon and Somerset Railway by Daniel Climie, October 1864'.

The Reverend W. Burdett offered up a prayer. Lady Poltimore then proceeded to perform the interesting ceremony of the day; at this moment the sun which had been clouded during the morning shone out with effulgence shedding his glorious radiance on the scene.

Her Ladyship (with the assistance of Mr Birch, the engineer) having lifted three sods in the barrow, wheeled them steadily to the end of the platform, tipping them out in a truly workman like manner. A voiciferous cheer followed and, at a given signal, the band struck up the royal anthem.

Mr Karslake asked the assemblage to express at once their interest in the work so propitiously begun.

Lady Poltimore was conducted to a seat by the Mayor and the open-air proceedings terminated.

The police arrangements were very defective; a rush from an eager crowd of rustics well nigh marred the proceedings, but happily the principal ceremony was performed without interruption.

The Processions returned in order to the Market Square, the band playing – 'Here's a health to all true lasses'.

A dinner took place in the spacious New Market at 4 o'clock under the presidency of Lord Poltimore. The dinner which gave great satisfaction was provided by Mr Joshua Gould, of the George Hotel. Covers were laid for 500 and the tables were fully occupied. The Hall was decorated with flags and evergreens, and at the back of the Chairman's seat was a well-executed representation of the Company's seal, with the name of the company in a circle, the respective arms of the three principal towns on the line – Barnstaple, Southmolton and Taunton – and the motto 'Labor omnia Vincit'; the handiwork of a clever workman of Southmolton. The Rev W. Burdett performed the devotions.

There followed the usual loyal and constitutional toasts and speeches, nineteen in all, including the Chairman, John Locke, John McMillan, Rev Burdett, Mr Karslake, Russell M. Riccard, Eugenius Birch and the Mayors of Southmolton and Barnstaple.'

Appendix 7
Review of Traffic and Revenues on the D&SR 1873-1901

The table attached summarises the passenger, goods, parcels and mail revenues in the period 1873-1901, the latter being the year of takeover by the GWR. These revenues are the 50% of gross receipts payable under the 1865 agreement initially with the B&ER and then the GWR. Overall, the percentage of passenger revenues was 53%, goods 41%, parcels 6% and mail 1%. However, it makes sense to look at the trends and fluctuations within selected years. For this purpose, the years 1876, 1880, 1885, 1890 1895 and 1900 have been chosen but mails receipts have been ignored, as there was a flat monthly payment for these, as shown in the main tables.

General Comment

There is a clear trend for all years analysed; passenger revenues dip in February and then climb to their peak in August, before dropping back by the end of the year. Clearly the holiday season played a substantial part even in the early days of the railway. Goods traffic has no such obvious peak, revenues being much more even, albeit fluctuating, month by month. The total revenues broadly showed steady but undulating growth, the most pronounced reductions being apparent in 1879, 1884 and 1885, and 1894 and 1895. It is no surprise that the biggest revenue year for all traffic types was 1900, the last full year.

Passenger revenues increased overall by 17.6% from 1874 (1873 was a part year) until 1900, with goods revenues posting a 64.4% increase. Admittedly that was starting from a much lower base (£9,258) compared with the passenger revenues from 1874 (£14,943), the 1900 amounts being £17,586 (passenger) and £15,221 (goods). Parcels showed an increase of 155% from its 1874 base but being such a small percentage of overall traffic (around 4-8% in the period), it was never going to impact on the overall numbers.

1876 (broad gauge)

The percentage of passenger receipts was 57% to 39% goods. With total revenues of £25,874, more that half the passenger revenues were earned in May-September but goods showed a more consistent monthly return, with low totals in January, July and December.

1880 (broad gauge)

The percentage of passenger receipts was 53% to 42% goods. With tota revenues of £26,879, this showed an increase of 3.88% on the 1876 results. Receipts were up on a month by month basis compared with the previous year, with only November showing a decline. The biggest increase was in July which posted increased revenues on 1879 of £419 1s 0d.

1885 (narrow gauge)

The percentage of passenger receipts was 54% to 40% goods. With total revenues of £27,405, this showed a much lower percentage increase on 1880, a mere 1.95%. The months of January, February, April, July, August and September showed reductions compared with the previous year. There was substantial parcels revenue in April and October compared to regular flows in other months. It is suspected that this was a settlement arrangement but that has not been confirmed.

1890

The percentage of passenger receipts was 55% to 39% goods. Total revenues were now £31,543 showing a 15.1% increase from the 1885 numbers. Five months showed reductions on the previous year with the biggest being in July and November. There was substantial parcels revenue in April and October compared to regular flows in other months.

1895

The percentage of passenger receipts was 52% to 42% goods. Total revenues were £31,153, a reduction of £410 (1.22%) on 1890. The first five months of the year all showed reductions in revenue compared with the previous year, with increases for the remaining seven months based on the previous year's monthly revenue. This was the first year after the GWR fare reduction (*see Chapter 1*) and it took time for revenues to recover. There was substantial parcels revenue in April and October compared to regular flows in other months.

1900

The percentage of passenger receipts was 50% to 43% goods. The total revenues were £35,493, an increase of £4,087 on the 1895 figures (13.9%), showing the impact of the reduced GWR fares. Again six months (March, April, June, July, September and November) posted reductions compared with the previous year. There was substantial parcels revenue in April and October compared to regular flows in other months.

RECEIPTS FROM PASSENGER, GOODS, PARCELS, ETC, 1873 TO 1901 (30TH JUNE)

YEAR ENDING 31ST DEC.	PASSENGER £	GOODS £	PARCELS £	MAIL £	TOTAL £	NOTES
1873	1,934	1,276	105		3,315	1
1874	14,943	9,258	1,056		25,257	
1875	13,952	8,204	1,106		23,262	2
1876	14,672	10,045	1,157	200	26,074	
1877	14,650	9,925	1,319	200	26,094	
1878	14,948	10,579	1,382	200	27,109	
1879	13,772	10,177	1,321	200	25,470	
1880	14,244	11,303	1,332	200	27,079	
1881	14,085	11,020	1,370	200	26,675	
1882	14,553	11,410	1,449	200	27,612	
1883	14,935	11,925	1,303	200	28,363	
1884	15,225	10,873	1,406	200	27,704	
1885	14,858	11,088	1,459	250	27,655	3
1886	15,048	11,615	1,545	250	28,458	
1887	15,813	11,825	1,539	250	29,427	
1888	15,928	11,807	1,580	250	29,565	
1889	16,954	12,590	1,666	250	31,460	
1890	17,409	12,390	1,744	250	31,793	
1891	17,362	12,361	1,726	250	31,699	
1892	17,355	12,502	1,870	250	31,977	
1893	17,037	12,738	1,829	250	31,854	
1894	16,204	12,853	1,887	250	31,194	4
1895	16,197	12,983	1,973	250	31,403	
1896	16,171	14,383	2,041	250	32,845	
1897	16,841	15,193	2,186	250	34,470	
1898	17,189	14,564	2,244	250	34,247	
1899	17,575	15,140	2,529	250	35,494	5
1900	17,586	15,221	2,687	250	35,744	
1901	6,542	7,353	1,714	125	15,734	6
TOTAL	433,982	332,601	46,525	5,925		
AVERAGE	15,781	12,095	1,692	215		7

NOTES
1. Part year
2. Excludes April
3. New Mail agreement
4. GWR fare changes (see text)
5. Year in which Passenger Revenues recovered above level of the fares pre GWR fare changes
6. To 30th June 1901, so half year only
7. Average over 27.5 years.

STATEMENT OF ACCOUNT – RECEIPTS & EXPENDITURE 1871

INCOME (£ S D)

MONTH	PASSENGER	PARCELS	MERCHANDISE
June	147 12 1	6 11 4	130 14 0
July	161 13 3	13 17 1	112 2 0
August	171 4 0	9 14 4	181 4 10
September	154 7 2	7 19 10	125 13 2
October	132 10 7	7 12 4	134 19 9
November	110 19 4	8 1 2	135 12 8
December	130 10 11	6 9 9	97 5 1
TOTAL	1,008 17 4	60 5 10	917 11 6

EXPENDITURE (£ S D)

MONTH	MOTIVE POWER	INTEREST ON LOCO STOCK	USE OF CARRIAGE STOCK	SUNDRY TRAFFIC CHARGES	PASSENGER DUTY
June	88 19 10	20 3 3	34 3 6	102 1 7	6 16 5
July	115 17 8	27 3 7	38 9 11	114 14 0	7 7 10
August	120 5 4	27 3 7	41 19 1	114 14 0	7 14 5
September	113 16 0	26 6 1	38 16 5	111 0 0	7 0 5
October	111 10 7	27 3 7	37 2 2	114 14 0	6 0 1
November	111 10 11	26 6 1	36 13 9	111 0 0	5 3 4
December	109 15 1	27 3 7	38 1 9	114 4 0	5 10 5
TOTAL	771 15 5	181 9 9	265 6 7	782 7 7	45 12 11

TRAIN MILES 1871-1878

6 MONTH PERIOD	PASSENGER	GOODS	TOTAL
31st December 1871	Not recorded	Not recorded	16,080
30th June 1872	13,572	2,247	15,819
31st December 1972	13,818½	2,276½	16,095
30th June 1873	13,460½	2,229½	15,690
31st October 1873*	9,338	1,537	*10,875
30th June 1874	82,941	27,330	110,271
31st December 1874	85,627	26,341	111,968
30th June 1875	84,133	25,961	110,094
31st December 1875	83,765	25,675	109,440
30th June 1876	84,359	26,298	110,657
31st December 1876	85,167	27,311	112,478
30th June 1877	89,930	34,531	124,461
31st December 1877	83,879	42,263	126,142
30th June 1878	83,345	41,518	124,863
31st December 1878	Not received		

*This was only a 4 month period

Selected Annual Analysis of Traffic Revenues month by month

1876	Passenger	Goods	Parcels	Per year change +/-
January	918	717	62	
February	726	838	56	
March	884	939	72	
April	1,083	801	87	
May	1,157	979	102	
June	1,415	902	95	
July	1,702	743	110	
August	2,062	894	108	
September	1,848	1,011	146	
October	1,074	804	105	
November	790	846	122	
December	1,013	571	93	
TOTAL	14,672	10,045	1,158	
1880				
January	898	794	84	+183
February	678	729	68	+61
March	937	929	80	+216
April	1,008	1,051	94	+70
May	1,161	1,108	137	+204
June	1,111	968	83	+104
July	1,722	1,005	124	+419
August	1,944	906	140	+119
September	1,759	1,048	161	+189
October	1,247	1,020	124	+84
November	810	929	126	-87
December	969	814	111	+49
TOTAL	14,244	11,301	1,332	
1885				
January	891	800	62	-42
February	655	824	65	-75
March	849	1,024	79	+174
April	1,035	939	216	-27
May	1,245	994	87	+19
June	1,258	1,035	80	+157
July	1,739	891	91	-28
August	2,157	857	129	-192
September	1,903	989	154	-113
October	1,279	1,073	302	+60
November	810	844	81	+6
December	1,037	818	112	+124
TOTAL	14,858	11,088	1,458	

1890	Passenger	Goods	Parcels	Per year change +/-
January	1,037	858	69	-13
February	754	901	55	+27
March	915	1,067	63	+52
April	1,184	1,022	451	+60
May	1,419	1,128	96	+169
June	1,395	1,117	81	+33
July	1,957	1,010	96	-214
August	2,717	1,132	113	-20
September	2,339	1,106	166	+276
October	1,722	1,200	368	+175
November	989	927	98	-197
December	981	922	88	-9
TOTAL	17,409	12,390	1,744	
1895				
January	878	845	76	-83
February	646	732	75	-336
March	860	989	88	-218
April	1,137	1,121	505	-90
May	1,285	1,240	103	-37
June	1,476	1,150	98	+114
July	1,804	1,038	124	+56
August	2,586	1,313	133	+314
September	2,152	1,204	142	+76
October	1,493	1,263	397	+217
November	923	1,138	110	+131
December	956	950	122	+62
TOTAL	16,196	12,983	1,973	
1900				
January	935	1,156	148	+128
February	714	1,081	105	+57
March	937	1,287	131	-35
April	1,141	1,275	666	-26
May	1,481	1,565	156	+379
June	1,462	1,295	126	-41
July	1,889	1,183	127	-163
August	3,001	1,260	168	+64
September	2,433	1,366	197	-52
October	1,600	1,374	554	+15
November	938	1,312	135	-69
December	1,055	1,067	173	+57
TOTAL	17,586	15,221	2,686	

Dulverton station circa 1969, minus the signal box, footbridge and Down side building and thus showing the structures which remain to this day. However, the Down platform has also since been removed (levelled) and the Up platform cut back to the goods shed, the gardens here now being at what was formerly rail level. ***Courtesy Richard Antliff and Amyas Crump***

BIBLIOGRAPHY & SOURCES

I am grateful to those who have trodden the path of research previously and acknowledge my debt to that work by listing my reference sources. Where possible I have sought to research primary documents and merely cross-check, in some circumstances, by reference to others' work, where relevant and available. Nonetheless, I set out below an acknowledgement to those whose prior research and publication has significantly helped me make this book more comprehensive and complete. Please note this list is common to both volumes and will thus not be repeated in Volume 2.

Geography/History

A History of the Forest of Exmoor, E.T. MacDermot, David & Charles, 1973
A Lazy Contentment. The History of the Carnarvon Arms Hotel, Sophia & Julian Watson, Lonsdale Press, 1999
Barnstaple: Town on the Taw, Lois Lamplugh, Phillimore, 1983
'Mining in North Devon', John Rottenbury, *Exmoor Review*, Exmoor Press, (and his thesis at Somerset Records Office)
Strong's Industries of North Devon, H.W. Strong & B.D. Hughes, David & Charles, 1971 ed.
The Book of Dulverton, Dulverton & District Society, Halsgrove 2002
The Book of South Molton, Jonathan Edmunds, Halsgrove 2002
Thorough Guides, North Devon and North Cornwall, C.S. Ward, Dulau & Co, 1892

Railways

A Pictorial Record of Great Western Architecture, Adrian Vaughan, OPC, 1977
A Pictorial Record of Great Western Engines, Vols 1 & 2, J.H. Russell, OPC, 1986
A Pictorial Record of Great Western Signalling, Adrian Vaughan, OPC, 1984
An Historical Survey of Great Western Engine Sheds 1947, E.T. Lyons, OPC, 1972
An Historical Survey of Selected Great Western Stations, Vols 1 & 3, R.H. Clark, OPC 1981
Back Along North Devon's Lines, Victor Thompson, Badger Books, 1983
Beeching – 50 years of the Axeman, Robin Jones, Morton's Media Group Ltd, 2011
Beeching – The Inside Track, Robin Jones, Morton's Media Group Ltd, 2012
Britain's Railways in Wartime, Kevin Robertson, OPC, 2008
British Locomotive Catalogue 1825-1923, Vol. 3A: Midland Railway and its constituent companies, Bertram & David Baxter, Moorland Publishing 1982
British Rail Standard Diesels of the 1960s, David N. Clough, Ian Allan, 2009
British Railways First Generation DMUs, Hugh Longworth, OPC, 2011
British Railways Steam Locomotive Allocations, Hugh Longworth, OPC, 2011
Devon Railway Stations, Mike Oakley, Dovecote Press, 2007
Devonshire Railways, Colin G. Maggs, Halsgrove, 2010
Dr Beeching's Axe 50 Years On, Julian Holland, David & Charles, 2013
Great Western Coaches 1890-1954, Michael Harris, David & Charles, 1972
Great Western Coaches (Official Drawings No. 3), John Lewis, Wild Swan, 1998
Great Western Railway Halts Vol. 1, Kevin Roberston, Irwell Press, 1990
Great Western Railway Halts Vol. 2, Kevin Roberston, KRB Publications, 2002
GWR Engineering Work 1928-1938, R. Tourret, Tourret Publishing, 2003
GWR Goods Wagons, A.G. Atkins, W. Beard & R. Tourret, OPC, 2013
Great Western Infrastructure 1922-1934, David Wallis & Kevin Robertson, Noodle Books, 2014
Great Western Locomotive Allocations For 1921, Ian Harrison, Wild Swan, 1984
Great Western Locomotive Allocations For 1934, Nigel Pocock & Ian Harrison Wild Swan, 1983
Great Western Way, John Lewis, Historical Model Railway Society, 2009
History of the Great Western Railway, Volumes 1, 2 & 3, E.T. MacDermot, C.R. Clinker, O.S. Nock, Ian Allan, 1982 ed.
Industrial Railways and Locomotives of South Western England, Roger Hateley, Industrial Railway Society, 2012
North Devon Railway Report, David St. John Thomas, David & Charles, 1963
Railway Passenger Stations in England, Scotland and Wales. A Chronology, M.E. Quick, Railway & Canal Historical Society, 2002 ed.
Railways In and Around Taunton, Somerset & North Devon, Michael J. Fox, Foxline Publishing, 1999
Railways of Britain – Devon and Cornwall, Colin & David McCarthy, Ian Allan, 2008
Railways Round Exmoor, Robin Madge, Exmoor Press, 1975
Signal Box Diagrams of the Great Western and Southern Railways, Vol. 8, G.A. Pryer
Signal Box Register; Vol. 1; Great Western, Signalling Record Society, revised ed. 2011
Somerset Railway Stations, Mike Oakley, Dovecote Press, 2002
Summer Saturdays in the West, David St. John Thomas & Simon Rocksborough Smith, David & Charles, 1973
Taunton to Barnstaple, Vic Mitchell & Keith Smith, Middleton Press, 1995
The Barnstaple & Ilfracombe Railway, Colin G. Maggs Oakwood Press, 1988
The Complete UK Modern Traction Locomotive Directory, Colin J. Marsden, TheRailwayCentre.Com, 2011
The Day of the Holiday Express, Richard Woodley, Ian Allan, 1996
The District Controller's View, No. 14 North Devon, Xpress Publishing, 2011
The Exe Valley Railway, John Owen, Kingfisher, 1985
The Heyday of GWR Train Services, P.W.B. Semmens, David & Charles, 1990
The Locomotives of the Great Western Railway, various vols, Railway Correspondence & Travel Society
The Lynton & Barnstaple Railway, G.A. Brown, J.D.C.A. Prideaux & H.G. Radcliffe, David & Charles, 1980
The Minehead Branch 1848-1971, Ian Coleby, Lightmoor Press, 2006
The North Devon Railway, The Southern Route between Exeter and Ilfracombe, John Nicholas & George Reeve, Irwell Press, 2010
The Railway Clearing House Handbook of Railway Stations 1904, David & Charles Reprints, 1970
The Reshaping of British Railways, British Railways Board, HMSO, 1963
The Taunton to Barnstaple Line, Colin Maggs, Oakwood Press, 1980
Track Layout Diagrams of the GWR & BR/WR, Section 15: North Devon, R.A. Cooke, 1977
Train Formations & Carriage Workings of the Great Western Railway, W.S. Beckett, Xpress Publishing, 2002
Western Change – Summer Saturdays 1957-1995, Paul Chancellor, RCTS, 1995
West Country Railway History, David St. John Thomas, David & Charles, 1973

Magazines & Journals

Exmoor, The Country Magazine, Issue 64, Aug. 2013, Rosemary Lauder, Hoar Oak Publishing Ltd, Venn Cross Gardens, Waterrow
Great Western Railway Magazine, various vols, GWR
Great Western Railway Journal, 'Barnstaple', Chris Turner, No. 42, Spring 2002, Wild Swan
Railway Observer (various editions), RCTS
Steam Days, Dec. 1997, 'Special Traffic – Animal Farm – livestock, feedstuffs, agricultural shows and farm removals', Michael Harris.
Steam Days, No. 24, 'With Stop Watch, Camera and Notebook in Devon and Somerset in 1958', James G. Tawse
Steam Days, Nov. 2009, 'A Summer Saturday at Paddington', Alan Teatherton
The Broadsheet, Journal of the Broad Gauge Society, No. 43, Spring 2000, 'The State of the North Devon Broad Gauge, 1850', Mike Hutson
West Somerset Railway Journal (various editions)

Local & Other Newspapers

Illustrated London News
North Devon Journal
North Devon Herald
Somerset Gazette
Western Morning News
West Somerset Free Press

Ex-GWR 'Mogul' No. 5336, which we last saw at Dulverton a few weeks prior to this (page 164) heads east across the Tone Viaduct on 5th September 1964, with a summer Saturday train bound for Taunton. The viaduct had almost become lost in the landscape since the days of its construction over ninety years earlier (see page 67), the undergrowth masking its true height, the structure rose 100 feet off the valley floor and was in fact taller than its sister at Castle Hill. Having covered the history of the Devon & Somerset Railway in this book, the second volume will look in detail at the stations and infrastructure, and will illustrate the line in all its scenic beauty courtesy of a quite superb range of photographs such as this. *Michael J. Fox, courtesy Rail Archive Stephenson*

CONTENTS – VOLUME 2
THE LINE, ITS STATIONS AND SERVICES

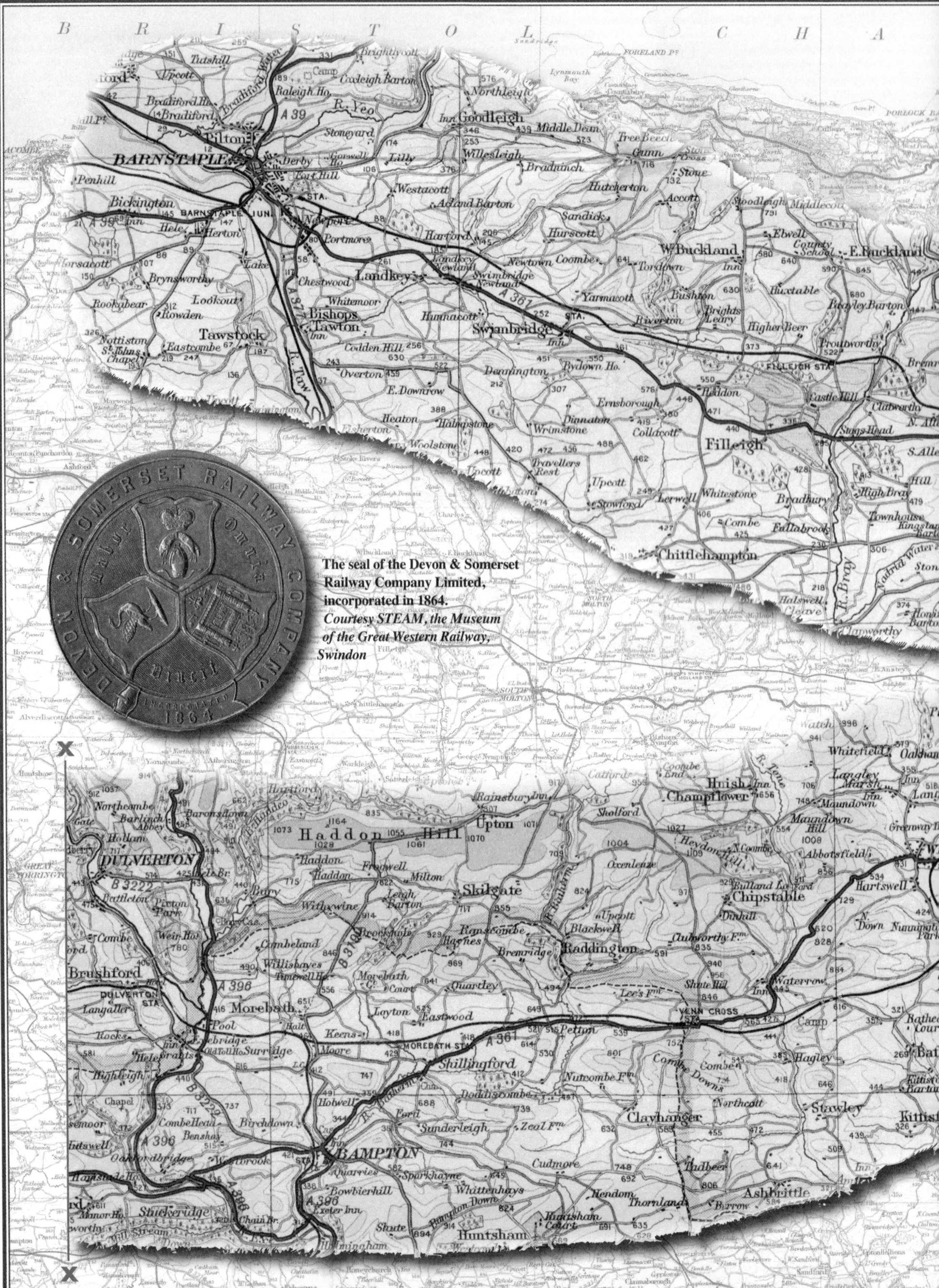

The seal of the Devon & Somerset Railway Company Limited, incorporated in 1864.
Courtesy STEAM, the Museum of the Great Western Railway, Swindon